THE JEWS IN THE MODERN AGE

Providing a broad as well as a pointillist overview of modern Jewish history on a global scale from the eighteenth century to the present day, this book analyzes how the Jewish people have been dramatically transformed by the forces of social, economic, political, technological, and demographic change.

Now in a new edition as a split volume, this second volume of a comprehensive history of the Jews includes topics such as the impact on Jewish society of the Enlightenment as well as its Jewish equivalent, the Haskalah; religious innovations in eastern and central Europe; the processes of emancipation and Jewish acculturation; the modern economic history of the Jewish people, which includes their embourgeoisement in central and western Europe, and the growth of a giant Jewish proletariat in eastern Europe; the emergence of an antisemitic politics that sought to roll back Jewish gains; and the variety of Jewish responses to those illiberal forces, especially in the form of vibrant Jewish political cultures, among them Zionism, socialism, and mass migration. Middle Eastern Jewish communities were likewise impacted by the forces of modernity in ways particular to them, and that history is addressed, as is the emergence and consolidation of the state of Israel in the wake of the Holocaust and the dissolution of Jewish communities across the Muslim world. Currently, illiberal forces are again on the march from both the right and the left, helping to foster a global upsurge of antisemitic violence and online hate.

The book is useful not just for those interested in the Jews themselves but also for readers open to learning about global history from the vantage point of an ethnic minority deeply impacted by modernity, both its blessings as well as its horrors.

John M. Efron is Koret Professor of Jewish History at the University of California at Berkeley. He specializes in the cultural and social history of German Jewry. He is the author of *German Jewry and the Allure of the Sephardic* (2016) and *All Consuming: Germans, Jews, and the Meaning of Meat* (2025).

THE JEWS IN THE MODERN AGE

John M. Efron

FOURTH EDITION

Routledge
Taylor & Francis Group

NEW YORK AND LONDON

Designed cover image: Composition 1911 by Otto Freundlich 1878–1943. German painter and sculptor of Jewish origin and one of the first generation of abstract artists. In 1943 he was arrested and deported to Majdanek Concentration Camp, where he was murdered on the day he arrived. Photo12/Ann Ronan Picture Library (Alamy)

Fourth edition published 2025
by Routledge
605 Third Avenue, New York, NY 10158

and by Routledge
4 Park Square, Milton Park, Abingdon, Oxon OX14 4RN

Routledge is an imprint of the Taylor & Francis Group, an informa business

First edition published by Pearson Education Inc, 2009
Third edition published by Routledge, 2019

Library of Congress Cataloging-in-Publication Data
Names: Efron, John M. author | Efron, John M. Jews.
Title: The Jews in the modern age / John M. Efron.
Description: Fourth edition. | Abingdon, Oxon ; New York, NY : Routledge, 2025. |
    Part of two volumes that were originally published as one book titled
    "The Jews: a History" by John Efron and Matthias Lehmann in 2009. |
    Includes bibliographical references and index.
Identifiers: LCCN 2024058495 (print) | LCCN 2024058496 (ebook) |
    ISBN 9781041007814 hardback | ISBN 9781041008033 paperback |
    ISBN 9781003611608 ebook
Subjects: LCSH: Jews—History | Judaism—History
Classification: LCC DS117 .E33 2025 (print) | LCC DS117 (ebook)
LC record available at https://lccn.loc.gov/2024058495
LC ebook record available at https://lccn.loc.gov/2024058496

ISBN: 978-1-041-00781-4 (hbk)
ISBN: 978-1-041-00803-3 (pbk)
ISBN: 978-1-003-61160-8 (ebk)

DOI: 10.4324/9781003611608

Typeset in Minion Pro
by Apex CoVantage, LLC

CONTENTS

FIGURES

MAPS

INTRODUCTION

John M. Efron
University of California, Berkeley

THIS IS NOW the fourth iteration of my history of the Jews in the modern period, the first appearing in 2009. The three previous versions constituted the final section of a book called *The Jews: A History*, a study that spans the ancient, medieval, and modern periods. That book was co-written by Professors Steven Weitzman, Matthias Lehmann, and me. Steve and Matthias wrote the ancient and medieval/early modern sections, respectively. Routledge's decision to publish a fourth edition of *The Jews: A History* opened up the opportunity to re-think our previous efforts, as gratifying and as well-received as they have been. It was determined that the large single volume be split up into two separate books: *The Jews: From Ancient Canaan to a Global Culture* and *The Jews: A Modern History*.

One of the compelling reasons to prepare two separate volumes is governed by the nature of the source material. Simply put, we have infinitely more sources for the last 300 years of Jewish history than we do for the preceding 3,000. One consequence is that in writing a modern history of the Jewish people, there are seemingly infinite topics that can be covered, and in remarkable detail. Today, the historical profession, like, say, medicine and law, is peopled by an army of specialists. The many thematic, temporal, geographic, and methodological approaches make for an exhilarating

yet daunting body of knowledge. My own area of specialty is modern German Jewish history. Entire libraries have been written about the truly spectacular achievements, failures, and tragedies of a community that peaked at only around 600,000 Jews between 1871 and 1933, that is, between the emancipation of German Jews and their disenfranchisement with Hitler's ascent to power. It is difficult for a specialist to keep up, even within a rich but relatively small field such as mine. While specialization is an absolute necessity, and a natural consequence of the discipline's development, we must be mindful of the fact that the average reader, no matter how enamored of history they may be, is unlikely to wade through the specialist journals or read narrow monographs. And yet there remain very large numbers of people wishing to read the latest works of history presented in a general format. This is what I have set out to achieve here, to present an as up-to-date and engaging an account of modern Jewish history as is possible.

Within Jewish studies, modern Jewish history is one of the largest, if not the largest, subfields. It is what makes it so exciting and so challenging. The attempt to keep up with the latest scholarship is a Sisyphean task. In practical terms, what this means for you, the reader, is that it is impossible to cover everything. For one reader, I will have spent too much time on

DOI: 10.4324/9781003611608-1

1

one subject. For another reader, I will have only scratched the surface or not dealt at all with a subject they deem essential. I have had to make choices, using my discretion. There is no other way to tell the history of a people found all over the globe. Most histories are written from the perspective of the nation-state or, in the case of nations with imperial holdings, for example, Britain, France, or Ottoman Turkey, through the prism of empire. Jews were imperial subjects and, sometimes, even officers of the empire. They were also ordinary citizens of nation-states. They lived in different countries that were themselves at very different stages of economic, social, and political development, and as a country goes, so, too, do its Jews. Some Jewish communities were well along the path of acculturation in the nineteenth century (France), while others remained religiously and culturally traditional (Russia); meanwhile Jews in England and Italy managed to exhibit both tendencies. Some Jewish communities became highly politicized and intensely fractured (interwar Poland), while Germany possessed no Jewish political parties save the short-lived Jewish People's Party during the Weimar Republic. In the Ottoman Empire, there was an indigenous Jewish community in nineteenth-century Palestine that was deeply religious and largely impoverished, while Iraqi Jews, especially those in Baghdad, were deeply immersed in Arabic culture and largely middle-class.

It is thus extremely difficult to make sweeping generalizations about modern Jewry. And yet we must bring the threads of the tapestry together and turn it into a recognizable image, something that makes sense to us. Of course, the past does not unfold as a neat, easily comprehensible string of events. This is true for all peoples, but especially widely dispersed diasporic communities such as the Jews. If history, in this case Jewish history, were to

be rendered as a painting, it seems as though the chaotic Abstract Expressionism of Jackson Pollock would serve as a more accurate depiction than the deeply emotional yet visually accessible post-Impressionism of, say, van Gogh. The historian's job is to portray the past by finding a happy medium between the non-linear movement of history and the necessary tethering provided by chronology and orderly description, which, by necessity, must be vivid and engaging.

To do this, I proceed in rough chronological order but cannot be confined by that alone. At times, it has made more sense to have the reader be guided along by a thematic approach. Certain large themes recur with relative frequency. These include subjects such as emancipation, acculturation, antisemitism, Jewish politics, religious diversity, language choice, migration, the Holocaust, as well as the near contemporary dissolution of Jewish life in Arab lands and the subsequent emergence of the state of Israel, as well as other post-Holocaust centers of Jewish life.

When writing a general history such as this, particularly when preparing the latest edition, it is tempting to bring the story as close to contemporary events as possible. To do so, however, is to be beset by problems. The first is that historians need the passage of time to build upon the work of earlier historians when seeking to analyze a period or an event. To bring the historians' skills to bear on contemporary affairs runs counter to the sensibilities of the historian. We look at the past from afar. To draw too close is to enter into the realm of journalism. Indeed, it was the editor of *The Washington Post*, Philip L. Graham, who is purported to have said, "Journalism is the first rough draft of history." In this book, the closer I come to the present, the more I feel the text reads like journalism, and thus a first rough draft of history. No self-respecting historian would ever dream of making a rough first draft of their scholarship available to the public. However, sometimes, dictums like Graham's need to be honored in the breach—at least a little bit.

As I write these lines, one of the largest Jewish populations left in Europe, the Jews of Ukraine, finds itself in the midst of a horrendous, unprovoked war. I can only acknowledge that fact here in the introduction but cannot further historicize it beyond this. Similarly, Israel is currently at war in Gaza and Lebanon. As a historian, I cannot include an analysis of current events in a book such as this and call it history. What I am prepared to say is that two aspects of the current conflict in the Middle East are without historical precedent and will surely capture the attention of future historians. The first is the October 7, 2023, infiltration of southern Israel by Hamas terrorists from Gaza and the savage pogrom they unleashed. With at least 1,200 Jews and non-Jews slaughtered, countless women raped and mutilated, and babies murdered, as well as the taking of at least 200 hostages, nothing like it had ever happened in Israel's history before. With the lack of precedent shattered, the massacre brought to Israel an all-too-common millennium-long historical experience suffered by Diaspora Jews. The second thing that future historians will most surely take note of has been the venomous global outpouring of opprobrium directed at Israel and Jews more generally. Antisemitism has exploded, with few inhibitions, whether on the street, on college campuses, and of course, online. Mass demonstrations all over the world have even been characterized at times by the celebration of Hamas's frenzied and depraved slaughter of Jews. The most extreme voices have even charged Israel with staging the rapes that were perpetrated on October 7. Living as we do in a "Me Too" world, the dismissal of accounts of

the rape of Jewish women is especially devastating, for behind the charge is the belief that there is no limit to the lies Jews will tell to gain some sort of advantage.

The championing of Hamas's actions began prior to the start of Israel's devastating military response. Considering the well-known fact that Hamas's foundational charter of 1988 expresses its intent to obliterate Israel as it simultaneously trumpets the movement's implacable hatred of all Jews, the embracing, the excusing, and even the denial of some of what occurred on October 7 have left Jews bewildered and feeling isolated. The sight of demonstrators in the West gleefully parroting Hamas's genocidal intent by calling for an end to Israel's existence has been deeply traumatic for most of world Jewry.

Individual Jews have been attacked from Los Angeles to Paris, while in Sydney, a crowd of demonstrators stood outside the city's iconic opera house, chanting, "Gas the Jews." Jewish communities the world over feel besieged and set upon by the unleashing of vile and unchecked public expressions of antisemitism. That said, history does not repeat itself, and contrary to the anguished expressions of Jews all over the world, this is not the 1930s all over again. Most importantly, in the Christian world, there are no government-imposed antisemitic laws anywhere. But we need not compare what is happening today to the greatest catastrophe in Jewish history. The events have been sufficiently shocking that future historians will indeed take special note of the unprecedented nature of Hamas's actions and the global responses to them of Israel's detractors and defenders alike. Of that, one can be certain.

Our narrative begins in the eighteenth century and ends around the time Donald Trump became president of the United States in 2016. Many of the observations I made in the previous edition about his coming to power and its impact on Jews sadly still hold true, while remarks I made about Israel, the Palestinians, as well as the designs of Hamas, Hezbollah, and other non-state terrorist groups appear to be references to what is currently transpiring. Instead, much of what was transpiring as the twenty-first century was entering its second decade can be seen as presaging events as they are currently unfolding.

Berkeley, California
October 2024

CHAPTER I

THE STATE OF THE JEWS, THE JEWS AND THE STATE

IN TRADITIONAL JEWISH fashion, we begin with a question: When does the modern period in Jewish history begin? The answer would seem to be self-evident: with the onset of modernity, of course. A notoriously difficult term to define, *modernity*, in one sense, can be defined as the state of conscious recognition that the present is unique, original, and meaningfully different from previous eras. Of course, since time immemorial, children and young adults have thought of their parents as old-fashioned or stuck in their ways and have believed their age to be different from previous eras. But *modernity* is not merely a technical term for the ancient expression of youthful rebellion. While young people have always tended to seek out new fashions and experiment with new trends, the world most people inhabited until the eighteenth century was not too radically different from that which their parents and grandparents knew. While there were many changes in the past, including technological advancements and even the emergence of new social classes and the decline of others, social change was nonetheless slow and often barely perceptible. The same holds true of the economic circumstances of human existence. Concentrating on Europe, economic historians have concluded that income for almost everyone remained

stagnant and at about the same level from at least the year 1000 until the mid-nineteenth century.

Modernity, by contrast, saw the rise of entirely new, clearly visible cultural and intellectual sensibilities that were conditioned by tangible changes in the economic, technological, political, and social environment. The kinds of changes we reference first took place in Europe and include monumental historical developments, such as the Enlightenment, the rise of modern science, the decline of the aristocracy and absolute monarchy, and the emergence to political and economic power of the middle classes—or bourgeoisie. They also include the beginnings of industrialization and the rise of the factory system, as well as large-scale migration from the countryside to the cities and the formation of distinctive urban sensibilities and lifestyles.

In the nineteenth century, both the bourgeois champions of free trade and the working classes that were the productive backbone of the capitalist order became highly politicized. Even the shrinking landed aristocracy emerged from the upheavals as a class with a new self-awareness and now demanded political representation to protect its interests. To tap into the disparate hopes and frustrations

DOI: 10.4324/9781003611608-2

of all these groups, mass political parties emerged to represent them. For the first time, the issues that motivated the creation of these new political entities were debated in constitutional assemblies, legislative bodies, and parliaments. Some of these institutions, which emerged as early as the seventeenth century, came into being either through Revolution, internal reform, or a combination of both. For example, we see such developments in England in 1688 and 1830; the United States in 1776; France in 1789, 1830, 1848, and 1870; and Canada, Australia, and New Zealand in the second half of the nineteenth century. While the various forms of representative democracy still limited participation, excluding, among others, women, Blacks, and Aboriginal peoples, these developments nonetheless mark the increasing democratization of society.

All these political transformations of the social order were preceded and, to a large extent, inspired by the intellectual revolution of the eighteenth century known as the Enlightenment. The leading figures of the Enlightenment—men such as the French philosophes Montesquieu, Rousseau, and Voltaire; the English economist Adam Smith; and the German philosopher Kant—proposed a refashioning of society based on reason, progress, faith in human ingenuity, and an abiding belief in the capacity of all people for improvement. In fact, this was a mantra of the Enlightenment, but it applied especially, it must be said, if one were a White, European, and Christian male. Inspired by the scientific revolution of the seventeenth century and its inner logic and practice of close observation and experimentation, the philosophers rejected all truths based on tradition and religious authority, championing instead a world where individuals, exercising their natural right to liberty, created new

economic, political, and social structures for the benefit of both individuals and the greater good. These ideas also gave rise to individualism, the self-conscious recognition that people have personal identities that, while shaped by the larger culture of which they are part, are nonetheless products of personal experience, of individual decisions and opportunities both taken and missed.

The emergence of Enlightenment thought and the liberal political and economic structures that followed in its wake throughout the course of the eighteenth and nineteenth centuries also saw the development of critiques of these rapid changes to traditional modes of existence. In Britain, conservative thinkers such as Edmund Burke advanced a political theory hostile to the French Revolution. In France, monarchists continued to resist the new Republic. Others began to reject the egalitarian ideology of the Enlightenment and the French Revolution by claiming that historical development was determined by the relative superiority and inferiority of certain races. In the political realm, the French Revolution spawned collectivist ideologies, including nationalism, whose exclusivist passions ensured conflict based on ethnic, national, or linguistic identity, thereby again challenging the universalistic tendencies of the Enlightenment. Imperialism and colonialism further inflamed nationalist chauvinism.

Romanticism, an artistic and intellectual movement that first emerged in the eighteenth century but that increased in appeal following Napoleon's defeat in 1815, further cemented particularism by stressing national difference based on the perception that various ethnic groups possessed certain instincts and drives drawn from language, history, folk culture, and race. In Germany, Karl Marx advanced a theory of history that predicted the abolition of private property and the bourgeoisie through proletarian revolution, which would eventually lead to the creation of a classless society. In Austria, psychiatrist Sigmund Freud challenged what he regarded as the hypocrisy of the moralistic bourgeois order by pointing out the effects of irrational impulses and sexual urges that contributed to the formation of individual personalities.

Finally, those wishing the destruction of bourgeois society employed one of the key characteristics of the age—mass politics—to bring about their aims. By the twentieth century, Communism, Fascism, and Nazism had all become revolutionary systems of violence and oppression dedicated to the ruthless destruction of enemies, the decimation of parliamentary democracy, the abolition of freedom of expression, the eradication of individualism, the celebration of violence, and in the case of Nazism, the promotion of racism. The modern period thus sees the emergence of mighty historical forces, many vying implacably with one another, to reinvent society.

Modernity has left its trace on all groups, to greater and lesser degrees. For Jews, its impact has been acute. Many of the key markers of the modern age—urbanism, trade, literacy and numeracy, the acquisition of higher education—were developments that Jews pursued with great enthusiasm. Modernity has seen the rise of the professional with expertise in a specialized area of knowledge. In the modern period, in addition to commerce, notable areas of such expertise have been law, medicine, and journalism—known as the "liberal professions." Over the last 200 years, Jews the world over have produced lawyers, doctors, scientists, journalists, entertainers, and businesspeople in numbers wildly disproportionate to their percentage of the population. Just as the word "doctor" became a term of opprobrium in post-expulsion Spain, for it was used as a euphemism for "Jew," the practice of the free professions in modern Europe likewise became synonymous with the Jews.

Similarly, whether one celebrated or derided modern arts and entertainment, Jews were in the thick of producing them. From experimental modernist poetry, with a small and rarefied audience, to the Hollywood blockbuster seen by millions, Jews have been central figures in the creation of modern culture. Finally, if the modern world has seen the emergence of groups espousing ideologies wishing to overturn contemporary society and remake it anew, Jews emerged as both expert revolutionaries and victims of revolution par excellence. Often, Jews found themselves at the center of those messianic and maniacal attempts to reinvent the world.

In large measure, the modern period in Jewish history is characterized by the dynamic of successful cultural, economic, and social integration on the one hand, and on the other, a backlash against those successes, producing social anxiety and hostility toward Jews. At the interstices of those opposing developments is an energizing and creative friction that serves as the motor of the modern Jewish experience. Even as Jews could not but bring with them into their encounter with modernity their ancient cultures, collective sentiments, indeed their psychology, their transformation since 1700 has been radical and total. The period bears witness to the development of new forms of Judaism and Jewishness, both religious and secular, the birth of various Jewish political ideologies, geographical dispersion on a global scale, genocide, displacement, the establishment of the State of Israel, and greater social, economic, and cultural integration than ever before in Jewish history. Of course, while the entire world has also been demonstrably transformed over that same time, Mark Twain is reputed to have once remarked, "The Jews are just like everybody else, only more so." How that came to be the case is the story that follows.

Changing Boundaries in the Eighteenth Century

In 1700, the Jews of Europe were easily distinguishable from their non-Jewish neighbors. They dressed differently, ate and drank differently, spoke differently, and read and wrote (and even thought) from right to left. They were still governed by and lived within the structures of Jewish autonomy, a self-contained world that had begun to crack by the eighteenth century. *Kehillot*, autonomous communities, functioned on the basis of Jewish law and were served by a vast network of Jewish social welfare institutions and fraternities—*hevrot* (sing. *hevrah*)—that provided for their members from cradle to grave. The elementary school (*heder*) and the rabbinic academy (*yeshiva*) provided education for boys and men in sacred sources and religious values and ensured the transmission of Jewish culture from one generation to the next. Jewish separateness, however, did not mean cultural insularity, as Jews shared the culture of their surroundings, even if they sometimes modified that culture to suit Jewish tastes and sensibilities. This also means that Jews were highly distinguishable from one another, for their dispersion endowed them with great inner diversity.

Jews also earned a living in ways that distinguished them from non-Jews, most of whom were peasants engaged in agricultural production. All over Europe, Jews suffered under the yoke of occupational restrictions and myriad taxes. In western Europe, nearly 90 percent were engaged in low-level commerce, generally earning a living from trading, artisanry, and peddling. Ascher Lehmann, who was born in 1769, was rather typical for the age. In his autobiography, he tells us of the difficulties he encountered trying to earn a living when he departed from his hometown of Zeckendorf, Germany, to study in Prague, a distance of 36 miles. His parents were poor and sent him off with a mere five gulden, knowing that he would be assisted along the way by fellow Jews. Jewish society had developed a system to take care of itinerant travelers and students. Destitute, Ascher obtained a *blett*, which was a billet or coupon that entitled him to food and lodging from Jews along the way. "I accepted the first *blett*, and it turned out to be as good as the man had said. One has to spend money not only for food, but in every town and borough, I had to pay 10, 12, and even 18 kreuzers as a poll tax." It was expensive to be a Jew: Town entrance taxes, poll taxes, Jewish community taxes all cut deeply into meagre livelihoods. Arriving at the small town of Eger on a Friday afternoon, Ascher went to the synagogue and was, in turn, invited back to the home of a well-to-do congregant.

> And he had a table the likes of which I've never seen again in all my days: a long dining room, in front of every person two large silver candelabra, each with eight branches, for every person two silver plates, for soup and roast, everything made of silver, several forks and spoons. It was the same with the food; there were all kinds of dishes, and on *Schabbes* afternoon, too, there were double portions of *kugel* [pudding] made with *lokschen* [noodles], and with the very best fruit, fruit of every kind.

Ascher soon had to leave, and needing to earn a living, he took on a number of odd jobs, tutoring commissions, and eventually turned to peddling, which

> was not restricted in those days . . . [but] when [he] came to the acquaintances of [his] father and offered [his] wares, with one voice the Catholic peasants, their wives, and [their] daughters said: "Oh, you pretty fellow, what a pity you will go to hell and purgatory. Get yourself baptized!"

When he arrived at a Lutheran town, he wrote:

> I couldn't sell a thing. One found villages with some forty to eighty peasants who didn't have a penny's worth of goods bought from a merchant in their houses. They wore nothing but what they had made themselves of wool or linen.

The tolerant spirit advocated in Enlightenment tracts had yet to make itself felt in the German countryside. There the Jew, though familiar to all, remained an alien figure (*see box*, "Friedrich Wilhelm I of Prussia and the Jews").

There was an important exception to the social marginalization of the Jews in eighteenth-century central Europe. Among the well-to-do, there was increasing fraternization among Jews and non-Jews. Deep friendships, platonic relationships, and romances characterized a new form of Christian–Jewish contact. Love matches and personal ambition also led to conversions. In the opening decades of the century, the majority of the apostates were to be found among the Sephardic communities of western Europe. By the end of the eighteenth century and into the opening decades of the nineteenth century, the majority of converts were to be found among Ashkenazim.

In central Europe, many of these conversions were undertaken for a variety of overlapping reasons: frustration with continued anti-Jewish discrimination, to escape what many felt was the stigma of being Jewish, to improve one's social status, to fulfill occupational desires, or to marry a Christian. In Germany, about 22,500 people converted throughout the course of the nineteenth century. In Berlin, converts tended to come from among the wealthier Jews. Between 1770 and 1830, nearly 1,600 Jews in Berlin were baptized (according to the card file of converted Jews compiled by the Nazis in the 1930s), over 1,200 of them in the first three decades of the nineteenth century. (In truth, at least 400 of Berlin's converted Jews were not Jewish according to Jewish law, as their mothers were not Jews at the time they were born.) Many of those baptized were illegitimate children born to mixed Jewish Christian couples. What is clear is that in the eighteenth century, women were more frequently represented than men among Berlin's Jewish converts, which in turn led to a rise in the number of Jewish men who underwent baptism in the early nineteenth century. While the waves of conversions amounted to only about 27 people per year in Berlin, it nevertheless alarmed German Jewish leaders—they referred to it as a "baptism epidemic"—because among the converts were many distinguished names. By contrast, in Russia, where a significant number of conversions took place in the 1840s and 1850s, there was no panic about apostasy, because those converting tended to be socially and economically marginal Jews.

In Berlin, the misgivings of some prominent figures about being Jewish underscored the self-doubt many Jews felt once they had come into close contact with the non-Jewish world. Though conversion was a radical response, a sense of Jewish cultural inferiority

FRIEDRICH WILHELM I OF PRUSSIA AND THE JEWS

Friedrich Wilhelm I, who reigned from 1713 to 1740, was ill-disposed toward Jews, especially poor ones. As with his predecessors, he extracted large sums from Jews for the privilege of living in his domains by selling them expensive Letters of Protection. Not long after Friedrich Wilhelm ascended the throne, he sought to limit the number of Jews in his kingdom by charging those with more than one child exorbitant sums for residence permits. A second child cost 1,000 talers, and a third child 2,000 talers. Beyond this, he imposed on Jews marriage, birth, death, divorce, travel, and occupational taxes; a special tax for his coronation; and in 1714, a tax to avoid having to carry a red hat while in Berlin. An edict of October 26, 1719, stipulated which gates foreign Jews had to use to enter Berlin, and on November 13, 1719, another edict was promulgated that forbade Jewish beggars from entering Prussia altogether. In 1725, the Berlin Jewish community had to contribute 7,000 talers to the building of a church in nearby Potsdam. An edict of 1727 prohibited Jews from selling goods made of spun wool. In 1728, Jews were required to pay taxes and fees collectively instead of on an individual basis. The cost of Letters of Protection alone was raised to 15,000 talers for all of Prussia. The 1728 tax "reform" edict also prohibited Jews from trading in spices and working in most handicrafts, and it also stipulated that goods taken in by Jewish pawnbrokers could only be sold after a two-year wait. The various prohibitions against Jews increased their general poverty. With Jews reduced to dealing in used clothes and bric-a-brac, as well as begging, the issue of their so-called "unproductive labor" became a major topic, both of the emancipation debates and the Jewish Enlightenment, and Zionism thereafter. All parties, seeing a link between occupation and character formation, sought to alter the economic and occupational structure of Jewish life to "regenerate" what was widely considered a "degenerate" Jewish existence.

gripped the Jewish world from the eighteenth century on, especially in central Europe. Rahel Levin Varnhagen (1771–1833) was born into a wealthy, religiously observant family in Berlin. A brilliant intellectual, she turned her home into a literary salon, as did a number of other Jewish women in Berlin and Vienna. There, for the first time in the modern era, Jewish women facilitated a fascinating encounter. Into their homes they invited distinguished poets, authors, artists, philosophers, and political figures, Jews and non-Jews together in a spirit of friendship, religious harmony, and intellectual exchange.

Rahel had long lamented the fact that, because she was a woman, the gates to formal higher education were locked to her, and that her Jewish coreligionists still had to enter cities through a separate Jews' gate. She confronted a double discrimination and described her whole life as a "slow bleeding to death." In order to marry a minor Prussian diplomat, in 1819, Varnhagen converted to Protestantism. On her deathbed, she confessed her sense of "how painful to have been born a Jewess . . . to which [she] can ascribe every evil, every misfortune, every vexation that has befallen [her]."

Figure 1.1 The document pictured here is one of the scores of regularly published edicts in eighteenth-century Prussia that attempted to regulate the movement of Jews. Issued by Friedrich Wilhelm I on January 10, 1724, this edict declares "that all Jews who do not have a letter of passage must leave the country at once."

Source: Photo Scala, Florence/bpk, Bildagentur fuer Kunst, Kultur und Geschichte, Berlin.

The sentiments of Abraham Mendelssohn (1776–1835), the son of the Berlin philosopher Moses Mendelssohn, illustrate perfectly the deep anxieties of prominent Jews. Abraham and his wife raised their two children as Protestants so that greater social opportunities would be opened to them. Moses had been unable to impart to his son his own firmly held belief that conversion was too high a price to pay for political emancipation. In a letter Abraham wrote to his daughter upon her confirmation into the Lutheran Church in the summer of 1820, one can detect that he was first and foremost convinced of the efficacy of conversion. The fact that he also viewed Christianity as a religion that preached decency accorded with his humanitarian spirit:

> We have educated you and your brothers and sister in the Christian faith, because it is the creed of most civilized people, and contains nothing that can lead you away from what is good, and much that guides you to love, obedience, tolerance, and resignation.

Two years later, Abraham and his wife converted to the Lutheran faith. While most Jews remained within the fold, in the era of emancipation, social pressures and seductions led a small but nonetheless influential cohort of upper-class Jews in Germany to abandon Judaism.

In France, prior to the Revolution of 1789, about 3,500 Sephardim, mostly merchants, resided in the south and southwest of the country. They were involved in international trade, had a solid and far-flung network of fellow Sephardic merchants with whom they dealt, and operated a guild structure not dissimilar from that of their non-Jewish counterparts in the cities of southwest France. They were also, to a great extent, well acculturated in terms of language, dress, and overall deportment. However, the bulk of the French Jewish population was the approximately 30,000 Ashkenazim who lived in the northeastern regions of Alsace and Lorraine. They were wholly unlike the Sephardim of Bordeaux and Bayonne. The chief economic activities of this traditional Yiddish-speaking community were petty trade and moneylending. With great linguistic, cultural, religious, and economic differences in relation to their peasant neighbors, Alsatian Jews in some way typified the radically distinctive character of a Jewish community on the eve of the French Revolution.

By the mid-eighteenth century, as many as 8,000 Jews were in England, about 6,000 of them Ashkenazi immigrants who had come to Britain from the continent to join the previously established Spanish and Portuguese Jews. Between 1750 and 1815, a further 8,000–10,000 Jews arrived. These two waves of Ashkenazi settlers, mostly from Germany, Holland, and Poland, formed the basis for the modern Jewish community of Britain. (A modest number of Sephardim fleeing the Inquisition's renewed persecution in Spain and Portugal between 1720 and 1735 also contributed to the growth of the Jewish community.) Once in England, the new

immigrants, both Sephardim and Ashkenazim, joined the Jews of London and earned a living from selling a wide array of goods, ranging from oranges and lemons to watches and belt buckles. In particular, Jews became identified with hawking secondhand items, especially used clothing. Their calling out to prospective customers and aggressively pursuing them—competition was extremely tight—was a common cause of Christian complaint. London alone had hundreds of such Jewish merchants. The sight and sound of Jews, unfamiliar with the English language, calling out to Christian customers and dealing in goods that often came from dubious provenance heightened the perception of Jewish otherness. This same scene played out all over the continent.

The Jewish urge to emigrate developed because, with the exception of a handful of wealthy Jewish families in each country, the vast majority of eighteenth-century Jews were impoverished. Germany alone had nearly 10,000 Jews who were officially classified as *Betteljuden* ("beggar Jews"). In Holland, the material success enjoyed by the Sephardic community in the seventeenth century suffered reverses in the eighteenth century, with the closing of the United East India Company and the overall decline in Dutch trade. By 1799, the situation had gotten so bad that 54 percent of Dutch Sephardim lived off assistance from the Jewish community. Things were even more dire among the Ashkenazim, the vast majority of whom earned a living either as peddlers of secondhand clothes or as cattle dealers, butchers, and purveyors of various foodstuffs. None of this was sufficient to provide an adequate means of support, and at the close of the eighteenth century, a staggering 80 percent of Ashkenazim in Holland received welfare.

Sephardic Jews in the Ottoman Empire hardly fared any better, and they, too, experienced significant economic decline by the end of the eighteenth century. Prior to this time, however, fundamental changes in world trade resulted in an increasing share of international shipping going to Dutch, English, and French fleets in the Atlantic. Balkan trade routes and the Jews who were so heavily involved in the commerce that went through them became increasingly marginalized. As Jews were global traders and merchants, a downturn in one area could have a far-flung impact elsewhere. In Greece, the Salonikan textile industry, which was largely in Jewish hands and was a major source of income for Balkan Jews, went into severe decline, impoverishing many of the city's 30,000 Jews and those in communities far from Salonika itself. Arbitrary taxation, epidemics, the competitive rise of Greek and Armenian merchants, the inability of Jewish traders to adapt and develop new economic strategies, as well as the overall decline of the Ottoman Empire exacerbated the increasing impoverishment of Ottoman Jewish communities.

In Italy, too, the economic situation of the Jews was perilous. There, Jewish communities in Venice and Rome saw their Jewish populations shrink by about half throughout the course of the eighteenth century. Between 1700 and 1766, the Jewish community in Venice fell to about 1,700, while that in Rome dwindled to 3,000 by 1800. Other communities such as Mantua, Verona, and Padua merely stagnated. At the same time that Jewish poverty and demographic decline deepened, economic theories of wealth and poverty shifted, from mercantilism, with its emphasis on the accumulation of capital and government protectionism, to physiocracy, the economic idea that national wealth and productivity derived primarily from agriculture. This shift away from trade and toward domestic self-sufficiency would have an important impact on the way European social commentators viewed Jews and their participation in the economy. In the context of the new economic theory, Jewish poverty was seen as symptomatic of deeper moral inadequacies, thus making the physiocratic critique of trade that much more potent.

Aside from religious differences, Jewish poverty and its supposed links to criminality created an impression of the Jews as outside the bounds of respectable society. In his *Discourse on the Diseases of Workers* (1700), the Italian physician Bernadino Ramazzini observed that Jews, who were involved in tailoring, mattress restoration, and selling old linen and canvas for the manufacture of paper, "are a lazy race, but active in business." He complained that "they do not plough, harrow, or sow," and wryly added, "but they always reap." In England, both Jewish and Christian dealers in secondhand goods became infamous for purchasing stolen wares, and Jews became linked to various kinds of criminal activity, such as passing counterfeit coins, pickpocketing, shoplifting, burglary, stealing from carts and warehouses, assault, robbery, and even murder, as was the case in 1771, when nine London Jews broke into a premises in Chelsea with intent to rob but also shot dead the servant of the house. And in Germany, where Jews were largely restricted to pawnbroking and trade in secondhand clothes and other used items, they came into contact with members of the underworld and joined them in criminal activity. Some Jews formed bands of highway robbers, holding up stagecoaches in daring armed robberies. Other bands, with names such as the "Long Hoyum" and the "Great Dutch," specialized in commercial and residential burglaries. Jewish bands tended to be almost entirely male (sometimes, women could be found among Christian bands) and religiously observant, and the bandits continued to live in Jewish communities. Still other bands were composed of Christians and Jews. Significantly, prior to emancipation (and for quite some time thereafter), these mixed robber bands were among the first venues outside of intimate relationships in elite circles where religious difference was not a hindrance to genuine Christian–Jewish social interaction.

In the largest Jewish community in the world, that of Poland-Lithuania, the situation was quite different. By the eighteenth century, the Jewish population was 750,000 (550,000 in Poland and 200,000 in Lithuania). Since the Middle Ages, Jews had been encouraged to settle and trade there, while others took refuge in Poland in times of distress. After the Jews were expelled from the German city of Braunschweig in 1546, Eliezer Eilburg, a rabbi and medical practitioner, arrived in the Polish city of Poznan and declared it to be a place "where the Jews live in safety, each one under his vine and his fig tree, and there is none to make them fearful." In 1565, a visiting papal diplomat was astonished to observe that Jews

> possess land, engage in commerce, and devote themselves to study, especially medicine and astrology. . . . They possess considerable wealth and they are not only among the respectable citizens, but occasionally even dominate them. They wear no special mark to distinguish them from Christians and are even permitted to wear the sword and to go about armed. In general, they enjoy equal rights.

While it is unclear what the Vatican's man meant by "equal rights," Jews agreed that their situation was good. The eighteenth-century mystic Pinhas of Korets expressed the widely shared view among Jews that "in Poland exile is less bitter than anywhere else."

Indeed, the kinds of residential and occupational restrictions and humiliating distinctions that were the lot of western European Jews were largely unknown or unenforceable in premodern Poland, particularly in the areas of greatest Jewish settlement. Jews lived all over, but especially in the densely Jewish urban centers of the east and the south. In those places, Jews lived among Christians and not separate from them, exhibiting a preference, however, for living directly on or very near the market square, a sign of their deep involvement in the urban economies. Up to 75 percent of all Polish Lithuanian Jews lived in cities, towns, and villages owned by aristocrat-magnates, whose estates were the backbone of the economy. (By contrast, in lands held by the Crown, residential and occupational restrictions were in force, while lands owned by the Church sought to exclude Jews altogether. Catholic clergymen often expressed opposition to Jews living in marketplaces because they tended to be where church processions took place.) Fear that Jews would leave due to mistreatment or in search of better conditions elsewhere meant that the owners of the private towns where most Jews lived encouraged toleration, often in defiance of the wishes of the local Christian residents who resented Jewish competition. Magnates protected the welfare and security of the Jews in return for their managerial and financial skills. Thus, Jews enjoyed an important measure of power and protection from arbitrary abuse.

The central role of Jews in the magnate economy can be measured by the fact that Jews comprised 80–90 percent of merchants in many Polish towns, often making them the only inhabitants involved in commercial activities. Up to 60 percent of all domestic trade was in Jewish hands, while in the area of international trade, Jews were likewise prominent. By 1775, the ratio of Polish Jewish merchants to Polish Christian merchants attending the international commercial fairs in Leipzig was 7 to 1. The Jewish merchants exported furs, skins, textiles, and metal goods. (Into the twentieth century, these would remain traditional items of trade among Jews the world over.) They worked as jewelers, haberdashers, tailors, butchers, bakers, and bookbinders. At the beginning of the eighteenth century, one Christian municipality complained that instead of confining their commerce to their own street, as they were obliged to by law, Jews "brew beer and mead, sell wine, grain, fish, salt, candles, meat, etc., in [Christian] marketplace. They even sell pork, which they do not eat." The diversified nature of the Polish Jewish economy stood in marked contrast to that of western European Jews, who tended to earn a living exclusively through petty trade or small-scale commerce.

Unlike their coreligionists in western Europe, the Jews of Poland were more closely tied to the rural economy, trading in agricultural goods, between estates and local markets, where they were suppliers to villages. While many dealt in luxury goods prized by the nobility, such as gold, silver, gemstones, and furs, the unique feature of the Polish Jewish economy was the *arenda* system. This involved the leasing of large estates by Polish lords to Jews, who, in return for paying rent to the nobleman, were granted the monopoly on a host of commodities and methods of raising revenue. Jewish lessees earned income from tax and toll collection and sales of grain (often to court Jews in Germany), salt, and grain-based alcohol, one of the most important sources of income

for at least one-third of Poland's Jews in the eighteenth century. Vodka became as popular a drink among Polish commoners as beer, with income from sales of vodka on royal estates rising from 6.4 percent in 1661 to 40 percent after 1750.

Although the nobles retained most of the profits, the Jews were the ones most visibly associated with the alcohol trade. The Jewish innkeeper became a prominent figure in the region's social and cultural life. In his novel *The Slave*, the great twentieth-century Yiddish author Isaac Bashevis Singer described the Jewish *arrendar* (leaseholder) and his relation to the serfs, as it existed in Poland following the Chmielnicki massacres (1648–1650):

> Josefov by day was a confusion of sounds: chopping, sawing; carts arriving from the villages with grain, vegetables, fire wood, lumber; horses neighing, cows bellowing; children chanting the alphabet, the Pentateuch, the commentaries of Rashi, the Gemara. The same peasants who had helped Chmielnicki's butchers strip the Jewish homes now turned logs into lumber, split shingles, laid floors, built ovens, painted buildings. A Jew had opened a tavern where the peasants came to swill beer and vodka. The gentry, having blotted out the memory of the massacres, again leased their fields, woods, and mills to Jewish contractors. One has to do business with murderers and shake their hands in order to close a deal.

By the last third of the eighteenth century, the economic security of Polish Jewry started to deteriorate as the Polish aristocracy began to respond to calls to limit Jewish involvement in the alcohol trade. These demands often came from the lower (and sometimes impoverished) gentry, who saw themselves as competing with Jews for the favor and leases of the wealthy aristocratic landholders.

JEWS AND BOXING IN GEORGIAN ENGLAND

The emergence of Jewish prizefighters in the eighteenth century is testimony to the class character of the Jews in England. The greatest of these boxers was the champion Daniel Mendoza (1763–1836), who proudly fought under the moniker "Mendoza the Jew." His story testifies to the particular nature of Anglo-Jewish integration and identity. Mendoza tells us in his memoirs that his parents, who "were by no means in affluent circumstances," sent him "at a very early age to a Jews' school," where he "was instructed in English grammar, writing, arithmetic. [He] was also instructed in the Hebrew language, in which, before [he] quitted school, [he] made considerable progress."

Mendoza was a sports superstar, beloved by Jews and gentiles alike. No Jew on the continent could have expected to be embraced in this way by the public at large. In what was perhaps the earliest manifestation of sports merchandising, non-Jewish porcelain and crockery manufacturers produced commemorative pitchers and mugs bearing Mendoza's likeness. That Mendoza was a Jew and openly proud of it seemed to make little difference to the English public and certainly did not prevent him from occupying an important place in the popular culture of Georgian England. Songs were even composed about Mendoza and, in particular, the monumental battles he fought with his principal opponent, Richard Humphreys, whom Mendoza fought three times. One of these songs referred to the challenge Humphrey issued to Mendoza at the latter's boxing school and Mendoza's

comprehensive victory when their third and final fight took place at the end of September 1790:

My Dicky he went to the school, that was kept by this Danny Mendoza,

And swore if the Jew would not fight, he would ring his Mosaical nose, Sir,

His friends exclaimed, go-it, my Dicky, my terrible, give him a derry;

You've only to sport your position, and quickly the Levite will sherry.

Elate with false pride and conceit, superciliously prone to his ruin,

He haughtily stalk'd on the spot, which was turf'd for his utter undoing;

While the Jew's humble bow seem'd to please, my Dicky's eyes flash'd vivid fire;

He contemptuously viewed his opponent, as David was viewed by Goliath.

Now Fortune, the whimsical goddess, resolving to open men's eyes;

To draw from their senses the screen, and excite just contempt and surprise,

Produced to their view, this great hero, who promis'd Mendoza to beat,

When he proved but a boasting imposter, his promises all a mere cheat.

For Dicky, he stopt with his head,

Was hit through his guard ev'ry round, Sir,

Was fonder of falling than fighting,

And therefore gave out on the ground, Sir.

In 1768, pressure from the Church and lower gentry led the *Sejm*, the Polish parliament, to forbid Jews from keeping inns and taverns without the consent of municipal authorities. Though many estate owners ignored the legislation, Jewish

involvement in the alcohol trade slowly began to decline.

In addition to the economic incentive to push Jews out of the liquor trade came the accusation that they deliberately sought to ply

Figure 1.2   On May 6, 1789, Daniel Mendoza knocked out Richard Humphrey after 35 minutes.

Source: Art Collection 2/Alamy Stock Photo.

On May 6, 1789, Daniel Mendoza knocked out Richard Humphrey after 35 minutes. Mendoza, wanting to give Humphrey a sporting chance, allowed his opponent to rest for half an hour, only to resume the fight and knock him out again. This engraving, by an unknown non-Jewish artist, bore the caption "The Christian Pugilist proving himself inferior to the Jewish Hero, as Dr. Priestly when oppos'd to the Rabbi David Levi." Levi had offered the natural philosopher and theologian Joseph Priestly a ringing and learned defense of Judaism. The comparison between Levi and Mendoza sees the boxer become the physical, as opposed to spiritual, defender of his people. In the popular nineteenth-century boxing magazine *Boxiana*, Pierce Egan wrote in 1812 that Daniel Mendoza, "'though not the Jew that Shakespeare drew,' . . . was that Jew, the acknowledged pride of his own particular persuasion."

peasants with vodka to keep them drunk. This became a staple of eastern European antisemitic discourse, later compounded by expressions of political and national antagonism. Already by the start of the eighteenth century, Polish Jews were being painted as enemies, or at least as not being genuinely Polish, for to be Polish was to be Catholic.

The superior economic condition and greater occupational diversity of Polish Jewry found its analogue in the political sphere. After 1550, Polish Jewry enjoyed the most elaborate form of communal autonomy to be found anywhere in Europe. In each town, local Jewish government was led by a partnership of wealthy merchants and leaseholders on the one hand and the rabbinic elite on the other. Their authority existed by virtue of the fact that they paid most of the taxes; it was this that gave them the right to vote and hold office. By contrast, the general population of the community (*kehillah*) was excluded from participating in political affairs. The disenfranchised included all women, single men, and the poor, the latter group determined by how much one paid in taxation. (This was by no means unusual. Even after the French Revolution of 1789, the only people eligible to vote were males who paid a certain amount in taxes, while French women did not get the vote until 1945.) In the early modern Polish Jewish communities, the leadership employed a system of electors to appoint candidates to all official positions. The officers of the communal council (*kahal*) included executive officers (*parnasim* or *roshim*), assistants to the executives (*tovim*), treasurers (*ne'emanim*), auditors (*ro'eh heshbon*), committee heads (*gaba'im*), judges (*dayanim*), and tax assessors (*shama'im*).

Among their activities, the councils maintained religious institutions and courts, gave some support to schools, and provided charity, welfare, and loans. They were also responsible for the appointment of rabbis, the regulation of social and economic behavior, and dealing with the Polish authorities. The funds required to provide all these services were substantial and were raised through internal Jewish community taxes. The community was also served by a vast network of voluntary associations, many dedicated to the performance of specific religious commandments: burial, visiting the sick, and providing dowries for brides. Jewish community governments met at local and regional assemblies. Above these stood the Council of Four Lands (*Va'ad arba aratsot*). Established in 1580 and effectively a Jewish national parliament, it met twice annually at the great fairs in Lublin in the early spring and in Jaroslav in the late summer. By the eighteenth century, the council was composed of a lay assembly and a council of rabbis. These two bodies formed the two "houses" of Parliament, with the lay leadership proposing various plans and measures to tackle particular problems, while the rabbis then formulated the corresponding legislation or edict in strict accordance with the demands of Jewish law. The council represented Polish Jewry before the king, the Polish parliament (*Sejm*); formulated responses to attacks on Jews; and through the office of the *shtadlan* (intercessor), lobbied the *Sejm* to not pass legislation that was harmful to Jews.

The trend toward state centralization in the eighteenth century meant that bodies representing different estates, as well as ethnic and religious groups within the state, were increasingly considered unnecessary and an impediment to the creation of a rationalized bureaucracy. In 1754, Empress Maria Theresa abolished the first of the regional Jewish councils, that of Moravia. In Poland, the process of administrative centralization only compounded the main issue that confronted the Council of Four Lands, namely, the apportionment and collection of taxes owed by Jews to the Polish treasury. Generally, the council calculated a figure and paid the government in one lump sum and then extracted sums from local communities. The nobility had long complained that this was to their disadvantage, preferring instead a head tax. In 1764, Poland's last king, Stanislaw August Poniatowski, ascended the throne and implemented fiscal reforms, one of which was to make the state responsible for calculating the Jewish poll tax. With its principal task now taken from it, the Council of Four Lands was deemed redundant and was officially dissolved.

In contrast to Polish Jewry's economic importance and even social interaction with the majority, there was the social and economic marginalization of central and western European Jewry at the dawn of the modern era. However, this should not be mistaken for insularity. While these Jews may have had very limited social contact with non-Jews, they were, as Jews had always been, intimately aware of the world around them. Acculturation into contemporary mores long preceded the lifting of legal disabilities. In England, which had no real Jewish intellectual class to agitate for religious modernization, the process took root early, gradually, in a secular fashion, and perhaps more un-self-consciously than in other places. Uniquely in England, the majority of Jews began to adopt the social conventions of the English poor, while on the continent, Jews tended to imitate the fashions of the middle and upper classes.

Where English Jewry's modernization took place without open rebellion against communal leadership, the situation on the continent was different. There, communal authorities attempted to both ban Jewish participation in non-Jewish culture and curb the wayward behavior of community members. Take the case of the north German communities of Hamburg, Altona, and Wandsbek. An ordinance issued by the Hamburg *kahal* (community council) in 1726 declared, "Jews of both sexes are prohibited from walking to public houses or inns, or from visiting bowling alleys, fencing schools, or comedies on the Sabbath and holidays. Women under no circumstance should attend the opera."

Other ordinances castigated Jews for wearing the latest fashions from Paris, including the application of false beauty spots by women. Yet another warning sought to regulate the boisterous Jews of Hamburg in synagogue. There, things seem to have gotten out of control:

> [It is forbidden] under penalty of 10 Reichsthaler, that on certain holidays, no one is allowed to shoot gunpowder or launch rockets in the synagogue. [They must] also abstain from hitting and throwing, punishable by a fine of 4 Reichsthaler; therefore, everyone in the community is obligated to warn his children and servants that they should obey this order.

This indicates not only the rowdiness of Jewish synagogue worship at that time but also that in this period, the baroque age, when fireworks became a staple of European celebrations, Jews, too, incorporated them into their own religious festivities in imitation of their Christian neighbors.

The rabbis despaired of these trends, constantly complaining that they were losing their authority over a community that was regularly attending concerts, visiting bars, going to bowling alleys, wearing fashionable clothes, and embracing vernacular culture. In Venice, Rabbi Shmuel Aboab (1610–1694) warned not only against Jews attending the theater but also against an initiative to open their own "theatres and circuses, establishments which turn kosher Jewish maidens into prostitutes." In Germany, Rabbi Jonathan Eybeschütz (1690–1764) passed a ruling that:

> The Israelites are to keep away from places of [ill-repute] or other places in which transgressions are a common habit, and more so from places known as Schauspiel [theater], comedy, opera, and where plays are performed, since Our Sages of Blessed

Memory said: sitteth not in the seat of the jesters, these are the houses of theatres, namely those places in which comedians entertain.

Indeed, Jewish participation in non-Jewish culture was increasingly in evidence prior to emancipation. It becomes all the more intriguing to consider that just as some Jews were clearly becoming more visibly European, eighteenth-century Christian thinkers began to consider the extent to which that process would succeed, and even whether such a transformation was fully possible or even desirable.

JEWS THROUGH JEWISH AND NON-JEWISH EYES

When Europeans debated whether to award Jews civic equality and admit them to citizenship, discussions were often couched in ethnological and anthropological descriptions and assessments of Jews and Jewishness. Just who and what were the Jews? Could they become real Europeans? Opinion was mixed.

One of the most vivid descriptions of an eighteenth-century Jewish community comes from the German author Johann Wolfgang von Goethe (1749–1832), who ventured into the Frankfurt ghetto. The Judengasse, or Jews' Street, as the ghetto was called, was home to 3,000 inhabitants and was one of the largest, poorest, and most densely packed Jewish quarters in all of Europe. It was in these humble circumstances that the Rothschild family emerged. Mayer Amschel Rothschild (1743–1812), scion of the family, sent his sons to five European cities—Frankfurt, London, Paris, Vienna, and Naples—where they proceeded over the course of the nineteenth century to build the largest private banking house in the world and to amass a vast fortune. The Rothschild name had not yet become synonymous with modern capitalism and fabulous wealth when Goethe visited the Jewish quarter. The majority of Frankfurt's Jews were then simply very poor. In his autobiography, Goethe tells us:

> [T]he confinement, the dirt, the swarm of people, the accents of an unpleasant tongue, all made a disagreeable impression, even when one only looked in when passing outside the gate. It took a long time before I ventured in alone; and I did not return easily after once escaping the obtrusiveness of so many people untiringly intent on haggling, either demanding or offering. . . . And yet, they were also human beings, active, obliging, and even in the stubbornness with which they hung on their customs, one could not deny them respect.
>
> Besides this, the girls were pretty and quite liked it if they encountered a Christian boy on the Fischerfelde on the Shabbat, who proved himself friendly and attentive. I was extremely curious to learn their ceremonies. I did not leave until I had repeatedly visited the school, attended a circumcision, a wedding, and observed the festival of Sukkot. Everywhere I was welcomed, well entertained, and invited to return.

Goethe's amazement that the Jews were genuine "human beings" was not mere hyperbole. The accumulated impact of social and economic marginalization born of 1,700 years of Christian teaching—which portrayed the Jews as cruel and inhuman, responsible for the crucifixion of Jesus, doomed to eternal wandering, enjoined to murder Christian children to use their blood to bake matzah, and bent on cheating and extorting Christians—led Europeans, both learned and illiterate alike, to question the very humanity of the Jews and inspired attempts to find out what made them appear to be so fundamentally different from non-Jews.

In the eighteenth century, European expansion and the development of modern branches of science and the arts converged to help shape the way educated Europeans saw Jews. One of the fundamental principles of the Enlightenment was that all people were created equal. This notion, however, came into question with the increasing contact White Europeans had with other races as a result of slavery, imperialism, and the great voyages of discovery. The observation that human groups differed physically from one another could be translated into the spurious notion that humans could be lined up on a scale reflecting racial superiority and inferiority. In the eighteenth century, anthropologists and biologists initially concerned themselves with the task of classifying human groups. Soon, however, they sought to explain the reasons for such differences among humans. The father of modern anthropology, Johann Friedrich Blumenbach (1752–1840), believed that *Homo sapiens* had originated in the Caucasus and that human difference was the result of degeneration from the original human type—the Caucasian. (In Blumenbach's day, that group was said to include a wide range of peoples, among whom were Europeans, Jews, Arabs, and even Black Africans.) The further away from the Caucasus a group of people ended up settling, the greater their degeneration and, hence, their difference from the original Caucasians.

Blumenbach, a liberal and a man of the Enlightenment, rejected any notion of permanent racial characteristics and instead held that differences in human appearance were conditioned by climate, and those qualities were susceptible to alteration when geographic relocation had occurred. He wrote:

Unless I am mistaken, there are instances of peoples who after they have changed their localities and have migrated elsewhere, in the process of time have changed also their original form of countenance for a new one, peculiar to the new climate.

In 1795, Blumenbach turned his attention to Jews and observed that they were an exception to the "rules" of nature. Their wide geographic dispersion notwithstanding, different environments had been unable to effect a change in Jewish appearance:

Above all, the nation of the Jews, who, under every climate, remain the same as far as the fundamental configuration of [the] face goes, [are] remarkable for a racial character almost universal, which can be distinguished at the first glance even by those little skilled in physiognomy, although it is difficult to limit and express by words.

Could it be true that all Europeans were subject to change except the Jews?

According to other thinkers, the inalterability of the Jews had to do with their peculiar biology. In 1812, a Dutch anatomist who studied the skull of a 30-year-old Jewish man noted the peculiarly "large nasal bones," the "square chin," and the specifically Jewish "bony impressions on both sides of the lateral orbits." This, he argued, was due to the fact that "among Jews, the muscles primarily used for talking and laughing are of a kind entirely different from those of Christians." In 1812, the year the Jews were first emancipated in Prussia, the Berlin anthropologist Karl Asmund Rudolphi (1771–1832) remarked on the consistency of Jewish physical features, characteristics that set them apart from the European majority:

Under Julius Caesar [the Jews] were almost as deeply rooted in Rome as they are today in some states of Germany and in Poland,

and in a word, have become indigenous. . . . [But] their form has not changed. Their color is here lighter, there darker, but their face, their skulls everywhere have a peculiar character.

It is in the context of these sentiments that we must understand Goethe's astonishment that not only were the Jews "human" but that also their women were "pretty" as well. To be sure, behind this latter comment was Goethe's thrill of having entered into the "Oriental" world of the ghetto. He was drawn to the exotic beauty of the *other*. But more significant here than Goethe's visual seduction is the fact that his remarks are truly a departure from the norm. Most Christians had never thought about Jews in terms of beauty and humanity; rather, Jews represented religious enemies and economic rivals. It even took Goethe a few attempts to overcome his reticence and to stay and observe the ghetto and not run away, repulsed as he was by the sights and sounds of the *Judengasse*.

Certainly, some Christians may have seen fashionably attired Jews at the theater; some may even have shared the odd joke with them in the vernacular. But the majority of Christians saw Jews, prior to their emancipation, as impoverished, unintelligible, and unappealingly different. The French philosopher Denis Diderot spoke for many when he excoriated the Jews as an "angry and brutish people, vile and vulgar men, slaves worthy of the yoke [Talmudism] which [they] bear." He continued,

Go, take back your books and remove yourselves from me. [The Talmud] taught the Jews to steal the goods of Christians, to regard them as savage beasts, to push them over the precipice . . . to kill them with impunity and to utter every

morning the most horrible imprecations against them.

While Diderot may have been among the most intolerant thinkers in the so-called "age of toleration," it was his contemporary Voltaire who best summed up the Enlightenment's ambivalent attitude toward the Jews: "In short, they are a totally ignorant nation who have combined contemptible miserliness and the most revolting superstition with a violent hatred of all those nations which have tolerated them. Nevertheless, they should not be burned at the stake." The source of Voltaire's clemency was his enlightened belief that all people, including the Jews, had the capacity for improvement.

One of the principal arguments concerning the Jews was whether they were capable of becoming productive members of society. For many, their occupations and religious obligations rendered the Jews at best useless and at worst pernicious. Would they remain mired in petty trade and endless study, or would they be able to contribute to the general welfare? Some pointed out that the principal responsibility for the condition of the Jews lay with Christian society. In Germany in 1781, the Prussian bureaucrat Christian Wilhelm Dohm (1751–1820) published *On the Civic Improvement of the Jews*. He argued that the Jews be emancipated, for it would make them "happier, better people, more useful members of society." Dohm's remedy was typical of the German solution to the problem; while heartfelt, it was piecemeal. He wished to remove economic restrictions on Jews to encourage them to farm and to pursue arts and science. However, he wished to limit petty trade among them because he considered it corrupting, and finally, he insisted that Jewish access to government service jobs be restricted until such time as they had demonstrated that they had changed. This approach meant that the Jews were to be placed under constant surveillance and inspected for measurable improvement before they could be emancipated. Other German supporters of Dohm's fundamental position advocated a lengthy period of re-education for the Jews prior to emancipation. In Germany, Jewish progress toward emancipation was bound up with the gradual political development of German society. In France, by contrast, as we will see, emancipation was theoretically unconditional, coming as it did as a by-product of the Revolution.

On the continent, Dohm's tract, which ushered in the debate and spawned a vast number of publications on the Jewish question, was the first text that advocated the emancipation of the Jews based on the Enlightenment proposition that Jewish difference and deficiency (when he compared them to Christians) were historical rather than innate. In other words, nothing was inherently wrong with the Jews that would prevent them from fulfilling their obligations to the state. If Christians treated them well, then Jews would respond in kind, for, after all, declared Dohm, "the Jew is more man than Jew." Preceding Dohm in making such a claim was the Englishman John Toland. His tract of 1714, *Reasons for Naturalizing the Jews in Great Britain and Ireland on the Same Foot with All Nations*, expressed the conviction that "the Jews . . . are both in their origin and progress not otherwise to be regarded than under the common circumstance of nature." Whether in England or on the continent, such sentiments were relatively novel in that they downplayed Jewish difference and stressed the common humanity that Jews shared with non-Jews.

Not everyone was convinced. The German Hebrew Bible scholar Johann David Michaelis (1717–1791) strenuously objected to Dohm's position. Michaelis questioned both the capacity of Jews to become citizens and the wisdom of those who advocated for it. For Michaelis, the Jews were simply criminals. He even quantified it, claiming that they were "twenty-five times as harmful or more than the other inhabitants of Germany." Not just their individual behavior but their religion made "citizenship and the full integration of the Jew into other peoples" impossible. According to Michaelis, the Jew "will never be a citizen with respect to love for and pride in his country . . . and he will never be reliable in an hour of danger." Michaelis charged that Jews in a Christian army would neither eat the rations nor fight if the country was attacked on the Sabbath. Now it would seem from this that Michaelis was really advocating changes in Jewish behavior, suggesting that if Jews gave up, say, keeping kosher, then they could fit in. But Michaelis remained suspicious of Jewish "hypocrisy," on moral grounds; he claimed, "[W]hen I see a Jew eating pork, in order no doubt to offend his religion, then I find it impossible to rely on his word, since I cannot understand his heart." Here we can see how neither the traditional nor the assimilated Jew was acceptable to Michaelis. Until this point, Michaelis's brief against Jewish emancipation was made on cultural grounds. However, to cement his case against Jewish emancipation, he included another line of argumentation, concluding that "modern warfare requires a specific minimum height for the soldiers . . . [and] very few Jews of the necessary height will be found who will be eligible for the army." Here was a nonbehavioral feature that the Jews could never change. In other words, ultimately, their physical nature, rather than any cultural differences, prevented them from becoming German citizens.

In 1793, the German philosopher Johann Gottlieb Fichte (1762–1814), who admitted the Jews were worthy of human, if not political, rights, combined a moral argument against the Jews with the proposal for a physical solution to the "problem." Claiming that the Jews constituted a "state within a state," Fichte desired to eliminate Jews as a potentially subversive group: "I see absolutely no way of giving them civic rights; except perhaps, if one night we chop off all of their heads and replace them with new ones, in which there would not be one single Jewish idea." A radical solution, it indicates the extent to which some saw Jews as fundamentally at odds with the creation of modern society.

Despite the warm reception in some circles that Dohm's ideas received, resistance to full Jewish political emancipation in Prussia prevailed until the last quarter of the nineteenth century. More immediately, however, a major policy change took root in neighboring Austria. There, in 1782, the reform-minded emperor Joseph II issued his *Edict of Toleration*, which sought to "make the Jewish nation useful and serviceable to the State mainly through better education and enlightenment of its youth." The edict promised many social benefits to Jews. They would be permitted, even encouraged, to attend non-Jewish primary and secondary schools, learn crafts and new trades, and even train with Christian masters. The edict also repealed the law mandating Jews to wear beards, as well as distinctive and humiliating clothing. It also abolished body and town entrance taxes and eliminated the prohibition against Jews leaving their homes before noon on Sundays and (Christian) holidays.

To reap the benefits, Jews had to agree to some changes in their own behavior. They were to adopt German surnames, and most invasive of all, they were expressly forbidden to use Yiddish in written business and legal transactions.

To facilitate aesthetic and cultural changes prior to their attendance at state schools, Jews were to enroll in German-language Jewish schools. Joseph II hired a Jewish educator from Bohemia, Herz Homberg (1749–1841), to be director of these institutions. Homberg encountered stiff opposition from both rabbis and lay leaders, who denounced him to the authorities as a revolutionary and an atheist.

The overall intention of the edict was to wean Jews away from Jewish culture as part of the empire's goal of Germanizing its subject populations. To that end, the General School Order of 1774 made mass education a goal, while in 1785 the Habsburg monarchy opened German-language Jewish schools in the newly won territory of Galicia. The goal of these schools was to promote Galician Jewry's productiveness and acculturation. The *Edict of Toleration* was issued under the assumption that Jews were morally and aesthetically defective and required re-education. Behind its passage lay Joseph II's belief that by fostering educational, occupational, and linguistic changes, the Jews could be reformed and turned into worthy and virtuous citizens.

The promotion of policies designed to change Jewish culture came not only from non-Jewish society. Increasing numbers of Jews also sought to effect such changes. So as to encourage Jews to accept the *Edict of Toleration*, the enlightener Naftali Herz Wessely (1725–1805) published a Hebrew tract titled *Divrei shalom ve-emet (Words of Peace and Truth)* (1782). Wessely claimed that there were two distinct varieties of knowledge: *torat ha-adam*, secular knowledge, and *torat ha-elohim*, religious knowledge. He held that familiarity with the former would enhance the capacity of Jews to appreciate better the divine teachings. According to Wessely, secular knowledge "comprised etiquette, the ways of morality and good character, courtesy, proper syntax, and purity of expression." Wessely's work elicited a firestorm of protest, and in many places, it was literally burned. The Polish rabbi David ben Nathan Tevele of Lissa, one of the harshest of Wessely's many critics, referred to him as "a sycophant, an evil man, a man poor in understanding, the most mediocre of mediocre men," and described *Words of Peace and Truth* as "eight chapters of bootlicking." Reversing Wessely's formulation, Tevele declared, "[O]ur children shall study the sciences as an adornment; however, the foundations of their education will be in accordance with the command of our ancient sages of the Talmud." And then the Polish rabbi delivered the coup de grâce: "Wessely, a foolish and wicked man, of coarse spirit, is the one who lacks civility. A carcass is better than he!" The traditional Jewish aesthetic, with its own notions of beauty and propriety, now stood in stark contrast with those of the Christian and, more recent, Jewish bourgeoisie. The battle lines in Jewish society were drawn. For the time being, in central Europe, the traditionalists won the day, as very little came of Joseph's reforms. Their importance lay in their symbolic value, as an expression of the desire to change Jewish morality and aesthetics. But all over western and central Europe, Jewish society and culture were about to change radically—and nowhere more so than in France.

On the eve of the Revolution in 1789, the debate over what to do with the Jews also engaged French intellectual circles. In 1785, the primary French advocate of Jewish emancipation, the Abbé Grégoire (1750–1831), entered an essay contest sponsored by the Royal Academy of Metz. It posed the question, "Are there possibilities of making the Jews more useful and happier in France?" Grégoire, a liberal Jesuit priest, titled his response *An Essay on the Physical, Moral, and Political Regeneration of the Jews.* Following a principle already laid down by Dohm, Grégoire declared, "Let us

reform their education, to reform their hearts; it has long been observed that they are men as well as we, and they are so before they are Jews." For Grégoire, the reason that Jews stood in need of "regeneration" was that they had been made degenerate because of mistreatment by the Christian government. They differ from their non-Jewish neighbors because "they [had] never been treated as children of the country" in which they live but suffer from "the load of oppressive laws under which they groan." Grégoire counseled the opponents of Jewish emancipation: "You require that they should love their country—first give them one."

Nevertheless, even Grégoire's staunch support of the Jews was laced with ambivalence. As a man of the Enlightenment, he pushed for Jewish liberation while at the same time claiming that Jews displayed multiple "marks of degeneration." Many of these were physical. He pointed to their uncleanliness; the prevalence of skin disorders among them; a diet that "is more suited to the climate of Palestine than to ours"; the endogamy of the Jews, which "causes a race to degenerate, and lessens the beauty of individuals"; and the practice of early marriage, a moral failing with physical consequences "prejudicial to both sexes, whom it enervates." Some charges were even sexual. Provocatively, Grégoire claimed that Jewish women were nymphomaniacs and that Jewish men were chronic masturbators. Still, he believed that an open heart, kind treatment, and French citizenship would lead to the "physical, moral, and political regeneration of the Jews."

JEWS AND THE FRENCH REVOLUTION

The historical changes that would facilitate the practical implementation of a program of regeneration were unleashed during the

French Revolution. In 1789, the subject of both Protestant and Jewish emancipation came up for debate in the French National Assembly. With the Protestants soon admitted to citizenship alongside the Catholic majority, the question of Jewish eligibility became more urgent. Amid heated opposition, Count Stanislas de Clermont-Tonnerre, a Parisian deputy to the National Assembly and a Freemason, rose in the house on December 23 and declared, "The Jews should be denied everything as a nation, but granted everything as individuals." This justly famous phrase meant that Jews would be granted citizenship at the cost of communal autonomy, something many Jews would object to, even while welcoming the lifting of heavy taxes and other discriminatory impositions. The Jews could not maintain a state within a state, while the revolutionary state guaranteed them their rights as individuals. They would be granted liberty and equality on the condition that they become French and relegate religious practice to the private realm.

Despite the declarations on behalf of the Jews, the debate on Jewish citizenship was postponed because of the vociferous complaints of Alsatian deputies that the Jews from their region were unfit for citizenship. The relationship between Jews and non-Jews in Alsace-Lorraine was particularly tense. The peasants were constantly in debt to small Jewish moneylenders, while occupational restrictions forced Jews into competition with their Christian neighbors. These factors, combined with age-old cultural antipathies, led a deputy from Lorraine to ask the chamber, "Must one admit into the family a tribe that is a stranger to oneself, that constantly turns its eye to [another] homeland, that aspires to abandon the land that supports it?"

At this point, the Sephardic community saw that its chances for winning civic emancipation

would be improved by disengaging from the Ashkenazim of northeastern France. They turned to the authorities, invoking the letters of patent that they had held since the sixteenth century, guarantees that had effectively extended civic rights to this acculturated community for nearly 200 years. On January 28, 1790, the French National Assembly made the following declaration:

> All of the Jews known in France, under the name of Portuguese, Spanish, and Avignonese Jews, shall continue to enjoy the same rights they have hitherto enjoyed, and which have been granted them by letters of patent. In consequence thereof, they shall enjoy the rights of active citizens.

With this, the Sephardim of France became the first Jews in Europe to enjoy complete equality.

This situation meant that the Ashkenazim remained unemancipated and politically isolated. However, revolutionary politics aided their cause. The radical Jacobin faction had assumed increasing dominance in Paris, which, in turn, became decisive in the National Assembly. In January 1791, the Jews of Paris, dressed in their National Guard uniforms, argued their case before the Paris Commune, which, in turn, informed the assembly that "general will" demanded that the Jews be emancipated. The issue played out a while longer until September 28, 1791, when the Ashkenazim were finally granted citizenship. All the Jews of France had now been emancipated.

Radical revolutionary politics had worked to the benefit of Jewish emancipation, as the Jacobins countered their critics by declaring that whosoever was opposed to Jewish emancipation was, in effect, an enemy of the Revolution. Even prior to the onset of what is known as "The Reign of Terror," few risked turning their backs on the Revolution. It would be wrong, however, to simply assume that the legislative decision to emancipate the Ashkenazim was motivated by fear of the Jacobins; rather, the Jews were emancipated in France because of their symbolic significance. Considered degenerate and corrupt, Jews were the ideal sample group for those wishing to test the Revolution's ability to transform the "degraded and corrupt" into model revolutionary citizens. No class had so far to rise, and no group in Europe would so challenge the Enlightenment's and the Revolution's optimistic claims about human nature's capacity for improvement as the Jews. The Jews were thus part of a grand "thought experiment."

Although, as elsewhere, the process of Jewish acculturation in France had already begun at least a century before the Revolution, in the wake of their emancipation, Jews rapidly and eagerly adopted French customs and habits. They also took up arms in large numbers in defense of the nation, served in government posts, increasingly sent their children to French schools, and became deeply integrated into the economy of France. They did all this and remained true to Judaism. Jewish emancipation went wherever Napoleon led his armies. Like the Jews of France before them, these Jewish communities would also enter uncharted territory as they sought to synthesize the demands of citizenship and Judaism.

Napoleon's Jewish Policy

As the Revolution gave way to empire, Napoleon Bonaparte set about conquering Europe, and Jews were emancipated wherever French armies were victorious: Holland in 1796, northern and central Italy in 1796–1798, and the western regions of Germany in 1797. While this was in keeping with the political goals of the Revolution, Napoleon, who seized power as the First Consul of France in 1799, also enacted policies that ran counter to the radical ideals of liberty, equality, and fraternity. One area where his conservatism was in evidence was his Jewish policy.

The emancipation of French Jewry did not end the debate on the Jewish question. Serious doubts lingered about whether the Jews could be regenerated. As ever, the focus fell on the Jews of Alsace. Tensions between Jews and peasants had always been high in this eastern province, but ironically, they increased with the new opportunities both groups came to enjoy as a result of the Revolution. When the National Assembly sold off the confiscated lands of émigré nobles, Alsatian peasants were free to make land purchases. Short of funds, they borrowed money from Jewish moneylenders, and quite soon, some 400,000 peasants were in deep debt to a few thousand Jews. This situation only got worse when Napoleon changed France's currency, making the money that had been lent to the peasants useless. How would they pay off their loans to their Jewish creditors? They could not. Between 1802 and 1804, Alsatian courts foreclosed on new peasant holdings and passed the aristocratic estates to Jewish lenders. Simmering hatred for Jews erupted into full-scale confrontation.

Seizing on this situation, and buoyed by Napoleon's increasingly autocratic and regal pretensions, royalists speaking on behalf of the aggrieved peasantry accused Alsatian Jews of profiteering from the Revolution. In this charge lay the origins of a European-wide canard that described Jews as beneficiaries of modernity, conspiring to orchestrate historical developments to their own advantage, while "true nationals" suffered the consequences. For modern antisemites, many of whom had a romantic attachment to the distant collective past, the claim that Jews were responsible for bringing about the destabilizing conditions of modernity became one of the central charges against them. Antisemites celebrated the mythical time prior to Jewish emancipation as an age of alleged perfection, an era to which they wished to return. Everything they loathed and considered rotten about contemporary society could be and was often attributed by them to the emancipation of the Jews, the most immediately visible beneficiaries of the emancipation of European society.

Indeed, Napoleon saw the emancipation of Alsatian Jewry as a failed political experiment. Neither the spirit of the Enlightenment nor the power of the Revolution had been able to effect the anticipated regenerative changes. Complaints against Jews did not die out. Inundated with peasant grievances, Napoleon, who had not hitherto given much consideration to Jews and was inherently hostile to commercial culture, now turned to the Jews, whose traits he felt revealed the socially disruptive effects of trade. In 1806, to assuage the hostility of the Alsatian peasantry, Napoleon suspended all debts owed to Jews for one year. Although he rejected a recommendation that the Jews be expelled, and another that emancipation be rescinded, the debt suspension was merely the beginning of Napoleon's reaction. His Jewish policy became part of his larger plans for scaling back the gains of the Revolution and embarking upon the administrative restructuring of France. His goal was to bring both the Catholic and Protestant Churches under centralized control. Likewise, the Jewish community would also be subject to the discipline of the state.

To effect the integration of Jews into the life of the nation, and to assert greater control over them, Napoleon first set out to learn about the Jews, a group about which he knew barely anything. Like earlier Enlightenment-inspired investigations, this attempt was also ethnographic and sociological in nature. On July 29, 1806, Napoleon convened an Assembly of Jewish Notables, a body of 112 distinguished lay and clerical Jewish leaders from France and French-controlled Italy. The emperor put before the delegates a list of 12 questions designed to ascertain the relationship of French Jews to the state and to their fellow citizens. Reflecting the atmosphere of mistrust, Count Molé, a member of the Council of State and an opponent of Jewish emancipation, introduced the questions to the assembly with a most threatening preamble:

> The conduct of many among those of your persuasion has excited complaints, which have found their way to the foot of the throne: These complaints were founded on truth; and nevertheless, His Majesty has been satisfied with stopping the progress of the evil, and he has wished to hear you on the means of providing a remedy.

Napoleon's wishes were further clarified by his minister:

> Our most ardent wish is to be able to report to the emperor, that, among individuals of the Jewish persuasion, he can reckon as many faithful subjects, determined to conform in everything to the laws and to the morality, which ought to regulate the conduct of all Frenchmen.

Here was the first serious loyalty test administered to the Jews by a modern state. The stakes were enormous.

The questions were as follows: (1) Is it lawful for Jews to marry more than one wife? (2) Is divorce allowed by the Jewish religion? (3)

Can Jews and Christians marry? (4) In the eyes of Jews, are Frenchmen considered brethren or strangers? (5) What conduct does Jewish law prescribe toward Frenchmen not of their religion? (6) Do Jews born in France and treated by the law as French citizens consider France their country, and are they bound to defend it and obey its laws? (7) Who names the rabbis? (8) What kind of police jurisdiction do the rabbis have among the Jews? (9) Are the forms of elections of the rabbis and their police jurisdiction regulated by Jewish law, or are they only sanctioned by custom? (10) Are there professions from which Jews are excluded by their law? (11) Does Jewish law forbid Jews taking usury from their brethren? (12) Does it forbid or allow usury toward strangers?

In August of 1806, the assembly gave its official response. Some of the questions were easy to answer. Insisting that Jews considered Frenchmen their brothers, the assembly asserted that Jews were loyal to France and its laws and were prepared to defend it. Indeed, Jewish law mandated that non-Jews be treated as equals. True to the spirit of enlightened toleration, the assembly claimed, "[W]e admit of no difference but that of worshipping the Supreme Being, everyone in his own way." In a departure from the tradition of communal authority, the assembly averred that rabbinical authority extended only into the spiritual realm. The question concerning intermarriage proved far trickier. The rabbis could not sanction marrying outside the faith, so they gave a subtle and carefully crafted response to avoid giving offense. They replied that the Torah did not prohibit Jews and Christians marrying and explicitly enjoined against unions only with the seven Canaanite nations, as well as Amon, Moab, and Egypt. With regard to marriage to French men and women, the rabbis noted that Jewish marriages, to be considered valid, required only a betrothal ceremony called *kiddushin*, as well as special benedictions. These can only be performed if both bride and groom "consider[ed] these ceremonies as sacred." Without the blessings, the assembly concluded the marriage was civilly but not religiously binding. Shrewdly, the rabbis observed, "Catholic priests themselves would [not] be disposed to sanction unions of this kind"—that is, unions that had no sacramental character.

Of particular interest is the first question, regarding polygamy. While few would have known that polygamy among Ashkenazim was expressly forbidden in a ban issued by Rabbi Gershom ben Yehuda (ca. 960–1028), a towering German Talmud scholar and communal leader, most people, even those as ignorant about Judaism as Napoleon, would have observed that Jewish men took only one wife. Why, then, would this have been the first question to which he sought an answer? If we bear in mind that the questionnaire was designed to test the ability of the Jews to become Europeans, the interest in Jewish marriage customs reveals the extent to which Judaism was seen as Oriental, its practices exotic and non-Western. With its titillating implications of a harem, few rituals challenged Christian notions of morality to the extent that polygamy did. Aberrant sexuality and racial inferiority are two tropes of a shared discourse. Recall the pro-emancipationist Abbé Grégoire's claim that Jewish men and women were hypersexualized beings, or Goethe's fascination with Jewish beauty. Sexuality became central to the modern discourse on Jews and Judaism. Indeed, the physical character of Jews, perhaps even more than their religious identities, would take the leading role in non-Jewish and Jewish discussions of Jewish status and Jewish fate in the modern period.

Napoleon was satisfied with the answers he received and correctly assumed that the Jews of France constituted a loyal community that wished to serve him and the nation. Not content to leave it at that, Napoleon sought to make the ratification of the assembly's responses a grand affair, one that would confirm his own magnanimity and imperial rule. To this end, he convened a Grand Sanhedrin, named after the supreme religious and judicial body of Jewish antiquity. Its seeming revival after 1,700 years sent a surge of messianic excitement through the Jewish world. Ever the keen strategist, Napoleon called the Sanhedrin not merely to exact the loyalty of Alsatian Jews. By 1807, after defeating the Prussians, the French established the Duchy of Warsaw as a semi-independent Polish commonwealth. With military supplies in great demand, Napoleon turned to eastern European Jewish army contractors, who made available to him the military supplies his troops needed. As Napoleon correctly envisioned, in the aftermath of the meeting of the Sanhedrin, eastern European Jews greeted him with enthusiasm as an enemy of Polish backwardness and Russian autocracy. The Grand Sanhedrin confirmed the widespread Jewish belief that Napoleon had been "chosen [by God] as an instrument of His compassion." The Italian representative at the Grand Sanhedrin, Rabbi Salvatore Benedetto Segre (1757–1809), even declared that Napoleon was a greater man than any figure from the Bible. By 1812, when Napoleon failed to bring liberation to the Jews of eastern Europe, they turned against him, and like most Europeans, eastern European Jewry likewise saw Napoleon as a tyrant to be crushed, a symbol of a failed revolution.

Meanwhile, the Sanhedrin, Count Molé claimed,

> [would] bring back the Jews to the true meaning of the law, by giving interpretations, which shall set aside the corrupted glosses of commentators; it will teach them to love and to defend the country they inhabit; but will convince them that the land, where, for the first time since their dispersion, they have been able to raise their voice, is entitled to all those sentiments which rendered their ancient country so dear to them.

France, in other words, would be the Jews' new holy land, and they were to love it and serve it as loyally as they did the original. The 71 members of the Grand Sanhedrin concurred that the Torah was both religious law and political constitution and was fully consistent with French law. The former was immutable, but the latter was only in use "for the government of the people of Israel in Palestine when it possessed its own kings, pontiffs and magistrates; . . . these political dispositions are no longer applicable, since Israel no longer forms a nation." Judaism would be reconstructed as a privately held faith, and Jewish identity would be reconstituted to create Frenchmen of the Mosaic persuasion—the self-conception that western European Jews would embrace in the nineteenth century.

Napoleon was not yet finished with the Jews. In 1808, as part of his administrative centralization of France, Napoleon established the Consistory, the formally constituted representative of French Jewry to the national government in Paris. It continues to function to this day as the chief administrative body of French Jewry. At the same time, Napoleon extended the anti-Jewish measures of Alsace. New laws, known among Jews as the Infamous Decrees, limited their residence rights and suspended all debts owed to them for ten years. This was a retrograde step that, while not rescinding emancipation, certainly contravened the spirit of the Enlightenment and the Revolution.

Following Napoleon's defeat and the restoration of the Bourbon monarchy to the throne, the Infamous Decrees were not renewed, and Judaism was accorded complete equality with Christianity in 1831. The state paid the salaries of Consistory officials, something the Revolution had guaranteed for Christian denominations but not for Jews. As far as French Jews were concerned, practice had finally caught up with the egalitarian sentiment that had swept the nation since 1789.

THE ANGLOPHONE WORLD

While no formal emancipation occurred in the English-speaking world, the story of the attainment of equal rights in England should be seen in the larger context of European Jewish emancipation, for it will permit us to see what was unique about the fate of Jewish communities in Britain and the wider Anglophone world. In England, resolution of the "Jewish question" was bound up with the process of according religious "dissenters" their civic rights. The quest in England focused on the right to hold political office; Jews had been naturalized in British common law since the end of the eighteenth century and had already long enjoyed most freedoms. This also held true for dissenting Protestants and Catholics, but when they each were accorded full rights to hold office in 1829, only the anomalous situation of the Jews remained exceptional. Between 1830 and 1833, emancipation bills that came before Parliament were passed in the House of Commons but rejected in the House of Lords.

Facing few social or legal restrictions, Anglo-Jewry became increasingly anglicized and materially comfortable. However, community elites resented the discrepancy between their anomalous political status and their cultural and economic position. As one of the leaders of the drive for Jewish emancipation put it in 1845, the Jews

desired to be placed on an equality in point of civil privileges with other persons dissenting from the established church not so much on account of the hardship of being excluded from particular stations of trust or honor, as on account of the far greater hardship of having a degrading stigma fastened upon us by the laws of our country.

Over time, Jewish legal disabilities were lifted. In 1830, Jews were able to open shops in the city of London; in 1833, they were free to practice as barristers; and in 1845, the Municipal Relief Act permitted Jews to take up all municipal offices. In 1854 and 1856, respectively, Jews were permitted to study at Oxford and Cambridge. Despite the strides made in the third and fourth decades of the century, the one hurdle Jews in England were still unable to straddle was that of assuming a seat in Parliament. The issue was put to test several times by Lionel de Rothschild (1808–1879). He had repeatedly been elected to Parliament by the City of London but steadfastly refused to swear the obligatory Christian oath. Eventually, a compromise was reached whereby each house of Parliament could determine its own oath, and in 1858, Rothschild took a nondenominational oath that allowed him to become England's first Jewish member of Parliament. The last act in the drawn-out legislative drama came in 1871, when the final barriers against Jews holding faculty and administrative positions at Oxford and Cambridge were lifted. In all, English Jews were never as vigorous as their continental coreligionists in demanding the lifting of legal barriers because, over the course of the nineteenth century, very few Jews felt aggrieved

AN OLD LANGUAGE FOR A NEW SOCIETY: JUDAH MONIS'S HEBREW GRAMMAR

The story of the first Hebrew grammar to be published in the United States reflects a deep ambivalence toward Jews in colonial America. Judah Monis (1683–1764) was America's first Hebrew teacher and taught at Harvard College from 1722 to 1760. Born in either Italy or North Africa into a family of Portuguese *conversos*, Monis migrated first to New York and then moved to Cambridge, Massachusetts, and received his MA from Harvard in 1720, becoming the first Jew to receive a college degree in the American colonies. At that time, all Harvard upperclassmen were required to study Hebrew. As part of his graduation requirements, Monis wrote *A Grammar of the Hebrew Tongue*, and in 1720, he submitted a handwritten copy of it to the Harvard Corporation for its "judicious perusal." On April 30, 1722, the corporation "[v]oted, [t]hat Mr. Judah Monis be approved instructor of the Hebrew Language." The positive attitude of Harvard toward Hebrew was offset by its requirement that all members of its faculty be professing Christians. One month before taking up the appointment, Monis converted to Christianity. For this act, he was severely criticized by both Jews and Christians, both parties seeing him as an opportunist. Monis argued for his sincerity with the publication of three books defending the deep faith that lay behind his conversion. Nevertheless, he was greeted with great suspicion, and the records of the Cambridge First Church record that he secretly observed the Jewish Sabbath on Saturdays. Both Church and Harvard records refer to Monis as "the converted Jew," "the converted rabbi," and "the Christianized Jew."

In 1724, to save his students from the burden of copying it by hand, Monis petitioned the Harvard Corporation to publish his *Grammar*. After much procrastination, Hebrew type was shipped from London, and in 1735, 1,000 copies of Monis's *Grammar* were published. It was the first Hebrew textbook published in North America.

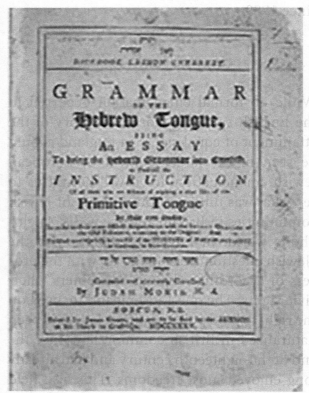

Figure 1.3 Frontispiece of Judah Monis's, *A Grammar of the Hebrew Tongue, Being an Essay to Bring the Hebrew Grammar into English, to Facilitate the Instruction of All Those Who Are Desirous of Acquiring a Clear Idea of This Primitive Tongue by Their Own Studies*. Judah Monis. Dickdook Leshon Gnebreet: A Grammar of the Hebrew Tongue. Boston, 1735. Hebraic Section, African and Middle Eastern Division, Library of Congress (042.00.00)

Source: Library of Congress (042.00.00).

by the remaining disabilities in England. In fact, the majority thrived in its relatively tolerant atmosphere. Compared to the situation on the continent, the good fortune of Anglo-Jewry was enviable.

Away from Europe in the rest of the English-speaking world, the situation was somewhat different, for official decrees of emancipation were not required. In 1654, Portugal conquered Dutch Brazil and expelled the small Jewish community of Recife. Some of the exiles went to Suriname, Curaçao, and Jamaica, while 23 of them made their way to New Amsterdam (later renamed New York)—they were the first Jews to come to North America. Though opposed to admitting them, Governor Peter Stuyvesant yielded to the directors of the Dutch West India Company, who granted the Jews the same "civil and political liberties" enjoyed by their coreligionists in Holland. Later, under British rule, the Plantation Act of 1740, which granted naturalization to foreign Protestants and Jews throughout the British Empire, saw Jews in the American colonies gain the full array of civil liberties, except for restrictions on holding public office in Maryland and New Hampshire. Those bans were lifted in 1826 and 1877, respectively.

The 2,500 Jews in the United States in 1776 had been guaranteed liberty within the general constitutional context. The security enjoyed by American Jews was enshrined in law in Article VI of the Constitution of 1789, which declared, "[N]o religious test shall ever be required as a qualification to any office or public trust under the United States." Of course, unofficial social restrictions against American Jews entering certain venues, institutions, and fields of endeavor prevailed into the twentieth century, but this rarely vitiated

Jewish enthusiasm for America. On August 17, 1790, Moses Seixas, the warden of Congregation Kahal Kadosh Yeshuat Israel, better known as the Hebrew Congregation of Newport, Rhode Island, wrote to George Washington, welcoming the newly elected first president of the United States on his visit to that city. Washington responded warmly to the invitation and, in so doing, took the opportunity to lay out the fundamental American principles of religious freedom and separation of church and state:

> May the Children of the Stock of Abraham, who dwell in this land, continue to merit and enjoy the goodwill of the other Inhabitants; while every one shall sit under his own vine and fig tree, and there shall be none to make him afraid.

Annually, Newport's Congregation Kahal Kadosh Yeshuat Israel, now known as the Touro Synagogue, re-reads Washington's letter in a public ceremony. (*See box*, "An Old Language for A New Society: Judah Monis's Hebrew Grammar.")

In Canada, where the first Jewish settlement dates to 1759, Jews mostly settled in Montreal and were engaged in the fur trade. While free to practice their religion and run for office, they were not able to actually hold office until 1832, when legislation was enacted to scrap the mandatory Christian oath for those wishing to take their seat in Parliament.

In Australia, where White settlement dates to 1788, at least eight Jews were among the convicts on the First Fleet transported to Botany Bay in Sydney. By 1830, about 300 Jewish convicts had arrived, and by 1845, that number had swelled to 800. Most were freed after serving short sentences and took their place in the life of the colony without hindrance. The unique feature of the Australian Jewish community in the era of emancipation is that Australia is the only country in the world that had a Jewish population from the very first day of its European settlement. Jews were therefore not seen as immigrants or interlopers. Their right to reside in Australia was never questioned. A pioneer society at great remove from Europe, Australia provided Jews with a level of freedom and acceptance rarely equaled elsewhere. From the beginning, Jews enjoyed full civil rights, were free to vote and sit in Parliament, and received grants of Crown land for

cemeteries and synagogues. Jacob Levi Saphir, a European rabbi who sojourned in Australia between 1861 and 1863, recorded the following in his Hebrew travelogue *Even Sapir (The Sapphire Stone)*:

There is no discrimination between nation and nation. The Jews live in safety, and take their share in all the good things of the country. They also occupy Government positions and administrative posts. In this land [Australia] they [gentiles] have learnt that the Jews also possess good qualities, and hatred towards them has entirely disappeared here.

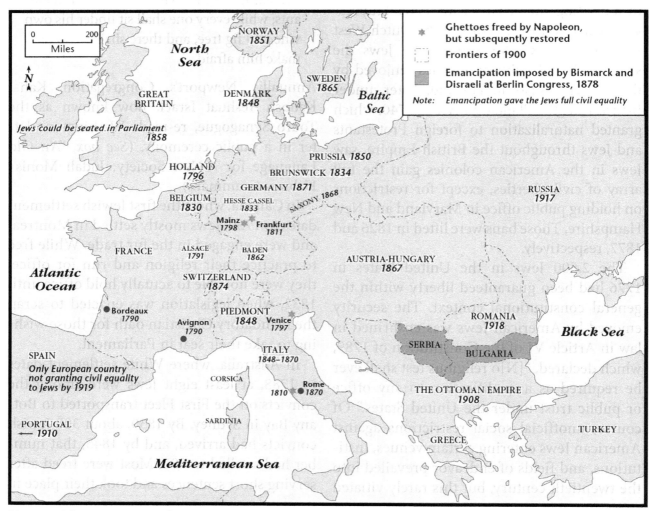

Map 1.1   The Emancipation of European Jewry, 1790–1918. Civic emancipation was a protracted process that began with the French Revolution and continued into the era after World War I. The variety of dates on this map reflects the uneven process of Jewish emancipation.

In South Africa, Jews, too, enjoyed religious and civic freedom from the early nineteenth century. Only in the Dutch territories, where being a member of the Reformed Church was a prerequisite for holding office, were Jews (and very often Catholics) summarily and periodically excluded from full participation.

JEWISH EMANCIPATION IN SOUTHERN AND CENTRAL EUROPE

An important feature of the emancipation process is the extent to which it differed from place to place. As we have seen, in France and the territories it conquered with its revolutionary armies, emancipation was extended to the Jews as part of the legacy of the French Revolution. In the English-speaking world, emancipation was granted through the passage of discrete pieces of legislation, which followed naturally upon common law or was granted automatically without any formal declaration or legal process (*see* Map 1.1).

Italian Jewry experienced yet another kind of emancipatory process, one that was unique to it. When the Jews of Italy were first emancipated in 1797 by Napoleonic forces, they were still a largely traditional community living in ghettos first established in the sixteenth century. However, they quickly embraced the social and economic opportunities that came in the wake of emancipation. This rapidly transformed Italy's 40,000 Jews, making them an integral part of the country's minuscule bourgeoisie. After their newly won freedoms were rescinded in the wake of Napoleon's defeat, Jews were drawn to the Italian liberation movement, and many became deeply involved in secret revolutionary societies, or "Carbonari." These groups promoted a liberal agenda of civil rights and an end to clerical and aristocratic rule.

Thus, the revolutionaries seeking to unify Italy—who finally succeeded in 1859—saw Jews as reliable and ideal allies in the struggle against the forces of reaction. During the Risorgimento, the period of national revival extending from 1830 to 1870, when the ideological and military battles for unification were fought, Jews by the thousands actively participated in the struggle, many earning honor and distinction along the way.

Secular and deeply embedded in modern Italian culture, Italian Jews were heavily invested in the project of Italian nation-building. The architects of Italian unification, Giuseppe Mazzini (1805–1872), Giuseppe Garibaldi (1807–1882), and Count Camillo Cavour (1810–1861), all recognized the political, military, and financial contributions made by Jews. They considered Jews to be central to the foundation of the Italian republic and championed their emancipation, the progress of which followed on the heels of nationalist military victories, with the Jews of Rome the last community to be liberated in 1870. Italian Jews displayed a degree of loyalty and patriotism that set them apart from other continental Jewries in two ways. First, neither Sephardic nor Ashkenazic, Italian Jews practiced the Apam rite of prayer, so-called because the Hebrew initials of four Italian communities—Asti, Fossano, Alessandria, and Moncalvo—form the word *Apam*. Second, Italian Jewry's distinctiveness was reinforced in the political realm; it was only in Italy that the nationalist leadership sided with the Jews. In most of Europe, nationalist forces looked upon Jews with suspicion, if not outright hostility. The acceptance of Jews by Italian nationalists makes the case unique. Italy saw the election of Europe's first Jewish minister of war, Giuseppe Ottolenghi

(1838–1904), and was the first nation in Europe to have a Jewish prime minister, Luigi Luzzatti (1841–1927), who served in that role from 1910 to 1911, after sitting in parliament for many years. Already by 1871, 11 Jews had been elected to the Italian parliament, a greater number than in any other country in Europe.

In central Europe, Germany presents us with a somewhat-different model of Jewish emancipation. The process was shaped by the fact that Germany did not become a unified state until 1871. When in 1782 Dohm launched the emancipation debate with his *On the Civic Improvement of the Jews*, Germany was made up of 324 separate principalities. The progress of emancipation was uneven, with some German Jewish communities being recipients of civic rights, thanks to French conquest. This left vast numbers of Jews behind. Even after the Congress of Vienna set about restructuring Europe in the wake of Napoleon's defeat in 1815, Germany was still made up of 38 different principalities. This ensured that disparities in political status would continue to characterize the situation.

The problem confronting proponents of Jewish emancipation in Germany was two-fold. First, unlike the situation in France, Holland, and the English-speaking world, emancipation remained conditional. Rather than simply granting emancipation by decree, German authorities sought to micromanage the progress of emancipation with a carrot-and-stick approach. Upon detecting signs of "improvement," authorities exhibited greater inclination to "reward" the Jews. This only served to enhance optimism and frustration and, eventually, create disappointment. Having instituted cultural, religious, and occupational changes, Jews considered themselves to have done enough to warrant full freedom. By contrast, seeing some improvement, German

authorities now insisted on more. In this situation, they were able to continually move the metaphorical "finish line," while Jews were forever chasing it. Results-oriented as opposed to ideologically committed, the Germans could not, as the French had done, leave it to the Enlightenment and the liberal political system it spawned to "regenerate" the Jews. Emancipation was thus not considered an inherent right but a reward for a self-regenerative job well done.

The second structural problem that impeded full-scale Jewish emancipation in Germany stemmed from the challenge of emancipating a group within a society that was not yet fully emancipated. The political structures that made for Jewish emancipation in England, the rest of the English-speaking world, and France were absent in Germany. It was not a unified state, a constitutional monarchy, a liberal republic, or a revolutionary nation.

The rocky path of Jewish emancipation in Germany can be divided into three distinct stages:

1. *Between 1781 and 1815*, the "Jewish question" was debated and certain legislative measures were enacted, such as the edict of 1812 that made Jews "natives and citizens of the Prussian state" with "the same civic rights and liberties as those enjoyed by Christians."

2. *Between 1815 and 1848*, in the wake of the post-Napoleonic reaction, the emancipation that Jews in formerly French territories in western Germany had enjoyed was annulled. Popular sentiment, informed by a general anti-French, anti-Enlightenment, and reactionary Christian attitude, staunchly opposed Jewish emancipation. This attitude manifested itself most dramatically in 1819 with the Hep Hep riots, so-called because the rampaging mobs

shouted out "Hep Hep, Jud' vereck!" (Hep Hep, Jews drop dead!). The violence first erupted in the city of Würzburg among rioting university students, then rapidly spread to southern and western Germany, and then north to Hamburg and Copenhagen, and even south to Cracow. Ostensibly a response to the emancipation debate, the riots indicate the passions that the subject evoked. Würzburg, with its tiny Jewish population of 30 families, is a measure of how radically hostile the opposition to the idea of Jewish equality was. Though local governments offered physical protection to Jews, authorities noted that the extension of civil rights to Jews was so inflammatory that withholding emancipation was the most prudent course.

3. *Between 1871 and 1933*, Germany went from being a unified nation for the first time to being ruled by the Nazis. During this period, the country's 600,000 Jews were finally emancipated and became central to the Germany's intellectual, social, cultural, and commercial life. The year 1933 marks the date that emancipation was rescinded.

While Jewish emancipation in Germany was tied to state-building, just as it had been in Italy, the intensity of the debate was far greater in Germany. The respective national liberation movements also viewed Jews differently. While German nationalists tended to see Jews as an impediment to the creation of a homogenous Christian nation, in Italy the nationalists saw Jews as valuable and loyal allies in their struggles, while in France there was no other way to organize the state other than to grant citizenship to all.

Jewish emancipation in central Europe was more than a strict change in legal status.

It came with the expectation of and desire for acculturation. After 1871, most middle-class Jews in western and central Europe expressed their Jewishness through their voracious consumption of European high culture. Whether through the attainment of a university education or by becoming aficionados and patrons of opera, theater, and classical music, Jews celebrated and participated in European culture to a greater extent than ever before. The majority was able to do this while still retaining a sense of Jewish distinctiveness. *Acculturation* did not mean assimilation or disappearance into the majority; rather, it meant, for many, becoming secular and combining European culture with Jewishness, as opposed to strict Jewish observance. When Sigmund Freud declared himself to be a "godless Jew," he was describing a modern form of Jewish identity, one not derived from religious practice but one steeped in ethnic self-consciousness.

STATUS OF THE JEWS UNDER OTTOMAN RULE

At the same time that Italian and German Jews were emancipated, the 150,000 Jews in the Ottoman Empire also saw their legal status change. In that region, Jews lived in a vast area that included Turkey, parts of the Balkans, and cities along the Aegean. As a monotheistic religious minority, Jews (as well as Christians) living under Islamic rule were regarded as *dhimmi*, protected and tolerated, yet socially and legally inferior to Muslims. Under Ottoman rule, the non-Muslim community was divided into *millets*, administrative units organized on the basis of religion. The four non-Muslim millets were Armenian, Catholic, Jewish, and Greek Orthodox, and each group enjoyed considerable cultural and social autonomy in this arrangement.

As the Ottoman Empire began to slip into decline by the end of the eighteenth century, administrators looked to emulate European forms of state organization in order to modernize and reassert central control over an increasingly fractious realm. Ottoman elites turned to France, seeing it as a model of a robust, centralized nation-state. The reorganization of the Ottoman state was partly triggered by the recognition that the status of non-Muslim minorities could not remain unchanged. In 1839, the sultan announced the Noble Rescript of the Rose Chamber, a series of reforms (*Tanzimat*) that guaranteed the life, honor, and property of "the people of Islam and other nations." Equality had not been clearly articulated but was implicit in the decree. With the Reform Decree of 1856, equality was explicitly granted to Jews and Christians. This was amended once more in 1869, with the passage of a new citizenship law that defined all Ottoman citizens as subjects of the sultan, irrespective of their religion. Although the constitution was granted in 1876, it was not really implemented until the Young Turk Revolution of 1908.

Legal and social practice, however, lay far apart. Because Ottoman modernization was uneven and halfheartedly implemented, so, too, was emancipation. Western ideas and practices did not displace indigenous modes of governing but rather overlapped with them. Without a thoroughgoing process of Ottomanization, characterized by state-sponsored education and linguistic change, Jews never developed the kind of attachment to Turkey and its language that their coreligionists formed vis-à-vis their respective countries, and neither did its other minorities. Further contributing to the alienation, the conservative Muslim establishment

succeeded in maintaining the discriminatory *jizya*, or *poll tax*, levied on non-Muslims. The regime also shut Jews and Christians out of the bureaucracy, ensuring an almost-complete Muslim monopoly on all bureaucratic positions of importance within the state. Despite the granting of equal rights in 1856, Jews were not subject to compulsory military conscription until 1909. Until that time, attitudes toward *dhimmi* remained unchanged, severely compromising the 1869 law that had granted citizenship and equality.

The rise of nationalist movements toward the end of the nineteenth century, the disintegration of the Ottoman Empire, and the impact of Western colonialism created massive changes for the Sephardic Jews of southeastern Europe and Asia Minor. Once imperial subjects, the Sephardic communities now found themselves residing in one of many new nation-states that emerged in the wake of the empire's collapse. Belgrade and Monastir, which had significant Sephardic populations, were now ruled by Serbia, while the Jews of Sarajevo became subjects of the Habsburg Empire. In that same year of 1878, Bulgaria came into existence and extended its authority over most of the Jews of northern Thrace and those south of the Danube. Greece, which became independent in 1830, had a small Jewish population, but after it annexed Salonika during the Balkan Wars of 1912–1913, it inherited a large Jewish community. This was the heartland of Sephardic culture and the Ladino language. Like their Ashkenazic coreligionists, who would suffer the loss of collective protection afforded by living in multinational empires, Sephardic Jews in the eastern Levant had to construct a new relationship to the nation-state and negotiate its homogenizing impulses.

The end of the Ottoman Empire and the advent of modern Turkey in 1923 was a time of increased Jewish marginalization. The genocide of Armenians during the war and the transfer of the Greek population back to Greece in exchange for Turks living in Greece saw the virtual disappearance of the Christian minority, leaving the Jews alone and isolated as the major *dhimmi* population. Intensely nationalistic, the Turkish state embarked on a program of "Turkicization" that intruded on the traditional educational curriculum of Jews. Under Mustafa Kemal Atatürk, the father of modern Turkey, the state rededicated itself to implementing the French model of administration, with a strong central government, but dispensed with intermediary structures such as the millet. Atatürk also brought about the formal separation of mosque and state in 1928, when Islam ceased to be the official religion. Even though these factors could have ensured Jewish integration into the modern Turkish state, they did not. Rather, as with the rise of nation-states in Europe between World War I and World War II, Ottoman Jews saw their political and cultural autonomy curtailed, while they experienced official exclusion at the national level.

RUSSIAN JEWRY AND THE STATE

In the nineteenth century, Russia was home to the world's largest Jewish population—approximately 5 million. By the 1870s—when most of central, southern, and western European, Ottoman, and Anglo Jewries had been legally emancipated—the vast majority of the world's Jews, those in eastern Europe, remained unemancipated, a condition that would prevail until 1917. The path to emancipation taken by Russian Jewry was longer and more arduous than that of other Jewish communities.

Over the course of the nineteenth century, many of the same issues that animated the emancipation debate in western and central Europe also came to the fore in Russia. But differences, particular to the Russian context, also conditioned government discourse and actions. Unlike states in the rest of Europe, virtually no Jews were in Russia until the eighteenth century. The large-scale Jewish presence there came about with the Polish Partitions of 1772, 1793, and 1795. Over those two decades, Poland was dismantled and divided between Austria, Russia, and Prussia.

The encounter between Polish Jews and the respective empires that came to govern them in the wake of the partitions determined the various paths to modernity taken by eastern European Jewry. Overnight, Polish Jews found themselves accidentally in or deliberately migrated to other parts of Europe, spreading their culture and their sensibilities. By the same token, while the traditional culture of Polish Jews remained intact for quite some time, the exposure to new forms of European culture also began to leave its mark on eastern European Jews.

With the partition of 1772, Russia inherited the lion's share of Polish Jewry, approximately a half million, and thus began the tsarist administration of the Jews. Initially, coming under Russian control did not significantly alter Jewish existence. Jews continued to enjoy considerable social and cultural autonomy and lived as a separate estate among a host of other ethnic minorities in the western borderland regions of Russia. This situation only began to change after the middle of the nineteenth century, when ever more Jews became Russian speakers and official policy underwent a change designed to handle the rising number of Jews.

Russia inherited its Jews so late that it was not until the 1860s, after Russification had begun to make an impact, that the term *Russian Jew* first became popular. Nevertheless, even after this time, the overwhelming majority of Jews in Russia retained their own languages, Yiddish, the lingua franca, and Hebrew for religious purposes; maintained their own forms of dress and occupation; and operated a vast network of legal, educational, and charitable institutions, all of which went to ensure a deep sense of religious and ethnic distinctiveness.

Russian policy toward the Jews was dictated by St. Petersburg's need to deal with this large influx of foreigners. Successive tsars enacted policies characterized by a mixture of confusion, contradiction, ineptitude, bigotry, and a genuine desire for reform. We must be cautious before branding Russian policy toward the Jews as driven by antisemitism pure and simple. Sometimes it was, but at other times, Jews were treated no differently (even if badly) than other groups in Russian society. Russia was an autocracy, and the tsar, who monopolized all political power and decreed all laws, was, in theory, answerable only to God. No one in Russia enjoyed rights either as individuals or as part of a collectivity that were not expressly granted by the sovereign. In the nineteenth-century Russian context, the Jewish situation was not so anomalous, especially when one considers that most of the population consisted of serfs and remained so until the abolition of serfdom in 1861.

Russia's first great acquisition of Polish Jews occurred during the reign of Catherine the Great, who ruled from 1762 to 1796. At first amenable to the Jews, she, somewhat like Napoleon, was also responsive to complaints about them from various quarters, especially merchants. In 1764, when Catherine issued an invitation to foreigners to settle in Russia, she explicitly excluded Jews. But wishing to promote the growth of towns and cities, in 1786, she decreed that the newly acquired Jews be registered as urban residents, with all the privileges that entailed. No such inclusion of Jews into the estate structure had ever occurred before in Europe. Still, the decree meant little real change, for the *kahals*, the governing boards of Jewish communities, were not disbanded, since the government saw them as valuable sources of revenue. So Jewish autonomy remained intact, negating the potential impact of the inclusion of Jews into Russia's estate system. Also, too many Jews lived outside of urban areas to make the decree meaningful. Finally, complaints from Christian merchants about Jewish competition and Catherine's fears of social reform in the wake of the French Revolution led to the passage of a law in 1791 that confined Jews to the newly acquired territories.

The vast area in which Jews were required to reside later became known as the Pale of Settlement. Nearly all five million of Russia's Jews lived in the Pale. There they comprised about 12 percent of the area's total population. With a distinct preference for living in towns and cities, they were often the absolute majority of residents in those places. By contrast, Jews were never an absolute majority in any place in western Europe. Overall, by the end of the nineteenth century, Jews were the fifth-largest ethnic group in the Russian Empire, behind Russians, Ukrainians, Poles, and Belorussians. They were the empire's largest non-Slavic, non-Christian group. Encompassing much of the western provinces acquired from the Polish Partitions and home to half the world's Jews, the Pale was a vast area covering 386,100 square miles, approximately the size of France, Germany, and Austria combined. By way of an American comparison, the size of the Pale was equivalent to the combined area of California, New York State, and Florida. The Pale was only abolished with the February Revolution of 1917.

The starting point for an analysis of Russian laws pertaining to Jews must begin with the recognition that the government ruled according to a highly complex legal system in which, by the late eighteenth century, people were divided into numerous groupings, of which some were estate-based and some were nationally based, each of which was ruled according to distinct laws. Unlike western Europe, Russia never had a feudal system, so legal emancipation on the French or central European models could never have taken place before 1905, when Russia received a constitution. Before then, Jews could not have been incorporated into any citizenry as equals. Russian governments consistently struggled with the question of how to fit the country's newly acquired Jewish population into this complex legal matrix.

Successive tsarist regimes established commissions designed to provide them with information about and recommendations for the reform of Jews and Jewish life. These reports, some of which were deeply hostile to Jews, were nonetheless often issued in the spirit and language of western European eighteenth-century enlightened opinion. Just such a mixture of liberal intent and harsh application characterized the Statute of 1804 Concerning the Organization of the Jews, the preamble of which noted that "the following regulations are in accord with our concern for the true happiness of the Jews and with the needs of the principal inhabitants of those provinces."

The statute was Russia's first basic law pertaining to Jews, but little in the way of happiness was experienced, thanks to this legislation. The goal of the statute was to fit the Jewish population into one of the existing legal categories of farmer, factory worker, artisan, merchant, or townsman. According to its provisions, Jews were to be admitted to municipal councils and could gain entrance to Russian schools; were required to use either Russian, German, or Polish in commercial or public documents; and were to be granted tax exemptions, land, and loans to establish agricultural colonies. Finally, the statute insisted on elections for Jewish community leadership positions every three years to prevent mini dictatorships arising. Other provisions, however, made the lot of the Jews worse. In particular, because Jews had been consistently blamed for promoting the drunkenness and exploitation of the Russian peasantry, they were banned from selling alcohol in villages, which, until then, had been a major source of income for large numbers of Russian Jews. This led to the threat of large-scale expulsion from the countryside. While the departure of many contributed to the process of urbanization, it also created new difficulties as Jews struggled to earn a decent living in the poorly developed urban economies. The government also failed to promote and financially support the occupational change it claimed it wanted to see. Many of the provisions of the 1804 statute were never effectively enforced. In sum, the reforms had little impact, and Jewish society continued to find itself in desperate straits. At the same time, Jews remained a remote and somewhat insignificant foreign population on Russia's western frontier. They did not yet constitute an important group within the minds of the tsar or his ministers.

The Jewish policies of successive tsarist regimes were confused and confusing and ranged from benevolent paternalism that aimed at integration of the Jews to crueler forms of forced assimilation. There were harsh decrees issued to integrate and Russify the Jews, and equally harsh decrees designed to drive Jews out of Russia. For Jews (and others), beneficent paternalism could have the same devastating impact as cruel autocracy.

The reign of Tsar Nicholas I (1825–1855) exemplified the tension between the integrationist efforts and conversionist agenda of various imperial governments. While Catherine II and Alexander I tried to implement administrative integration, Nicholas promoted official enlightenment, encouraging conversion to Orthodoxy using the military. Nicholas imposed compulsory military service—Russia's vast school of imperial socialization—on many of the groups inhabiting Russia's newly acquired Polish territories in the west of the country. Whereas Jews previously had been exempt from military service upon payment of a tax, in 1827, Nicholas withdrew that option for the majority of them. Now most Jews were subject to conscription for a period of 25 years, beginning at age 18. But unlike most other groups, a disproportionate number of underage Jewish children were taken, some as young as ten years old—the average age was 14—for a preparatory period prior to the beginning of their 25-year service. They were known as cantonists, and while the policy of recruitment was in force between 1827 and 1855, about 50,000 Jewish boys found themselves serving as forced recruits in the tsar's army.

The impact of this was devastating on the children in question and their distraught families. Nicholas's ultimate goal of Jewish service in the cantonist battalions was conversion. Unlike non-Jewish cantonists and children of Russian soldiers who were quartered with their families, Jewish cantonists lived in barracks and were likely never to see their families again. The young recruits were subject to physical and psychological pressure. Floggings (applied ecumenically in the Russian army), constant threats, miserable conditions, and forced baptisms were the lot of these young Jewish boys. For those who sought a way out, self-mutilation became an all-too-common tactic; if one shot oneself in the foot (literally), or cut off a few fingers, one was thrown out of the army. Others simply fled into the forests. For the close-knit families, many often lit mourning candles in the expectation that they would never see their sons again. Finally, Jewish communities were fractured by the policy because the tsar left the recruiting up to the Jewish communities. Under pressure from the government, in the last two years of the draft, communal authorities sent out *khappers* (Yiddish for "catchers") to apprehend young Jewish boys. According to the Hebrew account of Yehudah Leib Levin, "[O]ne afternoon, a cart pulled by two majestic horses drew up to a house. Six heavy-set men with thick red necks entered the house and soon emerged holding a six-year-old boy who was screaming and flailing his arms." As with countless such episodes, it was common for the grieving parents to "thrust into the hands of their sons books of Psalms, sets of *tefillin* (phylacteries), whatever small religious objects they had in their possession. Stay a Jew! They entreat their boys. Whatever happens, stay a Jew!" Indeed, Jewish conversion rates among draftees were lower than among other sectarian groups. An official government memorandum noted, "Jews do not abandon their religion during army service, in spite of the benefits offered to them for doing so."

The communal administration of the draft bred corruption. Wealthy Jews paid for replacements, while the poor had no resources with which to secure the release of their sons. Resentment, trauma, and class conflict among eastern European Jews exacerbated social divisions created by the advent of new religious movements and the Jewish

Enlightenment. One popular Yiddish folk song of the era stresses the theme of class conflict as it evokes the bitterness and suffering the children, the families, and the communities experienced:

Tots from school they tear away
And dress them up in soldiers' gray.
And our leaders, and our rabbis,
Do naught but deepen the abyss.
Rich Mr. Rockover has seven sons,
Not a one a uniform dons;
But poor widow Leah has an only child,
And they hunt him down as if he were wild.
It is right to draft the hard-working masses;
Shoemakers or tailors—they're only asses!
But the children of the idle rich
Must carry on, without a hitch.

Communal solidarity was severely compromised, and all over Russia, revolts against the kahal authorities broke out. When Rabbi Eliyahu Shik stood up to the authorities in the town of Mir, according to one account,

> [t]here was a great tumult when he proposed that the community revolt against the kahal leaders, wreak havoc upon their community house and raze it to the ground. Everyone grabbed a hatchet or an ax and followed the rabbi to the kahal building, broke down the doors, cut the bonds of the captives and freed them.

Nicholas I's goal of using the military to promote the integration of ethnic minorities into Russian society was, by and large, a failure, especially as it pertained to Jews. By law, Jewish and non-Jewish soldiers were distinguished from one another; Jews were barred from joining certain units and were subjected to different criteria for promotion. Because Nicholas had formally established the Pale of Settlement in 1835, which reaffirmed the residence restrictions on Jews established by

Catherine, Jewish soldiers were required to return to the Pale upon completion of their military service, even though many had served in Russia's interior. The army as brutal reform school failed to draw most Jews closer to Russian society.

The cantonist experience left deep psychological scars upon Russian Jews and their descendants. In part, this was because of the central role the cantonists assumed in Jewish popular culture. Novelists, playwrights, autobiographers, and songwriters all used the motif of the suffering youngsters to portray the heavy yoke that was Jewish life in Russia. Some authors used the cantonist experience to reflect the changing nature of Russian Jewry or their own personal transformation upon leaving Russia. Yehezkel Kotik's Yiddish autobiography, *My Memories* (*Mayne Zikhroynes*, 1912), recounted how brutal army service led many recruits to undergo radical personality changes. Kotik recalled that a cantonist friend of his, Yosele, entered his grandfather's house after an absence of many years:

> [He was] barefoot, clad in a large, coarse peasant shirt that reached down to his ankles but without any pants. . . . [H]is face was swollen and pale, like that of a corpse. . . . I went up to him and said, "Yosele, Yosele!" But all my attempts to arouse him were futile—he didn't respond. He had become like a log. . . . They brought him a glass of tea and a sweet roll, but he refused to eat or drink. It was a lost cause.

Yosele had been forcibly converted. But no Jew in these accounts emerged from their time in the army unchanged, and their experience, in turn, impacted other Jews. The memoirist Mary Antin recalled, "There were men in Polotzk [her hometown] whose faces made you old in a minute. They had served Nicholas I, and came back unbaptized." To this very day, many descendants of Russian Jewish immigrants continue to testify that their ancestors may have arrived in New York harbor in 1900 to avoid conscription for a period of 25 years—this despite the fact that the policy was abandoned in 1855. It is all the more ironic, then, that after introduction of universal conscription in 1874, Jews enlisted in the Russian army for a regular six-year term out of all proportion to their numbers in the general population.

Even while the senior officials of Nicholas I were carrying out his policy of military recruitment, the more liberal-minded among them also adopted a different approach that was realized only after the tsar's death in 1855. Under the leadership of P. D. Kisilev, Minister of State Domains and the person responsible for peasant affairs; S. S. Uvarov, Minister for Public Education; and Count A. G. Stroganov, Minister of Internal Affairs, a committee was established in 1840 with the telling title "Committee for the Determination of Measures for the Fundamental Transformation of the Jews in Russia." It determined that the Jews could never be fully integrated into Russia without first undergoing a moral and cultural transformation. Kisilev was influenced by Enlightenment ideas of human malleability and perfectibility. He believed that human nature could be transformed through education, noting that "the estrangement of the Jews from the civil order, and their moral vices do not represent some sort of particular or arbitrary deficiency of their character, but rather became firmly established through [their] religious delusions." Kislev was determined to use Jewish schools to eliminate the civic and moral imperfections of Russia's Jews. Seeking to emulate the situation in France with Napoleon's calling

of the Sanhedrin in 1807, Kisilev noted, "[T]he Jewish clergy [in France] has been turned into an instrument of the government in the execution of its policies."

As would so often be the case in Russia, Kisilev's committee, which concluded its work in 1863, failed to realize its ambitions. To make effective use of the schools and rabbinate required that the kahals be abolished. This happened in 1844. And yet Russian law and Russian social reality were often in conflict, as many kahals continued to operate clandestinely. Moreover, the government-sponsored Jewish public schools did not attract the anticipated number of Jews and, thus, like the army recruitment program, became a failed experiment for the integration of Russia's Jews.

Toward the end of the nineteenth century, during the reigns of the last three tsars—Alexander II (1855–1881), Alexander III (1881–1894), and Nicholas II (1894–1917)—Russian policy toward the Jews changed from the integrationist models of the early tsars, however imperfect they may have been, to exclusionary ones. Despite the fact that Alexander II forbade the conscription of child recruits and allowed Jewish professionals and students to reside outside the Pale, his policies toward the Jews basically continued the failed attempts of his predecessors, as he, too, was unprepared to entertain any basic restructuring of the social order that would lead to the recognition of individual rights. However, under him, the process of Russification intensified along with an increase in the number of Jews attending state-sponsored Jewish schools, Russian gymnasia, and universities. In 1865, a mere 129 Jews (3 percent of the total number of students) were enrolled at Russian universities, whereas two decades later, that number had risen to 1,856, or 14.5 percent of all university students. Just prior to World War

I, when 80 percent of Russians were illiterate, almost all Jewish boys and most Jewish girls could read and write Yiddish. Tellingly, by 1900, over 30 percent of Jewish men and 16 percent of Jewish women could also read Russian.

A significant feature of the slow but discernible integration of Jews into Russian society, albeit without emancipation, was the emergence of new Jewish communal leaders. The official end of the kahal in 1844 and the impact of the drafting of child recruits led to a crisis of communal authority. New leaders arose who bore different credentials from the previous leaders of eastern European Jewry. They were not drawn from the rabbinic elite but were, rather, wealthy young merchants. It is true that the overwhelming majority of Russian Jews were poor (as were the majority of Russians), but it bears emphasis that a substantial merchant class also existed among Jews in Russia. By the mid-nineteenth century, the 27,000 officially registered Jewish merchants comprised 75 percent of all the merchants in the Pale. When Nicholas I centralized the system of taxation gathering, the principal source of which was alcohol sales, great opportunities opened up for Jews, already heavily involved as they were in the alcohol trade. The wealthiest such Jewish merchants were also permitted to operate in the vast regions outside the Pale, thanks to a decree of 1848. Dealing almost exclusively with non-Jewish merchants and state officials, these Jewish "tax-farmers," as they were called, amassed significant wealth. Influenced by the ideals of the Jewish Enlightenment and their frequent contact with non-Jews, they became Jewish communal leaders of a very different cast from their rabbinic predecessors. While some may have been indifferent to Jewish custom and community, others—such as Evzel Gintsburg—were major philanthropists and promoters of the *Haskalah*, or

Jewish Enlightenment. Other merchants, such as Izrail Brodsky, a pioneer of the sugar industry, and Samuil Poliakov, a railroad baron, achieved enormous success and thus influence. The merchants, who were recognized by the state for their services, began to have increasing influence with Russian officialdom, which sometimes sought advice from them in formulating Jewish policy.

As important as this group was, it was unable to substantially alter the economic or political lot of most Jews. Following the assassination of Alexander II in 1881, Alexander III set out to stymie the integration of Jews into Russian society and especially curb Jewish access to higher education and entrance into the professional elite, a development increasingly apparent in the previous reign of Alexander II. While the treatment of Jews up until that time was not exactly anomalous, with harshness characteristic of the treatment suffered by many groups, Alexander III's policies and those of his successor, Nicholas II, marked a significant and overt attempt to use laws and ordinances to reverse the integration of Jews into Russian society.

The establishment of a quasi-constitutional monarchy in 1905 resulted in an odd situation, whereby Jews, who were granted the electoral franchise and permitted to organize political parties, were elected to the Duma, or Parliament. Once there, they joined non-Jewish colleagues in demanding Jewish civic equality. The presence of Jews in the Parliament betokened the unusual situation whereby Jewish political rights in Russia were attained before civil rights: the exact opposite of the situation in western Europe. The monarchy and conservative forces, as well as the uncooperative stance adopted by the Left, succeeded in undermining the 1905 Revolution, and the goal of Jewish emancipation remained unfulfilled.

Despite the reactionary policies of both Alexander III and Nicholas II, Jewish social and cultural integration proceeded apace without the granting of formal emancipation. Finally, it took the overthrow of the tsar and the installation of the Russian Provisional Government to usher in the emancipation of Russian Jewry. On April 2, 1917, the "Decree Abolishing Religious and National Restrictions" proclaimed, "All restrictions on the rights of Russian citizens which had been enacted by existing laws on account of their belonging to any creed, confession, or nationality, shall be abolished."

The fall of the Provisional Government and the Bolshevik seizure of power did not mean an immediate reversal of recent Jewish fortune. Jewish emancipation was enshrined in law and was reinforced by Lenin's decision to recognize the Jews as a nationality with distinct cultural and political rights. Jewishness became a category recognized in Soviet nationality law. Despite this, as in eighteenth-century France, Soviet Jews would be denied everything as Jews and granted much as Soviet citizens.

Between the French and the Bolshevik Revolutions, the political status of world Jewry changed drastically. For over a century, the Jewish struggle to attain civic rights was a protracted and complicated one. In central and eastern Europe, in particular, seeming advances were quickly followed by reversals. As such, one cannot speak of Jewish emancipation as a unitary phenomenon. There were different kinds of emancipation, each bearing the mark of specific features, such as country, region, and political conditions. As this chapter has demonstrated, the state of the Jews often determined the state's attitude toward the Jews, as did the state of the state. Over the period that Jewish civic status changed, the political struggle was accompanied by a Jewish cultural revolution, one that profoundly and permanently changed the Jewish people. It is to these developments we now turn.

For Further Reading

On the problem of periodization in modern Jewish history, see Michael Meyer, "When Does the Modern Period in Jewish History Begin?" *Judaism* 24 (1975): 329–338.

For selected general histories of Jews in specific countries or regions, see Todd Endelman, *The Jews of Britain, 1656–2000* (Berkeley: University of California Press, 2002); Paula Hyman, *The Jews of Modern France* (Berkeley: University of California Press, 1998); Michael A. Meyer, ed., *German-Jewish History in Modern Times*, 4 vols. (New York: Columbia University Press, 1996); William O. McCagg, *A History of Habsburg Jews, 1670–1918* (Bloomington: Indiana University Press, 1989); Hillel J. Kieval, *Languages of Community: The Jewish Experience in Czech Lands* (Berkeley: University of California Press, 2000); Raphael Patai, *The Jews of Hungary* (Detroit: Wayne State University Press, 1996); Israel Bartal, *The Jews of Eastern Europe, 1772–1881* (Philadelphia: University of Pennsylvania Press, 2002); Zvi Gitelman, *A Century of Ambivalence: The Jews of Russia and the Soviet Union, 1881 to the Present* (New York: Schocken Books, 1988); Esther Benbassa and Aron Rodrigue, *Sephardi Jewry: A History of the Judeo-Spanish Community, 14th–20th Centuries* (Berkeley: University of California Press, 2000); Stanford J. Shaw, *The Jews of the Ottoman Empire and the Turkish Republic* (New York: New York University Press, 1991); André Chouraqui, *Between East and West: A History of the Jews of North Africa* (Philadelphia: Jewish Publication Society of America, 1968); Nissim Rejwan, *The Jews of Iraq* (London: Weidenfeld and Nichloson, 1985); Hasia Diner, *The Jews of the United States, 1654–2000* (Berkeley: University of California Press, 2004); Suzanne

D. Rutland, *Edge of the Diaspora: Two Centuries of Jewish Settlement in Australia* (Sydney: Collins, 1988); Judith Elkin, *The Jews of Latin America* (New York: Holmes & Meier, 1998); and Alan Dowty, *The Jewish State: A Century Later* (Berkeley: University of California Press, 1998).

On emancipation, see David Sorkin, *Jewish Emancipation: A History Across Five Centuries* (Princeton: Princeton University Press, 2019); Pierre Birnbaum and Ira Katznelson, eds., *Paths of Emancipation* (Princeton, NJ: Princeton University Press, 1995); Salo Wittmayer Baron, "Ghetto and Emancipation," *Menorah Journal 4*, 6 (1928): 515–526; Frances Malino, *The Sephardic Jews of Bordeaux: Assimilation and Emancipation in Revolutionary and Napoleonic France* (Tuscaloosa: University of Alabama Press, 1978); Ronald Schechter, *Obstinate Hebrews: Representations of Jews in France, 1715–1815* (Berkeley: University of California Press, 2003); Jacob Katz, *Ghetto and Emancipation: The Social Background of Jewish Emancipation, 1770–1870* (Cambridge: Harvard University Press, 1973); Frances Malino and David Sorkin, eds., *Profiles in Diversity: Jews in a Changing Europe, 1750–1870* (Detroit: Wayne State University Press, 1998); Artur Eisenbach, *The Emancipation of the Jews in Poland* (Oxford: Basil Blackwell, 1991); and Michael C. N. Salbstein, *The Emancipation of the Jews in Britain: The Question of the Admission of the Jews to Parliament, 1828–1860* (Rutherford, NJ: Fairleigh Dickinson University Press, 1981).

On the social and economic conditions in various Jewish communities in the eighteenth and early nineteenth centuries, see Yosef Kaplan, *An Alternative Path to Modernity: The Sephardi Diaspora in Western Europe* (Leiden, The Netherlands: Brill, 2000); Todd Endelman, *The Jews of Georgian England: Tradition and Change in a Liberal Society* (Philadelphia: Jewish Publication Society, 1979); John Klier, *Russia Gathers Her Jews: The Origins of the "Jewish Question" in Russia, 1772–1825* (DeKalb: Northern Illinois University Press, 1986); Gershon Hundert, *The Jews in a Polish Private Town: The Case of Opatów in the Eighteenth Century* (Baltimore, MD: Johns Hopkins University Press, 1992); Gershon Hundert, *Jews in Poland-Lithuania in the Eighteenth Century: A Genealogy of Modernity* (Berkeley: University of California Press, 2004). Murray Jay Rosman, *The Lords' Jews: Magnate-Jewish Relations in the Polish-Lithuanian Commonwealth during the Eighteenth Century* (Cambridge, MA: Harvard University Press, 1990); Glenn Dynner, *Yankel's Tavern: Jews, Liquor, & Life in the Kingdom of Poland* (New York: Oxford University press, 2014); Mordechai Breuer and Michael Graetz, *German-Jewish History in Modern Times*, vol. 1: Tradition and Enlightenment, 1600–1780, ed. Michael A. Meyer (New York: Columbia University Press, 1996); Steven M. Lowenstein, *The Berlin Jewish Community: Enlightenment, Family, and Crisis, 1770–1830* (New York: Oxford University Press, 1994); and J. S. Levi and G. F. J. Bergman, *Australian Genesis: Jewish Convicts and Settlers, 1788–1850* (Melbourne, Australia: Melbourne University Press, 2002).

CHAPTER 2

MODERN TRANSFORMATIONS

THE JEWISH PEOPLE were energized by their encounter with modernity, stepping forward to meet its challenges by trying to refashion themselves and their faith to suit the demands of changing times. Jewish thinkers, writers, and ordinary people produced a dizzying array of cultural and political options that reflected the prodigious diversity of the Jewish people. The relationship of Jews to modernity was not merely reactive; it was also proactive. In the process of refashioning themselves, Jews also contributed to the creation of modern sensibilities. What made for the rich variety of responses was the fact that beginning in the early modern period but becoming even more pronounced in the eighteenth century, the Jewish world, particularly in Europe, began to fracture. This was especially the case among Ashkenazim, the majority faction among world Jews. Despite certain differences in *halakhah* (Jewish law) and *minhag* (Jewish custom) between western and central European Jews on the one hand and those from eastern Europe on the other, the pan-Ashkenazic religious culture had been relatively uniform. Beyond this, there was what has been termed a "meta-Ashkenazic interconnecting web of [family and business] relationships." But in the eighteenth century, whatever religious and social cohesion had existed began to unravel as Ashkenazic communities that extended from England to Russia became increasingly different from one another.

Radically divergent policies across eighteenth-century Europe also left a deep impact on the character of various Jewish communities. In liberal England, the small Jewish population became increasingly English, whereas, at the same time on the continent, Empress Maria Theresa expelled the Jews of Prague in 1744 as if they constituted a foreign body. What a contrast to the situation in France, where the Revolution transformed Jews into French citizens. At the same time, German Jews, while becoming ever more German and middle-class, were still denied the full benefits of civic freedoms. Within the Jewish world, moderate and radical Sabbateans (followers of the seventeenth-century false messiah, Shabbetai Tsvi) fought bitterly with each other, while small but significant numbers left Judaism altogether, choosing apostasy. Eastern European Jews, while politically disenfranchised, nevertheless expressed great cultural vibrancy with the advent of Hasidism and its opposition movement, Mitnagdism. Proponents of the Haskalah or Jewish Enlightenment further contributed to the splintering

DOI: 10.4324/9781003611608-3

of eastern European Jewry. The Ashkenazic world split into a variety of types, courtesy of both larger historical forces and Jewish attempts to confront, adapt, and often anticipate change. Jews who initiated transformations in Jewish society often did so in reaction to contemporary developments, but it would be inaccurate to claim that Jews were merely playing catch-up. The modern Jewish proponents of the reform or regeneration of Jewish life also acted just as Jews always had, as agents of their own destiny, filled with new ideas born of Jewish needs and experience.

PARTITIONS OF POLAND

In eastern Europe, Jewish life began to undergo a period of radical change in the last quarter of the eighteenth century. Of the many developments to have an impact on Jews, the Partitions of Poland proved to be of utmost significance. Poland, not for the last time in its history, became a battleground for European power struggles and succumbed to economic crisis, political impotence, and war. Austria, Prussia, and Russia partitioned Poland among themselves on three occasions during the eighteenth century: 1772, 1793, and 1795. Having inherited the Jews of the now-defunct Polish state, Russia took in approximately 750,000 Jews, while Austria became home to 260,000, and Prussia, 160,000.

As a consequence of the partitions, Polish Lithuanian Jewry divided along the imperial frontier. In Austria and Prussia, Jewish elites became more Europeanized, learning to speak local vernaculars, such as German, Hungarian, and Czech. Religiously, they embraced liberal forms of Judaism, and culturally, they became increasingly secular, exposed to Western ideas and, eventually,

political emancipation. Cities such as Berlin, Vienna, Prague, and Budapest became major Jewish centers, cities where Jews threw themselves into the hurly-burly of modern culture. However, the majority of Jews were to be found in eastern Europe, and they remained steeped in traditional Jewish culture and were overwhelmingly poor. The splitting of Ashkenazic Jewry, occasioned by the partitions and the subsequent cultural and economic relationship between German Jews and their eastern European counterparts, forms a central and fascinating transnational theme in modern Jewish history.

In Russia, which inherited the bulk of Poland's Jews, there were barely any liberal trends, and no one was emancipated. Economic opportunities were uneven, with a bustling entrepreneurial culture in Ukraine and pockets of deep poverty in the northwest. But even there, pockets of great wealth and a small, emerging middle class were to be found. The Jewish encounter with modernity in Russia developed differently from the way the situation unfolded in east-central Europe. While some Jewish elites were deeply attracted to European culture, transformation among most Jews in eastern Europe tended to be more a product of internal processes that first manifested themselves within the context of religious innovation.

FRANKISM

In the wake of the Sabbatean movement, various new religious experiments emerged among Polish Jews. One of the most subversive was Frankism, named after its leader, Jacob Leibowitz, a Jew from the Polish province of Podolia who, during a sojourn in the Ottoman Empire, took on the name Yakov Frenk, or Frank. The term "Frank" was used to refer to a European in the Orient (for Polish Ashkenazim, it also denoted Sephardim visiting Poland from Turkey). "Frankism" was originally a derogatory term directed at the descendants of Frank's followers who converted to Roman Catholicism and attempted to conceal their Jewish backgrounds. Jacob Frank (1726–1791) preached certain doctrines and engaged in a number of practices that were in deep conflict with Judaism. These included the rejection of rabbinic authority and the Talmud, belief in the Trinity, acceptance of the New Testament, and a belief in the kabbalistic notion of "purification through sin," which, in the case of the Frankists, involved sexual orgies. While the Frankists initially thought of themselves as a branch of Judaism, they eventually came to see themselves as a separate religious group, largely independent from both Judaism and Christianity.

On January 27, 1756, Frank and his followers, many of whom were Sabbatians, were caught engaging in antinomian activities in the village of Lanckorona near Krakow. These included reading banned Sabbatian books, wife swapping, and other acts considered hedonistic. A Jewish religious court in Brody began proceedings against the group and, after obtaining admissions of guilt, issued a *herem* (writ of excommunication) against them. Not content with this outcome, the rabbis sought the assistance of the bishop of Kamenesk-Podolsk, Mikoiaj Dembowski, informing him that the group's practices were an affront not only to Judaism but to Christian morals as well. For their part, the Frankists claimed that their study of Kabbalah led them to the conclusion that there are three persons within one God and that the rabbis were persecuting them because their teachings resembled those of Christianity. The rabbis' tactic failed, as Dembowski, instead of condemning them,

threw the full weight of the Polish Church behind the Frankists and arranged for a public disputation between them and the rabbis, which took place from June 20 to 28, 1757. Referring to themselves as the Contra-Talmudists, the Frankists were declared the victors. The rabbis were fined, those Jews in Lanckorona who were said to have caused the furor to begin with were sentenced to be flogged, and the Talmud was ordered to be burned in the city square. The court also designated Sabbatians as Contra-Talmudists and granted them the same legal status as other Jews living in Poland.

With Dembowski's sudden death in 1757, the Frankists lost their protector, and the rabbis reignited their campaign against Frank and his followers, many of whom fled to Turkey. Things took a radical turn, however, with the emergence of Kajetan Ignacy Sołtyk, a Polish priest who served as the bishop of Kiev and, later, Krakow. In 1753, he had initiated a charge of ritual murder against Jews of Zhitomir, which saw 14 of the accused sentenced to death. By 1757, Sołtyk had become embroiled in a number of political scandals, including charges of bribery, forgery, and even murder. To deflect attention from himself, he sought to revive the subject of Jewish ritual murder, believing that if he could provide Jewish witnesses who would verify claims that Jews did, in fact, ritually use the blood of Christian children, he would emerge as a hero, his personal problems would disappear, and his political opponents would be vanquished. To do so, he obtained a royal invitation for the Frankists to return to Poland and then arranged for their participation in another public disputation, where they would affirm Sołtyk's accusations. In preparation for the event, they submitted a list of seven debating points, the last one reading: "The Talmud teaches that Jews need Christian blood, and whoever believes in the

Talmud is bound to use it." This was the evidence Sołtyk needed—one group of Jews testifying that another group engaged in ritual murder.

The disputation took place in Lwów from July 17 to September 19, 1759. This time, however, the result was inconclusive, in part because the Vatican, which had never accepted the charge of ritual murder, was again unconvinced and displeased. During the disputation, the Church ceased considering the Frankists to be a Jewish sect and instead regarded them as Jews on the cusp of conversion. Two days before the conclusion of proceedings, on September 17, 1759, Jacob Frank was baptized in Lwów Cathedral and assumed the name Jakub Josef. He was baptized again the following day in Warsaw; his godfather was none other than Augustus III, King of Poland and Grand Duke of Lithuania. Thereafter, before large public assemblies attended by many dignitaries, approximately 3,000 Jews converted in Lwów, Lublin, and Warsaw. Many nobles acted as godparents, while some of the newly converted Jews were immediately ennobled courtesy of a Lithuanian statute of 1588 which awarded such privileges to baptized Jews and their children.

Following Frank's death in 1791, Warsaw became the most important Frankist center. An anonymous pamphlet printed in 1791 claimed that there were 6,000 baptized Frankists living in the city, while in Poland, as a whole, there were 24,000. Toward the end of the eighteenth century, Frankism had lost much of its energy and unity. Although Frankists existed as an identifiable social group into the 1880s, by this time, the founder's doctrine was neither taught nor animated the group any longer. Instead, in nineteenth-century Warsaw, Frankism survived as a mutual aid society, and what bound members to each other was no longer Frankist

Sabbatianism but business connections. While Frankism's direct impact on Judaism was negligible, its mere existence was testament to a new spiritual ferment among Polish Jews. However, Frank's contemporary and fellow Podolian, Israel Ba'al Shem Tov, also led a religious revival. This was one that sublimated the messianic and kabbalistic dimensions of Frankism, shunned its transgressive practices, and remained firmly within the bounds of normative Judaism. That movement was called Hasidism, and unlike Frankism, it was a monumental success.

HASIDISM

One of the most profound developments in the religious history of the Jewish people took place with the advent of Hasidism in the eighteenth century. Originating among small elite groups of Torah scholars and kabbalists in the southeastern Polish province of Podolia in the 1750s, Hasidism was an expression of religious revival based on charismatic leadership as well as mystical teachings and practices. Podolia, which had been occupied by the Turks from 1672 to 1699, was a multiethnic, multi-religious environment which was characterized by a high degree of religious tolerance. The emergence of a new social expression of pietistic revival would have been in keeping with this most religiously diverse part of eastern Europe. Never a movement insofar as it never had a central authority or organization, Hasidism is a collective term used to denote a highly diverse number of groups that, while sharing much in common, were also distinct from one another on ideological and cultural grounds and because of allegiance to different dynasties or courts. Hasidism emerged against a background of dramatic change in eighteenth-century Poland—its political partition, the dissolution of the Council of Four Lands, the increasing social tensions among Jews, and the ongoing ramifications of Sabbatianism and Frankism. Where previous generations of historians once contended that Hasidism emerged in the context of communal crisis, new research has established that eighteenth-century Polish Jewry was growing demographically and enjoyed a firm economic base. It was not in decline. To be sure, the partitions created some uncertainty, and there was considerable antisemitism stemming from the peasantry and the Church, which accused Jews of medieval crimes, such as ritual murder and host desecration. On the whole, though, at the time Hasidism emerged, Polish Jewry was culturally vibrant, enjoyed considerable autonomy, and was socially as well as economically quite secure.

Hasidim's beginnings are associated with Israel ben Eliezer, known as the Ba'al Shem Tov (1700–1760). A Ba'al Shem Tov was a wonder-worker, especially renowned for his healing talents. Known by his acronym, the BeShT, Israel ben Eliezer was a kabbalist, a faith healer, a writer of amulets designed to ward off illness, and an exorcist. While the traditional view of the BeShT was that he was an unlearned but pious man, he was, in fact, a scholar, a prominent and respected figure in his community. It was in the last 20 years of his life, 1740–1760, when residing in the Mezhbizh, one of the largest towns in the Ukrainian part of Poland and an important commercial and military center, that his spiritual message began to attract a following, especially in elite pietistic circles. Within the community, at the *bet midrash* (house of study), he headed a group of rabbinic scholars who were also kabbalistic adepts. He also became acquainted with a wide cross

section of Christians, among them nobles, priests, and even criminals, serving them as their healer, just as Jews also frequented Christian shamans when in need of a cure, a potion, or an incantation. The BeShT also turned to Christians when he needed them to assert their authority and provide protection for the Jewish community. The need for assistance derived from the fact that despite the tradition of religious tolerance in this region, beginning in the sixteenth century, Roman Catholic forces, fearing the spread of Protestantism, began a hunt for heretics and blasphemers. Jews, as well as Christians, were targeted.

Among the BeShT's earliest followers were ritual slaughterers, cantors, and teachers. While always mindful of and attentive to the needs of the lower classes, the Ba'al Shem Tov did not include them in his inner circle. Those places were reserved for the elite. Similarly, despite what would become the enormous popularity of the BeShT's religious teachings, they were not intended for mass consumption. That would come in later Hasidic generations.

At the core of the BeShT's theology, there was an emphasis on certain kabbalistic concepts. Central among them were *let atar panui mineh* (the idea that all creation contains the Divine presence), and that one can therefore worship God through *avodah be-gashmiyut* (corporeal methods). This meant that God's presence could be felt in mundane activities, such as eating, working, and having sex; accordingly, in their performance, it is possible to build a relationship with God. That said, the BeShT also taught the importance of adopting an attitude of *hishtavut* (indifference) to the material aspects of human existence.

In the generation following his death, his adherents referred to themselves as Hasidim.

Traditionally, this was a term reserved for kabbalists or the deeply devout, such as the Hasidei Ashkenaz of twelfth- and thirteenth-century Germany. It was never a term to be applied to Jews en masse, and as such, use of the word in this way was both novel and highly contentious. One further innovation of the Ba'al Shem Tov and his followers was their introduction of the Sephardic prayer book, attributed to the sixteenth-century kabbalist Yitzhak Luria and his disciples.

We know little about the BeShT's personal life, since he did not leave a written record, save for a handful of letters. Most of what we do know comes from the miraculous stories and the legends attributed to him by his disciples. The most famous collection of such stories, over 200 of them, is known as *Shivhei ha-BeShT* (*In Praise of the Baal Shem Tov*), which first appeared in 1815. Beyond this, there was a proliferation of texts claiming to be the BeShT's oral teachings. In fact, *In Praise of the Baal Shem Tov* tells us more about his followers and the way they sought to represent their leader than it does about the BeShT. In these tales, supernatural occurrences take place with great frequency, the Ba'al Shem Tov performs miracles, and the world appears not as it is but as it should be. Typical for hagiographies, the hero meets with considerable opposition wherever he goes, but through the power of his message and his personal charisma, he begins to win over those who once scorned him.

Of the many themes that appear in the tales, stories that teach the importance of reconciliation, repentance, and economic justice prevail. Hasidism proclaims the need for Jewish unity, and one story in particular stresses the role played by the BeShT in bringing this about. Two disputants arrive at reconciliation after accepting the judgment of the BeShT, his Solomonic wisdom leading the story's editor to say of the litigants, "Both the guilty and the innocent agreed with [the BeShT] because in his great wisdom he appealed directly to their hearts, so that all were satisfied." In a Poland torn apart by great power struggles, with a Jewish community that had lost its governing body in 1764, this message stressing unity and togetherness was met with great receptivity. The *Shivhei ha-BeShT* had an impact far beyond Hasidic circles. It elevated storytelling to a high art in Hasidic culture, and because many of the masters of modern Yiddish and Hebrew literature came from Hasidic environments, and even as they left those places behind, they took with them the precious legacy of Hasidic storytelling, later adapting it to secular culture. Hasidic music also came to play a role in Jewish musical forms in synagogues, across denominational lines, and in Jewish secular music, particularly klezmer. Seemingly, secular expressions of Jewish culture cannot always be completely divorced from religion's impact.

In its formative period, Hasidism went through three distinct phases. The first was during the lifetime of the BeShT, when a small clutch of disciples followed his path. But it must be stressed that the BeShT neither consciously created a movement nor founded any institutions or held office; he never even formally taught. Most likely, because of this, there was never any opposition to him during his lifetime. That would begin in earnest a little over a decade after he died. In the second generation, a leading figure did emerge. Rabbi Dov Ber of Mezrich (d. 1772) was not the designated successor to the BeShT but was one of a number of equally important Hasidim. However, his emergence was nonetheless a vitally important development, because his erudition challenged the contemporary (though unfounded) critique of Hasidism by its opponents that it neglected Torah study.

Dov Ber, an ascetic, was widely recognized as an accomplished Talmudist. His advent did not mean a radical change in the nature of Hasidim; rather, the ecstatic character and theology of Hasidism were further theoretically refined. For example, he and his followers gave serious consideration to the necessity of mental preparation prior to prayer and the place of song within it. But Dov Ber also expressed disapproval of the more exuberant behavior of some of his students. For example, he rebuked Rabbi Avrom of Kalisk, who, together with his circle of Hasidim, had taken to somersaulting during prayer. Dov Ber and his fellow intellectuals' emphasis on Torah study ensured that Hasidism remained within the bounds of normative Jewish tradition, all the while maintaining what was new and exciting about it.

In theological terms, Dov Ber's important contribution to Hasidism was his emphasis on the concept of the *shekhinah*, or Divine presence in the world, something already found in the teachings of the BeShT. Dov Ber elaborated on the medieval kabbalistic tradition that posited that the *shekhinah* was to be found everywhere, even in "the lower realms," and thus all living creatures are but one part of the *shekhinah*. Moreover, the *shekhinah* represents the core of being and is encased in an outer shell or husk. From this, Dov Ber believed that both the inner essence and the outer casing were actually one indivisible unit. God is thus in everything and in union with everything. With distinctions thus erased, Dov Ber allowed for the idea that heaven and earth are actually one and the same. His is a cosmic theory of unification. Hasidism came to emphasize and celebrate the omnipresence of the Divine both in thought and in deed, encouraging its followers to come to know God, an essential goal in the quest for moral self-perfection, which, in

turn, was a necessary precondition for attaining the ultimate state of being—the negation of the self. A perfect state of spiritual being is one in which the world, the self, and God come together as One.

While Dov Ber was not a man of the people—he was a bedridden intellectual—he succeeded in spreading Hasidism by moving his "court," known in Yiddish as a *hoyf*, from the fairly remote southeastern province of Podolia further north to Volhynia (*see* Map 2.1). From Volhynia, Hasidism spread rapidly, north to Belorussia and Lithuania and west into Galicia. Because Russian and Austrian authorities did not regard Hasidism as a separate movement, Hasidim were not required to obtain government permits to open new synagogues and study houses. Ignored by the authorities, Hasidism was free to branch out. With the strategic move of his court to a more central location, Dov Ber dispatched his emissaries, young men, to a very wide geographic area, where they preached and won over many new adherents, especially students. The latter then traveled back to Dov Ber's court and, from there, went out as foot soldiers of Hasidism in search of new recruits. After the Magid's death in 1772, Hasidism displayed the qualities and energy of a genuine movement.

The Magid of Mezrich had a number of disciples who emerged as leaders even while Dov Ber was still alive. Important Hasidic communities were led by Aron ha-Godol ("the Great") in Karlin and Menachem Mendel of Vitebsk. The demographic boom experienced by eastern European Jewry in the nineteenth century also spurred the expansion of Hasidism and the formation of Hasidic courts, which, in turn, made for considerable intellectual and ritual diversification within Hasidism. Among leading figures after Dov Ber's death in 1772 were Ya'akov Yosef of Polnoye (d. 1783) and Pinhas

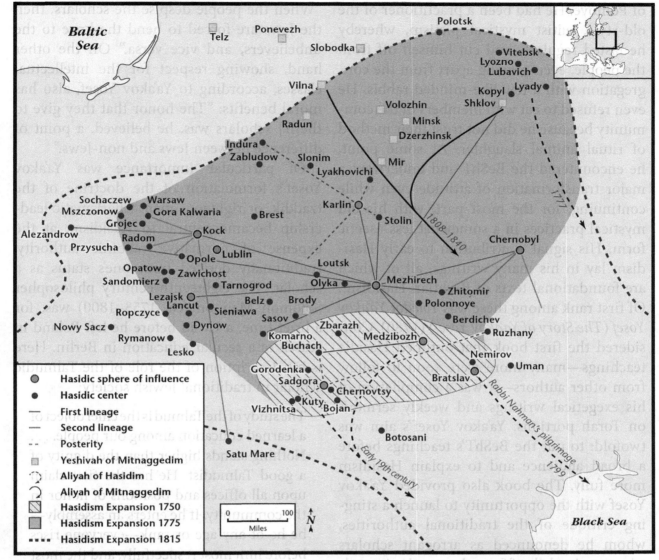

Map 2.1 The spread of Hasidism and Mitnagdism in the eighteenth and nineteenth centuries. This map depicts those cities and towns that became major Hasidic centers as well as those Mitnagdic locations where opposition to Hasidism was strongest.

Shapiro of Korets (d. 1790). Diversity notwithstanding, one important cultural characteristic bound all Hasidim together, and that was language. From its beginnings in the eighteenth century and then well into its growth phase in the nineteenth, Hasidism was adopted almost exclusively among eastern European Yiddish-speaking Jews. In places where Jews spoke European vernacular languages—Hungarian in Budapest, German or Czech in Prague, and

German in Poznan—Hasidism did not take root. Similarly, in geographic terms, Hasidism never crossed the border into Germany. Differences in religious culture and language were among the most decisive markers of the radical split that took place within modern Ashkenazic culture, between eastern and central Europe.

The missionary aspect of Dov Ber's leadership was augmented by Rabbi Ya'akov Yosef of Polnoye. He had been a practitioner of the old-style, elitist mystical pietism, whereby he fasted regularly and cut himself off from the people, even praying apart from the congregation with a few like-minded rabbis. He even refused to eat with members of the community because he did not trust their method of ritual animal slaughter. At some point, he encountered the BeShT and underwent a major transformation of attitude even while continuing, for the most part, with his old mystical practices in a somewhat less-ascetic form. His signal contribution to early Hasidism lay in his many writings, all of which are foundational texts of Beshtian Hasidism. Of first rank among these was *Toledot Ya'akov Yosef* (*The Story of Ya'akov Yosef*) (1780). Considered the first book that outlined Hasidic teachings—many more were soon to follow from other authors—it was a compilation of his exegetical writings and weekly sermons on Torah portions. Ya'akov Yosef's aim was twofold: to put the BeShT's teachings before a broad audience and to explain Hasidism more fully. The book also provided Ya'akov Yosef with the opportunity to launch a stinging critique of the traditional authorities, whom he denounced as arrogant scholars who remained aloof from the people. According to Ya'akov Yosef:

> Because of their divisiveness they were bereft of Torah. . . . [Because the function of scholars is] to go before the people and light their way with Torah, showing them the proper path to follow, but because of their coarseness of spirit the rabbis disdained to lead them.

However, Ya'akov Yosef was himself an elitist and chastised the uneducated classes for being disdainful toward the rabbis, warning of the dire consequences of such an attitude:

"When the people despise the scholars, then the Jews are forced to bend the knee to the unbelievers, and vice versa." On the other hand, showing respect for the intellectual classes, according to Ya'akov Yosef, also has moral benefits: "The honor that they give to the[ir] scholars was, he believed, a point of difference between Jews and non-Jews."

Of particular importance was Ya'akov Yosef's formulation of the doctrine of the tzaddik, or righteous man. Charismatic leadership became central to Hasidism, at the expense of normative rabbinic authority, traditionally derived from one's status as a scholar. The eighteenth-century philosopher Solomon Maimon (ca. 1753–1800) was, for a brief time, a Hasid before he left Poland in search of a secular education in Berlin. Here is his description of the role of the Talmudic scholar in traditional Jewish society:

> The study of the Talmud is the chief object of a learned education among our people. . . . Nothing stands higher than the dignity of a good Talmudist. He has the first claim upon all offices and positions of honor in the community. If he enters an assembly— be he of any age or rank—everyone rises before him most respectfully, and the most honorable place is assigned to him. He is director of the conscience, lawgiver and judge of the common man.

The *tzaddik*, by contrast, derives his authority from what were believed to be his Divine powers. According to Hasidic teachings, the *tzaddikim* are variously described as "emissaries of God," capable of "sustaining the entire world," of existing on a level that is "higher than the angels," possessing the "power to transform Divine judgment into Divine mercy." Such is his power that Hasidic teaching declares, "Whatever God does, it is also within the capacity of the *tzaddik* to do." Ya'akov Yosef saw the *tzaddik* as a communal leader, which was a new and innovative understanding of his role and thus a departure from the BeShT's thinking on this subject. So influential was Ya'akov Yosef's conception that from this time on, the social structure of Hasidism was formed around the primary relationship between the *tzaddik* and the masses.

The third phase of Hasidism's early growth was characterized by decentralization. Between the last quarter of the eighteenth and the beginning of the nineteenth centuries, the pattern of succession for Hasidic leadership was established and became dynastic. It was believed that the *tzaddik* could bequeath his religious charisma to his sons. Characteristic of the Ashkenazic world as a whole in the eighteenth century, Hasidim also underwent a certain splintering (sometimes bitter), with a wide variety of separate groups or courts emerging, all with various ritualistic, theological, and even sartorial differences. Hasidism grew rapidly in this third phase, thanks to the decision by the Russian government in 1804 to legalize Hasidic prayer houses and restrict the anti-Hasidic forces, known as the Mitnagdim. The other reason for the growth of Hasidism was the work of Rabbi Shneur Zalman of Lyady (1745–1812). He developed a distinct brand of Hasidism called HaBaD, the largest of all contemporary Hasidic sects. The word is an acronym of three key concepts: *hokhmah* (wisdom), *binah* (reason), and *da'at* (knowledge). For Shneur Zalman, intellect and reason were considered as legitimate paths to God, along with mystical and deeply emotional devotion. His teaching also emphasized the need to nurture social bonds, with an emphasis on brotherly love, charity, and kindness.

Shneur Zalman articulated a systematic theology which he set down in a book titled *Likutei Amarim* (*Collected Sayings*). Popularly known as the *Tanya*, the book, which is a guide to Hasidic practice and stresses the need for regular Torah study, first appeared in 1796 and remains a core Hasidic text to this day. In the *Tanya*, Shneur Zalman taught that through a personal relationship with a *tzaddik*, the average person, or *beinoni*, could achieve *devekut*, a state of "cleaving to God." This is a fundamental teaching of Hasidism and is derived from Lurianic Kabbalah, with its traditions of seeking mystical communion with the Divine. Indeed, Shneur Zalman emphasized the study of mystical texts to a greater degree than other contemporary Hasidic leaders. One of Hasidism's strengths is that the relationship between the *tzaddik* and his disciples is intimate and mutually necessary. As a mark of this intimacy, Hasidim use the more familiar and warmer-sounding word *rebbe* instead of the formal *rabbi* to refer to their *tzaddik*. Ya'akov Yosef of Polonye often referred to the *tzaddik* as the head or eyes of the body, with the Jewish people as the feet; only their unity represents cosmic completeness. Hasidism openly celebrates this co-dependency between rabbinic leadership, which Ya'akov Yosef called "men of form," and the masses, which he designated "men of matter." In *Toledot Ya'akov Yosef*, it is written, "I adjure you that there ought to be union between heaven—that is, the rabbis—and earth—that is, the masses of the people—so that one may influence the other, and so that truth and compassion may meet."

While the traditional rabbinate was initially alarmed at the rise of Hasidism, in the long run, Hasidism bolstered the waning control of religious elites. This happened in the economic realm, where Hasidism's emergence helped bring about a measure of social harmony and stability to the Jewish economy. When a Jew leased an asset of any sort from a Polish landlord, the price a Jew could pay was firmly fixed by the *kahal*, according to the laws of *hazakah* ("occupancy"). The point was to avoid a bidding war among Jews, keep prices in check, prevent the landlord from price gouging, and ensure some sort of equity of income and opportunity among Jews. The problem was that in the eighteenth century, many Jews were ignoring the prices set by the laws of *hazakah* and were outbidding their fellow Jews. Hasidic leaders were adamant that the system of *hazakah* be followed for the benefit of all and, with their charismatic leadership, were able to enjoin Jews to observe the dictates of the system. In so doing, they stabilized the Jewish economy and shored up their own authority by being seen as arbiters of fairness. In reality, Hasidic leaders were often in league with the rich and hence served to exacerbate class divisions, but the overall impression was that they were on the side of the people.

One of the keys to Hasidism's success was that it proved to be a "big tent," capable of encompassing Jews from all walks of life. Learned and uneducated Jews, rich and poor ones, rural inhabitants, and those in cities were all to be found among the ranks of followers. Another source of its success was the extent to which it introduced mysticism into everyday religious practice. After the failure of the Sabbatean revolt in the seventeenth century, unfulfilled messianic yearning still prevailed among the Jewish people. There was a great demand for Hebrew and Yiddish books that explained Lurianic Kabbalah. For large numbers of Polish Jews, Kabbalah was the best means through which to communicate with God and introduce the Divine into daily life. Kabbalistic passages were inserted into daily prayer, and certain kabbalistic practices became characteristic of Jewish life cycle events. Kabbalah was

thus already a well-established component of Jewish religious culture in Poland prior to the advent of Hasidism. However, when it emerged, Hasidism contributed to the spread and entrenchment of kabbalistic thought through its print culture, publishing a vast number of books for both the learned elite and the commoner alike, which made Kabbalah comprehensible and usable. Hasidism positioned itself as the keeper of the keys to Kabbalah and attracted many adherents, who believed the best path to Kabbalah came from the institutional authority and resources that Hasidism possessed. After all, the Ba'al Shem Tov himself was employed by his community as a practitioner of practical Kabbalah. Hasidism sought to channel the people's mystical longing and energy into the psychology of the believer, thereby neutralizing its destructive social impact. While it would not tolerate false messianic claims, neither did it discourage speculation about the coming messianic age. In fact, it openly encouraged people to perform the commandments in the spirit of messianic longing.

Hasidism emphasized mystical prayer as an efficacious way of connecting with God directly, and the BeShT taught that by praying with intense concentration (*kavanah*) on each one of the letters that make up Scripture as opposed to the words—one was supposed to see and hear them on an experiential, metaphysical level—the worshiper could attain a state of *devekut*. According to the historian Moshe Rosman, "this technique for communion with God therefore democratized Jewish worship and shifted the center of spirituality from study to prayer." Hasidic prayer was (and is) intended to bring about a state of ecstatic joy. As such, it is an extremely physical and raucous act, with overt gesticulations, swaying to and fro (known in Yiddish as *shokl*), hand clapping, foot stamping, singing, and dancing. The earliest Hasidim, as noted, even performed somersaults during prayer. In fact, prayer was sometimes regarded as an erotic act, with one Hasid boldly declaring, "Prayer is copulation with the *Shekhinah* ['Divine Presence']." Ya'akov Yitshok of Przysucha expressed another view. He asked rhetorically, "What is proper prayer?" and responded, "When you are so engrossed that you do not feel a knife when it is thrust into your body."

By stressing the presence of God even in the most mundane circumstances and acts, Hasidism endowed every human action with mystical and deep religious significance. According to Aryeh Leib Sarahs (1730–1791):

> I did not go to the Magid of Mezrich to learn interpretations of the Torah from him, but to note his way of tying his shoelaces and taking off his shoes. For of what worth are the meanings given to the Torah, after all? In his actions, in his speech, in his bearing and in his fealty to the Lord, man must make Torah manifest.

If God was to be detected in the mundane act of tying one's shoelaces, Hasidic theology held out the hope that even for the common folk, it was possible to come into immediate spiritual contact with the Divine.

Essential to Hasidic teaching was the need to ward off misery, which, it was believed, stood in the way of attaining *devekut*. Hasidism stressed that the way to God was through a joyous demeanor. The BeShT did not recognize a separation between body and soul and believed that both had to be elevated by being nourished with pleasure at one and the same time. One of the BeShT's disciples claimed that the master told him, "[S]top, for this way is dark and bitter and leads to depression and melancholy. The glory of God does not dwell where there is depression but where the joy in performing His mitzvah prevails."

Given that eighteenth-century Polish Jews lived in very close proximity to and in relative harmony with Christians, interacting with each other in many ways and at all levels of society, a fact attested to in Hasidic stories, it is intriguing to consider cultural borrowing in the realm of religious practice. Where did Hasidic rituals come from? While there is no direct evidence of Hasidism adopting aspects of the surrounding Christian religious cultures or Hasidic leaders even being in communication with Christian leaders, some Hasidic customs do bear certain similarities to those of nearby Christians. For example, some Orthodox Old Believers in Podolia, as well as Romanian mystics in the Carpathian mountains engaged in ecstatic prayer, replete with singing and dancing, reminiscent of Hasidism's intensity and exuberance of religious experience. While the Uniate and Orthodox churches have "holy hermits," charismatic individuals who operated as informal religious leaders, faith healers, and miracle workers, the Hasidic *tsaddik* sometimes approximated that sort of individual. Catholic pilgrimages to shrines have their analogue among the Hasidim as well. But pilgrimage is an essential practice in many, if not most, major religious traditions, and this should be taken as proof that what might look like cultural borrowing by the Hasidim are really just expressions of faith that are common to many religious traditions, some at great remove from one another. As an example, one might point to various central and northern European Protestant groups, such as Quakers and German Pietists, who sought to purposefully negate one's own personality during prayer. This would become an important feature of Hasidic worship but given that such Christian faith communities did not live near the Hasidim, we must again assert that Hasidism shares certain ritual features found in other religions, which are not necessarily the product of cultural transfer or imitation. The one exception to this phenomenon is the Hasidic court, which, in their opulence and household structure, have led historians to conclude that they were most likely created in conscious imitation of the houses of the nobility.

Israel Ba'al Shem Tov and his followers adhered strictly to the regnant rabbinic beliefs and practices of their day. However, they rebelled against the kabbalistic pietism that preceded them by taking it out of the exclusive hands of the elite, popularizing Kabbalah, and giving the average Jew access to it. In the BeShT's own time, the circle of followers was limited to about ten people, but in the generations that came after him, Hasidism would become a mass phenomenon. The incorporation of traditional kabbalistic practices into daily life and the emphasis on joy and spiritual ascent marked a crucial innovation in the history of eastern European Judaism. With these changes, the Hasidic movement won many new followers. It also garnered many new enemies.

MITNAGDISM

Hasidism and their putative enemies, the Mitnagdim ("Opponents"), have long been presented as diametrically opposed to each other insofar as Hasidism was presented as a breakaway sect, while the Mitnagdim saw themselves as the upholders of traditional Judaism. In truth, representatives of both camps came from the same scholarly elite. Both share an identical commitment to Torah and *halakhah* (Jewish law) and a reverence for Kabbalah. There were, however, differences, and quite

often they were bitter ones. Initially, Hasidism met with fierce opposition from learned elites, especially in Lithuania and Belorussia. One consequence of the battle is that Hasidim, who did not initially see themselves as a splinter group, gained a collective identity once the battle lines were drawn, while the Mitnagdim likewise crystallized into an identifiable group. The conflict was motivated by two principal grievances. The first involved matters of faith, while the second was political in nature. In the realm of religion, early disputes centered on the Hasidic introduction of Kabbalah into the daily life of the masses. Traditional authorities had previously held that such esoteric practices had to be confined to Talmudic masters and mystical adepts. Theological disagreements could also have social and economic consequences. Such was the case in the early dispute that centered on methods of animal slaughter. Hasidim had three principal concerns in this area: (1) that untrained slaughterers were operating in the villages, (2) that some of the slaughterers could be Sabbateans, and (3) that the knives then in use for slaughtering were insufficiently sharp. This latter issue was connected to the widespread belief in reincarnation and concern about the fate of a soul that transmigrated into an animal that had been rendered unkosher because the knife it had been slaughtered with was not properly honed and had torn, rather than cut, the animal's flesh. If a Jewish soul were to enter such an animal, then it, too, would be considered to have been "killed," because the meat would never be eaten by a pious Jew, and the soul would have no chance to re-enter a Jewish body. As such, Hasidim were especially strict about the need for the knife blade to be extremely sharp, smooth, and completely free of nicks. The degree of blade sharpness touched off a great dispute. Traditional rabbis maintained that the Hasidic blades were so sharp and thin that they could develop nicks that would tear the animal's flesh, rendering the meat unkosher. Such questions of theology also had an economic dimension, because growing numbers of Hasidim refused to eat meat slaughtered under the supervision of the *kahal*. The kosher meat tax was a crucial source of income for the community board, which stood to lose this revenue because large and increasing numbers of people were choosing to only eat meat slaughtered according to Hasidic standards.

The Mitnagdim had other complaints. They were appalled by the Hasidim's apparent lack of attention to Torah study (a false accusation), the establishing of their own places of worship, and their modes of prayer. Among other criticisms of the Hasidim were charges of sexual promiscuity, drunkenness, immodesty, and violations of the times set for communal prayer. The drinking and generally ecstatic nature of Hasidic practices were, for the Mitnagdim, frighteningly reminiscent of Sabbatean and Frankist deviancy.

The religious dispute led directly to the political insofar as the traditional rabbinic elite felt its authority threatened by the increasing popularity of Hasidic rebbes. The rabbis sensed that their grip over the people was losing out to the charismatic power and attraction of the *tzaddik*. The leading opponent of the Hasidim was the greatest Talmud scholar of his generation, Rabbi Eliyahu ben Shlomo Zalman (1720–1797). Known as the Vilna Gaon ("Sage of Vilna"), this exceptional man, who never held public office, was a revered figure. He earned a stellar reputation as a man of prodigious intellect and deep piety and, by the nineteenth century, had become an iconic figure among eastern European Jews. Descended from a family of scholars, he showed great promise at an early age and was sent away at the age of 7 to study with a leading Lithuanian rabbi. Soon unsatisfied, he preferred to study alone. At the age of 18, he left Vilna and entered a period of "exile," during which he visited Jewish communities throughout Poland and Germany. Upon his return, and for the rest of his days, he led an ascetic life of seclusion and study.

He is remembered for many achievements, not the least of which was his astounding memory. He could recite by heart the Torah, both the Babylonian and the more rarely studied Jerusalem Talmud, as well as the many commentaries. He worked at improving his memory by constantly reviewing legal literature; it is said that once a month for his entire life, he went over the Babylonian Talmud. Unlike other scholars of that day, who tended to concentrate solely on the *halakhic* or legalistic dimension of rabbinic literature, he also mastered the literary component of the corpus in the form of Midrash and Aggadah. He wrote scores of commentaries on a vast array of subjects, from the Bible to the Talmud to Kabbalah to astronomy and algebra. All his treatises, however, represent the tiniest fragment of his accumulated knowledge. His commitment to solitary study was somewhat of an innovation in Judaism—it is a matter of contention as to what degree he even attended synagogue, believing that it was primarily a venue for the dissemination of gossip—as was his elevation of Torah study to an end in and of itself. While it would be incorrect to claim that the Gaon was a student of Enlightenment thought—he was most definitely not—he was nonetheless reflective of the age, where emphasis was placed on the individual and his capacity for improvement. Also, in promoting the personality of their father, we can detect in the Gaon's sons the power of a modernizing ethos that celebrates heroic individuality.

Most significantly, the Vilna Gaon led a major transformation in the way that Jews studied, initiating a shift away from a focus on codes of Jewish law to the Talmud. By endowing Talmud study with primacy over all other forms of Jewish learning, the Vilna Gaon ushered in an institutional and social revolution among Jewish intellectual elites. This change in focus and the advent of the modern yeshiva bespoke a particular road to modernization among observant circles in eastern Europe, one that was different from the secularized cast of modernization that took place among Jews in central Europe and later among those in eastern Europe. They would seek to throw off or modify what they saw as the burden of tradition, while pious circles recast, reconceptualized, and became more self-conscious about their orthodoxy. The emphasis on Torah study was not merely an idiosyncratic expression of the Vilna Gaon but part of a larger Mitnagdic theology he helped formulate in response to Hasidism. Rejecting the Hasidic concepts of the *beinoni* and *devekut* and their inherent promise that even the humblest Jew could attain mystical union with God, Mitnagdism insisted on the stark separation of the material and the spiritual worlds and emphasized that Torah study was the only legitimate way to approach God. Similarly, they considered the idea that God was present in the world of the mundane to be an affront.

Even the Vilna Gaon's dogged enemies, the Hasidim, acknowledged and continue to recognize the man's greatness. So large did he come to loom in the culture of eastern European Jewry that Jews from across the political and cultural spectrum—traditionalists, Mitnagdim, and Maskilim (Jewish proponents of the Enlightenment)—all tended to see him as their intellectual ancestor. Ironically, for his

followers, the devotion that he engendered meant that he inadvertently played a role somewhat akin to a Hasidic *rebbe* or *tzaddik*.

The Vilna Gaon considered Hasidism a Jewish heresy and sought its eradication. He was uncompromising and refused all overtures by the Hasidim to meet and work through their differences. When Shneur Zalman of Liady and Menachem Mendel of Vitebsk went to Vilna to meet with him, he left the city rather than give them an audience. With his troops inspired to zealotry, the battle began in earnest in 1772 when in two communities—Vilna and Brody—the Mitnagdim seized and burned Hasidic texts, had their leaders arrested, and forbade their followers all contact, especially of a religious nature, with the Hasidim. The key act in this first wave of organized opposition was the Vilna Gaon's issuance of a writ of excommunication (*herem*) against his Hasidic enemies. From the wording, we can clearly see the Mitnagdic belief in Hasidic separatism, rejection of traditional authority, and disregard for accepted religious practices:

[They] meet together in separate groups and deviate in their prayers from the valid text for the whole people. . . . [They] conduct themselves like madmen. . . . The study of Torah is neglected by them entirely. . . . Owing to our many sins they have succeeded in leading astray in many locales the sons of Zion. . . . They consistently mock the angels of the Lord and desecrate the men of greatness in the presence of ignoramuses. . . . When they pray according to falsified texts, they raise such a din that the walls quake . . . and they turn over like wheels [somersaults]. . . . Yet all this is only a little fraction, only a thousandth part of their disgusting practices. . . . Therefore, we do declare to our brethren in Israel, to those near and far. . . . All leaders of our people must wear the garment of zealotry, zealotry for the Lord of Hosts, to extirpate, to destroy, to outlaw and excommunicate them. And with God's help we have already uprooted their evil belief from among us, and just as we have uprooted it here, may it be uprooted everywhere.

Issued at the conclusion of Passover in 1772, the *herem* was signed by 16 leading rabbis of Vilna, including the Vilna Gaon, and circulated throughout many communities. The Gaon, who was firmly supported in his campaign by the Vilna *kahal* (official community), followed this up with another letter, detailing other Hasidic practices that he considered transgressive. These included not praying at the appointed times, carelessness with prayers, the insertion of new or mispronounced words, adoption of Isaac Luria's Sephardic rite of Kabbalah instead of the Ashkenazic rite, as well as shouting and bellowing during worship. The second letter included a particularly bitter denunciation of Hasidic attire, such as the *shtrayml*, or fur hat. He also characterized the wearing of white on Sabbath and festivals as a blatant attempt to appear saintly. In all, the Gaon saw Hasidic garb as an ostentatious display of piety. He surely knew, however, that both the *shtrayml* and the wearing of white preceded the advent of Hasidism. He was infuriated by what he thought were excessive expressions of joy, charging Hasidim with frivolousness, made most manifest in their constant smoking of tobacco. Later critics also lambasted the Hasidim for their supposedly excessive alcohol consumption. So intemperate were the denunciations of the Hasidim that they were accused of homosexuality and bestiality. Still others condemned swaying while worshipping, which they considered lascivious, and in this vein, they even accused the Hasidim of ejaculating during prayer. For those communities outside of his native city, the Vilna Gaon urged that they, too, ostracize and excommunicate the Hasidim, which they did. In Judaism, the *herem*—in its most extreme application—was a kind of social death, where all contact, including speaking with the excommunicated party, was prohibited. For Jews, who lived on the social margins of European society to begin with, the consequences of being driven away from one's own community were dire.

The conflict with the Hasidim reached a peak between the years 1785 and 1815, becoming so extreme that Mitnagdic leaders forbade "intermarriage" with Hasidim. They also turned to the tsarist government, denouncing Hasidim as political subversives and spies, demanding that they be arrested and jailed. The Russian authorities often obliged. (The prison release dates of incarcerated Hasidic leaders, such as Shneur Zalman of Lyady, became days of celebration, some still observed to this day.) It also needs recalling that both Russian and Austrian authorities refused to outlaw Hasidism. Without the support of the state, beyond the *herem*, Mitnagdim had few coercive mechanisms at their disposal with which to crush the Hasidic movement. In their responses to the Vilna Gaon, the Hasidim maintained a stance of great respect, even covering for him by claiming that his evaluation of Hasidism was based on having been fed faulty information. The Hasidim did not want to create a rupture with either the traditional Jewish community or the *kahal* itself, as evidenced by the fact that Shneur Zalman of Liady counseled his followers to be moderate in their behavior and attitude toward the Mitnagdim.

In the end, all the writs of excommunication, as well as the bans and the denunciations, issued continually until the first quarter of the nineteenth century, came to naught. One reason is that most of the Mitnagdic objections to Hasidic practice had no basis in Jewish law, something the Vilna Gaon surely knew. The extravagant accusations by the Mitnagdim were reminiscent in tone to those directed toward Sabbatians and Frankists, a reflection of the fact that this was simply the way one was supposed to denounce so-called "heretics." The death of the Vilna Gaon in 1797 also severely weakened the Mitnagdic campaign, which was never as big as its actions and denunciations would suggest. In the vanguard were relatively few rabbis, and most of them were from Lithuania. The religious revival that was Hasidism continued to blossom; within about three generations of its founding, Hasidism became a mass movement, capturing the hearts and minds of much, but not a majority, of eastern European Jewry. In fact, most eastern European Jews did not identify with either camp. Another reason the battle petered out is that the Mitnagdim and the Hasidim eventually made peace, each considering the other to be Torah—true upholders of the faith. Their reconciliation allowed them to form a united front against that which both groups considered to be the greatest internal enemy facing the Jewish people—the Haskalah or Jewish Enlightenment.

THE VOLOZHIN YESHIVA

While the Mitnagdim drew spiritual inspiration from the Vilna Gaon, they followed the practical lead of his most talented student, Rabbi Hayim of Volozhin (1749–1821). Although Hayim was opposed to the Hasidim, he did not regard them as heretics, as his revered teacher had done. He considered them sincere and God-fearing Jews, albeit in error. Hayim's great contribution was to build an institution which gave practical expression to the Mitnagdic position. In 1803, he founded what would become Lithuanian Jewry's most prestigious Talmud academy, the Volozhin yeshiva. More than just a venue in which to continue the battle against the Hasidim, Volozhin represented an entirely new Jewish institution—the self-supporting, independent yeshiva. Previously, Torah study generally took place in a *bet midrash*, a study hall adjacent to a synagogue and under the auspices of the local rabbi. By contrast, before the Volozhin yeshiva opened, Hayim sent out a call to all of Lithuanian Jewry to offer financial support to the project. He sent emissaries far and wide to collect funds, and in so doing, the Volozhin yeshiva was not seen as the product of a single community but, rather, an institution that belonged to the whole nation.

The Volozhin yeshiva recast the religious culture of eastern European Jewry. Students came from great distances to study there, and it helped shape a national elite in the same way that Oxford and Cambridge universities did in England. According to the Hebrew poet Hayim Nahman Bialik (1873–1934), who was a student at the Volozhin yeshiva, it was the "school where the soul of the nation was formed." A vast array of Jews, from those who remained in the world of Torah Judaism to those who would later make major contributions as writers, philosophers, poets, and Zionists, were educated there.

The yeshiva of Volozhin resembled the great European universities in another way. Its pedagogy offered a Torah-centric version of a liberal arts education. Volozhin did not train young men to become rabbis. Talmud study was undertaken for its own sake (*torah lishma*) and not for the purpose of making legal decisions or in the name of ecstatic and mystical fulfilment, as was the case among the Hasidim. Rather, in intellectual terms, the goal of Torah study was to arrive at a clear comprehension of the text. This stood in stark contrast to the complicated dialectical method previously common among Torah scholars, *pilpul* (from the Hebrew word for *pepper* and a reference to the often-fiery mode of Talmudic argumentation). Never before in the history of Judaism had such intellectual purism dominated Torah study. But Hayim also taught that there was a spiritual reward to Torah study, observing that the Torah is an embodiment of God, and as such, the more intensively one studies it, the closer one is drawn to becoming one with God. His emphasis on the value of Torah study as a means of achieving communion with God is a synthesis of Mitnagdic and Hasidic values. Volozhin became the prototype for all the great Talmudic academies of eastern Europe, such as those in the towns of Mir, Brisk, Slobodka, and Telz.

At its peak at the end of the nineteenth century, the Volozhin yeshiva was home to approximately 450 students from all over Europe and the United States. Despite its size, a highly selective admissions process made acceptance into Volozhin extremely competitive. Life was rigorous for the students, mostly single men aged between 18 and 25. They were deeply immersed in Torah study, which took place six days a week, with some students beginning their day as early as 3:00 a.m., breaking at 8:00 a.m. for morning prayers, after which they studied until 1:00 p.m. Lunch and a further break would follow until 4:00 p.m., when studies were resumed and lasted until 10:00 p.m., with some students even continuing until midnight.

Students lived off stipends granted by the yeshiva, which had raised funds for that purpose. This was a modern innovation that no previous yeshiva had undertaken. Traditionally, the local community supported such institutions, and residents provided for the students' room and board. The financial independence that the young scholars at Volozhin enjoyed, thanks to the stipend, was very important in their own maturation process. They were no longer infantilized, as young Torah scholars had once been. Students were also encouraged to organize themselves into *vaadim* (councils) for the purpose of raising supplementary funds and exercising a whole host of organizational functions at the yeshiva. This also helped their sense of self-worth to blossom. Another source fed their growing self-confidence: Because students were no longer dependent on handouts from townspeople, the locals adopted a much more respectful tone and manner toward the Volozhin students, for they were fast becoming a new elite.

For most of the students at Volozhin, it was their first time away from home, and the diverse origins of the student body gave the yeshiva a somewhat cosmopolitan feel. Moreover, the impact of the separation from family and familiar surroundings and the new forms of community, independence, and male bonding they experienced left a permanent impression on the students. Almost all of them studied together in the great hall and, encouraged by the heads of the yeshiva, did so in pairs (*hevruta*). They worked on different texts at the same time. While study was not coordinated, the method of study—with its high-decibel singing, hypnotic chanting, foot stamping, and bodily swaying—lent a uniformity and an intensity to the experience that made the participants feel as though they were part of a single great spiritual, social, and intellectual undertaking. Impressions of the study hall at Volozhin remained with students forever. Decades after leaving, Eliezer Isenstadt recalled vividly:

> Imagine a building of large proportion, all of which—barring the large vestibule—is one massive auditorium filled with tables and benches. The tables are covered from corner to corner with oversized and heavy tomes. The benches are occupied by three hundred to three hundred and fifty gyrating young men, swaying back and forth, immersed in Torah study, which they sing. This was not the first time I had ever seen such a phenomenon: in our *bet midrash* on the High Holidays those who prayed would gyrate from side to side and their variegated tunes would echo through the building. But what I saw [at Volozhin] with my own eyes and with my own ears was beyond anything I could imagine.

The transformative nature of all these new social and cultural arrangements was augmented by new intellectual challenges. At Volozhin, as well as at other similar institutions, there was considerable innovation in the method of Talmud study, with emphasis put on the logic of a Talmudic argument, the plain meaning of the text, and the linguistic structure of a Talmudic passage. Ironically, with its stress on abstraction and intellectualism, the Volozhin methodology bred a certain skepticism. Stressing critical analysis above received wisdom, Volozhin fostered the questioning of authority, albeit in the circumscribed and tightly controlled culture of the yeshiva. Chaim of Volozhin even declared, "[A] disciple is forbidden to accept the statements of his teacher when he questions them, and sometimes the truth is on the side of the disciple, just as a small tree ignites a large one." In a world dominated by tradition, this encouragement of independent thought marked a significant concession to the age and to the sensibilities of modern culture.

In the late nineteenth century, the tsarist government began to impose itself on the yeshiva, demanding that secular subjects, taught in Russian, be introduced into the curriculum. The yeshiva reluctantly complied and offered the minimum amount of Russian-language study acceptable to the government. A dispute over succession to the position of head of the yeshivah (*rosh yeshiva*) in the early 1890s fractured the relation between the institution and the tsarist regime; fearing that the mood could turn the Volozhin yeshiva into a hotbed of political radicalism, the place was closed down in 1892, on the pretext that it had failed to properly implement the teaching of Russian-language subjects. Although it reopened a few years later, the Volozhin yeshiva never regained its pre-eminence.

ISRAEL SALANTER AND THE MUSAR MOVEMENT

While pure intellectualism was one of the defining features of the modern yeshiva, in the rest of the Jewish world, increasing laxity of religious practice, the attraction to Haskalah, revolutionary politics, and Zionism also began to take root in nineteenth-century eastern Europe. To counter some of these modernizing trends, Rabbi Israel Salanter (1810–1883) formed the *Musar* (self-improvement through virtue-based ethics) movement. Preaching the goal of ethical self-perfection and self-restraint, something he considered inseparable from Torah study, Salanter hoped to foster a spiritual and ethical revival within Lithuanian Jewry. The Musar movement developed its own method of instruction, which eventually came to dominate the world of the Lithuanian yeshiva and competed with the intellectual approach of Volozhin. Students read the ethical literature of Judaism in addition to those passages of the Bible and Talmud that taught ethical lessons. They would read such stories, even singing them to evocative melodies in dim light to heighten the experience. While Salanter did not argue against the ultimate importance of Talmud study, he elevated personal introspection to a level at least equal to, if not above, scholarly achievement. Some rabbis even ordered their students to keep a journal to record their personal failings. Salanter's stress on the cultivation of the individual personality, while owing nothing to the formal teachings of modern psychology, was nevertheless reflective of the modernizing age in which he lived, with its emphasis on self-analysis and personal growth.

As with Hasidism and Mitnagdism, the Musar movement was not homogeneous. After Salanter's death, different streams emerged, ranging from the deeply emotional forms of practice at the Slobodka yeshiva founded in 1881 to the stringently ascetic Musar culture of the Novaredok yeshiva established in 1896. This movement, too, was not without its critics. In 1897, students at both the Telz and Slobodka yeshivot rose in revolt against Musar itself, which they increasingly came to see as an infringement on their Talmud study as well as on their personal lives. The flames of rebellion and reaction were stoked when both sides resorted to making their respective cases in the Hebrew press. The recourse to newspapers among Orthodox Jews for the purpose of carrying on a religious dispute became commonplace in the twentieth century, and the debate over Musar was one of the earliest manifestations of this distinctly modern practice.

Despite the vibrant inner life of traditional Jewish elites, increasing secularism was proving attractive to many such Jews. One of the earliest creative responses to this came from Rabbi Esriel Hildesheimer (1820–1899). In 1851, in the Hungarian town of Eisenstadt (Kismarton in Hungarian), he opened the first yeshiva to include secular subjects in the curriculum. Hildesheimer encountered considerable hostility and left Hungary in 1869 for the more liberal environment of Berlin. There he became leader of the separatist Orthodox community, and in 1873, he established the Orthodox rabbinical seminary, whose ethos lay in training rabbis equally committed to Orthodox Judaism and the modern methods of critical scholarship.

For some rabbis, the times demanded even greater concessions to non-Jewish culture. In 1905, Rabbi Isaac Jacob Reines (1839–1915) opened eastern Europe's first modern yeshiva in the town of Lida. Fearing that the tide was shifting away from tradition, Reines declared: "[S]oon, the vital and vivid Judaism we still find among the Jews of Russia will suffer a fate like that which befell her in France. A dreadful disaster is imminent!" To prevent such a catastrophe, Reines moved away from the intellectualism of Volozhin and the *Musar*-centered yeshivot of Lithuania, offering students practical education in addition to Torah study. Incorporating Hebrew language and grammar, as well as Jewish history, into the curriculum, Reines promised that his

> yeshiva will provide its students with a secular education equal to that of the public schools. They will be taught to speak and write Russian fluently, and will study Russian and world history, geography of the five continents, arithmetic, geometry, algebra, and some natural sciences.

Neither the Torah nor ethics was left behind, but instead, both were joined with a secular curriculum to produce Jews faithful to both Jewish and Russian culture.

By the early nineteenth century, the feud between the Hasidim and the Mitnagdim lessened in intensity. With the emergence of such new secularizing trends as the Jewish Enlightenment, the once-bitter enemies found common cause. In defense of religious practice and Torah study, the two most powerful forces of eastern European Judaism formed a unified front to combat what the rabbis and the rebbes saw as the dangers of modernity. In making the self-conscious decision to counter the secularizing trend of the Haskalah, both Hasidim and Mitnagdim came to reject all secular study to an ideological extent that was new in Jewish history. Rabbis in the medieval and early modern period were, far more than their ultra-Orthodox modern counterparts, open to the acquisition of secular wisdom. Yet in the self-conscious opposition to modernity, even the new forces of tradition in eastern Europe proved to be inherently modern movements.

INCIPIENT MODERNITY IN SEPHARDIC AMSTERDAM

Unlike in eastern Europe, the principal challenge faced by the Jews of western Europe at the start of the modern period was the claim that Jewish society was stuck in the past and that the Jewish religion was wedded to outmoded traditions and needed to be radically modernized. This was not just an expression of Christian antipathy. Individual Jews, too, had internalized many of the negative impressions. This was the case among certain Sephardic Jews in western Europe, some of whom were in the vanguard of changing Jewish attitudes to Judaism. In Amsterdam, Uriel da Costa (c. 1585–1640) and Baruch Spinoza (1632–1677), both descendants of families forced to convert to Catholicism on the Iberian Peninsula, challenged some of the most fundamental teachings of Judaism as well as the authority of the community's rabbis.

Da Costa, who, together with his family, fled Portugal for Holland in 1617, was never able to adjust to the Judaism he saw in Amsterdam, for it conflicted too radically with the biblical Judaism he was drawn to, and that made him seek a return to his ancestral faith. He dismissed rabbinic Judaism as nothing more than a coercive system for the performance of meaningless rituals, devoid of spirituality. After seven long and lonely years, he recanted, promising to quietly conform or, as he derisively put it, "become an ape among the apes." Unable to remain silent, he fell afoul of the rabbis again and, in 1640, was forced to submit to a humiliating public ceremony which included the public recantation of his opinions, 39 lashes across his bare back, and being forced to lie on the threshold of Amsterdam's Great Portuguese synagogue so that all in the congregation could tread on him as they left. Traumatized by the event, he went home, wrote a few pages of his autobiography, and not long thereafter, shot himself to death.

Like Da Costa, Spinoza embraced a rationalist critique of Judaism, which led to his rejection of all revealed religion. He denied the idea of Divine Providence and the immortality of the soul and held that the Torah was not literally given by God to the Jews. Rather, he believed that the ceremonial laws of Judaism were the articles of the constitution of a now-defunct state, namely, ancient Israel. As such, they were no longer binding upon Jews. Spinoza, who rejected the authority of the rabbis, was excommunicated in 1656 at the age of 23.

Harshly worded but altogether formulaic, the *herem* read as follows:

The Lords of the *maamad* [Sephardic council of elders], having long known of the evil opinions and acts of Baruch de Espinoza, have endeavored by various means and promises, to turn him from his evil ways. But having failed to make him mend his wicked ways, and, on the contrary, daily receiving more and more serious information about the abominable heresies which he practiced and taught and about his monstrous deeds, and having for this numerous trustworthy witnesses who have deposed and born witness to this effect in the presence of the said Espinoza, they became convinced of the truth of the matter; and after all of this has been investigated in the presence of the honorable *chachamin*, they have decided, with their consent, that the said Espinoza should be excommunicated and expelled from the people of Israel. By the decree of the angels, and by the command of the holy men, we excommunicate, expel, curse and damn Baruch de Espinoza, with the consent of God, Blessed be He, and with the consent of all the Holy Congregation, in front of these holy Scrolls with the six-hundred-and-thirteen precepts which are written therein, with the excommunication with which Joshua banned Jericho, with the curse with which Elisha cursed the boys, and with all the curses which are written in the Book of the Law. Cursed be he by day and cursed be he by night; cursed be he when he lies down, and cursed be he when he rises up; cursed be he when he goes out, and cursed be he when he comes in. The Lord will not spare him; the anger and wrath of the Lord will rage against this man, and bring upon him all the curses which are written in this book, and the Lord will blot out his name from under heaven, and the Lord will separate him to his injury from all the tribes of Israel with all the curses of the covenant, which are written in the Book of the Law. But you who cleave unto the Lord God are all alive this day. We order that no one should communicate with him orally or in writing, or show him any favor, or stay with him under the same roof, or within four ells of him, or read anything composed or written by him.

After the issuance of the *herem*, Spinoza left Amsterdam and never sought readmission to the faith or the community. Although he abandoned the practice of Judaism, he did not convert to Christianity. Refusing membership in a religious community was not yet a viable social option in Spinoza's day. It was, in fact, a recipe for an individual's social isolation and loneliness. Still, by choosing the path he took, Spinoza embraced what would later become one of many alternative forms of Jewishness, and that included rejecting Judaism without the formal adoption of another religion. It is this stance that has led many to refer to Spinoza as the first modern Jew.

The Sephardic converso experience that led to a radical critique of Judaism differed significantly from the contemporary Ashkenazic experience. While the former constituted the reactions of troubled and disaffected individuals, Ashkenazic intellectuals, first in Germany, and later in eastern Europe, formed a loyal opposition, a movement for Jewish cultural and religious change, with a clearly articulated ideology.

The reformist project known as the Haskalah, or Jewish Enlightenment, is one of the most important developments in the entire history of European Jewry. It began in central

Europe in the 1740s, and like the European Enlightenment, which was its inspiration, its followers stressed the primacy of the individual and his capacity for self-improvement. Seeking to wrest control from the rabbis, who held a monopoly on knowledge and education, the Maskilim (proponents of the Haskalah) succeeded in creating the first of what would turn out to be many competing secular ideologies that captured the hearts and minds of modern Jews. The Haskalah served as a "gateway ideology" through which Jews traveled to arrive at liberalism, Jewish nationalism, socialism, Orthodoxy, Reform Judaism, and even in rare cases, apostasy.

In Germany, the Haskalah sought to reform Jews and Judaism by harmonizing religious and social life with the ideals of bourgeois culture. Maskilim sought to cultivate those necessary virtues they believed to be absent in the core principles of rabbinic Judaism. Already in the premodern era, there was heated debate over secular knowledge in the form of philosophy and its compatibility with the Torah. The Haskalah saw the re-emergence of this kind of debate, but now the focus was squarely on the desirability of acquiring a scientific education, European languages, and cultural mores. The Maskilic Jewish project in the West, and then in the East, can be seen as an attempt to transform Jews and Judaism: physically, sartorially, linguistically, morally, theologically, liturgically, politically, and occupationally.

THE HASKALAH IN CENTRAL EUROPE

The emergence in Germany of an elite that stood apart from the rabbis was a consequence of the repressive legal code, the Jewry Regulation (*Juden-Reglement*), issued by Frederick

II in 1750. By subordinating the Jewish community to the demands of the centralized state, the authority of the *kehillah* was greatly diminished. Contemporaneously, new economic policies led to the emergence of a small band of Jewish entrepreneurs who supported a cadre of Jewish intellectuals. In close contact with Prussian officials whose dedication to cameralist economics and Enlightenment values they shared, the wealthy and the wise of Berlin Jewry rose to lead in place of the rabbis and sought to promote cultural changes among the Jews, reflective of their own improved status. Despite the concern expressed by some Maskilim that the moneyed elites were thoughtlessly aping Christian culture, both groups saw their respective Europeanization as not merely a matter of individual choice but an exemplary path for the advancement of the Jews as a whole.

The Berlin Haskalah emerged just at that time when Jews were absorbing secular European culture to a greater extent than ever before; it was also the moment when Europeans began to debate the issue of Jewish emancipation. The Haskalah constituted an elaborate Jewish response to these historical developments. In their self-conscious attempt to create a new Jewish culture, the Maskilim arrogated to themselves a form of authority previously held by the rabbis, and as such, they constituted a new social group in Jewish society. Prior to the emergence of the Haskalah, there had been grumblings about the need to break the monopoly on education, knowledge, and communal authority held by the rabbis, but little came of it. One of the truly innovative features of the Haskalah, however, was that it broadened the demands of a few individuals into a movement that disseminated its demands in German-language periodicals, as well as in Hebrew prose, Yiddish plays, and literary salons, forming what one historian has called a new Jewish "republic of letters."

Nevertheless, this challenge to the rabbis did not make the Maskilim enemies of religion. On the contrary, unlike the anticlerical sentiments of the French philosophes, contemporary Jewish (and non-Jewish) enlighteners in Germany were mostly conservative men respectful of religious belief and religious morality. The Maskilim were dedicated to reforming Jews to better prepare them to assume their place as citizens in a modern state. This did not demand the abandonment of religion. Their ultimate goal was to change the Jewish character, to create a new kind of Jew—in Hebrew, *ish yehudi shalem*, an ideal of perfected, integral Jewish manhood. The new Jew would be a person who adhered to both Judaism and modern culture.

Moses Mendelssohn

In Germany, the most visible symbol of the possibility of a Jew living in two worlds—the traditional Jewish and the modern secular—was the Berlin philosopher Moses Mendelssohn (1729–1786). The son of a Torah scribe, Mendelssohn had first been exposed to secular knowledge in the form of Maimonidean philosophy by his tutor and intellectual mentor, Rabbi David Hirshl Fränkel of Dessau. When Fränkel moved to Berlin to take up the post of chief rabbi, Mendelssohn, aged 14, followed him there. Working as a bookkeeper in a Jewish silk factory by day, Mendelssohn, who had arrived in the capital speaking only Yiddish and knowing only Jewish texts, soon learnt Latin, Greek, German, French, and English. He also studied various branches of contemporary and ancient philosophy. Consequently, his reputation soared, and he earned the title of the "Jewish Socrates." In 1763, the Berlin Jewish community honored him by relieving him of paying Jewish communal taxes.

Mendelssohn was a genuine celebrity in Berlin's intellectual world. He was sought out for his character as much as for his intellect. His closest non-Jewish friend, the man who first encouraged him to publish, was playwright Gotthold Ephraim Lessing (1729–1781), whose drama *The Jews* (1749) was the first of at least 50 German-language plays between 1750 and 1805 to portray the Jews in a positive light. This was no small thing. According to Mendelssohn, the critics objected to Lessing's main Jewish character because "he was much too noble and generous." They claimed that it was an "improbability" that such a Jew could really exist. And as if to prove the point that such Jews could and really did exist, 30 years later, Lessing used Mendelssohn as a model for the character Nathan in his classic play *Nathan the Wise* (1779). (Lessing also created Nathan as a counterpoint to Shakespeare's Shylock.) Nathan was a spokesman for the Enlightenment values of universal brotherhood and tolerance. When publisher and poet Friedrich Nicolai wrote to Lessing, "I am indebted to [Mendelssohn] for the most cheerful hours of the past winter and summer. I never left him, regardless of how long we were together, without becoming either better or more learned," he was expressing a truly revolutionary sentiment. Rarely had a non-Jew spoken so warmly of a Jew. It was, for most non-Jews, inconceivable that one's wisdom or moral character could be improved by friendship with a Jew. This was because the idea that the Jews were degenerate was so deeply a part of the European mindset that only Jewish improvement could be imagined stemming from intimate Christian–Jewish relations. Few Christians thought that they could benefit either morally or intellectually from close contact with Jews, especially devout ones, which is what Mendelssohn remained his entire life.

With his hunchback and unattractive appearance, Mendelssohn was an unlikely cultural icon. For those non-Jews who laid eyes on him for the first time, he evoked the kind of contempt that most Jews had learned to expect. We can see this from the vivid description of a Christian university student who saw Mendelssohn when the philosopher visited the University of Königsberg in 1777. His physical appearance alone, especially in a university lecture hall, was enough to incite the crowd. However, people are often judged by the company they keep, and the negative and hostile expressions Mendelssohn aroused soon gave way to feelings of awe when the students realized the purpose of his visit:

> Without paying attention to those present, but nonetheless with anxious, quiet steps, a small, physically deformed Jew with a goatee entered the lecture hall and stood standing not far from the entrance. As to be expected there began sneering and jeering that eventually turned into clicking, whistling and stamping, but to the general astonishment of everyone the stranger stood with an ice-like silence as if tied to his place. . . . Someone approached him, and inquired [why he was there], and he replied succinctly that he wanted to stay in order to make the acquaintance of Kant. Only Kant's appearance could finally quiet the uproar. . . .
>
> At the conclusion of the lecture, the Jew pushed himself forward with an intensity, which starkly contrasted with his previous composure, through the crowd to reach the Professor. The students hardly noticed him, when suddenly there again resounded a scornful laughter, which immediately gave way to wonder as Kant, after briefly looking at the stranger pensively and exchanging with him a few words, heartily shook his hand and then embraced him. Like a brushfire

there went through the crowd, Moses Mendelssohn. "It is the Jewish philosopher from Berlin." Deferentially the students made way as the two sages left the lecture hall hand in hand.

Mendelssohn was engrossed in the study of philosophy and, in particular, ethics, aesthetics, and language. His concern, like that of his disciples and so many more modern Jews, involved a linking of these three areas of philosophical speculation and using them as the basis for a new Jewish educational curriculum. Mendelssohn began his publishing career in 1758 with the Hebrew weekly *Kohelet Musar* (*The Moralist*). In this publication, the first ever journal in Hebrew, Mendelssohn sought to establish a code of morals and ethics based upon his commentaries of classical Hebrew sources. He also encouraged his readers to contemplate nature and beauty and to appreciate a higher aesthetic. Nature, which was God's creation, and as well as poetry and art, the product of man's artistic genius, were to be equally embraced and celebrated.

In Mendelssohn's understanding of aesthetics, he often had in mind poetry and the formal rules of rhetoric. It is with this that his ideas about language came to play such a decisive role in the Haskalah. In 1778, to assist with the transformation of Jewish youth and lead them to an aesthetic awakening, Mendelssohn began the publication of his own German translation of the Bible (in Hebrew characters) with an accompanying Hebrew commentary called the *Bi'ur*. The book's proper name was *Sefer Netivot Hashalom* (*Book of Paths to Peace*). The text and commentary were both faithful to tradition and employed the exegetical modes of medieval Sephardic rabbis, who focused on the recovery of the authentic text at the expense of elaborate midrash. Originally intended for the use of his son, Joseph, who, Mendelssohn said, "has all but given up his Hebrew studies," the translation into German became a staple of the Haskalah educational system. Mendelssohn saw it as a vehicle for exposing traditional Jews to modern culture, getting unobservant Jews to return to Judaism, as well as weaning Jews from the general use of Yiddish and their reliance on Yiddish translations of the Bible, two of which had appeared just a few years before the *Bi'ur*. Indeed, this is precisely what rabbi Ezekiel Landau (1713–1793), chief rabbi of Europe's largest Jewish community, Prague, and one of Mendelssohn's most bitter critics, derided about the translation. He claimed that it served to degrade the Torah "into the role of handmaiden to the German language." Mendelssohn, a native Yiddish speaker, came to reject Yiddish (except when writing to his wife), speaking of it disparagingly and in a way that inspired generations of Jewish ideologues to also reject it. He detected a cause-and-effect relationship between the lowly status of the Jews and their vernacular: "I fear," he declared, "that this jargon has contributed not a very little to the immorality of the common man and I expect a very good effect from the increasing use of pure German idiom." Obviously, Mendelssohn failed to note that Yiddish had never compromised his own ethical makeup. Nevertheless, Mendelssohn's emphasis on language meant that it became central to the Maskilic goal of transforming the Jewish character. While he became a champion of Hebrew and German, as the Haskalah moved eastward, Maskilim in other lands would come to promote Hebrew, Yiddish, as well as Russian and Polish.

EDUCATIONAL REFORMS IN BERLIN

The earliest Maskilim were drawn from three groups—autodidacts, physicians, and rabbis—and while they emphasized different things in their call to reform Jewish education, they all had one thing in common: a raging sense of inadequacy. In his algebra textbook of 1722, physician Anschel Worms said that he published it in order "to open the gates of understanding to the nation [the Jews] which walks in the dark." All Maskilim repeatedly presumed Jewish intellectual inferiority and pleaded with their fellow Jews to acquire the rudiments of secular wisdom. Typical was the cry from Moyshe Marcuze, a Jewish doctor from Poland, who had taken his medical degree in Germany. In his Yiddish *Seyfer Refues* (*Book of Remedies*) (1790), he urged his readers to "take a leaf out of the pages of the Gentiles" and learn science and modern medicine.

In central Europe, the Haskalah first spread through individual initiative and not through an organized movement. Before the establishment of government schools that offered a dual curriculum, private tutors employed in the homes of the wealthy introduced a new pedagogic agenda, instructing students in secular as well as religious subjects. Then in Berlin in 1778, the first of the new Maskilic schools opened for instruction. Called the Jewish Free School, it offered courses in Hebrew, German, French, arithmetic, mechanics, geography, history, and natural science. Jewish schoolteachers were the first group to propound Enlightenment principles beyond their own circles.

Along with tutors and schoolteachers, physicians constituted the other group advocating changes in Jewish society. Medical doctors were the vanguard of new cultural currents among central European Jews because they were the first aspiring Jewish intellectuals to not attend a yeshiva, choosing, instead, to enter medical school. As a consequence, Germany acquired a scientifically trained, skeptically inclined Jewish elite that served as a role model for future generations of German Jews.

Moses Mendelssohn's Jerusalem

Since the 1770s, Mendelssohn had been formulating his position that Judaism constituted the principles of natural religion (belief in the existence of God, in the immortality of the soul, and in Divine Providence) combined with a singular revelation of the law to Jews. In 1783, he laid out the philosophical position of the Haskalah in his book titled *Jerusalem*. In two separate parts, Mendelssohn presented his vision of the ideal society. In the first section, he declared the state to be pluralistic and tolerant. Only secular authorities could compel action; Mendelssohn rejected all religious instruments of coercion, such as excommunication and censorship. "Let everyone be permitted to speak as he thinks, to invoke God after his own manner." Like his contemporary Thomas Jefferson, who declared in his *Notes on Virginia* (1781), "[I]t does me no injury for my neighbor to say there are twenty gods or no god," Mendelssohn held religious beliefs to be a strictly private matter and advocated freedom of conscience, as well as the separation of church and state.

In the second part of *Jerusalem*, Mendelssohn turned his attention specifically to Judaism, outlining an ideal form of the religion to conform to his image of the ideal state. An ideal Judaism was, like the state, tolerant and rational, and he drew upon the metaphor of a house to illustrate Judaism's relationship to the larger society. On the ground floor resided all of humanity, or at least that large portion that accepted natural religion. In saying that Jews and Christians occupied the same moral ground, Mendelssohn meant that both communities shared fundamental beliefs and were socially compatible. However, he also added that Jews dwelt on the top floor or in the attic of the metaphorical house. There they performed their ceremonial laws derived from revelation, which applied to them alone.

According to Mendelssohn, Judaism did not constitute a revealed religion but revealed legislation. He maintained that adherents of other faiths have their own means of achieving moral goodness; Judaism's path is the way of the Torah. Thus, it is imperative that the commandments be maintained and observed, because they have eternal moral value and are "absolutely binding on us as long as God does not revoke them with the same kind of solemn and public declaration with which He once gave them to us." Ceremony, he believed, also provided for communal distinctiveness and the retention of Jewish identity.

In arguing that Judaism was eternally relevant and compatible with philosophical ethics, Mendelssohn expressed the opinion that Judaism was the ideal religion for the secular state because it was free from supernatural dogma, embodying as it did the rationalistic principles of the Enlightenment. *Jerusalem* represents something very new in the history of the Jewish book. It presents Judaism as a religion for readers seeking to learn more about it. Traditional Jewish scholarship engages the Torah according to a variety of methodologies—legalistic, mystical, exegetical, to name but three. The rabbis had not, however, produced texts outlining Judaism as though it were a religion that could be explained in a primer. In doing that, Mendelssohn's *Jerusalem* and similar books that followed were distinct inventions of modernity.

While Mendelssohn was a pillar of German Jewry, he was not a vocal advocate of either Jewish emancipation or religious reform. While he doubtless would have welcomed it, he was not prepared to compromise Judaism for the sake of emancipation, believing it to be an inherent right, one that must be granted without strings attached. It was not a privilege, and thus, he declared at the end of *Jerusalem* that if the abandonment of Judaism was the price to pay for emancipation, then the Jews would have to reject the offer.

LITERATURE OF THE BERLIN HASKALAH

Mendelssohn's disciples were more active than their master in promoting the cause of the Haskalah. In addition to the new schools that were founded, new publications were dedicated to spreading the Jewish Enlightenment. The Hebrew-language journal *Ha-meassef* (*The Gatherer*), which appeared on and off between 1783 and 1811, was published by the Society of Friends of the Hebrew Language. Written in a highly ornamental biblical Hebrew that reflected the Enlightenment's general rejection of medieval culture and its preference for antiquity, *Ha-meassef* published poetry, biblical exegesis, and articles on natural science and philology. It also carried biographies of distinguished Jews, book reviews, and news concerning Jewish communities abroad. While the journal played an important role in the secularization of the Hebrew language, it did not last long because, as with the Maskilim's complaint that Yiddish separated Jews from non-Jews, Hebrew did no more to bring them together. Besides this, after the era of Mendelssohn's immediate disciples, fewer and fewer German Jews could understand the language.

For that reason, in 1806, the language of the Berlin Haskalah changed to German, heralded by the publication of the journal *Sulamith*. Bearing the revealing subtitle *A Periodical for the Promotion of Culture and Humanism among the Jewish Nation*, *Sulamith* signaled that its goal was to conduct a "civilizing" mission among the Jews. But more than this, the modernization of Judaism and the promotion of secular culture were objectives explicitly tied to the goal of emancipation. In the opening volume of the journal, the editor stated:

> Religion is the essential intellectual and moral need of a cultured man. It is the purpose of *Sulamith* to expose this religion to the highest light . . . [and it] wants to point up the truth that the concepts and commands contained in the Jewish religion are in no wise harmful to either the individual or to society [and] would never be an obstacle to any political constitution.

Harmonizing Judaism with European culture was the goal of the German Haskalah. And *Sulamith* was committed to the ideals of the Enlightenment. In its second issue, the periodical stated, "Enlightenment teaches us that we must think liberally and act humanely, not offend anyone who thinks differently or worships differently than we." No national group has ever been able to live up to such noble sentiments at all times, but that German Jews adopted them as a code by which to live came to define how they saw themselves and how they wished to be seen by others.

After Mendelssohn's death in 1786, the leadership of the German Jewish community passed to one of his disciples, a wealthy entrepreneur from Königsberg, David

Friedländer (1750–1834). In desiring religious reform, he was not seeking, like Mendelssohn, to forge a harmonious synthesis of traditional Judaism and modern secular culture. A man of wealth and taste, he had to contend with the fact that his political status was not commensurate with his social position. He spoke and wrote German, enjoyed classical literature, and was generally rooted in the European cultural landscape, a feature that would come to characterize German Jewry from that time on.

While Mendelssohn's principal objective was to share a common culture with Germans, for Friedländer and other second-generation Maskilim who had already been reared in German culture, their principal concern was the attainment of political equality. Wealthy, cultured, but politically disenfranchised, these men were concerned with the abolition of humiliating taxes imposed on Jews and their exclusion from state service and desired the repeal of the law that held well-to-do Jews responsible for paying off the debts of those Jews who had gone bankrupt or who had been found guilty of stealing property. To their dismay, when in 1790 Jewish community leaders approached the Prussian government to abolish this law, the regime refused.

While their worldview was shaped by the discrepancy between their wealth and political marginality, men such as Friedländer keenly felt the need for internal change. They feared that Jewish religious ceremonies, unless subject to reform, would continue to hinder the quest for civic emancipation. After Jews were emancipated in Prussia in 1812, Friedländer published a pamphlet arguing for religious reform. He called for the abandonment of Hebrew and of the study of the Talmud and demanded that all kabbalistic references from prayers be excised, along with calls for the restoration of Jerusalem. With these demands, Friedländer emerged as a radical. When in 1799 he had offered to convert to Christianity but then reversed himself, declaring Christian dogma contrary to reason, few in the Jewish community were perturbed, because this was a private affair. But there were great fears that his new proposals for the reform of Judaism might gain a foothold within the community. At the 1813 community elections, Friedländer was overwhelmingly defeated. He retreated into private life, becoming even more extreme in his demands. By 1815, he insisted that entirely new prayers for Jewish worship be composed, and that Sabbath services be conducted on Sundays instead of Saturdays, so as to better align Judaism with Christianity. Still, he never converted, wishing to remain within the fold. Despite his personal defeats, Friedländer's goal of changing the face of Jewish worship began to take root. Reform rabbis ultimately inherited the mantle of the Maskilim and continued to advocate from the pulpit for their ideal of philosophical, social, and aesthetic synthesis.

The Haskalah led to other innovations in Jewish thought and practice. Saul Ascher (1767–1822) was a Jewish book dealer from Berlin and a political journalist. A staunch defender of Jewish rights, Ascher challenged the right of Austria's Joseph II to enlist Jews into the army to fight the Turks in the absence of emancipation. In 1792, Ascher published *Leviathan*, a book that challenged Mendelssohn's synthetic conception of Judaism as a combination of natural religion and revealed legislation. Ascher's was also the first to attempt to discern an essence of Judaism, insisting that it contained dogmas.

According to Ascher, Judaism was in possession of unique truths, of which he identified 14. Ten, he said, were purely abstract articles of faith, while four were ceremonial practices. The ten abstract principles centered on three basic beliefs: (1) that God revealed himself to the people of Israel at Mount Sinai, (2) that Jews had to uphold their faith in messianic redemption, and (3) that the dead would be resurrected. The four essential ceremonies were circumcision, observance of the Sabbath, observance of holy days, and seeking God's favor through atonement. All these were immutable principles and practices and could not be abandoned. There were, however, 613 commandments in Judaism, while Ascher had identified only four that were indispensable. He claimed that both Jews and non-Jews had reduced Judaism to a cold legalism, with the laws being the end rather than the means to spiritual fulfilment. Arguing against Kant, who, like Spinoza, had seen Jewish law as the political constitution of a now-defunct state, Ascher was the first person to attempt to transform Judaism from a political and national ethos into a purely religious one. Ascher's aim, in keeping with the Enlightenment, was "to present Judaism in such a way that any enlightened man might embrace it, that it might be the religion of any member of society and that it would have principles in common with every religion." Later nineteenth-century reformers would attempt to further attenuate the ethnic dimension of Judaism in the name of pure religion. This was accompanied by changing terminology, such as using the word *temple* rather than *synagogue* because it was a universal word for a house of prayer, and describing Jews, for example, as Germans, Frenchmen, and Americans of the Mosaic persuasion.

THE SEPHARDIC HASKALAH

Mendelssohn's translation project was part of a larger literary trend, for the eighteenth century saw a flowering of translations of canonical Hebrew works into vernacular languages. Not only in the Ashkenazic world were the Bible and other texts translated into German and Yiddish, but seminal religious texts were also rendered into Ladino in the Sephardic Diaspora.

These Ladino publications were part of a larger global phenomenon. Most Jews knew little or no Hebrew and were increasingly reliant on the vernacular as a means of retaining their allegiance to Judaism and its print culture. In fact, such publishing domesticated Jewish practice by democratizing access to Jewish sources. Just as Yiddish began with Middle High German and added elements of other languages, notably Hebrew, Aramaic, and Slavic words, Ladino began with Spanish as its base and later incorporated Hebrew, Turkish, and Greek, eventually forming a distinct Jewish language. It developed to become the lingua franca of the Jewish communities of the Ottoman Empire, principally those in the Balkans and Asia Minor.

In the era of print, spoken Ladino was augmented by the creation of modern literary texts. This not only heralded Ladino's arrival as a literary language but also proved central to the modernization of the Sephardic Jews. The most important of these works was Jacob Huli's (1689–1732) *Me-am Loez*. One of the great achievements of rabbinic literature, this multivolume compendium of rabbinic lore and Bible commentary began appearing in 1730, and after Huli died in 1732, other authors wrote subsequent volumes. This effort went on well into the nineteenth century.

Although the book was initially greeted with skepticism by the rabbis, its popular success eventually won it rabbinic approbation, especially because Huli wrote, "[B]ecause of our sins . . . there are very few who know how to read a verse [of Bible] correctly." While his was a time-honored literary convention to be sure, one signaling a gap between rabbinic ideals and social reality, more Ladino works were required, and Huli's *Me-am Loez* inspired other Ladino authors. Between 1739 and 1744, Abraham Asa translated the Bible into Ladino, replacing the first such translation of 1547. In 1749, Asa also provided a new translation of important portions of the authoritative code of Jewish law, the *Shulhan Arukh*. The translations of such foundational texts saw other Ladino authors produce a diverse corpus of literature that included religious poetry, Purim plays, and ethical works. By the nineteenth century, religious treatises in Ladino included the full range of rabbinic literature; works on *halakhah*, however, continued to appear in Hebrew.

In the eighteenth century, Sephardic intellectuals and merchants came into contact with expatriate Italian Jews, known as Francos. They lived in some of the Ottoman Empire's important port cities, and the secular ways of these Francos began to have an important impact on Sephardic Jews. In Livorno, David Moses Attias wrote the first book in Ladino that rehearsed the basic themes of the European Haskalah. In his *Guerta de Oro (Garden of Gold)* (1778), he encouraged his fellow Sephardim to adopt Western learning and European languages. His book also included an introduction to the Italian language. Attias inspired other authors, and throughout the nineteenth century, many textbooks appeared offering Jews instruction in various European languages, Turkish, Hebrew, geography, and mathematics. Just as the Haskalah

journal *Ha-meassef* dedicated itself to telling the story of "the great men of our nation," nineteenth-century Ladino authors began to produce biographies of distinguished Jewish personalities from the secular world, such as Moses Montefiore, Adolphe Cremieux, and the Rothschilds. Even the classic authors of contemporary Yiddish literature, such as I. L. Peretz, Sholem Aleichem, and Sholem Asch, were translated into Ladino and were extremely popular.

THE HASKALAH IN EASTERN EUROPE

The Haskalah in eastern Europe was both similar to and different from its counterpart in western Europe. As in the west, eastern European Maskilim wished to bring about occupational and moral reform through the introduction of secular knowledge into the Jewish school curriculum. Eastern European ideologues similarly displayed a nagging sense of Jewish inferiority. Already in the eighteenth century, some individuals sought out knowledge beyond the Pale of Settlement. Rabbi Baruch Schick of Shklov (1740–1810), a disciple of the Vilna Gaon, translated Euclidian geometry into Hebrew in accordance with the Gaon's teaching that "if one is ignorant of the secular sciences in this regard, one is a hundredfold more ignorant of the wisdom of the Torah, for the two are inseparable." Many eastern European Jewish critics lamented that Jews were ignorant of the sciences, fearing that they were laughingstocks before the gentile world. The Lithuanian Talmudist turned Maskil and German philosopher Solomon Maimon (1753–1800), who criticized the traditional education system among his fellow eastern European Jews, said that after discovering the world of science, he had found a key to all the secrets of nature, as [he] now knew the origin of storms, of dew, of rain, and such phenomena. [He] looked down with pride on all others who did not yet know these things, laughed at their prejudices and superstitions, and proposed to clear up their ideas on these subjects and to enlighten their understanding.

Yet these and other like-minded scholars remained lone individuals. They embraced enlightened principles but did not promote a systematic program of curricular and behavioral change. The Haskalah in eastern Europe did not really emerge in full force until the 1820s, but when it did, significant differences from its German predecessor became apparent.

First, among eastern European Jews, there was no substantive and intellectually prominent elite that pushed for greater contacts with non-Jews. Jewish merchants, physicians, and intellectuals who promoted the Haskalah were not part of a social circle that included non-Jews. There were no salons of the variety that existed in Berlin and Vienna, where Jews, especially women, socialized and exchanged ideas with non-Jews. Second, the languages of the Haskalah in eastern Europe were Hebrew and Yiddish, even though many eastern European Maskilim knew French, German, Russian, and Polish. Aside from a couple of Yiddish plays and a significant, though small, number of publications in Hebrew, the Berlin Haskalah soon switched to German. Third, the eastern European Jewish community, compared to the Jewish community in Germany, was more hostile to deviations from traditional behavior. The Haskalah in eastern Europe did not merge with Reform Judaism as it later did in Germany; there, Maskilim and later Reformers worked in opposition to Jewish tradition. Fourth, where Prussian authorities were wary of the Haskalah and Reform Judaism, for fear that they could soon turn into expressions of political radicalism, the government played a very different role in Russia. Because the Russian Maskilim faced a large and implacably hostile community, led by Hasidim and Mitnagdim, they turned to the Russian authorities to support their quest for reform. The government of Nicholas I (r. 1825–1855) advocated the Haskalah among Jews, hoping that it would lead to their integration into Russian society. In actuality, Nicholas I sought the conversion of the Jews, and nearly all Russian Jewry knew it. Hence, the alliance between Maskilim and the state served to cast great popular suspicion on the Maskilim and often alienated them from Jewish society. Fifth, the particular social and cultural circumstances that prevailed in Galicia also ensured that the Haskalah there looked very different from its German forerunner. Socially, for example, a wide gulf separated Maskilim from the Jewish masses. While the bulk of German Jewry became middle class and therefore came to share the social aspirations and cultural inclinations of German Maskilim, most eastern European Jews remained extremely poor throughout the course of the nineteenth century and thus socially distant from the Maskilim in their midst. No Maskilic role model emerged whose behavior eastern European Jews wished to emulate. None of the eastern European Maskilim, for example, ever attained the paradigmatic status that was accorded Mendelssohn in Germany.

The Galician Haskalah

After Berlin and Königsberg, the Haskalah spread into Galicia, a region of Poland that had been annexed to the Austrian Empire in 1772. This area, which lay between Germany and Russia, had a Jewish population of around 300,000. In its major cities, such as Brody, Lemberg (Lvov), and Tarnopol, the Haskalah found a home. In all these places, and later in certain port cities of southern Russia, most notably Odessa, an emerging Jewish commercial class welcomed the winds of Europeanization.

Many of the most prominent Galician Maskilim came from well-to-do families or were supported by the social and economic elite of Galician Jewry. As in Germany, they were preoccupied with the process of embourgeoisement. This helped give the Haskalah a conservative cast. Even though the Maskilim were often derided as radicals by both the traditional Jewish leadership and the Christian authorities, the Haskalah was, in fact, a conservative social experiment. Tolerance was a hallmark of Enlightenment and Haskalah ideology. However, this did not mean that the Haskalah was characterized by libertinism or an "anything goes" attitude, but rather, it was tempered by demands for conformity. Bourgeois self-discipline became a substitute for traditional religious and communal discipline.

However, Brody was not Berlin. Unlike the Prussian capital, Galicia was heavily Hasidic and mostly Yiddish-speaking. Both characteristics would leave their mark on the Haskalah in this region. In terms of Maskilic texts, those from Galicia differed from those that had been produced in Berlin in the areas of language, genre, and object. Despite Joseph II's reforms of 1782, which included a ban on the use of Yiddish in official documents, the language persisted, indeed thrived. As such, Maskilim, seeking to have an impact upon the people, used the Jewish vernacular in their writing from the very outset.

The kinds of genres that marked the literary output of the Galician Haskalah were also new. Here, the beginnings of a secular Jewish national culture in both Yiddish and Hebrew developed with the production of plays, novels, poetry, and periodicals. Short-run Hebrew journals such as Yosef Perl's *Tsir ne'eman* (*Faithful Envoy*) (1813–1815) or the longer-lived journal *Kerem Khemed* (*Vineyard of Delight*) (1833–1843, 1854, 1856) were devoted to scholarship, polemics, and exegesis. *Kerem Khemed* was the earliest periodical devoted to scholarly analysis and critical reviews of Hebrew literature and medieval poetry and philosophy of history. It was also a vehicle for the publication of satire, either in translation or original works in Hebrew.

Satire assumed great social and artistic importance in the Galician Haskalah. By contrast, satire and humor more generally played almost no role in the Berlin Haskalah. The main object of Galician satire was the rabbinate in general and Hasidism in particular. While Moses Mendelssohn indignantly but solemnly attacked the rabbis' power to coerce and excommunicate and David Friedländer cautiously questioned the need for ceremony in Judaism, Galician authors drew devastatingly biting and witty portraits of Hasidic life. Their criticism was deeply personal, as many of the Maskilim in the Galician, and later Russian Haskalah, came from Hasidic backgrounds. They shared an internalized anticlericalism of the sort that eighteenth-century French philosophes, who were mostly from Catholic backgrounds, adopted in their attacks on the Catholic Church. But unlike men such as Voltaire, who became deeply anti-Christian, the Maskilim did not seek to destroy Judaism; rather, they sought only to extirpate what they believed were the most obscurantist and superstitious manifestations of contemporary Jewish religious culture.

The greatest exponent of the early form of Maskilic satire was Yosef Perl (1773–1839). Originally from a Hasidic family, Perl became a Maskil and, in 1813, established a Jewish school in the Galician city of Tarnapol. The school took as its model Mendelssohn's Jewish Free School in Berlin. Shortly thereafter, Perl, seeking to spread enlightenment among the Jews, began to publish calendars that contained scientific information, interspersed with relevant Talmudic passages. Perl's most important literary activities coincided with the spread of Hasidism into Galicia and the publication of the *Shivhei ha-Besht* and the writings of Nachman of Bratslav. An implacable enemy of Hasidism, Perl wrote many entreaties to the Austrian authorities, in which he lambasted Hasidism for its backwardness and implored the government to ban the movement. Of particular significance was a memorandum Perl wrote in German between 1814 and 1816, titled *On the Essence of the Hasidic Sect* (*Über das Wesen der sekte Chassidim*). Perl sent the manuscript to the governor of Galicia, Franz von Hauer, explaining that his goal was to expose Hasidic customs, claiming that his depictions of Hasidic life were drawn directly from their own books. Referring to it as a "sect," Perl observed that Hasidism was growing "from hour to hour like the disease of cancer," and that it was retarding the cultural development of the Jewish people. Aware of the storm of outrage its publication would cause, the censor did not permit Perl to print the text, but nonetheless, the government was sympathetic to Perl's claims and maintained close surveillance over the Hasidim.

In 1819, Perl published his most significant literary work, *Revealer of Secrets* (*Megaleh Temirin*). He wrote two versions of this novel: one Hebrew and one Yiddish; the latter did not appear in print until 1937. Aimed at the Hasidim and written in the form of letters—there are 151, plus an epilogue—the book tells the story of Ovadyah ben Psakhyah, a Hasidic hero who, through his magical powers—he could make himself invisible and self-transport from place to place—takes possession of a cache of letters that reveal a number of plots, the most important one being the search for a German-language book (it was Perl's *On the Essence of the Hasidic Sect*) that was said to contain all the secrets of Hasidic life. Perl's story, a hilarious comedy of errors, reveals the various intrigues and no-holds-barred tactics employed by the Hasidim to gain possession of the book and thus keep their secrets from the outside world. In the first letter, Reb Zelig Letitchiver writes to Reb Zaynvl Verkhievker, instructing him:

> For now, I'm informing you that first of all you should do whatever you can to get hold of this *bukh*, so that we can know what's written there and so we'll know the name of the *bukh*, so as to direct our Faithful to buy the *bukh* and burn it up and wipe it out, and also to find out who the author is so as to take revenge against him. In case the author's name isn't written in the *bukh*, maybe it contains the author's picture, the way the sinners print their picture at the beginning of their trashy books. Then, even if he's from another country, our *rebbe* will look at his picture and punish him just by looking. So don't be lazy about this! Be quick to get hold of the *bukh* and send it to me.

Perl painted such a vivid picture of Hasidic life that most contemporaries took *Revealer of Secrets* to be a genuine account rather than a satire. One other aspect of Perl's book came to have an unintended consequence—the extent to which he turned the Hasidim into appealing characters. He had them speak Hasidic

Hebrew, which, while not grammatically correct, was full of vitality and rang true to Perl's readers. By peppering their language with Yiddish witticisms, Perl created Hasidim who were worldly, wise, and full of humor. Perl's panoramic Jewish comedy became a standard trope for much Jewish literature and theater that blossomed at the end of the nineteenth century. Considered by some to be the first Hebrew novel, *Revealer of Secrets* was the first text in the genre of Maskilic anti-Hasidic satire and became the gold standard for all similar works that followed throughout the nineteenth century.

In the work of Nahman Krochmal (1785–1840), the Galician Haskalah also produced a significant attempt to outline a philosophical approach to Jewish history. Jewish philosophers of note virtually disappeared after Moses Mendelssohn and did not emerge again until the end of the nineteenth century; Krochmal was a singular exception. Born into a merchant family from Brody that maintained traditional values and customs, Krochmal was married off at the age of 14 and, like Moses Mendelssohn before him, earned a meager living as a bookkeeper while privately studying European languages and philosophy.

In his book, *A Guide for the Perplexed of Our Time* (*Moreh nevukhe ha-zeman*), which appeared posthumously in 1851, Krochmal outlined an idealist philosophy of Jewish history. (He borrowed the title from Maimonides's philosophical treatise on Judaism, *A Guide for the Perplexed*). Krochmal claimed that the spirit of Judaism differed from that of other religions because it embodied a unique relationship to the Absolute Spirit. Thus, the evolution of Jewish history revealed with greater clarity than did other cultures the development of the Absolute Spirit of world consciousness, a concept he borrowed from Hegel. Krochmal identified three distinct historical stages of Judaism: (1) growth, from the time of the patriarchs to the conquest of Canaan; (2) maturity, the settlement of Israel until the death of King Solomon; and (3) decline, the history of the divided kingdoms of Israel and Judea. But the story does not end with decline and demise, since the Jews are an "eternal people." Krochmal posited that following the period of decline, Israel entered into a series of cycles, each marked by rebirth or growth and characterized by an ever more intensified and introspective relationship with the Absolute Spirit. This, in turn, was followed by a period of maturation and another phase of decline. He concluded that the turn to philosophy and kabbalistic speculation in the Middle Ages constituted yet another stage of rebirth.

Krochmal was the first modern Jewish thinker to place historical development at the center of a philosophical understanding of Judaism. In so doing, he sought to establish the continuing relevance of a tradition that to many seemed at odds with the modern world. By endowing Judaism with eternal purpose and reason, Krochmal produced a philosophical alternative both to Hasidism and to traditional rabbinic culture. Claiming that Judaism remade itself over the course of its history, Krochmal also challenged the contemporary notion among some gentile critics that Judaism was an archaic, if not dead, religion. For Krochmal and his disciples, Judaism was a vital force whose eternality depended on its capacity to adapt and change.

The Russian Haskalah

From the Galician center of Brody, the Haskalah moved into the Russian Empire, where it went through three identifiable phases: from the early nineteenth century to the 1840s, from the 1840s to 1855, and from 1855 to the early

1880s. The founding document of the eastern European Haskalah was a book by Yitzhak Ber Levinzon (1788–1860), titled *Testimony in Israel* (*Teudah be-Yisrael*). Written in Hebrew and published in 1828, with the support of the tsar, *Testimony in Israel* argues for the relevance of natural sciences and foreign languages to the Jewish school curriculum and urges Jews to change their occupations from commerce to crafts and agriculture.

Levinzon, in fact, said nothing that other Maskilim had not already said. In fact, *Testimony in Israel* is quite similar to Wessely's *Words of Peace and Truth* (*Divre Shalom ve-Emet*), except that it goes to extreme lengths to justify the Haskalah in light of Jewish tradition, claiming that nothing in the program ran counter to traditional Judaism and, in fact, that the Haskalah drew its inspiration and strength from the Torah. The real significance of the book lay in the way it reflected the particular nature of the Russian Haskalah and its close ties to the state. Even though it bore the obligatory approbation of the rabbis, Levinzon did the unthinkable and dedicated his book to Nicholas I. He did this as an expression of gratitude, for the tsar granted Levinzon a subvention of 1,000 rubles to assist with the publication.

The impact of *Testimony in Israel* was enormous, because its appearance signaled a break between the moderate Haskalah and Talmudic circles in Vilna. Mitnagdic and Maskilic criticisms of Jewish culture were similar in the early nineteenth century. Even Levinzon's demand for secular wisdom was replete with rabbinic justifications for this innovation, and the study of sciences was permitted in certain Maskilic circles. Yet the tsar's patronage and the increasing tendency of the Haskalah toward secularization contributed to a sharpening of the battle lines between opponents and proponents of the Haskalah. Opposition between these two camps reached a peak in the 1840s, with the advent of the Russian government–sponsored Haskalah.

During the second phase from the 1840s until 1855, the Haskalah spread thanks to the establishment of modernized, state-run Jewish schools. Already during the reign of Alexander I (r. 1801–1825) and continuing under Nicholas I (r. 1825–1855), it was determined that the authority of the state and Christianity must be strengthened through the school system. To illustrate the point, the ministry of education was merged with the ministry of public worship. Consequently, Jews were fearful of sending their children to Russian schools. In 1840, out of 80,017 children attending elementary and secondary schools in Russia, only 48 were Jewish. However, Jews who were inclined to provide their children with a secular education could send them to a small number of privately established modern Jewish schools in cities such as Riga and Odessa. Beginning in the 1840s, as part of his carrot-and-stick approach to the social integration of Russian Jewry, Nicholas ordered his Minister of Education, Sergei Uvarov, to promote a program of "official enlightenment." This led to the creation of a network of reformed Jewish schools; two government-sponsored rabbinical seminaries, one in Vilna, the other in Zhitomir; and the enactment of a set of regulations restricting certain customs deemed superstitious and a barrier to enlightenment. These included prohibitions on traditional Jewish garb and early marriage. The law instituting this reformist program was passed in November 1844.

To bring the program to fruition, Uvarov cultivated the support of local Maskilim as experts, schoolteachers, and advisors. An admirer of the integration efforts of German Jewry, he sought out the assistance of the director of the modern Jewish school in Riga, Max Lilienthal (1814–1882), to introduce the project to the Russian Jewish masses. Uvarov dispatched Lilienthal on a tour of the Pale of Settlement to ascertain the attitude of Jewish communities to the government's new educational policies. Almost everywhere he went, Lilienthal, a German-speaking, clean-shaven, short-coated "reformer," was greeted with suspicion and hostility by Jewish communal leaders, who were steeled against both the government and the Maskilim. Only in Odessa, which would later become a center of the Hebrew language revival, did local Jewish enlighteners warmly accept Lilienthal. In search of new economic opportunities, Lilienthal soon left Europe for the United States, where he became a communal leader, first in New York, and then most notably in Cincinnati, where he was instrumental in the development of American Reform Judaism.

Although Nicholas's reform project found nearly universal support among Russian Jewish enlighteners desirous of using the prodigious resources of the state to implement their own social vision and oust the existing elites (especially the Hasidic rebbes), most Jews associated "official enlightenment" with the conversionary goals of the conscription decree. Indeed, for Nicholas—the proponent of official nationalism, dynastic patriotism, and Orthodox discipline—the line between integration and conversion was blurred, if not an impossibility. In a secret memorandum, the tsar averred that "the purpose of educating the Jews is to bring about their gradual merging with Christian nationalities, and to uproot those superstitions and harmful prejudices which are instilled by the teachings of the Talmud." Even though the curriculum of the new schools offered all Jewish subjects, including Talmud, most Jews balked

at sending their children to these institutions. They simply did not appreciate that there was any distinction between "school service" and "military service." Lilienthal admitted that any program of Jewish Enlightenment would have to overcome Jewish hostility to government intervention in Jewish affairs—hostility that extended also to the Maskilim. He declared that "an honest Jewish father will never agree to train his child for conversion."

Altogether, about 3,000 Jewish children were educated at the government schools, a figure that is proportionately similar to the 80,000 Russian children receiving elementary and secondary-level schooling. Despite their paltry numbers, those who emerged from these institutions made significant contributions to Jewish culture. The first cohort of graduates from Nicholas's Jewish schools, as well as from the two modern, rabbinical seminaries, produced the generation that founded modern Russian Jewish culture and politics. At the same time, the profound opposition of the majority of Jews to all forms of non-traditional education fueled mass resistance to government schools. The Maskilic rabbis who graduated from the government-run yeshivot failed to win the respect of the masses. The source of their education plus the fact that they hardly made any significant contributions to rabbinical literature were another measure of Nicholas I's failed program. In sum, too many Jews remained rightly suspicious that the government's Jewish educational program was intended to promote Jewish conversion to Christianity.

The final phase of the Haskalah coincided with the liberal, reformist reign of Alexander II (r. 1855–1881). It began with great hope, with certain discriminatory laws against Jews rescinded and residence restrictions for some groups of Jews relaxed. But after Russia had crushed the Polish uprising of 1863, reaction set in, and the state embarked on an intensified program of Russification. The country's nascent industrialization and modernization, which held out the promise of new opportunities and employment, also contributed to the Russification of the Jews, because command of the national language became a prerequisite to obtain better-paid jobs. When the social benefits of secular schooling became evident—a university degree was the passport out of the Pale of Settlement—Jewish students began to seek entry into Russian institutions of higher learning in large numbers, something that had never occurred prior to this. What emerged as a result of these developments was, for the first time, a university-educated, Russian-speaking Jewish intelligentsia. This cohort began, as their Maskilic predecessors had done in Germany, to promote the ideas of the Haskalah in the vernacular, and so, for the first time, they began to publish Russian-language Jewish newspapers.

It was during the third and final phase that, in the 1860s and 1870s, the Russian Haskalah entered into its most radical period. With many Maskilim stemming from traditional backgrounds, writers such as Sholem Yankev Abramovitch (Mendele Moykher-Sforim), Yehudah Leib Gordon, Moshe Leib Lilienblum, and Peretz Smolenskin were profoundly influenced by contemporary Russian literary and political trends. Already by the middle of the nineteenth century, the *shtetl* (small town), where the majority of eastern European Jews lived, had begun to go into economic decline. The emancipation of the serfs in 1861 and the spread of railroads in Russia saw the beginnings of a great flight from the land. Far from train lines and rendered economically marginal, the *shtetlekh* (pl.) seemed to be left behind by history, but in fact, they remained heavily populated until they were destroyed during the Holocaust.

The great and recurring theme in the work of these Maskilic writers was the grinding poverty of the Jewish masses. This saw them reject the agenda of the Maskilim of the previous generations. Hebrew philology, biblical exegesis, and the dispute with the Hasidim were now considered luxuries that Russian Jewry could not afford to waste time on. Instead, they sought to represent in their literary works the terrible material destitution and cultural backwardness of Russian Jewry, with a view to alleviating its lot. They were activist authors who bitterly criticized traditional Jewish education, the economic and political structure of Jewish communities, and even the institution of arranged marriages. The rabbi, the *melamed* (elementary schoolteacher), and the community leader were held up as figures of ridicule and contempt, men who represented all that was wrong with Jewish life in Russia. Similarly, the *shtetl* was described not only as a real place where millions of Jews lived but also as a symbol of their parochial backwardness. The *shtetl* was not a mere place of residence but a state of mind. In Yiddish literature of the Haskalah, a narrow-minded Jew who had not seen much of the world was referred to as *kleynshtetldik* (small-townish). Mendele typified the radical Maskilic critique of traditional Jewish society, with unvarnished portrayals of *shtetl* life in Yiddish classics such as *Dos vintshfingerl* (*The Magic Ring*, 1865), *Fishke der krumer* (*Fishke the Lame*, 1869), *Di klyatshe* (*The Nag*, 1872), and *Masoes Binyomin hashlishi* (*The Travels of Benjamin the Third*, 1878). By contrast, the heroes in the literary works of this generation of Maskilim were always the young men, those who longed to break out of the *shtetl*, make their way to the big city, acquire secular wisdom, and master European languages.

In the end, Jewish society could not be reformed so long as economic and political discrimination remained the lot of Russian Jews. In fact, after the 1870s, conditions only became more restrictive. In terms of promoting Haskalah, the Maskilim can only be said to have been partially successful insofar as those who became most radicalized tended to gravitate toward Russian language and culture, rejecting both Hebrew and Yiddish. Even the Maskilic champions of Hebrew began to despair for the future of the language. In his poem of 1871 "For Whom Do I Toil?," Yehuda Leib Gordon (1831–1892), a leading Hebrew poet, asked achingly, "Alas, who will probe the future, who will tell me, whether I am the last of the poets of Zion, whether you are not the last readers?" On the other hand, the majority of Jews rejected the Haskalah and the radical critique of their way of life and continued to speak Yiddish and pray in Hebrew. However, that was far from the end of it, for the impact of the Haskalah among eastern European Jews was profound. It was just not immediate; rather, the Maskilim provoked a delayed reaction. Eventually, the Haskalah led to total cultural renewal, creating a path to Jewish modernization, the birth of modern Hebrew and Yiddish culture, Jewish politics, and secularization.

HASKALAH AND LANGUAGE

Language formed a key component of the modern Jewish experience. Four essential Maskilic positions reflected a welter of Jewish cultural predispositions, generational and socioeconomic realities, and political inclinations. In both central and eastern Europe, early Maskilim favored the use of Hebrew. In the initial prospectus of the Haskalah journal *Hameassef*, the emphasis on Hebrew was made in the following way. Explaining the contents of a section titled "Essay and Disquisitions," the editors noted:

At the source will be the words of men who are learned in languages in general and in the wisdom and character of Hebrew in particular. This section will illuminate subjects in Hebrew grammar, clarify problems of phraseology and rhetoric, chart a path in Hebrew poetry, and teach the reader to recognize the meaning of the individual root words.

In the Russian Haskalah, a similar sentiment predominated. What began as a standard Maskilic position later became one of the central planks of Zionism, the followers of which became the staunchest advocates of Hebrew culture. In 1868, the Hebrew novelist Peretz Smolenskin (1840–1885) founded a journal with the optimistic name *Ha-shahar* (*The Dawn*). More explicitly political than the editors of *Ha-meassef*, Smolenskin declared:

When people ask what the renewal of the Hebrew language will give us I shall answer: It will give us self-respect and courage. . . . Our language is our national fortress; if it disappears into oblivion the memory of our people will vanish from the face of the earth.

Many doubted the moral appropriateness of using Hebrew for modern, secular culture, while others questioned the project on aesthetic grounds. Did Hebrew have a vocabulary and syntax that could be modernized? The issue of whether it could really be done successfully was answered with the work of the Lithuanian-born Abraham Mapu (1808–1867). Regarded as the father of the modern Hebrew novel, he turned explicitly to Israel's past as a source of inspiration for modern Jewish renewal. Influenced by the French Romantic school, Mapu's *Love of Zion* (1853) was written in sparse language interwoven with biblical passages. With its evocative descriptions of ancient Israel's terrain, the novel tells of the romance between Amnon and Tamar in the days of King Hezekiah and the prophet Isaiah. Mapu's utopian depiction of life in ancient Israel was extremely popular with eastern European Jewish readers, who, leading lives of great material hardship, were swept away in an escapist Jewish fantasy.

Other eastern European modernizers rejected the idea that the language of the Bible could best carry Jews into the modern age and likewise dismissed the idea that Judaism and Jewishness could only be fashioned in Hebrew. Maskilic populists argued that for strategic, political, and cultural reasons, change should be propounded in the dominant language of the people: Yiddish. In the Russian census of 1897, 97 percent of Jewish respondents claimed that Yiddish was their mother tongue. Yiddish was the language of millions, indeed the most widely spoken vernacular in Jewish history. The great author Sholem Yankev Abramovitch (1836–1917)—known by his popular pseudonym Mendele Moykher Sforim ("Mendele the Bookseller")—is considered to be *der zeyde* ("the grandfather") of modern Yiddish literature. Abramovitch, the founder of modern Jewish prose in both Hebrew and Yiddish, spoke out against the Hebraists: "Those of our writers who know Hebrew, our Holy Tongue, and continue to write in it, do not care whether or not the people understand it." Despite the dire warnings of his friends, he abandoned Hebrew prose for Yiddish because "[his] love for the useful defeated false-pride." He went on to publish in the first successful weekly Yiddish newspaper, *Kol Mevasser* (*The Herald*), founded in Odessa in 1863. According to Abramovitch, his novella *The Little Man* (1864), a satire about the backward state of the Jews in the Pale of Settlement, "laid the cornerstone of modern Yiddish literature. From then on, [his] soul desired only Yiddish." By the turn of the twentieth century, Yiddish no longer only served the cause of the Haskalah but was also the language of Jewish literary modernism and political expression.

Hebraists faced stiff competition not only from Yiddish as a language but also from Yiddishism as an ideological movement which was begun in the 1860s by Alexander Zederbaum (1816–1893) with the publication of *Kol Mevasser*. Though Yiddish was already at least 800 years old, *Kol Mevasser* marked the emergence of Yiddish as a modern literary language, for it standardized Yiddish orthography and provided an opportunity for the best young Yiddish writers of the day to publish their works.

By the modern period, Hebrew and Yiddish were engaged in an unfortunate language war. What should never have been an either/or choice saw militants pit one language against the other. Some, like the Zionist author Micha Yosef Berdichevsky (1865–1921), did not believe it had to be that way. There was room and, indeed, necessity for both tongues, something the average eastern European Jew would have instinctively believed. Hebrew was, for Berdichevsky, the language of Jewish tradition and texts, but so too was Yiddish:

The [Yiddish] language is still so indivisible from the Jew, so thickly rooted in his soul, that all we can say about it is, this is how a Jew talks. . . . You see, anyone can learn Hebrew, provided that he confines himself to his desk for a few years, stuffs himself with the Bible and grammar, and reads some *melitse* (satire). . . . The mastering of Yiddish, however, is a gift; a faculty one must be born with. I am speaking, of course, of the real thing, of radical, authentic Yiddish.

SHOLEM ALEICHEM

Sholem Aleichem (1859–1916) was one of the most gifted of all Jewish writers. Like his equally talented contemporaries Mendele Moykher Sforim and I. L. Peretz, Sholem Aleichem had begun as a Hebrew writer but switched to Yiddish in order to speak to his people in their own language. To a greater extent than his fellow Yiddish authors, Sholem Aleichem wrote in such a way as to perfectly capture the nuance and cadence, as well as the rhythms and patterns, of spoken Yiddish. Doing this created an intense intimacy with the reader that few authors in any language have been able to enjoy. Readers heard themselves or their neighbors in Sholem Aleichem's characters.

Sholem Aleichem was a brilliant humorist and created beloved characters, such as Tevye the Dairyman and Menachem Mendl, the latter a ne'er-do-well schemer, into whose mouths he put expressions and aphorisms that were so appealing that they were quickly incorporated into Yiddish. The Tevye character, upon whom the Broadway musical *Fiddler on the Roof* was based, was famous for his running monologues with God, arguing with him in a time-honored Jewish tradition. In the story "Tevye Strikes It Rich," we see another characteristic aspect of Sholem Aleichem's style, as Tevye's words flow in a torrent of stream-of-conscious prevarication:

> Well, to make a long story short, it happened early one summer, around Shavuos time. But why should I lie to you? It might have been a week or two before Shavuos too, unless it was several weeks after. What I'm trying to tell you is that it took place exactly a dog's age ago, nine or ten years to the day, if not a bit more or less.

Sholem Aleichem wrote biting (and, late in life, rather dark) social commentary. In 1909, he published the short story "Talk about the Riviera," a brilliantly witty satire on the emergence of middle-class values among Jews and, in the process, their adoption of gentile habits. In this case, Jews going on vacation become the object of ridicule and self-parody as the narrator mocks his own plight—being stuck at an expensive European holiday resort:

> Talk about the Riviera?—Thanks but no thanks. . . . Because the Riviera is the kind of place they've got over in Italy that doctors have thought up only to squeeze money out of people. The sky is always blue there. Same old sky as back home. Sun is the same too. Only the sea, that's the worst part! Because all it does is heave and crash about and make a great thundering nuisance of itself—and, by God, you never stop paying for it either. Why pay for it? Oh, no reason. No reason at all. . . . One good thing about the place, though—give credit where credit is due—it's warm there. It's always warm there, the whole blasted year. Both summer and winter. Yes, but what's the point? The point is the sun keeps you warm. Well, yes, but what's the point? Keep a good fire going at home and you won't be cold either.

For Berdichevsky, who wrote mostly, but not exclusively, in Hebrew, Yiddish was "purely Jewish [for] in it is expressed and revealed the soul of a people." For the Hebrew poet Bialik, Hebrew and Yiddish were a "match made in heaven." Yiddish played a pivotal role in the creation of modern Hebrew, although that is something hardly any of the Hebraists would dare admit. In addition to being a living repository of Hebrew words and expressions, Yiddish also provided Hebrew with vocabulary,

"Air __ __," they say. Well, yes, the air isn't too bad as air goes. Doesn't smell too bad either. Got kind of a fragrance to it. Only it's not the air that smells, it's the oranges that smell. Out there, they grow oranges. But I don't know if that's enough reason to be traveling all that way for it. Seems to me there is air all over. And you can buy oranges at home, anyway.

Enjoying international fame, Sholem Aleichem was a genuine hero, read by Jews the world over. As the literary critic Irving Howe put it, "[e]very Jew who could read Yiddish, whether he was orthodox or secular, conservative or radical, loved Sholem Aleichem, for he heard in his stories the charm and melody of a common *shprakh*, the language that bound all together." When Sholem Aleichem died on May 13, 1916, over 100,000 people lined the streets of New York City to pay their respects. To this day, it remains one of the largest funerals the city has ever seen.

Figure 2.1   Frontispiece of Sholem Aleichem's three-volume work *Tevye the Dairyman and Other Stories* (1912).
Source: John M. Efron.

syntax, and intonation, serving to modernize and animate the ancient language. (Modern Hebrew would also borrow liberally from other European languages.) As a vernacular Jewish tongue, Yiddish also served as a model and source of hope for those seeking to turn Hebrew into a daily language for millions of Jews.

The prestige of Yiddish grew immeasurably in the nineteenth century, especially thanks to the creation of a towering literary canon. Due to the dazzling talents of Mendele, I. L.

Peretz (1852–1915), and Sholem Rabinowitz, better known as Sholem Aleichem, Yiddish prose and poetry were elevated to the status of a great European literature. This gave hope to the ideological proponents of the language while it gave untold pleasure to millions. Yiddish also gained currency as the language of a vibrant newspaper, periodical, musical, theater, and later, film culture (*see box*, "Sholem Aleichem").

The principal theoreticians of Yiddishism were the Jewish nationalist Nathan Birnbaum (1864–1937), who also coined the term *Zionism*, and the philosopher, literary critic, political activist, and architect of secular Jewish culture Chaim Zhitlovsky (1865–1943). Together, they developed sophisticated theories of Diaspora nationalism and, in 1908, organized the First Yiddish Language Conference in Czernowitz, at which Yiddish was declared "a national language of the Jewish people." Though the language was expressive of the Jewish soul, as Berdichevsky said, the great author I. L. Peretz declared at Czernowitz that Yiddish was to be the means by which Jews would draw closer to non-Jews:

> We no longer want to be fragmented, and to render to every Moloch nation-state its tribute: There is one people—Jews, and its language is Yiddish. And in this language, we want to amass our cultural treasures, create our culture, rouse our spirits and souls, and unite culturally with all countries and all times. . . . If Yiddish is to become a full member in the family of the languages of the world, it must become accessible to the world.

It is in such expressions that the universalism of the Yiddishists appeared to clash with the more parochial sentiments of the Hebraists. In truth, however, both languages were so deeply Jewish that neither one became "accessible to the world."

The Orthodox likewise embraced Yiddish. Unlike Jewish political revolutionaries or modernists, they used Yiddish to stem the tide of secularization. While they reserved Hebrew for liturgy and Torah study, Yiddish was now the product of self-conscious choice and thus an expression of Orthodoxy's own antagonistic encounter with modernity. For Rabbi Akiba Joseph Schlesinger (1837–1922), who officially defined the ideology of ultra-Orthodoxy (*haredi*, in Hebrew), Yiddish was elevated to the status of a sanctified language. In his work of 1864 *The Heart of the Hebrew*, the Hungarian Schlesinger invoked the authority of his teacher, Moses Sofer.

> Our sainted ancestors, who were forced not to speak Hebrew, changed the language of the nations into Yiddish. . . . Thus we have to understand Rabbi Sofer's command that we must not change the language (that is, replacing Yiddish with another language) since our Yiddish is, from the viewpoint of Jewish law, just like Hebrew.

Yiddish was not merely spoken in the Orthodox world but was used in religious scholarship and books in that language constituted about 8 percent of the library holdings of the Volozhin yeshiva. The old canards about Yiddish being the language of Jewish women and unlearned men simply do not comport with social reality. Yiddish readers in eastern Europe had access to a vast array of reading matter, both religious and secular. Yiddish literacy was nearly universal, an astonishing development in light of the fact that on the eve of the Russian Revolution, Russian literacy stood at a mere 20 percent.

Finally, there were those Maskilim who insisted that Jews learn European vernaculars.

LINGUISTIC BORDER CROSSING: THE CREATION OF ESPERANTO

A noteworthy linguistic innovation was the invention of Esperanto by a Polish Jewish ophthalmologist, Ludwik Lazar Zamenhof (1859–1917). Raised in Bialystok, Zamenhof was reputedly troubled by the animus that existed between the city's three main ethnic groups: Poles, Belorussians, and Yiddish-speaking Jews. He believed that if only they shared a language, much of the hostility they felt toward each other would dissipate. To that end, in 1887, he published the first book in *Esperanto*, a word that means "one who hopes." This was an apt description for Zamenhof, because his utopian goal was to create a language that was easy to learn and would become a universal second language. His ultimate hope was that it would promote peace and international understanding.

Even while the Berlin Haskalah sought to revitalize Hebrew, its proponents simultaneously extolled the virtues of learning German. Mendelssohn even claimed that it would be of ethical benefit to the Jews to learn the language, since Yiddish was morally corrupting. After the Ashkenazic Jews of France had been emancipated in 1791, the communal leader and merchant Berr Isaac Berr (1744–1828) sent a letter to the Jews of Alsace and Lorraine, in which he exhorted his Yiddish-speaking coreligionists: "French ought to be the Jews' mother tongue since they are reared with and among Frenchmen." Wherever the Haskalah began to make an impact, voices were to be heard encouraging Jews to learn the language of the majority. In the first Russian-language Jewish weekly, *Razsvet* (*The Dawn*), the author Osip Rabinovich pointed out, "In other European countries the Jews speak the pure language of their Christian brothers, and that fact does not hinder them from being good Jews." For his own community, he stressed, "The Russian language must serve as the primary force animating the masses, because, apart from Divine providence, language is the constitutive factor of humanity. Our homeland is Russia—just as its air is ours, so its language must become ours."

Important though they were, the positions we have outlined were those of cultural ideologues. Other prominent Maskilim counseled Jews to be bearers of more than one culture. In his 1866 poem "Awake My People!," the Russian Jewish poet Judah Leib Gordon exhorted his readers, "Be a man abroad and a Jew at home," by which he meant, when in public, be sure to express oneself in the culture of the majority, while Judaism and Jewishness must shape the culture of the home. Generally speaking, most eastern European Jews would have concurred. They were not content with monolingualism and often deployed a variety of languages in different social, intellectual, and political settings (*see box*, "Linguistic Border Crossing: The Creation of Esperanto"). All over Europe and in the Ottoman Empire, Ashkenazim and Sephardim inhabited polyglot worlds where they had facility with three or four languages, at least two of which were Jewish. Because they could speak several languages, Jews adapted well and quickly to changing economic and political circumstances. This stood them in particularly good stead in the era of mass migration. Combined with vastly superior literacy rates compared to non-Jews, multilingualism also made vast amounts of

JEWISH WOMEN IN DOMESTIC SERVICE

Unlike the cantonists, merchants, rabbis, and maskilim, women as well as the subject of gender relations have not received the attention they deserve from historians of eastern European Jewry. One important social category in particular, that of "maidservant," has been almost entirely ignored in Jewish historiography. The reasons for this are that Jewish history has, to a disproportionate extent, been written from the perspective of intellectual history, that "maidservants" did not display a specific class identity or consciousness, and that they were women. But Jewish women as domestic servants and the sheer number of them speak for a most important aspect of the life of the modern Jewish family.

Aside from earning a living, one of the main reasons Jewish women went into domestic service was their need for a large dowry. Although there were special funds and institutions established in Jewish communities to provide dowries to young women in need, the amounts available were unequal to the demand. Thus, young women who either lacked a well-to-do relative or were without access to meager communal funds sought work as domestic servants so as to save enough in order to provide a dowry for themselves. In fact, already in the seventeenth century, Jewish communal records in Lithuania show that young Jewish women applying for a dowry were required to demonstrate that they had worked as a maid for at least three years. Self-reliance was thus a critical prerequisite to obtaining communal assistance. If such proof were unavailable, the communal authorities would assign the woman to a wealthy household, where she would work to earn her dowry. Beyond this, Jewish communal institutions strictly regulated the terms of service for female domestics, which included a kind of sickness insurance whereby employers were mandated to care for servants for one full month should they fall ill. Employers were also expected to contribute toward the dowries of unmarried Jewish girls. By contrast, such regulations did not exist in the relations between non-Jewish servants and their Jewish employers.

However, that is not to say that such provisions were not offered on a voluntary basis.

Whatever the motivation to become a domestic servant, it was the path taken by very large numbers of young Jewish women. In the eighteenth century, in the Polish town of Opatow, one study has demonstrated that half of all Jewish homes with five people or more employed a Jewish domestic servant, while according to the census of 1897, some 35 percent of Jewish women in the Russian Empire claimed they worked as domestic servants. Even in the United States, where, by the end of the nineteenth century, there were greater economic opportunities than in the old country, there were still not enough permanent industrial, manufacturing, or clerical jobs for all the Jewish women seeking employment. As such, in 1900, some 12 percent of Jewish women worked as domestic servants. Although they worked 12-hour days and were responsible for cleaning, cooking, shopping for the family, and taking care of sick family members, many young Jewish women saw the work as respectable, preferable to working in a sweatshop or, as was the case for many women, working alone in a room with a male employer who did not own a factory but ran his business out of his apartment.

Respectability was not always the defining characteristic of relations between domestic servants and their employers. The young women were often vulnerable and taken advantage of. They were frequently used for sex, which, in some cases, was consensual, but nevertheless, things could go terribly wrong. Such was the case of Leia Vaismanova. In 1869, she told a Russian court that she had lost her virginity to a Jewish soldier who was a guest in the home of her employer. She had become pregnant, but instead of keeping his word and marrying Leia, he abandoned her. Rape was not uncommon. Perpetrators could be either men in the family or those who came into contact with the servant while she was carrying out her domestic duties. Ryfka Gierszeniowna was a Russian Jewish woman who was twice raped by the local butcher when she went to buy meat for the family. Not infrequently, the housemaids were impregnated. Yet even when the father was a single man, he rarely married the woman.

In late nineteenth-century Russia, Jewish women who engaged in premarital sex took huge risks. Public humiliation, social ostracism, and the right of a bridegroom to abrogate a commitment to wed an unmarried woman found not to be a virgin were just some of the serious social and legal consequences such a woman may face. In traditional cultures—and Jewish culture in nineteenth-century eastern Europe was no exception—the community was highly unlikely to punish the man who reneged on the promise of marriage. While there were a few cases of Jewish women suing their lovers for seduction or charging men with having raped them, most women did not pursue those men through legal channels. According to the historian ChaeRan Freeze, who has studied marital and sexual relations between Jews in late nineteenth-century Russia, this is understandable, "given the onerous process and the dismal prospects of success." In the case of reneging on a promise of marriage, "the plaintiff had to prove that her lover had expressed a 'serious intention' of marriage." This was extremely difficult, given that these relationships were usually secret, with no third party who could support the woman's claim. The other fact that discouraged women from seeking redress in the courts was that despite the fact that if found guilty a man could face a prison sentence of up to two years, the sentence did not include the stipulation that he marry the woman. As such, her material and social circumstances would have remained unchanged.

Because of social pressures and expectations, sexual relations were not merely a private matter but also often a public one. Soured relations between domestic servants and their employers could sometimes lead to public scandal because both men and women wishing to ruin the reputation and standing of a person against whom they bore a grudge could level charges of sexual impropriety. In 1885, the domestic servant Rakhil

Krupen accused her employer, Girsh Kolodnyi, of raping her. She filed a petition to the procurator of the Moscow court, claiming that "he took advantage of [her] weakness and violently deprived [her] of [her] virginity and honor." She went on to claim that after "observing the signs of pregnancy in [her] and wishing to hide his vile behavior [he] dismissed [her] from the house." She concluded her accusation with a simple request: "I humbly ask Your Excellency . . . to investigate my case and bring Girsh Kolodnyi to trial for his action." A police investigation was initiated, and a number of men and women, Jewish and Christian, were interviewed, and their testimonies entered into the record. One person after another testified that Kolodnyi was not guilty of the accusations laid by Krupen. More than this, however, Krupen's own behavior and morality became the focus. According to the Christian peasant woman Praskovia Ivanova Kondakova, who had lived at the Kolodnyis' as a wet nurse for about four months, "[a]ll this time she [Krupen] behaved like a street walker . . . [and] carried on with the servants and the yard men." Another witness, a 22-year-old Jewish man named Gesel Borukhovich Itskovich, declared that he knew Krupen for about a year and a half when she stayed at the Kolodnyis', claiming that "she is absolutely an immodest girl who became involved with various people." Apparently, Itskovich's proof of Krupen's immodesty was rooted in the fact that "he sometimes remained to spend the night at the Kolodnyis' and had sexual relations with Krupen, who herself persuaded him [to do so]." According to the police report, Itskovich "had nothing good to say about her. Her slander against Kolodnyi was raised on instructions from people who are ill-disposed to the Kolodnyis." Irrespective of whether accusations of a sexual nature were true or false—and there were most certainly both—domestic service provided very large numbers of poor Jewish women with much-needed income while, at the same time, often rendering them vulnerable to the people they served and the severe cultural norms that shaped the contours of Jewish social life.

information accessible to Jews. The acquisition of such knowledge both threatened tradition and prepared Jews better than most for the demands of modernity.

Domestic servants were considered to be more than just employees. They were thought of as members of the family, privy to and participants in the intimate details of family life. Given the entangled and sometimes unseemly nature of some of these relationships, the historian Rebecca Kobrin has rightfully suggested that historians expand "our focus from the Jewish family to the Jewish household" in order to "appreciate more fully how issues of class, gender, and sexuality shaped the daily life experiences and inner worlds of the East European Jewish 'family' in the last two centuries."

WISSENSCHAFT DES JUDENTUMS (ACADEMIC STUDY OF JUDAISM)

One of the catalysts for the emergence of new Jewish cultural expressions and religious streams within Judaism was the rise of historical consciousness in the nineteenth century. The discipline of history, as we understand it, the desire to grasp the meaning of historical development, to separate myth from reality and record "what really happened," as the historian Leopold von Ranke (1795–1886) said, is a product of modernity. Beginning in the second decade of the nineteenth century in Germany, the first Jewish historians began to appear. Dedicated to casting a reflective and introspective eye on the Jewish past, they sought to apply critical methods of scholarly analysis to those texts that had once principally been the focus of religious devotion and

exegesis. Urgency for such a project also came from a violent outburst of antisemitism in Germany. The Hep Hep riots of 1819 inspired a group of largely assimilated German Jewish university students to join together with some aging Maskilim to defend Jews against a host of charges that surfaced during the riots. They believed that their mightiest weapon in the forthcoming cultural battle was the writing of objective history. To this end, in 1819, they founded the Society for Culture and the Academic Study of the Jews, thus inaugurating modern Jewish scholarship, known as the academic study of Judaism, or by its German name, *Wissenschaft des Judentums*.

The old method of Jewish learning was no longer sufficient to satisfy the needs and sensibilities of these young Jewish intellectuals. They had been the first Jews to study anything other than medicine at the university level, and armed with the critical academic skills they acquired in the study of history and philology, they sought to define the place of Judaism in the modern world. The proponents of the academic study of Judaism were motivated by two main impulses. The first was the wish to have Jewish studies (and, by extension, the Jewish people) accorded the respect of inclusion in the university curriculum. They believed that only through education could bigotry be eliminated. Secular Jewish scholars were of the opinion that civic equality for Jews that was not accompanied by the formal recognition of the cultural value and richness of Judaism would be without value and would, in fact, compromise the legal gains made by individual Jews. Emancipation without respect would ring hollow. Second, prominent figures in the academic study of Judaism movement feared that rapid and increasing social

THE NEW ISRAELITE HOSPITAL IN HAMBURG

On the occasion of the laying of the hospital's foundation stone in 1841, author Heinrich Heine (1797–1856), nephew of the hospital's patron, Salomon Heine, wrote the following poem, in which he considered the inheritability and indelibility of Jewish identity. Heinrich, who had converted to Protestantism in 1825

Figure 2.2 The New Israelite Hospital in Hamburg was founded in 1841 by the Jewish merchant and philanthropist Salomon Heine (1767–1844), in memory of his wife, Betty. Germany had a tradition of establishing Jewish hospitals. The first modern one was opened in Berlin in 1756 and survived the Nazi era. It remains open today.

Source: Leo Baeck Institute.

because he was unable, as a Jewish law graduate, to gain admission to the bar, never stopped thinking of himself as Jewish:

> A hospital for sick and needy Jews,
>
> For those poor mortals who are triply wretched,
>
> With three great evil maladies afflicted:
>
> With poverty and pain and Jewishness.
>
> The worst of these three evils is the last one,
>
> The thousand-year-old family affliction,
>
> The plague they carried from the Nile valley,
>
> The old Egyptian unhealthy faith.
>
> Incurable deep-seated hurt! No treatment
>
> No surgery, nor all the medications,
>
> This hospital can offer to its patients.
>
> Will Time, eternal goddess, someday end it,
>
> Root out this dark misfortune that the fathers
>
> I do not know! But meanwhile let us honour
>
> By pouring timely balm upon the lesions.

integration meant that not only non-Jews but also Jews themselves needed to learn about Jewish religious culture. But they were not optimistic. In his programmatic study *On Rabbinic Literature* (1818), historian Leopold Zunz declared that in Germany, post-biblical Hebrew literature was "being led to the grave," while bibliographer Moritz Steinschneider declared sarcastically that Judaism needed to be studied so as "to give it a decent burial."

As Joel Abraham List (1780–c. 1848), a Jewish elementary school director and one of the founders of the Society, remarked, "Jews one after another are detaching themselves from the community. Jewry is on the verge of complete disintegration." Conversion to Christianity was the most extreme expression of this "disintegration," which, beginning in the eighteenth century, increased dramatically. When the poet Heine converted, he called his baptismal certificate "the ticket of admission to

European culture." Heine forever regretted his conversion and told a friend some years later, "I make no secret of my Judaism, to which I have not returned, because I never left it" (*see box*, "The New Israelite Hospital in Hamburg").

When members of the Mendelssohn family and other famous Jewish personalities began to convert, it bespoke a crisis born of the unfulfilled hopes Jews invested in emancipation. This was the internal motivation for the founders of the academic study of Judaism, who believed that through scholarship, "the bond of science, the bond of pure rationality [and] the bond of truth" would unite Christians and Jews by erasing the differences between the two groups. As Eduard Gans (1798–1839), a jurist, historian, and founding member of the Society for Culture and the Academic Study of the Jews, put it in 1822,

> everything passes without perishing, and yet persists, although it has long been consigned to the past. That is why neither the Jews will perish nor Judaism dissolve; in the larger movement of the whole they will have seemed to have disappeared, yet they will live on as the river lives on in the ocean.

In other words, the Jews would become invisible, while Jewishness would persist. Quoting philosopher Johann Gottfried von Herder, Gans predicted, "There will be a time when no one in Europe will ask any longer, who is a Jew and who is a Christian?"

Nothing in this outlook constituted a program for stemming the tide of Jewish assimilation and conversion. In fact, Gans's own fate confirmed the reality that insurmountable political barriers stymied the progress of talented Jews. Denied an appointment in the law faculty at the University of Berlin because he was Jewish, Gans traveled to Belgium, England, and France seeking a similar appointment. He was unsuccessful. Fed up, he was baptized in Paris in 1825 and returned

to Berlin, where he was immediately offered the position for which he had been initially turned down because he was a Jew.

Nonetheless, the academic study of Judaism remained enormously influential in three ways. First, it inaugurated the critical, secular study of Judaism and Jewish history. Second, despite the defection of the founders of the academic study of Judaism, subsequent generations of scholars emerged, who remained wedded to the goal of preserving Judaism. And third, later innovations in Judaism, such as Reform, modern Orthodoxy, and positive-historical Judaism, owe their existence to the fact that the leading figures in such developments were imbued with the spirit and methodological innovations ushered in by *Wissenschaft des Judentums*.

THE RISE OF MODERN JEWISH HISTORIOGRAPHY

Leopold Zunz (1794–1886) was a historian of Judaism and one of the founders of the *Wissenschaft des Judentums* movement. Typical of a new generation of Jewish scholars, Zunz, who studied philology at the University of Berlin and obtained a doctorate from the University of Halle, studied Jewish texts, employing secular, critical methods. His overriding ambition was to obtain command over the entire corpus of medieval Jewish literature and historically situate each work. Within a few years of founding the Society for Culture and the Academic Study of the Jews, he became the editor of the important but short-lived *Journal for the Academic Study of Judaism*, the first publication in the field of Jewish studies. His initial contribution was a biography of the medieval biblical exegete Rashi. Zunz was ordained as a rabbi and served for two years as preacher in the New Synagogue in Berlin, a Reform congregation, but eventually left because he was too wedded to tradition to accept the innovations of Reform Judaism. This became a feature of his scholarship when, for example, he wrote an essay extolling the high ethical value of wearing *tefillin* (phylacteries). However, his disenchantment with Reform Judaism did not mean any abandonment of Reform's sense of Judaism's historical development over time. Uncovering that process remained for him a noble and necessary goal.

Zunz was a very productive scholar, writing on a vast array of subjects, including synagogue liturgy and practice and Jewish religious poetry, as well as an important study of Jewish names. His preeminent scholarly work, *The Sermons of the Jews, Historically Developed* (1832), is a masterful study of the history of Jewish preaching and constitutes one of the first attempts to describe the development of the entire Midrash. Just as the Haskalah was connected to politics, so too was Zunz's scholarship. His *Sermons of the Jews* convinced the German authorities that were wary of religious innovation—they felt it was but a short step to political rebellion—not to ban Jewish preaching in German. Zunz demonstrated that Jews had preached sermons in the vernacular since the rabbinic period, and thus, contemporary German Jewry's doing so was in a time-honored tradition. Zunz was convinced that Jews had to apply the critical tools of modern scholarship to the examination of Jewish texts in the same manner that Christians were doing for their own sources. It was this, Zunz believed, that would mark the Jews as full participants in German culture, because through their use of history, they would be treading an intellectual path similar to that of their Christian neighbors.

To a great extent, Zunz was a literary historian. He produced little in the way of a history of the Jews. The first great exponent of that genre was Isaac Marcus Jost (1793– 1860), a boyhood friend of Zunz. Between 1820 and 1828, he published his nine-volume *History of the Israelites from the Maccabean Period to Our Own Day*. This was the first modern history of the Jews, one that focused on their relationship to their host societies. Jost had received a traditional Jewish education and also studied history at university. For most of his life, he taught in Jewish schools, especially at those institutions that can be considered progressive heirs of Berlin's Jewish Free School. Though little read today, Jost's historical work was a significant achievement, for it was the first to apply the methodological principles of modern history writing to the Jewish past. Written in an impartial tone and in a simple, unadorned style, Jost's work was directed to common Jew and Christian statesman alike. Its principal thrust was to demonstrate the loyalty Jews had displayed to their host societies throughout history. Beyond this, Jost's goal was to show that histories of European states were incomplete if the Jewish dimension to national life was ignored. Though highly learned, Jost's *History of the Israelites* was flat and apologetic and owed more to the rationalism of the Enlightenment than to the more vivid nationalist sensibility of the Romantic era, in which he actually lived. In later works, however, Jost first raised important questions about the Jewish past that have preoccupied historians ever since. In 1832, he wrote the *General History of the Israelite People*, a two-volume summary of his magnum opus, in which he tracked the uniqueness of the Jewish march through history. If in Jost's day history writing generally focused on high politics and war written by the victors, could one write the history of a group on the margins? As Jost asked, "Can there be a history of a slave?" Today, we might refer to such an attempt as "a history of the subaltern." Being a member of a long-reviled group on the periphery of

European society made Jost especially attentive to the special nature of writing the history of the "Other."

Jost also initiated a more programmatic approach to the study of the past. He urged fellow Jewish historians to use all available sources to write Jewish history:

> [T]he historical sources are scattered far and wide. . . . One is confronted by an immense number of deeds, speeches, laws, disputes, opinions, stories, poems, legends, and other phenomena affecting the lot of the Israelites. This is to say nothing of the many different places, times, and thinkers. One must consider as well human inclinations, cultural variations, historical setting, and in general the prevailing circumstances of entire nations, districts, and individuals, to say nothing of natural predispositions, emotions, and intellectual movements. All this is necessary to arrive at a certain historical understanding and to derive fruitful results and just evaluations.

While Jost may have pioneered the writing of a comprehensive history of the Jews, it was Heinrich Graetz (1817–1891) who brought such a project to its apogee. The leading Jewish historian of the nineteenth century, Graetz has as his greatest scholarly achievement his 11-volume *History of the Jews*, published between 1853 and 1876. This work differed markedly from that of his predecessor. Where Jost's language was cold and dry, Graetz's was flamboyant and deeply impassioned, and where Jost seemed detached from his subject, Graetz was an advocate for the Jewish people against the prejudice that had followed them throughout history. His passions sometimes got the better of him, and he often lost all semblance of objectivity. He was merciless toward those he deemed enemies of the Jews.

These included entire peoples, such as the Romans, the Christians, and the Germans, as well as individual antagonists, such as Martin Luther and Voltaire. Graetz was nothing if not ecumenical in drawing up his list of enemies, for on it he included Hellenized Jews, such as Herod and Josephus, early modern apostates, such as Johannes Pfefferkorn, and contemporary Reformers of Judaism, such as Abraham Geiger. Graetz also utterly rejected the historical importance of the mystical tradition in Judaism and was deeply hostile toward eastern European Jewish culture, in particular, Hasidism.

Displaying virtuosic erudition, Graetz wrote Jewish history as no one had before. It has been called "suffering-and-scholarship history" because he focused almost exclusively on the history of anti-Judaism and later antisemitism and the history of rabbinic culture. Writing in a highly emotive style, Graetz observed, "This is the eighteen-hundred-year era of the diaspora, of unprecedented suffering, of uninterrupted martyrdom without parallel in world history. But it is also a period of spiritual alertness, of restless mental activity, of indefatigable inquiry." In keeping with the way national histories were written in his day, Graetz's magisterial sweep rarely offered a glimpse of the social world of the Jewish people. He concentrated on Jewish intellectual life and the impact on Jews of the host societies' policies. He painted a bleak picture of Jewish life yet, at the same time, evoked the grandeur of Jewish tenacity and creativity. Conceptually, Graetz's great innovation was to depict the Jews in national terms. Where previous practitioners of the academic study of Judaism saw the Jews as a religious community, Graetz was a Romantic; he described the Jews as an "ethnic group" and maintained that their history possesses a "national character."

In contrast to Jost and Geiger, Graetz characterized the post-Talmudic era as

> by no means the mere history of a religion. . . . Its object is not simply the course of development of an independent people, which, though it possesses no soil, fatherland, geographical boundaries, or state organism, replaced these concrete conditions with spiritual powers. Though scattered over the civilized portions of the earth and attached to the land of their hosts, the members of the Jewish race did not cease to feel themselves a single people in their religious conviction, historical memory, customs, and hopes.

THE RISE OF REFORM JUDAISM

After some brief French-inspired attempts at transforming the synagogue service in Holland (1796) and in the kingdom of Westphalia (1808) and the establishment of a private congregation in Warsaw in 1802 called *Di Daytshe Shil* (Yiddish for "The German Synagogue"), the focus of religious reform shifted to Germany. The first synagogue there to introduce some aesthetic changes was the private service founded in Westphalia by the man known as the father of Reform Judaism, Israel Jacobson (1768–1828). Jacobson's temple not only met with Jewish opposition but, in 1817, was also forced by the Prussian government to close. The authorities were of the opinion that the willingness to abandon religious tradition might translate into a desire to institute radical political change. Jacobson left Berlin and moved to the more hospitable environment of Hamburg.

There, in 1818, the New Israelite Temple Association founded the Hamburg Temple. The association wished "to restore public worship to its deserving dignity and importance." As an early defender of the temple stated, "Look at the Gentiles and see how they stand in awe and reverence and with good manners in their house of prayer." Inspired by Jacobson's first efforts at reforming the style of synagogue services, the board of the Hamburg Temple insisted on strict decorum; emphasized the Saturday-morning service (at the expense of the normal thrice-daily services) and limited it to two hours; allowed for a choir and organ; instituted a confirmation ceremony for boys and girls; mandated weekly sermons in German, time for which was made by eliminating the traditional weekly reading of the prophets; introduced a German-language prayer book, which most significantly eliminated references to the coming of a personal messiah; and removed prayers that called for an end to Jewish exile and a return to Zion.

The rabbinical court of Hamburg immediately published a volume of responsa that set out its opposition to the temple. Then rabbis from across Europe rose up in indignation. The most important opponent of the Hamburg Temple was Rabbi Moses Sofer (1762–1839). Popularly known as the Hatam Sofer, in 1806, he was appointed rabbi of Pressburg, at that time the most important Jewish community in Hungary. He was a renowned Talmudist, his yeshiva the epicenter of the battle against Reform Judaism. Leading the forces of traditional Jewry, he opposed any changes in Judaism, his battle cry encapsulated in dire warnings such as this:

> May your mind not turn to evil and never engage in corruptible partnership with

those fond of innovations. . . . Do not touch the books of Rabbi Moses [Mendelssohn] from Dessau, and your foot will never slip. . . . The daughters may read German books but only those that have been written in our own way [Yiddish], according to the interpretations of our teachers. . . . Be warned not to change your Jewish names, speech and clothing—God forbid. . . . Never say: "Times have changed."

Institutionally, it took two generations for Reform Judaism to become firmly established in German congregations. After the founding of the Hamburg Temple, Reform houses of worship were not built in significant numbers until the 1830s. Thereafter, Reform Judaism spread, even becoming a palpable presence in rural areas. In 1837, the small village of Walldorf had 1,580 inhabitants, 567 of whom were Jewish. Moritz Siegel was born in the village and was the son of a well-to-do textile merchant. His description of Jewish religious life in the German countryside indicates the extent to which religious reform was bound up with other factors, including Jewish contact with Christian society, exposure to general education, and one's social status and class. Essentially, two groups of Jews resided in Walldorf, one poorer and traditional, the other wealthier and religiously progressive:

In the years of my youth, these two factions also went their own ways socially, so that on holidays, for example, the Festival of Weeks [Shavuot] or the Festival of Booths [Sukkot], the celebrations were held separately. In our social circle there prevailed a highly proper tone, within the boundaries of the most refined customs and manners, and to be included in our circle was a privilege. Already at the time we celebrated our balls with a gay dinner and lively conversation, with speeches and wine, and although our menus did not conform to the precepts of ritual law, this was no cause for us to enjoy ourselves less. The dietary laws were not strictly observed by the younger generation, most of whom had seen the world and thereby departed from the old customs. I remember quite well, already as a seven-or eight-year-old boy, seeing young grown-ups from my family circle or other circles smoking their cigars on Saturday and eating at the inns. This was at the end of the 1840s. To be sure, the fact that many young people had received their training in the outside world contributed to this; the growing association with non-Jews and attendance at secondary schools also bore part of the blame; and, in addition, liberal thinking in Christian circles at that time carried over to the Jewish population. What had once been regarded as inadmissible, that is, writing on Saturday, was permitted by Rabbi Hofmann [the Reform rabbi of Walldorf], and was also not objected to by his successors, so that gradually one custom after another crumbled away and . . . Walldorf soon gained a reputation for being very liberal among communities that were more hesitant in their reforms.

Most of the new Reform schools and temples that opened in Germany largely in the second half of the nineteenth century expressed the universalistic sentiments of the Enlightenment, touting the way such ideals harmonized with Judaism. As Gotthold Salomon, the preacher at the Hamburg Temple, put it, "[t]he summons to be an Israelite is the summons to be a human being." But the most important development that facilitated the growth of Reform theology and practice was the appearance in the 1830s of a new kind of rabbi. University-educated and familiar with the secular disciplines of history, philology, philosophy, and classics, the new German rabbi was heir to the Haskalah and often a proponent of *Wissenschaft des Judentums*. Neither in eastern Europe nor in other parts of western Europe did rabbis with PhD degrees appear on the religious landscape. Of particular significance is the fact that such rabbis appeared among German Orthodox as well as Reform rabbis. This feature made Judaism in Germany distinct, marking it as a unique innovation in Ashkenazic civilization.

The new rabbinical elite brought a fresh sensibility to the practice and theology of Judaism, one born of their own intellectual encounter with secular studies. Typifying the new outlook was Abraham Geiger (1810–1874). The product of a traditional Jewish education, Geiger was the spiritual leader of Reform Judaism. After attending the University of Bonn, where he studied Near Eastern languages and philosophy, Geiger spent a lifetime in scholarship, writing the history of Judaism. He employed historical scholarship to demonstrate that instituting reforms was not anathema to Judaism, because Jewish culture was constantly in flux, engaged with its surroundings, and flexible enough to respond to the demands of the times.

Geiger's contribution to the writing of Jewish religious history was novel in a number of ways. Methodologically, his approach was truly comparative; he made a genuine attempt to historicize religious origins, seeking to discover the relationship between the three great monotheistic faiths: Judaism, Christianity, and Islam. Moreover, Geiger sought to elevate new textual sources of rabbinic Judaism to their proper place in the development of Christianity and Islam. In Geiger's estimation, both the Gospels and the Koran bore the unmistakable stamp of Midrashic and Talmudic wisdom.

Geiger integrated Reform innovations into a coherent ideology and subjected the Jewish religious canon to the dictates of modern textual criticism. In contrast to Graetz, Geiger strenuously denied the national element in Judaism. Only ancient Israel could be characterized as a national entity, but even then, Judaism as an idea did not really require the trappings of nationhood: a common language, a territory, and national institutions. For Geiger, Judaism's greatness and its survival through the ages lay in the fact that it transcended national-political externalities. Rather, Judaism was free to grow as a pure expression of faith in God. This formulation suited Jews who wished to proclaim their loyalty to Germany and remain true to Judaism.

As someone who saw the history of Judaism in evolutionary terms, Geiger divided its development into four conceptual periods: (1) revelation, a period "which extends to the close of the biblical era, which cannot be said to have ended at the time of Exile, for its outgrowths continued well beyond that date"; (2) tradition, "the period during which all biblical material was processed, shaped, and molded for life," which stretches from "the completion of the Bible to the completion of the Babylonian Talmud"; (3) legalism, when "the spiritual heritage was guarded and preserved, but no one felt authorized to reconstruct it or develop it further"—this period extended from the completion of the Babylonian Talmud into the middle of the eighteenth century; and (4) critical study, a period of liberation "marked by an effort to loosen the fetters of the previous era by means of the use of reason and historical research." Geiger saw this final period as characterized by the attempt to "revitalize Judaism." In so doing, he endowed his own age with the character of creative vitality akin to the first and second periods of Judaism's initial genius and subsequent growth. Geiger regarded it as scholarship's task to reverse the atrophy of the third period and revitalize Judaism.

Rabbinical Conferences

Despite Geiger's efforts to provide Reform Judaism with a solid intellectual and philosophical grounding, divisions soon began to appear, not just between Reformers and their opponents, but among the Reformers themselves, split between lay Reformers and rabbis. To heal the fissures and to facilitate the broad acceptance of Reform Judaism, the rabbi and author Ludwig Philippson (1811–1889) proposed that those dedicated to Reform meet to confer about the most pressing issues facing the movement. To that end, rabbinic conferences were held in Germany in 1844, 1845, and 1846. It is noteworthy that similar divisions between traditionalists and Reformers also appeared among German Catholics and Protestants in the 1840s. Jewish religious leaders were not alone in seeking to define the role of religion in the modern world.

The first of the conferences took up a variety of issues, some of which produced broad consensus among the participants. For example, all agreed on abolishing the demeaning oath that Jews were still required to swear in courts in certain German states. On the subject of Jewish patriotism, one delegate concluded, "[T]he Jew acknowledges every man as his brother. But he acknowledges his fellow countryman [the Germans] to be one with whom he is connected by a particular bond." The proponent of radical Reform, Samuel Holdheim (1806–1860), seeking to denationalize the links

between Jews, likewise declared, "The doctrine of Judaism is thus, first your compatriots then your co-religionists."

At the second conference of 1845, the 30 participants devoted themselves to the question of language and Jewish liturgy. Just as language posed a problem for Maskilim and their opponents, so too did the debate over language concern religious reformers. On the one hand, increasing use of German at home left fewer and fewer Jews with a command of Hebrew; on the other, the continued use of what was once the Jews' national language might compromise the conferees' claims to German patriotism. A split emerged between those who supported retaining the centrality of Hebrew prayer and those who felt it both practical and necessary to pray in German. Abraham Geiger declared Hebrew to be his mother tongue but nevertheless declared solemnly, "[A] German prayer strikes a deeper chord than a Hebrew prayer." Ultimately, Geiger held the opinion that Hebrew was dispensable because "anyone who imagines Judaism to be walking on the crutches of a language deeply offends it."

Geiger encountered opposition from Zacharias Frankel (1801–1875), the founder of positive-historical Judaism, later called Conservative Judaism in the United States. For Frankel, who favored moderate reforms, Hebrew was essential for "it is the language of our Scripture which . . . is a constant reminder of our Covenant with God." Frankel also feared that dispensing with Hebrew meant that it would become the intellectual property of the rabbis alone; this would bring about a breach with the people and thus, as far as Frankel was concerned, could not have been God's intention. In fact, maintaining the centrality of Hebrew was so self-evident to Frankel that he resisted a law to ensure that Hebrew would be the language of liturgy, because no one had "ever thought of abandoning the Hebrew language." A narrow majority determined that the retention of Hebrew was a subjective claim by its proponents and that it was probably not necessary. At this point, Frankel walked out of the conference.

Two other issues occupied the attendees at the second conference: Sabbath observance and messianism. The radical Samuel Holdheim found himself almost entirely alone in his recommendation that the Sabbath be shifted from Saturday to Sunday, the day chosen by his congregation in Berlin and, later, among some classical Reform congregations in the United States. The overwhelming majority insisted on Saturday as the Jewish Sabbath. Messianism was reaffirmed as a central tenet of Judaism but was declared a universal conception, divorced from any projected return of the Jews to the Land of Israel.

WOMEN AND EARLY REFORM JUDAISM

The final conference of 1846 was a less-charged affair than the previous two, but it also achieved less. Though it was never put to a vote, apparently due to "a lack of time," the most important thing to come out of the assembly was the report it heard on the status of women in the synagogue. From its beginnings, the new Reform movement was concerned with the relationship of women to Judaism. They were determined to make Judaism significant for women and include them as active participants. They saw a reformed, modernized religious service and a proper religious education as essential to the creation of a well-rounded, moral individual. To that end, they championed greater gender equality, and in their desire to Westernize Judaism, they proposed the elimination of those religious practices they considered "Oriental."

Back in 1786, the maskil Isaac Euchel and the religious reformer and community leader David Friedländer published translations of parts of the liturgy into German specifically for women, who, generally speaking, did not have sufficient competency in Hebrew to understand the service. In truth, this was increasingly the case for men as well. The Hungarian advocate of Reform Judaism, Rabbi Aaron Chorin, articulated the movement's position on women thus: "Women must not be excluded from the soul-satisfying experiences which come to us through a solemn worship service."

There were also new ceremonies created specifically for girls, which were intended to include them more fully in the devotional life of the congregation. In 1814, the first confirmation ceremony for girls took place in Berlin. Intended to be the female equivalent of the Bar Mitzvah, it quickly spread throughout Germany and, soon thereafter, across Europe. The egalitarianism inherent in introducing confirmation ceremonies for girls did not completely overturn traditional gender roles but could be interpreted by proponents as a means of reinforcing them. For Rabbi David Frankel of Rybnik, a city that today is in southwest Poland but that had been part of Germany until 1918,

> religious instruction has become a necessity for girls as much as for boys. Indeed, in regard to their future profession as mothers and educators, [he] consider[s] it [the religious education of girls] as even more urgent, since it depends on them [the women] whether the house of the Israelite can be regarded as truly Jewish.

The education of young girls and boys focused on the moral and ethical teachings of Judaism and on the biblical history of ancient Israel. Many congregations even replaced the Bar Mitzvah ceremony with confirmations. In practical terms, this meant that where receiving honors in the synagogue had previously been the preserve of male congregants, girls could now publicly pledge their allegiance to Judaism, be blessed by the rabbi, and be counted as full members of the Jewish community.

As early as 1837, Abraham Geiger had argued for women's legal majority and formal equality in Jewish law as well as the abrogation of the morning prayer thanking God "*she lo asani ishah*" (who has not created me as a woman). The latter prayer was soon removed from Reform prayer books. Geiger was also opposed to various traditional laws pertaining to weddings, marriage, and divorce. He utterly rejected as primitive the idea that a man "acquires" a wife and that she legally "belongs" to him. Interestingly, Geiger was not willing, however, to change the formulaic wedding ceremony, because "nobody is thinking about what it once meant." He also objected to Jewish divorce law that prevented a wife from annulling a marriage against the husband's will. He maintained that secular divorce law replace Jewish divorce law. Still, Geiger's position on women in Judaism was only radical in relation to Orthodoxy. He still very much believed that the inherent differences between men and women determined the role they could play in Jewish life. By contrast, the radical reformer Samuel Holdheim demanded a complete change in the wording and even the choreography of the Jewish wedding ceremony. He, too, was offended by the notion of the groom "acquiring" the bride and proposed eliminating the traditional formula whereby the groom and he alone says, "Be thou consecrated unto me with this ring." Instead, Holdheim insisted that both bride and groom say to each other, "I consecrate myself to thee." The elimination of the word

"ring" reflected the fact that Holdheim wanted to do away with rings altogether because, in Jewish law, they symbolized acquisition.

At the Reform conference of 1846, rabbis prepared a "Report of the Committee on the Religious Status of Women in Judaism," which demonstrated that they had scoured biblical and rabbinic literature to make the case for women's equality in Judaism; recommended the emancipation of women from the binds of traditional *halakhic* categories; abolished differences in terms of rights and obligations; called for women to be counted in a *minyan*, the prayer quorum traditionally composed of ten males over the age of thirteen; abolished the male prayer wherein the male worshipper thanked God for not having made him a woman; and suggested new educational programs tailored to women's needs. However, they never voted on any of the proposals. Significantly, issues to do with marriage, divorce, and women assuming leadership roles in the synagogue were not discussed. All the positive talk and sincere belief in egalitarianism did not lead to immediate practical change. In fact, even something as relatively non-contentious as seating arrangements did not reflect the high-minded talk of the Reformers. Seating in the new egalitarian atmosphere of Reform Judaism conformed to traditional arrangements. Unlike in the United States, Reform services in Europe retained separate seating for men and women into the twentieth century. The first synagogue to introduce mixed seating was the Jewish Religion Union in London in 1902, followed by the Union Libérale Israélite in Paris in 1907. It was not until 1930 that the first major synagogue in Germany allowed men and women to sit together.

However, although the Reformers failed to enact deep-seated changes in the *halakhic* status of women, German Jews succeeded in creating a new religious language, one that reflected a new religious consciousness in which, according to Geiger, emphasis was placed on "the beneficial influence of the feminine heart." He spoke, albeit in essentialist terms, of the way women were constitutionally receptive to deep religiosity thanks to what he called their "true female sentiments." Those who advocated for a change in women's status within Judaism did not employ the language of human, civic, or religious rights to argue for equal treatment with men. In refraining from such language, Jewish Reformers merely reflected the general outlook of German society. In other words, just as feminism gained little traction in nineteenth-century German society, so too did it make little headway in German Jewish society. Instead, bourgeois culture in Germany considered women the moral sex, compassionate, caring, and with an innate sense for "the beautiful and the lofty." According to historian Benjamin Baader, the impact of this general sentiment on Jews saw women move from "a marginal to a more central position in Jewish culture." Crucially, this was not due to a changed understanding or reinterpretation of Jewish law but, rather, the impact of bourgeois culture on German Jews, and as such, "the modern Jewish culture that welcomed women was a non-Torah and non-Halakhah centered modern Judaism."

Certain historians have referred to the changes that took place as the "feminization" of Judaism in nineteenth-century Germany, and there is no doubt, according to the historian Michael Meyer, that with the adoption of bourgeois values, there came an increased emphasis on "sentiment, emotion, morality and aesthetic experience." Meyer even points out that the move of men to recite prayers in German is reminiscent of the traditional practice of women praying in Yiddish, but he also identifies other features at work that complement the "feminization" thesis. Among these, he notes that the emphasis on morality was less about the impact of feminine qualities on a reformed Judaism but was more a conscious response by Reform rabbis to the harsh challenge Judaism faced from prominent thinkers, like the philosopher Immanuel Kant, who had decried Judaism for lacking all morality. In addition, the conversion to Christianity by prominent Jewish salon women who claimed that Judaism was spiritually barren may also have spurred Reform Judaism's "internalization of bourgeois values," including an emphasis on emotion. Finally, Jewish men, like women, sought a more emotional religious experience, which, rather than deriving from men adopting behaviors believed at that time to be characteristic of women, Meyer attributes to the impact of a highly emotional Romanticism, which had a deep impact on important Jewish intellectuals. In the end, there is no doubt that the face of Judaism in Germany was largely changed by a combination of factors that were a consequence of German Jewry adopting middle-class values, greater attentiveness by rabbis to the role women might play as participants in the religious life of the community, and the need felt by many Jewish men to move from an orthopractic Judaism to one that emphasized Judaism's spiritual, moral, and ethical attributes.

In the end, the conferences enjoyed mixed success. The new rabbinate certainly made its presence felt and initiated a serious discussion about the future of Judaism. Over time, some of the assemblies' proposals were instituted in various communities both in Germany and abroad. These included the introduction of the organ, new prayers in lieu of those calling for the restoration of temple sacrifice, the use of the vernacular in liturgy, and equality for women. We must stress, however, that the aesthetics, ideology, and sensibility of European Reform Judaism did not resemble current Reform practices in the United States. Rather, Reform Jewish congregations in nineteenth-century Europe, for the most part, still had segregated seating; they were not confronted with the issue of widespread intermarriage and the place of non-Jews among the congregants; and they were far more insistent on the denationalization of Judaism. While nineteenth-century Reform and Orthodox Judaism in Europe staunchly opposed Zionism, contemporary Reform congregations are equally staunch supporters of the national idea in Judaism and identify strongly with Israel.

NEO-ORTHODOXY

The increasing prominence of the Reformers inspired the growth of conservative reaction. The term *Orthodoxy* is itself a product of the modern period and does not appear until 1795. By the nineteenth century, it was used as a term to distinguish traditional from Reform Jews. In response to the Reform assemblies, 116 German and Hungarian rabbis circulated a letter of protest, decrying the actions of the Reformers. Sensing that Judaism was imperiled, the Orthodox not only led a defensive reaction but also went on the offensive as well. The leader of what became known as Neo-Orthodoxy was Samson Raphael Hirsch (1808–1888) from Hamburg. Though Hirsch's family members voiced opposition to the Hamburg Temple, they were in favor of many aspects of the Haskalah. After receiving a traditional Jewish education, Hirsch went to a non-Jewish high school and then to the University of Bonn in 1829, where he studied classical languages, history, and philosophy. It was there that he met Abraham Geiger, and the two formed a Jewish debating society.

Figure 2.3   Modern Orthodoxy, of which Samson Raphael Hirsch was the founder.

Source: Vinard Collection/Alamy Stock Photo.

Modern Orthodoxy, of which Samson Raphael Hirsch was the founder, was just as keen to change Judaism's aesthetic as was Reform Judaism. A premium was placed on appearing appropriately attired in a manner befitting someone communing with God. In the mid-nineteenth century, modern rabbis, of whatever denominational stripe, were characterized by their having attended university. In this portrait, note Hirsch's collar and academic gown, which were also typical of contemporary Christian clerical dress. He is also sporting a very closely trimmed beard, and while one can assume Hirsch's head is covered, his skullcap is not visible in this picture.

Between 1830 and 1841, Hirsch served as the rabbi of a principality in north Germany. During this time, he began to formulate his response to what he saw as the crisis besetting modern Jews. In 1836, he published his important *Nineteen Letters on Judaism*, and a year later, he published *Choreb: Israel's Duties in the Diaspora*. Both of these works sought to establish the essential harmony between traditional Judaism and modernity.

The more famous of the two works, *The Nineteen Letters*, inaugurated a new form of Judaism, a self-consciously modern Orthodoxy that embraced rather than rejected modernity. The book is a passionate defense of traditional Judaism written in the form of an epistolary exchange between two young Jews—Benjamin, the spokesman for the "perplexed" of his generation of Jewish intellectuals whose faith was waning, and Naphtali, the representative of traditional Judaism. Naphtali responds to the skeptical questions of Benjamin in the form of 18 answers that explore the relationship of Jewish to secular culture. Hirsch articulates the belief that it is the task of human beings to actualize the infinite good inherent in the Deity. But the exercise of free will prompts people to confront the choice between good and evil. Here, according to Hirsch, an entire community needs to be dedicated to the mission of teaching humanity to strive for goodness and obedience to God's will. Such a daunting task requires a collectivity with distinctive laws and customs that would illuminate the path for individual Jews, making it possible for them to guide the rest of humanity. The universal applicability of Jewish ethics was a belief shared by all streams of German Judaism. As one of the correspondents writes in the *Nineteen Letters*:

> Consider for a moment the image of such an Israel, living freely among the nations, striving for its ideal! Every son of Israel a respected, widely influential priestly exemplar of justice and love, disseminating not

Judaism—which is prohibited—but pure humanity among the nations!

Unlike Moses Mendelssohn, who saw Judaism and secular culture as compatible yet distinctly separate spheres, Hirsch sought to integrate the two in a practical way. He coined the term *Mensch-Jissroeïl*, thereby linking the German words for *human being* (*Mensch*) and *Israel* (*Jissroeïl*) to designate a Jew who fully and with equal gusto celebrated both aspects of his personality, the general and the specifically Jewish. From 1851 until his death, Hirsch served as the rabbi of the Israelite Religious Society, a separatist Orthodox community in Frankfurt, which was a city whose Jewish residents had largely accepted classical Reform Judaism. Through Hirsch's talent and efforts, the flourishing congregation was made up of about 500 families. At both the synagogue and the two schools he opened, Hirsch practiced what he preached, providing an education that combined secular subjects and Torah. This method was expressed in a Hebrew concept that he coined, *Torah im derekh erets*, the fulfilment of which was to combine a commitment to Torah with active participation in the life of the state and society. This is but one way that Hirsch's brand of Judaism differed from the traditional Orthodoxy that preceded it.

Another important area of difference had to do with the role of women in Judaism. Throughout history, the study of rabbinic texts has been the almost-exclusive preserve of men. Only quite recently has this begun to change within Orthodox communities. Whenever the issue of women studying classical Jewish sources was brought up in traditional communities, rabbis tended to rely on biblical expressions, such as "The king's daughter is all glorious within," which rabbis of the Talmud understood as meaning that a woman's place was in the domestic sphere, the word "within" being a euphemism for *home*. Elsewhere in the Talmud, there is the verse "And you shall teach them to your children [*l'vanekha*]." However, the literal translation of the last word does not mean *children* but rather "sons." This was understood to mean that a father's obligation was to teach his sons Torah and not his daughters. Finally, another proof text used to deny women access to the study of Torah was the Talmudic warning that "[a]nyone who teaches his daughter Torah, it is as if he taught her sexual licentiousness."

Along with Hirsch, the other leading figure of modern Orthodoxy in Germany was Esriel Hildesheimer (1820–1899), founder of the first Orthodox rabbinical seminary in Germany. Like Hirsch, Hildesheimer was also raised in a somewhat enlightened Orthodox environment, attending Hasharat Zvi, which opened in 1796 and was the first Orthodox elementary school in Germany to teach secular as well as Jewish subjects; it even became co-ed in 1827. Most unusual for an Orthodox rabbi, Hildesheimer, in 1844, earned a doctorate in the field of biblical studies. In addition to their openness to secular subjects, Hirsch and Hildesheimer proved to be trailblazers in another area. They argued that girls and women were permitted and required to study Torah. In championing this, they not only diverged sharply from the traditional Orthodox position but also were closer to the Reformers than either would have cared to admit, for they were vehement opponents of Reform Judaism.

According to the scholar of German Orthodoxy David Ellenson, Hirsch's call for women's education came in the larger context of his belief that to lead a proper Jewish life, it was incumbent on men and women to "study in order to practice." Opposed to the academic study of Judaism, with its propensity to undermine rather than undergird tradition, Hirsch

believed that action without learning was meaningless, and that throughout Jewish history women have performed heroically to save the Jews. In this age of secularism and assimilation, Judaism was under threat, and as in the past, it would again fall to women to save the Jews, but that was only possible if action was informed by learning. In his book *Choreb*, he wrote:

> No less should Israel's daughter's learn the content of the Written Law and the duties which they have to perform in their lifetime as daughter and young woman, as mother and housewife. . . . The deliverance from Egypt was won by the women and it is by the pious and virtuous women of Israel that the Jewish spirit and Jewish life can and will be revived.

The first line of defense against the forces of assimilation was to be the Jewish home, and thus, for Hirsch, it was essential that Jewish women be educated in Torah, so that they can pass it on to their children. According to Hirsch, however, Torah study for women was to be confined to the five books of Moses, the Prophets, and the Writings. These books offered lessons for a practical life. The more theoretical works of Judaism, the Talmud and Oral Law, were to remain off-limits to Jewish women. For Hirsch, what most Jewish women as well as men needed was to study those texts that promote a "fear of the Lord and the conscientious fulfilment of our duty."

Hildesheimer adopted a similar position to Hirsch, wherein he stressed the importance of the home as the space where children would be inculcated with Jewish values and a love of Torah and that women would play a central role in the education and formation of the Jewish child. To do this effectively, women needed to learn Torah. Here, Hildesheimer turns to the expression "The king's daughter is all glorious within," but not to draw from it the idea that women should be kept from Torah study, but the exact opposite. The socialization of children in the ways of Judaism that begins in the home demanded a Torah-literate mother. As he observed in his tract *A Few Words Regarding the Religious Instruction of Girls* (1871), "if it is true that knowledge is power, then the Jewish knowledge of our wives and young ladies will contribute to an invincible Jewish power."

Neither Hirsch nor Hildesheimer viewed women in anything but traditionally gendered ways. To a great extent, this is also the way that most of the Reformers, even those who championed greater gender equality, saw Jewish women. However, both the Reformers as well as the proponents of modern Orthodoxy shared a deep concern with Jewish continuity. While the views of both camps on how to secure Judaism for future generations differed markedly, both agreed that inculcating a love for Judaism must begin at home. While these men of the nineteenth century still continued to believe that a woman's place was in the home, they reimagined the place of domicile, elevating its importance and the centrality of the woman's role in it. To carry out Hirsch's task of practical action effectively required that a wife and mother first receive a formal Jewish education. Thus, even as they reaffirmed traditional gender roles, Hirsch's and Hildesheimer's creation of modern Orthodoxy made them, along with the Reformers, important early contributors to what would become changing conceptions of gender in Judaism.

Positive-Historical Judaism

The third significant stream of Judaism to emerge in the middle of the nineteenth century was termed positive-historical Judaism.

Zacharias Frankel (1801–1875) was the founding figure of what would later emerge in the United States as Conservative Judaism. He came from a family of distinguished Talmudists but was, like Samson Raphael Hirsch, imbued with the values of the Enlightenment. He attended the University of Budapest and received a PhD in the natural sciences, philosophy, and philology. The term *positive-historical* refers to Frankel's belief that the essence of Judaism was "positive," divinely revealed, and therefore could not be changed but by rabbinic fiat. But he also recognized that Judaism developed within history; thus, its traditions and entire postbiblical development were subject to alteration and continual reinterpretation.

Frankel rejected unbending Orthodoxy as well as radical Reform. Instead, he was in favor of moderate accommodation. As to the question of authority, unlike the Reformers, who took it upon themselves to institute changes, and the Neo-Orthodox, who considered the entire corpus of Jewish law to be inviolable, Frankel considered modifications only if they did not run counter to the sensibilities of the majority of Jews. For Frankel, who saw his brand of Judaism as stemming from Neo-Orthodoxy, religious practice, as established by the people, was a form of Divine revelation and thus could not be easily dismissed. However, to save Judaism from wholesale rejection by the people, Jewish leadership must "take into consideration the opposition between faith and conditions of the time. True faith, due to its Divine nature, is above time . . . but time has a force and might, which must be taken account of." Espousing a democratic position, Frankel asserted that change was permissible in Judaism, but that it was the people's sensibilities that would determine when "certain practices [would be allowed to] fall into disuse. . . . Only those practices from which it [the Jewish people] is entirely estranged and which yield it no satisfaction will be abandoned and will thus die of themselves." Frankel's mission was to determine the rate and nature of change in Judaism, his goal being to prove that Jews and Jewish law had been flexible throughout history and that being so in his day was in keeping with the well-established tradition of innovation in Judaism.

In his magnum opus, *Darkhe ha-Mishnah* (*The Paths of the Mishnah*) (1859), Frankel historicized the work of the ancient rabbis, described the place and time in which they worked, and gave them credit for innovative legal thinking and practice. Coincidentally appearing in the same year as Charles Darwin's *On the Origin of Species*, Frankel's work posited a theory of evolution as it applied to *halakhah*, maintaining that Judaism was the product of development and not the result of spontaneous creation. While previous depictions of the rabbis focused on their role as vehicles for transmitting *halakhah*, Frankel represented them as active figures rising to meet the challenges of the present. According to Frankel, the rabbis "instituted ordinances in accordance with the condition of the state and of human society in their days." *Darkhe ha-Mishnah* emerged from the lectures that Frankel gave as head of the Jewish Theological Seminary, founded in Breslau in 1854. Similar to a yeshiva in that it taught traditional Jewish texts, it also included Jewish history in the curriculum, thus combining positive-historical Judaism's reverence for tradition with its belief in the power and utility of historical investigation. Both symbolic and representative of this goal was the presence of historian Heinrich Graetz on the faculty. The Jewish Theological Seminary in Breslau was the precursor to Conservative Judaism's New

York institution of the same name, which was established in 1886.

RELIGIOUS REFORMS BEYOND GERMANY

Liberal Judaism spread to other parts of Europe, usually in a far more conservative manner and at a much slower pace than in Germany. One important exception was Hungary, where developments moved rapidly. Prior to 1867, the year Hungary's 542,000 Jews were emancipated, every Jew in Hungary, according to civil law, had to belong to a local congregation, all of which were Orthodox. After Hungary gained autonomy from Habsburg Austria in 1867, the government called upon all Jewish leaders to meet and form a single nationwide religious organization. This resulted in a schism that led to the emergence of three distinct groups, each organized separately in civil law. The Neologs, who emerged in 1868, were traditional in practice but were open to some religious and many substantial aesthetic innovations; the radical Orthodox, who were "ultra-religious," were exceptionally scrupulous in their devotion to Jewish law and were opposed to any and all reforms; and a third group represented the status quo ante. These were the Orthodox Jews of the pre-1867 era.

Some of the more significant reforms and aesthetic innovations also took hold among traditional Jews. In England, two synagogues broke from the establishment. The West London Synagogue of British Jews was established in 1810. The congregation's most important social innovation was to bring together Ashkenazim and Sephardim as congregants; in the domain of religion, the synagogue took the novel but hardly radical step of abrogating the second day of the four major festivals: Pesach,

Sukkot, Shavuot, and Rosh Hashanah. The Manchester Reform Association, composed of many German Jews, began to conduct its own services in 1856. Never as radical as their coreligionists in Germany, the association members used the prayer book of the West London Synagogue but retained the second day of festivals.

In France, reforms were undertaken under the auspices of the Central Consistory. This meant that, based on law, French Jewish communities retained their hierarchical structure and national cohesion. Still, synagogues that were nominally Orthodox adopted reforms such as confirmation ceremonies, the use of organs and choirs, and rabbis wearing vestments that were nearly identical with those of the Catholic clergy. Synagogue officials even donned uniforms with gold braid, epaulets, and the famous three-cornered hat, such as the one worn by Napoleon. In the British Empire, Orthodox rabbis were called "reverend," and the leading cleric became known as the chief rabbi, a position modelled on that of the Anglican archbishop of Canterbury. In 1844, Nathan Adler became the first such chief rabbi and instituted many of the changes in decorum characteristic of Reform Judaism, although in terms of Jewish law, practice remained strictly orthodox.

NEW SYNAGOGUES AND THE ARCHITECTURE OF EMANCIPATION

Typical of new trends and changing sensibilities were innovations in synagogue architecture. Across the world, Jewish congregations, Orthodox included, were imbued with the spirit of emancipation and religious reform. Increasingly middle class and keen to display social prominence, as well as to assert their status as citizens with equal rights, Jews began to build monumental synagogues that served as architectural declarations of their residential permanence, as well as announcing to their neighbors that they were both proud of their Jewish identities and that their Jewishness was completely compatible with being loyal citizens of their nations.

From the mid-nineteenth century to World War I, such synagogues were to be found around the globe. Prior to emancipation, synagogues had generally been small places of worship and study, while the new synagogues, very often recalling the size and grandeur of the Temple in Jerusalem, were enormous structures built in eclectic styles, often modelled on churches or neo-Islamic forms. The "architecture of Emancipation" and the modern aesthetic of the synagogue service that were initiated by Reform Jews spread to other denominations and far beyond the confines of Germany. In Budapest, the Great Synagogue in Dohány Street, also known as the Dohány Synagogue, or the *Tabac-Shul* (the Yiddish translation of *dohány* is *tabac*, or *tobacco*), was built between 1854 and 1859 by the Neolog Jewish community. One of the largest in the world, the synagogue is grand, with a capacity of 2,964 seats (1,492 for men and 1,472 in the women's galleries). The building is more than 174 feet long and is 87 feet wide. The design of the Dohány Street synagogue is principally neo-Islamic but also features a mixture of Byzantine, Romanesque, and Gothic elements. The western façade boasts arched windows with carved decorations and brickwork in the heraldic colors of the city of Budapest: blue, yellow, and red. Above the main entrance is a stained-glass rose window. The gateway is flanked on both sides by two polygonal towers with long arched windows and crowned by copper domes with golden ornaments. The towers soar to a height of 143 feet each, their decoration featuring carvings of geometric forms and clocks, while atop the façade sit the Ten Commandments. The synagogue's interior is adorned with colored and golden geometric shapes. The Holy Ark is located on the eastern wall, while above it sits the choir gallery. A gigantic 5,000-pipe organ, exquisite enough to have been played by Franz Liszt, bespoke the congregation's commitment to making beautiful music central to the synagogue service. Distinguished cantors from the Great Synagogue in Dohány Street earned worldwide acclaim.

While the Dohány Street synagogue was built by the reformist Neologs (various Reform congregations built similar edifices in other European and American cities), the Orthodox likewise built similar houses of worship. In fact, Orthodox congregations built the majority of such synagogues. Like their reform-minded coreligionists, Orthodox Jews also strove to present a form of Judaism to the world that was stately, solemn, and modern.

The names of new synagogues frequently bore the word "Great" or "Grand." This was the case in Paris, Rome, and Sydney. In 1878, exactly 90 years after the first Jews landed in Australia, the Great Synagogue of Sydney was consecrated. Designed by the distinguished architect Thomas Rowe, it is a glorious structure, a harmonious blend of Byzantine and Gothic styles. The interior is spacious, the height of the synagogue accentuated by cast-iron columns that reach up to plaster decorations, arches, and a paneled and groined ceiling covered with gold leaf stars and other elaborate decorations. Further enhancing the grandeur is the abundance of sunlight that pours through magnificent stained-glass windows. When built, the 90-foot-high twin sandstone towers made the synagogue the tallest building in the city. Although skyscrapers have now dwarfed the Great Synagogue, the fact that well

into the twentieth century a Jewish house of worship was the tallest building in Australia's largest metropolis spoke to the community's confidence in itself and in the nation that it called home. And in apparent fulfilment of Saul Ascher's dream that Judaism, if presented in an enlightened way, "might be the religion of any member of society," a Christian minister from Melbourne reported after a visit to the Great Synagogue in 1896:

The galleries are well filled, so is the amphitheatre like floor space. Facing the ark-alcove, but separated from it by a wide unoccupied space, is the Almemmar, or tribune, a highly ornamented wooden structure with seats for the Rabbis and presiding officials of the synagogue, and a spacious reading stand on which to repose the roll of the Torah, and up to which the successive readers of the lessons advance, supported on either hand by prominent members of the congregation. . . . All the males in the body of the synagogue wear the tallithim [prayer shawls] and have their hats on. As I took my seat the sweet musical voice of the second minister rose clear, plaintive, voicing the heart-cry of the children of the dispersion to their fathers' God to remember Zion and the set time to favour her. The musical Hebrew had a sobbing plaintiveness, indescribably charming, ever and anon the congregation took up the responses. The venerable Chief Rabbi—the Reverend A.B. Davis—now takes his place at the reading stand; the sacred roll is unwound; the aged man, his natural force scarcely abated, in clear, ringing tones, a kind of semi-chant, recites the law of the Lord; the great congregation are on their feet. This is the psychological moment. . . . Rabbi Davis, raising the sacred scroll high in the air, descended from the tribune, and with slow and stately step, marched up the broad steps to the Ark, in which he deposited the Law of the Lord. . . . Then the Chief Rabbi, taking his stand at the top of the flight of steps, in front of the Ark, preached his sermon; a wonderful effort for an aged man, delivered ore rotundo, with wonderful fire and passion. . . . As I passed into the life of the streets, and nineteenth century feeling again asserted its potency, I felt like one who had been in Dreamland, and had heard things which it is not lawful for a man to speak to the fool multitude.

With the recognition by this Christian clergyman that the Jews engaged in "majestic worship," the elders of Sydney's Great Synagogue might have been well satisfied that the aesthetic changes they rang in were having a positive social and ecumenical impact. In the United States, the Touro Synagogue (1763) in Rhode Island resembled congregational meetinghouses of the colonial era, while synagogues in the South, such as Beth Elohim (1792) in Charleston, South Carolina, looked very similar to the Georgian churches found in the same city. The latter was rebuilt in Greek Revival style in 1841 after a fire in 1838 destroyed the original building. At the inauguration ceremony for the new Beth Elohim, Reverend Gustavus Poznanski observed in the fashion typical of Reform Jews of his era, "This synagogue is our Temple, this city our Jerusalem, and this happy land our Palestine."

In Rome, the majestic Great Synagogue was modelled on the Roman- and Byzantine-styled Grand Synagogue of Paris, built between 1867 and 1874. Inaugurated in 1904, the synagogue in the Italian capital was constructed in an eclectic blend of Roman, Greek, Assyro-Babylonian, and Egyptian styles. Its location was of great significance, for it was built on the site of the Roman ghetto and thus represented the emancipation of Italian Jews from an enclosed world marked by restrictions and physical confinement. At the inauguration, in the presence of Italy's most important political dignitaries, the Jewish community president, Angelo Sereni, blended republican political hopes and Jewish religious sensibilities (a symbol of the ideal nineteenth-century synthesis) when he declared:

The construction of this Temple is not only a manifestation of the religious feelings of one part of the citizenry who alone may take pleasure in it. It is also an affirmation, a solemn pronouncement that gives cause for rejoicing to all those, with no distinction whatsoever, who harbor high and noble ideals of liberty, equality, and love.

As this chapter has shown, Jews in the eighteenth and nineteenth centuries responded creatively to the challenges of modernity. In the realms of religious and secular culture, innovation was the order of the day, from Hasidism in Poland to Mitnagdism in Lithuania, from Reform Judaism, Neo-Orthodoxy, and positive-historical Judaism in Germany to secular Sephardic culture in Italian port cities. Everywhere, Jews were either claiming to be maintaining tradition or were consciously breaking with the past. Everywhere, they were reconsidering Judaism and their individual Jewish identities in light of the changing times. Beyond religious and cultural innovations, late nineteenth-century Jewish life underwent significant change in the social and economic realms. Many of these changes, long advocated by non-Jewish society, nevertheless led to unexpected hostility on the part of non-Jews, which in turn gave rise to innovations in both non-Jewish and Jewish political culture. It is to such developments that we turn in the following chapter.

For Further Reading

On religious life in Poland, see Gershon Hundert, *Jews in Poland-Lithuania in the Eighteenth Century: A Genealogy of Modernity* (Berkeley: University of California Press, 2004); David Biale et al., eds., *Hasidism: A New History* (Princeton: Princeton University Press, 2017); Immanuel Etkes, *The Gaon of Vilna: The Man and His Image* (Berkeley: University of California Press, 2002); Immanuel Etkes, *Rabbi Israel Salanter and the Mussar Movement: Seeking the Torah of Truth* (Philadelphia: Jewish Publication Society, 1993); Ada Rapoport-Albert, ed., *Hasidism Reappraised* (London: Vallentine Mitchell, 1996); Eliyahu Stern, *The Genius, Elijah of Vilna and the Making of Modern Judaism* (New Haven: Yale University Press, 2013).

On religious life in central Europe, see Michael A. Meyer, *Response to Modernity: A History of the Reform Movement in Judaism* (New York: Oxford University Press, 1988); Mordechai Breuer, *Modernity within Tradition: The Social History of Orthodox Jewry in Imperial Germany* (New York: Columbia University Press, 1992); Jacob Katz, *A House Divided: Orthodoxy and Schism in Nineteenth-Century Central European Jewry* (Hanover, NH: University Press of New England, 1998); and Michael Brenner, Steffi Jersch-Wenzel, and Michael A. Meyer, *German-Jewish History in Modern Times*, vol. 2: *Emancipation and Acculturation, 1780–1871*, ed. Michael A. Meyer (New York: Columbia University Press, 1996).

On the Haskalah, see David Sorkin, *The Transformation of German Jewry, 1780–1840* (New York: Oxford University Press, 1987); Shmuel Feiner and David Sorkin, eds., *New Perspectives on the Haskalah* (Portland, OR: Littman Library of Jewish Civilization, 2001); Shmuel Feiner, *The Jewish Enlightenment* (Philadelphia: University of Pennsylvania Press, 2004); Shmuel Feiner, *Haskalah and History: The Emergence of a Modern Jewish Historical Consciousness* (Portland, OR: Littman Library of Jewish Civilization, 2002); Michael Brenner, *Prophets of the Past: Interpreters of Jewish History* (Princeton: Princeton University Press, 2010); David Fishman, *Russia's First Modern Jews: The Jews of Shklov* (New York: New York University Press, 1995); Michael Stanislawski, *For Whom Do I Toil? Judah Leib Gordon and the Crisis of Russian Jewry* (New York: Oxford University Press, 1988); Steven Zipperstein, *The Jews of Odessa: A Cultural History* (Stanford: Stanford University Press, 1991); Shaul Stampfer, "Gender Differentiation and Education of the Jewish Woman in Nineteenth-Century Eastern Europe," in Antony Polonsky, ed., *From Shtetl to Socialism: Studies from Polin* (London and Washington: Littman Library of Jewish Civilization, 1993), 187–211; Olga Litvak, *Haskalah: The Romantic Movement in Judaism* (New Brunswick: Rutgers University Press, 2012); Matthias Lehmann, *Ladino Rabbinic Literature and Ottoman Sephardic Culture* (Bloomington: Indiana University Press, 2005); and Aron Rodrigue, "The Ottoman Diaspora: The Rise and Fall of Ladino Literary Culture," in David Biale, ed., *Cultures of the Jews* (New York: Schocken Books, 2002).

CHAPTER 3

THE POLITICS OF BEING JEWISH

AMONG THE MOST salient features of Jewish life in the modern period were the changes in residential patterns and the astronomical growth in the Jewish population. By the last decades of the nineteenth century, the village Jew of Alsace, Bavaria, and Bohemia in western and central Europe was disappearing. In eastern Europe, the shtetl Jew, though still in evidence until the Holocaust, had become an increasingly less-visible figure on the Jewish social landscape. Rather, what typified and conditioned much of Jewish existence in the modern period was the move to cities. The increase in the sheer number of Jews and in Jewish population density put pressure on local economies. In search of economic and educational opportunities, Jews left their smaller towns for expanding urban areas. Population growth and mobility shaped every aspect of Jewish life, including occupational choice, residential patterns, and emigration, as well as political affiliation and organization. Often, the choices Jews made occasioned a host of responses and reactions among their gentile neighbors that ranged from sympathetic to hostile. The reactions depended on whether one saw Jewish social mobility and increasing prominence in European affairs as a positive

or a negative development. More pointedly, feelings about Jews proved to be a litmus test for feelings about modernity. Quite often, those disenchanted with it blamed Jews.

Over the course of the nineteenth century, the number of Jews in the world increased dramatically. In Europe, the Jewish population grew from 716,000 in 1700 to 2.7 million in 1825 and then reached 4.1 million in 1850. That number rose to 8.7 million in 1900 and 9.5 million in 1939. Taking the whole world, in 1880, there were 7.8 million Jews, a number that increased to 13.5 million by the outbreak of World War I in 1914.

This population explosion meant that the Jewish rate of growth was greater than that of any other European people. By 1900, approximately 82 percent of all the world's Jews lived in Europe. Nearly 50 percent of those Jews, approximately 5.2 million, lived in the Russian Empire, with a further 20 percent, nearly 2 million, residing in what, after 1867, became the Austro-Hungarian Empire. By the late 1870s, just over 10 percent lived in North America and South America (1 million), and a total of about 7 percent lived in the Middle East and Asia (432,000) and Africa (340,000). Prior to the outbreak of war in 1914, most of the world's Jews were subjects of multiethnic empires: the

DOI: 10.4324/9781003611608-4

Russian, Austro-Hungarian, Ottoman, French, or British.

What contributed to Jewish population growth were high birth rates and low death rates. The trend originated in the eighteenth century, though exact numbers are hard to come by for that period. We can be more precise about the period between 1850 and 1880; in eastern Europe, there were 17 more Jewish births than deaths for every 1,000 people. Even in places where the Jewish birth rate remained relatively low, such as in western Europe, the low death rates due to the higher survival rate among Jewish infants ensured a positive Jewish demographic balance. As one Jewish journal article on the subject proudly noted in 1910, "[t]he death rate among Jewish children in the unhealthy, narrow confines of the Frankfurt ghetto is lower than the rate among the city's [Christian] patricians."

Statistics the world over showed the Jews to have been an extraordinarily healthy people. They tended to live longer than non-Jews, had a significantly lower infant mortality rate, had a lower death rate, and seemed to be far less susceptible to the most common diseases of the day, particularly childhood illnesses, such as measles, scarlet fever, and diphtheria. Contemporary doctors and social critics offered several explanations for this. First, they all suggested that the virtual absence of alcoholism among Jews, a disease that ravaged Europeans, especially in eastern Europe, proved to be a great advantage. Second, having fewer offspring meant that Jewish parents could divide their material resources among a smaller number of children. Fewer mouths to feed made for a higher caloric intake per individual, and therefore a greater survival rate. Third, contemporary physicians noted that Jewish mothers in both

eastern Europe and America breastfed their children to a greater extent, and for a longer period of time, than did non-Jewish mothers. This was widely considered to be advantageous for the baby. Fourth, Jewish mothers, especially in western Europe, tended not to work outside the home after marriage; thus, they were on hand to tend to their children. And even in eastern Europe, where Jews were more closely tied to rural economies, the grinding agricultural work done by peasant women was largely unknown among the Jewish population. Fifth, medical opinion at the turn of the twentieth century unanimously credited Jewish hygiene habits, particularly regular handwashing, with stemming the spread of infectious disease. Sixth, by the late nineteenth century, Jews, especially those in western and central Europe, were better educated, were better remunerated, and overall, enjoyed higher standards of living than non-Jews. The vast majority of Jews displayed a host of bourgeois customs and habits that, in the areas of hygiene and nourishment, worked to minimize infant mortality and improve and extend the life of adults. Of course, most eastern European Jews and immigrants from that part of the world who settled in New York and London were decidedly poor and working-class, but they, too, lived longer and healthier lives than their Slavic, Irish, or Italian neighbors did and had a significantly lower incidence of infant mortality. There is no doubt that the modern period produced healthy, vibrant Jewish communities.

By the outbreak of World War I, the Jewish population explosion had begun to run its course. Greater affluence, increased use of birth control, rising levels of assimilation that, in certain instances, extended to apostasy, mixed marriage, emigration, and aging all took a significant demographic toll, especially in western Europe. In Germany, for example, the Jewish community was only demographically replenished by the influx of eastern European Jewish immigrants. Jewish birth rates declined not only in western Europe but also in Russia, Hungary, Poland, and Romania.

THE MOVE TO CITIES

Despite the decline in the rate of population growth, Jews remained highly visible due to urbanization, a process that began among Jews before it reached the general population. By 1925, more than a quarter of the world's Jews lived in a mere 14 large cities, and just prior to the outbreak of World War II, half of all Jews lived in cities with populations of over 100,000. This led the distinguished Jewish historian Salo Baron to observe that "one may thus speak of the metropolitanization rather than the urbanization of the Jews."

"Metropolitanization" began in earnest toward the end of the nineteenth century, when neighborhoods with significant Jewish populations began to proliferate throughout European capitals. Often, this was the result of eastern European Jewish migration. London's Jewish population, heavily crowded into the East End, rose from 40,000 in 1880 to 200,000 by 1914 thanks to the arrival of Russian Jews. Internal Jewish migration from rural or provincial areas to the capital and major cities also contributed to metropolitanization. Sigmund Freud's Jewish Vienna grew from 72,000 in 1880 to 175,000 in 1910, largely as a result of migration from Galicia. In 1808, the year Napoleon passed his Infamous Decrees, the Jewish population of Paris stood at a mere 8,000. By 1900, the Jewish population of the city had grown to 60,000, largely due to Jews moving to the capital from Alsace. Crowded into the Marais district, the area was also known by its Yiddish name, the *Pletzl* (Little Place). Amsterdam's Jewish community also grew as a result of migration from the Dutch provinces to the capital. While the Jews of Amsterdam totaled 20,000 in 1800, that number had expanded to 90,000 by the turn of the twentieth century. Here, the Jewish presence was so pronounced that Amsterdam itself was known as *Mokem* (the Yiddish pronunciation of "makom," the Hebrew word for "place"). Among all Amsterdamers, whether Jewish or gentile, *Mokem* remains the colloquial word for the Dutch capital. In Germany, when the Second Reich was founded in 1871, its capital city, Berlin, had a Jewish population of 36,000. In a mere 40 years, that number had quadrupled, and by 1910, Berlin had 144,000 Jewish residents. As was the case with other European capitals, much of the growth was due to the arrival of eastern European Jews, a large percentage of whom resided in the slum area known as the Scheunenviertel.

The same pattern was to be seen among Sephardic Jews in the Mediterranean region. In Greece, Salonika became one of Europe's largest Jewish cities, earning it the exalted Hebrew title of *Ir ve'em be-Yisrael* ("Metropolis and Mother of Israel"). The city was a haven for Jews after their expulsion from Spain in 1492, and Jews continued to come to the city over the centuries. By 1900, Salonika was home to nearly 90,000 Jews, a full half of the entire population. With more than 50 synagogues, 20 Jewish schools, the largest Jewish cemetery in Europe, and a full range of Jewish institutions, the city was a vibrant Jewish center. As with cities elsewhere, Salonika's Jewish population increased in the last quarter of the nineteenth century due to the arrival of eastern European Jewish immigrants. The beginnings of decline of Jewish Salonika, however, are not attributed to declining birth rates, as was the case elsewhere, but to the rise of Greek nationalism. In 1917, a massive fire swept through the city, leaving 53,000 Jews homeless. In the aftermath of the devastation, Greek nationalists saw their chance to confiscate substantial tracts of land from the fire-ravaged Jewish quarter and impose a draconian program of Hellenization on Jews and other non-Greek minorities who had displayed allegiance to the imperial rulers of the city, the Ottoman Turks. Many Jews began to leave, and by 1939, the Jewish community of Salonika had shrunk to 56,000.

In eastern Europe, Jews were leaving their *shtetlekh* (small towns) and villages and moving to nearby large cities. The image of Sholem Aleichem's protagonist Tevye the Dairyman as the prototypical Russian Jew corresponded less and less to the social reality of eastern European Jewish life. Between 1897 and 1910, the Jewish urban population of Russia increased by about 1 million, or 38.5 percent. Of the 5.2 million Jews in the Empire, 3.5 million lived in cities. Between 1869 and 1910, the Jewish population of the imperial capital, St. Petersburg, grew from 7,000 to 35,000, while in the Black Sea port city of Odessa—a lively Jewish intellectual and commercial center, home to Yiddish, Hebrew, and Russian writers—the Jewish population rose dramatically from 55,000 in 1880 to 200,000 in 1912. Over this period, the percentage of Jews among the total population went from 25.2 to 32.3 percent. In Warsaw, which would become the largest Jewish city in Europe, the Jewish population stood at 12,000 in 1804 and rose to 43,000 in 1850. By 1910, however, that number had climbed dramatically to 337,000, or 38 percent of the total population. This increase was the result of mass

migration from the Pale of Settlement; it first began in the 1860s and increased substantially over the rest of the nineteenth century. Approximately 150,000 Jews from Lithuania, Byelorussia, and Ukraine moved to Warsaw (*see* Map 3.1).

Even in cities where the absolute number of Jews was not large, their percentage of the total population stood well above 50 percent. Cities such as Bialystok, Berdichev, Grodno, Pinsk, Lvov, Lodz, Lublin, Cracow, and Vilna all had relatively small Jewish populations as late as 1880, but by 1900, Jewish immigrants, mostly from surrounding areas, had poured into these towns, substantially changing their character. At the turn of the century, Berdichev was 87.5 percent Jewish; Pinsk, 80 percent; Brody, 75 percent; Bialystok, 66 percent; and Vilna, 40 percent. Jews made up between 25 and 50 percent of the total populations in scores of towns and cities in the Russian Empire. Towns like these constituted the provincial heartland of eastern European Jewry.

Outside of Europe, similar trends were in evidence by the start of the twentieth century. In a very short period of time, New York City grew into the largest urban Jewish center in history. A mere 10,000 Jews lived in the city in 1846. Between 1881 and 1917, mass migration mostly from Russia and Galicia saw the Jewish population grow to 1,503,000. By that point in time, Jews comprised a full 26.4 percent of the total population of America's largest city. In the Southern Hemisphere, with relatively small Jewish populations, the results of urbanization were perhaps even more striking. By 1900, nearly all Australian Jews were to be found in either Sydney, Melbourne, or Adelaide. Nearly half of Argentina's Jews resided in Buenos Aires. Brazilian Jews were to be

Map 3.1   The Pale of Settlement, 1791–1917. By 1897, approximately 5 million Jews lived in the Pale of Settlement, a vast area covering over 386,000 square miles.

found almost exclusively in Rio de Janeiro or São Paulo, while Uruguay's Jews lived mostly in the capital, Montevideo.

In the Muslim world, too, where large numbers of Jews lived in small villages in countries such as Morocco and Yemen, the tendency toward urbanization was also evident. Across North Africa from Morocco all the way to Iran, Jews were mostly to be found in cities. Jewish artisans and merchants were highly visible in Casablanca, Fez, Mogador, Algiers, Constantine, Oran, Tunis, Baghdad, Teheran, and Istanbul.

Living in large cities had a significant impact on Jewish society and culture. The profile of the urban Jew was one of a people alienated from the land. This image shaped the ideas of political ideologues from divergent backgrounds, Jewish and gentile, who latched on to this feature of Jewish life, seeing it as especially pernicious. Zionists sought to transform Jews by returning them to agricultural work, while enemies of the Jews pointed to their urbanization as a symbol of their divorce from the rural, and thus "authentic," heart and soul of the nations in which they lived. City life also had a decisive impact on the occupational choices of Jews. Their preference was to work in the industrial and commercial sectors and in the professions. Cities also provided Jews with an array of cultural and intellectual offerings, exposing them to ideas and ideologies that would challenge in significant ways both Jewish practices and Jewish beliefs. Making the most of opportunities afforded them by their move to cities, Jews became extremely prominent in all spheres of commercial and intellectual activity. An unforeseen response to Jewish success and cultural integration was the explosive growth across Europe of antisemitism.

Modern Antisemitism

In the modern period, Jews became heavily involved in politics. This engagement, however, was not always voluntary, for Jews sometimes got caught up in political movements against their wishes. The politics of antisemitism is one such case. Antisemitism, an ideology that sought to attribute contemporary social ills to the Jews, actually led some Jews into politics, where they hoped to forge robust responses to the wide variety of accusations directed at them.

Modern antisemitism is characterized by ideological claims and organizational features that make it different from traditional anti-Judaism. Ideologically, it is a mostly secular faith, although not exclusively so, and grounds its claims in two core beliefs: first, that there exists a Jewish conspiracy to control the world and, second, that the Jews are a distinct race possessed of physical and psychological characteristics unique to them. Organizationally, the nineteenth century saw the advent of antisemitic political parties in central and western Europe. Ideologues and politicians who subscribed to antisemitism often turned hatred of Jews into full-time jobs. They were backed by a vast array of associations, clubs, organizations, and lobby groups that espoused antisemitic views, whether based on economic, religious, or racist principles. While these groups disagreed about much, they generally concurred that the Jews were responsible for all that ailed the modern world. Promising a cure, politicians and cultural critics emerged on both the Right and the Left of the political spectrum. The new radical right, composed of monarchists, clerics, nationalists, university students, and members of the struggling lower middle classes, was especially receptive to antisemitism. On the other hand, while the Left was not immune to Jew hatred, it was more likely to focus on attacking individual Jews, such as the capitalist Rothschilds, or commercial occupations that attracted large numbers of Jews, such as banking, the stock market, or even petty trade and peddling. Antisemitism was an ideology that was often able to unite Europeans ordinarily divided along class, religious, and national lines.

The "Jewish Question"

Over the course of the nineteenth century, the movement of central and western European Jews into European culture and out of insular Jewish communities led to the emergence of a new Europe-wide discourse about Jews known as the "Jewish question." The term, which applied to the new problem of the secular Jew, was first used in France in 1833 but was popularized by the German Protestant theologian Bruno Bauer in an 1843 essay of that title. Bauer decried what he saw as the Jews' wish to enter the modern world without surrendering their distinctive culture. Their refusal to disappear had been, according to Bauer, the cause of gentile opposition to them. Blaming Jews for the hostility they inspired, Bauer noted:

In history, nothing stands outside the law of causality, least of all the Jews. . . . The will of history is evolution, new forms, progress, change; the Jews want to stay forever what they are, therefore they fight against the first law of history—does this not prove that by pressing against this mighty spring they provoke counter-pressure?

Reversing Christian Wilhelm Dohm's firm contention that "the Jew is more man than Jew," Bauer now declared:

[A]s long as he is a Jew, his Jewishness must be stronger in him than his humanity and keeps him apart from non-Jews. He declares by this segregation that this, his Jewishness, is his true, highest nature, which has to have precedence over his humanity.

Bauer's claim that Jews possess an immutable collective loyalty and essence and plot against the rest of the world lies at the heart of modern antisemitism. But such tropes are themselves of ancient provenance. In classical antiquity, writers such as Tacitus and Juvenal denounced the Jews for being misanthropic. The Catholic Church taught a theological version of these secular claims, decrying Jewish obstinacy for refusing to accept Jesus and fomenting hatred against all Christians. The Church Father, Origen, in the third century, claimed that the Jews had "formed a conspiracy against the human race." Muslim thinkers said similar things about the Jews' refusal to accept the message of Prophet Muhammad. Still, it was only in the modern period that such claims became the stuff of politics.

Antisemites drew on ancient and modern as well as religious and secular prejudices against Jews to create a potent mix of charges that emerged with surprising strength in the closing decades of the nineteenth century. The reason for the popularity of antisemitism rests on the fact that it is not only about Jews and their alleged flaws. While Jews are its principal targets, modern antisemitism also levels a broader critique at the nature of modern society. Antisemites believe that a Jewish presence lurks behind every aspect of modernity that they find objectionable, and since modernity is multifaceted, the Jews can be accused of anything and blamed for everything, including unbridled capitalism, Marxism, liberalism, Communism, ethnic exclusiveness, cosmopolitan universalism, parliamentary democracy, the uprooting of the peasantry, the demand for workers' rights, the campaign to enfranchise women, the White slave trade in women, the "taking over" of various European cultures, being disloyal to the nation, being excessively patriotic, and above all, plotting to start a race war against their enemies. In 1890, Isaac Rülf, a German Jewish teacher, journalist, and philosopher, astutely observed:

> Everywhere this anti-Semitic fury signi-
> fies nothing more and nothing less than
> the beginnings of the social revolution.
> Let it be clearly understood by all who
> support anti-Semitism openly or secretly,
> or who merely tolerate it; it is not a ques-
> tion of the Jews at all, it is a question of
> subverting the entire order of life, society
> and the state!

Still, Jews are not merely scapegoats. Genu-ine antisemites truly believe their accu-sations against Jews. The belief in Jewish culpability is as real as the antisemites' sense of grievance.

By the 1860s and 1870s, legal emancipation throughout western and central Europe was a fact. European Jews, historically suspicious of their Christian neighbors, were increas-ingly secure and confident of their place in a secular political order. Most central and western European Jews, having accepted the fundamental premises of Enlightenment dis-course that they stood in need of regenera-tion, energetically dedicated themselves to the project of Europeanization. Believing that

they had succeeded, Jews now expected that the reward for their efforts would be the end of Jew hatred. Many Christians, however, were disappointed with the results of emancipation or were never truly convinced it could change the Jews. During the 1848 Revolution, the composer Richard Wagner (1813–1883) was a supporter of Jewish emancipation. Neverthe-less, his commitment to it was half-hearted. In his paradigmatic antisemitic essay of 1850 *Judaism in Music*, he wrote: "[W]ith all our speaking and writing in favour of the Jews' emancipation, we always felt instinctively repelled by any actual, operative contact with them." While Jews, especially those in urban areas, did move closer to European culture, most proved unwilling or unable to erase the communal and psychological characteristics of Jewishness or, more radically, do what Wag-ner called on them to do, namely, to engage in an act of "self-extinction."

The persistent refusal of the Jews to dis-appear frustrated many Europeans—both antisemites and even philosemites. Jews con-tinued, for the most part, to marry among themselves, to live in Jewish neighborhoods, and to work in largely Jewish sectors of the economy, such as commerce, manufacturing, and the liberal professions. The fields of jour-nalism, art, and popular entertainment also proved extremely attractive to Jews. Their rapid acculturation had been remarkable, and Jews genuinely believed they had done all that could be reasonably asked of them. For many Jews (and for some non-Jews), the "Jewish question" had been solved. But it alarmed many that these radical social and cultural changes the Jews underwent failed to diminish their strong sense of collective iden-tity, which, to many observers, appeared to be an indelible vestige of their ancient tribal identity. Jewish particularity, combined with remarkable professional success, engendered hatred and envy. For Jews, the backlash came as a great shock.

Charges of Jewish distinctiveness and harmfulness were central to four critical discourses of the nineteenth century: those of urbanization, capitalism, international politics, and race. Urbanization and the concomitant flight from the land led many Europeans to long romantically for a return to pre-industrial society. Reactionary nationalists, most of whom lived in cities, glorified the peasant and the soil. Antisemites held Jews in contempt for exemplifying the kind of lifestyle typical of increasing numbers of Christians—urban and cosmopolitan. As the prominent German antisemite and "rural romanticist" Otto Glagau declared in 1879, "all Jews and persons of Jewish descent are born opponents of agriculture." Antisemitic nationalists projected their own misgivings about their alienation from the nation's rural roots onto modern Jews. Absent ties to the land Jews were never able to convince non-Jewish critics of their authentic attachment to it. Zionists, too, would see the Jewish return to agriculture as an essential ingredient in the creation of the new Jew.

In western Europe, Jews, as supporters of a liberal, capitalist, democratic order, were seen as benefiting from social changes other groups considered to be detrimental. Liberalism and free commerce abetted social mobility, and those who wished to preserve the ordered hierarchy of society, even if they occupied a low rung on its ladder, hated Jews for their upward rise. There was the old nobility anxious about the loss of long-standing privileges, and new commercial elites protective of their recently won wealth and status, and the vast petit bourgeoisie made up of state bureaucrats, schoolteachers, small shopkeepers, shopworkers,

and artisans. All these groups became increasingly disaffected by the social changes then underway. In response, they formed political interest groups to redress their particular resentments. Agitating against Jews was core to their various missions. One such group was the National Union of Commercial Employees, which was founded in Hamburg in 1893 and, by 1913, had nearly 150,000 members. It claimed that German commerce was made up of "two nationalities, Germans and Jews." The latter were barred from membership in the National Union because of their "unpleasant Jewish qualities, namely lack of courage, greed for profits, sultry sexuality, lack of honesty and cleanliness.... The German concepts of fidelity and faith [are] essentially different from Jewish concepts of commercial honesty." Many among these same groups also rebelled against mass society and consumer culture, for which they also held Jews responsible. One of their most hated symbols was the department store, an innovation they associated with Jews. As a new social institution, it symbolized the mass market and signified the end of settled cultural norms such as close relations between storekeepers and customers. It also signaled the end of artisanship, which appeared lost with the advent of mass production techniques. In the violent riots against Jews in France in 1898 during the Dreyfus Affair, a particular target of the demonstrators were Jewish-owned stores. In at least 30 different towns, the windows of large stores were smashed, and the contents pillaged. In Poitiers, the local Ligue Antisémitique du Commerce, which had over 200 members, launched a campaign urging women, "[f]or the honor and the salvation of France, [to] buy nothing from the Jews." One delegate to the Ecclesiastical Conference held at Reims in 1896 referred to Jews when he declared, "We know only too well about the merciless war waged on small traders by big department stores, those immense bazaars selling the produce of the whole world under one roof."

In the nineteenth century, international politics, as well as military, economic, and colonial competition between England, France, and Germany, became increasingly intense. Aggressive jingoism, nationalism, and racism contributed to the combustible atmosphere prior to World War I. In Russia, while the autocratic rule of the tsar remained tenuously intact, radical groups continually sought the destruction of the old order. At the same time, the multinational Austro-Hungarian Empire began to totter under the sway of competing nationalist aspirations, while the Catholic Church reacted with hostility and fear at the rising tide of liberalism, modern science, and socialism. Antisemitism proved a unifying ideological component of the agendas of these ofttimes-competing political and social forces.

Finally, race science provided antisemites with the ability to endow their demagoguery with a veneer of scientific authority. Antisemitism tended increasingly toward secularization, and the use of scientific discourse animated and gave substance to what was called the "Jewish racial question." It focused upon determining the physical and psychological characteristics of the Jews in order to ascertain whether these differed fundamentally from those of non-Jews. A typical such description comes from the Austrian physician August Weisbach, who, in 1867, observed that

the [European] Jews have a small stature, have mostly straight, but also curly, hair, of predominantly dark, not rarely also red, color, usually grey and light brown eyes,

and a lively pulse. They have a large, mesocephalic (more often dolicho-than brachycephalic) head . . . , a long face which is moderately wide between the cheeks, very narrow at the top, and narrow between the corners of the lower jaw, with a moderately high forehead. . . . The nose starts out very narrow at its root, is in general very big and of considerable length and height, but at the same time very narrow.

Whether one maintained that there was a single Jewish race or two—Sephardim and Ashkenazim—Jews were always said to be easily identifiable. According to the geographer and ethnologist Richard Andree, writing in 1881,

anthropologically, the Jews are the most interesting objects, for no other racial type can be traced back through the millennia with such certainty as the Jews. And no other racial type displays such a constancy of form, withstanding the influences of time and environment as does this one.

Physical anthropologists began to build an enormous data bank, accumulating statistics about the Jewish body by measuring skull size, chest circumference, height, as well as the range of eye and hair color. Antisemites used such statistics to merely reaffirm their belief in Jewish difference, and hence incompatibility with Europeans. At its most extreme, the racial antisemites argued not only for Jewish difference but also for their extermination.

Beginning in the 1870s, antisemites in western and central Europe dedicated themselves to reversing the gains that Jews had made as a result of their legal emancipation. While the general charges against Jews were echoed in one country after another, each variant had specific causes and characteristics that were driven by local concerns.

Antisemitism in Germany

Germany provided many of the tropes and much of the organizational structure of the modern antisemitic movement. In the nineteenth century, the major supporters of the German antisemitic parties came from the lower middle classes and the small farmers; both groups were particularly hard-hit by the economic depression of 1873, for which they blamed Jews. Parallel to the increased social and economic vulnerability of the lower middle classes was the rise of the Jews, who, especially after their emancipation in 1871, made extraordinarily rapid social, economic, educational, and cultural strides. Within a very short period of time, most German Jews became solidly middle class, earned more than their non-Jewish neighbors, achieved far higher levels of education than Germans, and played a vital role in the cultural life of the nation. Despite the fact that there were only about 600,000 German Jews (about 1 percent of the total population), the visibility of successful individual Jews and the disproportionate presence of Jews in certain fields inflamed the feeling that Jews had commandeered modern Germany.

Europe's first antisemitic political party—the Christian Social Workers Party—emerged in Berlin in 1878. At its head was Adolf Stöcker (1835–1909), court preacher to the kaiser. Stöcker's initial goal had been to form a political party that would curb the Social Democrats' influence on workers. His platform stressed Christian ethics and reconciliation between the state and the working classes. Stöcker enjoyed very little success, as social democracy continued to spread among the German proletariat, but the introduction of antisemitic rhetoric into his speeches produced political traction. In 1879, Stöcker gave an inflammatory speech at a party rally that signaled his shift in strategy. It was titled "What We Demand of Modern Jewry." Stöcker insisted, "Israel must renounce its ambition to rule Germany," and that the "Jewish press become more tolerant." He declared that Jewish capital should be curbed by the abolition of the "mortgage system in real estate and property should be inalienable and unmortgageable," and that quotas be put in place "to find out the disproportion between Jewish capital and Christian labor." Quotas should likewise be extended to limit the "appointments of Jewish judges in proportion to the size of the population" and to ensure the "removal of Jewish teachers from our grammar schools." Stöcker offered a bleak prognosis should these steps not be taken: "Either we succeed in this and Germany will rise again, or the cancer from which we suffer will spread further. In that event our whole future is threatened and the German spirit will become Judaized." Stöcker's slogan was "A return to a Germanic rule in law and business, a return to the Christian faith."

Stöcker was a demagogue, and his powerful oratory attracted a faithful, albeit small, following. However, after 1879, the larger movement to channel widespread social discontent into antisemitism snowballed, and many groups and parties emerged, coalescing into what was called the Berlin movement. Antisemitism had become so widespread that the party of the traditional elites, the Conservative Party, feared that if it did not declare its tacit antisemitism openly, it would lose ground to the radicals. In 1892, the Conservative Party therefore adopted the Tivoli Program. In the name of Christianity, monarchy, fatherland, and anti-capitalism, paragraph 1 of the Tivoli Program declared, "We combat the widely obtruding and decomposing Jewish influence on our people. We demand a Christian authority for the Christian people and Christian teachers for Christian pupils."

In their attacks on Jews, the conservatives were joined by associations such as the powerful Agrarian League, both a political party and a rural lobby group; the nationalist Pan Germans, who demanded union with Austria; and the Reform Clubs, whose grassroots members dedicated themselves to the battle against liberalism. It is no accident that antisemites jointly opposed liberalism, while, by contrast, 85 percent of German Jews voted for liberal and social democratic political parties. These alliances demonstrated that antisemitism could mobilize a party representing social elites alongside organizations that promised to deliver large numbers of disgruntled lower-middle-class voters. Antisemitism proved to be a great political unifier.

German political parties helped make antisemitism acceptable and, in some quarters, even respectable. Everywhere, antisemitic discourse was out in the open. Pamphlets, posters, books, cartoons, and magazines deriding Jews, accusing them of all sorts of conspiracies, and caricaturing their physical features were to be found all over Europe. But Germany, with its highly literate population and its prominent publishing industry, produced the lion's share of such material. The German antisemitic movement was extremely well organized, spreading propaganda through clubs, societies, and fraternities, many of which were hardly fringe groups but, rather, respectable organizations at the center of German society. Many were not specifically antisemitic. They ran the gamut from colonialist organizations with close government connections to a vast array of right-wing clubs promoting such pursuits and lifestyles as occultism, vegetarianism, nudism, sun

worship, and hiking. In most of these, Jews were not welcome. With their emphasis on the perfection of Aryan bodies, often juxtaposed with Jewish ones, or their pseudo-pagan practices, often grounded in the celebration of the country's pre-Christian, Germanic roots, Jews were excluded, regarded as essentially different, if not the enemy.

Seeing Jews as racially alien, antisemites went so far as to predict that Jewish and German friction would result in an apocalyptic race war. Wilhelm Marr (1819–1904) invented the term *antisemitism*. In his seminal text *The Victory of the Jews over the Germans, Considered from a Non-Religious Point of View* (1879), Marr refrained, as his subtitle suggested, from attacking Judaism the religion, an important departure from previous manifestations of anti-Jewish sentiment. He claimed that it was "idiotic to blame Jews for the crucifixion, a performance staged, as we all know, by the Roman authorities." Marr, in fact, defended the Jews from religious persecution and blamed the medieval Church for relegating Jews to a marginal and despised economic role. He praised Jews for being "highly gifted and talented, tough, of admirable endurance and resilience." Presenting a counter-image of the Jews as weak, humiliated, and rejected by God, Marr actually claimed that Jews were much stronger than the Germans. The source of their vigor lay in their racial characteristics, which permitted them to "triumphantly resist the western world for 1,800 years. [The Jews then] rose in the nineteenth century to the position of the number one major power in the West." More powerful than Britain or France, not to mention Germany, the Jews, according to Marr, had achieved dominance over the West, and since this had been the pre-eminent power, it meant that Jews were now the most powerful force on Earth.

Marr believed Jewish racial peculiarities made it impossible for non-Jews to live on an equal footing with them. Of the inevitable race war, Marr predicted that the Jews would win:

> Of tougher and stronger fiber than we, you Jews remained the victor in this people's war which you fought by peaceful means while we burned and massacred you but did not possess the ethical strength to confine you to yourselves and to intercourse among yourselves.

For Marr, the problem was no longer the separateness of the Jews but their post-emancipatory integration into German society. This historical process, he believed, had led to Jewish material success. Once granted civic freedom, the Jews were able to deploy their superior racial qualities to great advantage. The granting of emancipation, according to Marr, represented German ethical weakness. This largesse had backfired, for all the freedoms accorded Jews only translated into misery for the Germans. Marr's antisemitism was a product of his cultural pessimism. He saw Germans as powerless to defeat the Jews and concluded his book with an anguished cry: "Finis Germaniae!" Germany is finished!

Not all antisemites shared Wilhelm Marr's pessimism. Some were hopeful that emancipation could be scaled back. In 1880–1881, the infamous Antisemite's Petition was presented to German Chancellor Otto von Bismarck. With a quarter of a million signatures, the petition demanded immigration restrictions; the dismissal of Jews from government jobs, the judiciary, and higher education; and the separate registration of Jews according to religion in all surveys. Bismarck refused to accept it.

Thanks to the organizing power of the German antisemites and the wide appeal of their message, the year 1882 saw over 300 people, Adolf Stöcker among them, attend the First International Antisemites' Congress in Dresden. Held at a prominent hotel in the center of the city, the congress issued a "manifesto to the governments and peoples of the Christian countries, which are in danger because of Jewry." Like Wilhelm Marr's *The Victory of the Jews over the Germans*, the "Manifesto to the Governments" also lamented the course of modern history and its consequences:

> The victorious ideals of the French Revolution—liberty, equality, and fraternity—have torn down the barriers against the Jewish race that had been erected for the protection of the Christian peoples. . . . The emancipation of the Jews . . . which decades ago raised the expectation in Europe that the Jewish clan would assimilate into the Christian nations, has resulted in an absolute disaster. It has merely served to convince any thinking person that it is completely impossible for the European nations to be able to establish a *modus vivendi* with the Jewry living in their midst.

Attendees at the convention demanded the establishment of a "universal Christian alliance" to combat Jewish influence. With the threat of violence, they concluded, "[T]he Jewish question can only be solved to satisfaction once and for all by following the manner in which the Arab, Tartar, and Turkish questions were solved in the past by the European states under attack."

At the Dresden conference, a picture of the alleged victim of the 1881 Tiszaeszlar

(Hungary) blood libel fraud hung behind the speaker's podium. It was a striking link between modern antisemitism and medieval anti-Judaism. At the end of the nineteenth century, the medieval charge that Jews ritually killed Christian children and used their blood to bake matzah was resurrected. Between 1891 and 1900, at least 79 such charges were laid against Jews across central and eastern Europe, plus one in America.

While finding a home in the vast political and associational life of Germany, antisemites drew on the nation's intellectual strengths. Science and philosophy combined to produce a new racial antisemitism. Prior to World War I, the idea of race as the chief organizing principle in the battle against Jews received its most elaborate treatment in the work of the economist and philosopher Karl Eugen Duehring (1833–1921). One of the principal architects of modern racial antisemitism, Duehring produced an influential polemic titled *The Jewish Question as a Racial, Moral and Cultural Question* (1881), in which he declared that race, and not religion, defines the Jews. Even those who had abandoned Judaism and converted to Christianity remained, for Duehring, "racial Jews." In fact, he claimed that it was through conversion and assimilation that Jews entered German society in order to undermine it from within. Indeed, between 1880 and 1919, 25,000 German Jews converted to either Protestantism or Catholicism, while the intermarriage rate also grew in the period after emancipation, rising from 4.4% in the period between 1876 and 1880 to 20.8% between 1916 and 1920. Thus, for Duehring, keeping Jews and Germans entirely apart was, therefore, absolutely necessary for German well-being.

No one better typified the blending of racist antisemitism and pseudo-philosophy than Houston Stewart Chamberlain (1855–1927). An English Germanophile, Chamberlain was one of Germany's most prominent and well-connected antisemites. His influential *Foundations of the Nineteenth Century* (1899) was Adolf Hitler's bedside reading, and Hitler visited Chamberlain when the latter was on his deathbed. Chamberlain was also Richard Wagner's son-in-law and a member of the antisemitic circle at Bayreuth, presided over by the composer's wife, Cosima. Together with the Wagners, Chamberlain provided the libretto for racist antisemitism, based upon a cultural critique that alleged the Jews were biologically incapable of producing beautiful culture. Instead, they mimicked, commodified, and debased European art.

Embracing Nietzsche's myth of the superman, Chamberlain championed the theory of Nordic supremacy, depicting history as a cataclysmic struggle between the Aryan and the Semite. He described the former as creative and noble, and the latter as destructive and barbaric: "Not only the Jew, but also all that is derived from the Jewish mind, corrodes and disintegrates what is best in us." The Jews were, in Chamberlain's view, a powerful threat because "this alien people has become precisely in the course of the nineteenth century a disproportionately important and in many spheres actually dominant constituent of our life." Everywhere, antisemites evoked this dark fantasy, namely, that they were losing control of their nations to the Jews they had emancipated. Chamberlain was a crucial figure in the antisemitic pantheon. The emperor Wilhelm II read Chamberlain aloud to his children, and *Foundations of the Nineteenth Century* became standard reading in military officers' schools. Antisemitism became part of the ruling ideology. For emphasizing Teutonic racial and moral superiority, urging Germany to exert itself as a world power, Chamberlain was hailed as a hero and a visionary by German militarists and conservatives. Hitler referred to him as a "Prophet of the Third Reich."

It is important to recall that despite the widespread antisemitic sentiment that swept over Germany, it was not matched by any retraction of the Jews' newly won legal rights, nor was there any diminution in their social and economic gains. At this very same time in America, for example, quotas were in place against Jews attending universities, and restrictions prevented them from living in certain neighborhoods, working in various firms, getting medical and legal internships, or even staying at certain hotels and resorts. By way of a further comparison, in eastern Europe, there was violence against Jews. None of this occurred in Germany, where, paradoxically, the blossoming of the antisemitic movement coincided with German Jewry's own flowering. Many Jews were not even fully aware of the antisemitic movement, or if they were, they dismissed it as a fringe phenomenon. Now, after the Holocaust, we need to be mindful of this question: If things were so bad for Jews in nineteenth-century Germany, how was it that they were so good? Strangely, what drove antisemitism in Germany was the fact that Jews had done exactly what was demanded of them. They became German, participating fully and eagerly in the cultural and economic life of the nation, but they had done it to such an extent and so successfully that it occasioned an envy-driven backlash.

Antisemitism in Austria

The cradle of modernism, turn-of-the-century Vienna was an exciting and frenetic city. In fields such as art, music, psychology, and modern politics, the glittering culture of the Austrian capital broke new ground. Vienna had one other distinction: It was also the most intensely antisemitic city in central Europe, with antisemitic politicians holding the reins of power in the Vienna municipal government for two decades. There was also a vast array of rabid nationalists, racists, and occultists who, while not in political office, repeatedly and persuasively argued that the Jews were responsible for the aging Habsburg Empire's problems. These ideologues produced a heady brew of hate, their literature and antisemitic cartoons readily available all over Vienna. Their discourse was an important element of the city's background chatter. Young men, including Adolf Hitler, proved especially susceptible to the anti-Jewish sentiment then swirling around the imperial capital.

In 1880, 72,500 Jews lived in Vienna, but by 1910, that number had swollen to 175,000, and Jews constituted about 8.77 percent of the city's total population. With their numerical increase came greater visibility. The Jews of the city were principally of two cultural types. The first was the acculturated German-speaking minority that included famous writers such as Arthur Schnitzler and Stefan Zweig, musicians such as Gustav Mahler and Arnold Schoenberg, and renowned physicians such as Sigmund Freud. The second group, by far the majority, was composed of the Yiddish-speaking Jews who had moved to Vienna from the Austrian hinterland, primarily Galicia. Both groups proved worrisome to the antisemites—the former because they were too much a part of Austrian culture, the latter because they remained too foreign. As in Germany, anti-Jewish hostility seemed to increase as Jewish participation in the cultural and economic life of Vienna deepened.

The Empire's social problems, rooted in class divisions, rural–urban splits, the discontent of urban workers, the impoverishment of the peasantry, and the rise of aggressive nationalism, both German and Slavic, found expression in Viennese politics. Social divisions pitted Left against Right and German Austria against the various Slavic nationalist movements seeking independence from the multiethnic Habsburg Empire. Jews, trusted by neither side, were caught in the middle of this historic struggle. Culturally, they tended to identify with the German elite, while politically, as elsewhere in Europe, they were liberals, an inclination that originated during the Revolutions of 1848, when, together with industrial workers and students, Jews supported the progressive cause.

In this environment, antisemitism emerged as virulent and all-pervasive, serving to unify a society that was coming apart at the seams. Politicians and rabble-rousers quickly capitalized on the widespread social discontent to point the finger of blame at Jews, who, as a religiously different and professionally successful minority, were seen as the cause of Austria's woes. In his newspaper, *The Fatherland*, the conservative Catholic intellectual Karl von Vogelsang (1818–1890) summed up the views of many who still resisted the liberating changes ushered in by the French Revolution. Its masthead read, "Our Battle Is Against the Spirit of 1789." Vogelsang held Jews responsible for the exploitation and impoverishment of peasants, artisans, and industrial workers, a position that became widespread in Viennese antisemitic circles.

The Prussian victory over France in 1870 inflamed nationalist passions. At the forefront of the new Pan-German movement, which called for the unification of all German speakers, was the radical antisemite Georg von Schönerer (1842–1921). Leader of the German Nationalists, von Schönerer had his politics resting on two principles. The first was his call for the breakup of the Habsburg monarchy and the push for Austrian union with Germany. The second element of his political agenda was his radical antisemitism. More than any other individual, von Schönerer changed the tone and nature of Austrian politics. Debate gave way to verbal abuse and street fighting.

Von Schönerer unleashed powerfully aggressive antisemitic sentiments. With his massive ego, he portrayed himself as a militant medieval knight come to save the German people from the Jews. He held huge rallies, gave bloodcurdling speeches about the "harmful Jewish plutocracy," and attacked Jews for their alleged control of the press. He claimed that "the removal of Jewish influence from all fields of public life is indispensable." Von Schönerer invited other racists to the podium; their recommendations included higher taxes on Jewish income, marriage and occupational restrictions, and violence. He amassed support from broad elements of the Viennese population, ranging from the lower middle classes to artisans to student fraternities. Changes to electoral rights in 1884 prompted the enfranchisement of many more artisans and small businessmen. They now came out in large numbers to support von Schönerer and other antisemites running for office, one of whom campaigned to have Jews murdered. Von Schönerer championed the latest racist ideas, his crude slogan being "Let the Jew believe in what he may, racially he is a swine."

Von Schönerer's political success came to an end in 1888 when he led a violent demonstration against the offices of a liberal daily newspaper. Jailed for four months, he was stripped of his parliamentary seat for five years. While his own career was in tatters, the Austrian antisemitic movement that von Schönerer unleashed did not die. His principal political adversary, Karl Lueger (1844–1910), immediately sensed an opportunity. Drawing on the same pool of student, artisan, and lower-middle-class support as von Schönerer, Lueger expanded his electoral base by appealing to schoolteachers, white-collar workers, state and municipal bureaucrats, and Catholics. Where von Schönerer had been a Protestant and dismissed the Church, Lueger sought to empower religious institutions, playing on fears of Catholic decline in the face of increasing secularization. He often held his own antisemitic rallies in churches. When the emperor Franz Josef appealed to Pope Leo XIII to condemn Lueger officially, the Pontiff not only refused but also gave Lueger his blessing.

Lueger was enormously successful, and his career pointed to the future of modern politics. He developed the politics of the crowd with his demagoguery and spellbinding oratory, while constantly harping on the pernicious role of Jewish plutocrats and financiers. That the bulk of Austrian Jews were extremely poor, especially those in the provinces, seemed to matter little to him or his followers. His principal theme was Jewish power: "Whenever a state has allowed the Jews to become powerful, that state has collapsed." No concrete example was given, because to his audience, the claim appeared self-evident.

In the municipal elections of 1897, Lueger's campaign motto paraphrased a line from Karl Marx's *The Communist Manifesto* when, instead of "workers of the world," it called on all antisemites to unite. Liberals were outvoted ten to one. After having twice previously refused to appoint Lueger, this time Emperor Franz Josef, beloved by Jews, could no longer resist. Karl Lueger became mayor of Vienna, the first major city in Europe to be governed by a declared antisemite. With his enormous public support, Lueger made antisemitism a respectable and winning political formula. When, for example, the Viennese city councilor Hermann Bielohlawek took to the floor of the House in 1902 and in Lueger's presence declared, "Yes, we want to annihilate the Jews. We are not ashamed to say the Jew must be driven from society," the parliamentary record noted that there was "approval and applause." This was the kind of discourse that Lueger fostered. His own oratory, charisma, political skill, and radical agenda proved especially appealing and paradigmatic. Between 1908 and 1913, Adolf Hitler resided in Vienna and saw for himself the power of antisemitic political demagoguery. Both von Schönerer and Lueger proved inspirational to him. From both he imbibed political antisemitism and the power of emotional and brutal rhetoric, the necessity of presenting oneself as a savior of the German people, as well as the value of tapping into popular frustration and social discontent.

The other significant source of Viennese antisemitism was a fringe group of occultists led by Guido von List (1848–1919) and Lanz von Liebenfels (1874–1954). List—who would become a major influence on the head of the Nazi SS, Heinrich Himmler—rejected Christianity because of its Jewish roots and urged a return to paganism, especially the religions of ancient Europeans. He was also a proponent of the mystical interpretation of the Runic alphabet, the script of the ancient Germanic tribes. While List's mysticism, paganism, and cult of Odin may seem marginal, when the establishment of a Guido von List Society was proposed in 1905, over 50 prominent Germans and Austrians signed up. By the time the society was officially founded in 1908, many more public figures had joined.

Lanz von Liebenfels, a former monk and publisher of the antisemitic *Ostara: Newsletters of the Blond Champions for the Rights of Man*, was one of the most influential of Austria's occultist antisemites. A pornographic pamphlet widely available at newsstands across Vienna, *Ostara* depicted a struggle between blond Aryans and a race of hairy ape-men. In 1904, von Liebenfels published his book *Theozoology*, in which he advocated the sterilization of the "sick" and "lower races" while extolling the virtues of the "Aryan god men." Von Liebenfels was a major influence on Hitler and represented an extreme secular antisemitism. He extolled racial purity, supported eugenics and selective breeding, and declared Jews to be subhuman, recommending that they be castrated.

Austrian antisemitism of the fin de siècle pointed the way to the future. In terms of organization, crudeness, ubiquity, and acceptability as public discourse, it had few peers. The utilization of violence, the demagoguery, and the realization of political power in its name only served to highlight the singular contribution of Austria to the counter-Enlightenment political culture of the late nineteenth century.

Antisemitism in France

While much of the social criticism inherent to German and Austrian antisemitism also appeared in France, other factors informed French antisemitism. Principally, there have been two major sources of antisemitism in modern France: a right- and a left-wing tradition. A third source, tied to French imperial politics, emerged later and somewhat less frequently. Antisemitism proved to be a regular feature of post-Revolution French politics. Right-wing antisemitism originated in royalist and conservative Roman Catholic or Protestant circles, primarily in the political philosophies of men such as Count Joseph de Maistre (1753–1821) and Viscount Louis de Bonald (1754–1840). Hostile to the French Revolution, reactionaries such as these longed for the restoration of the monarchy, the nobility, and the Church. In particular, they lamented that the Revolution had liberated the Jews, whom they deemed as parasites and whose cunning they predicted would soon conquer France. Jewish emancipation symbolized everything that seemed wrong and "unnatural" about 1789.

From the early nineteenth century, French antisemitism also issued from left-wing and secular politics. In Charles Fourier (1772–1837), Pierre-Joseph Proudhon (1809–1865), and Alphonse Toussenel (1803–1885), socialism and anarchism found their most strident and influential antisemitic voices. Concerned with identifying the cause of proletarian misery, socialists identified the Jews as the source of the plight of the French underclass, both rural and urban.

For Fourier, Jews epitomized the danger of capitalism and predatory commerce. He lamented their emancipation, an act he decried as "shameful," and claimed that Jews stood poised to dominate France. Only their small numbers prevented the country from becoming "one vast synagogue." Fourier believed the Jews were incapable of change. In contrast to the Enlightenment idea of Jewish "regeneration," Fourier declared:

They will reform, say the philosophers. Not at all: They will pervert our morals without altering theirs. Besides, when will they reform? Will it take a century for them to do so? . . . The Jews, with their commercial morality, are they not the leprosy and perdition of the body politic? . . . Let the Jews remain in France for a century and they . . . will become in France what they are in Poland and end by taking commercial industry away from the nationals who have managed it without the Jews thus far. . . . Wherever they are conspicuous, it is at the expense of the nationals.

Fourier insisted that, for the sake of France, the number of Jews residing there had to be strictly limited, and their freedom of movement within the nation's borders restricted, so that they could be forced into "productive" labor. Ultimately, Fourier wanted the Jews expelled from France, and he even entertained the fanciful idea of Rothschild resurrecting the Jewish nation under his kingship in the Land of Israel.

Proudhon, the anarchist, famous for his expression "Property Is Theft," maintained that Jewish financiers (and Protestant merchants) were bleeding France. But the sins of the Jews extended beyond their involvement in commerce. Echoing the radical secularism of philosophers such as Diderot and Voltaire, Proudhon accused the Jews of being "the first authors of that evil superstition called Catholicism in which the furious, intolerant Jewish element consistently overwhelmed the other Greek, Latin, barbarian, etc. elements and served to torture humankind for so long." But in a contradictory fashion, Proudhon echoed de Bonald and de Maistre by drawing on Christian tropes, saying that Christians were justified in calling the Jews "deicides." And like Fourier, he also wished to be rid of the Jews, a people he described as "unsociable" and "obstinate":

The Jew is the enemy of humankind. The race must either be sent back to Asia or exterminated. . . . By the sword, by amalgamation, or by expulsion the Jew must be made to disappear. . . . Those whom the peoples of the Middle Ages loathed by instinct, I loath upon reflection, irrevocably. Hatred of the Jew, as of the Englishman, needs to be an article of our faith.

With Toussenel, a student of Fourier, the link between anti-capitalism and antisemitism was made explicit. He was best known for depicting the contemporary Jewish financier as a modern version of the medieval usurer. Eliding the distinctions between medieval moneylending and modern capitalism, Toussenel decried that France was gripped by "economic feudalism," of which the Jews were the new nobility. In his seminal book *The Jews: Kings of the Epoch* (1845), Toussenel railed against government corruption and social unrest, blaming the Jews for both. Their "economic feudalism . . . entrenches itself in the soil more deeply each day, pressing with its two feet the throats of the royalty and the people." Toussenel thundered that "the Jew reigns and governs France" and recommended "the king and the people . . . unite in order to rid themselves of the aristocracy of money."

In the late nineteenth century, France's leading antisemitic agitator was Edouard Drumont (1844–1917). A journalist and onetime parliamentary deputy representing Algiers, Drumont penned the scurrilous, thousand-page, two-volume work *Jewish France* (1886). Reissued in over a hundred editions, it was one of France's most widely read books and one of the best-selling antisemitic screeds of all time. A mélange of racist, paternalist-socialist and anti-capitalist thinking, *Jewish France* depicts the historic clash between Aryans and Jews. Drumont's Aryans were, of course, from Gaul, chivalrous, idealistic, and brave, traits, he claimed, that were inherited by contemporary Frenchmen. Pitted against them were the Jews, who he characterized as cunning, avaricious, treasonous criminals with repugnant physical features.

Drumont juxtaposed the dire social and economic conditions of French workers and peasants with the success of Jewish bankers and entrepreneurs. Hyperbolically, he claimed, "The Jews possess half of the capital in the world." The same, he said, was true for France. To solve the problem and redistribute wealth more equitably, Drumont suggested taking a cue from the Revolution's expropriation of noble and ecclesiastical riches. He called for the establishment of "The Office of Confiscated Jewish Wealth," justifying the organized theft by claiming that Jewish wealth was "parasitical and usurious [because] it is not the carefully husbanded fruit of the labor of innumerable generations. Rather, it is the result of speculation and fraud." Dispensing with the Jews was central to the counterrevolution against the French republic that Drumont proposed:

> With a government scorned by all and falling apart at the seams, 500 determined men in the suburbs of Paris and a regiment surrounding the Jewish banks would suffice to carry out the most fruitful revolution of modern times. Everything would be over by the end of the day.

Placing special emphasis on the destructive influence of Jews over France after 1870, the year it was defeated by Prussia, Drumont blamed the Jews for France's decline rather than placing responsibility for the defeat on the nation's military and political elites.

With the popularity of Drumont, antisemitism became central to the republican-radical versus royalist-clerical split in France, sharpened as it was by the Dreyfus Affair, one of the nineteenth century's most dramatic manifestations of antisemitism. In 1894, a Jewish army officer, Alfred Dreyfus (1859–1935), was falsely accused of spying for Germany. The charges were based on forged documents and a massive cover-up in the military. All the while protesting his innocence, Dreyfus was found guilty of treason in a secret court-martial, during which he was denied the right to examine the evidence against him. The army stripped him of his rank in a humiliating public ceremony that included having his epaulets torn off his uniform and his sword broken. He was sentenced to life imprisonment on Devil's Island, a penal colony located off the coast of South America.

The Dreyfus Affair took on even greater significance in 1898 when the famous author Emile Zola resurrected the cause of Dreyfus's innocence in his newspaper article titled "J'accuse!" It was a stunning denunciation of the army, which he charged with responsibility for the cover-up. Among doubts as to the justice of the verdict and amid unleashed popular passions, the army conducted a new trial. Again, Dreyfus was found guilty, but this time with "extenuating circumstances." Although returned to Devil's Island in 1899, Dreyfus was granted a presidential pardon when the real identity of the traitor and details of the cover-up emerged. Despite the pardon, public furor forced a delay in his full exoneration, which did not occur until 1906.

Figure 3.1 shows an election poster for Adolphe-Léon Willette. Willette (1857–1926) was the self-declared "Antisemitic Candidate" for Paris's 9th arrondissement in the legislative elections of 1889. In the picture, a bare-chested Marianne stands above a host of French types,

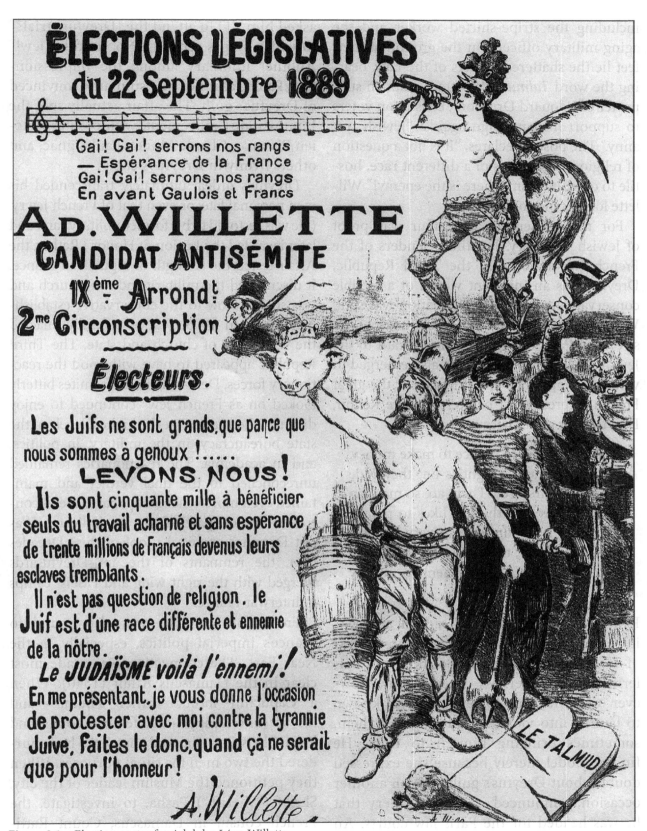

Figure 3.1 Election poster for Adolphe-Léon Willette.

Source: John M. Efron

including the stripe-shirted worker and the aging military officer. On the ground at their feet lie the shattered Tablets of the Law, bearing the word *Talmud*. Willette, a staunch supporter of Edouard Drumont, calls upon voters to support his campaign against "Jewish tyranny." The poster declares, "It is not a question of religion. The Jew is of a different race, hostile to ours. Judaism—here is the enemy!" Willette lost his bid for election.

For the antisemites, the affair was proof of Jewish treachery. For the defenders of the French Revolution and the Third Republic, Dreyfus was an innocent victim of a terrible conservative conspiracy. The nation was split. While a mob estimated at 100,000 took to the streets of Paris in 1898, crying, "Death to the Jews," intellectuals and artists also emerged to voice their opinions on Dreyfus. For the great French Impressionist painter Auguste Renoir, Dreyfus was guilty because

> [the Jews] come to France to make money, but the moment a fight is on, they hide behind the first tree. There are so many in the army because the Jew likes to parade around in fancy uniforms. Every country chases them out; there is a reason for that, and we must not allow them to occupy such a position in France.

Renoir was joined by the radical antisemite Edgar Degas, the master Impressionist of so many delicate scenes of beautiful ballerinas. His tenderness deserted him, however, when it came to Jews. He was known to launch into violent tirades against them, sometimes bringing himself to tears. He fired a model merely because she expressed doubts about Dreyfus's guilt and, on another occasion, announced in an art gallery that he was headed for the Paris law courts. An art dealer in attendance was reported to have

asked him, "[T]o attend the [Dreyfus] trial?" to which Degas replied, "No, to kill a Jew!" Another luminary among the Impressionists, Paul Cézanne, was similarly convinced of Dreyfus's guilt. The affair actually split the Impressionist movement, with painters Lucien Pissarro, Claude Monet, Paul Signac, and others firmly in Dreyfus's camp.

Dreyfus's ordeal ultimately transcended his own personal fate, or even that of French Jewry. (He was restored to his former military rank and later awarded the Legion of Honor.) Rather, the Affair tested the strength of republican France. It discredited the military and the Church and was such a blow to the conservative establishment that, in 1905, France officially enacted the separation of church and state. The Third Republic appeared to have withstood the reactionary forces. Defeated, the antisemites bitterly looked on as French Jews continued to enjoy distinguished careers at the highest levels of the state bureaucracy, in the military, in politics, and in academia. The reactionaries remained unreconciled to the final verdict and maintained even more vehemently that the Jews controlled France, particularly the judiciary. Was not Dreyfus's acquittal proof of this? Decades later, the remnants of the anti-Dreyfusards merged with the right-wing and Fascist camps in interwar France.

French antisemitism was also bound to France's imperial politics, especially in the Near East. The connection was made most clear in the Damascus Affair (1840). When a Capuchin monk—Father Thomas—and his servant disappeared, fellow monks and local Christians claimed that Jews had murdered the two men for ritual purposes. When they petitioned the Muslim leader of the city, Sharif ("Sheriff") Pasha, to investigate, the French consul in Damascus, Count Ratti-Menton, suggested to the sheriff that Jews killed the two men so as to use their blood to bake matzah. Mass arrests followed the ransacking of the Jewish quarter. About 70 men and 60 boys, most between the ages of 5 and 12, were taken into custody. Some of the city's most notable Jews had their beards set on fire and their teeth pulled out. One of the accused was murdered in custody, while another converted to Islam under duress. To bring an end to their suffering, a Jewish barber named Negri confessed. Thereafter, a riot broke out, during which a synagogue was ransacked and the Torah scrolls desecrated.

The matter soon escalated into an international incident with competing imperial ambitions coming into play. England and Austria attempted to use the case to undermine French interests in the Near East, while the Austrians were also aggrieved by the fact that one of the arrested Jews was an Austrian citizen. The United States, while quite disconnected from events in Syria, seems to have been moved to protest the torture of Jews on humanitarian grounds. The Damascus Affair demonstrates the extent to which an antisemitic episode can, in fact, actually have little to do with Jews, although their fate was central to the drama. In fact, the day before Father Thomas's disappearance, a Muslim had threatened to kill him for allegedly having blasphemed against the prophet Muhammad. Ratti-Menton had fabricated the story of Jewish guilt because (even if he had sincerely believed the story) blaming anyone in the Muslim community would have upset France's imperial relations with Muhammad Ali, the Egyptian ruler of Syria and ostensibly France's protégé. Father Thomas and his servant effectively went missing on Muhammad Ali's watch, reason enough for the latter to have colluded with Ratti-Menton. Significantly, the ritual murder charge was easily accepted by the Muslim community, even though the accusation was unknown in the Islamic world and was imported along with French imperialism.

Public meetings in support of the Jews were held in London, Paris, New York, and Philadelphia. The lawyer Isaac Crémieux and the Orientalist Solomon Munk, both French Jews, and Sir Moses Montefiore, the leading figure of British Jewry, were sent on a mission to secure the release of the falsely accused Jewish prisoners. After several meetings with Muhammad Ali, despite his initial obstinance, the delegation secured from him the unconditional release of the men and a full recognition of their innocence. Tragically, the exonerations came too late for several of the accused. The affair had begun in February and concluded in August, by which time only 9 remained alive of the 13 originally imprisoned.

Beyond the sphere of international relations, the Damascus Affair was also of great significance within the Jewish world. The episode contributed to the emergence and growth of the popular Jewish press. Written in European languages and therefore open to general scrutiny, newspapers such as the German *Allgemeine Zeitung des Judenthums* (*General Newspaper of Jewry*), founded in 1837; the French *Archives Israelite de France* (*Jewish Archives of France*), first published in 1840; and England's *Jewish Chronicle*, established in 1841 (and still in existence), were joined by a host of other Jewish publications from across Europe and the United States, all of which helped spread word of the Damascus Affair. The Jewish press transformed a local issue into a modern, international media event.

The advent of a vigorous Jewish press heralded the onset of modern Jewish public opinion and became an important means of discussing the "Jewish question." Journalism and newspaper publishing also became a common career path for modern Jews. Invariably, in the West, wherever Jews owned newspapers, whether for principally Jewish or non-Jewish consumption, such as the *Berliner Tagblatt* (*Berlin Daily*) or *The New York Times*, they promoted liberal politics. In the early twentieth century, mass-circulation newspapers—such as the Yiddish dailies from Warsaw *Der Moment* (*The Moment*) and *Der Haynt* (*Today*), New York's *Forverts* (*The Forward*), and the biweekly Ladino newspaper from Istanbul *Il Tiempo* (*The Times*)—exposed Jewish readers to world news and politics. They also made Jews feel as though they were part of a global Jewish community.

The Damascus Affair had other important consequences. Montefiore and Crémieux, as well as the Rothschilds, represented a handful of Jews with access to seats of power and political influence. While the affair testified to Jewish vulnerability, the presence of strong and well-placed Jewish advocates also reflected this new source of Jewish collective vigor. The affair also seems to have altered Jewish sensibilities. Perhaps because the injustice was perpetrated in France, the liberal nation that most loudly proclaimed the values of liberty, equality, and fraternity, the sense of betrayal Jews felt was especially keen. The events in Damascus spurred Jews into collective action. They were unwilling to suffer silently; they would now protest injustices with all the means at their disposal. The international dimensions of the affair thus inculcated a new sense of Jewish mutual responsibility. Philanthropy emerged as a major goal of western Jews, prepared more than ever to assist their needy coreligionists in the Middle East and, eventually, in eastern Europe.

Finally, it should be noted that in France, just as in Germany and Austria, the antisemitic movement did not succeed in disenfranchising Jews, and their integration and embourgeoisement across western Europe continued apace. Nevertheless, there were lasting consequences of the campaign of French antisemites in that they provided forces on both the Right and on the Left of the political spectrum with a new language of social and cultural criticism.

Antisemitism in Italy

In contrast to Germany, Austria, and France, antisemitism was not a constitutive factor of political life in modern Italy. In 1938, when Mussolini imposed race laws, the unprecedented move aroused opposition not only among many ordinary Italians but also among many loyal Fascists. While political antisemitism barely existed in Italy, there was religious antipathy, and it originated within the Vatican. On one occasion, it exploded and had a major impact on political affairs and the formation of the modern Italian state. The Mortara affair (1858) evinces the effects of antisemitism even in the near absence of Jews, as was the case in the great struggle between Catholic and secular, nationalist forces in Italy.

On the evening of June 23, 1858, in the city of Bologna, papal police broke into the home of the Mortara family and snatched six-year-old Edgardo from his distraught and bewildered mother. According to Inquisition authorities in Rome, the family's Catholic housekeeper had Edgardo secretly baptized when he had fallen very ill at the age of one. The police had the law on their side, for the abduction of Edgardo, the most infamous example of several such cases in nineteenth-century Italy, was sanctioned by canon law, according to which a child, once baptized, even involuntarily, had to be removed from his or her Jewish home. Edgardo was taken away in haste, and his Catholicization began immediately. Frantic efforts to have the child released came to naught; his parents were repeatedly told, however, that they could be reunited with their son provided they themselves converted. Despite the storm of international protest, both popular and diplomatic, Pope Pius IX refused to relent and, in fact, raised Edgardo as his own "adopted" son. Edgardo Mortara eventually joined the priesthood in 1873. A celebrated preacher, he failed, despite consistent efforts, to induce his parents to convert. He died in a Belgian abbey on March 11, 1940, two months before the Nazis invaded.

Beyond the immediate family tragedy, the event had profound historical repercussions. Count Camillo Cavour, the architect of Italian unification, and Napoleon III of France, both of whom sought to undermine the temporal authority of the papacy, used the affair to agitate against Vatican rule. In Britain, a leading Jewish figure, Moses Montefiore, took up the cause, while in Austria, Emperor Franz Josef appealed to the Pope in vain. Protestants across Europe and the United States, where *The New York Times* ran more than 20 editorials demanding Edgardo's release, mobilized against the obscurantism of the Catholic Church. The plight of Edgardo also catalyzed liberal Catholic protest against the conservative papacy of Pius IX.

The Mortara affair emerged against the backdrop of the Vatican's waning authority in the modern, secular world. While it smacked of medievalism, the kidnapping of Edgardo Mortara and the international responses, characterized by the mobilization of outraged political, public, and editorial opinion, mark it as a distinctly modern episode. While Edgardo was lost to his family and the Jewish community, in the long term, the aftermath of the abduction diminished the power of the papacy, for it galvanized the forces promoting liberalism, nationalism, Italian unification, and anticlericalism. In 1870, Italian troops entered Rome, and the temporal power of the popes, which had lasted for a thousand years, came to an end.

Antisemitism in Russia

Although prior to the 1880s many of the harsh decrees of the tsars that pertained to Jews appear to have been driven by antisemitism, very often it was more the desire for reform rather than retribution that drove such policies. However, after 1881, the state purposefully sought to exclude Jews, and their situation among Russia's minorities became anomalous. From that time until the fall of the Romanovs, a series of laws and ordinances, outbreaks of violence, and new kinds of accusations constitute a transformed response to Jews, one where Russia joined the ever-rising chorus of antisemitic sentiment heard across Europe, but with more dramatic, devastating, and long-lasting consequences.

Whether popular or official, nineteenth-century Russian antisemitism was a curious blend of the premodern theological variety with some distinctly modern innovations. Along with official government policy that targeted Jews, popular sentiment also hardened. Among the Russian masses, the ever-present religious hatred of Jews was joined by a new development—violence. This marked Russian antisemitism as unusual in the context of late nineteenth-century antisemitism. Not since the outbreak of the German Hep Hep riots in 1819 had Jewish communities been physically attacked on a level comparable to the violence that erupted in 1881, when a series of riots swept through southern Russia. (Two smaller outbreaks of violence against Jews had already occurred in Odessa in 1859 and 1871.) These riots were known by the Russian word *pogrom*, a term that connotes wanton violence, havoc, physical attacks against members of a particular group, and the destruction of property.

The pogroms were one product of the turbulent political situation in late nineteenth-century Russia. Following the accession to the throne of Alexander II (son of Nicholas I) in 1855, the new tsar charted a somewhat liberalizing course, all the while asserting his autocratic rule. Among his achievements were the emancipation of the serfs (1861) and the institution of far-reaching reforms of military and governmental administration. But the changes he wrought made him too radical for the reactionary forces and too moderate for liberals and the burgeoning revolutionary movement. Unsatisfied with the reforms, radical activities increased among the intelligentsia, which, in turn, prompted Alexander to respond with heightened repression. When a populist movement (*Narodnichestvo*, "Going to the People," or Narodism) arose in the late 1860s, the government arrested and prosecuted hundreds of students.

Many of the radicals turned to terrorism, and on March 1, 1881, a member of the terrorist group People's Will (*Narodnaya Volya*) assassinated Alexander with a hand-thrown bomb. Among the plotters was Hessia Helfman, a Jewish woman who, for many Russians on the Right, came to symbolize what they saw as a Jewish plot against Russia. With religious tensions already high because of the convergence of Easter and Passover that year, the assassination furthered the division between those who wept for the fallen tsar and those who did not. The assassination saw the outbreak in mid-April of attacks against Jews in southern Russia, which spread like wildfire and raged until 1883, with approximately 200 pogroms leaving some 40 Jews killed, and

thousands wounded, homeless, and destitute. Rape was also widespread. The pogroms began in the town of Elizavetgrad, where a government report noted:

> The city presented an extraordinary sight: streets covered with feathers and obstructed with broken furniture which had been thrown out of residences; houses with broken doors and windows; a raging mob, running about yelling and whistling in all directions and continuing its work of destruction without let or hindrance, and as a finishing touch to this picture, complete indifference displayed by the local non-Jewish inhabitants to the havoc wrought before their eyes.

The Jewish memoirist Mary Antin reported how the violence began:

> Somebody would start up that lie about murdering Christian children, and the stupid peasants would get mad about it, and fill themselves with vodka, and set out to kill the Jews. They attacked them with knives and clubs and scythes and axes, killed them or tortured them, and burned their houses. This was called a "pogrom." Jews who escaped the pogroms came to Polotzk [her hometown] with wounds on them, and horrible, horrible stories, of little babies torn limb from limb before their mothers' eyes. Only to hear these things made one sob and sob and choke with pain. People who saw such things never smiled any more, no matter how long they lived; and sometimes their hair turned white in a day, and some people became insane on the spot.

Written after she had immigrated to the United States, Antin's account is most likely exaggerated. The vivid description "of little babies torn limb from limb before their mothers' eyes" echoes motifs drawn from much earlier accounts of anti-Jewish violence in eastern Europe. It is also improbable that "people who saw such things never smiled any more." However, her general description of the pogrom as a brutal attack by drunken rioters using deadly weapons against Jews is correct. Antin's compelling account, even if not precise in all its historical details, is most valuable, however, because it is a genuine reflection of the terror and trauma the pogroms evoked among Jews, perhaps especially among those who were not there. The pogroms did more than any other event to shape Jewish views of Russia thereafter.

Although the government did not orchestrate the pogroms, local authorities rarely intervened, and only light sentences were meted out for those perpetrators who were arrested. The new tsar, Alexander III, immediately set out to destroy the revolutionary movement. Jews, who right-wing agitators identified as conspirators against Mother Russia, were subject to harsh legislation. The May Laws (1882), promulgated in the wake of Tsar Alexander II's assassination, demanded that Jews leave villages and rural settlements and move into urban areas. In their new locations, Jews had few prospects for employment, and the general economic and social conditions were bleak. Jews could not buy or rent property other than their own residences, were ineligible for civil service jobs, and were forbidden to trade on Sundays and Christian holidays. Specific laws targeted the Jewish intelligentsia. Beginning in 1882, the first Jewish quota was introduced at the Military Medical Academy, limiting Jews to just 5 percent of all students. This was followed by the imposition of quotas at a variety of institutions, until in 1887, the Russian Ministry of Education established a formal, Russia-wide *numerus clausus*, or

quota: 10 percent within the Pale of Settlement, 5 percent outside it, and 3 percent in both Moscow and St. Petersburg. This led to an exodus of Russian Jewish students to Germany. By 1912, over 2,500 Russian Jews were studying at German universities and technical schools. Of the Russian Jews at Prussian universities, 85 percent studied medicine, while the figure was 90 percent at non-Prussian institutions. In 1889, the Russian Ministry of Justice ordered that all "non-Christians," meaning Jews, would only be admitted to the bar upon permission granted by the minister. For the next 15 years, no Jew was registered as a barrister in the Russian court system. Over subsequent years, ever more restrictions were added, further degrading the conditions of life for Russia's 5 million Jews. Tsar Alexander III's tutor and overprocurator of the Holy Synod, an architect of conservative reaction, Konstantin Pobedonostsev, was said to have remarked that the only way for the "Jewish question" to be solved in Russia was for one-third to emigrate, one-third to convert to Christianity, and one-third to perish.

The impact of anti-Jewish state policies was intensified by enormous demographic growth and rising population density among Jews. Hunger, poverty, and a future that seemed hopeless led many to immigrate abroad and even more to move to Russia's bigger cities. For the masses of poor Jews, the policies of the last two tsars had a profoundly negative impact on the Jewish economy. While historians debate whether some Jews actually benefited from or were victims of Russian industrialization, what cannot be denied is that pauperization among most Jews was spreading. In 1898, approximately 20 percent of Jews in the Pale of Settlement applied for Passover charity, while in Odessa, 66 percent of Jews were buried at the community's expense. By 1900, up to 35 percent of Russian

Jewry was receiving poor relief of one sort or another. Poverty and despair also led many Jews to agitate for revolution, thinking that perhaps socialism or Zionism, or a combination of the two, could offer a panacea for the plight of Russian Jewry.

Of course, it was not just Jews who led lives of material deprivation in Russia. When the last tsar, Nicholas II, assumed the throne in 1894, peasants, workers, and students rioted and continued to agitate for change. In 1902, Nicholas appointed a new Minister of the Interior, Vyacheslav Plehve, to deal with the situation. In a speech given in Odessa in 1903, Plehve, referring to Jews, stated pointedly and threateningly:

> In Western Russia some 90 per cent of the revolutionaries are Jews, and in Russia generally—some 40 per cent. I shall not conceal from you that the revolutionary movement in Russia worries us but you should know that if you do not deter your youth from the revolutionary movement, we shall make your position untenable to such an extent that you will have to leave Russia, to the very last man!

Incitement continued against Jews, marked by a campaign that depicted them as menaces to Christianity and the settled social order. It culminated in a pogrom that erupted in the town of Kishinev (in present-day Moldova) on April 6, 1903. The Kishinev pogrom lasted for three terrifying days. Both Russians and Romanians joined in the riots in a scenario where old prejudices blended with new methods. Just a week prior to the pogrom, a letter was circulated around the teahouses of the city, claiming that Jews performed ritual murder and that, with Easter fast approaching, the Jews would again sacrifice a Christian child. The rumors were spread by a local

journalist, Pavel Krushevan, who sought to whip up both his readers and his newspaper sales.

Beginning with the claims of human sacrifice, the circular continued with more modern charges, observing that killing young Christians

> is the way of their jeering at us, Russians. And how much harm do they bring to our Mother Russia! They want to take possession of her. . . . [T]hey publish various proclamations to the people in order to excite it against the authority, even against our Father the Tsar, who knows the mean, cunning, deceitful and greedy nature of this nation, and does not let them enjoy liberties. . . . But if you give liberty to the *Zjid* [a pejorative term for Jew], he will reign over our holy Russia, take everything in his paws and there will be no more Russia, but *Zjidowia* [Jewland].

Russians were dispatched to Kishinev from surrounding towns, with students from theological seminaries, high schools, and colleges leading the charge. While some soldiers and police warned Jews of impending pogroms, most issued no warning and offered no assistance. This was true of the garrison of 5,000 soldiers stationed in the city. Although they could have easily turned back the mob, they remained in their barracks.

As was the case in 1881, the government did not orchestrate the pogroms, contrary to popular Jewish opinion, but its antisemitic policies and refusal to intervene created the climate wherein pogroms could and did flourish. According to official statistics, in Kishinev, 49 Jews were killed, 587 were injured, scores of women and girls were raped, 1,350 houses and 600 businesses and shops were looted and destroyed, and about 2,000 families were left homeless. It was estimated that material losses amounted to 2,500,000 gold rubles—a huge sum in those days, and especially for a community that was poverty-stricken even before the pogrom.

International protest was immediate, akin to the reaction to the Damascus blood libel and the Mortara affair. Kishinev's Jews were especially adept at spreading word about the pogrom through the world's press. So too did Jews throughout the world quickly mobilize philanthropic support for the victims. A variety of prominent people in Russia, inspired by a host of differing political agendas, protested on behalf of the Jewish victims, even if they offered competing accounts of what had taken place. The famed novelist Leo Tolstoy spoke out, as did the Jewish historian Shimon Dubnov, the Zionist Ahad Ha-Am, and the Hebrew poet Hayim Nahman Bialik, while other Jews founded the Historical Council in Odessa, the purpose of which was to investigate the Kishinev pogrom. Bialik was called upon to collect oral testimonies and other documentary material for a report on the events. Though the report was never published, Bialik's work provided the source material for his epic Hebrew poem *Be-Ir ha-Haregah* ("In the City of Slaughter"). The poem, which became a catchcry for the Zionist revolt against the conditions of exile, opened with an anguished summons to the reader:

Arise and go now to the city of slaughter;
Into its courtyard wind thy way;
There with thine own hand touch, and with the eyes of thine head,
Behold on tree, on stone, on fence, on mural clay,
The spattered blood and dried brains of the dead.

Soon, however, Bialik's pain turned to rage when, instead of saving his invective for those who perpetrated the atrocities, he blamed the victims, in particular, the men, for their apparent passivity in the face of the attackers. Challenging Jewish manhood, Bialik "outed" the once-proud Jews, calling them cowards:

Come, now, and I will bring thee to their lairs
The privies, jakes and pigpens where the heirs
Of Hasmoneans lay, with trembling knees,
Concealed and cowering—the sons of the Maccabees!
The seed of saints, the scions of the lions!
Who, crammed by scores in all the sanctuaries of their shame
So sanctified My name!
It was the flight of mice they fled,
The scurrying of roaches was their flight;
They died like dogs, and they were dead!

The impact of the poem on the nascent Zionist movement was enormous. With translations into Yiddish by Bialik and into Russian by Vladimir Jabotinsky, the poem obtained a wide audience and established Bialik as the Jewish national poet.

Figure 3.2 depicts the burying of Torah scrolls after the Kishinev pogrom (1903). At the turn of the twentieth century, Jews made up approximately one-third of Kishinev's population of 145,000. An important element in the city's industrial sector, Jews were largely employed in crafts, many as skilled artisans. Agricultural work, especially of the seasonal variety, provided a living for many Jews, as did peddling. Poverty was widespread and increasing and can be measured by the number of families that applied for Passover relief: 1,200 in 1895; 1,142 in 1896; 1,450 in 1897; 1,494 in 1898; 1,505 in 1899;

Figure 3.2   Burying Torah scrolls after the Kishinev pogrom (1903).

Source: From the archives of the YIVO Institute for Jewish Research, New York.

and 2,204 in 1900. Aside from the general poverty of the area, economic restrictions on Jews further exacerbated an already-precarious economic situation. An important social welfare network of charity provided assistance to the city's Jews, and in 1898, all such charitable institutions were united under the name of "The Society in Aid of the Poor Jews of Kishinev."

After a period of mounting economic, religious, and political tensions, on April 6, 1903, a pogrom broke out. In addition to the loss of life and the destruction of residential and commercial properties, there was also widespread desecration of synagogues. Here, men are posing for the camera with desecrated Torah scrolls, which have been placed on stretchers prior to burial. The custom of burying unusable sacred texts follows from a discussion in the Babylonian Talmud, Tractate Shabbat 115, a–b.

For antisemites long convinced that the Jews enjoyed undue influence and control

and sought the downfall of Christianity and especially Russia, the activist, global response to the Kishinev pogrom only reinforced their view that the Jews worked in league with each other in a most coordinated and malicious way, stopping at nothing to achieve their goal of taking over the world. Even the world's response to the pogrom was "proof" of Jewish cunning, for the Jews had planned it that the world would react sympathetically. Who else but Jews could and would orchestrate such a thing?

The Kishinev pogrom of 1903 left more than just suffering in its wake. That event gave birth to an even more devastating legacy, one that retains its terrible power to this very day—*The Protocols of the Elders of Zion.* In terms of a foundational document, it is Russia's most influential and catastrophic contribution to modern antisemitism. It was first published four months after the pogrom in late August 1903 in nine newspaper installments by the aforementioned Pavel

Krushevan; he most likely also wrote or co-wrote it. *The Protocols* are a notorious forgery that purport to be the minutes of a meeting of Jewish elders plotting world domination. The alleged "discovery" of *The Protocols* was the "unimpeachable" documentary evidence that proved the "truth" of everything antisemites in Russia and beyond had long been saying. No longer were the accusations limited to this or that particular country; instead, *The Protocols* portrayed Jews as conspiring on a global scale to foment the most hated forces of modernity: liberalism, parliamentary democracy, capitalism, Marxism, and anarchism. In the wake of the 1903 pogroms, Krushevan's original serialized newspaper articles titled "The Program of World Conquest by Jews" were read by few. However, after the pogroms of 1905, those articles were issued in book form as *The Protocols* and received a wider audience, one that grew by leaps and bounds in the 1920s. Both the Russian Revolution of 1917 and Germany's defeat in the First World War turned *The Protocols* from being just another antisemitic text into the "bible" for antisemites the world over. Reactionaries circulated *The Protocols* during the Russian Civil War to charge that the overthrow of the tsar was in fact a "Jewish revolution." In postwar Germany, *The Protocols* was used by the Nazis to "prove" that the Jews were promoters of a Judeo-Bolshevik conspiracy to conquer the nation. After World War I, the book enjoyed wide success in western Europe and was published in the United States by the automobile magnate Henry Ford under the title *The International Jew*. Today it is used to claim that Israel is the seat of the Elders of Zion. The central theme of *The Protocols*, that there exists a gigantic Jewish conspiracy against the world continues to resonate with large numbers of people from different cultures. It especially resonates in the Muslim world, where it is a bestseller and was even adapted into a 41-part Egyptian television series. And after having sunk into obscurity for decades, Krushevan is currently heralded as a hero among Russian nationalists and pro-Russian, anti-Western forces in eastern Europe.

Throughout 1905–1906, Kishinev and some 300 other towns were again struck by pogroms as the country erupted in revolution. Mainly organized by the monarchist Union of Russian Peoples, and with the cooperation of local government officials, the pogroms left over a thousand Jews dead and many thousands more wounded. Reactionary forces blamed Jews for the revolution, for the constitution that the tsar reluctantly granted in October of 1905, and for the general political turbulence then rocking Russia. They openly called for the extermination of the Jews.

While the violence of the pogroms did not have its analogue in the west, the reasons for them were entirely familiar and identical to the sorts of complaints heard elsewhere in Europe—Jewish economic competition and a totally unfounded but widespread sense that Russia was being taken over by Jews. Here, the government did play a role in that it promoted this line of thinking to marshal the people against revolutionary radicalism, in which many Jews were active. The tsar failed to so much as condemn the pogromists, let alone compensate Jews for their losses. All requests for the merest display of compassion were rebuffed. It is little wonder that Jews joined others in feeling abandoned by Mother Russia.

The ritual murder charge brought against Mendel Beilis (1874–1934) in 1911 in Kiev confirmed the continued presence in Russia of older, more familiar forms of antisemitism. In February 1911, liberals in the Third Duma (parliament) introduced a proposal to abolish the Pale of Settlement. A tidal wave of right-wing and monarchist organizations vehemently objected. Armed with government subsidies, they embarked on an anti-Jewish campaign. When in March 1911 the body of a young Christian boy was found in Kiev, the tsarist authorities charged Mendel Beilis, the Jewish manager of a Kievan brick kiln, with ritual murder. This occurred despite the fact that the authorities already knew the identity of the criminal gang that had killed the boy.

For more than two years, Beilis remained in prison on trumped-up charges, while the government built its case, largely through producing forged documents as well as buying off and threatening witnesses. Entirely novel in this whole episode was the decision of the prosecutor to go beyond Beilis and also put Judaism and world Jewry on trial, calling "expert" witnesses to affirm the reality of the blood libel. Beilis's plight became symbolic of the larger struggle between the regime and opposition forces. The liberal and revolutionary press exposed the machinations of the minister of justice, including the fact that throughout the trial, he had reported to the tsar, who had kept a close watch on the proceedings. The Beilis case not only drew international attention to the plight of the Jews in Russia but also united the conservative Octobrists and the radical Bolsheviks in their opposition to the government. Eventually, to the surprise of the regime and the world, Beilis was acquitted by a jury of illiterate peasants. The fate of Judaism was less clear than that of Beilis. The jury failed to deliver a clear-cut verdict on the blood libel, unable to decide whether Jews were obliged to practice it.

THE PATHS JEWS TOOK

The impact of massive Jewish population growth and urbanization; the desperate economic circumstances in eastern Europe; the rise of organized, violent antisemitism; and the emergence of nationalist ideologies and mass political movements influenced Jews in the way they assessed their current situations and imagined their futures. Under the sway of such forces, the Jewish people began to set out in new social and political directions. The decisions taken by millions of Jews concerning where they would live, what politics they favored, what languages they would speak, and what, if any, Jewish ritual they would practice began to take shape in the last third of the nineteenth century.

At that time, the bulk of the Jewish people, especially those in eastern Europe, lived, for the most part, in small towns or cities in crippling poverty under a regime that combined hostility with callous indifference to their plight. In the west, material conditions among Jews were sound, indeed getting increasingly better, but the tone and stridency of the antisemitic movement were alarming and confusing precisely because they seemed to grow in tandem with Jewish acculturation. The different social, economic, and cultural conditions in various European countries also determined the variety of Jewish responses to the "Jewish question." There was no unitary Jewish response. However, if one general statement can be made, it is that nowhere did Jews sit passively in the face of economic misery and antisemitism. The last two decades of the nineteenth century saw the flowering of nationalist sentiment among the various ethnic and language groups of east-central

Europe. Jewish nationalism also began to grow in the last two decades of the nineteenth century, as a reaction to both antisemitism as well as internal developments whose origins can be traced to the changing nature of Jewish consciousness that originated with the Haskalah. Many of the developments that historians once saw as being a direct response to the events of 1881 actually began long prior to that date—community rupture, the turn to political radicalism, and the less dramatic but powerful process of acculturation that began as early as the 1780s.

In the period between 1881 and 1921, from the outbreak of the pogroms until the aftermath of World War I, Jews organized, resisted, accommodated, and adapted themselves to the circumstances in a host of ways. Essentially, we can identify three major Jewish responses to these events: (1) the rise of modern Jewish politics, basically socialism or nationalism; (2) an activist response among western European Jews characterized by the development of Jewish advocacy and philanthropic organizations; and (3) mass migration out of Europe.

The Rise of Modern Jewish Politics

Toward the end of the nineteenth century, young Jews, energized by frustration and inspired by hope, turned to mass politics. Some sought salvation in socialism, others in nationalism, and still others in a combination of the two. Despite or because of their disenfranchisement and the fact that the Jewish population in the Pale of Settlement increased at a staggering rate of 22 percent from 1881 to 1897, or approximately 100,000 per year, Jews in Russia were far more involved and invested in political activity than their emancipated coreligionists in western Europe, although important figures in the West, such as Theodor Herzl, came to have an enormous impact on Jewish political culture.

The burgeoning revolutionary ferment sweeping across Russia in the last decades of the nineteenth century attracted Jewish students to socialism. Many young Jews believed that the "Jewish question" could only be solved in the context of the larger social question, and that meant getting rid of the old order. Both cruel autocracy and oppressive capitalism would have to be eliminated for both the Jewish and non-Jewish underclasses to be free. Later, preferring not to throw themselves into the general revolutionary movement then raging in the Russian Empire, other Jews articulated a specific Jewish socialism, believing it to be the key to a secure Jewish future.

Others saw no future for the Jews in Europe at all. Jewish nationalists regarded antisemitism as an incurable cancer, poverty an inescapable fact of life, and assimilation a scourge that would lead to the disappearance of the Jews. They held out that the return of the Jews to their ancestral homeland in Palestine was the only solution to the Jewish dilemma. Still others embraced the establishment of Jewish communal autonomy in the Diaspora. Jews not only adopted socialism, Zionism, and territorialism, but also the boundaries between them were often fluid. What emerged was a syncretistic mixing of ideological positions and political experimentation that proved rich and was reflective of the energy but also the fragmentation and divided nature of modern Jewish culture and society.

Jewish Socialism

Jews first became involved in left-wing politics in central Europe. Almost all German Jewish socialists came from comfortable middle-class homes and were rarely concerned with specifically Jewish needs. Ferdinand Lassalle (1825–1864), who, as a 15-year-old, expressed deep dismay at what he characterized as the submissiveness of Jews in the face of the Damascus Affair, never entered the field of Jewish politics but instead became an organizer of German workers and founder in 1863 of the General German Workers' Association. Similarly, the socialist thinker Eduard Bernstein (1850–1932) was principally concerned with the lot of impoverished German workers. Whenever such men did consider the "Jewish question," the response of Bernstein was rather typical: "I believed that the solution would be found in the Socialist International." Writing after the calamity of World War I, Bernstein concluded, "To this belief I still adhere, and it is more important to me than any separatist movement."

What was true in Germany was also true in eastern Europe, where socialists such as Rosa Luxemburg (1871–1919), founder of the Social Democratic Party of Poland and Lithuania, claimed in 1916 to have "no room in [her] heart for Jewish suffering." She felt "equally close to the wretched victims of the rubber plantations in Putamayo, or to the Negroes in Africa with whose bodies the Europeans are playing catch-ball." Leading Bolshevik and commander of the Red Army, Leon Trotsky (1879– 1940), whose real name was Lev Davidovitch Bronshteyn, was similarly committed to international socialist revolution. He believed it would solve all of humanity's problems, including the plight of the Jews. "The Jews do not interest [me] more than the Bulgarians," he declared in 1903 to a Jewish delegation that had come to him for assistance. And while this was an honest appraisal, his report on the 1905 pogroms, titled "The Tsarist Hosts at Work," bears similarities to Bialik's poem "In the City of Slaughter." Trotsky wrote evocatively of "the crying of the slaughtered infants, the frenzied stabbed mothers, the hoarse groaning of dying old men and wild wailings of despair." If Trotsky only allowed himself occasional expressions of parochial sympathy, the same cannot be said for the bulk of Russian Jewish socialists, who were passionately driven by their concern for the needs of Jewish workers in the Pale and elsewhere.

The Bund

Although anarchist and socialist ideas had long proliferated in Jewish immigrant centers in London and New York and strike activity and revolutionary agitation had begun among Jewish workers in the Pale of Settlement in the 1890s, the key moment in the history of Jewish socialism occurred in 1897 in Vilna with the founding of the Bund, short for Algemayne Bund fun Yidishe Arbeter in Rusland, Poyln un Lite (General Association of Jewish Workers in Russia, Poland, and Lithuania). Many of the Bund's early leaders were revolutionaries estranged from their Jewish roots. However, observing the deteriorating Jewish economy, which saw Jews shut out of higher-paying jobs in the industrial sector, confined to sweatshop labor in terrible conditions that included an average workday of between 16 and 18 hours, and ongoing discrimination, many began to agitate among their people.

Under the leadership of Aleksandr (Arkadii) Kremer (1865–1935), the Bund did not officially regard itself as a separate political party but rather as part of the Russian

Social Democratic Party. However, there was always ambiguity on this point. Why organize at all if there was not tacit recognition of a specific need to lead Jewish workers? As Kremer declared, "Jewish workers suffer not only as workers but also as Jews, and we must not and cannot remain indifferent at such a time." Despite claims to the contrary, the Bund, by virtue of its very existence, was from its inception a nationalist organization speaking the language of international revolution. Even if the leadership did not see it this way, the Jewish rank and file did. And not only them. The future leader of the Bolshevik Revolution, Vladimir Lenin, correctly characterized the Bund as a national Jewish party with a specifically Jewish character. By 1903, the plight of the Jews in Russia had become clearer to the Bund leadership, and demanding autonomy, they wanted the Social Democrats to regard them as "the sole representative of the Jewish proletariat." Leading Jewish Social Democrats such as Trotsky opposed this, and the Bund seceded from the party.

The Bund's influence grew quickly among Jewish workers, particularly in the northwest. For most Jews in the Russian Empire, a predilection for left-wing politics was more than just a matter of individual choice. For many rank-and-file Jewish socialists in eastern Europe, politics was deeply bound up with their own sense that the Jews were a distinct nation and that the "Jewish question" could not be solved within a larger framework of world revolution. With a mission beyond the purely political, the Bund sought to address a variety of cultural issues that related specifically to the needs of the Jewish worker. Among the Bundists' earliest activities was the organization of Jewish self-defense units during the period of pogroms between 1903 and 1907. By creating a sort of de facto national army, the Bund was the first Jewish political organization to encourage and support the idea that Jews should take up arms to protect Jewish life and property. While it was a secularist movement, the Bund's membership was more conservative than the leadership in its approach to religion. Only the most radical of Jews would have been in accord with the feelings expressed by the socialist Yiddish poet David Edelstadt:

Each era has its new Torah—
Ours is one of freedom and justice. . . .
We also have new prophets—
Börne, Lassalle, Karl Marx;
They will deliver us from exile,
But not with fasts and prayers!

By 1905, the Bund had 35,000 members and was the largest Jewish political party in eastern Europe. In command of a powerful constituency, the Bundist leadership attempted to return to the ranks of the Russian Social Democratic Party. Within a few years, the partnership began to flounder. Bitter internal debates and constant attacks from Russian Social Democrats drove the Bund to openly break with the party and promote the idea of national cultural autonomy as part of its continued commitment to socialist revolution. Bundists expected that after the revolution, the dictatorship of the proletariat would transfer responsibility for culture, education, and law to democratic institutions elected by the various national minorities. Jewish institutions, the Bund maintained, would conduct their work in the national language of the Jewish masses—Yiddish.

By the end of 1917, the Bund began to split between those who wished to remain within the framework of the Russian Social Democratic Party and those who were keen to join the Bolsheviks. (Jewish members of the latter group obtained important positions within the newly established Soviet government but, in the 1930s, were, for the most part, liquidated in Stalin's purges.) With the consolidation of the Russian Revolution, political parties other than the Bolsheviks were eventually banned, and the Bund was eliminated. The exiled Russian Bundists joined their comrades in newly independent Poland, where, first under the leadership of Vladimir Medem (1879–1923), the Bund became the largest and best supported of all Jewish political parties. While it was fiercely anti-Zionist, it could hardly ignore the increasing popularity of the movement, and in response, Medem refined what would become a central element of Bundist ideology—*doikayt*, the Yiddish word for "here-ness." Medem held that the Jewish people could not turn their backs on the places where their history and culture had unfolded. Not only was it important to preserve that past, but he also asserted that building upon it "here," by which he meant the Diaspora, was the key to a successful Jewish future. Central to the Jewish cultural patrimony was Yiddish, and the Bund represented itself as the guardians of secular Yiddish culture. The organization portrayed its principal opponents, the Zionists, as unrealistic and irresponsible in wishing to wrench Jews from their homes, move them to Palestine in a risky endeavor, and turn Jews away from Yiddish language and culture and toward Hebrew, which it claimed was the language of backward religiosity.

In terms of electoral politics, the Bund had some notable successes in the interwar period. In the first city council elections held in Poland in 1919, 160 Bundists won seats on various municipal councils. In Warsaw and Łódź, cities with large Jewish working-class populations, the party received 20 percent of the Jewish vote. Yet despite such successes at the local level, in terms of national politics, the Bund was quite unsuccessful. The main reason for this was the party's staunch refusal to form strategic alliances with other Jewish parties. This ideologically rigid stubbornness prevented the Bund from fulfilling much of its promise.

By contrast, the Bund's great achievement was to offer working-class Jews a Jewish alternative to radical politics. Bundism tapped into the vast reservoir of *Yiddishkayt* (Yiddish cultural identity) that informed the sensibilities of eastern European Jewry by celebrating all things Yiddish, the language spoken by the majority of Jews well into the twentieth century. In so doing, the Bund fostered Jewish nationalism (while claiming not to). It is little wonder that the non-Jewish Russian Marxist theoretician Georgi Plekhanov quipped that the Bundists were "Zionists with sea sickness."

Jewish Nationalism

Because of the political and cultural success of Zionism, with the establishment of the State of Israel and the regeneration of Hebrew as a daily spoken language, there has been a tendency to equate Jewish nationalism with Zionism. But doing so has meant that alternative forms of Jewish nationalism have been forgotten and, indeed, written out of the narrative of modern Jewish history. When considered at all, these other expressions of Jewish nationalism have been dismissed as utopian. However, for large numbers of eastern European Jews in the period before World War I, other forms of Jewish nationalism proved attractive, meaningful, and as far-fetched as they may seem today, realistic. Zionism, precisely because it seemed the most utopian and radical of all political programs, took considerable time to become a popular political option among Jews, and even then it was mostly confined to those in eastern Europe, and only in the interwar period did its appeal begin to blossom among the Jewish masses. The widespread acceptance of Zionism by world Jewry today is a post-Holocaust phenomenon. Until that time, there were other options.

Yiddishism

All varieties of Jewish nationalism had to confront the question of "Here or there?" Where would the "Jewish question" best be solved? In the Diaspora or in Palestine? Diaspora nationalism was one of the most intriguing and influential of all Jewish political ideologies. In the beginning was Chaim Zhitlovsky (1865–1943), a Russian Jewish intellectual who formulated a socialist and nationalist ideology premised on the idea that it was the Yiddish language that endowed Jews with their national identity.

In 1904, Zhitlovsky arrived in the United States as an unknown emissary of the Russian Party of Socialist Revolutionaries. Within a few short weeks, he had written articles, publicly debated, and lectured to audiences that he by turns inspired and enraged. Such was the force of his arguments and personality that he could not be ignored. He stayed for 18 months, left, and returned to America permanently in 1908, an indefatigable promoter of a new Jewish politics that he called *yidishe kultur* (Yiddish culture). Zhitlovsky promoted the idea that not only among the Yiddish-speaking Jews of eastern Europe but also among American Jews did the future lie with the creation of an autonomous Yiddish culture replete with a full network of schools and social institutions. He believed that were

it not to do so, American Jewry was destined to disappear into the larger environment. He was aware, of course, that not all Jews spoke Yiddish, but believed that those who did not could learn it. This son of a student of the Volozhin yeshiva, Zhitlovsky considered the resurrection of Hebrew to be an unattainable fantasy, while other Jewish languages, such as Ladino, were not spoken by sufficient numbers of Jews to serve as the foundation upon which a Jewish future could be built. His demand that Jewish students be reared upon a diet of progressive nationalism made him the first Jewish political figure of any orientation to argue for a fully developed Jewish school system.

With great philosophical sophistication, Zhitlovsky tackled the difficult theoretical problems that lay at the core of modern Jewish identity formation. In his voluminous writings, he examined whether the Jews were a religious group or a nation, a religious or a secular nation; whether they required their own country or whether national aspirations could be fulfilled in the Diaspora; and whether all these questions could best be answered through Zionism or by some form of territorialism.

Most crucially, Zhitlovsky was moved to consider the fate of a people that, while it had once been solely defined in religious terms, had now, to an increasing extent, abandoned its faith in God. And even for those who remained pious, Zhitlovsky believed that religion was a private affair and had no place in the public sphere. Yet without religion, what force was it that made for Jewishness? At the end of the eighteenth century, argued Zhitlovsky, Western society was shaken by the rise of freethinking and science, both of which undermined the authority of religion. This shook the self-conception Jews had of themselves as well, namely, that they were a group bound by faith. But what happens if that faith is lost? Zhitlovsky's analysis made him the architect of Jewish secularism. In August 1939, he reiterated that which he had argued for a long time:

> Jewish secular culture in its modern form is Yiddish. It is not the first form of secular Jewish culture in our history. But it has brought a new feature into Jewish life. Previously, belonging to the Jewish people was associated with belonging to the Jewish faith. Leaving the Jewish faith meant leaving the Jewish people. Today, any Jew who lives with his people in the Yiddish language sphere, whether he believes in the Jewish religion or whether he is an atheist, belongs to the Jewish people. When a Jew satisfies his spiritual-cultural needs in Yiddish—when he reads a Yiddish newspaper, or attends a Yiddish lecture, or sends his child to a Yiddish secular school, when he holds a conversation in Yiddish-he is without doubt a Jew, a member of the Jewish people.

Although largely forgotten today, Zhitlovsky was a major modern Jewish intellectual. That his contemporary anonymity is due to the fact that the political vision he promoted was never realized cannot be in doubt. While his dreams for Yiddish did not come to pass, his belief that the Jewish people formed a Jewish nation based on a Jewish language was not altogether different from that of Zionists, who imagined a Jewish national future in Hebrew, and perhaps not as far-fetched when it is recalled that, unlike Yiddish, very few Jews were able to speak Hebrew until well into the twentieth century. For all newcomers to Palestine, and later Israel, Hebrew was a foreign language that had to be learned. While never a member of the Bund, Zhitlovsky was a great inspiration to it and was a driving force behind its developing a nationalist consciousness and for its acceptance of an ideology that saw nationalism and internationalism as compatible. In other words, Jewish nationalism, whether Diasporic or Palestino-centric, could be combined with a commitment to progressive, left-wing politics. This vision of Zhitlovsky's came to be shared by secular Jews of all political stripes. And finally, while his hope for a Yiddish-speaking American Jewry did not come to fruition beyond a generation or two, his belief that American Jewry could blossom into a vibrant and creative community on its own soil was most certainly realized.

The Folkspartey

While Zhitlovsky did not form a political party, many of his ideas were implemented by the Bund and the short-lived Folkspartey. Founded in St. Petersburg in 1906 and led by the distinguished historian Shimon Dubnov (1860–1941), the Folkspartey occupied the political center. One of the greatest historians of the Jewish people, Dubnov specialized in the history of eastern European Jewry. Unlike his predecessor, Heinrich Graetz, who focused on the long history of Jewish intellectual life and the history of antisemitism, Dubnov concentrated on the social life of the Jewish people, especially their politics and communal institutions. For him, the Jews, especially those in eastern Europe, had built themselves up into a nation. His political vision was informed by his interpretation of Jewish history as well as his experience of eastern European Jewish life. The ideology of the Folkspartey proceeded from the assumption that the Jews were a national group with their own unique institutions, language(s), religion, and worldview. The party's political platform stood for democracy, national minority assemblies, national minority rights, cultural autonomy, and the establishment of autonomous national or ethnic territories within the Russian Empire. The Folkspartey was particularly sensitive to Jewish mass culture, and instead of trying to change Jews, as the Maskilim or the acculturationists had sought to do, it was respectful of Jewish culture as it existed. As such, it insisted on the right of Jews to use Yiddish as the official language in the public life of the anticipated Jewish autonomous territory. Here, Jews would elect their own representative organs to control their state-budgeted school system and cultural institutions. These would function in Yiddish, possibly in combination with Hebrew.

Despite Dubnov's stature and the force of his ideas, the Folkspartey had some inherent weaknesses. It was small and lacked the funds and infrastructure to grow into a big political party. Beyond this, its increasing hostility to both Bundism and Zionism saw it lose ground to both. Catering to the political center and with middle-class support, the Folkspartey considered the Bund too narrow and not sufficiently independent of the general socialist movement. It demanded a more uniquely Jewish response to the Jewish problem than the offer of paradise on earth after the workers' revolution. It alienated the Left, which was its natural ally in the program to build a network of Yiddish secular schools, a system which would be at the core of national cultural autonomy. On the other hand, its advocacy of Yiddish ensured the hostility of Zionists, who had their sights set on the establishment of a Hebrew-speaking homeland. On class grounds, as a bourgeois party, the Folkspartey also competed with any number of Zionist parties for middle-class votes, and finally, its staunch secularism alienated the Orthodox.

Zionism

The earliest expressions of Jewish nationalism were heavily indebted to the notion of messianic redemption and restoration of the Jewish people to the Holy Land. Yehuda Alkalai (1798–1878), a rabbi from Sarajevo, and a Prussian rabbi, Zvi Hirsch Kalischer (1795–1874), called upon Jews to return to Palestine to affect the divine salvation of the Jewish people. Kalischer demanded that Jews take history into their own hands rather than wait for redemption. They were to seize the moment, just as Italian, Polish, and Hungarian nationalists had done. This combination of redemptive imperative, secular inspiration, and a desire to actively shape Jewish history became the credo of Zionism.

Like some Bundists, the earliest advocates of Jewish nationalism were Jews estranged from their Jewish heritage. In 1862, a onetime socialist and colleague of Karl Marx, Moses Hess (1812–1875), published *Rome and Jerusalem*, the title being a reference to the connection between the unification of Italy, which took place in 1859, and the hope that Jerusalem would again rise as the national capital of the Jewish people. Hess broke with the then prevalent view among German Jews that being Jewish was merely a matter of religion. Rather, Hess saw the Jews as a distinct national group and challenged the idea that they could ever or would ever want to be absorbed into the majority, "for though the Jews have lived among the nations for almost two thousand years, they cannot, after all, become a mere part of the organic whole." Anticipating Zionism, Hess interpreted the "Jewish question" through the lens of nationality and—typical for his age—race rather than religion. A secular Marxist, he rejected religion, but unlike Marx, he no longer considered class essential either. Collective identity and hostility to

Jews were the products of deeper national and biological divisions: "The German hates the Jewish religion less than the race; he objects less to the Jews' particular beliefs than to their peculiar noses."

Hess's understanding of modern antisemitism's secular nature was prescient but resonated very little with his contemporaries. Up until the last two decades of the nineteenth century, Jewish nationalism attracted very few adherents, since deeply religious circles rejected the idea of short-circuiting the divine plan of Jewish dispersion, while secular, middle-class Jews in the West anticipated that the current liberal era would soon see them emancipated. Radical Jews in eastern Europe were mostly drawn to socialism.

In the 1880s, nationalism began to penetrate eastern European Jewish intellectual circles. Triggered into action by the pogroms of 1881–1882, a new movement, called *Hibbat Tsiyon* ("Love of Zion"; its members were *Hovevei Tsiyon*, "Lovers of Zion"), emerged with hundreds of chapters organized into a loose federation in Russia and Romania. Their goal was to see the Land of Israel settled by Hebrew-speaking Jewish farmers and artisans. With their political program short on details and their organization desperately strapped for funds, Hibbat Tsiyon remained a small movement. It was rejected by most Orthodox Jews, who opposed its Maskilic leadership, which included the lapsed Orthodox Talmud scholar Moshe Leib Lilienblum (1843–1910) and the Russian-speaking doctor Leon Pinsker (1821–1891).

Hibbat Tsiyon was a somewhat-sputtering, hamstrung movement lacking effective organization. In fact, its first settlement efforts in Palestine (1881–1904), known as the First Aliyah ("First Ascent"), can, in practical terms, be regarded as a failure. Nevertheless, the ideology

of Hibbat Tsiyon represented the first phase of what would become central to later Zionist ideology—the movement of secular Jews to the Land of Israel. Hibbat Tsiyon did not call for the establishment of a Jewish state; that would come later. Rather, it more vaguely promoted the idea of an ingathering and remaking of Jews in the Land of Israel.

Zionism was a revolutionary movement, for it entailed a rejection of traditional religious, family, and social values. In the first instance, Zionism rebelled against the traditional concept of waiting for the Messiah to usher in the return of the Jews to Zion. It was a self-conscious effort to realign Jewish history, to stage-manage it by being proactive and not fatalistic. Second, Zionism was also a revolt of the youth against their parents. Finally, it meant a rejection of the most fundamental fact of Jewish social life—living in the Diaspora. Like all revolutions, Zionism required the energy and support of the masses, but in all revolutions, certain individuals emerge through the force of their ideas or their charismatic personalities to shape those revolutions. In Zionism's formative phase toward the end of the nineteenth century, Leon Pinsker, Theodor Herzl, and Ahad Ha-Am, respectively, provided the movement with a reason, an élan, and a mission.

Leon Pinsker

Leon Pinsker (1821–1891) was one of Zionism's most important early figures. Although he was head of Hibbat Tsiyon, his reputation was not built on his leadership qualities. In response to the pogroms, Pinsker wrote his German-language manifesto, *Auto-Emancipation* (1882). It was the very first great theoretical work of its kind. Like many educated Russian Jews who were deeply shocked by the pogroms, Pinsker abandoned the idea that

Jewish integration into the larger society was either possible or desirable. The reason was antisemitism:

> Though you prove yourselves patriots a thousand times . . . until some fine morning you find yourselves crossing the border and reminded by the mob that you are, after all, nothing but vagrants and parasites, without the protection of the law.

In *Auto-Emancipation*, Pinsker offered one of the earliest psychological and sociological analyses of antisemitism. While many had claimed that the pogroms were a display of medieval hatred, Pinsker asserted that they were distinctly modern. Antisemitism, he said, existed because Jews were incapable of being assimilated into the majority. They were terminal strangers. Ethnic tension was exacerbated by economic competition, wherein Jews were shut out of local economies and preference was given to members of one's own ethnic group. Pinsker maintained that every society had a saturation point when it came to Jews, and that once there were too many of them, economic and social discrimination emerged to limit their opportunities. At its most extreme, violence would erupt.

In addition to being a lawyer, Pinsker took a medical degree at the University of Moscow and practiced medicine in Odessa. It is noteworthy that in *Auto-Emancipation*, he called antisemitism "Judeophobia," an extreme fear or dread of Jews. He claimed that Europeans perceived Jews as disembodied, as ghosts, or as frightening apparitions. "A people without a territory is like a man without a shadow, a thing unnatural, spectral." Though it was an ancient Greek word, "phobia" was rarely used in ordinary speech at the end of the nineteenth century and was a word that Pinsker would most likely have learned in his medical studies. *Judeophobia*, he claimed, was a psychopathology, "an inherited aberration of the human mind" passed through the generations. It was, according to Dr. Pinsker, incurable. The only way to mitigate the effects of the disease was for the Jews to emancipate themselves from Christian society. For Pinsker, the transformation entailed the return of the Jews to a national home of their own; he did not specify where. This process required that the Jews develop a genuine sense of national self-awareness. While emancipation had been a gift bestowed upon western Jews, the changes he was advocating in Jewish self-consciousness could only come from within through an act of "auto-emancipation." Modifying a traditional version of Jewish history, Pinsker concluded his work by saying, "Help yourselves and God will help you."

Pinsker wrote his manifesto in German to appeal to western Jews. For the most part, they either ignored or dismissed it. Even in the east, despite translations into Yiddish, Hebrew, and Russian, his ideas gained little popular acceptance. However, among Jewish intellectuals who shared Pinsker's post-pogrom disenchantments, the response was much more enthusiastic.

Theodor Herzl

Jewish nationalism was predicated on two essential points: (1) that all Jews, irrespective of where they lived, were part of a single nation with a common heritage and that they shared the same hopes for a national future built on a shared cultural patrimony, and (2) that the Jewish people were to build the institutional framework through which they would develop their goal of an autonomous Jewish homeland. These two principles formed the ideological core of political

Zionism, the chief architect of which was Theodor Herzl (1860–1904).

Born and raised in Budapest, Herzl, and his family, moved to Vienna, where he established his career. Although a lawyer by training, he devoted himself to playwriting and journalism. Several of his plays had runs in Vienna theaters, and eventually, he became the Paris correspondent for the liberal daily *New Free Press*. Herzl was an unlikely leader of the Zionist movement. Born into an assimilated family that, like many others in central Europe, celebrated Christmas with greater enthusiasm than they did any of the Jewish holidays, Herzl attended the University of Vienna, where he joined the German nationalist student fraternity Albia. When, however, that organization began to espouse antisemitism, he quit. His own experience of the increasingly raucous tone of German and Austrian racism led Herzl to entertain wild fantasies in search of a solution to the "Jewish problem." In 1893, he envisioned a mass conversion of Jews to Catholicism. He wrote in his diary, "[A]s is my custom, I had thought out the entire plan down to all its minute details," something that would be characteristic of his later political activities: "The conversion was to take place in broad daylight, Sundays at noon, in St. Stephen's Cathedral, with festive processions and amidst the pealing of bells. Not in shame, as individuals have converted up to now, but with proud gestures." He portrayed himself as a Moses figure, leading young Jews to the promised land of conversion, one that he did not intend to enter: "I could see myself dealing with the Archbishop of Vienna; in imagination, I stood before the Pope—both of whom were very sorry that I wished to do no more than remain part of the last generation of Jews."

As the level of antisemitism in Vienna increased, Herzl questioned more deeply his previous commitment to assimilation. In 1894, he introduced the subject of antisemitism into one of his plays for the first time. Titled *The New Ghetto*, the drama was a savage critique of the assimilated Jewish bourgeoisie of Vienna, who had relinquished their Jewish identities without fully becoming Austrians. At the play's conclusion, the hero, Jakob, dies in a duel. For young Jewish men, to participate in a duel was to partake of a particularly seductive aspect of Christian culture, one bound up with honor and machismo, two characteristics the antisemites constantly accused Jews of lacking. By 1896, all 44 Austrian dueling fraternities had passed resolutions denying Jews the right to duel. According to an official resolution, "there exists between Aryans and Jews such a deep moral and psychic difference [that] no satisfaction is to be given to a Jew with any weapon, as he is unworthy of it." Seeking satisfaction, Herzl's Jakob character dies, a consequence of his futile attempt to participate in gentile culture.

In 1894, two episodes in particular led Herzl to a new awareness about the "Jewish question": the Dreyfus Affair and his deep shock that it took place in France, beacon of liberty, and the election of Karl Lueger as mayor of Vienna, the first major political victory for the antisemites. For Herzl, this signaled an ominous development. During the September mayoral election campaign of 1895, he wrote chillingly in his diary:

I stood outside the polls on the Leopoldstadt on election day to have a close look at some of the hate and anger. Toward evening I went to the Landstrasse district.

A silent, tense crowd before the polling station. Suddenly Dr. Lueger appeared in the square. Wild cheering. . . . The police held the people back. A man next to me said with loving fervor, but softly: "That is our Führer." More than all the declamations and abuse, these few words told me how deeply antisemitism is rooted in the heart of the people.

More determined than ever, Herzl sought out wealthy philanthropists to support what would be his greatest production—the establishment of a Jewish national homeland. He needed finances and approached the Rothschilds, as well as Baron Maurice de Hirsch, a man already supporting Jewish agricultural colonies in Argentina and Palestine. Neither Hirsch nor the Rothschilds were Zionists and wanted nothing to do with Herzl. Nevertheless, out of notes he prepared for the meetings with the two financiers, Herzl composed the

tract that would become his political manifesto, *The Jewish State: Attempt at a Modern Solution of the Jewish Question* (1896).

Figure 3.3 shows a satirical cartoon depicting the process of Jewish assimilation. *The Schlemiel: An Illustrated Jewish Humor Magazine* ran from 1904 to 1923. The magazine was founded in Berlin by Leo Winz, a Jew from Ukraine. With his other publications, such as *Ost und West (East and West)*, Winz's declared aim was to "reverse" the process of assimilation and make it acceptable to give public expression to Jewishness in Wilhelmine Germany. In this 1904 cartoon titled "Darwinism," taken from *The Schlemiel*, which depicts the evolution of a Hannukah menorah into a Christmas tree, the caption reads, "How the menorah of the goatskin dealer named Cohn from Pinne [a Polish city that came under Prussian rule in 1793] developed into the Christmas tree of Kommerzienrat Conrad in Berlin's Tiergartenstrasse." A Kommerzienrat

Figure 3.3 Satirical cartoon depicting the process of Jewish assimilation.

Source: Photo Scala, Florence/bpk, Bildagentur fuer Kunst, Kultur und Geschichte, Berlin.

was an honorary title conferred on distinguished financiers or industrialists. And "Conrad's" address in Berlin is an exclusive one. The joke depicts the assimilatory process befalling eastern European Jews as they move away geographically and socioeconomically from their roots.

Three thousand copies were printed and sent to leading figures in the press and politics, and the slender volume was soon translated into several languages. It was met with ridicule. With Herzl as a Jew in Freud's Vienna with unimaginably grandiose plans, it should come as no surprise that (in some quarters) he was considered mentally deranged. His claim "We are a people, *one* people" upset those western Jews who had placed all their hopes on emancipation and being accepted as citizens of their respective countries. Among the Jews of eastern Europe, however, the impact of Herzl's ideas was immediate and electric, despite the fact that the Russian censor had banned the publication of *The Jewish State*. In the east, Herzl was seen as a prodigal son returning to his people and a messianic figure, a persona he did much to cultivate.

Herzl's analysis of modern antisemitism was similar to Pinsker's. Concluding that it was ineradicable, he stated his goal: "Let sovereignty be granted us over a portion of the globe large enough to satisfy the rightful requirements of a nation; the rest we shall manage for ourselves." To this end, Herzl recommended the establishment of two agencies: the "Society of Jews," which "will do the preparatory work in the domains of science and politics" and "will be the nucleus out of which the public institutions of the Jewish State will later on be developed," and the "Jewish Company," which "will be the liquidating agent of the business interests of departing Jews, and will organize trade and commerce in the new country." Before any Jews moved to the new state, Herzl insisted that Jewish sovereignty be "assured to us by international law."

In both *The Jewish State* and then in his utopian novel *Altneuland* (*Old New Land*, 1902), Herzl painted a picture of what the new state would look like. He considered how the land would be purchased, the nature of workers' housing, compensation for labor, the nature of government, "an aristocratic republic," one where both army and priesthood "must not interfere in the administration of the State." Like Switzerland, the Jewish state would be politically neutral and similarly multilingual, a place where "every man can preserve the language in which his thoughts are at home." As for Hebrew, Herzl never imagined it could be resurrected, for "who amongst us has a sufficient acquaintance with Hebrew to ask for a railway ticket in that language?" The inhabitants would speak "the language which proves itself to be of the greatest utility for general intercourse." The people would rally around a flag that would be white, with seven gold stars, white symbolizing "pure new life; the stars are the seven golden hours of the [Jewish] working-day." Beyond this, a Jewish state would be open to "men of other creeds and different nationalities," with all accorded "honorable protection and equality before the law."

To realize his ambition, Herzl set about assembling a Zionist conference to discuss his ideas. He sought to hold it in Munich, but after the Jewish establishment there, both Reform and Orthodox, formed a united front of opposition, the venue was shifted to Switzerland. The First Zionist Congress opened on August 29, 1897, in Basel. Ever the impresario, Herzl insisted that the 200 attendees wear formal attire to give the proceedings an air of solemnity. Even the 80 Russian Jews in attendance, not generally accustomed to wearing such finery, agreed to Herzl's demand. He was producer, director, scriptwriter, and star of the Basel conference. Herzl ascended to the podium and gave flight to his soaring oratory, demanding the establishment of a Jewish homeland that would be "openly recognized" by the world and "legally secured" by what were then the Great Powers. Those in attendance were awestruck.

The success of the conference buoyed his already-supreme self-confidence. On September 3, he noted in his diary:

> Were I to sum up the Basel Congress in a word—it would be this: At Basel I founded the Jewish State. If I said this out loud today I would be answered by universal laughter. Perhaps in five years, and certainly in fifty, everyone will know it.

By the Jewish New Year in 1897, within the space of five weeks, the two greatest modern Jewish political movements, Bundism and Zionism, had been born.

Much more work needed to be done, however. Herzl had long believed that Zionism could not be a politically marginal movement but had to have the full backing of the international community to fulfil its aims. He turned to feverish diplomatic activity. Herzl obtained an audience in Constantinople in 1898 with the German emperor, Wilhelm II, hoping that the kaiser would influence the sultan to sign a charter granting permission to Jews to settle in Palestine. The emperor seemed sympathetic and promised to take up the matter when he next met the sultan. Later in the year, Herzl followed the imperial retinue to Palestine and again met with Wilhelm and again was led to believe that he was amenable to the idea of a Jewish homeland in Palestine. Months passed, nothing happened, and Herzl finally realized he was being strung along. A later meeting with the sultan ended in disappointment; the best the sultan would offer was his government's approval of Jewish settlement throughout the Ottoman Empire, without guarantee of a separate Jewish entity in Palestine. While Herzl's diplomatic missions, which included meetings with both the British colonial and foreign secretaries, all ended in failure, Zionism began to grow. The number of associations increased rapidly from 117 at the time of the Basel Congress to 913 within a year. The congresses became important annual events, passing further resolutions, each one taking nascent state-building steps despite the absence of any ceded territory.

Though still a minority position on the Jewish political landscape, the growing success of Zionism was accompanied by vigorous internal criticism. For all his brilliance and energy, the critics complained that Herzl had neglected one crucial issue—the Jewishness of his imagined state. Russian Zionists expressed profound concern that Herzl's universalist vision took no account of the Jewish character of his proposed homeland. In *Altneuland*, Herzl imagined the land crisscrossed with electric trolley cars, dotted with the latest scientific research institutions, and full of people engaging in modern commerce. There would be English boarding schools, French opera houses, and Viennese coffee shops. Everywhere in this pan-European paradise, people would chat away in their native tongues. Tel Aviv would be just like any major European capital, only with a sunny climate and an ocean view. Above all, there would be no pogroms. After its founding in 1909, Tel Aviv did, in many ways, come to resemble Herzl's vision.

But for many eastern European Zionists, creating a Jewish state was always about more than merely finding a place of refuge. For them, nationalism involved the creation of a new Jew and a new Jewish culture, expressed in Hebrew. In Odessa, the Russian Empire's second-largest Jewish city and a center of Maskilic activity, Herzl's un-Jewish vision for a Jewish state met with great resistance. The issue turned on whether Herzl wanted to establish a Jewish state or merely a state for Jews. Proponents of a Jewish cultural renaissance grounded in Hebrew—Moses Leib Lilienblum, Hayim Nahman Bialik, and a young ex-Hasid from Ukraine, Asher Ginsberg, better known by his nom de plume, Ahad Ha-Am ("One of the People")—imagined something far different from that which Herzl sketched out in *Altneuland.*

At the 1901 Zionist Congress, splits within the movement became apparent, prompting the emergence of the Democratic Faction. Inspired by the philosophy of Ahad Ha-Am and led by the man who would become the first president of the State of Israel, Chaim Weizmann (1874–1952), the group sought to place greater emphasis than Herzl had ever done on Jewish culture. Though they never officially split from Herzl, their cultural mission became central to the Zionist enterprise thereafter.

Through indomitable will and charisma, Herzl led the movement in its earliest phase. Though he died prematurely in 1904 at age 44, Herzl's lasting legacy was the creation of the World Zionist Organization (WZO). The WZO was a democratic and progressive body that housed the nation-building institutions, such as the Jewish Colonial Office and the Jewish National Fund. These were the agencies charged with the purchase and rational management of land in Palestine on behalf of the Jewish people. Questions of Jewish culture, politics, and the work of state building would be taken up by those who followed Herzl.

Ahad Ha-Am

If Herzl was the representative of political Zionism, Ahad Ha-Am (Asher Ginsberg) (1856–1927) became the great spokesman and theoretician of cultural Zionism. Bitterly opposed to Herzl's diplomatic activities, emphasis on Jewish settlement, and cavalier attitude to Jewish culture, Ahad Ha-Am recalled the First Zionist Congress at Basel thus: "I sat alone among my brothers, a mourner at a wedding banquet."

Where Herzl was concerned to protect the physical safety of the Jews, Ahad Ha-Am had been long dedicated to their spiritual welfare. A brilliant Hebrew stylist steeped in Jewish culture, Ahad Ha-Am rejected the state-building efforts of Herzl, insisting that nation building required the establishment of a Hebrew-speaking vanguard who would create a spiritual center in the Land of Israel. According to Ahad Ha-Am, the new Hebrew culture would radiate out to the Jewish world to invigorate a moribund and decadent Diaspora Jewry.

Long before Herzl appeared on the world stage, Ahad Ha-Am had been a fierce critic of Jewish settlement efforts in Palestine. While a member of Hibbat Tsiyon, Ahad Ha-Am penned a famous critique of the organization in 1889 titled "This Is Not the Way." In this essay, he expressed his dissatisfaction with settlement efforts. He objected to pioneering that only served the interests of those immediately involved in colonization efforts but failed to move the spirit of all Jews to the Zionist idea. In an oblique reference to Hibbat Tsiyon, Ahad Ha-Am wrote, "The demon of egoism—individual or congregational—haunts us in all that we do for our people, and suppresses the rare manifestations of national feeling, being the stronger of the two." Instead of immediately settling in Palestine, he intimated, "[they] ought to have made it [their] first object to bring about a revival—to inspire men with a deeper attachment to the national life, and a more ardent desire for the national well-being." Pessimistic about the disorganized and haphazard nature of Jewish settlement, Ahad Ha-Am insisted that

> every step needs to be measured and carried out with sober and considered judgment, under the direction of the nation's statesmen and leaders, in order that all actions be directed to one end and that individuals do not, in their private actions, upset the apple-cart.

What was needed was "unified and orderly action."

With his emphasis on the rebirth of the Hebrew language and the need to cultivate enthusiasm for the Zionist idea among Diaspora Jews, Ahad Ha-Am became the champion of Russian Zionists. Although after the Basel conference the name Hibbat Tsiyon was dropped in favor of the term *Zionism*, Ahad Ha-Am saw the advantages of the former. In his 1897 essay "The Jewish State and Jewish Problem," he wrote:

> Zionism, therefore, begins its work with political propaganda; Hibbat Tsiyon begins with national culture, because only through the national culture and for its sake can a Jewish State be established in such a way as to correspond with the will and the needs of the Jewish people.

Ahad Ha-Am was also one of the first Zionists to call attention to the reality of Palestine's Arab population and the real prospect of a confrontation between them and Zionists. In his "Truth from Eretz Yisrael" (1891), a scathing critique of local conditions, he warned against ignoring the Arab population: "If the time comes when the life of our people in Eretz Yisrael develops to the point of encroaching upon the native population, they will not easily yield their place."

When, in 1922, he finally moved to Tel Aviv, the modern world's first Hebrew-speaking Jewish city, Ahad Ha-Am was surrounded by his beloved Odessa circle, which included the poet Bialik and Tel Aviv's first mayor, Meir Dizengoff. Instrumental in advising the latter on the shape the city should take, Ahad Ha-Am was the inspiration for Tel Aviv's main academic institution, the Herzliyah Gymnasium. (He also helped found the Hebrew University of Jerusalem.) One of his closest confidants was Moshe Glickson, an editor of Tel Aviv's first daily newspaper, *Ha'aretz* (*The Land*), the official line of which often reflected Ahad Ha-Am's own views.

Ahad Ha-Am's importance lies in the fact that he was both Zionism's chief theoretician and its greatest critic. His sober realism stood in marked contrast to the fantasies and grandiose plans of political Zionists. Whether questioning Herzl's leadership, attempts at Great Power diplomacy, the nature of agricultural produce on Zionist settlements, or the thorny problem of the Jewish character of the state, he provided something essential to the nascent movement—an internal Zionist critique and a cultural vision.

The Uganda Proposal and Territorialism

The other political development that went directly to the heart of the problem besetting political Zionism and its relation to the question of Jewish culture in any possible Jewish state emerged during the controversy over Uganda. In the wake of the Kishinev pogrom of 1903, the British government offered parts of Uganda to the Zionist movement for the purpose of Jewish autonomous settlement.

At the Sixth Zionist Congress of 1903, Herzl suggested Uganda as a temporary refuge for Russian Jews. Still committed to Palestine as the only proper place for a Jewish state, Herzl called Uganda a "night asylum." Nevertheless, his unwise use of the name "Uganda proposal" saw Herzl meet strenuous opposition, especially from eastern European Jews. Still, he managed to secure a vote of 295–178 in favor of sending an "investigatory commission" to determine the suitability of Uganda. Although the Zionist movement formally rejected the plan in 1905, some members remained committed to finding a place of immediate refuge for Jews under threat. To this end, a body called the Jewish Territorial Organization (ITO) was established, dedicated to "obtaining a large tract of territory (preferably within the British Empire) wherein to found a Jewish Home of Refuge." Its president was the British author and Zionist Israel Zangwill (1864–1926). Its members were known as Territorialists, or ITO men. The ITO considered many places, including Australia and Canada, both vast and with much vacant territory. While nothing came of these plans, both nations did eventually become places of refuge for Jews, although mainly after the Holocaust. One undertaking prior to World War I that met with some success was the Galveston project. With financial support from the American Jewish banker Jacob Schiff, some 9,300 Jews settled in Texas between 1907 and 1914.

An essential part of all nationalist movements, Zionism developed its own graphic culture. Ephraim Moses Lilien (1874–1925) was a Galician illustrator and photographer. A Zionist, he produced many of the movement's most classic and widely disseminated images. In addition to taking the renowned photograph of Theodor Herzl looking out in solitary contemplation from the balcony of his hotel room at the First Zionist Congress in Basel in 1897, Lilien produced many pen-and-ink images in the Art Nouveau style celebrating Zionism. It was Lilien who was largely responsible for the popularization of symbols such as the menorah, the Star of David, and the olive branch, depicting them as quintessentially Jewish and Zionist. At the Fifth Zionist Congress in Basel in 1901, Lilien organized an exhibition with other Jewish artists, in which his style represented a new, modernist Jewish aesthetic. This striking illustration was one of the most widely reproduced Zionist images. Titled *From Ghetto to Zion*, it was the semi-official picture of the Fifth Zionist Congress and was used subsequently by the Jewish National Fund, turned into postcards, and issued as a stamp by the Israel Postal Service in 1977. An elderly religious Jew sits forlorn, enveloped in thorns, a symbol of his diasporic imprisonment. Over his shoulder stands an androgynous angel, with a Star of David on the tunic, pointing the way to Zion, where, in the distance, another religious Jew, rejuvenated by agricultural labor, walks in the sunlight behind a plow and oxen. At the base of the drawing, Lilien has quoted a verse from the Shemoneh Esreh prayer: "Our eyes will behold Your return to Zion in mercy."

The influence of the ITO was greatly reduced after the issuance of the Balfour Declaration in 1917 and Zangwill's passing in 1926. It eventually folded in 1943; however, before that time, with worsening conditions for Jews in Europe, territorialism entered a second phase with the founding in London in 1935 of the Frayland-lige far Yidisher Teritoryalistisher Kolonizatsye (Freeland League for Jewish Territorial Colonization). Increasingly violent antisemitism in Poland and the rise

הקונגרס החמישי של הציונים בבזל•תרסב

והחזינה עינינו בשובך לציון ברחמים

Figure 3.4 Ephraim Moses Lilien (1874–1925) was a Galician illustrator and photographer.
Source: John M. Efron.

to power of Hitler in Germany in 1933 again made urgent the need to find a place where large numbers of Jews could immediately settle. The violent riots between Arabs and Jews in Palestine that broke out in 1920 and again in 1929 convinced the Frayland-lige that Palestine would not prove a viable haven for Jews fleeing Europe. Britain's issuance of the white paper in May 1939 severely restricting Jewish immigration to Palestine also served to increase Jewish support for a non-Zionist territorialist response to the crisis facing European Jewry.

Hitler's invasion of Poland essentially ended any possibility of success for the Frayland-lige. The movement sputtered along during the war and, at its conclusion, sought to obtain an autonomous Jewish territory for the settlement of some 250,000 displaced persons. Zionist factions thwarted their every move, fearing the Frayland-lige would dissuade Jews from going to Palestine. In terms of active success, only a few small Jewish settlements in New Jersey and Argentina were established in the 1950s. Already by this point, settlement plans had given way to nurturing what remained of the destroyed culture of eastern European Jewry. In 1979, under the leadership of the Yiddish linguist Mordkhe Schaechter, the Frayland-lige changed its name to the Yidish-lige (League for Yiddish).

Varieties of Zionism

There were other varieties of Zionism beyond those previously outlined. Both Herzl and Ahad Ha-Am shared a vision of Zionism that was avowedly secular and bourgeois. In 1902, despite religious opposition to Zionism, Mizrahi was established as the chief political arm of religious nationalism. Seeking to counter the secularism of most Zionist streams, Mizrahi combined strict adherence to tradition and nominal acceptance of Zionism.

One of the most historically significant variants of Jewish nationalism came in the form of socialist Zionism. Its leading exponents were Nahman Syrkin (1868–1924) and Ber Borochov (1881–1917). Syrkin, the founder of labor Zionism, sought to combine utopian or prophetic socialism and Jewish nationalism. As such, he differed from Bundists, who believed that the "Jewish problem" would be solved when the general social revolution took place. Syrkin also maintained that the only viable socialist solution for Jews was the establishment of a socialist Jewish state in Palestine. In 1897, he led the socialist Zionist faction at the First Zionist Congress, and in 1898, he published "The Jewish Question and the Socialist Jewish State," in which he called for the establishment of cooperative settlement of the Jewish masses in Palestine. Syrkin was particularly attentive to the immediate needs of the Diaspora, urging the organization of self-defense among Russian Jews facing pogroms. Like Ahad Ha-Am, Syrkin was also a vociferous internal critic of Zionism, attacking virtually every stream, including what he called the "bourgeois and clerical" elements of the World Zionist Organization. He also fell out with Ahad Ha-Am over what he regarded as the latter's disregard for antisemitism and the immediate need for mass migration. He was, therefore, amenable to the Uganda proposal,

and he regarded Ahad Ha-Am's notion of Israel as a "spiritual center" as an unrealistic and unaffordable luxury.

Socialist Zionism also spawned a more radical wing of Marxist Zionists, whose great theoretician was Ber Borochov. By synthesizing class struggle with nationalism, he attempted to interpret Marxism in accordance with Jewish nationalism. Despite recognizing the growth of antisemitism, Borochov did not regard antisemitism as the impetus for Zionism, nor did he see Zionism as the principal motivation or means for spiritual renewal. Rather, he sought to usher Jews out of the abnormal socioeconomic condition of the Diaspora, which he considered the cause of Jewish economic and political powerlessness. Being a minority meant that the Jews would always lose out to the controlling interests of the ruling majority. Borochov was one of the founders of Poalei Tsiyon (The Workers of Zion), formed in 1906 and a forerunner of Israel's Labor Party. Poalei Tsiyon became the first socialist Zionist political party and had branches across eastern and central Europe, Britain, and the United States. (Various local branches of the party had existed as early as 1901.) Addressing the Russian Poalei Tsiyon at its first convention in December 1906, Borochov stated, "The Jewish nation in the Galut [Diaspora] has no material possessions of its own, and it is helpless in the national competition struggle." What was needed was for Jewish life to be made economically productive again, and this could only come about through mass migration to the Land of Israel.

Zionist Culture and the Founding Generation

As Zionist theoreticians of all stripes continued to theorize, idealistic pioneers, wishing to work the land, continued to arrive in Palestine prior to the outbreak of World War I. During the Second Aliyah (1903–1914), about 35,000 Jews settled in Palestine, taking the Jewish population to 85,000, or 12 percent of the total. The *aliyah* was not uniform in character. Middle-class Jews tended to live in Tel Aviv, whose population grew to 2,000 by 1914, while pious immigrants went to traditional religious centers. Although many of the immigrants left after a few weeks due to the difficult conditions, a group of about 2,000 to 3,000 Zionists who were ideologically committed to the idea of creating the new Hebrew-speaking Jew also arrived at this time. They had no intention of returning to Europe. Among this group were David Ben-Gurion (1886–1973), first prime minister of the State of Israel; Berl Katznelson (1887–1944), a leading figure of labor Zionism; and Yitzhak ben-Zvi (1884–1963), scholar of Oriental Jewish communities, a founder of the Jewish defense agency Ha-Shomer, and second president of the State of Israel.

Two of the more important developments that took place in Palestine in the period before World War I were the establishment of Jewish agricultural settlements and the revival of the Hebrew language. The first agricultural collective, known as a *kvutza* (group), was set up in Degania in 1910 along the shores of the Sea of Galilee. Ten men and two women formed an autonomous economic undertaking; they rejected private property, capitalism, and urbanism and made decisions on the basis of direct democracy. Later, the expansion of such settlements, where the inhabitants considered themselves an extended family, became known as kibbutzim (sing. *kibbutz*). The official Israeli legal definition of a *kibbutz* is "an organization for settlement which maintains a collective society of members organized on the basis of general ownership of possessions. Its aims are self-labor, equality and cooperation in all areas of production, consumption and education." Eventually, however, different ideological and cultural goals and even economic practices

would come to characterize the varieties of kibbutzim.

After World War I, more kibbutzim began to develop, and by the early 1940s, the kibbutz population had grown to 25,000 members, approximately 5 percent of the total Jewish population of Palestine. But more important even than the number of people living on kibbutzim was the ideology that informed them and, in turn, was employed to define the new nation. Aaron David Gordon (1856–1922) was the major theoretician of Jewish agricultural labor and stressed that the regeneration of the Jews could only come about if they worked with their own hands. As such, he spoke out sharply against the then practice of employing Arab workers on Jewish agricultural settlements. Jewish self-sufficiency was his catchphrase. It was during this time that the agricultural laborer became for Zionism what the cowboy was in American culture—a symbol of attachment to the land, a pioneer spirit, and an authentic representative of the nation. Arab opposition to Jewish settlement was apparent from the very beginning, and the existence of kibbutzim saw the need for the establishment of military guard units, such as Ha-Shomer, which came into existence in 1909. The Second Aliyah also saw the establishment of new political parties, such as Ha-Po'el Ha-Tsa'ir ("The Young Worker") (1905), which espoused the ideology of Gordon, and the Marxist-Zionist party Poalei Tsiyon (1906).

Zionist culture in Palestine at this time was also characterized by a deeply hostile attitude to religious Orthodoxy and especially Yiddish language and culture. Men such as Ben-Gurion made secularism and the bitter rejection of Yiddish central to the culture of the Yishuv (Zionist settlement in Palestine prior to 1948) and then the State of Israel. Many of the most fervent Zionists exchanged their names for new Hebrew ones and were single-minded in their devotion to the Hebrew language. To take the first three prime ministers as examples, David Ben Gurion ("Son of a Lion Cub") had been David Grün, Moshe Sharett ("Servant") had previously been Moshe Shertok, while Levi Shkolnik became Levi Eshkol ("Cluster of Grapes"), thereby denoting his link to the Holy Land's soil. Other Zionists took up last names such as Peled ("steel") and Tzur ("rock"). The hebraizing name change was intended to indicate a total transformation from Yiddish-speaking Diaspora Jew to the new Hebrew pioneer—tough, fearless, and reborn. This was not particular to Zionism. Such name changes also took place at the same time in the Soviet Union, where a new man, *Homo sovieticus*, was also being created. Joseph Dzhugashvili became Joseph Stalin ("steel"); his protégé, Vyacheslav Mikhailovich Skryabin, became Molotov ("hammer"); while the onetime chairman of the Politburo, Lev Kamenev ("rock"), had previously been Lev Rosenfeld.

Although modern Hebrew fiction's origins can be traced to Europe—first with Maskilim in eighteenth-century Berlin, and then nineteenth-century eastern European authors who explored pastoral themes set in ancient Judea or the spiritual life of the shtetl—it was during the Second Aliyah that the political and literary elite saw to it that Hebrew would become the lingua franca of the new Jew. This gave rise to a modern Hebrew literature, with writers such as Micha Yosef Berdichevsky (1865–1921), Saul Tchernichovsky (1875–1943), Yosef Chaim Brenner, (1881–1921), and Shmuel Yosef Agnon (1884–1970), all of whom arrived in Palestine with the Second Aliyah. Deeply influenced by the German philosopher Nietzsche, many hardcore Zionists were committed to the "transvaluation of Jewish values." They were revolutionaries who

wished to overturn the culture of the Diaspora and create the new Hebrew man and woman. Some made the distinction between Jews and Judaism a point of ideology. According to Berdichevsky, "[o]ur hearts, ardent for life, sense that the resurrection of Israel depends on a revolution—the Jews must come first, before Judaism—the living man, before the legacy of his ancestors." Brenner was harsher, asserting that Jewishness in the absence of religion is possible and natural:

> We, the living Jews, whether or not we fast on Yom Kippur and whether or not we eat meat and milk [together], whether or not we hold to the morality of the Bible, and whether or not we are in our world view students of Epicurius, we do not stop feeling that we are Jews. . . . The best of our people here and abroad are fighting, and they don't believe in the Messiah and they have nothing to do with traditional theological Judaism.

The most extreme among Hebrew writers and Zionist ideologues promoted an ideology of *shlilat ha-Golah*, "negation of the Diaspora."

Shmuel Agnon, who was the greatest of the authors to arrive in Palestine before World War I, did not share the religious rejectionism of some of his fellow Hebrew writers of the Second Aliyah. Born into a Hasidic family in the Galician town of Buczacz, and remaining personally observant, Agnon often returned to the conflict between tradition and modernity in his works. He wrote evocatively of shtetl life, but never in a nostalgic or maudlin way, charting instead its demise, particularly in the wake of World War I, as he did in his 1938 novel *A Guest for the Night*, which was inspired by a return visit to his hometown. Agnon's talents were such that he won the Nobel Prize for Literature in 1966, an award he shared that year with the German Jewish poet Nelly Sachs.

The man most associated with the rebirth of Hebrew was Eliezer ben Yehuda (1858–1922), who insisted that his family only speak Hebrew after they immigrated to Palestine in 1881, despite the fact that they barely spoke the language. Still he persisted, believing that children held the key to the revival of Hebrew. If they could learn it, then it would flourish. He observed:

> The Hebrew language will go from the synagogue to the house of study, and from the house of study to the school, and from the school it will come into the home and . . . become a living language.

For it to become a language of the street, it needed a new vocabulary, and ben Yehuda toiled away at what would become his 17-volume work, *A Complete Dictionary of Ancient and Modern Hebrew*. He invented hundreds of words for a language that was not yet suited to modernity but soon would be. Inspired to give his own young son a Hebrew vocabulary, ben Yehuda invented the Hebrew words for *bicycle*, *doll*, *ice cream*, and *jelly*—the very kind of words that young children needed if they were to live their lives in Hebrew.

The Second Aliyah was far more successful than the First. These pioneers built new political, military, and economic institutions and a Hebrew culture, all of which proved durable. Nevertheless, Jewish settlement in Palestine remained vulnerable. Most of the 85,000 Jews who lived there, by 1914, were poor, and the local economy had difficulty sustaining such numbers. Beyond this, the 700,000 Arabs of Palestine were increasingly opposed to Jewish settlement, as were the Ottomans, the region's political overlords. In Europe, however, the aftermath of World War I would see antisemitism intensify and the call of Zionists become ever more urgent.

Philanthropy and Acculturation

The second significant response to the "Jewish question" entailed a robust assertion of Jewish rights combined with philanthropy and a redoubled commitment to acculturation. Together with the Damascus blood libel, the Mortara affair made Jews aware of the need for a central body to represent their interests, and in 1860, in Paris, they founded the Alliance Israélite Universelle. Under the leadership of Adolphe Cremieux, the organization's motto, taken from the Talmud, was "All Israel is responsible for one another." In addition to actively combating discrimination against Jews wherever it occurred, the Alliance also built a vast network of schools throughout the Ottoman Empire to Westernize the Jews of the Balkans and the Islamic world and provide them with modern, secular education. At its peak, the Alliance ran 183 schools with 43,700 students across an area stretching from Morocco to Iran. Instruction was in French, while Jewish subjects, taught according to modern pedagogic methods, reflected the cultural sensibilities of Franco-Judaism. An especially important undertaking of the Alliance was its commitment to providing a modern education to Jewish women, who came to enjoy social mobility and increased status as a result. The Alliance contributed to the breakdown of traditional Jewish communities across North Africa and the Middle East, and as increasing numbers of Jews became acquainted with French, they oriented themselves toward Europe and secular culture. Moreover, the Alliance contributed to the development of a Jewish bourgeoisie and overall increasing prosperity in Jewish communities throughout the Middle East and Asia

Minor, particularly in cities such as Istanbul, Salonika, and Izmir.

Philanthropy, in both monetary and educational terms, became a central feature of Jewish communal life in the nineteenth century. In fact, philanthropy became the basis for a Jewish social policy that was administered by experts in possession of modern economic and diplomatic skills. Before the advent of the Alliance in 1860, Jewish philanthropy in the form of charity was directed at the poor within one's own community. After this time, however, philanthropy was channeled outward to the needy of other lands. This coincided with two changes: the rise in income levels of Western Jews, which enabled them to donate money to Jews in distress, and the rise of mass Jewish immigration due to dire economic circumstances and pogroms in Russia and Rumania, which brought poor, helpless Jews into direct contact with the Jews of western Europe. As such, western European Jews established large organizations to assist and educate their less-fortunate coreligionists in eastern Europe and the Near East. After the Alliance was established, it became a model for similar organizations, such as Great Britain's Anglo-Jewish Association (1871), the Israelitische Allianz zu Wien (Israelite Alliance of Vienna) (1872), and in Germany, the Hilfsverein der deutschen Juden (Aid Association of German Jews) (1901). All sought to alleviate Jewish poverty at home and abroad and, where possible, to promote educational programs to secularize and Westernize Jewish youth.

Philanthropy also supported Jewish agricultural schemes. Through his Jewish Colonization Association, Baron de Hirsch funded Moisesville, a Yiddish-speaking agricultural settlement in Argentina. It began in 1889 with the arrival of 824 Russian Jews. Most of the 81,000 Jews who immigrated to Argentina between 1901 and 1914, however, settled in cities. In Palestine in 1880, out of a total population of 450,000, 25,000 were Jews, two-thirds of whom lived in Jerusalem, while the rest resided in Safed, Tiberius, and Hebron, cities with religious significance. Known as the Old Yishuv (settlement), the Jewish population was roughly split evenly between Sephardim and Ashkenazim, the former arriving in the wake of the expulsion from Spain and the latter toward the end of the eighteenth century. Both communities were deeply religious and desperately poor, surviving on charity sent from abroad (see box, "Bertha Pappenheim and the League of Jewish Women").

Philanthropy also made a deep psychological impact. Those in receipt of aid felt cared for, sensing that they were not being forgotten, while donors derived an important sense that their largesse was deeply meaningful, a fitting testament to the nations where they prospered to the point of being able to offer assistance. This further enhanced their sense of gratitude to those nations where they had been free to succeed. The large Jewish philanthropic network throughout the world also created a conscious sense that the Jews, though globally dispersed, were a united people, with a sense of mutual responsibility for each other's welfare.

While considerable friction could be found between organizations, antagonisms of a kind that mirrored the larger national tensions between countries, the aid associations worked together for the greater Jewish good, co-sponsoring and jointly funding many projects ranging from schooling to refugee repatriation. Socioeconomically and ideologically, the leaders of these Jewish organizations and the larger communities they represented shared much in common. Economically secure and solidly middle class, their members were unified in their attachment to their respective lands, to emancipation, to acculturation, and to Europe.

Just as philanthropy was an important expression of middle-class Jewish values, so too was the establishment of Jewish self-defense organizations to combat antisemitism. In fact, philanthropic and self-defense activities often engaged the same community leaders. In 1893, the Central Union of German Citizens of the Jewish Faith was founded; its goal was to safeguard Jewish civil and social equality and combat antisemitism. It did so vigorously, using public relations campaigns, the media, and the court system. It repeatedly sued antisemites for libel and enjoyed great success in the German courts. In the United States, the Anti-Defamation League was established in 1913. With a similar mission to that of its German counterpart, the League's charter states:

> The immediate object of the League is to stop, by appeals to reason and conscience and, if necessary, by appeals to law, the defamation of the Jewish people. Its ultimate purpose is to secure justice and fair treatment to all citizens alike and to put an end forever to unjust and unfair discrimination against and ridicule of any sect or body of citizens.

The Pursuit of Happiness: Coming to America

Unlike those Jews in eastern Europe who turned to Jewish politics, or those in western Europe who built strong Jewish communities based on bourgeois values, a third path taken by millions of Jews was to leave for the West. In response to economic distress and discrimination, vast numbers left eastern Europe in search of opportunity. Between 1881 and 1924, nearly 2.5 million Jews fled eastern Europe in what was a largely non-ideological response to persecution and stifling economic conditions. Nearly 85 percent of those Jews went to the United States, or, as the immigrants called it in Yiddish, the *goldene medineh*, the "Golden Land." Demographically speaking, American Jewry's rise was spectacular. In 1800, approximately 10,000 Jews lived in the United States. That number had grown to 300,000 by 1870, but by 1880, the number had risen to 1.7 million, and by 1915 America was home to over 3 million Jews.

In the mid-nineteenth century, America underwent a population explosion with the arrival of vast numbers of immigrants from central and northern Europe. Among them were impoverished young Jewish men from rural Germany. While most came principally in search of economic opportunity, they were further motivated to depart Europe due to a host of antisemitic restrictions, among them limitations on the number of Jewish marriages, laws against opening businesses, and others against the entrance of Jews into various professions. The sense of dismay after the failure of the liberal revolutions of 1848 and the prosecution of Jewish revolutionaries prompted others to leave Germany. Between 1830 and 1860, perhaps as many as 200,000 central European Jews arrived in America. Though, as we will see, there were important distinctions and tensions between the elites of the two Jewish immigrant groups—central and eastern European—and important cultural differences as well, the reasons for the mass of Jews leaving Europe and coming to the United States, their successful integration once there, and the forms of Judaism they came to practice have much in common. We can see the period of 1820 to 1924 as a century-long time of Jewish immigration out of Europe's poorer regions to the relative abundance of the West.

Uptown Jews: The Rise of the German Jews in America

Moving on quickly from their ports of embarkation, German Jewish immigrants, mostly single men, settled in Midwestern cities, such as Cincinnati, St. Louis, and Chicago. Some headed farther west to San Francisco. Most earned a living, as they had in Europe, as itinerant peddlers. With astonishing speed, these immigrants soon gave up their carts and packs for small stores and businesses, and in some cases, such as that of Lazarus Straus, they turned those little shops into large department stores. From modest beginnings, they created global brands, such as Levi's, named after the German Jewish immigrant Levi Straus, who, together with another immigrant, Jacob Davis, took out a patent to manufacture pants with copper-riveted pockets for working men. Still others began as peddlers in the Midwest and the Deep South and became captains of finance in New York. In the 1850s and 1860s, they opened businesses, some of which are still in operation today. Among the itinerant salesmen who wandered the American countryside selling such items as shoelaces, fabric, clothes, and pots and pans was Marcus Goldman, the founder of Goldman Sachs; Henry Lehman and his siblings, who formed Lehman Brothers; Joseph, William, and James Seligman, who formed J. and W. Seligman & Co.; and J. S. Bache, whose

BERTHA PAPPENHEIM AND THE LEAGUE OF JEWISH WOMEN

In central Europe, Jewish philanthropic efforts were generally directed by men, though middle-class Jewish women were heavily involved in the work. A notable exception was the role played by Bertha Pappenheim (1859–1936). From an Orthodox Viennese family, she early on became committed to feminism and social welfare, trying to marry the two to Jewish concerns. More famously known as the patient Anna O. in Josef Breuer and Sigmund Freud's *Studies on Hysteria*, Pappenheim worked as a soup kitchen volunteer, nursery school administrator, and headmistress of a Frankfurt orphanage. In 1902, she founded the "Care for Women Society," whose objective was to place orphans in foster homes, educate mothers in childcare, and provide vocational counselling and employment opportunities for women.

Pappenheim's greatest legacy was the League of Jewish Women, which she founded in 1904 and presided over for 20 years. The League had three main objectives: the international campaign against the prostitution and "White slavery" of young Jewish women from eastern Europe and the Near East; the promotion of the full participation of Jewish women in the political structures of the Jewish communities; and vocational training, so that Jewish women could enjoy financial independence. While seen as a radical by her opponents, Pappenheim was in fact quite conservative. Women were trained in traditional female occupations, such as nursing, social work, and housekeeping. Pappenheim also remained committed to religious tradition and made instruction about Jewish family observances central to the training she offered on running a proper Jewish home. Her traditionalism aside, Pappenheim was a maverick, and the league she created was an important vehicle for the self-assertion of Jewish women.

brokerage house eventually became Prudential Bache. Having made it in America, these families and others, such as the Guggenheims and the Schiffs, formed the backbone of the American Jewish establishment. While these were certainly exceptional success stories, the overall experience of the German Jewish migration to America was one in which the vast majority became solidly middle-class, productive citizens.

The process of Americanization accompanied the immigrants' movement into the middle class. Their embourgeoisement also provoked renewed interest in their religious life, something that had initially been neglected as the immigrants struggled to make a living in rural America in communities with few Jews and no Jewish leaders. Now they sought to build new Jewish institutions and, in so doing, created a uniquely American Judaism. With considerable hyperbole, the German-born rabbi Adolf Moses of Mobile, Alabama, declared, "From America salvation will go forth; in this land [not in Germany] will the religion of Israel celebrate its greatest triumphs."

One of the first steps in the consolidation of American Judaism was the organization of the scattered frontier communities under a more centralized form of leadership. The most important institution established for this purpose was the Union of American Hebrew Congregations (UAHC), founded in 1873. Under the leadership of the Cincinnati rabbi Isaac Mayer Wise (1819–1900), the Union called for the establishment of institutions that would provide instruction in "the higher branches of Hebrew literature and Jewish theology." To this end, Hebrew Union College (HUC) was established in 1875 for the training of Reform rabbis (*see box*, "A Meal to Remember: The 'Trefa Banquet'"). Wise served as president of HUC from its opening until his death in 1900.

The UAHC's initial constitution also called upon the organization to "provide means for the relief of Jews from political oppression and unjust discrimination, and for rendering them aid for their intellectual elevation." To a great extent, this became an imperative for those German Jews who had come to America in search of opportunity and had struck it rich. In addition to funding various institutions for the benefit of all the residents of cities such as New York, Chicago, St. Louis, and San Francisco, German Jewish notables offered much-needed assistance to Jewish newcomers through a network of charitable and social institutions. Until 1881, the demands on these charities were modest, but with the massive influx of eastern European Jews, the situation changed radically, as did the face of American Jewry.

Downtown Jews: Eastern European Jewish Immigrants

While some 15 percent of eastern European Jews went to Germany, France, England, Palestine, South Africa, Canada, Argentina, and Australia, 85 percent went to the United States. More than any other country, moving there was on the minds of potential immigrants. As one of those immigrants, Mary Antin, recalled:

America was in everybody's mouth. Businessmen talked of it over their accounts; the market women made up their quarrels that they might discuss it from stall to stall; people who had relatives in the famous land went around reading their letters for the enlightenment of less fortunate folk ... children played at emigrating; old folks shook their sage heads over the evening fire, and prophesied no good for those who braved the terrors of the sea and the foreign goal beyond it; all talked of it, but

A MEAL TO REMEMBER: "THE TREFA BANQUET"

In July 1883, over 200 Jews and non-Jews gathered at Cincinnati's exclusive Highland House restaurant to celebrate Hebrew Union College's ordination of its initial graduating class of four American-trained rabbis. The college's founder, Isaac Mayer Wise, a man who strove for unity among American Jews, nonetheless presided over an evening that brought about anything but solidarity. Together with his close friend the traditionalist Reverend Isaac Leeser, both men sought to emphasize commonalities among American Jews rather than those things that separated them. But there were already deep fissures in the Reform camp. The traditionalists like Wise were confronted by radical reformers, men who had attended the mid-century Reform rabbinical conferences in Germany and were determined to rid Judaism of what they considered antiquated practices.

The dinner that evening, with its lavish French menu, became immediately infamous. The first course was littleneck clams, followed by soft-shell crabs, shrimp salad, various meats, ice cream, and cheese. It is unclear whether Wise was responsible for the fiasco or whether some of the radicals, seeking to do mischief, had "gotten" to the caterer, Gus Lindeman. Wise, who kept a kosher home, claimed he knew nothing about it and had, in fact, ordered Lindeman to serve kosher meat. How the shellfish and dairy products came to be served is uncertain. A subsequent investigation by a panel of rabbis from the Union of American Hebrew Congregations (UAHC) cleared Wise of wrongdoing, but the damage was done.

The "Trefa Banquet," as it came to be known, was but one step in the division of the American Reform movement into radical and more traditional camps. In the years after the banquet, a series of debates between radical rabbi Kaufmann Kohler and traditionalist rabbi Alexander Kohut set out the position of both parties. In 1885, the UAHC conference in Pittsburgh, dominated by radicals, adopted the Pittsburgh Platform, which described observance of traditional Jewish laws governing diet and dress as "altogether foreign to [their] mental and spiritual state" and "apt rather to obstruct than to further modern spiritual elevation."

The various divisions among American Jews were soon institutionalized with a formal split into Reform, Conservative, and Orthodox camps, with many variations within each branch. The "Trefa Banquet" of 1883, while not the cause of such divisions, was profoundly symbolic of them.

scarcely anyone knew one true fact about this magic land.

Jews scrimped and saved, selling off all their possessions for a ticket in steerage. The conditions were deplorable on a journey that lasted anywhere from ten days to three weeks. The voyage, wrote the immigrant George Price, was "a kind of hell that cleanses a man of his sins before coming to the land of Columbus." Having had little to eat once their kosher food quickly ran out, nauseated from seasickness and the open latrines they used on board, the immigrants disembarked, mostly in New York harbor, starved, fatigued, fearful, and discombobulated. Numbered and lettered before they disembarked, the immigrants were led into the redbrick buildings of Ellis Island (opened in 1892), where they were subject to medical inspections and a host of intimidating questions, unsure whether their answers would assist or hinder their entry. Once admitted, they received assistance from Jewish charitable organizations, such as the United Hebrew Charities, founded in 1874, and the Hebrew Immigrant Aid Society (HIAS), founded in 1881. Established by Russian Jews and still in operation today, HIAS provided temporary housing to those without relatives, ran soup kitchens, and provided clothing for needy Jews. It has proven to be a lifeline to millions.

Unlike their German Jewish predecessors, between 70 and 90 percent of the eastern European Jews remained in New York. Aside from the fact that they had little money with which to travel beyond the city, New York had industries that required a skilled workforce. After 1900, a greater percentage of Jews were skilled industrial workers than were any other immigrant group, beneficiaries of the process of industrialization that had already begun in eastern Europe. While Jews were only 10 percent of immigrants between 1900 and 1925, they constituted 25 percent of all skilled industrial workers entering the United States in that period.

Cultural reasons compelled many Jewish immigrants to stay in New York. They often had family members who had preceded them to America. Here they found the necessary institutions of Jewish life, such as synagogues, ritual bathhouses, and kosher butchers, in abundance. They were able to converse with fellow speakers of Yiddish, read a lively Yiddish press, and for entertainment, attend the Yiddish theater, which attracted millions. Between 1890 and 1940, at least a dozen Yiddish theater companies performed on the Lower East Side, in the Bronx, and in Brooklyn, with another 200 traveling companies performing all over the United States. Plays often dealt with themes of generational conflict between immigrant parents and their American children, and Old World versus New World culture and values. The theater also produced Yiddish versions of European classics by authors such as Shakespeare, Oscar Wilde, Goethe, and Ibsen, and even a much-loved production of Harriet Beecher Stowe's American classic *Uncle Tom's Cabin*.

The leading light of the Yiddish theater was Abraham Goldfaden (1840–1906). A Hebrew and Yiddish poet and playwright, Goldfaden had a revolutionary innovation that was to adapt Western popular theater, an art form that was alien to Judaism, and to transform it in such a way as to make it acceptable to and popular among Jews. In single-handedly creating the entire enterprise of Jewish show business, Goldfaden trained Jewish actors and created opportunities for Jewish set and costume designers, makeup people, musicians, librettists, playwrights, and many others. He also helped reconfigure the Jewish economy through its heavy involvement in show business.

The cultural impact of the Jewish theater under Goldfaden was enormous. According to a recent account, Goldfaden "turned show business into an integral part of Jewish culture, and [thus] contributed tremendously to the secularization and acculturation of Ashkenazi Jews." Though largely unknown today, Goldfaden's importance was recognized by contemporaries, and not just in the world of Yiddish theater. When he died, *The New York Times* reported on the funeral of "the 'Yiddish Shakespeare' and bard of the Jewish stage":

Fully 75,000 Jews turned out yesterday morning for the funeral of Abraham Goldfaden, the Yiddish poet, playwright, and Zionist, who died on Wednesday at his home, 318 East Eleventh Street. All the streets through which the funeral procession of 104 coaches passed on its way to Washington Cemetery, in Brooklyn, were thronged with mourners. Even the fire-escapes were crowded.

Eastern European Jewish immigration between 1881 and 1914 differed from contemporary non-Jewish immigration in important ways. Above all, this was to be a permanent settlement. A smaller percentage of Jews returned to Europe than any other immigrant group. Nearly 95 percent of Jews stayed, while the comparable number for non-Jews was 66 percent. Jewish immigration involved families. While the Italians, the Irish, and the German Jews of the mid-century came as single males, Jews from Russia at the end of the nineteenth century came with much larger percentages of women and children. Between 1899 and 1910, 43 percent of Jewish immigrants were women, while 25 percent were children under the age of 14. The fact that 70 percent of Jewish immigrants were between the ages of 14 and 44 is a measure of the extent to which young Jews anticipated starting entirely new lives in the United States.

The relative youth of the Jewish immigrants also meant that the way they built families is a crucial part of the history of Jews in the United States. And here we see how changing gender norms changed the Jewish family as a unit, the character of the burgeoning Jewish community as a whole, and even the larger role played by Jewish women with the impact they would come to have on American society. The leader of the birth control movement in America was Margaret Sanger (1879–1966), a non-Jewish woman who, on October 16, 1916, opened her first birth control clinic in the heavily Jewish, working-class, and socialist Brownsville section of Brooklyn in New York.

According to Sanger, it was Jewish women who pleaded with her to open her clinic in their neighborhood. Society's resistance to Sanger and the birth control movement gave it a political character. In fact, it was Jewish women active in socialist circles who were among the first in the United States to draw attention to the subject of women's reproductive rights. Already in 1900, the radical Emma Goldman (1869–1940) began lecturing Yiddish-speaking audiences on the importance of contraception. She became affiliated with Sanger and her campaign on behalf of making contraception legal and readily available to the women of America. Similarly, Rose Pastor Stokes (1879–1933) was a poor Jewish immigrant from eastern Europe who worked in a Cleveland cigar factory. A member of the Socialist Party, and then later on a member of the Communist Party's Central Executive Committee, she had also previously been a widely read New York journalist for the *Yidishes Togblat* (Jewish daily news). In that role, she became involved with multiple social causes, including the campaign for women's access to contraception, and became financial secretary of the National Birth Control League (NBCL), an organization dedicated to legalizing the publication and distribution of birth control information.

From the beginning, Margaret Sanger published articles advocating birth control in the left-wing press. (Goldman eventually broke with Sanger because of her refusal to go along with Goldman's commitment to anarchism.) The distribution of birth control information also contravened Article 1142 of the New York Penal Code, and so it was also a potentially criminal matter as well. Neither of these things deterred the Jewish women activists, who offered Sanger their wholehearted support. Both the radical Yiddish secularists as well as Orthodox Jewish women were open to the use of contraceptives, and in this respect, eastern European Jewish women who came to America would soon follow the fertility patterns of their Jewish sisters in western and central Europe who had, by the early twentieth century, reduced their fertility rates through contraceptives and abortions.

Sanger's relationship with Jewish women had already been forged in the 1910s when she worked among immigrants on the Lower East Side as an obstetric nurse for Lillian Wald's Visiting Nurses' Association. She had witnessed the ill effects of too frequent childbirth as well as the material struggle to feed, clothe, and educate the children of the poor immigrants. Sanger was also moved to do something about the often-deadly abortions that were all too common. In 1917, it was determined that only one-third of immigrant women on the Lower East Side knew of any other method of contraception aside from abortion, with many immigrant women having more than ten of them during their childbearing years. Aside from abortion, some women also knew of condoms and the withdrawal method, both of which placed the onus on the man. Eventually, the widespread use of contraception among Jewish (and other) women restored a good measure of control over childbearing to women themselves. In addition to the efforts of Sanger and other Jewish activists, the idea of contraception became integral to Jewish popular culture and was publicized in the many Yiddish versions of Sanger's newspaper column on health and sex education, titled "What Every Girl Should Know." New York's Yiddish theater, which both reflected and helped shape the outlook of immigrant Jews on a host of social issues, also promoted the idea that contraception was essential. In 1916, Harry Kalmanowitz's play *Birth Control, or Race Suicide*

brought the issue of contraception and safe family planning to the Yiddish stage. In fact, Jews became so identified with the birth control movement that it was the National Council of Jewish Women that pioneered the establishment of birth control clinics, usually referred to as Mother's Health Bureaus, during the 1920s and 1930s. Though Jews in New York City had the highest number of children per marriage of any immigrant group in 1915, by the early 1930s, Jewish fertility rates compared favorably to the national average.

Once newly arrived Jewish immigrants found work, it was mostly in the garment industry, centered in New York. Many arrived from Europe with knowledge of basic crafts, like tailoring. Jews made up over 50 percent of skilled workers in the clothing trades, and a further 40 percent in the production of leather goods. Many Jewish immigrants worked out of their apartments in the densely packed Lower East Side of Manhattan. Dirt and disease and a generally foul atmosphere were the consequences of terrible overcrowding. By way of comparison, the heavily Jewish tenth ward of Manhattan had 626 persons per acre, while Prague had 485 inhabitants per acre, and Paris only had 125. By 1910, 540,000 Jews lived in the one and a half square miles that constituted the Lower East Side.

The conditions in the tenement flats were deplorable—overcrowded, cockroach-infested, with fetid air, poor lighting, substandard plumbing, and intensely hot in summer. Where they could, upper-class German Jews, such as the financier Jacob Schiff, who described *philanthropy* as the "ideal and aim of Judaism," offered assistance. Others made alleviating the plight of the immigrants their life's work. In 1895, the nurse Lillian Wald (1867–1940) founded the Henry Street Settlement, a meeting place for workers offering them nursing, social, educational, banking, and cultural facilities. A tireless fighter for improvements in public health nursing, housing reform, suffrage, and the rights of women, children, immigrants, and working people, Wald recalled how one of her first visits to a tenement set her on her life's mission:

> Over broken asphalt, over dirty mattresses and heaps of refuse we went. . . . There were two rooms and a family of seven not only lived here but shared their quarters with borders. . . . [I felt] ashamed of being a part of society that permitted such conditions to exist. . . . What I had seen had shown me where my path lay.

Pragmatic considerations also played a role in motivating German Jews to assist. As stated in the newspaper *The American Hebrew*: "All of us should be sensible of what we owe not only to these . . . coreligionists, but to ourselves, who will be looked upon by our gentile neighbors as the natural sponsors for these, our brethren."

With no division between workplace and home, hours were crushingly long. Inspectors in 1891 reported that during the slack season, clothing workers put in a minimum workweek of between 66 and 72 hours. During the busy season of 1904–1905, it was up to 19 hours per day, seven days per week. According to Bernard Weinstein, who arrived in America in 1882,

> [t]he front room and kitchen were used as workrooms. The whole family would sleep in one dark bedroom. The sewing machines for the operators were near the windows of the front room. The basters would sit on stools near the walls, and in the center of the room, amid the dirt and dust, were heaped in great piles of materials. On top of the sofas several finishers would be working. . . . Old people . . . using gaslight for illumination, would stand and keep the irons hot and press the finished coats, jackets, pants and other clothes on special boards.

Thanks to newly established unions, hours grew somewhat shorter for work done in factories, tellingly called "sweatshops." In 1894, after the cloak-makers' union went on strike, workers were rewarded with a ten-hour day. By 1901, clothing union workers in factories put in a 59-hour workweek. Exploitation was rife, and pay was extremely low, around $3.81 per week for men and a miserable $1.04 per week for women. Conditions in the factories were also hazardous, something that became tragically apparent in the massive Triangle Shirtwaist Fire, which erupted near closing time on March 25, 1911. With the fire spreading rapidly, an illegally locked door prevented the women workers from escaping down the stairs. Many waited in vain at the windows, only to see that the fire department ladders reached just to the fifth floor and the fire hoses likewise proved too short. At that point, many chose to jump out of the ninth floor. An eyewitness, Benjamin Levy, described the harrowing scene:

> I was upstairs in our workroom when one of the employees who happened to be looking out of the window cried that there was a fire around the corner. I rushed downstairs, and when I reached the sidewalk the girls were already jumping from the windows. None of them moved after they struck the sidewalk. Several men ran up with a net, which they got somewhere, and I seized one side of it to help them hold it.
>
> It was about ten feet square and we managed to catch about fifteen girls. I don't believe we saved over one or two however. The fall was so great that they bounced to the sidewalk after

striking the net. Bodies were falling all around us, and two or three of the men with me were knocked down. The girls just leaped wildly out of the windows and turned over and over before reaching the sidewalk.

I only saw one man jump. All the rest were girls. They stood on the windowsills tearing their hair out in the handfuls and then they jumped.

In the end, 146 young women workers, mostly Jewish and Italian, lost their lives. Across the political spectrum, the city reeled with righteous indignation. Demands from all corners came for improvement in working conditions, and the governor of New York State appointed a Factory Investigating Commission, which, for the next five years, examined working conditions in factories. The result was the passage of important factory safety legislation. In the Jewish community, the fire redoubled the commitment to trade unionism and progressive politics more generally.

Even before the fire, agitation against bosses for improved conditions was actually a source of internal Jewish conflict, for of the 241 clothing factories in New York City in the 1880s, 234 were owned by German Jews, including the Triangle Shirtwaist Factory. As a trade union leader observed, "[t]he early class struggles in the modern clothing industry in New York were *Jewish* class struggles; both masters and men were of the Hebrew race." These class struggles were, however, far more than just a history of Jewish "masters and men."

There is an important gender dimension to this story and to the Jewish immigrant experience more generally. While Jewish women shared many of the social and familial characteristics of other immigrant women, they also differed in crucial ways. Jewish women were far more likely than their gentile counterparts to participate in public life as well as attend night school. In the garment industry, Jewish men and women worked side by side and, as such, did not earn a living in separate spheres, as was commonly the case among other immigrant groups. While still patriarchal, Jewish society took on a different cast because of shared work experience. Jewish men tended to be far more committed to the idea of gender equality and women's rights, and this included women's suffrage, where Jewish men in New York stood solidly with women in their struggle to win the right to vote. The refusal of working-class eastern European Jews to be exploited extended beyond the garment industry and their relations with German Jewish factory owners. In May 1902, Jewish women organized a successful kosher meat boycott in response to a sudden price hike that saw meat go from 12 cents to 18 cents per pound. The boycott committee of 19 women demanded that meat wholesalers reduce their prices, leading as many as 20,000 protesters on marches and demonstrations through the Lower East Side. For one month, the agitation continued and spread throughout the city, with men joining the women. On June 5, the strike was officially ended when, in a compromise, prices were rolled back to 14 cents per pound. It is important to recall that most of the adult eastern European Jews arrived in America already highly politicized, having been participants in the class and cultural struggles that had so gripped and energized them back in Europe.

The "uptown" German Jews and "downtown" eastern European Jews were not just divided along employer–employee lines; there were deep cultural differences as well. The sincere compassion of German Jews was often mixed with condescension toward their coreligionists.

They were especially ashamed of the immigrants' appearance, dress, language, cultural institutions, and preference for left-wing, if not socialist, politics. German Jews also feared that antisemites would see them in the same light as they saw the immigrants, challenging the very Americanness of German Jews. Similar anxiety gripped Jews in Germany, who feared that the recent arrival of eastern European Jews compromised them. German Jews sought to "civilize" the eastern European newcomers by sponsoring English classes, courses on American culture, and vocational training.

For their part, eastern European Jews, though grateful for the assistance, never felt a sense of inferiority and were resentful of the condescension. They did not care much for the ways of their "uptown" coreligionists, especially what many considered to be the lax religious practices of these overwhelmingly Reform Jews. Especially galling was the fact that prior to immigrating, many of the eastern European Jews had been distinguished scholars and leaders revered in their communities. Now they were reduced to seeking handouts from Jews who did not respect them. As a contemporary observed:

> In the philanthropic institutions of our aristocratic German Jews you see beautiful offices, desks, all decorated, but strict and angry faces. Every poor man is questioned like a criminal, is looked down upon; every unfortunate suffers self-degradation and shivers like a leaf, just as if he were standing before a Russian official. When the same Russian Jew is in an institution of Russian Jews, no matter how poor and small the building, it will seem to him big and comfortable. He feels at home among his own brethren who speak his tongue, understand his thoughts and feel his heart.

As soon as it was possible, eastern European Jews sought to establish self-help organizations and created a network of *lantsmanshaftn*, the Yiddish word for *mutual aid societies*, which were organized around the eastern European city of one's origin. They sprang up as soon as the great wave of migration began, and by 1914, at least 534 of them in New York were providing the immigrants with insurance, sickness benefits, interest-free loans, and coverage of burial costs. The arrivals from eastern Europe also founded a network of Jewish charities, orphanages, hospitals, a school for deaf-mutes, and societies to provide for the Jewish blind and physically handicapped. A Passover Relief Committee provided free matzah to the poor. But where poverty was rife, so too was crime, and large numbers of Jewish women were led into prostitution on the Lower East Side. Other Jewish immigrants went into petty crime, and by the last decade of the nineteenth century, there were enough Jewish inmates to warrant the establishment in 1893 of a Jewish Prisoners' Aid Society.

Reflective of the many-faceted nature of new Jewish life in America, the Lower East Side was also an intensely religious place. Hundreds of synagogues and, by 1903, at least 307 heders and several yeshivas operated on the Lower East Side, including the Yeshiva Isaac Elchanan, which was opened in 1896 and would later grow into Yeshiva University, the premier institution for the training of men for the modern Orthodox rabbinate. Ten years before, in 1886, two Sephardic rabbis had founded the Jewish Theological Seminary as an institution to train men for the Conservative rabbinate.

Jewish life was further strengthened by the tight bonds of ethnic solidarity. Intermarriage was almost non-existent, and in the early years of immigration, Jews were even averse to marrying other Jews from different European towns. Still, as time passed, it was difficult for the immigrants to re-establish anything like the all-encompassing religious life they enjoyed in Europe. The distance from centers of tradition, the demands of working seven days a week to make ends meet, the lure of socialism, and the seductions of American life all made adherence to tradition increasingly difficult. With time, the revolt against tradition saw German Jews, eastern European Jews, and even the small Sephardic population begin to put aside their ethnic and cultural differences, melding into one larger community as they gradually left Europe behind in the process of becoming American. By the outbreak of World War I, there were millions of American Jews where only decades before there had been relatively few. In a mere 30 years, America had become home to one of the biggest, most vibrant Jewish communities in the world, and in 1917, New York City became the largest center of Jewish life in history, with a Jewish population of 1.5 million.

For Further Reading

On modern antisemitism, see Jacob Katz, *From Prejudice to Destruction: Antisemitism, 1700–1933* (Cambridge, MA: Harvard University Press, 1980); Shmuel Almog, *Nationalism & Antisemitism in Europe, 1815–1945* (Oxford and New York: Pergamon Press, 1990); Peter G. J. Pulzer, *The Rise of Political Anti-Semitism in Germany & Austria* (Cambridge, MA: Harvard University Press, 1988); John M. Efron, *Defenders of the Race: Jewish Doctors and Race Science in Fin-de-Siècle Europe* (New Haven, CT: Yale University Press, 1994); John Weiss, *The Politics of Hate: Anti-Semitism, History, and the Holocaust in Modern Europe* (Chicago: Ivan R. Dee, 2003); George L. Mosse, *Toward the Final Solution: A History of European Racism* (Madison: University of Wisconsin Press, 1985); Richard S. Levy, *Antisemitism in the Modern World: An Anthology of Texts* (New York: D.C. Heath, 1991); and Edward H. Judge, *Easter in Kishinev: Anatomy of a Pogrom* (New York: New York University Press, 1992).

On politics, see Ezra Mendelsohn, *On Modern Jewish Politics* (New York: Oxford University Press, 1993); David Vital, *A People Apart: A Political History of the Jews in Europe, 1789–1939* (Oxford: Oxford University Press, 1999); Eli Lederhendler, *The Road to Modern Jewish Politics: Political Tradition and Political Reconstruction in the Jewish Community of Tsarist Russia* (New York: Oxford University Press, 1989); Jonathan Frankel, *Prophecy and Politics: Socialism, Nationalism, and the Russian Jews, 1862–1917* (Cambridge, England: Cambridge University Press, 1981); Michael Stanislawski, *Tsar Nicholas I and the Jews: The Transformation of Jewish Society in Russia, 1825–1855* (Philadelphia: Jewish Publication Society of America, 1983); Michael Berkowitz, *Zionist Culture and West European Jewry Before the First World War* (Cambridge, England: Cambridge University Press, 1993); Arthur Hertzberg, *The Zionist Idea: A Historical Analysis and Reader* (Philadelphia: Jewish Publication Society of America, 1959); Michael Brenner, *Zionism: A Brief History* (Princeton, NJ: Markus Wiener, 2003); Steven J. Zipperstein, *Elusive Prophet: Ahad Ha-Am and the Origins of Zionism* (Berkeley: University of California Press, 1993); Amos Elon, *Herzl* (New York: Schocken Books, 1975); and Jehuda Reinharz, *Fatherland or Promised Land: The Dilemma of the German Jew, 1893–1914* (Ann Arbor: University of Michigan Press, 1975); Noam Pianko, *Zionism and the Roads Not Taken: Rawidowicz, Kaplan, Kohn* (Bloomington: Indiana University Press, 2010); Joshua M. Karlip, *The Tragedy of a Generation: The Rise and Fall of Jewish Nationalism* in Eastern Europe (Cambridge: Harvard University Press, 2013).

On Jewish society and culture in the nineteenth-century, see Steven E. Aschheim, *Brothers and Strangers: The East European Jew in German and German Jewish Consciousness, 1800–1923* (Madison: University of Wisconsin Press, 1999); John M. Efron, *Medicine and the German Jews: A History* (New Haven, CT: Yale University Press, 2001); John M. Efron, *German Jewry and the Allure of the Sephardic* (Princeton: Princeton University Press, 2016); Mirjam Zadoff, *Next Year in Marienbad: The Lost Worlds of Jewish Spa Culture* (Philadelphia: University of Pennsylvania Press, 2012); Derek J. Penslar, *Shylock's Children: Economics and Jewish Identity in Modern Europe* (Berkeley: University of California Press, 2001); Roni Aaron Bornstein, *Schnorrers: Wandering Jews in Germany, 1850–1914* (Tel Aviv: Dekel, 2013); Steven Beller, *Vienna and the Jews, 1867–1938: A Cultural History* (Cambridge, England: Cambridge University Press, 1989); Marsha L. Rozenblit, *The Jews of Vienna, 1867–1914: Assimilation and Identity* (Albany: State University of New York Press, 1983); David Feldman, *Englishmen and Jews: Social Relations and Political Culture, 1840–1914* (New Haven, CT: Yale University Press, 1994); Nancy L. Green, ed., *Jewish Workers in the Modern Diaspora* (Berkeley: University of California Press, 1988); Nancy L. Green, *The Pletzl of Paris: Jewish Immigrant Workers in the Belle Epoque* (New York: Holmes & Meier, 1986); Irving Howe, *World of Our Fathers* (New York: Harcourt Brace Jovanovich, 1976); Tony Michels, *A Fire in their Hearts: Yiddish Socialists in New York* (Cambridge: Harvard University Press, 2005); Jeffrey S. Gurock, *When Harlem Was Jewish, 1870–1930* (New York: Columbia University Press, 1979); Marion A. Kaplan and Deborah Dash Moore, *Gender and Jewish History* (Bloomington: Indiana University Press, 2011); Benjamin Nathans, *Beyond the Pale: The Jewish Encounter with Late Imperial Russia* (Berkeley: University of California Press, 2002); ChaeRan Y. Freeze, *Jewish Marriage and Divorce in Imperial Russia* (Hanover, NH: University Press of New England, 2002); Olga Litvak, *Conscription and the Search for Modern Russian Jewry* (Bloomington: Indiana University Press, 2006); Jeffrey Veidlinger, *Jewish Public Culture in the Late Russian Empire* (Bloomington: Indiana University Press, 2009); Hillel J. Kieval, *The Making of Czech Jewry: National Conflict and Jewish Society in Bohemia, 1870–1918* (New York: Oxford University Press, 1988); Benjamin Harshav, *Language in Time of Revolution* (Berkeley: University of California Press, 1993); Robert Alter, *Hebrew and Modernity* (Bloomington: Indiana University Press, 1994); Dan Miron, *A Traveler Disguised: The Rise of Modern Yiddish Fiction in the Nineteenth Century* (Syracuse: Syracuse University Press, 1996); Carole B. Balin, *To Reveal Our Hearts: Jewish Women Writers in Tsarist Russia* (Cincinnati: Hebrew Union College Press, 2000); Marion A. Kaplan, *The Making of the Jewish Middle Class: Women, Family, and Identity in Imperial Germany* (New York: Oxford University Press, 1991); George L. Mosse, *German Jews beyond Judaism* (Cincinnati: Hebrew Union College Press, 1985); Aron Rodrigue, *Jews and Muslims: Images of Sephardi and Eastern Jewries in Modern Times* (Seattle: University of Washington Press, 2003); and Aron Rodrigue, *French Jews, Turkish Jews: The Alliance Israélite Universelle and the Politics of Jewish Schooling in Turkey, 1860–1925* (Bloomington: Indiana University Press, 1990).

CHAPTER 4
A WORLD UPENDED

T HE TWENTIETH CENTURY was an age of extremes. Advances in medicine, science, public services, education, labor and safety laws, women's and minority rights improved the lot of millions. At the same time, unprecedented levels of carnage, brutality, and cruelty likewise characterize the era. Across the globe, perpetrators and victims alike came from all racial, ethnic, religious, and class backgrounds.

The twentieth century can be said to have begun with World War I. Up until 1914, the broad patterns of nineteenth-century life—its pace, manners, social hierarchies, and imperial political structures—still prevailed. With the onset of war, however, it soon became apparent that the scale and nature of the conflagration were such that nothing of the old order would survive. Along with millions of young men, it, too, died in the trenches.

Already transformed by the great nineteenth-century historical processes of secularization, acculturation, politicization, migration, and urbanization, Jewish society was further shaken to the core by World War I and its aftermath. Jews in eastern Europe suffered violence and communal devastation during the war, while those in central and western Europe experienced initial patriotic euphoria, the camaraderie soon shattered by the intensification of antisemitism as the war began to go badly for the Central Powers. Yet inspired by nationalism and spiritual revival, Jews in the interwar period created vibrant, modern Jewish cultures that bespoke self-confidence and faith in the future. Others participated in the majority cultures as scientists, entrepreneurs, writers, journalists, musicians, actors, and directors. Their work was not Jewish in any definable way, but the disproportionate presence of Jews in these fields of endeavor nevertheless saw them bring to their creative activities the attitude of the marginalized—a willingness to not follow conventions and to create something entirely new. Sigmund Freud, typical of such Jews, declared in a 1926 address to the B'nai B'rith Lodge (of which he was a member) that what he found most appealing about Jews and what he shared with his people was their fierce independence, born of their being outsiders: "As a Jew I was prepared to join the Opposition and to do without agreement with the 'compact majority.'" Indeed, whether as young Zionists rebelling against their father's assimilation, Communist revolutionaries trying to remake the world, modernist Hebrew poets rebelling against the canon, or

DOI: 10.4324/9781003611608-5

psychoanalysts unearthing the hidden secrets of bourgeois respectability, young Jews in the interwar period very often stood in opposition to the forces of authority, both Jewish and non-Jewish.

WORLD WAR I

World War I erupted on August 1, 1914, and what all Europeans imagined would be a short war dragged on until November 11, 1918. The Allied Powers—made up of the British Empire, France, Russia, and after 1917, the United States—defeated the Central Powers, composed of the German Empire, the Austro-Hungarian Empire, and the Ottoman Empire. At the conclusion of hostilities, the war had completely transformed the map, culture, politics, mentality, and importance of Europe. Approximately nine million people were slaughtered, while nearly 22 million were missing or left crippled and mutilated. European economies were left in tatters, and four empires—the Austro-Hungarian, German, Russian, and Ottoman—had collapsed. To many, European civilization appeared to have completely crumbled.

The impact of the war was felt for decades to come. An entire generation was lost, and for winners and losers alike, the war was an unmitigated disaster. Due to its massive losses, France sought revenge against Germany and exacted a harsh settlement in the Versailles Treaty. Germany's defeat and subsequent humiliation contributed to the climate of resentment responsible for the rise of Nazism. The war also contributed to National Socialism's culture of violence and lust for vengeance. Italian Fascism, too, was a product of the war, while in Russia, with a staggering casualty toll of nine million, the war also provided the opportunity for the Bolshevik

victory. Indeed, many returning soldiers and civilians alike were not only physically damaged but also left brutalized and susceptible to the aggressive messages and exhortations to further violence of radical ideologues, such as Lenin, Mussolini, and Hitler.

Also for European Jewry, the war was a disaster. Like their fellow Europeans, Jews flocked to enlist. Approximately 1.5 million Jewish men fought for their respective homelands. Many died, many more maimed and missing in action. In eastern Europe, there were also substantial losses of Jewish property. In short, the war undermined the very existence of Jewish life—in different ways in both eastern and western Europe.

JEWS ON THE EASTERN FRONT

On the eastern front, the war raged in the heart of the Pale of Settlement and Galicia, home to almost 4 million Jews. In these regions, antisemitism was already strong but was exacerbated by the war, as the local population accused Jews of assisting the enemy. In addition to being denounced and robbed by Poles and Ruthenian peasants, Jewish civilians were treated brutally by Russian and Cossack troops. Despite the fact that some Jews served as officers in the Russian and Rumanian armed services, they were unable to prevent the violence meted out to Jews by invading Russian forces. Jews suffered pogroms, mass rape, theft, forced labor. Implementing a "scorched-earth" policy, the Russians destroyed Jewish homes, businesses, synagogues, and schools. Shtetlekh and villages were particularly hard-hit, especially if the small communities were unable or unwilling to pay protection money to the Russians. In several towns in the heavily Jewish Kielce province, more than 90 percent of the buildings were destroyed. By the spring of 1915, about 100 Jewish communities in the Kingdom of Poland had been completely devastated. Decrees outlawed publishing and theater performance in Yiddish and Hebrew, along with bans on telephone use. Jews were taken hostage and were subject to semi-judicial executions and outright murder, while forced expulsion of Jews also occurred on a massive scale. A Jewish soldier with the Austro-Hungarian army reported thus:

> Whenever the Russians came through, the Christians would put icons in their windows. If there was no icon, the house was therefore Jewish, and the soldiers could destroy it without fear of punishment. When our brigade marched through one village, a soldier spotted a house on a hill, and told our commander that it was probably the home of Jews. The officer allowed him to go and have a look. He returned with the cheerful news that Jews *were* indeed living there. They opened the door and found some twenty Jews half dead with fear. The troops led them out, and the officer gave his order: "Slice them up! Chop them up!" I didn't stay to see what happened next.

Somewhere between 500,000 and 1 million Jews were expelled and moved east behind Russian lines, many given a mere 24 to 48 hours' notice to leave their homes. The Russians took Jewish hostages to ensure that Jewish communities complied with the evacuation orders. Forced deportations precipitated a refugee crisis of enormous proportions. In May 1915, over 100,000 homeless Jews poured into Warsaw alone. Other expulsions, such as those from Galicia and Bukovina—both in the Habsburg Empire—saw vast numbers of Jews driven into the capital cities of Vienna and Budapest, where they existed

in terrible conditions in refugee camps. Jews were unable to return home because eastern Galicia and Bukovina remained in Russian hands until 1917. Central and western Galicia fared even worse, as those areas were so devastated that Jews who fled often had no homes, businesses, or communal institutions to which they could return. The massive international outcry against Russian mistreatment of Jews had the unintended effect of stiffening Russian resolve and increasing the persecution.

The social and material conditions of eastern European Jewry lay in ruins. At least 500,000 Jews served in the Russian army, and about 70,000 men, often the family's sole breadwinner, were killed, while many thousands went missing in action. This left thousands of *agunot* (women whose husbands are either unwilling or unable to grant a bill of divorce). *Agunot* became a serious problem for Jewish society, as rabbinical courts refused to accept proof of widowhood, and thus, remarriage under Jewish law was impossible. For the Jews of eastern Europe, World War I was a defining moment. It devastated economies, fractured families, destroyed Jewish communities, and exposed the vulnerability of eastern European Jewry to violence and persecution on a local and state level.

Jews on the Western Front

Unlike Jews in eastern Europe, those in western and central Europe, like their gentile compatriots, greeted the war with great enthusiasm. Everywhere, Jews flocked to enlist. In Germany, 100,000 men, or 18 percent of the total Jewish population, served; 12,000 of them were killed, and 35,000 were decorated. In the Austro-Hungarian army, some 275,000, or 11 percent of all Jews, fought. On the opposing side, about 41,500 Jews from across the empire fought for

Britain. Of the 10,000 who enlisted as volunteers prior to the institution of conscription in May 1916, 18 percent fought as officers, double the proportion of voluntary recruits to officers in the rest of the British army. The highest-ranking Jewish soldier of World War I was Sir John Monash (1865–1931), commander of the Australian forces. No other Great Power so lavishly rewarded Jews for their heroic efforts. Jews of the British Empire received 5 Victoria Crosses, 50 Distinguished Service Orders, and 240 Military Crosses. In all, approximately 15 percent of Britain's Jewish population fought in the war, in contrast to 11.5 percent for the general British population. In France, 35,000 Jews, or 20 percent of the total Jewish population, joined the army. Jewish women from all over western Europe moved beyond the confines of bourgeois domesticity and volunteered for service, mostly working in clinics, military hospitals, and welfare agencies.

For German Jews, the war was an especially auspicious event, because this was their first opportunity since their legal emancipation in 1871 to make the ultimate sacrifice for their country. They were swept up in the patriotic frenzy that attended the outbreak of hostilities. On Wednesday, August 5, 1914, German Jews of all denominations heeded the emperor's call for a day of prayer. Throughout Germany and Austria, Jews poured into synagogues to celebrate special war services. Over the course of the war, German and Austrian Jewish newspapers of all orientations stressed their patriotic duty. A Zionist newspaper in Vienna declared, "In these trying days the Jews are the truest of the true. No other Austrian nationality is as willing to sacrifice as the Jews." Journalists drew on biblical imagery to bolster Jewish morale, with one Austrian Jewish newspaper telling

its readers on Rosh Hashanah 1914 that the war was a holy one for Jews, and they should recall the *akedah*, the binding of Isaac by his father Abraham, both because it was the New Year and because the patriarch Abraham and Austrian Jewry were alike, as both had been called upon to sacrifice their sons. Jewish soldiers were often described as modern Maccabees. In a eulogy for a Berlin rabbi who fell in battle, the speaker said of the dead chaplain, "German courage and Maccabean heroism came together in his worldview." The book of Psalms was also an inspiration. In 1914, an article titled "The War and the Psalms" appeared in the German-language newspaper *The Truth* and quoted Psalm 144: "Send forth Your hand from on high; redeem me and save me from the mighty waters, from the foreigners' hand, whose mouth speaks falsely, and whose right hand is a right hand of lies." Here, Austrian Jews depicted themselves as biblically sanctioned saviors of Russian Jews. To some extent, the notion that the German and Austrian armies were liberators possessed a grain of truth. They certainly posed as such, even printing posters in Yiddish announcing themselves as liberators. Eastern European Jews, however, were rarely fooled, even when the German general Erich Ludendorff issued a proclamation in Yiddish titled "To My Dear Jews in Poland" (*An mayne libe Yidn in Poyln*). In it he promised Jews protection, freedom, and equality after Germany had won the war. The Jews were right to be skeptical. Freedom and equality did not come their way, and after Germany's defeat, Ludendorff became a radical antisemite and an early supporter of Hitler.

All German and Austrian Jews spoke of duty and service, but perhaps none more enthusiastically than the Orthodox Jew Joseph Wohlgemuth. He drew parallels between Germans and Orthodox Jews, explaining how both were culturally adapted to fighting a patriotic war:

> The fact that Germans, more than other nations, have learned how to obey has made it possible for their leaders to prepare for the anticipated victory and carry it out. The adherent of traditional Judaism possesses this inclination toward lawfulness to an even greater degree. His entire life is oriented to subservience to the law. . . . Always loyal to the law, now too he has fought like a hero and died like a hero, just as the law demands.

A small number of prominent Jews spoke out against the war. After initially supporting the cause, the philosopher Martin Buber (1878–1965) became an opponent, while the scholar of Jewish mysticism Gershom Scholem (1897–1982) and the psychoanalyst Sigmund Freud (1856–1939) were against the war from the start. Scholem's father threw his son out of the house for his pacifism. In a lecture to B'nai B'rith, Freud said that the war was proof that even in the best people, aggressive and egotistical impulses were merely repressed but never entirely absent. The war, he told his audience, truly displayed that even the most cultured Europeans "have not descended as deeply as we fear because they had not risen as high as we believed."

The heady feelings of patriotism experienced by most German Jews soon gave way to disappointment and disillusionment. Just as Jews had drawn on biblical symbolism to justify their efforts and draw closer to their gentile compatriots, non-Jewish Germans drew on Christian symbols to exclude Jews. As the nationalist author Walter Flex observed, "the sacrificial death of the best among our people is but a divinely ordained repetition of the most profound miracle of which the earth knows, the vicarious sufferings of Jesus Christ. The wine of Christ is prepared from German blood."

As the war dragged on and frustration became mixed with chauvinism, German Jewry began to find itself out of touch with prevailing sentiment. Although it was a young Jew, Ernst Lissauer, who wrote "The Hate Song Against England," one of the war's most popular poems and a personal favorite of the kaiser's, the predominately liberal and Anglophile Jewish community rejected it. On the battlefield, too, differences between German and Jewish soldiers began to show. In the trenches, one Jewish soldier wrote, "The Jewish comrade suddenly realized that he felt as if he were discovering an unknown world." That world, according to another Jewish soldier, was one where "the average German simply does not care for the Jew. [He doesn't] want to be anything here but a German soldier—and yet [he is] given no choice but to believe that it is otherwise."

The increasing sense of distance came to a head with the "Jew count" (*Judenzählung*) of 1916. As the war ground on and Germans began to demand explanations for why the quick victory they had been promised had not materialized, accusations came from antisemitic quarters that German military efforts had been compromised because Jews were dodging the draft and shirking service at the front. German Jews were incredulous that they, of all people, could have their loyalty questioned. The Prussian War Ministry conducted the Jew Count, a census to determine whether the charges of draft dodging were true or not. Noting that Jews were serving at the front in disproportionately large numbers, the War Ministry never published the results.

For some, the Jew Count shattered the Jewish illusion that non-Jewish Germans had accepted the process of Jewish acculturation and social integration. The sense of frustration led to greater efforts at Jewish self-assertion. The majority remained patriotic to Germany, but many rededicated themselves to their Jewishness as well. For many young German Jews, the process of reclaiming their Jewish identities had already begun to occur when they encountered Jews on the eastern front. Young German Jews idealized these Polish Jews as authentic representatives of Jewish peoplehood.

A cult of the eastern European Jew developed in the interwar period. For other German Jews, Zionism beckoned in the aftermath of the Jew Count. According to the philosopher Ernst Simon (1899–1988):

> The dream of commonality was over. The deep abyss, which had never disappeared, opened up once more with terrible force. . . . Our vital energy would have drained away completely . . . if Judaism had not spread out its arms to take us back. . . . We had come home; we had once more become Jews. . . . Now we were Zionists, at first without wanting or realizing it.

British Jewry

In Britain, the war allowed for Christian–Jewish social tensions to surface. British Jewry was heterogeneous. The establishment was middle-class, anglicized, and religiously liberal. After 1881, mass emigration from Russia brought about 60,000 working-class, Yiddish-speaking Orthodox Jews to England. Most settled in London's East End, with smaller numbers going to Manchester, Leeds, Liverpool, and Glasgow.

When war broke out, Jews from the British establishment signed up enthusiastically, identifying themselves with the national cause. The official voice of the community was the world's oldest Jewish newspaper, *The Jewish Chronicle*, founded in 1841. As late as 1914, the paper favored neutrality, but when war was declared, the paper changed its stance, declaring on August 7, 1914, "England has been all she could be to Jews, Jews will be all they can be to England."

Still, great discomfort with the cause persisted among Jews. Most members of the native Jewish community had their roots in Germany. Many still had family and business interests there. Some community leaders, such as Lord Rothschild and Lucien Wolf, openly objected to Britain's entente with the hated tsarist regime. Antisemites attacked them, and despite professions of loyalty as well as a rash of name changes to more English and less German-sounding ones, hostility against Jews was on the rise. In May 1915, when the British ship RMS *Lusitania* was sunk by a German submarine, East Londoners rioted for three days, smashing and looting German- and Austrian-owned shops. Charges of Jewish cowardice and shirking accompanied anti-German hostilities. This tense situation was compounded by the refusal of many immigrant families to volunteer their sons for the army. Few Russian Jewish immigrants wished to risk their sons' lives, defending Russia, Britain's ally.

With the imposition of conscription in April 1916, British-born sons of immigrants were called up, but not men of military age (18 to 41) who had been born in the Russian Empire. Approximately 30,000 Jewish men were thus exempt, classified as friendly aliens. This discrepancy exacerbated tensions between native and immigrant Jews and between Jews and non-Jews. In June 1917, a pogrom took place in Leeds. A mob numbering several thousand destroyed Jewish homes and looted shops in the city's Jewish section. By the Jewish New Year, tensions were so inflamed that, in September, about 3,000 Jews and gentiles fought each other in the streets with bats and iron bars.

While the war exposed fault lines within the Jewish community and the vulnerability of Jews to popular animosity, the state continued to promote and defend Jews, never countenancing the attitude of the mob. Moreover, a British victory would spell the end of Ottoman dominance in the Middle East. The Zionist movement would be the great beneficiary of these developments as it was moving to the center stage in British Jewish communal politics.

THE JEWS OF INTERWAR EUROPE

After the end of World War I, Zionism, Bundism, territorialism, and other forms of Jewish nationalism captured the hearts of European and Middle Eastern Jewry. Under grave threat in the new states that emerged in the wake of the war, Jews from Europe to the Middle East were subjected to exclusion, economic boycott, discrimination, and physical violence. They responded in a number of ways, including establishing self-defense units, immigration, political activism within a Jewish sphere, and also as part of central and eastern European revolutionary movements. Some promoted Jewish territorial separation, while others embarked on an intense engagement with Jewish culture conducted at a high level and at a feverish pace. It is one of the great paradoxes of the modern

Jewish experience that as Jews were faced with increasing threats, discrimination, economic ruin, and violence in both central and eastern Europe, they were phenomenally productive in the cultural sphere. In particular, secular Jewish culture flourished in Germany, Poland, and the Soviet Union. In Poland, Jewish religious culture also continued to thrive.

After the Paris Peace Conference of 1919 that rearranged the map of Europe, new states emerged from the ruins of the German, Austro-Hungarian, Russian, and Ottoman Empires. Among the new states were Poland, the Soviet Union, Czechoslovakia, Hungary, Lithuania, Latvia, Estonia, Rumania, Greece, and Yugoslavia. Though all were founded on democratic and universal principles, the majority failed to live up to the ideals enshrined in their written constitutions and, by the 1930s, had become authoritarian regimes. (The only exception was Czechoslovakia.) Right-wing nationalists preached an integral nationalism that tended to favor the dominant ethnic, religious, and language groups in the country. As a result, Jews were increasingly shut out of the new economies and societies by a systematic process of discrimination. In Russia, the situation was markedly different, as the Bolshevik Revolution completely changed the nature of Jewish life, opening up many avenues of opportunity for social and cultural integration and shutting many others in terms of Jewish culture and politics.

Violence against Jews also marked the interwar period. In Poland, over a hundred pogroms occurred by 1919, the biggest in Lvov, where 70 Jews were murdered. Similar outrages occurred in Hungary and Lithuania. The scale of carnage was greatest, however, in Ukraine. Despite the facts that minority rights were guaranteed; that Jews were represented in the central government, or Rada; that they enjoyed considerable autonomy; and that Yiddish was even printed on the Ukrainian currency, the locals everywhere accused Jews of spying for the Bolsheviks. In a time of food shortages, requisitions, and fear of the Bolsheviks, Ukrainian peasants and Cossacks turned on Jews. The pogromists had different reasons for hating the Jews. According to historian Jeffrey Veidlinger, some blamed them "for the communist onslaught, some blamed the Jews for the war; some blamed the Jews for the economic collapse, and others blamed the Jews simply for being Jews."

Whatever the reason, looting, rape, and murder took place on an unprecedented scale. The situation was so horrific that the Federation of Ukrainian Jews in America held a convention in New York to draw attention to the atrocities. Attended by 800 delegates, the goal of the attendees was to mobilize assistance for the victims as well as to garner the political and diplomatic support of the government of the United States. Reporting on the gathering, the headline in *The New York Times* on September 8, 1919, bore the ominous words, "6,000,000 Are in Peril," which had been drawn from the dramatic statement made to the convention by the president of the Federation, Joseph Seff:

We come out now before the world with the determined slogan "Those pogroms must stop." It is only a question of holding these facts continually before the civilized world; we must not permit the world to slumber. This fact that the population of 6,000,000 souls in Ukrainia and in Poland have received notice through action and by word that they are going to be completely exterminated—this fact stands before the whole world as the paramount issue of the present day.

Between 1919 and 1921, at least 100,000 Jews were killed in pogroms, and at least that many girls and women were raped.

Among Jews, Ukrainian Minister of Defense Semion Petlura was widely regarded as responsible for the pogroms, for while he never ordered them, he never attempted to halt them either and even went so far as to justify them. In an act of vengeance, Sholom Shvartsbard, a Jewish refugee from the pogroms in Paris, who had lost 14 family members in a pogrom, murdered Petlura in the French capital in 1926. Shooting him on the street three times, Shvartsbard exclaimed with each pull of the trigger, "This, for the pogroms; this, for the massacres; this, for the victims." He was tried and acquitted by a French jury, which held that he had committed a "crime of passion."

Everywhere, Jews tasted new freedoms yet, paradoxically, saw antisemitism on the rise. In 1918, the German Empire collapsed, Kaiser Wilhelm fled to Holland, and the Weimar Republic (1919–1933)—Germany's first real experiment in liberal democracy—came into existence. Under Weimar, the last vestiges of exclusion were lifted and the nation's 564,000 Jews enjoyed unprecedented access to coveted positions in the state and society. Some Jews placed their hopes in socialist revolution. On November 7, 1918, Kurt Eisner overthrew the Bavarian government and became prime minister. Eisner declared Bavaria a socialist republic, but one that, in contrast to what the Bolsheviks had done in Russia, would protect private property. He was assassinated by the nationalist Anton Graf von Arco auf Valley in 1919, while Ernst Toller, who was later found guilty of high treason for assisting Eisner, became one of the most important pacifists, poets, and playwrights of the interwar period. Not long after the Nazis rose to power and Toller fled Germany (he committed suicide in

1933), the propaganda minister, Josef Goebbels, declared, "Two million German soldiers rise from the graves of Flanders and Holland to indict the Jew Toller for having written: 'the ideal of heroism is the stupidest ideal of all.'" The Jewish anarchist Gustav Landauer also preached a new pacifist dawn and was assassinated for it. Standing at the center of the political spectrum, the Jewish lawyer Hugo Preuss wrote the liberal constitution of the Weimar Republic, which was often referred to by Nazis and other right-wing parties as the *Judenrepublik* ("Jew Republic"). In 1922, the Jewish industrialist Walter Rathenau became foreign minister, an unprecedented achievement for a Jew. But his assassination by right-wing extremists that same year also indicates the fragile nature of Jewish life in the public eye. As radicalism took root and Left and Right battled each other for supremacy in the unstable political and economic conditions of postwar Germany, those on the Right were particularly keen to hold Jews responsible for Germany's defeat and postwar suffering. In this environment, antisemitism reached vicious heights.

Interwar Jewry: The Numbers

As a result of the combined impact of mass immigration, the social and economic dislocation caused by World War I, and the economic warfare waged against Jews in the interwar period, European Jewry declined as a percentage of the European population but, remarkably, increased in sheer numbers. In 1900, 82 percent of all Jews lived in Europe. By 1925, it was 62 percent, while, by 1939, only 57 percent of Jews were to be found there. Despite this important trend, more than nine million Jews lived in Europe in 1925. Nearly everywhere, they were a very visible presence in society and the economy. In the fields of law and medicine, Jews were especially prominent. Jews were drawn to them because, as professions, they were open to Jews and because they were high-status avenues into the middle class. Since they were members of a long-marginalized and derided minority group, becoming a doctor or a lawyer conferred respectability upon a generation of Jews desperate for social acceptance. In Budapest, they were 51 percent of the lawyers, 49 percent in Odessa, and about 40 percent in Berlin. In Vienna and Budapest, respectively, 63 percent of all doctors were Jews. In Germany in the 1920s, medical specialties were still in their relevant infancy. However, while 26 percent of gentile doctors were specialists, that figure for Jewish physicians was 52 percent. This led to wild charges that Jews were destroying the holistic nature of medicine as it had been traditionally practiced. That was the view of antisemites and many in the medical establishment. By contrast, specialized knowledge may explain why large numbers of non-Jews in major cities were quite likely to have had a Jewish doctor. Even though interwar Polish Jewry can be classified as having been lower-middle-class and proletarian, Jewish professionals and intellectuals, perhaps totaling 300,000 people altogether, were important and highly visible. In 1931, of all of Poland's physicians, 56 percent were Jews (4,488). In Polish cities, the picture is even more startling. In Cracow, Jews constituted 61 percent of physicians, 66 percent in Warsaw, 71 percent in Lvov, 74 percent in Vilna, and 83 percent in Lodz, Poland's second-largest city. Jews constituted 43 percent of Poland's teachers, 33 percent of her lawyers, and 22 percent of her journalists (*see* Map 4.1).

Across Europe, Jews were also highly visible in the business sector, with 60 percent of all German Jews engaged in commerce, compared to about 16 percent for non-Jews. In 1920, Budapest's 215,000 Jews formed

190
THE JEWS IN THE MODERN AGE

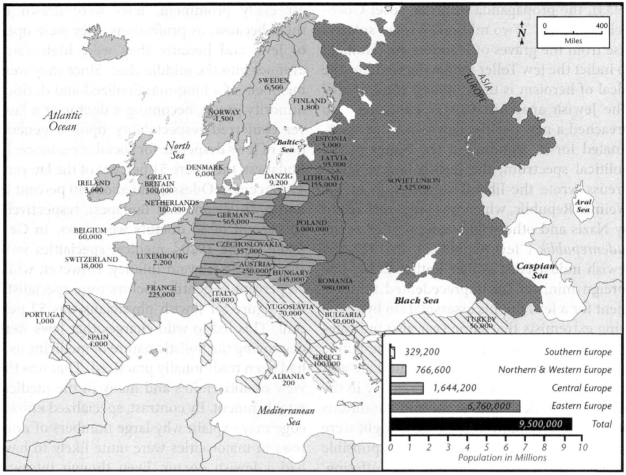

Map 4.1 The Jews of interwar Europe. In 1933, the total world Jewish population was 15.3 million. Of this number, 60 percent, or 9.5 million, lived in Europe. Of the 9.5 million, about 5.5 million Jews lived in Poland and Russia.

Europe's second-largest Jewish community. (Only Warsaw with 219,000 had a bigger Jewish population, a number that swelled to 352,659 by 1931.) In the Hungarian capital, Jews made up 23 percent of the total population but controlled 60 percent of the city's commerce. Nearly 65 percent of all bankers and executives in the financial sector were Jewish, while 88 percent of the members of the stock exchange were Jewish. Perhaps as much as 90 percent of all Hungarian industry was financed by privately owned Jewish banks. By contrast, while 60 percent of Hungarians were involved in agriculture, only 4

percent of Jews were, and while 44 percent of Jews were involved in trade, only 4 percent of Hungarians were similarly engaged. In Czechoslovakia, Romania, Italy, and Greece, the proportion of Jews involved in commerce was similarly high. In Poland, most Jews who were not members of the professions were employed in the commercial and industrial sectors. In certain areas, such as Galicia, Jews constituted almost the entire commercial class. On the whole, however, none of this served to make the Jews wealthy. Families such as the Rothschilds and the Sassoons were exceptions. Rather, the economic activities of Jews made most in western and central Europe comfortable, while the majority in eastern Europe and the Middle East remained poor. Yet despite economic realities, interwar political and economic conditions across Europe made all Jews objects of envy and hatred by nationalist political groups.

In terms of trade, Jews were to be found concentrated in leather goods, textiles, clothing, and shoe manufacture. One field that attracted Jews was cosmetics. Firms such as Max Factor and Helena Rubenstein, though founded before World War I, all became internationally famous in the interwar period. In Germany, Nivea, the skin cream invented in 1911 by the Jewish scientists Isaac Lifschütz and Paul Unna, was repackaged in 1925 in the now-famous blue-and-white container and soon became a household product worldwide. Another commercial phenomenon closely associated with Jewish entrepreneurs was the department store. In Paris, Berlin, and Vienna, these consumer emporiums provided shopping opportunities for middle-class customers. What these professional and commercial characteristics show is that by the interwar period, Jews had made very significant economic strides, especially in western Europe.

In eastern Europe, despite the desperate conditions caused by World War I, Jews remained integral to the local postwar economies, and in the Soviet Union, they enjoyed a level of occupational freedom that they had not previously known. The 3.3 million Jews of Poland, who comprised about 10 percent of the total population, paid approximately 40 percent of all taxes: little wonder, given the fact that in 1931, in a small city such as Tarnopol, of the 19,667 economically active persons in the city, 92.5 percent were Jews. In the larger city of Bialystok, of the 16,354 people involved in commerce, 84.5 percent were Jews, while in the capital, Warsaw, 33,910 people were actively involved in commerce, of whom 75 percent were Jews. In Romania (662,779), Hungary (450,000), Lithuania (157,500), Latvia (95,675), and Estonia (4,500), the Jews of east-central Europe were essentially the productive and commercially active middle class. By contrast, in nearly all these countries, the majority of non-Jews were still tied to rural economies.

Not only did Jews differ from non-Jews occupationally; their patterns of domicile also differed significantly from the majority. By 1930, nearly 30 percent of all Jews were to be found in a mere 19 cities worldwide. Few ethnic groups were as resolutely urban as the Jewish people. By the 1930s, 90 percent of Latvian, 85 percent of German, 80 percent of Hungarian, 75 percent of Polish, and 70 percent of Rumanian Jews lived in cities. Very often, they were found in capitals: Copenhagen (92 percent), Paris (70 percent), Vienna (67 percent), and London (67 percent). Though not the capital of the United States, New York, by the interwar period, was 25 percent Jewish, thus making it the largest Jewish city in the world. In all, prior to World War II, only 1 to 2 percent of all Jews earned a livelihood from agriculture.

Soviet Russia Between the Wars

In November 1917, Vladimir Lenin and Leon Trotsky led the Bolshevik Revolution, and tsarist Russia was transformed into the Soviet Union. The Revolution was a mixed blessing for Jews. Never before had so much oppression been inflicted alongside the granting of so much liberation, especially in the early phase—the February Revolution—which saw the Jews of Russia finally emancipated and the Pale of Settlement abolished forever. Judaism and secular Jewish culture fared less well than did Soviet Jews as individuals, who now enjoyed access to new occupations, professions, and education in a way unimaginable to their forebears in tsarist Russia. They also enjoyed a good measure of physical protection too, as the Red Army sought to save Jews from pogroms. Throughout the 1920s, the Soviet regime actively fought against antisemitism, which it saw as a primitive by-product of capitalist exploitation.

But political expressions of national Jewish identity were dealt with severely. As was the case with politics in general, all Jewish political activity was crushed as the Bolsheviks grabbed the monopoly on power and shut down the Russian branch of the Bund and various Zionist parties. Further alienation was caused by the Marxist atheism of the Bolshevik Revolution, which led to a direct assault on traditional Judaism. By the early 1920s, the Jewish section of the Communist Party (Yevsektsia) had systematically closed down about 1,000 Hebrew schools and 650 synagogues and religious schools. Jewish religious life was essentially snuffed out or forced underground. In the most radical expression of the goals of the French Revolution, the Jews were to disappear as a religious-ethnic collectivity but enjoy rights as individual Soviet citizens. Despite its zeal and commitment to Communism, the Yevsektsia was always suspect in the eyes of Soviet authorities. It was shut down in 1930, charged with Jewish nationalism, and most of its leaders were eventually imprisoned or executed during the Stalinist purges of 1936–1938. The suffering of Jews and Judaism under the Soviets led many to quip, "The Trotskys make the revolution and the Bronshteyns pay for it," a reference to Trotsky's original family name—Bronshteyn.

In the 1920s, the Soviet Union, which believed that language, more than any other characteristic, defined nationhood, poured considerable resources into promoting social, political, and cultural institutions in the languages of its many ethnic groups. The aim was to indoctrinate each minority in the teachings and ways of the new state. While the Soviets dismissed Hebrew and Zionism as expressions of Jewish reaction, Yiddish culture thrived in the interwar period. Admittedly, much of it was of dubious worth, as Yiddish writers and journalists produced propaganda, often virulently anti-religious, in the service of the Revolution. Yiddish writers and linguists even changed the orthography of Yiddish so as to erase the Hebrew spelling of those words in Yiddish that were derived from Hebrew. Still, there was much that was of high quality, and the Soviet Union was the only country in the world to have state-sponsored Yiddish institutions, among them, schools, courts, and publishing houses.

Alongside the pedestrian outpourings of Soviet propaganda in Yiddish, brilliant works of art appeared, especially Expressionist literature and poetry. A thriving Yiddish publishing industry emerged. In 1924, only 76 books and pamphlets appeared. By 1930, that number had increased to 531. Over the same period, the number of Yiddish newspapers increased from 21 to around 40. An important site of Soviet Jewish cultural production was the State Jewish Theater in Moscow. With Jewish actors such as Shlomo Mikhoels, one of the greatest interpreters of *King Lear* in any language, and the celebrated artist Marc Chagall as set designer, the Soviet Jewish Theater produced stunning works while introducing Jewish themes into Soviet culture. In so doing, it promoted a "distinct Jewish identity." Once seen by historians as a mere propaganda tool, the theater's deployment of "national forms—languages, myths, archetypes, and symbols—were semiotic systems that aroused pre-existing emotions and expectations among [Jewish] audiences familiar with the codes." Because the productions were in Yiddish, Soviet Jews often interpreted them as being more than mere propaganda. They were seen as distinctly and authentically Jewish. Just as the Soviet Union was in the process of creating a new man, *Homo sovieticus*, so too were the interwar producers of Soviet Yiddish culture creating a new form of Jew, the Soviet Jew. In 1926, the leading figure among Soviet Yiddish writers, Dovid Bergelson, declared in his article "Three Centers" that the Soviet Union, in contrast to assimilationist America and decaying Poland, would be the future homeland of Jewish culture.

In the field of Soviet Yiddish literature, Yiddish modernism began in 1917–1918 in Kiev with the group *Eygns* (Our Own). After that time, Yiddish avant-garde groups were to be found in Moscow, Warsaw, and Berlin—in writers' circles, such as *Yung Yidish* (*Young Yiddish*), *Khalyastre* (*The Gang*), and *Shtrom* (*The Current*); and among those who published journals such as *Oyfgang* (*Ascent or Sunrise*) and *Milgroym* (*Pomegranate*). Until 1932, when the Communist Party forced all writers into the Union of Soviet Writers, great artistic and ideological diversity had been the norm among Yiddish writers in the Soviet Union. The demand for conformity compromised what had been an exciting quest for artistic experimentation.

Those Jews who produced Soviet Yiddish culture occupied a particularly delicate position. On one hand, they were both part of the state apparatus and proponents of the regime; on the other, by working in the Yiddish language, Jewish cultural activists played an important role in reaffirming and preserving a distinct form of Jewish identity. As adherents of Soviet language theory, many Yiddishists believed that the language reflected Jewish identity. As Esther Frumkina, a Soviet

Yiddish activist, observed in 1923, "[w]hether it is beaming or laughing, serious and harsh or soft and dreamy, dry or damp—[Yiddish] is always a divine work of art, always a picture of the people that created it."

Yet despite state support, Yiddish culture showed signs of decline, as young Soviet Jews displayed a preference for Russian. Sales of Yiddish newspapers were poor; by the end of the 1920s, total circulation of the three largest dailies was only 28,000. Few people read the works of the prominent Yiddish modernists, the Yiddish-reading public still preferring the classics of Yiddish literature and even Yiddish translations of European classics above the latest avant-garde Yiddish offerings. With the destruction of the religious school system, the only Jewish educational alternative were the secular Yiddish schools, with 366 such institutions in 1924 and 1,100 in 1930. Student enrollment over that period increased from 54,000 to 130,000, but these children tended to be in Ukraine and Belorussia. In the Russian Republic, which had few Jews before the large postrevolution migration, less than 17 percent of Jewish students were enrolled in Yiddish schools. Even religious Jews tended to send their children to non-Jewish schools because there the atheist message denigrated all religions and not especially Judaism, as was the case in Yiddish schools. A prominent slogan displayed in Yiddish schools read, "He who does not work, does not eat," a reference to the "unproductive" Torah scholar. That Yiddish schools only existed at the elementary level further discouraged Jewish parents from sending their children to such institutions. Entrance to secondary schools (and, naturally, university) required Russian. Even though some party cells, courts, and trade unions conducted their affairs in Yiddish, most operated in Russian. Increasingly, Jews considered Russian prestigious, while Yiddish and Hebrew were thought of as cultural remnants from the shtetl. Advancement in all spheres of Soviet society was dependent on mastery of Russian, and that is the cultural route upon which most Jews embarked. It was not just educated Jews who took seriously the message that, by abandoning Yiddish and adopting Russian, social rewards lay in store. As a Jewish porter remarked at a transport workers' union meeting in 1924: "For many years I have carried hundreds of pounds on my back day in and day out. Now I want to learn some Russian and become an office worker." Deepening acculturation among Soviet Jews was another reason that the Yevsektsia was dismantled in 1929. There was simply no longer a need for a Yiddish-speaking section of the party.

Until World War II, Jews tended to enjoy more favorable treatment within the context of Soviet nationality policy than other ethnic groups. Like Poles and Germans, Jews were seen as Western. A large intellectual class and a very high literacy rate meant that, in Soviet eyes, Jews were "advanced." Significant numbers had been convinced socialists even before the Bolshevik Revolution, and thus, they were granted greater autonomy than those ethnic minorities the Soviets considered more backward and in greater need of cultural re-education. One problem for Soviet theoreticians of nationality policy was the landlessness of Jews. Here, they were said to resemble "gypsies" more than Germans. Members of the Yiddish intelligentsia—and here they concurred with their archenemies, the Zionists—also found the Jews' lack of territory problematic. To solve the anomalousness of the Jewish situation, Yiddish intellectuals pushed for the formation of a Jewish territory in the Soviet Union. The regime also saw merit in the idea.

In 1928, Stalin implemented his Five-Year Plan, a program of agricultural collectivization and rapid industrialization, designed to quickly modernize Russia. Stalin also sought to encourage socialism among the nationality cultures through a mixture of compulsion and reward. To attract Jews to the agricultural aspect of the scheme, the Soviets decided to create a Jewish territory in the vast, isolated area called Birobidzhan. It lay on the Soviet border with China. This region was chosen for four reasons: (1) to redirect recently arrived Jewish farmers away from agricultural settlements in Ukraine, Belarus, and Crimea, where their presence agitated locals; (2) to buffer the Soviet Union from Chinese and Japanese expansionism by creating Soviet settlement in Russia's far east; (3) to exploit the region's natural resources; and (4) to gain international recognition for the Soviets having established the very first Jewish national homeland.

A massive social engineering project, Birobidzhan was elevated in 1934 to the status of a Jewish Autonomous Region (JAR). In addition to those from Russia, Jews from Argentina, Lithuania, and the United States came and settled, desiring to participate in the great experiment. Ultimately, the Communist Party's goal was to establish an autonomous Jewish territory that promoted secular Jewish culture rooted in both Yiddish and socialist principles. The idea was to provide an alternative to Zionism and settlement in Palestine. Birobidzhan boasted Yiddish schools, newspapers, and cultural institutions. The regional government also printed street signs, railway station signs, and postmarks in both Yiddish and Russian. In 1935, the government decreed that all government documents, including public notices, announcements, posters, and advertisements, had to appear in both Yiddish and Russian, and in 1946, the city's main thoroughfare was renamed Sholem Aleichem Street. But the dismal conditions failed to attract large numbers of Jews. (The Jewish population peaked in 1948 at about 30,000, one-quarter of the total population.) Land had been neither surveyed nor drained and was mostly unsuitable for farming, and as such, by 1939, less than a quarter of the Jews worked in agriculture, most having moved into traditional Jewish occupations in the service industries. In the end, Stalin's purges of 1936–1938 destroyed the Jewish experiment, as the JAR's Jewish leaders were arrested for "counter-revolutionary" activities. Even the wife of the region's Jewish Communist Party head, Matvei Khavkin, was imprisoned, accused of spiking her homemade gefilte fish with poison and feeding it to the secretary of the Central Committee of the Communist Party, Lazar Kaganovich, during his visit to the JAR in 1936. From an internal Jewish perspective, the Birobidzhan project was always doomed to failure, as the rapidly assimilating Jewish youth of the Soviet Union were uninterested in returning to what looked to many like a latter-day version of the Pale of Settlement.

Yet with all the opportunity and temptation offered by the Soviet state also came danger. With members of the Russian intelligentsia fleeing in the wake of the Revolution, a substantial number of men of Jewish background filled the ranks of revolutionary leadership. Among them were Leon Trotsky, basically second in command to Vladimir Lenin; Gregory Zinoviev, leading theoretician, head of the Comintern, and one of the most powerful men in the Soviet Union following Lenin's death in 1924; Yakov Sverdlov, head of the All-Russian Executive Committee; and Lev Kamenev, a member and chairman (1923–1924) of the party's five-man ruling Politburo. The apparatus of Stalinist coercion, the Soviet secret police, or NKVD, also had a disproportionate Jewish presence. In January 1937, 42 of the top NKVD officials were Jews. The NKVD was divided into 20 separate directorates; 12 of them (60 percent) were run by Jews. Until 1938, the Soviet Foreign Service was almost exclusively Jewish. The reason for the disproportionate Jewish presence in the government and secret police had nothing to do with a particular Jewish penchant or desire to exact revenge on those who had discriminated against their ancestors in the Pale of Settlement. Rather, the prominence of Jews was a result of their having made the most of opportunities for advancement that opened up after the Revolution. Despite their origins, Jews in positions of power had next to no regard for Judaism or sympathy for the plight of the Jewish people. Nevertheless, their prominence ensured that the Bolshevik Revolution would be associated with Jews in the minds of the Revolution's enemies and antisemites thereafter. The fact that 72 percent of Bolshevik Party members in 1922 were ethnic Russians, and that it was Latvians who provided the highest rate of ethnic overrepresentation, counted for little in terms of Russian and foreign perceptions of the revolution. Everywhere, it was seen as a Jewish plot.

Although the Bolsheviks failed to win the support or sympathy of the Jewish masses, Jews took advantage of the new freedoms and opportunities that came their way, especially in the revolution's early phase. The changed circumstances made for the creation of a new form of radically secular Jewish identity, and a sort of Jewish subculture emerged. Soviet Jews came to occupy a disproportionate presence in the intellectual, scientific, and cultural life of the nation. In this respect, Soviet Jewry, in a strictly sociological sense, came to replicate German or American Jewry, even considering the vast political, social, and economic disparities among these examples.

The changes to Jewish life engendered by the Revolution were dramatic and transformed the face of Russian Jewry. Jews were no longer prevented from living in certain areas. By 1939, 40 percent of Jews had left the area that had been the Pale of Settlement. About 1,300,000 Jews lived in parts of Russia that had been off-limits to them as recently as 1917. In 1912, Moscow had a Jewish population of 15,300. In 1939, it was about 250,000. On the eve of World War II, 87 percent of all Soviet Jews were urban dwellers, and half of them were to be found in the largest 11 cities. Urbanization was accompanied by economic advancement, thanks to Lenin's introduction of the liberalizing New Economic Policy of 1921. While they were less than 2 percent of the total Soviet population, Jews were 20 percent of all private traders by 1926. They were also 40 percent of artisans (mostly tailors). The industrialization of the first Five-Year Plan also altered the social profile of Jews, as they left areas of traditional Jewish settlement for the Soviet Union's new industrial cities. Between 1926 and 1935, the number of Jewish salary and wage earners tripled, reaching a high of 1.1 million in the latter year.

More literate than Russians—85 percent compared to 58 percent in 1926—Jews were well prepared to take advantage of the opportunities the Revolution afforded. With free access to education and the elimination of the pre-revolutionary elite, the Soviet Union became an intellectual meritocracy for members of the formerly "exploited classes," a category in which many Jews found themselves. By 1939, 26 percent of all Soviet Jews had a high school education, compared to 8 percent of the total population. Jews were to be found in the two upper grades of Soviet high schools at a rate of 3.5 times their share of the general population. At universities, even though the proportion of Jewish students declined with the overall opening up of admissions and the implementation of certain programs that gave preference to "indigenous" nationalities in non-Russian republics, Jews continued to disproportionately fill the ranks of university students. Between 1929 and 1939, the number of Jews attending university rose from 22,500 to 98,000, 11 percent of the total or five times their percentage of the total population.

Where discrimination had kept Jews away from state employment under the tsars, urbanization, education, and loyalty to the Bolshevik regime saw Jews become white-collar state employees after the Soviet Revolution. Considering all bureaucrats who had served the tsarist regime as untrustworthy, highly literate and well-educated Jews were seen as indispensable to the Revolution. Lenin observed:

> The fact that there were many Jewish intelligentsia members in the Russian cities was of great importance to the revolution. They put an end to the general sabotage that we were confronted with after the October Revolution. . . . It was only thanks to this pool of a rational and literate labor force that we succeeded in taking over the state apparatus.

By 1939, 82 percent of all employed Jews in Moscow and 63 percent of those in Leningrad were in state service. In all, there were 364,000 such Jewish workers in the Soviet Union on the eve of World War II. They were mostly bookkeepers, technicians, engineers, teachers, and those classified as "cultural and artistic workers."

Soviet Jews also filled the ranks of the professional classes. By 1939, in Moscow and Leningrad, Jews comprised about 70 percent of all dentists, nearly 60 percent of pharmacists, 45 percent of defense lawyers, 40 percent of physicians, 31 percent of all writers, journalists, and editors, and just under 20 percent of all scientists and university professors. In the performing arts, nearly 25 percent of all musicians and 12 percent of artists, actors, and directors were Jews. The presence of Jews in the public life and culture of the Soviet Union was unmistakable.

The state's official support of Yiddish culture in the interwar period notwithstanding, the Soviet Union quickly advanced the Russification of the Jews, a process that was already underway toward the end of the nineteenth century. In 1926, only a quarter of the Jews declared Russian as their "native language." By 1939, that number had risen to 55 percent. Urbanization, increased educational opportunities, the atheism of the Revolution, and the campaign against antisemitism all contributed to increasing contact between Jews and Russians. This, in turn, led to a dramatic rise in the intermarriage rate. Between 1924 and 1936, the rate of mixed marriages for Jewish men increased from 2 to 12.6 percent in Belorussia, from 3.7 to 15.3 percent in Ukraine, and from 17.4 to 42 percent in the Russian Republic. By the outbreak of World War II, most Russian Jews were, to varying degrees, literate in both Russian and Jewish culture, the latter in either its secular or religious forms. The Nazi war of annihilation left millions of these Yiddish-speaking Jews dead. Those Russian Jews not immediately caught in the onslaught tended to be the more Russified Jews, those who lived in big cities, deeper inside Russia's interior. This, too, sped up the process whereby Soviet Jews became less identifiably Jewish through traditional markers, such as language use and religious practice. As in western Europe, however, the intellectual and cultural presence of Soviet Jews was so noticeable that they retained the appearance of a distinct caste.

Soviet Jewish distinctiveness extended to relations with Jews abroad. Throughout the 1920s, contact had been maintained through American aid organizations that assisted Soviet Jews. In the 1930s, as the Great Purge (1934–1939) spread fear and terror through the Soviet Union, Jews found themselves increasingly isolated. Even though the purges were not aimed at Jews per se, and many of those who conducted purges were Jewish (they later became victims themselves), Jews were always particularly vulnerable to charges of "internationalism" and disloyalty. With relatives abroad, they had to be particularly careful about contact with the outside Jewish world. Displaying too great an interest in Jewish culture, which was increasingly dismissed as "petit bourgeois nationalism," was also extremely risky. All Jewish political and cultural expressions were scrutinized for "errors" and "deviations" from orthodox Marxist-Leninist principles. With so many Jews in positions of political and cultural prominence, they were also disproportionately represented among those purged. The liberation experienced by Russian Jewry during the first phase of the Bolshevik Revolution was eventually supplanted by fear, discrimination, and persecution. This was the lot that faced most Russians under Stalin and beyond, but the sense that they had been betrayed by the Revolution was especially acute among Jews, because few ethnic groups in Russia had experienced such a meteoric rise after the events of 1917.

Poland Between the Wars

In the new postwar national economies, fear of Jewish competition and propaganda about Jewish exploitation led to economic discrimination and the imposition of quotas against Jews. According to the 1931 government census, there were 3.1 million Jews in Poland, the largest Jewish population in Europe outside of Soviet Russia. Economically, the periods 1919–1923 and 1936–1938 were especially bad. Jews were usually the only link between the village producer in Poland and more distant markets. Peasants did try to sell some goods in the nearest towns, but those markets were too small, and the peasants had neither the know-how nor the connections to compete in more distant markets. The consequences of the worldwide Depression created an economic crisis in western Poland, the country's more industrially developed region. The shrinking economy prompted consumer demand for cheap goods, and Jewish peddlers were well situated to roam the countryside, selling their wares door to door. In these difficult economic circumstances, Jewish merchants and peddlers, with low operating costs, competed for the small customer base with non-Jews, thereby exacerbating long-standing cultural and religious tensions.

The overall structure of the Polish economy was fragile, and both Jews and Poles struggled to make ends meet. Outright discrimination made the Jewish situation especially precarious. Already in 1919, the Parliament had declared Sunday to be an official day of rest, meaning, that Jews would not trade on Saturdays and could not trade on Sundays. In retaliation for their heavy presence and as part of the scheme to nationalize industries, Jews were dismissed from government jobs. All but 400 of the 4,000 Jews who worked on the Polish railroads were fired, while all 6,000 employed in the lumber industry likewise lost their jobs. Of 20,000 people employed by the city of Warsaw, whose Jewish population was 30 percent of the city's total, only 50 Jews were employed in government service. The situation was so bad that thousands left, especially to Palestine, Australia, and Latin America, significantly changing the face of Jewish life the world over. In 1934, the chief rabbi of

Radzilow, Yehoshuah Gelgor, wrote a desperate letter to Nehemiah Rozenbaum in Australia. Rozenbaum had migrated to the country town of Shepparton, 120 miles north of Melbourne, where, in the 1930s, there was a thriving community of Polish Jewish orchardists. The rabbi's letter to Rozenbaum gives a vivid sense of the terrible circumstances of one family but reflects the larger crisis confronting Polish Jewry:

I do not know you, seeking your compassion for your nephew Zundel, son of your brother Yitzchak from Grajewo, who is in frightful condition, simply dying from hunger and cold. He is sick and bedridden, unable to earn anything. Our shtetl is very poor because of the crisis prevailing in Poland. Thus we cannot help him, and since I am a neighbour of his, I cannot witness his poverty and destitution and not write it down on paper. It is very upsetting when one enters his home. He is above all a sensitive man; he is embarrassed to talk about his situation. He keeps silent, but as a neighbour I know of his poverty. My conscience dictated that I should ask him for an address of friends abroad and write to them telling how their friend Zundel, son of Yitzchak, Rabbi of Grajewo, is naked and barefoot and hungry and his entire family is starving. He has three nice grown marriageable daughters who all sit at home with nothing to do. They would want to work but there is no work and there are no proposed matches since no one wants to marry a poor girl. Every young man wants a woman with a dowry. These girls don't even have proper clothing, and on top of everything, now is the terrible winter with a great frost and he doesn't even have fuel with which to heat the oven. His situation is very sad.

So it is my holy duty to alert and awaken pity for him and his whole family and not allow him and his whole family to die of hunger and cold and be evicted from his residence since he doesn't have money to pay rent. Therefore you must know that if you direct your *tzedokeh* [charity] to this place, you will simply save people from dying of starvation.

Following the military coup d'état of 1926 by Marshal Josef Pilsudski (1867–1935), political conditions improved somewhat for Poland's Jews. He personally opposed antisemitism, as did the Polish Socialist Party (PPS) that he once led, and in 1927, the military government accorded legal status to Jewish communal organizations, the *kehillot*, and these became the channel for funding Jewish institutions and social services. But the death of the marshal in 1935 saw the radicalization of Polish politics, which became increasingly ethno-nationalist. The Endek Party, headed by Roman Dmowski (1864–1939), led the antisemitic campaign. For him, the Jews could never be Poles because

> in the character of this race so many different values, strange to [Poles'] moral constitution and harmful to [Polish] life, have accumulated that assimilation with a larger number of Jews would destroy [Poles], replacing with decadent elements, those young creative foundations upon which [Poles] are building the future.

Like other right-wing Polish nationalists, Dmowski was bitterly opposed to the Treaty of Versailles, in large part because of its Minorities Treaty, which held that Poland must guarantee "total and complete protection of life and freedom of all people regardless of their birth, nationality, language, race, or religion." He also wished to redraw the border with Germany that he believed had not been placed far enough west. Maintaining that Jews were responsible for the treaty, he claimed it was the product of an "international Jewish conspiracy."

Pilsudski was more accommodating on the issue of Poland's minorities than his bitter rival, Dmowski, who believed that Germans and Jews were threats to Poland and that to be Polish was to speak Polish and be Catholic. In his Poland, there was no room for minorities, especially Jews. But in truth, during the interwar period, the political center and the Left came to hold similar views, even if the antisemitism of the latter was not expressed as crudely as was that of the Right. Neither Pilsudski nor the Polish Socialist Party favored the possibility of any form of Jewish national autonomy and was wholly committed to Jewish assimilation. One way this was sought was by not funding the Yiddish or Hebrew school systems, despite the obligation to do so in the Minorities Treaty. Jews, and not the state, were responsible for the costs. To make matters worse, the state denied graduates of such institutions admission to Polish universities. This served to guarantee that a national network of Jewish schools would fail, and indeed, it did. The majority of Jewish children attended Polish schools in the interwar period.

In the economic realm after 1936, the nationalists orchestrated a campaign of boycotts against Jewish businesses. Despite the fact that Jewish merchants barely made enough to survive, a widespread propaganda campaign harped on the themes of Jewish exploitation and responsibility for Poland's economic plight. The fact that Jews in interwar Poland were overwhelmingly poor, with about 30 percent of them receiving welfare, seemed to have little impact on those who propagated the myth that Jews were enriching themselves at the expense of "true Poles." The impact of the boycott on the Jewish economy was devastating. Jewish businessmen had great difficulty obtaining government-backed loans, while Jewish artisans could not get licenses. Official Polish unions of shopkeepers and artisans even promoted a program to resettle Christian merchants and artisans in western and eastern regions with large Jewish populations. While the program was a failure, with probably only 1,000 Catholic shopkeepers and artisans making the move, the plan revealed the extent to which nationalists would go to remove Jews from the Polish economy.

Throughout the interwar period, Jews were increasingly denied admission to universities, and enrollment declined dramatically, from about 25 percent in 1921 to just over 8 percent in 1938. In addition to the 1937 imposition of quotas on Jews, antisemitic violence and the constant threat thereof characterized the atmosphere at universities across Poland. Jews were sometimes made to sit on "ghetto benches" at the back of classrooms, and at some universities, Jews were attacked and thrown through windows from the upper floors. Violence against Jews was spreading, and between 1935 and 1937, pogroms again swept through Poland, claiming the lives of 79 Jews and leaving about 500 injured. The prevailing atmosphere was summed up by Cardinal Hlond, Primate of Poland, who, in a pastoral letter of February 29, 1936, declared:

> A Jewish problem exists, and will continue to exist as long as the Jews remain Jews. . . . It is a fact that the Jews fight against the Catholic Church, they are free-thinkers, and constitute the vanguard of atheism, and of revolutionary activity. The Jewish influence upon morals is fatal, and the[ir]

publishers spread pornographic literature. It is also true that the Jews are committing frauds, practicing usury and dealing in white slavery.

In favor of boycotting Jewish businesses but opposed to anti-Jewish violence, Hlond advised Poland's Catholics:

> One ought to fence oneself off against the harmful moral influences of Jewry, and to separate oneself against its anti-Christian culture, and especially to boycott the Jewish press. . . . But it is not permissible to assault Jews. . . . When divine mercy enlightens a Jew, and he accepts sincerely his and our Messiah, let us greet him with joy in the Christian midst.

Romania Between the Wars

Romanian Jewry in the interwar period was extremely diverse, some communities Western in orientation, with a Germanized elite, a majority Yiddish-speaking eastern European type, a Hungarian-speaking community, and other communities that were variations on these essential types. However, irrespective of such internal differences—and they were significant—they mattered little to Romanians. Jews in Romania faced similar forms of discrimination as those meted out in Poland. Although this new state was formed in 1919, it resisted granting legal equality to Jews until 1923.

In 1930, of 757,000 Jews in Romania, 318,000 earned a living from commerce, and as was the pattern elsewhere in eastern Europe, Romania's overwhelmingly poor Jews were held responsible by nationalist elements for the state of the economy and the suffering of the masses. Parties across the political spectrum promoted a policy of restricting what they called "Jewish capital." Rejecting the nation's obligation under law to protect minorities, a professor at the University of Iasi, Alexandru C. Cuza, head of the violently antisemitic League of National Christian Defense, declared on July 14, 1926:

> It is monstrous that the constitution should speak of the rights of the Jews. The solution ought to be to eliminate the Jews by law. The first step ought to be to exclude them from the army. Leases of forests granted to Jews should be canceled. All land held by Jews should be expropriated. Likewise, all town houses owned by Jews should be confiscated. I would introduce a *numerus clausus* in the schools.

Cuza was particularly successful in winning support among university students, who agitated repeatedly during the interwar years for a total ban on admission of Jewish students. In 1922, medical students at a number of universities sought a prohibition against Jews dissecting Christian cadavers. Violent demonstrations at universities were common; the 1926 murder at the University of Cernauti of a Jewish high school student while he inquired about admission was only the most extreme manifestation of the hatred then gripping Romania.

The National Liberal Party, the National Peasant Party, and the National Christian Party were all stridently antisemitic, while the Fascist Iron Guard Party, founded in 1927, like the Nazi Party in Germany, elevated violent antisemitism to the center of its ideology. Its leader, Corneliu Zelea Codreanu, combined a bloodthirsty antisemitism with fascism and mystical Christianity. By 1938, Codreanu's rivals, the National Christian Party, under the short-lived dual leadership of the poet Octavian Goga and the professor Alexandru Cuza, imposed antisemitic laws, inspired by Germany's Nuremberg Laws. Even though King Carol crushed the Goga–Cuza government two months after it took power, anti-Jewish measures were not rescinded, and by 1939, at least 270,000 Romanian Jews had lost their citizenship. In 1940, the passage of more antisemitic legislation, which now defined Jews in racial terms, tightened the noose around Romanian Jewry. Property was confiscated, Jewish institutions were closed down, newspapers were shut, and Jews were, by and large, excluded from the nation's economy and society. In the late 1930s, desperate to leave Romania, Jews actively sought ways to enter Palestine. But British policy and the deteriorating conditions in Romania, including the closure of Zionist organizations that attempted to facilitate the departure of Jews, stymied the plan. In 1935, only 3,616 Romanian Jews immigrated to Palestine, a figure that was significantly reduced in the following years.

Hungary Between the Wars

In Hungary, the loss of the war, which precipitated the demise of the Austro-Hungarian Empire, left the nation brutalized and dispirited. The country underwent a Communist Revolution in March 1919 under the leadership of Béla Kun (1886–1938 or 1939). His disastrous management of the nation and the economy led to widespread suffering. After a failed anti-Communist coup attempt in June 1919, Kun organized a Red Terror campaign with the aid of the secret police and revolutionary tribunals. Hundreds were executed, which, in turn, increased antisemitic sentiments, as Kun was never permitted to forget the fact that his father had been Jewish. As a result, all Jews in Hungary were held responsible for Kun's actions and Hungary's woes. In retaliation, right-wing extremists in a White Terror campaign between 1919 and 1920 murdered hundreds of Jews. Having been previously accepted as Hungarians, as evidenced by the large numbers that had been ennobled and the high intermarriage rate, Jews were no longer considered truly Hungarian. Antisemitism dominated the political culture until the destruction of Hungarian Jewry in the Holocaust.

In 1920, there were 473,355 Jews in Hungary, approximately 6 percent of the total population. They were to be found disproportionately in all areas of commerce and the professions. Little wonder, then, that Budapest was known derisively as "Judapest." In that same year, the government of Admiral Nicholas Horthy introduced the quota system at the universities, restricting the Jewish presence to a maximum of 6 percent of all students. While outright pogroms ceased because the economy was still dependent on Jewish businessmen, the refugee civil servants from the lost territories, along with the lower middle classes and the small gentile middle classes, were determined to push Jews out of Hungarian public and commercial life. By 1938, there were 35,000 baptized Jews in Hungary, and when combined with a declining birth rate and immigration spurred on by the government assault on Jews, the overall size of the Jewish population went into decline, sinking to 444,567, or 5 percent of the total population. On May 24, 1938, the Hungarian Parliament instituted race laws. Among other provisions, the law limited the employment of Jews in private businesses to 20 percent. A year later, the law was supplemented by further discriminatory measures, which included more stringent application of the *numerus clausus*, confiscation of Jewish landed property, and denial of citizenship through marriage, naturalization, or adoption.

The Balkans Between the Wars

The principal issues facing the Jews of the Balkans in the wake of the demise of the Ottoman Empire after World War I were poverty and discrimination, the two being closely linked. While the small Ashkenazic communities in the Balkans tended to be comparatively better off than the majority Sephardim, both communities were adversely affected by the overall decline of the Balkan economy, which had been ravaged by the war. Social and economic dislocations also resulted in a rightward political drift so that the Jews of the Balkans faced similar difficulties to those encountered by other European Jewish communities in this period. Though Jews had been guaranteed equal rights in places such as Serbia, Bulgaria, and Greece, enforcement varied widely, and the multiethnic tensions of the region saw Jews increasingly marginalized. In these relatively small communities—in the interwar period, Turkey, Greece, Yugoslavia, and Bulgaria were home to about 82,000, 75,000, 68,000, and 48,000 Jews, respectively—economic and social pressure from nationalist forces proved a constant problem. Across the region, the creation of peasant cooperatives, government use of specially designated state import–export agencies, and the desire in Turkey to create a Muslim middle class to replace the role previously filled by Jews, Greeks, and Armenians all had devastating consequences for Jews. Finally, the impact of the Great Depression of 1929 did severe damage to the Jewish economy in the Balkans. In the 1920s in Greece, Jews involved in the sugar, rice, coffee, and tobacco trades increasingly shut down their businesses or transferred operations abroad. In Salonika, where the 61,000 Jews were one-sixth of the total population, they were responsible for a fifth of all economic activity. Their exclusion from economic life would allow many "true" Greeks to fill the commercial void. In Greece, two Jewish banks, the Amar Bank and the Union Bank, continued to operate in the interwar period, and loans to Jews were available, but the overall trend in this once-thriving community was toward increasing poverty, as it was across the Balkans. In Bulgaria, Jews organized as best as they could. With the assistance of the American Joint Distribution Committee, Jews formed their own cooperatives and loan banks, called *kasas*. They were helpful in small measure, but the community faced increasing pauperization. By 1940, about 17 percent of the Jews of the Bulgarian capital, Sofia, were receiving financial assistance from Jewish communal funds.

As elsewhere in the Balkans, the social marginalization of Jews was nonetheless accompanied by increasing Westernization and secularization. This is most apparent in the area of language use. In 1895, only 2.8 percent of Serbian Jews claimed to speak Serbo-Croatian. That figure had jumped to 49 percent by 1931. Conversely, over the same period, those who spoke Ladino went from 80 percent down to 30 percent. In Bulgaria, a cradle of Ladino culture, nearly 90 percent of Jews claimed the language as their mother tongue in 1926, a figure that declined to just below 40 percent in 1934. Ladino usage had also fallen markedly due to the impact of the ideology and education system of the Alliance Israélite Universelle, which discouraged Jews from speaking the language. (In Bulgaria, by contrast, the slow but steady Bulgarization of the Jews was due in large part to the disappearance of the Alliance schools.) Also, the nationalist movements that emerged in these new countries insisted that all citizens speak the national language, and the fact that Ladino had its detractors, even among Jewish journalists and intellectuals who wrote in the language, further compromised its standing. In the 1920s, Atatürk's Latinization of the Turkish alphabet was accompanied by the Latinization of Ladino script. Subsequent to

this and the general decline in Ladino usage in Turkey, Ladino publishing was greatly diminished. In Sarajevo, where in 1931 51 percent of Jews still spoke Ladino, Serbo-Croatian was increasingly used in the administration of Jewish community institutions and even came to replace those newspapers previously published in Ladino. Even in Salonika, the largest Ladino-speaking community, Greek was increasingly used, in large part because of the state's rigorous and uncompromising Hellenization program. All over the Balkans, social and economic advancement required that Jews adopt the dominant languages and relegate Ladino to the domestic sphere. As with Yiddish, the Holocaust destroyed the last remnants of Ladino culture, while those who survived the Nazi genocide and made their way to Israel confronted a burgeoning nation-state that was singularly focused on the promotion of Hebrew, committing few, if any, resources to maintaining other Jewish languages.

JEWISH CULTURAL LIFE IN INTERWAR CENTRAL EUROPE

In contrast to the state-sponsored Yiddish culture of the Soviet Union, Jewish cultural activities that took place elsewhere in interwar Europe were private initiatives. Two of the most important centers were Germany, where secular Jewish culture was produced in the German language, and Poland, where Yiddish predominated but was not exclusive, as Polish and Hebrew were also used in the production of what was both high and mass secular Jewish culture.

Interwar Jewish Culture in Weimar Germany

A combination of the encounter with their brethren on the eastern front during World War I, a growing antisemitism after the war, and a rejection of the assimilatory path of their parents' generation saw young German Jews between the wars turn energetically to Jewish culture in the attempt to reclaim what had been lost in the process of becoming German. But the German Jewish engagement with Jewish culture was not a mere process of reclamation; instead, an attempt was made to create a specifically modern Jewish culture, one that looked to the past but did not seek to take German Jews back into it. Such a move would be impossible. Rather, the Jewish encounter with Judaism in Weimar Germany would foreshadow most contemporary approaches by Jews to gain access to their own cultural treasures by the "invention" of new traditions.

Prior to World War I, certain German Jews, some very detached from Judaism, were already beginning to express an intense interest in their religious and ethnic heritage. Gershom Scholem, who left Germany for Palestine in 1923 and became one of the most formative figures in Jewish intellectual life in the twentieth century, turned to the study of Jewish mystical texts. In Prague, Franz Kafka began attending the Yiddish theater and studying Hebrew, while Franz Rosenzweig, a man so alienated from Judaism that he was on the brink of conversion, recaptured his faith and became a Jewish philosopher of renown. Together with Martin Buber, Rosenzweig prepared a new translation into German of the Hebrew Bible. Many such figures were in youthful rebellion against what they considered the stultified Judaism of their middle-class parents. Kafka's bitter letter to his father exemplified such revolt:

> But what sort of Judaism was it that I got from you? . . . It was indeed, so far as I could see, a mere nothing, a joke—not even a joke. Four days a year you went to the synagogue, where you were, to say the least, closer to the indifferent than to those who took it seriously . . . so long as I was present in the synagogue . . . I was allowed to hang around wherever I liked. And so I yawned and dozed through the many hours (I don't think I was ever again so bored, except later at dancing lessons) and did my best to enjoy the few little bits of variety there were, as for instance when the Ark of the Covenant was opened, which always reminded me of the shooting galleries where a cupboard door would open in the same way whenever one hit a bull's-eye; except that there something interesting always came out and here it was always just the same old dolls without heads. Incidentally, it was also very frightening for me there . . . because you once mentioned in passing that I too might be called to the Torah. That was something I dreaded for years. . . . That's how it was in the synagogue; at home it was, if possible, even poorer, being confined to the first Seder, which more and more developed into a farce, with fits of hysterical laughter,

> Still later, I did see it again differently and realized why it was possible for you to think that in this respect too I was malevolently betraying you. You really had brought some traces of Judaism with you from the ghetto-like village community; it was not much and it dwindled a little more in the city and during your military service. . . . Basically the faith that ruled your life consisted in your believing in the unconditional rightness of the opinions of a certain class of Jewish society, and hence actually, since these opinions were part and parcel of your own nature, in believing in yourself. Even in this there was still Judaism enough, but it was too little to be handed on to the child; it all dribbled away while you were passing it on.

Most central European Jews were secular, so for those looking to "return" to their Jewish roots, something other than religious practice would have to necessarily constitute their Jewish identities. They became what have been called "post-assimilatory" Jews. Rather than revive and mimic authentic traditions, they sought to construct new ones. In some ways, what Jews were doing after World War I in Germany was similar to what non-Jews were doing—namely, trying to explore and recapture the spirit of cultures that were no more, thanks to the social and economic impact of modernity. Additionally, German Jewry turned increasingly to their Jewish identities in the wake of increasing antisemitism in the postwar period. For others, the enthusiasm brought about by the political success of Zionism, which had secured the Balfour Declaration, as well as the intense encounter with eastern European Jews, both on the battlefront and with those who came as immigrants to Germany, energized and enthused those German Jews seeking to reject what they considered to be the sterile bourgeois Judaism of their assimilated parents.

The changes that occurred were most dramatic in the area of youth culture. In Imperial Germany, most Jews attended public schools and, where permitted, joined German youth groups. By contrast, in the Weimar period (1919–1933), Jewish schools were established, and the Jewish youth movement blossomed. In cities such as Frankfurt, Hamburg, and Cologne, over 50 percent of Jewish children attended a Jewish school. Munich and Nuremberg opened Jewish schools that had been closed for lack of attendance decades earlier. In Weimar Germany, Jews were now mostly excluded from the German youth movements. In response, by the 1920s, a third of Jewish youngsters were members of a broad array of Jewish youth organizations, from Zionist to right-wing German nationalist. Gershom

Scholem and his siblings typified this better than most families. Gershom was a Zionist, Werner was a Communist, Erich was a liberal, and Reinhold was a German nationalist. Jewish hiking and scouting groups became extremely popular, with even the most secular ones insisting on taking kosher food with them on their trips, more as an act of rebellion against their acculturated parents than an expression of faith. Others attempted to play games in Hebrew.

At the center of the "renaissance of Jewish culture," a term coined by the philosopher Martin Buber in 1900, was the Lehrhaus. Established in Frankfurt in 1920 by the philosopher Franz Rosenzweig (1886–1929), the *Lehrhaus* was a school of Jewish adult education. Although its name is derived from the Hebrew *bet midrash* ("study house"), the Lehrhaus, characteristically for the larger project of inventing Jewish tradition in Weimar, was not a replica of the traditional *bet midrash* but was modeled on the vast network of contemporary German adult education schools.

The goal of the Lehrhaus was to offer a systematic "reappropriation" of Jewish knowledge through the teaching of classical Jewish texts and traditions. Pedagogically, the most original concept of the Lehrhaus was what Rosenzweig called "learning in reverse order." He sought to offer a kind of instruction that was "a learning, no longer out of the Torah into life, but out of life . . . back into the Torah." By this was meant that the teachers themselves had only recently acquired Jewish knowledge, "returning" to Judaism from having been on its outermost periphery. In 1913, Rosenzweig was about to convert, a promise he had made to his already-converted cousins. He had written to his parents, "We are Christians in all things, we live in a Christian state, go to Christian schools, read Christian books, our whole culture is based on a Christian foundation." Still, he asked for a "time of contemplation" so that he might study more closely that from which he was departing. It was the ten-day period between Rosh Hashanah and Yom Kippur. Attending Yom Kippur services at an Orthodox synagogue in his hometown of Kassel, he is said to have undergone some kind of epiphany or mystical experience, though he never discussed it. He reversed his decision to leave the faith, calling the period his "ten days of return" to Judaism.

At the Lehrhaus, the relationship of teachers to students was more egalitarian than was the hierarchical norm in Germany, and teaching was to be in the form of a dialogue, not a monologue, with teachers only one step ahead of the students. The system was a great success. With branches across Germany, the Lehrhaus had enrollments of around 2,000 students per semester in Berlin and about 1,000 per semester in smaller cities. These were higher numbers than the corresponding enrollment figures for non-Jewish adult education schools.

The Lehrhaus was concerned with more than just imparting factual knowledge. A larger philosophical goal lay behind the enterprise. Though the Lehrhaus closed in 1930, three years before the Nazis came to power, one of the teachers, Richard Koch, summed up prophetically the aims of the Lehrhaus:

> If our historical suffering should recur one day, then we want to know why we suffer; we do not want to die like animals, but like humans. . . . Often enough others and we ourselves have told us that we are Jews. We have heard it too often. The *Lehrhaus* shall tell us why and for what purpose we are Jews.

As part of the "renaissance" of Jewish culture in the Weimar Republic, the era saw the production of two Jewish encyclopedias, the five-volume *Jüdisches Lexikon* and the ten-volume *Encyclopaedia Judaica*, which covered *A* through *L*. (The project had to be abandoned with the rise of the Nazis.) These works covered all fields of the Jewish experience, but the editors were especially guided by the desire to introduce to German Jews the rich variety of Jewish culture, to re-establish the leading position of German Jewish scholarship—prior to World War I, great multivolume Jewish encyclopedias had appeared in English, Russian, and Hebrew—and to contribute to the creation of a modern Jewish consciousness among German-speaking Jews by presenting Judaism and Jewish history in the distinctly modern form of the reference book. Also, these works deviated from the model of scholarship established by the *Wissenschaft des Judentums* in that they concentrated less on texts and concerned themselves with the social history of the Jewish people. They contained lengthy entries on taxes, workers, Jewish communities, trades, and the Jewish press, but there were also entries by the literary critic Walter Benjamin on "Jews in German Culture" and Gershom Scholem's seminal entry on "Kabbalah," a decisive inclusion of a subject studiously avoided by previous generations of German Jewish scholars embarrassed by that tradition in Judaism. The more popular *Jüdisches Lexikon* was a lavish production that covered Jewish sociology, folklore, art, costume, and music and included superb maps, inserts of Jewish sheet music, and facsimiles of letters by famous personalities. Each of its five volumes had a print run of 10,000.

As part of the turn to Jewish culture in Weimar, a number of individuals began to use contemporary Expressionist forms in the production of Jewish art but attempted to claim the new forms as inspired by ancient Jewish culture. For example, composers of Jewish atonal synagogue music claimed they based their compositions on ancient Oriental Jewish musical forms. Others, troubled by the assimilatory trend of German Jewry, turned with appreciation to eastern European Jews, who they prized as "authentic" Jews. Connected to this, German Jews involved in the reappropriation of Jewishness became enamored of Hebrew and Yiddish. While only a small vanguard made the actual effort to learn the languages, Hebrew, once ignored, and Yiddish, once reviled, enjoyed great prestige in this environment. The small number of German Zionists turned to the study of Hebrew, and by 1927, over 30 communities throughout Germany offered evening language classes. In addition, the early 1920s saw Berlin become an important center of Hebrew culture. Authors such as Hayim Nahman Bialik, Micha Yosef Berdichevsky, David Frischmann, Uri Zvi Greenberg, and the later Nobel laureate Shmuel Yosef Agnon lived there. Bialik even taught at the Lehrhaus, while YIVO (the Yiddish acronym for the Yiddish Scientific Institute, the major institution for the study of Yiddish and eastern European Jewish history and culture) was founded in Berlin in 1925 before making its home in Vilna and, later, New York.

Finally, Weimar Jews flocked to the theater to watch Yiddish Expressionist productions by the Vilna Troupe and the Moscow State Yiddish Theater. Moscow's Hebrew-language theater, *Habimah*, also drew appreciative audiences. With avant-garde set design and direction, what passed for "authentic" Jewish themes in the minds of German Jews was combined with their predilection for artistic modernism. In eastern Europe, at that time, Jewish audiences viewed such productions quite differently, as simply modern European theater, something at great and welcome remove from "traditional" Judaism.

The experiment of inventing a secular Jewish culture in interwar Germany was, of course, the product of a minority of Jews, but an impassioned one. How broad their impact in Germany might have become, we cannot say, for the storm clouds for German Jewry were fast approaching. But in the period from 1919 to 1933, German Jewry went very far toward creating a viable secular Jewish culture, one that embraced things Jewish in new and modernist forms, and with hindsight, they can be said to have produced a model of Jewish culture that, for the majority of Jews who are today secular, has become predominant in the Jewish world. (*See box*, "Jews in Austrian Culture.")

Interwar Jewish Culture in Poland

Despite the ruinous material conditions that existed for eastern European Jews in the interwar period, they managed to produce a glittering secular Jewish culture, especially in Yiddish, which reached its zenith before being abruptly cut short by the Holocaust. Polish Jewry at this time existed in what has been termed a *polysystem*—namely, a culture that was expressed in three languages: Yiddish, Polish, and Hebrew. One of the major differences between the secular Jewish culture produced in Germany and that to be found in Poland was that in the latter, politics played a much greater, if not the determining, role. Yiddish and Hebrew cultures were generally linked to Jewish nationalist positions—Bundism and Folkism in the case of the former, and Zionism in the case of the latter, with some overlap, considering that as Zionism grew in strength in the interwar years, some Zionist leaders and most rank-and-file supporters expressed themselves in Yiddish. Even though they were often bitterly split, the adherents of the two Jewish languages were united in their rejection of the idea that a real Jewish culture could be expressed in Polish—another contrast with the potential of a secular Jewish culture in German. That said, while the 1931 census demonstrated that 80 percent of Poland's 3 million Jews declared Yiddish as their mother tongue, with 12 percent claiming Polish and 8 percent claiming Hebrew, increasing numbers (among the Yiddish and Hebrew speakers) were beginning to speak Polish in the interwar period. These figures, however, are not a true reflection of reality, because there never were a quarter of a million Hebrew speakers (8 percent) in Poland, nor were there so many that had Polish as their mother tongue. Prior to the census, Zionists encouraged Jews to declare Hebrew as their first language in protest to the ongoing discrimination against Jews. Even the declared figure of 80 percent for Yiddish is subject to debate, for there was a protest element within that, as some Polish speakers may have registered as Yiddish speakers. Whatever the true case, the overwhelming majority of Polish Jews spoke Yiddish but were often bilingual and trilingual, and the trend appeared to be in the direction of the increasing Polonization of the Jewish population.

By the mid-1930s, about 500,000 elementary school–age Jewish children resided in Poland, about 100,000 of whom attended Jewish schools. Despite the increasing secularization of Polish Jewry, approximately 56 percent of all Jewish children were enrolled in religious schools, such as Horev and other yeshivot for boys, and the girls' school system, Beys Yaakov. At these institutions, classical Hebrew texts were studied, with Yiddish as the language of instruction. At the Tarbut and Yavneh schools, Hebrew was the language of instruction, with nearly 34 percent of children attending them, while in the small Shulkult schools, attended by 1.3 percent of Jewish children, a bilingual education in Yiddish and Hebrew was offered. Finally, in the TSYSHO (Central Yiddish School Organization), where 9 percent of children attended, classes were conducted in Yiddish. All these schools also taught Polish. The principal reason the other 400,000 elementary-age Jewish children attended Polish state schools, however, was that they were free of charge, unlike Jewish schools, so attendance there was less an ideological expression on the part of parents than it was an economic necessity. Moreover, to gain admission to state-run high schools—the Tarbut and TSYSHO systems also ran high schools—good Polish was required, and Jewish schools were not considered strong enough in this area of instruction.

In a variety of pursuits, such as literature, journalism, scholarship, theater, cabaret, music, the movie industry, and sports, secular Jewish culture in Poland blossomed. The field of Yiddish literature was especially vast, with genres ranging from cheap pulp fiction for the masses all the way to the experimental prose and poetry of the literary group *Yung Vilne* ("Young Vilna"), exemplifying the diverse nature of Polish Jewish thought. Established in 1929, the group published literary works, anthologies, and periodicals. Among its leaders were the poets Abraham Sutzkever, Chaim Grade, and Leyzer Wolf, who concluded his autobiography with a sentiment that spoke for many in the group, certainly before the Holocaust led to its destruction and the dispersal of surviving members. Wolf dreamt: "My distant ideal—a single nation. The world—a single land."

Among the jewels in the crown of interwar Yiddish culture in Poland was the theater. Operating on a shoestring budget, Yiddish theater was exceptionally popular and a genuine vehicle for national Jewish expression. Comedies, farces, and revues were staged by small theaters, such as Azazel and Folkste'ater (People's Theater); cabarets were performed at Ararat; Khad Gadyo put on avant-garde puppet theater; and Sambatyon was a theater grotesquerie founded in 1926 in Warsaw. Yiddish theater performed such Jewish plays as *The Dybbuk*, as well as works by Shakespeare, Molière, and Eugene O'Neill. A new art form came into its own in the interwar period—Yiddish stand-up comedy, particularly political satire. Performing at clubs such as the Qui Pro Quo and the Morskie Oko, the two greatest exponents of the form, Shimen Dzigan and Yisroel Shumacher, became cult figures, both in Poland and later in Israel, after the Holocaust. It is a significant comment on interwar Jewry and its relation to the theater that just as in the Soviet Union, where Shlomo Mikhoels was the unofficial head of Soviet Jewry, the theater director Mikhl Weichert played a similar role in Poland. During the war, he would become head of Aleynhilf, the Jewish social self-help organization. Jewish theater was not confined to Yiddish. Polish-language Jewish theater was also popular, a sure sign that increasing numbers of Polish Jews had facility with the national language.

Yiddish scholarship during the interwar period likewise flourished. Thanks in large part to the increasing number of Polish Jews with access to university educations, large numbers of scholars produced historical, linguistic, economic, folkloristic, and ethnographic studies of Polish Jewry. Much of the work was sponsored by YIVO, with its headquarters in Vilna, the city known as the "Jerusalem of Lithuania." Among YIVO's founding supporters were Albert Einstein and Sigmund Freud, while the driving organizational force behind it was its director, from 1925 until 1939, Max Weinreich (1893–1969), the distinguished linguist and historian of the Yiddish language. Under his guidance, the institute was dedicated to researching the history, language, literature, culture, sociology, and psychology of eastern European Jewry. From humble beginnings, it became one of the Jewish people's great repositories of knowledge. (After the outbreak of war, YIVO moved to New York in 1940, where it remains to this day.)

During the interwar period, the Bund, which was the most popular Jewish political party, was the staunchest promoter of Yiddish culture. It operated a vast network of cultural activities aimed in particular at future generations. Among these were two children's organizations, SKIF (The Union of Socialist Children) and Tsukunft ("The Future"). On the eve of World War II, youth membership in the Bund stood at 12,000. With Jewish life under assault, these associations gave young Jews venues wherein they could express their Jewish identities and develop invaluable leadership skills. Jewish youth culture was extremely well developed by the interwar period, with all Jewish political parties operating youth movements. In more than a hundred communities, the Bund also supported the Yiddish school network, which ran classes from kindergarten up through a teacher's training college. In all, more than 24,000 students attended. The Bund also operated summer camps for impoverished urban youth, providing thousands with wholesome food and a welcome sojourn in the fresh air of Poland's countryside. Other organizations, such as the Society for the Protection of Jewish Health (TOZ), funded largely by the Joint Distribution Committee in New York, likewise offered summer camps and published health magazines for young readers. Contributing to the deep sense of Jewish nationhood among Poland's Jews was the fact that the country had a vast network of Jewish social services that included hospitals, sanatoriums, orphanages, welfare offices, and a parallel network of institutions that serviced religious Jews.

Polish Jews were avid newspaper readers, and the Jewish press flourished in the interwar period. Here again, the Yiddish press outshone both the Hebrew and Polish Jewish press, publishing a wide array of genres from daily newspapers to specialist periodicals, such as children's newspapers, health and beauty magazines, and sports papers. In 1936–1937, Warsaw alone boasted 11 Yiddish dailies (there were 25 throughout Poland), covering all points on the political and religious spectrum. The sheer number of newspapers is reflective of the diversity of Polish Jewry. No group of 3 million people could be homogenous, and Polish Jewry was split along religious, political, linguistic, and cultural lines. Even among Yiddish speakers, a large linguistic, and therefore cultural, divide existed between those who spoke Lithuanian Yiddish (Litvish) and those who spoke Polish Yiddish (Poylish). While mutually intelligible, both forms of Yiddish are pronounced very differently, with accent being only the most immediately noticeable of the many cultural differences between the two groups. Amid all the secular activity, however, it should not be forgotten that the Jewish community of Poland remained an overwhelmingly traditional society deeply attached to its religious heritage. Hasidism and Mitnagdism continued to flourish, and Poland remained the center of religious scholarship.

Despite the dramatic growth of Zionism between the wars, and in contrast to Yiddish, Hebrew literature and culture actually went into decline in interwar Poland. The reasons for this were a declining readership plus the fact that many of the best Hebrew authors left Poland for Palestine during the Third Aliyah

(1919–1923) and the Fourth Aliyah (1924–1929), turning Palestine into the principal center of secular Hebrew culture. Despite several short-lived attempts, there was not one sustainable Hebrew daily or even weekly newspaper left, no Hebrew theater, while only 12.6 percent of Jewish elementary and 6.2 percent of Jewish high school students, respectively, received a Hebrew education. Commentators inside and outside Poland lamented the situation. On the absence of Hebrew literature in Poland, one of the country's last Hebrew writers, Z. Z. Weinberg, declared, "[T]he time has come for grave digging and burial," while an editorial from the newspaper *Ha'aretz* in Palestine asked, "Has the day come when Polish Jewry is fated to live like the other parts of our nation in America, Germany, Russia, etc.,— without the ring of a Hebrew word? The idea is a terrible one and difficult to accept." But as a measure of the cultural complexity of Polish Jewry, Hebrew for secular purposes was not entirely abandoned. The relatively small numbers that wished to read Hebrew literature and newspapers now read the material imported from Palestine. In a similar vein, Polish Jews, even if they did not understand Hebrew, flocked to the Hebrew theater to see performances by visiting acting troupes from Palestine, such as Habimah and Ohel. Still, Hebrew-language use trailed a distant third behind Yiddish and Polish.

With the establishment of an independent Poland after World War I, Polish was increasingly used as a daily language among Jews. A number of Polish-language Jewish newspapers existed, with the two leading ones in Warsaw having combined daily sales of 100,000. Rather than promote assimilation, most of the Polish Jewish newspapers were mildly Zionist in orientation, published the works of Yiddish and Hebrew authors in translation, and were staunch advocates for Jews in the face of antisemitism. Nevertheless, the Polish Jewish press faced considerable hostility from the champions of Yiddish and Hebrew, who decried Polish-language Jewish culture as inauthentic and assimilationist (*see box*, "Miss Judea Pageant").

A central element of interwar Jewish culture in Poland was the existence of a wide array of competing Jewish political parties. While the pattern and culture of Jewish politics were forged in late tsarist Russia, it came into its own in interwar Poland. Covering the entire spectrum of ideologies, there were Bundists and Poale Tsiyon on the Left, General Zionists and Folkists, represented by the smaller Folkspartey occupying the center, and Jabotinsky's Revisionist Zionists were situated on the right flank, as were, to some extent, Agudas Yisroel, the religiously devout, antimodern, anti-Zionist, yet nationalist party led by a coalition of Hasidic and non-Hasidic rabbis. These and a wide array of splinter parties vied for the allegiances of the Jewish people. In particular, they aimed at winning the support of Polish Jewish youth, who had become intensely politicized at this time. All political parties had youth groups attached to them, with very large memberships.

Figure 4.1 depicts youngsters at a Jewish summer camp in interwar Poland. TOZ, the Polish acronym for the social welfare organization Society for the Protection of Jewish Health, fought to eradicate the widespread incidence of tuberculosis, diphtheria, and trachoma among Jews in interwar Poland. One of the organization's mottos, "Air-Sun-Water," was intended to promote the benefits of all three. As the economic conditions among Jews deteriorated after World War I, disease became rampant due to the poor living conditions in the Jewish districts of Poland's overcrowded cities. To give children a respite from their dank living conditions, TOZ promoted summer camps across Poland that were attended by tens of thousands of youngsters. Here, before World War II, children at the TOZ summer camp in Pospieszka, just outside Vilna, sit in formation to spell the acronym TOZ.

The central feature of interwar Jewish politics was its divisiveness. Polish politics were similarly divided, but the Jewish situation—characterized by questions of "Here or there?," "Yiddish or Hebrew or Polish?," "Religious or secular?," "Socialist or bourgeois?," and combinations and permutations of all these positions—made Jewish politics intensely complex and fractured. The intensity and the bitterness of the splits were commensurate with the reality of Jewish political powerlessness. Jewish political parties were unable or unwilling to put aside differences or, at least, compromise with each other. Without a unified voice, they were largely rendered weak and ineffective in the context of Polish national politics.

By the mid-1930s, the three most powerful political forces in Jewish Poland were the Zionists, the Bundists, and Agudas Yisroel. In an environment of intense nationalism and antisemitism, the Zionist message was especially appealing, although its prestige was severely compromised by the fact that, in Palestine, the *Yishuv*—the Jewish community of Palestine before the establishment of the State of Israel—had proven incapable of absorbing large numbers of Jews, with only about 140,000 Polish Jews making it there in the interwar period. And within Poland, Zionism had yet to capture the trade union movement or large religious blocks. Still, Zionism, which had at times in the 1930s as many as 30 delegates in the *Sejm* (the Polish Parliament), did benefit from the fact that most Western governments in the interwar period blocked Jewish immigration, leading many Jews to

JEWS IN AUSTRIAN CULTURE

From the end of the nineteenth century, Jews, or people of Jewish descent, had been central to the modernist culture of Vienna. Sigmund Freud, Theodor Herzl, the composer Gustav Mahler, the playwright Arthur Schnitzler, and the writer and aphorist Karl Kraus are only the most well-known. In terms of cultural criticism, Jews ran the three most important Viennese cultural journals, while those who sat on the editorial boards of the major liberal dailies were also primarily Jewish. The importance of Jewish involvement in the arts continued into the interwar period. But the political context had changed, and where once there had been a multinational empire, there now was a republic, a diminished and fragile nation-state where antisemitism was rampant.

After World War I, some Jewish artists looked to the Catholic Church as a symbol of the multinational Habsburg Empire that had once afforded them stability, protection, and opportunities. In 1920, the Salzburg Festival opened, founded by the part-Jewish Hugo von Hofmannsthal, the Jewish theater director Max Reinhardt, and the non-Jewish composer Richard Strauss. Under Reinhardt's direction, the festival opened with a performance of *Everyman*, Hofmannsthal's version of a fifteenth-century English morality play.

Hofmannsthal, who only had one Jewish grandfather, had already been charged with seeking to undermine German culture with his 1906 drama *Oedipus and the Sphinx*, which critics dismissed as having been written in a "Jewish German way." At Salzburg, *Everyman* contained a Catholic redemptive theme, and Catholic liturgy was central to the play. Hofmannsthal even wrote the first publicity pamphlet for the festival in the form of a catechism. The antisemites reacted harshly, perhaps as much to the perceived Jewishness of Hofmannsthal as to his and Reinhardt's claim that they were merely attempting to draw universal and collective lessons from Catholic Baroque

theater, which, as Hofmannsthal hoped, would infuse the new republic with the spirit of the now-defunct Habsburg Empire. In truth, the festival was reactionary but was seen as anything but by the true custodians of reactionary culture, who would not associate Jews with that kind of political or cultural expression. Hofmannsthal drew on Jewish patronage to support the Salzburg Festival, further tainting it in the eyes of critics by reinforcing the sense that Jews were outsiders come to commandeer Austrian culture.

This was a sentiment that was further enhanced by the deep involvement of interwar Jews in the production of *Heimatoperette*, light operas with nationalist, Alpine themes, meant to emphasize the beautiful natural wonders and traditional values of Austria. The most famous of these was *The White Horse Inn* (1930), where the majesty of the Alpine landscape and nostalgia for the Habsburg Empire are juxtaposed with contemporary social and economic distress. The main composer, Ralph Benatzky, was not Jewish, but it did not matter, for scores of others who worked on the operetta were. For the antisemites, Jews, not being "true" Austrians, did not have the right to extol the virtues of the "real" Austria, the Austria of the Alps. In fact, the Austrian alpine tourist industry in the interwar period was an extremely conservative movement, as these regions attempted to modernize without industrializing. Alpine Austria sought to sell an image of itself to urban dwellers that glorified its stratified, rigid, social structure, its deeply conservative patterns of behavior, and its ethnic and religious homogeneity. Nevertheless, Jewish artists pursued Alpine themes, a classic example of this genre being the silent film *Romeo and Juliet in the Snow* (1920) by the German Jewish director Ernst Lubitsch. It is a retelling of Shakespeare's story, but with a happy ending, and is set among the traditional inhabitants of the Alps. Jews were most decidedly not a part of Alpine culture, and thus, their writing operettas and novels and making films about it were regarded as unforgivable transgressions.

The more Jews were deeply involved in European cultural life in the interwar period, the more some began to fear a backlash, imagining life in various European cities without Jews. The Austrian Jewish author Hugo Bettauer's *Stadt ohne Juden* (*City Without Jews*) of 1922, Artur Lansberger's "tragic satire" *Berlin ohne Juden* (*Berlin Without Jews*) of 1925, and the satirical comedy sketch by the Polish Yiddish comedian Shimen Dzigan "Der letster Yid fun Poyln" ("The Last Jew of Poland"), performed in Warsaw in 1935, all signaled a world where the antisemites had gotten their fondest wish—the departure of the Jews and the return of culture into Christian hands. These Jewish works all point to how boring and lifeless these cities had become without Jews. Bettauer, who had converted to Lutheranism, sold 250,000 copies of his utopian novel *City Without Jews* in its first year of publication. Written 16 years before Hitler annexed an approving Austria to Nazi Germany, Bettauer has the Viennese celebrate their triumph in expelling the Jews:

> For Vienna the last day of this year was a holiday unparalleled in the history of that gay and carefree city. By mobilizing all means of transportation, by borrowing locomotives from neighboring countries, and by interrupting all other traffic the authorities had succeeded on that day in sending out the last Jews, in thirty enormous trains. At one o'clock in the afternoon whistles proclaimed that the last trainload of Jews had left Vienna, and at six o'clock in the evening all the church bells rang to announce that there were no more Jews in all Austria. Then Vienna began to celebrate its great festival of emancipation. With his powerful voice, audible even at the opposite end of the square, the Chancellor [Dr. Kurt Schwerfeger] began to speak—briefly, coolly, but all the more effectively: "Fellow citizens, a gigantic task has been

completed. Everyone who is not Austrian at heart has left the territory of our small but beautiful country. Now we are alone, a single family. . . . We must show the world that we can live without the Jews. Nay, more—we must show that we will recover because we have removed the foreign element from our organism."
>
> In rapturous delight, the crowd yelled, "We promise. . . . Hail, the liberator of Austria!"

In the book, the Austrians are initially overjoyed at the expulsion of the Jews, but soon it becomes apparent just exactly what the Jews meant to the cultural and economic life of Vienna. Theaters and concert halls shut down, while department stores, cafés, hotels, and resorts suffer significant losses. Vienna's once-brilliant cultural life is no more. The economic downturn is so severe that there are calls to allow the Jews to return. Not only are they welcomed back, but also, no longer having Jews to blame for society's ills, the Nazi Party collapses, as it is they who are held responsible for having precipitated the crisis to begin with.

Bettauer was denounced by the right wing as a "Redpoet" and a "corruptor of youth." In 1925, three years after publishing *City Without Jews*, Bettauer was shot to death by a Nazi. At his trial, the murderer, Otto Rothstock, offered the defense that he killed the author in order to save German culture from Jewish degeneration. Declared insane, Rothstock was jailed but then set free after only 18 months. The *Wiener Morgenzeitung*, a Zionist paper, editorialized that the murder "was not directed against Bettauer alone, but against every intellectual who wrote for a cause." As in interwar Germany, the lenience of the Austrian courts in dealing with right-wing crimes was an ominous development.

World War I had exacerbated the widespread and long-held belief that the promotion of cultural modernism by Jews indicated the unbridgeable gulf that existed between them and "real" Austrians. In 1927, novelist Ludwig Hirschfeld published a humorous travel guide to Vienna and Budapest as part of a series of such guides to cities including London, Rome, Prague, and Cologne. Titled *What Isn't in Baedeker: Vienna and Budapest*, Hirschfeld's book contained a chapter titled "Peculiarities That One Must Get Used to in Vienna." One such oddity was the need to play the game "Is He a Jew?" According to Hirschfeld, this was the game that all Viennese played, and depending on the answer, residents of the capital then decided whether they liked the person or not. Since his is a guidebook, Hirschfeld tips his own hand by advising readers not to be "too interesting or original, otherwise you will suddenly, behind your back, become [mistaken for] a Jew." Indeed, in Germany, author Thomas Mann had expressed a similar sentiment: "It is a fact that simply cannot be denied that, in Germany, whatever is enjoyed only by 'genuine Teutons' and aboriginal Ur-Germans, but scorned or rejected by the Jews, will never really amount to anything, culturally."

Although Zionism grew in strength among Austrian Jews, especially among those from eastern Europe, the cultural activity of many Jews in interwar Austria was less specifically Jewish than the contemporary renaissance of Jewish culture in either Germany or Poland and tended to manifest itself more overtly in a liberal, pacifist humanism. Whether the creators were actually Jews—such as the authors Joseph Roth, Friedrich Torberg, and Stefan Zweig; the cabaret performer and composer of famous Wiener Lieder (songs about Vienna) Hermann Leopoldi; converts, such as the café house wit Hermann Broch; philosophers, such as Ludwig Wittgenstein and Karl Popper, whose parents had already converted to Protestantism before their sons were born; or gentiles, such as author Robert Musil—to the enemies of modernism, such important distinctions of identity made little difference. They branded everyone whose modernist culture they opposed as "Jewish," whether they were or were not. It would seem that all that was required, as Hirschfeld had said, was to be "too interesting or original."

warm to the idea of Jewish self-actualization through Zionism.

A special reason for Zionism's appeal was that it was an umbrella ideology that could make room for socialists, antisocialists, bourgeois centrists, secularists, and the religiously pious. Despite its commitment to Hebrew, there was even room for a left-wing Yiddish Zionist party, *Linke Poyley Tsiyen* ("Left Workers of Zion"). Zionists were split between two visions: a Palestino- and Hebrew-centric approach dedicated to immediate settlement in Palestine and the more pragmatic approach

adopted by the General Zionists, who wished to settle the Land of Israel, but also to contribute to Diaspora politics by ensuring that Jewish national rights in Europe were respected. The split was important, but not definitive. Sufficient agreement kept the movement intact. The virtue and appeal of Zionism was that it tapped into Jewish national feeling but also provided hope for some kind of eventual escape from existential threat and material want.

As large as the Bund was, its appeal was limited by the fact that its message was only

Figure 4.1 Youngsters at a Jewish summer camp in interwar Poland.

Source: From the archives of the YIVO Institute for Jewish Research, New York.

meant for eastern European, secular, and mostly working-class Jews, and like the Zionists, Bundists, too, were unable to alleviate the plight of the Jewish masses. But the movement nevertheless enjoyed success, especially among the Yiddish intelligentsia and in city elections. However, it never succeeded in getting a single deputy elected to the *Sejm*. Still, as the conditions grew increasingly worse for Polish Jewry, the nationalist dimension of the Bund's activities, which included self-defense units, became increasingly prominent as its internationalist agenda began to diminish. The Bund's great achievement was to offer an alternative to an assimilationist path. It did this by tapping into the vast reservoir of *Yiddishkayt* (Jewish pride and feeling) that

informed the sensibilities of eastern European Jewry and did so by celebrating all things Yiddish. In so doing, the Bund was a major force in fostering Jewish nationalism and keeping Jewish culture alive.

Agudas Yisroel was perhaps the most successful of the parties in that it was able to control local kehillah politics and it ran the largest of the private Jewish school systems. But the increasing secularization of Polish Jewry, the slow drift to the adoption of Polish language, and the fact that its natural constituency, the Hasidim, remained mired in desperate poverty all meant that Agudas Yisroel was unable to alter the larger cultural trajectory of Polish Jewry or care for the most basic material needs of the Jews it represented.

MISS JUDEA PAGEANT

While many Yiddish and Hebrew speakers considered those Jews who spoke Polish to be assimilationists, this was not actually the case. One example of the deep involvement in Jewish affairs and the promotion of Jewish popular culture by the Polish-language Jewish press occurred in February 1929. In the midst of economic crisis and intense anti-semitism, the newspaper *Nasz Przeglad* (*Our Review*), which was sympathetic to Zionism, sponsored a beauty contest, the Miss Judea Pageant. Hundreds of Jewish women, aged 18 to their early 20s, sent in photos of themselves to the editors. Just over 130 pictures were published, and readers were invited to choose the 10 they liked best. The finalists were then to attend a gala event at the exclusive Hotel Polonia in Warsaw, where a panel of Jewish journalists would crown the most beautiful Jewish woman in Poland. The Yiddish press was dismissive of the contest, claiming that it mimicked gentile culture, was superficial, assimilationist, and was part of an attempt to destroy "real" Jewish culture—Yiddish culture. Despite such charges, the Jewish public was thrust into feverish excitement by the contest, never once considering it an aping of gentile culture. In fact, the contest generated intense discussions about the notion of "Semitic beauty," with articles in *Nasz Przeglad* about the need to promote it. Most of the contestants, in fact, conformed to stereotypical notions of "Oriental" or "Semitic"

beauty. They were dark-haired and swarthy, exotic types, diametrically opposed to what passed for "typical" Polish good looks—blond hair, fair complexion, and blue eyes. It is noteworthy that it was this Polish-language Jewish newspaper that touted the "Semitic" ideal of beauty, promoting it as something distinct and superior. This was hardly an expression of assimilationism.

The 1929 winner of the Miss Judea Pageant was 20-year-old Zofia Oldak. In addition to becoming the toast of Jewish Poland, where she met the leading figures in Polish Jewish cultural and political life, Oldak was also the winner of numerous prizes, many of which were donated by some of Jewish Warsaw's premier boutiques. These included a fur coat, couture garments, perfumes, and a record player. But because *Nasz Przeglad* had promoted the winner as a Jewish national icon, the public reacted negatively, claiming that the prizes she won were inappropriate to her heroine status. The paper then promoted a Miss Judea Fund, to which readers could contribute for "educational opportunities" for Ms. Oldak.

The positive feelings generated by the beauty contest did not last long. The Miss Judea Pageant soon turned into a political cause célèbre. When Ms. Oldak went to a gala event hosted by the Warsaw *kehillah* (a quasi-governmental body comprised of different Jewish political parties), the president of the body, Hershl Farbstein, toasted her

ZIONIST DIPLOMACY BETWEEN THE WARS

Not long after World War I erupted in 1914, British Zionists led by Chaim Weizmann approached Whitehall with a proposal. Weizmann sought British government support for the establishment of a Jewish homeland in Palestine, which, in turn, would support British imperial interests in the region. Both the government and the Zionists were certain that the Ottoman Empire would collapse, and that Britain would come to dominate much of the Middle East. Intent on controlling the eastern by reciting "Song of Songs." Farbstein was a member of the religious Zionist party Mizrachi. His sworn enemies from the ultra-Orthodox Agudas Yisroel, who were also part of the governing board of the kehillah, attacked him viciously for reciting a sacred text to the winner of a beauty contest. Soon thereafter, upon the death of a leading figure of Agudas, Farbstein, as president of the kehillah, was scheduled to deliver a eulogy at the rabbi's funeral. Trouble broke out at the cemetery when Farbstein took to the podium to speak. His opponents shouted epithets at him, while his supporters broke into a chant of "Miss Judea, Miss Judea." The chanting then degenerated into an all-in brawl in the middle of the cemetery. The whole sorry affair became grist for the Jewish humorists' mill, as Yiddish satirists and cabaret performers produced stories, cartoons, cabaret sketches, and a musical recalling the whole affair. Because the events took place around Passover, even a parodic Haggadah was produced, with Miss Judea asking the Four Questions.

Figure 4.2 shows Zofia Oldak, winner of the Miss Judea Pageant, 1929. The event illuminates some of the most important social fault lines of interwar Polish Jewry—the struggle between secular and religious forces, among religious political parties, and between the Polish Jewish press and the Yiddish press. Here is "Miss Judea," Zofia Oldak, pictured on the front page of *Nasz Przeglad*, wearing a gown of silver lamé and an ermine wrap fashioned by M. Apfelbaum of 125 Marszalkowska Street, Warsaw.

Figure 4.2   Zofia Oldak, winner of the Miss Judea Pageant, 1929.

Source: From the archives of the YIVO Institute for Jewish Research, New York.

Mediterranean as well as shipping lanes to India, British authorities understood that a foothold in Palestine was necessary to that aim (*see box*, "Sporting Jews").

To achieve their geopolitical goals, the British concluded agreements with various parties, some of which were contradictory, and most of which were hazy in their details and obtuse in their language. Deals were struck with the Arabs, the French, and the Zionists. At the start of the war, the British cultivated an alliance with anti-Ottoman Arab nationalists through emir Husayn, sharif of Mecca and Medina. The British promised

Husayn an independent Arab state, one that Husayn believed would include Palestine, along with much of the Middle East. For his part, Husayn agreed to raise an Arab force to attack Britain's enemy, the Ottoman Turks. Led by his son, Feysal, attacks on Ottoman forces began in 1916. In that same year, the secret Sykes–Picot Agreement, named after a British cabinet member and a French diplomat, called for the postwar division of the Middle East between the two imperial powers. This agreement, of course, appeared to run counter to the promises made to Husayn. Meanwhile, some members of the British cabinet were convinced of the necessity of controlling the Suez Canal, the waterway to India, and believed that supporting the Zionists would give them a foothold in Palestine, which was the best way of realizing their imperial designs.

While some British officials were sympathetic to Zionism because they were evangelical Christians, others were drawn to Zionism out of an exaggerated sense that Jews wielded genuine economic and political power in the United States and Russia. They believed that Jews could force America, then still neutral, into the war, and that the Jews controlled the Russian government of the February Revolution. Other British officials feared that Germany, given its alliance with the Ottomans, might make some sort of offer to the Zionists, thus seducing world Jewry to the side of the Triple Alliance.

Weizmann, a supporter both of Ahad Ha-Am's cultural Zionism and the political activism of Theodor Herzl, matured as a leader during the war. A chemist of considerable renown at Manchester University, Weizmann was heralded during the Great War due to his advances in the production of acetone, which was used in the production of explosives and was crucial to the British war effort. As a result, Weizmann saw the doors of power opened to him. Possessed of great personal chemistry, this appealing Anglophile from near Pinsk, who mastered the English language, set about cultivating the British ruling classes.

Like Herzl, Weizmann often acted alone, to the dismay of his Zionist comrades, but to the delight of the larger Jewish public, who greatly admired him. Some Zionists believed that Weizmann's success could lead to Ottoman reprisals against a defenseless Yishuv. Like other Russian Jewish expatriates, they were deeply suspicious of the Russian–British alliance. Within British government circles, there was considerable opposition to the Zionist movement, but Weizmann's powers of persuasion paid off. In November 1917, the British War Cabinet issued what would later be called the Balfour Declaration, named after Foreign Secretary Arthur James Balfour. It stated:

> His Majesty's Government view with favour the establishment in Palestine of a national home for the Jewish people, and will use their best endeavours to facilitate the achievement of this object, it being clearly understood that nothing shall be done which may prejudice the civil and religious rights of existing non-Jewish communities in Palestine, or the rights and political status enjoyed by Jews in any other country.

The wording was painstakingly crafted and went through several drafts. In addition to the commitment safeguarding the rights of non-Jews in Palestine, as well as Jews in the Diaspora, most significant are two small words: "a" national home—designed to suggest that Palestine would be just one of many places Jews might live—and "in" Palestine—to indicate that a Jewish national home or state would not take up the entire area of Palestine, just a part of it. This declaration of support for Zionist aims by the world's greatest empire was the first major political achievement of the Zionist movement and a personal triumph for Chaim Weizmann. Despite Weizmann's singular achievement in securing the Balfour Declaration, the Zionist movement faced some of its greatest challenges from within.

Ze'ev (Vladimir) Jabotinsky and Revisionist Zionism

Leadership within the World Zionist Organization (WZO) was held by a group called the General Zionists. After Herzl's death in 1904, this group supplied a string of presidents to the WZO: David Wolfssohn (1905–1911), Otto Warburg (1911–1920), Chaim Weizmann (1920–1931 and 1935–1946), and Nahum Sokolow (1931–1935). As its name suggests, General Zionism represented a mainstream element within Zionism, free of stark ideological positions and committed to the primacy of establishing a Jewish state over any class, cultural, party, or personal interests. An opposing group known as the Revisionists, led by Ze'ev (Vladimir) Jabotinsky (1880–1940), emerged to strike a far more militant pose. Hailing from Odessa, Jabotinsky was an intellectual of considerable force, a respected translator, and a revered orator who captivated crowds in six languages.

Jabotinsky saw himself as heir to Herzl in that he, too, emphasized politics and diplomacy. And like Weizmann, Jabotinsky aligned himself with the British during the war, to help establish the Jewish Legion. The Jewish Legion was composed of three volunteer Jewish combat units who fought for the British. Totaling about 5,000 men, they formed the 38th, 39th, and 40th Battalions of the Royal Fusiliers. All had very different experiences. The 38th Battalion comprised of veterans from the Zion Mule Corps (created by Jabotinsky and Joseph Trumpeldor in 1915) as well as the British, Russian, and American armies, served as a true combat unit. The 39th Battalion, on the other hand, saw combat during the September 1914 offensive but also spent a great deal of time training in the desert. The 40th Battalion, known as the "Palestinians," included David Ben-Gurion, Levi Eshkol, and Yitzak Ben-Zvi. Ben-Gurion, known to his superiors as a poor and ill-disciplined soldier, even had his rank and pay reduced during his service. In contrast to the 38th Battalion, the 40th spent most of its time training in the desert and being "Anglicized" by British officers, who ordered them to participate in sporting events and educational courses.

Jabotinsky, a courageous commander of the 38th Battalion, was also a combative political figure. He brought his penchant for militarism into his political ideology, dismissing Weizmann's approach as too diplomatic and altogether too soft. He sought to convince the WZO to force Britain to uphold its pledge in the Balfour Declaration, which he took to imply the unrestricted immigration and settlement of Jews in all of Palestine, including the Transjordan. While labor Zionism was determined to expand Jewish settlement in Palestine, create a Jewish state, and establish a new Hebrew culture, it spoke the language of internationalism and socialism. It bore few outward traces of militant aggressiveness in its culture or rhetoric. This stood in marked contrast to the tenor of Jabotinsky's politics. Jabotinsky, a deeply cultured and cosmopolitan man, was also an admirer of Mussolini and was openly lured to Fascist symbols and rhetoric. (*See box,* "Zionist Culture.")

In 1925, Jabotinsky formed the World Union of Zionist Revisionists, the name of

SPORTING JEWS

One of the most important cultural developments in the modern period, and one that is directly tied to Jewish politics, was the participation of Jews in organized sports. Toward the end of the nineteenth century, Jews began to establish sports clubs, the first having been founded in 1895 by German Jews living in Istanbul after they had been expelled from the local German gymnastics club. A second Jewish gymnastics club, Ha-Gibbor (later called Samson), was founded in the Bulgarian city of Plovdiv. After 1897, clubs spread throughout Europe, the Americas, and eventually, the Middle East. By the interwar period, sports were one of the most eloquent and ubiquitous expressions of Jewish modernity and secularization. Inspired by Max Nordau (1849–1923), the Zionist leader who, in 1898, called for the creation of a "Muscular Judaism," Zionist sports clubs, such as Maccabi, Hakoah, and Ha-Gibbor, had branches all over Europe. The Zionists' rivals in Poland—the Bund—also promoted sports through its network of sports clubs, called Morgnshtern ("Morning Star"). In Hungary, the participation and success of Jews in both table tennis and fencing proved so spectacular that these two sports were identified as "Jewish." In the former, Viktor Barna (1911–1972), who won 32 World Championship medals, among them 23 gold, 6 silver, and 3 bronze, was described by Sir Ivor Montagu, president of the International Table Tennis Federation from 1926 to 1967, as "the greatest table tennis player who ever lived." Fencing, in particular, because of the upper-class milieu from which it sprang, was extremely popular among Hungarian Jews. Many of them were assimilated, others were raised as Catholics, and some were even converts. As was often the case, however, the disproportionate presence of Hungarians of Jewish extraction among national and Olympic champions only ensured

that they would be identified and stigmatized as Jews. Nevertheless, Hungarian Jews celebrated their achievements. In the United States, the Detroit Tigers' first baseman and power hitter, Hank Greenberg (1911–1986), who was open about and proud of his Jewish identity, was inspirational to American Jews. Especially in an era of widespread antisemitism, American Jews longed for a muscular sports hero of their own, and that Greenberg played the quintessential American sport at the highest level ensured his iconic status in the Jewish community. His refusal to play on Yom Kippur in 1934 further endeared him to American Jews. Greenberg's principled stance was immortalized by the prolific American poet and writer for the *Detroit Free Press* Edgar Guest:

Come Yom Kippur—holy fast day wide-world over to the Jew—And Hank Greenberg to his teaching and the old tradition true Spent the day among his people and he didn't come to play Said Murphy to Mulrooney, "We shall lose the game today! We shall miss him in the infield and shall miss him at the bat, But he's true to his religion—and I honor him for that!"

In the 1938 season, Greenberg came very close to overtaking Babe Ruth's record of 60 home runs in a single season. With five games remaining, Greenberg had hit 58. In those last games, several pitchers chose to walk him rather than give him a chance to break Ruth's record. Greenberg never complained, but many observers—and there were non-Jews among them—believed that Major League Baseball did not want a Jew breaking Ruth's record.

In two sports in particular—boxing and soccer—interwar Jewish identity was forged and energized. In Britain and the United States, in particular, the continued existence of a Jewish working class saw many Jews take up boxing. Most of them children of eastern European Jewish immigrants, Jewish boxers adopted colorful names and often fought with a Star of David on their trunks. Men such as Barney Ross, Benny Leonard, Jack "Kid" Berg, Ted "Kid" Lewis (Gershon Mendeloff), "Slapsie" Maxie Rosenbloom, and "Battling" Levinsky were world-class fighters and electrified a Jewish world that was suffering discrimination and violence and was desperately in search of heroes.

In Austria, Hakoah Vienna was an all-Jewish social-athletic club with 5,000 members. It sponsored a vast array of sports, but its soccer team was at the heart of the club and achieved the greatest renown. Competing in the Austrian league, the team finished second in the 1921–1922 season but won the Austrian National Championship in 1924–1925. Jewish players from all over the world made up the team, while Jewish fans the world over celebrated their glorious triumph.

Pictured in Figure 4.3 is Judah Bergman, aka Jack "Kid" Berg, aka "The Whitechapel Windmill" (1909–1991). During the interwar period, when Jews were still predominantly working-class and poor, they produced many fine boxers. In England and the United States, Jews were prominent in the sport, and a number of national and world champions were found in the lower-weight divisions. Perhaps the greatest of Jewish boxers, Gershon Mendeloff, aka Ted "Kid" Lewis (1894–1970), born in London's East End and known as the "Aldgate Sphinx," was the winner of nine official world and national titles. What especially endeared these boxers to the working-class Jewish public was that, like Daniel Mendoza in an earlier age, interwar Jewish boxers celebrated their Jewishness. They most often wore trunks emblazoned with Stars of

Figure 4.3   Judah Bergman, aka Jack "Kid" Berg, aka "The Whitechapel Windmill" (1909–1991).

Source: Getty Central Press/Getty Images.

David—Kid Berg also entered the ring wearing a prayer shawl (*tallis*)—and continued to live in the densely Jewish neighborhoods of London's East End and New York's Lower East Side. In the 1920s and the 1930s, when Fascism was on the rise across Europe and antisemitism became increasingly virulent, Jewish boxers became folk heroes, not only for their skills in the ring. Many of London's Jewish boxers associated with criminal gangs, including the notorious "Bessarabians," led by Max Moses, at one time himself an East End boxer. Jewish boxers and gangsters also took it upon themselves to be physical defenders of the Jews, especially against groups like Oswald Mosley's British Union of Fascists.

which was intended to indicate the corrective he wished to introduce into Weizmann's centrist Zionism. Revisionism was always more popular in the Diaspora than in the Yishuv, where labor Zionism held a tight rein on the political culture. Jabotinsky spent most of the interwar period in Europe, as he had been banished from Palestine by the British, who held the Revisionists chiefly responsible for the 1929 riots. He and his followers were convinced that some kind of a catastrophe, particularly economic, was about to befall European Jewry and that only unrestricted immigration to Palestine, coupled with the formation of a militarized Jewish nation, would be an effective response to the plight of the Jews. In Poland and other parts of eastern Europe, which in the 1930s were in the grip of ultra-nationalist and Fascist regimes with openly antisemitic agendas, Jabotinsky's message of aggressive Jewish militarism fell on receptive ears. Even though Revisionists carried out the important service of forming self-defense units against Polish pogromists, the presence of genuine Fascists in eastern Europe tended to moderate the behavior of Betar and the Revisionists in Europe.

In Palestine, by contrast, the Revisionists were on the political back foot as labor Zionism held sway. As such, the Revisionists there regarded themselves as a revolutionary cell. As a radical vanguard, they tended to extremism. In 1932, they formed the *Brit ha-Biryonim* ("League of Thugs"). The League made a virtue of violent protest, its anthem, written by Ya'akov Kahan, proclaiming:

War! War for our country, for freedom, war—
And if freedom dies forever—Long live vengeance!
If there is no justice in the land—the sword shall judge!

The volcanoes will be silent—We shall not be silent.
In blood and fire fell Judea
In blood and fire shall Judea rise!

In 1933, on a Tel Aviv beach, Chaim Arlosoroff, the leader of Israel's main labor party, Mapai, was assassinated. Right-wing assassins were tried for the crime, and radical groups like the Revisionists found themselves severely weakened. In genuine opposition to the conciliatory position of mainstream Zionism toward the British and the Arabs, Jabotinsky led the Revisionists out of the WZO in 1935 after the Zionist Executive rejected Jabotinsky's hard-line political program. He resigned from the Zionist movement and founded the New Zionist Organization (NZO). Its goal was to undertake political activity independent of the World Zionist Organization, lobby for unrestricted immigration of Jews to Palestine, and establish a Jewish state. Jabotinsky's militarism was not mere rhetoric; it split the Yishuv. In April 1937, during the Arab riots, members of the *Haganah*—the Zionist popular militia established after the Arab riots of 1920 and 1921—defected, with forces loyal to Jabotinsky forming the *Irgun Tzvai Le'umi* (The National Military Organization). Known also by its acronym, *ETzeL*, it was the military arm of the Revisionist movement. In support of Jabotinsky's rejection of the Haganah's policy of "restraint," *ETzeL* launched armed reprisals against Arabs, actions that served to further alienate the Revisionists from the Jewish Agency, which condemned such behavior. (In 1944, *ETzeL* would declare war on the British as well.) One of the significant achievements of Jabotinsky's military operations was bringing more than 40 boatloads of Jewish refugees from Europe to Palestine.

ZIONIST CULTURE

In 1923, Ze'ev Jabotinsky formed a militant youth league, Betar, an acronym for "Brit [Covenant of] Yosef Trumpeldor" ("League of Yosef Trumpeldor"), his goal being to imbue Jewish youth with the same martial values and spirit that typified the fallen hero of Tel Hai. Betar was also the place where the ancient warrior Bar Kochba fought his last stand against the Romans. This linkage of ancient and modern symbols of Jewish militancy became central to Zionist culture. It is for that reason that the festival of Hannukah was magnified in importance by Zionists and transformed from a minor religious holiday recognizing the eight-day divine miracle of the oil into a national holiday celebrating Jewish resistance to oppression. Masada, too, became an important symbol in the Zionist pantheon of sacred places. The ancient hilltop fortress where Jews were believed to have committed suicide rather than fall into Roman hands was venerated as an example of Jewish heroism. Today, in a solemn annual ceremony held atop Masada, some Israeli military cadets swear an oath to defend their country.

Zionism and the Arabs

Various Zionist groups had articulated different positions regarding the Arabs. Herzl took a typically European liberal line, believing that the local Arab population in Palestine would welcome Jews, who would bring economic and agricultural know-how to the land. In fact, Feysal's assurance in 1919 to the American Zionist Felix Frankfurter suggests a similar sentiment among some Arabs. Stressing bonds of kinship, Feysal wrote:

> We feel that the Arabs and Jews are cousins in race, having suffered similar oppressions at the hands of powers stronger than themselves, and by a happy coincidence have been able to take the first step towards the attainment of their national ideals together. The Arabs, especially the educated among us, look with the deepest sympathy on the Zionist movement.... We are working together for a reformed and revived Near East, and our two movements complete one another. The Jewish movement is national and not imperialist. Our movement is national and not imperialist.... Indeed, I think that neither can be a real success without the other.

Feysal later claimed he did not remember writing the letter, while Arab nationalists claimed it was a Zionist forgery. Most likely, it was written by Feysal at the Paris Peace Conference of 1919 to curry favor with the British and, because Palestine was of marginal importance to him, as he had set his sights more squarely on Syria.

In contrast to Herzl's attitude toward the Arabs, Ahad Ha-Am was extremely wary and more farsighted, noting as early as 1891 that Arabs were objecting to the presence of Jewish immigrants, particularly to their purchase of land from the Ottomans. Socialist Zionism of varying stripes was riddled with contradictions. Socialists tended to express sympathy for the Arabs, whom they identified as similar to themselves: an economically exploited class. But their desire to lead the class struggle that would unite Jews and Arabs, pitting them against two empires—the Russian and the Ottoman—meant that Jews would dominate and lead Arabs rather than form an egalitarian union with them. Many labor Zionists were convinced that only Jewish democracy would provide Arabs with an environment free of imperial oppression. Above all, the labor Zionist belief in "conquest by labor" meant that their position would lead them into conflict with indigenous Arabs, including the displacement of many through the Jewish attempt to own and control the land. Ben-Gurion's constant recourse to the historic claims of the Jewish people to the land was typical of this contradiction.

The position of Jabotinsky and the Revisionists differed starkly from the more accommodationist approaches of the General Zionist and socialist Zionist camps. Political maximalists, they sought to create a Jewish state on both sides of Jordan. In their vision, if Arabs were prepared to live under Jewish sovereignty, they were free to stay. If not, they were free to move to neighboring Arab lands. Jabotinsky believed that, given Jewish political and military weakness, it was crucial to redress the power imbalance between Arabs and Jews. Only from a position of strength would Jews be able to fairly negotiate with Arabs. Jabotinsky expressed sympathy for Arab nationalist claims but believed, in light of the threats facing Jews in Europe, that Zionist aspirations were morally compelling. Testifying before the Peel Commission in 1937, Jabotinsky observed:

> [I]t is quite understandable that the Arabs of Palestine would also prefer Palestine to be the Arab State No. 4, No. 5, or No. 6—that I quite understand; but when the Arab claim is confronted with our Jewish demand to be saved, it is like the claims of appetite versus the claims of starvation.

Mandate Palestine Between the Wars
In 1917, Britain invaded Palestine to defeat the Turks, and by September 1918, they were in complete control of the land. Palestine remained under British military administration until 1920. At the San Remo Conference, the Allied Powers divided up the former Ottoman Empire. Lebanon and Syria went to France, while Britain took control of Palestine and Iraq. British dependencies were called mandates, and according to President Woodrow Wilson's notions of national self-determination, the mandate governments were to lead their charges toward democracy.

By international agreement, and in accordance with the terms of the Balfour Declaration, Britain was to facilitate Jewish immigration to Palestine. Eventually, the vague language of the declaration gave way to the evasive and obstructionist policies of the British mandatory government. From the perspective of Zionist leadership, 1917–1920 was a period of growth. Britain dispatched Sir Herbert Samuel, a Jewish former cabinet minister, to be high commissioner of Palestine. With deep sympathy for Zionism, Samuel was permitted to deal with the Jewish Agency, the de facto Jewish government of the Yishuv. Jewish immigration to Palestine increased from 1,800 in 1919 to 8,000 in 1920–1921. In May 1921, Haj Amin el Husseini, a leading figure in Palestinian politics in the mandate period and a man appointed by Sir Herbert Samuel to the position of grand mufti of Jerusalem, instigated Arab riots in Jaffa and Petah Tikvah, which claimed the lives of 43 Jews. As a result, in 1922, the attitude of Whitehall to Jewish immigration changed. Winston Churchill, in his capacity as colonial secretary, declared in a white paper, "We do not intend for Palestine to become as Jewish as England is English." Britain then aimed to limit Jewish immigration to a level commensurate with the ostensible economic capacity of the country to absorb immigrants. The Zionists were content to place a limit on Jewish immigration, for they, too, agreed that the local economy could not support an infinite number of newcomers. They came to favor a policy of selective immigration. The

Arabs, on the other hand, were bitterly disappointed that the Balfour Declaration was not rescinded altogether and refused to countenance any form of Jewish settlement whatsoever. In 1925, there were 121,000 Jews in Palestine, a mere 14 percent of the total population, but by 1930, the number had risen to 175,000 Jews, or 17 percent of the total. The lower birth rate of Jews was offset by their lower death rate in comparison to the Arab population and the steady, though relatively small, influx of immigrants. During the mandate period, Arabs also immigrated to Palestine from surrounding countries.

In the immediate postwar period, the Zionist movement was beset by certain structural problems. The leadership of the movement was in Germany, while London occupied an increasingly important place. The majority of the Zionist rank and file, however, lived in eastern Europe, while the most important economic benefactors were to be found in the United States. Additionally, in the early 1920s, the funds and donations that the Zionist movement anticipated, especially from American Jewry, the largest financial supporter of Zionism, were not forthcoming. Beyond this, the number of immigrants, about 10,000 per year, was lower than expected, and Weizmann's leadership came under attack from various quarters—from Jabotinsky, who believed Weizmann was too accommodating to the British, and from far away in the United States. There, the leader of American Zionism was the distinguished lawyer Louis Brandeis (1856–1931), who headed the Federation of American Zionists from 1914 to 1916, when his appointment to the US Supreme Court forced him to give up that position of leadership. Nevertheless, he retained a lifelong attachment to the cause. Brandeis was a pragmatist and had little patience for the ideological schisms within the Zionist movement.

Because of Brandeis's intellectual and moral authority, Weizmann saw him as a competitor. Their falling-out was more than a failed relationship between two powerful, headstrong men but exemplified the fractured and weakened nature of the Zionist movement in the early 1920s. Brandeis, inspired by the political Zionism of Herzl, believed that the Balfour Declaration officially recognized Zionist aspirations and that attention now had to be placed on the construction of a sound economy in Palestine. Weizmann, by contrast, felt that the political work of Zionism was just beginning. He regarded the Zionist Organization as a provisional government, and the *Keren Hayesod* (Foundation Fund), the name of the fundraising campaign he launched in the United States in 1920, as the basis of a national treasury. Indeed, the workers' movement in the Yishuv drew funds from *Keren Hayesod* for salaries, agricultural settlements, public works, and industrial projects. Brandeis objected to this use of public funds. Although he supported trade unions and expected big business to act in a morally responsible manner, Brandeis saw the American Zionist organization as a business, obliged to seek out private investment, using public funds only for nonprofit initiatives, such as medical care and education.

In 1920, matters came to a head at the Zionist conference in London. Weizmann publicly confronted Brandeis, telling him, "I do not agree with your philosophy of Zionism We are different, absolutely different. There is no bridge between Washington and Pinsk." In many respects, Weizmann was correct: Brandeis and the eastern European Zionists were utterly different. Brandeis had no time for Zionist theorizing and argumentativeness, preferring to concentrate on rational organizing: "Members! Money! Discipline!" That is what Zionism needed. What further separated

Brandeis from the eastern European Zionists was that he was not overly concerned with the Jewish character of a future homeland and instead regarded the American ideals of Wilsonian national self-determination, cultural pluralism, and democracy to be at one with the needs of a Jewish state. For Brandeis, Zionism and Americanism were fully compatible. As he said in 1915, "[e]very American Jew who aids in advancing the Jewish settlement in Palestine, though he feels that neither he nor his descendants will ever live there, will likewise be a better man and a better American for having done so."

Under the British Mandate, the various institutions and political culture of a future Jewish state were established. Often Western-educated and fluent in English, Zionist leaders in Palestine were able to develop close working relations with the British high commissioners. Since Palestinian Arab leaders refused to sit on a joint Jewish Palestinian legislative council, Zionists were free to develop the structures and experience required for self-government on their own. Driven by military needs, the ruling British authority built Palestine's road, rail, telephone, and telegraph systems, as well as the port of Haifa. When the Jewish state was eventually established, it inherited a modern infrastructure, and its leadership had honed the administrative skills to run that state.

Still, despite permitting Jewish immigration, fostering Jewish political autonomy, and incorporating the weak economy of the Yishuv into that of the British Empire, British efforts were the fruit of self-interest. They did little to assist the Zionist Organization directly. Zionist settlement in Palestine remained tenuous, and to succeed required massive financial assistance from world Jewry, as well as a steady supply of immigrant labor. In contrast to other modern nationalist movements, all of which had an indigenous peasantry, whose labor formed the backbone of a local economy, Jews needed to import a labor force to create a national economy that could support an independent Jewish state. This was extremely difficult. Although an agricultural economy carried out on collective farms, such as the *moshav* or *kibbutz*, became mainstays of the Jewish economy in the 1920s, Jewish immigrants to Palestine remained an overwhelmingly urban people. By 1938, only about 15,000 people lived on 68 collective agricultural settlements. Still, the ideal of the Jewish agricultural laborer captured the imaginations of Palestinian and world Jewry alike.

The Third Aliyah (1919–1923), which brought about 35,000 Jews to Palestine, mostly from Ukraine and Russia, fostered a pioneer ethos that stressed themes of sacrifice, national rebirth, the anguish involved in preparing the soil, clearing malarial swamps, and defending the land. Central to the literature and music of the period was *halutziut* (pioneering), and the *halutz* (pioneer) became a revered figure in Israeli culture. The sentiments of this group were articulated by Uri Zvi Greenberg (1896–1981), a Yiddish, and then later a Hebrew, poet, whose uncompromising and sometimes violent imagery reflected the passions of those who made up the Third Aliyah. Building the land and defending it to the death were recurrent themes in Greenberg's work and in that of other Hebrew poets of that era. As he wrote in "With My God, The Blacksmith":

And over me stands my God, the blacksmith, hammering mightily.

Every wound that Time has cut in me, opens its gash and spits forth the pent-up fire in the sparks of moments.

This is my fate, my daily lot, until evening falls.

And when I return to fling my beaten mass upon the bed, my mouth is a gaping wound.

Then, naked, I speak to God: "You have worked so hard. Now night has come; let us both rest."

The Third Aliyah was similar to the Second in that at its core were young Jews with deep Zionist as well as socialist convictions. Their lasting achievements were to build some of the most important institutions of the Yishuv and what would become the State of Israel. In 1920, this generation of leaders founded the *Histadrut*, the major labor union. It built roads, housing, and expanded agricultural settlements. Beyond this, the Histadrut was also an all-encompassing cultural and social institution sponsoring sporting activities, a newspaper, book publishing, and medical insurance for Jewish workers.

The health-care facilities of the Histadrut were supplemented by the work of Hadassah, the largest Zionist women's organization. Established in 1912 by the American Jewish activist Henrietta Szold (1860–1945), Hadassah grew quickly and had over 40,000 American members by 1927. The large and energetic membership specialized in providing health care to both Jews and non-Jews in Palestine, and by 1930, Hadassah had opened four hospitals, a nurses' training school, and 50 clinics. With medical research laboratories, pharmacies, and prenatal and infant health centers, Hadassah was able to exert an enormous influence on the development of the Yishuv. It helped to drastically reduce the incidence of tuberculosis, malaria, trachoma, and typhoid. As a result, the Jewish mortality rate fell from 12.6 per 1,000 in 1924 to 9.6 per 1,000 in 1930. Jewish infant mortality in the Yishuv also declined sharply over that same period from 105 per 1,000 to 69 per 1,000.

Among the most important developments in the 1920s was the political triumph of labor Zionism. Under the leadership of Ben-Gurion and Chaim Arlosoroff (1899–1933), the Left abandoned its doctrinaire Marxism and made peace with the Yishuv's bourgeois elements. By 1930, the various streams of the Left coalesced into *Mapai*, an acronym for *Mifleget Poalei Eretz Yisrael* ("Land of Israel Workers' Party"). Rather than shun private capital, Mapai recognized it as essential to the welfare of the Yishuv. Though Brandeis had been defeated by Weizmann, the Americans' belief in the need for private enterprise and sound financial accounting found a footing in the policies of Ben-Gurion.

The Jewish Agency, founded in 1923, was responsible for facilitating Jewish immigration to Palestine, purchasing land from Arab owners, and formulating Zionist policy. It was largely controlled by Mapai and the Histadrut. After 1929, the Jewish Agency also took control of the Haganah. This effectively meant that Mapai, led by Ben-Gurion, who had become a de facto prime minister during the British Mandate period, now enjoyed the allegiance of most workers, had built a de facto government, and had a military force under its control. Ben-Gurion's special achievement lay in centralizing the political, economic, and military structures in Palestine, placing them under the control of his own party. All such institutions could now be put in the service of the Zionist revolution, and for Ben-Gurion, the goals of that revolution were nothing less than overturning 2,000 years of Jewish history, or at least his tendentious reading of it:

Galut [Diaspora existence] means dependence—material, political, spiritual, cultural and intellectual dependence—because we are aliens, a minority, bereft of a homeland, rootless and separated from the soil, from labor, and from basic industry. Our task is to break radically with this dependence and to become masters of our own fate—in a word, to achieve independence.

In its early stages, Zionism was a movement driven by secular Jews. By the 1920s, however, the voices of religious Jews in Palestine added an important dimension to Zionist ideology. Most crucial in this development was Avraham Yitzhak Kook (1865–1935), who, in 1921, was appointed the first Ashkenazic chief rabbi of Palestine. Kook forged an important alliance between Orthodox Jews, traditionally hostile to Zionism, and secular leaders of the movement. Kook, who in his youth had personally opposed Zionism and all forms of secular Jewish nationalism, began to see Zionism as part of a cosmic plan for divine redemption. Although he interpreted the work of labor Zionists in ways they personally rejected—he saw them as unwitting servants of the Lord—both factions accommodated each other. Thereafter, secular and Orthodox Jews in Palestine, and then in Israel, have reached a general consensus, deeply strained to be sure, but thus far workable, about how to live together. With the necessity that coalition governments in Israel be formed out of unions between secular and religious parties, both sides have regularly abandoned core principles for the sake of maintaining power.

The Fourth Aliyah (1924–1929) was of a different character than its predecessors. Restrictions on departure from the Soviet Union reduced the number of Russian Jewish immigrants to a trickle. At least half of the 67,000 Jews who came to Palestine in the mid- to late 1920s were middle-class shopkeepers and artisans from Poland. Fleeing the economic crisis that gripped Poland and the campaign to push Jews out of the national economy, they were not pioneering souls like those who made up previous waves of immigration; rather, they were urbanites who settled in cities, principally Tel Aviv, and expanded the economy of the Yishuv by introducing the commerce of leisure in the form of cafés, hotels, and restaurants, as well as new industries, particularly in the field of construction.

The development of urban culture (and economy) was reflected in changes that took place within Hebrew literary culture in the 1920s and the 1930s. Writers struggled to modernize the language by making it less ornate, having it reflect as well as energize the language of the street. A distinctly hard-edged urban poetry emerged that took account of modern life and its capacity to alienate. In his poem written after the State of Israel was established, "Said John Doe of His Neighborhood," Avraham Shlonsky (1900–1973) expressed the modernist poets' themes of fear, grief, agony, and boredom:

> The house I live in is 5 floors high, and all its windows yawn at their opposites, like faces of those standing before a mirror.
> There are 70 bus routes in my city, all chock-full, stifling with the stench of bodies; traveling, traveling, traveling, deep into the heart of the city, as if one couldn't die of boredom right here, in my own neighborhood
> The house I live in is 5 floors high—
> that woman who jumped from the window opposite only needed 3.

Here was modern Hebrew poetry that was neither biblical in its use of imagery, overly formal in its language, nor idealistically romantic in its subject matter. It constitutes a complete rejection of the lyricism of Bialik and the founding generation of modern Hebrew poetry.

While some may have felt psychologically estranged in their new land, the majority of those who faced difficulties were mostly victims of the economic crisis that hit Palestine in the mid-1920s. At least half of the 67,000 who arrived in 1926 left the country, while in 1927 more than 5,000 people departed, more than double the number that had arrived. Immigration stagnated in 1928, when only about 2,000 people arrived, with about the same number leaving. The Fourth Aliyah is generally considered to have ended in 1929, when Arab riots in Jerusalem erupted in protest against Jewish immigration.

More than 250,000 Jews came to Palestine in the Fifth Aliyah (1929–1939), with about 60,000 having fled Hitler's Germany and Austria and 94,000 from Poland. Most settled in urban areas, with over half going to Tel Aviv, which grew from 4,000 Jewish residents in 1921 to 135,000 in 1935. These central European immigrants expanded the commercial and light industrial sector of the economy. Most noticeably, this aliyah included many professionals, particularly physicians, lawyers, accountants, scientists, and scholars, all of whom greatly enhanced the intellectual life of the Yishuv.

Building Zionist Culture

Early Zionists sought to establish national cultural institutions, the most important of which opened in the interwar period. In 1903, Boris Shatz, a founder of the Royal Academy of Art in Sofia, Bulgaria, proposed to Theodor Herzl that a school of arts and crafts be established in the Land of Israel. In 1905, delegates to the Seventh Zionist Congress in Basel decided to establish the Bezalel School of Art, and a year later, the Bezalel Academy of Art and Design opened in Jerusalem. From its inception, Bezalel was intended to be a national academy of art, its goal being the creation of a new, national Jewish style that would be achieved by blending Middle Eastern and European forms. The Bezalel School artists used Art Nouveau to portray both biblical and Zionist subjects. Besides the attempt to create a new style, what further enhanced the concept of a national school of art were the diverse origins of artists at Bezalel. European and Middle Eastern Jews worked together at the academy. Particularly influential in creating a national style of decorative art were Yemenite Jews, who possessed a long tradition of jewelry making, silversmithing, and elaborate costume design. World War I cut Bezalel off from its executive committee in Berlin, as well as from its patrons and supporters across Europe. Due to lack of funds, the academy closed in 1929, but under the directorship of the Berlin print artist Josef Budko, Bezalel reopened in 1935 as the New Bezalel School for Arts and Crafts. Budko influenced a shift in Bezalel's emphasis to typography and graphic arts—particularly important in the public visual culture of the Yishuv, with its growing need for posters, signage, and graphics that were expressive of national development.

The arrival of numerous Jewish architects from Germany in the interwar years had a decisive impact on building styles and techniques in the Yishuv and, in particular, on Tel Aviv. Founded on sand dunes in 1909, Tel Aviv experienced significant growth in the interwar period. This coincided with the high point of modernist architecture's Bauhaus movement. Most of the architects working in Tel Aviv at this time were refugees from Europe and implemented Bauhaus designs, or what became known as the International Style. At least 17 of the city's architects had been students at the Bauhaus school in Dessau, Germany, which the Nazis closed on

April 11, 1933. Championing function over form, volume over mass, repetition over symmetry, Bauhaus architecture focused on the social dimension of building design and was especially preoccupied with creating a new form of social housing for workers. Some of the key design elements that were adapted for the climate in Palestine were the installation of small horizontal strip windows, called "thermometer windows," to balance the need for light and for keeping out the strong sun; the provision of balconies to take advantage of the moderate climate; the placing of buildings on stilt-type columns, which raised them off street level, thereby creating room for a garden area and providing for greater airflow; and finally, using a flat, as opposed to the traditional, European steeple, roof. The buildings were usually between two and four floors, constructed as a single building and covered with a shade of white plaster. In all, the style is characterized by asymmetry, functionality, and simplicity. The modernist style of the architecture helped establish Tel Aviv as the first Hebrew City. It was not beholden to historic styles but, rather, to the new, the modern, and the avant-garde. The style was an apt expression of Zionism's social and cultural goals—the emphasis on function over form, collective well-being over individualism, and new over old.

During the interwar period, the foundations of a national Hebrew theater were also erected. *Habimah* (The Stage) was the world's first Hebrew theater company, founded in Moscow in 1917. Out of the revolutionary and messianic atmosphere, which then had Russia in its grip, the country became a laboratory of both political and cultural experimentation. One such experiment was Hebrew theater and its use of the ancient, sacred tongue, for modern, secular culture. The language of the prophets also fit the language of revolution. David Ben-Gurion, who visited Moscow in 1923, was astonished. Knowing the opposition to Hebrew of the regime, and especially the Jewish section of the Communist Party, Ben-Gurion asked rhetorically:

> Does all this exist in the Moscow of 1923, where the state library does not allow Hebrew newspapers, and conceals many of its Hebrew books, where study of the Hebrew language is not permitted? . . . A sense of miracle grips me, a feeling of wonder, of rebellion against the laws of reality.

Bialik, who had also visited the theater in Moscow, was struck by how incongruous it was for there to be a Hebrew theater in the Soviet Union: "Perhaps under the strange circumstances of the Revolution in Moscow, . . . Habimah, too, drank from the intoxicating cup affecting others. I do not know if the masters of Habimah will be privileged to enjoy again such months and days." What Ben-Gurion and Bialik saw was actually a multicultural event. Habimah performed in Hebrew the classic Yiddish play by Ansky *The Dybbuk*, under the direction of the Armenian director Eugene Vakhtangov. Bialik was the Hebrew translator of *The Dybbuk*.

Led by Nahum Zemach, Habimah performed in Moscow for nearly eight years, until it left on a world tour in 1926 to perform *The Dybbuk*. The company never returned to the Soviet Union. In 1927, while in the United States, Habimah split. Some, including Zemach, stayed in America, while the others went to Palestine. Although many accomplished Hebrew prose stylists and poets were working in Palestine at this time, there were but few playwrights. The earliest plays staged by Habimah were the historical dramas *B'layil*

Zeh (On This Night, 1934), which depicted the destruction of the Temple in Jerusalem, and *Yerushalayim ve-Romi (Jerusalem and Rome*, 1939), about the ancient Roman Jew Josephus. By 1930, three professional Hebrew theater companies were active in the Yishuv. Habimah later developed into the National Theater of Israel.

As far back as 1884, Hibbat Tsiyon had proposed the establishment of a university where instruction would take place in Hebrew. This remained a goal of many within the Zionist movement, but funding and staffing such an institution took time. While the cornerstone of the Hebrew University in Jerusalem was laid in 1918, it was not until 1925 that the institution finally opened its doors. The faculty was comprised almost exclusively of academics from German-speaking Europe who had come in the Fifth Aliyah. The Technion in Haifa, dedicated to research and instruction in the sciences, was opened in 1924 by the German Jewish foundation known as Ezrah. In the 12 years between the laying of the cornerstone in 1912 and the beginning of classes, a bitter debate raged over the language of instruction. Ezrah, which had managed to open 20 other schools between 1912 and 1913, demanded that German be used at the Technion, for it was the preeminent language of science. The organization challenged the partisans of Hebrew, claiming that the ideas and practice of modern science could not be expressed in the ancient language. After Germany's defeat in World War I, instruction in Hebrew became the norm throughout Palestine. Both the Hebrew University and the Technion were more than places of higher learning—they were national institutions, established to educate leaders of a new, modern nation by providing them with a secular education in Hebrew. During the interwar period, the revolutionary and youthful leadership of the Yishuv was successful in building the institutions and essential characteristics of Zionist culture, one that was felt in all fields of the arts, scholarship, and public sector service. This new Jewish culture was vital, as it was informed by both European and Jewish elements fused in an entirely novel and experimental way.

Tensions with the Palestinian Arabs

At first, European Zionist aspirations were animated by the myth that the Land of Israel was empty of inhabitants. But those Jews who migrated there soon found out that this was far from the case. About 700,000 non-Jews were living in Palestine in 1914, a number that increased to nearly 1 million by 1939. Rather than the benign, cooperative relationship between Jews and Arabs that Herzl and many later labor Zionists imagined, the encounter was marked by hostility and a recurring cycle of violence. From the beginning of Zionist settlement, neither side has been willing to see the merits in the other party's claims. From the Zionist perspective, the young immigrant Jews harbored utopian and peaceful visions of a Hebrew future on the land. They assumed that Arabs would welcome their technological and scientific know-how and were convinced that Arabs would appreciate the material benefits of modern, productive land management. By contrast, Palestinian Arabs saw the Zionists as predatory colonialists from Europe come to dispossess them.

So long as the size of the Jewish population was negligible, so too was Arab protest against the Jewish presence. This changed during the interwar period, as the Jewish population of Palestine grew from about 85,000 in 1914, or 12 percent of the total population, to 475,000, or approximately 31 percent of the total population, on the eve of World War II. Growing Arab nationalism, hatred of the British mandatory authorities, and genuine fear of displacement due to the growing stream of Jewish immigrants—most of them refugees fleeing Europe and, to a lesser extent, a host of countries in the Middle East—led to increasing Arab frustration and anti-Jewish violence. In 1920, Arabs attacked the Jewish settlement in the Upper Galilee at Tel Hai and killed eight Jews, among them the Zionist leader and veteran of the Russo-Japanese War Yosef Trumpeldor (1880–1920). His last words were purported to be "Never mind, it is good to die for our country." Since Trumpeldor was revered by the political Right as an example of the muscular Jew who fought back and by the political Left as a defender of socialist agricultural settlements, his death became a national inspiration and a milestone in the development of Zionist collective memory.

On September 24, 1928, a minor incident at Jerusalem's Wailing Wall, which was under Muslim jurisdiction, led to rioting and substantial loss of life. Orthodox Jews erected a screen to separate Jewish male and female worshippers. Arabs considered this a provocative first step to a Jewish takeover of the Al-Aqsa Mosque on al-Haram al-Sharif, or the Temple Mount. Protests and counterprotests ensued. For nearly a year, tensions simmered, until August 23, 1929, when bands of armed Arabs marched on Jerusalem and attacked the Jewish quarter of the Old City. The rioting soon spread to Haifa, Jaffa, and Tel Aviv. For five days, the bloodletting continued. The result was 133 Jews killed, 60 of them massacred in Hebron. In repelling the rioters, the British killed 116 Arabs.

One of the most significant Zionist responses to increasing Arab militancy was the formation of the defense organization the Haganah. Originally a popular militia, established after the riots of 1920 and 1921 for the purposes of protecting agricultural settlements, the Haganah lacked a strong central authority, was poorly equipped, and lacked proper training. Thereafter, and particularly in response to the Arab Revolt of 1929, the Haganah was transformed into a better-trained and more effective armed force. By 1936, the Haganah had 10,000 men under arms and about 40,000 reservists. Soldiers were now equipped with arms purchased from overseas and with light weapons they had manufactured themselves.

The British response to the riots made it clear to the Yishuv that they were losing the confidence of Whitehall. The colonial secretary, Lord Passfield, issued a white paper in 1930 recommending that Jewish land purchases and immigration levels be restricted. Although the British prime minister, Ramsay MacDonald, essentially overturned the white paper in 1931, it was clear to Chaim Weizmann that doors, which had once been open to him, were now closing. Even Jewish deaths at the hands of the Arabs failed to arouse British sympathy. Beatrice Webb, Lord Passfield's wife, commented callously, "I can't understand why the Jews make such a fuss over a few dozen of their people killed in Palestine. As many are killed every week in London in traffic accidents, and no one pays any attention." At the official level, the British were beginning to realize that they could not adhere to the terms of the Balfour Declaration and accommodate Arab demands at the same time.

Constant Jewish immigration to Palestine throughout the 1930s exacerbated Arab opposition and led to increasingly organized protests, the most significant of which was the Arab Revolt of 1936–1939. In 1936, a loose coalition of Arab political parties, known as the Arab Higher Committee (AHC), was created. Led by Grand Mufti Haj Amin al-Husayni, it declared a national strike in April 1936, a boycott of all Jewish and British products, and a tax revolt in support of three basic demands: the cessation of Jewish immigration, an end to all further land sales to the Jews, and the establishment of an Arab national government. The protests soon turned violent, with attacks directed at both Jews and the British. With the aid of their regional Arab allies, the British were able to mediate a ceasefire, which fell apart in 1937. Between 1937 and 1939, Palestine was drenched in blood. With the aid of Syria, Iraq, and Egypt, Palestinian resistance to Zionism took on the character of a pan-Arab nationalist uprising. (Nazi and Italian Fascist agents also offered them encouragement and assistance.) Arab demands and expectations grew as the uprising became intertwined with a peasant revolt. Internecine feuds also erupted. Poverty-stricken *fellahin* attacked Palestinian landowners, British authorities, and Jews. The British responded with brutal force. By 1939, nearly 5,000 Arabs and 415 Jews had been killed, and thousands were wounded and imprisoned. The AHC was dissolved, and the grand mufti fled to avoid capture by the British.

During the Arab Revolt, the British Peel Commission (1937) issued its recommendation for the partition of Palestine into Jewish and Arab states. The Arab state, the larger of the two, was to be united with Transjordan and would consist of what is today the West Bank, the Gaza Strip, and the Negev. The Jewish state was to consist of the Mediterranean coastal plain and the Galilee. The zone between Jaffa and Jerusalem, including both of those cities, would remain under British control.

The Arabs rejected the partition plan; the Zionist leadership, while opposed to the proposed size of the Jewish state, nonetheless grudgingly accepted it. However, important Zionist factions rejected the partition, the most significant being the Revisionists led by Ze'ev Jabotinsky. A smaller group of religious Zionists also rejected partition, believing that God had promised the Land of Israel in its entirety to the Jewish people.

As the 1930s passed, it became increasingly clear to Britain that war with Nazi Germany was a distinct possibility. Of particular concern to the British was the fact that many Arab nationalists were attracted to Hitler's message, especially his antisemitism. Yet Britain could not chance alienating the Arabs by accommodating Zionist ambitions, and it could ill afford to jeopardize its access to oil, a resource that it would desperately need should the nation find itself at war. The British white paper of 1939 reflected a change in attitude to Zionism and fears for the health of the British Empire in the face of Nazi belligerence and Italian designs on North Africa and the Mediterranean. The British then renounced the idea of partition, declaring that Arab Palestine would become an independent state within ten years and that Jewish immigration would be limited to a further 75,000 people over the next five years.

Figure 4.4 shows "White City" in Tel Aviv (1930s), a district where the buildings are covered with a shade of white plaster, hence the name of the area. The buildings were mostly residential, but many commercial structures were also built in this style. Such buildings predominate Tel Aviv's architectural landscape, giving it the greatest collection of Bauhaus architecture in the world. In "White City," about 4,000 such buildings were constructed between the 1930s and 1948. Over half of them were constructed between 1931 and 1937, coinciding with the arrival of refugees from Nazi Germany. Lack of funds, the harsh beach weather, and a neglect of the buildings

Figure 4.4   "White City" in Tel Aviv (1930s).

Source: Library of Congress Prints and Photographs Division, LC-DIG-matpc-03593.

when the style fell out of fashion mean that today many of the buildings are in a state of disrepair. Approximately 1,100 of these international style buildings are slated for preservation. White City is considered such an architectural gem that in July 2003, UNESCO, the United Nations Educational, Scientific, and Cultural Organization, proclaimed the "White City" of Tel Aviv-Jaffa a World Cultural Heritage site.

The Jews of the Eastern Levant and Muslim Lands

In 1914, while nearly 90 percent of the world's Jews were of Ashkenazic origin, approximately 1 million Jews of Sephardic and Middle Eastern descent were still living in the Balkans and in Muslim lands, stretching from Morocco to Afghanistan. These communities were highly differentiated from one another culturally and socioeconomically, living under a variety of political regimes and religions. The massive changes that affected the Muslim world in the nineteenth and into the twentieth centuries are manifold. Internal and external causes were both driving political, social, and economic transformations, with the impact of European dominance in the area among the most important. Certainly, for Jews of the region, European, especially French, hegemony played a decisive role in changing the character of Sephardic and Middle Eastern communities. This historical influence was highly uneven, with communities such as those in Istanbul, Baghdad, and Tehran far more receptive to Westernization than Jewish communities in, say, Kurdistan, Afghanistan, and the interior of Yemen.

Language is an important marker of difference among these Jews. The Sephardic communities of western Europe retained Spanish and Portuguese into the eighteenth century. Neither was ever written in Hebrew script and can make no claim to being Jewish languages. Thereafter, descendants of European Sephardim adopted the local vernacular. By contrast, Sephardic Jewry in the Ottoman Empire, especially in the Balkans and in Turkey, developed Ladino into the Jewish vernacular. The Ottomanization of Balkan Jewry came at the expense of the indigenous, Greek-speaking Romaniote Jews, who largely disappeared, demographically swamped by the large Sephardic influx beginning in the sixteenth century. In the Balkans, Ladino retained Spanish as the core language but liberally incorporated Hebrew, Turkish, and Greek. Unlike other Jewish languages, it was written in Rashi script, originally a fifteenth-century form of cursive script used by Spanish Jews. Eastern Sephardim have used numerous names for their language in addition to Ladino: *Espaniol* (Spanish), *muestro Espaniol* (our Spanish), and *djudezmo.*

Ironically, Ladino culture flourished where French, thanks to the Alliance Israélite Universelle, made its greatest inroads. French became the language of high culture, but Ladino remained the language of the Jewish masses and catered to their tastes with scores of newspapers, novels, plays, and translations. At the same time, the number of religious texts appearing in Ladino went into marked decline, as Jews increasingly wanted their Ladino literature to reflect their secular sensibilities.

In the wake of the expulsion from Spain, across North Africa, the Sephardic population never exceeded that of the indigenous Jewish communities. Spanish soon died out, and Sephardim, like native-born Jews, began to speak Judeo-Arabic. (A few small communities in northern Morocco, such as Tangier and Tetuán, spoke a form of Judeo-Spanish called Haketia, which remained in use until the twentieth century.) In other Arab lands, such as Iraq, Syria, and Lebanon, Jews spoke Arabic. A neglected yet significant number of Arabic-speaking Jewish intellectuals emerged in the late nineteenth and early twentieth centuries, and their contributions mark a distinctly Middle Eastern Jewish encounter with modernity. Arabic writers such as Esther Azhari Moyal (1873–1948) in Beirut, and later Jaffa, who was an outspoken feminist and supporter of Arab women's rights, as well as a passionate defender of Jews, and the Egyptian nationalist playwright and journalist Ya'qub Sanu' (Jacob Sanua) (1839–1912) characterize an engagement between modern Jews and Arab culture that further illuminates the vast cultural differences that existed among Jews in the Muslim world. In Iran, Jews spoke Judeo-Persian until the twentieth century, at which time they shifted to Farsi. By contrast, a large proportion of Sephardic and Middle Eastern Jews became French speakers, thanks to the vast educational network established by the Alliance Israélite Universelle and thus felt a greater affinity for European culture and colonial authority.

In North Africa, Jews in Libya, Tunisia, Algeria, and Morocco comprised the only non-Muslim minority in the Maghreb, the area of Africa north of the Sahara Desert and west of the Nile River. Until the arrival of the European powers in the nineteenth century, Jews lived as *dhimmi*, second-class but protected subjects of the sultan. They paid an annual tax, the *jizya*, and lived under the strictures of the Pact of Umar, an eighth-century legal code intended to ensure Jewish subservience to the Muslim majority. At certain times, it was imposed more stringently than at others, depending on many variables, including who was in power and which Muslim religious forces were in the ascendancy. Jewish status was changed when the French took control of North Africa and extended French citizenship to Jews. The first beneficiaries were the 15,000 Jews of Algeria in 1830, thanks to the tireless efforts of Adolphe Crémieux (1794–1880), leading statesman, founder of the Alliance, and from 1834 until his death, vice president of the consistory. Tunisia's 25,000 Jews won citizenship in 1881, while the 100,000 Jews of Morocco gained their civil rights in 1912. Finally, in 1916, the 16,000-strong Jewish population of Libya (an Italian colony) was emancipated.

The majority of North African Jews were desperately poor, though for a significant number, socioeconomic conditions improved with the opportunities that came in the wake of European colonization. Christians, who were likewise *dhimmi*, benefited equally from European rule. By the twentieth century, like their Ashkenazic coreligionists, North African Jews tended to concentrate in urban centers or in port cities. Many engaged in commerce, while the majority were artisans and tradesmen. The officially constituted Jewish communities in Morocco were called *mellahs*, while in other parts of North Africa, they were called *haras*.

Across North Africa, violence and discrimination had plagued Jewish communities for centuries. A non-Jewish account of Jewish life in Tunisia shortly before the coming of the French painted a miserable picture:

> [The Jews] had to live in a certain quarter, and were not allowed to appear in the streets after sunset. If they were compelled to go out at night they had to provide themselves with a cat-o'-nine-tails . . . which served as a kind of passport to the patrols going around at night. If it was a dark night, they were not allowed to carry a lantern like the Moors and Turks, but a candle, which the wind extinguished every minute. They were neither allowed to ride on horseback nor on a mule, and even to ride on a donkey was forbidden them except outside the town; they had then to dismount at the gates, and walk in the middle of the streets, so as not to be in the way of Arabs. If they had to pass the "Kasba," they had first to fall on their knees as a sign of submission, and then to walk on with lowered head; before coming to a mosque they were obliged to take the slippers off their feet, and had to pass the holy edifice without looking at it. As Tunis possesses no less than five hundred mosques, it will be seen that Jews did not wear out many shoes at that time.

Muslim humiliation of and discrimination against Jews diminished significantly with the arrival of European rule. Thanks to the French presence, economic and educational opportunities became available, and even the health of Jews improved with the introduction of new systems of sanitation. By 1900, the lifespan of Algerian Jews was significantly higher than that of their Muslim neighbors, a feature in keeping with the rest of the Jewish world.

The largest Jewish community in North Africa lived in Morocco, a highly fragmented society whose Jewish population followed suit. There were Jewish city dwellers, village Jews in the Atlas Mountains, and Jewish Berbers, all making for a highly diverse population. According to the Moroccan census of 1936, three-quarters of Morocco's 161,000 Jews were bilingual in Berber and Arabic, and another 25,000 were exclusively Berber speakers. There were also Spanish-speaking Jews in the north of the country, which, for a while, was under Spanish control. As in other parts of North Africa, the Jewish population was also divided into what were known in Hebrew as *megorashim* (descendants of those expelled from the Iberian Peninsula) and *toshavim* (native-born Jews).

In Tunisia, the Jews were divided between an Arabic-speaking majority and an Italian-speaking minority. Where possible, they sought to remain separate. They attended different synagogues, were buried apart from each other, and turned to parallel community institutions. Little intermarriage occurred between the two groups. In certain circumstances, however, the lines between the two communities blurred, especially when a wealthier or more Westernized Arabic-speaking Jew returned from Europe and sought access to the Italophone community. The size of a Jewish community also played a decisive factor in this process. Where a *haras* was especially small, separate institutions made little sense and could, in fact, endanger the existence of the community. In those circumstances, there was a much greater degree of fraternization.

In Algeria, the Jewish population had grown considerably in the interwar period, from 74,000 in 1921 to 99,000 in 1936. The Crémieux Decree of 1870, which bestowed French citizenship on Algerian Jews, was a source of Muslim and Christian envy and hostility. The access to French education provided unprecedented opportunities for Algerian Jews, and their social and economic situation soon outstripped that of any other Jewish community in the Maghreb and tended to exceed that of their Muslim neighbors. By 1941, although they constituted only 2 percent of the total population, Jews were 37 percent of all Algerian medical students and 24 percent of all law students. Organized into the consistory system—in Algiers, Constantine, and Oran—Algerian Jews were linked directly to the central consistory in Paris and to the French administration in Algiers. The level of Jewish acculturation was extremely high, as the Jews rapidly became French speakers and often sent their children to Paris for study and work. By the interwar period, about 90 percent of the Jews were evenly divided among artisans, merchants, and salaried employees of the French state.

Libya was under Ottoman control from 1835 until 1911 and then was ruled as a colony by the Italians from 1911 until 1943, at which point the British captured it. In Libya, with a relatively small Jewish population of about 25,000 in the interwar period, Jews were nevertheless a notable presence. The 15,300 Jews who lived in Tripoli in 1931 formed about 20 percent of the capital city's total population. In the late 1930s, the situation of the Jews began to markedly deteriorate when Mussolini's Fascist government extended its antisemitic laws to Libyan Jews.

By the 1930s, the existence of the ancient Jewish communities found throughout the Middle East became increasingly precarious. In most cases, Arab nationalism and Muslim fundamentalism played their part in the decline. Even in Turkey, with the more favorable conditions under the rule of Atatürk, the Jewish population declined in the twentieth century, a process that began in earnest in the 1920s. In 1927, half of the 81,500 Turkish Jews lived in Istanbul. They were mostly

Sephardim, but there were Ashkenazic communities as well. Over the course of the next decade, significant numbers began to leave for the Americas and Palestine.

Iraq, where the Jews, mindful of their long tenure in that country, referred to themselves in Hebrew as Babylonian Jews, came under Ottoman control in 1638. Iraqi Jews were essentially divided into two main groups: the mountain Jews of Kurdistan, numbering up to 20,000 in the twentieth century, and the highly Arabized communities of the lowland regions, principally Baghdad. Originally one community, sometime in the fifteenth century, the Jews split into these two distinct communities. Mostly poor artisans, traders, and agriculturalists, Kurdish Jews were subject to the oppressive rule of local Kurdish chieftains, called *agas*. They spoke Judeo-Kurdish, an Aramaic dialect known as *Targum* by its speakers, and had their spiritual center in Mosul. The harsh conditions of Jewish life in Kurdistan became worse in the 1930s and the 1940s, when riots against Jews in the south of the country began to move northward. In response, many Kurdish Jews immigrated to Palestine.

Most Iraqi Jews, however, lived in Baghdad, a center of both Jewish religious and secular culture. Baghdad was home to one of the leading rabbinic authorities of the nineteenth century, Joseph Hayyim (1834–1909), a revered scholar, renowned for his *halakhic* flexibility and his receptivity to modernization. By 1927, Baghdad also had five Alliance schools, which Hayyim publicly opposed, believing that they would lead not merely to Jewish modernization, something he deemed important, but to Jewish secularization. His fears were not unfounded. Iraqi Jewry was faced with some of the same competing ideological trends that were readily apparent in other Jewish communities, and

its Western-educated elite likewise dominated communal affairs.

Like other Iraqis, the Jewish community was deeply affected by British rule. When the British captured the southern Iraqi city of Basra in November 1914, the governing Ottomans panicked, and their rule became arbitrary and often brutal, characterized by executions and extortion of Jews, Christians, and their fellow Muslims. Under these circumstances, many Jews fled. When the British occupied Baghdad in March 1917, the Jews of the city declared it a "Day of Miracle." Jewish communities in Mosul and Kirkuk did likewise. When the British took control of Iraq, Jews were granted civil rights and made equal to Muslims before the law.

When the British arrived in 1917, Baghdad was a noticeably "Jewish city." Jews were the single largest ethnic group in the capital. Of a total population of 202,800, 80,000, or 40 percent, were Jews. Sunnis, Shi'ites, and Turks totaled 101,000; Christians, 12,000; Kurds, 8,000; and Persians, 800. The Jews were a significant presence in nearly all walks of life. In 1926, when the Baghdad Chamber of Commerce was established, of the 15 members, 5 represented Jewish merchants, 4 Muslim merchants, 3 British-owned businesses, 1 each for Christian and Persian merchants, and 1 for the banks. The importance of the Baghdadi Jewish community went beyond its numerical superiority. Part of the strength of the Jewish merchant class, with the Sassoon and Kadoorie families most prominent, derived from its vast international trading networks, extending in one direction to London and in the other to India and on to the Far East.

Throughout the period of the British Mandate, 1922–1932, the Jews of Iraq continued to enjoy economic vitality and participate in government and national affairs. However, a rising chorus of Muslims, echoing the language of European Fascists, began decrying Jewish "control" of the Iraqi economy and the disproportionate Jewish presence in the country's administration. As Baghdad became a gathering point for Arab nationalists from Syria and Palestine, implacable hostility to Zionism further contributed to the increasingly delicate position of Iraq's Jews.

When Iraq gained full independence in 1932, Jews became Iraqi citizens. This did not, however, protect them from Arab hostility as much as they had hoped it would. In 1936, rising Arab nationalism broke out in violence against the Jews of Iraq. Three people were shot and killed around the Jewish New Year. The next day, which had been declared Palestine Day, was marked by violent protests, as antisemitic sermons rang out from mosques. As was the case elsewhere, when the loyalty of Iraqi Jews was questioned, the response was a ringing assertion of Jewish patriotism, a swipe at Europe, and a dissociation from Zionism. In 1936, the Jewish school principal, scholar, and writer Ezra Haddad proclaimed:

> The Arab Jew, when he makes his attitude to the Zionist question clear, feels in his innermost being that he does that of his own free will and motivated by considerations of justice, conscience and . . . well established facts. And when he speaks of the Arab lands, he speaks of homelands which from time immemorial surrounded him with generosity and affluence— homelands which he considered and continues to consider as oases in the midst of a veritable desert of injustices and oppressions which were the Jews' lot in many of the countries which boast of culture and civilization.

Not long before he published this piece, Haddad published another with the title "We Were Arabs Before We Became Jews." Haddad's declarations on behalf of Jewish Arabization reflected general community sentiment. The Jews of Iraq were indeed among the most Arabized of all Jewish communities in the region. Their level of cultural integration and modernization was enhanced by the Alliance education they received and, according to a report sent from the British consul general's office in Baghdad to the foreign office in London in 1910, contributed to further the process of secularization: "In contradistinction to past days, the clergy enjoy no influence over their co-religionists, and this may confidently be ascribed to the effect of education diffused among the classes of the community."

The secularization of the Jewish middle classes rapidly advanced among all Sephardic and Middle Eastern Jewries. Even poor Jews were not immune. Nothing so clearly illustrates the results of this process as the formal critique lodged in 1929 by an Alliance teacher, Monsieur L. Loubaton. He feared a complete "de-judaization" among the Jews of Tunisia:

> Hebrew instruction for children, which was highly valued in the time preceding the arrival of the Alliance, can be said to be non-existent. . . . The children are ignorant of all that represents the beauty and uniqueness of our doctrine; they have no notion of biblical history or Jewish history; they are totally unaware that a modern Jewish literature exists.

At the synagogues, Loubaton saw only impiety:

> I myself go out to the terrace for a moment. It is like entering a public meeting place. Everyone has closed his book, circles of

people have formed, and there is chatting, yawning, jesting, laughing. In the evening, more than three-fifths of those attending services are gathered on the terrace.

In the city of Sousse, the situation was the same: "Let us consider the cafés on a Saturday. They are literally invaded by Jews. With few exceptions, all are smoking, gambling—often for large sums of money—at cards or at backgammon, or discussing business." Loubaton also observed that "already, mixed marriages are becoming common." The only remedy that he envisioned was the "founding of yeshivot and for the encouragement of theological studies [and] the creat[ion] of a rabbinical corps."

This needed to be undertaken by the Alliance, for "the very preservation of Tunisian Jewry, which now shows so many signs of degeneration, depends on this undertaking."

Loubaton clearly failed to recognize or was unwilling to appreciate the cultural path that Middle Eastern Jewry had set out on. What he identified as a local Tunisian Jewish problem was, in fact, part of a general historical process that existed in modern Jewish communities, whether in Europe, the Middle East, or the Americas. The decline of traditional observance went hand in hand with rising educational and socioeconomic levels and the emergence of new, vibrant secular cultures.

For Further Reading

On World War I, see George L. Mosse, *The Jews and the German War Experience, 1914–1918* (New York: Leo Baeck Institute, 1977); David Rechter, *The Jews of Vienna and the First Word War* (London and Portland, OR: Littman Library of Jewish Civilization, 2001); Mark Levene, *War, Jews, and the New Europe: The Diplomacy of Lucien Wolf, 1914–1919* (Oxford, England: Oxford University Press, 1992); Tim Grady, *The German-Jewish Soldiers of the First World War in History and* Memory (Liverpool: Liverpool University Press, 2011); Derek J. Penslar, *Jews and the Military: A History* (Princeton: Princeton University Press, 2013).

On Jewish politics and culture in the interwar period, see Michael Brenner and Gideon Reuveni, eds., *Emancipation Through Muscles: Jews and Sports in Europe* (Lincoln: University of Nebraska Press, 2006); Michael Brenner, *The Renaissance of Jewish Culture in Weimar Germany* (New Haven, CT: Yale University Press, 1996); Steven Beller, *Vienna and the Jews, 1867–1938: A Cultural History* (Cambridge, England: Cambridge University Press, 1986); David Shneer, *Yiddish and the Creation of Soviet Jewish Culture, 1918–1930* (Cambridge,

England: Cambridge University Press, 2004); Jeffrey Veidlinger, *The Moscow State Yiddish Theater: Jewish Culture on the Soviet Stage* (Bloomington: Indiana University Press, 2000); Anna Shternshis, *Soviet and Kosher: Jewish Popular Culture in the Soviet Union, 1923–1939* (Bloomington: Indiana University Press, 2006); Yuri Slezkine, *The Jewish Century* (Princeton, NJ: Princeton University Press, 2004). Michael Steinlauf and Antony Polonsky, eds., *Polin 16* (2003); Zvi Gitelman, ed., *The Emergence of Modern Jewish Politics: Bundism and Zionism in Eastern Europe* (Pittsburgh, PA: University of Pittsburgh Press, 2003); Ezra Mendelsohn, *The Jews of East Central Europe between the World Wars* (Bloomington: Indiana University Press, 1983); and Jeffrey Shandler, ed., *Awakening Lives: Autobiographies of Jewish Youth in Poland before the Holocaust* (New Haven: Yale University Press, 2002).

On Zionism and the Yishuv, see Tom Segev, *One Palestine Complete: Jews and Arabs under the British Mandate* (New York: Owl Books, 2001); Anita Shapira, *Land and Power: The Zionist Resort to Force, 1881–1948* (New York: Oxford University Press, 1992); Anita Shapira, *Berl*

(Cambridge, England: Cambridge University Press, 1984); Yosef Gorni, *Zionism and the Arabs, 1882–1948: Study of Ideology* (Oxford: Oxford University Press, 1987); Yoav Gelber, "The Historical Role of the Central European Immigration to Israel," *Leo Baeck Institute Year Book 38* (1993): 323–339; Itamar Even-Zohar, "The Emergence of Native Hebrew Culture in Palestine, 1882–1948," in Jehuda Reinharz, and Anita Shapira, eds., *Essential Papers on Zionism* (New York: New York University Press, 1996), 727–744; Anat Helman, "Taking the Bus in 1920s and 1930s Tel Aviv," *Middle Eastern Studies 42, 4* (July 2006): 625–640; Anat Helman, "European Jews in the Levant Heat: Climate and Culture in 1920s and 1930s Tel Aviv," *Journal of Israeli History 22, 1* (2003): 71–90; David N. Myers, *Re-inventing the Jewish Past: European Jewish Intellectuals and the Zionist Return to History* (New York: Oxford University Press, 1995); Dan Horowitz and Moshe Lissak, *Origins of the Israeli Polity: Palestine under the Mandate* (Chicago and London: University of Chicago Press, 1978); and Hillel Cohen, *Year Zero of the Arab-Israeli Conflict 1929* (Waltham, MA: Brandeis University Press, 2015).

On Sephardic and Middle Eastern communities, see Aron Rodrigue, *Images of Sephardi and Eastern Jewries in Transition: The Teachers of the Alliance Israélite Universelle, 1860–1939* (Seattle: University of Washington Press, 1993); Esther Benbassa and Aron Rodrigue, *The Jews of the Balkans: The Judeo-Spanish Community, 15th to 20th Centuries* (Berkeley: University of California Press, 2000); Julia Phillips Cohen, *Becoming Ottomans: Sephardi Jews and Imperial Citizenship in the Modern Era* (New York: Oxford University Press, 2014); Julia Phillips Cohen, and Sarah Abrevaya Stein, eds., *Sephardi Lives: A Documentary History, 1700–1950* (Stanford: Stanford University Press, 2014); Aron Rodrigue and Sarah Abrevaya Stein, eds., *A Jewish Voice from Ottoman Salonica: The Ladino Memoir of Sa'adi Besalel a-Levi* (Stanford: Stanford University Press, 2014); Sarah Abrevaya Stein, *Making Jews Modern: The Yiddish and Ladino Press in the Russian and Ottoman Empires* (Bloomington: Indiana University Press, 2004); and David M. Bunis, ed., *Languages and Literatures of Sephardic and Oriental Jews: Proceedings of the Sixth International Congress for Research on the Sephardi and Oriental Jewish Heritage* (Jerusalem: The Bialik Institute, 2009).

CHAPTER 5

THE HOLOCAUST

THE GREATEST CATASTROPHE to befall the Jewish people in their long history occurred between 1933 and 1945. Due to the actions of the Nazis and their accomplices across Europe, Jews were robbed of their rights, dispossessed of their property, and slaughtered without pity. At the war's end, at least 6 million were dead, and both the Ashkenazic and Sephardic civilizations that had flowered on European soil over the previous millennium had been utterly destroyed.

The assault on European Jewry began with World War I. The war, which devastated Europe, took the lives of a generation of young men and left societies and economies in ruins. The violence and loss were translated by many returning veterans into a vicious political ideology bent on destruction and vengeance. Across the continent in the interwar period, Fascists either came to power or left their mark on Europe's political culture, preaching the virtues of integral nationalism, anti-Communism, militarism, violence, and antisemitism. After the war, Jews across Europe confronted virulent antisemitic rhetoric, economic boycotts, the imposition of quotas, and outbreaks of violence.

In Fascism's most extreme variant, Nazism, antisemitism was elevated to holy writ. Even if a majority of those who voted for Adolf

Hitler (1889–1945) did not do so because of the Nazi Party's antisemitism, the majority of Germans were indifferent to the endless harangues against Jews. While all too many applauded Hitler's threats to exact retribution against the Jews for Germany's defeat and humiliation in World War I, most dismissed them as bluster or paid no heed. Vast numbers, however, believed that "something had to be done about the Jews," even if they never considered anything beyond this vague demand. While the destruction of European Jewry by the Nazis was not inevitable and was not even foreseeable when they came to power, their radical antisemitism was apparent from the start. Jews were central to Hitler's political worldview, and in his war of world conquest, he saw them as Germany's principal enemy.

THE JEWS IN HITLER'S WORLDVIEW

The state-sponsored attack on German Jewry began when Adolf Hitler became chancellor of Germany on January 30, 1933. Upon taking office, Hitler unleashed a violent political program that targeted Jews, political enemies, and all groups he considered inferior. He was

242

DOI: 10.4324/9781003611608-6

driven by an unquenchable desire to avenge Germany's defeat in World War I and an ambition for world conquest. All these aspects of Hitler's political and cultural ideology were intimately linked.

Jews occupied the center of Hitler's worldview. Seeking to dehumanize them, in his speeches and in his political testament *Mein Kampf* (1925), Hitler repeatedly called Jews "parasites," "maggots," "cockroaches," "bacilli," and "cancer." These descriptors were not Hitler's invention; he merely borrowed them from the language and ideas of antisemites who had preceded him, especially those drawn from the circles of occult racists in Vienna, not one of whom had held the reins of political power. Hitler, by contrast, was determined to practice a "biological politics," using the nation's intellectual, economic, and military resources to forge a new world order. Once in office, Hitler had the means to implement a program predicated on the idea that Germans were biologically and morally superior to all other groups. In the racial hierarchy as set out in Nazi ideology, Germans were *Übermenschen* ("supermen"), while Jews were categorized as inferior *Untermenschen* ("subhumans") disguised in human form, though they were, in fact, held to be inhuman. "In the course of centuries, their exteriors had become Europeanized and human looking," Hitler once confided to an early supporter.

The Jew is the counter Man, the Anti-Man. The Jew is the creation of a different God. He must have grown from a different root of the human tribe. If I put the Aryan next to the Jew and call the former a man, then I have to call the other by another name. They are as far apart as the animal is from the human. Not that

I want to call the Jew an animal. He is farther removed from the animal than the Aryan. He is a being foreign to nature and removed from nature.

From the earliest phase of his political career, Hitler openly expressed a desire to do violence to Jews. In 1922, he was interviewed by the anti-Nazi journalist Josef Hell, who asked him, "What do you want to do to the Jews once you have full discretionary powers?" Hell recalled that until that point, Hitler had spoken calmly, but then something snapped and he was dramatically transformed:

His eyes no longer saw me but instead bore past me and off into empty space; his explanations grew increasingly voluble until he fell into a kind of paroxysm that ended with his shouting, as if to a whole public gathering: "Once I am really in power, my first and foremost task will be the annihilation of the Jews. As soon as I have power, I shall have gallows after gallows erected on the Marienplatz, in Munich, for example—as many of them as traffic allows. Then the Jews will be hanged one after another, and they will stay hanging until they stink. They will stay hanging as long as the principles of hygiene permit. As soon as they have been untied, then the next batch will be strung up and that will continue until the last Jew in Munich has been exterminated. Exactly the same procedure will be followed in other cities until Germany is completely cleansed of Jews."

Hitler's pathological hatred of Jews was such that he confessed to having an adverse physical reaction to them, claiming that they actually nauseated him: "The odor of these caftan wearers often sickened me," he wrote. But he judged their morality as being even more offensive than their smell. And it was with this that Hitler and the Nazis came to hold Jews responsible for all the ills of humanity:

> Was there any kind of filth or brazenness, particularly in cultural life, in which there was not at least one Jew participating? As soon as you cautiously cut into such an abscess, you would find, like a maggot in a rotting body, blinded by the sudden light, a little Yid!

Hitler set himself a political goal with religious-like fervor: to create a purified world ruled according to the laws of racist biology, wherein he played the role of high priest. Such an expansionist agenda, one that demanded war be waged on a global scale, was justified because, according to Hitler, "all occurrences in world history are only the expression of the races' instinct of self-preservation, in the good or bad sense." By starting and winning a preemptive war, the Nazis sought to defeat their eternal enemies and then remake the world anew.

According to historian Saul Friedländer, Hitler preached "redemptive anti-Semitism." Assuming for himself the role of crusader in a quasi-religious mission, Hitler observed, "I believe that by defending myself against the Jew, I am fighting for the work of the Lord." Essential to the creation of a pristine universe was the removal of the Jewish menace. Hitler believed that the Nazis were performing a service for all humanity by destroying the Jews, who, he was convinced, were bent on "world domination." The consequences of not taking on this task were dire: "[I]f . . . the Jew is victorious over the other peoples of the world, his crown will be the funeral

wreath of humanity and this planet will . . . move through the ether devoid of men." Hitler imagined his battle against the Jews—and Bolsheviks, categories he elided—to be an apocalyptic struggle on a global scale, and thus, he had to launch a world war, because the Jews lived everywhere.

Nazi ideology was also driven by its desire for vengeance for Germany's defeat in World War I and subsequent humiliation at Versailles. Because the Nazis regarded the loss as the fault of the Jews (and leftists), revenge would come through world conquest and the assertion of German hegemony. "Justice" would be delivered in the form of the destruction of the Jews. The Holocaust, then, was not a separate or discrete aspect of World War II but lay at the center of Nazi war aims.

For a long time, historians have debated just when Hitler took the fateful decision to exterminate European Jewry. One group of historians, referred to as "intentionalists," maintain that it was always Hitler's intention to embark on mass murder, a goal he had set himself sometime toward the end of World War I. Few historians subscribe to this view today. An opposing view is held by historians, referred to as "functionalists." They maintain that the decision to murder European Jewry evolved during World War II, with Germany controlling ever-increasing numbers of Jews as a result of territorial conquest. In this reading, genocide becomes somewhat of a practical solution to a logistical problem. While it is indeed most plausible that the decision was made during the war, the problem with the functionalist thesis is that it downplays the role of ideology, and thus, it would seem that the term "moderate intentionalism" best describes the Nazi's decision-making process that led them down the path to genocide. This position recognizes the centrality of antisemitism to Nazism and Hitler's determination to rid Germany of Jews, while it acknowledges that "removing" Jews did not originally mean murder but most likely dispossession and expulsion. In other words, Hitler's aim at first was to throw the Jews out of Germany and the territories she occupied, and only later was a policy change instituted that had genocide on a European-wide scale as its goal. As such, the history of the Holocaust can be divided into two periods: 1933–1939 and 1939–1945. The first phase sees the exclusion of Jews from the economic, social, and cultural life of Germany and Austria, while the second coincides with the war and the systematic plunder and extermination of European Jewry.

PHASE I: THE PERSECUTION OF GERMAN JEWRY (1933–1939)

Although Hitler's assault on Jews began upon his taking office, he had thought about it long before 1933. His promise to push the Jews out of German public life was a central plank of the Nazi Party's 25-Point Program (1920). Point 4 stated, "Only a member of the race can be a citizen. A member of the race can only be one who is of German blood, without consideration of creed. Consequently no Jew can be a member of the race." The implementation of this program was made possible by Hitler's rise to power and the increasing centralization of the Nazi state. Through a combination of intimidation, violence, weak opposition, and his personal popularity, Hitler gained control of the most important organs of state: the armed forces, the judiciary, the state treasury, and the press.

At the heart of the system of repression were the concentration camps. At first, only four specific groups were targeted for incarceration: political enemies, inferior races, criminals, and "asocial elements." The first concentration camp, Dachau, just outside of Munich, was opened in March 1933, and Jews were among the first inmates. In the early phase of the Nazi regime, Jews were taken to camps, frequently because they were socialists, not because they were Jews, and on signing a statement declaring that they had been well treated, they were often released. Other Jews, however, were killed outright in the camp. Over the course of the Third Reich, the camp system grew enormously large and was composed of a variety of different kinds of camps. Recent research has conclusively established that during the war, the camp system had mushroomed into something that was far greater than previously thought. There were, apparently, some 30,000 slave labor camps, 980 concentration camps, 6 extermination camps, 1,000 prisoner-of-war camps, and while not technically camps, about 500 brothels with sex slaves in territories the Nazis conquered during the war.

At first, anti-Jewish policy proceeded along two tracks. On one, stormtroopers from the SA, also called "Brownshirts," and other party activists physically attacked Jews and their property at random. Decisions on when and where to do this were taken at a regional and local level. On the other track, more conservative government officials sought likewise to persecute Jews but wished to do so in a way that was less obvious and would not harm Germany's international reputation and economic recovery. Thus, after the so-called "Night of the Long Knives," Hitler's purge of the SA in 1934, the anti-Jewish campaign was increasingly directed from Berlin, although local initiatives were still encouraged, provided they were in keeping with the government's goals. Whether regionally or centrally directed, the persecution of the Jews became an ongoing ritual within Nazi Germany.

The goal to remove the Jews from German public life and effectively rescind their emancipation began in dramatic fashion. On April 1, 1933, the Nazis led a boycott of Jewish-owned stores and businesses. At precisely 10:00 a.m. that day, all over Germany, jackbooted thugs stood vigil outside Jewish-owned businesses bearing signs that read, "Do not buy from Jews." They also painted antisemitic slogans on shop windows and harassed and intimidated German customers who wished to enter the premises of Jewish retailers and professionals. On April 4, 1933, Zionist leader Robert Welsch encouraged German Jews to turn the circumstances to their advantage. In an article he wrote in the *Jüdische Rundschau*, a Zionist newspaper, the headline read: "The Yellow Badge, Bear It with Pride!" Welsch was not referring to the wearing of a yellow badge as a distinguishing marker for Jews under Nazi rule. (That decree was first implemented on November 23, 1939, against Polish Jews over 10 years of age and for German Jews on September 1, 1941.) Rather, he was referring to the vandalism recently meted out by Nazi hooligans:

> Many Jews suffered a crushing experience last Saturday [the day of the boycott]. . . . The patrols moved from house to house, stuck their placards on shops and signboards, daubed the windows, and for 24 hours the German Jews were virtually placed in the stocks. In addition to other signs and inscriptions one often saw windows bearing a large

Magen David, the Shield of King David. It was intended to dishonor us. . . . *Jews, take up the Star of David and bear it with honor!* . . . We remember all those, who for five thousand years, were called Jews and were stigmatized as Jews. We are [now] reminded that we are Jews. We say, "yes [we are]" and bear that with pride too.

Welsch was imploring hitherto-assimilated Jews to seize the moment and return to the fold. For others, secure in and proud of their Jewishness, the events of April 1 occasioned a complete revaluation of who they were as people. Edwin Landau was 43 years old when the boycott took place. He was a working-class Prussian Jew who had been raised on a steady diet of German patriotism. He recalled that, on the day of the boycott, "[t]wo young Nazis stationed themselves outside of [their] establishment and prevented the customers from entering. [He] couldn't believe [his] eyes. [He] simply could not imagine that this was happening in the twentieth century." Landau's entire world caved in at this moment, and worse than the boycott's harm to his plumbing business was the sense that his service to and love of Germany had all been a colossal error:

> And we young Jews had once stood in the trenches for this people in the cold and rain and spilled our blood to defend our nation from its enemies. Were there no comrades left from this time who were disgusted by this behavior? We saw them pass by on the street, including many for whom we had done many a good turn in the past. They now wore smiles on their faces and could scarcely conceal their satisfaction. . . . What we were looking at now was Satanism and it was only the

beginning. I gathered my war medals and pinned them on, then I went into the street and visited the Jewish shops, where I was also stopped. But I was seething inside; I wanted to scream my hatred into the faces of these barbarians. Hatred, hatred—when had this emotion first taken hold of me? A change had come across me in the last few hours. This land and this people, which I had always loved and appreciated, had suddenly become my enemy. I was no longer a German, or at least I wasn't supposed to be one. Of course, it takes more than a few hours for that to happen. But all of a sudden I realized: I was ashamed that I had once been part of this people. I was ashamed of the trust I had placed in so many people who now revealed themselves to be my enemies. Suddenly even the street seemed strange to me. In fact, the entire city was strange. There are no words to describe the sensations I felt in these hours.

Landau was a member of the ultra-nationalist Reich Association of Jewish Frontline Soldiers, hence his reaching for his medals before venturing out onto the street. But unusually for a member of this organization, he was also an Orthodox Jew. On the Friday night before the following day's boycott, he went to the synagogue and returned home for Sabbath dinner:

As I began to celebrate the Sabbath in the circle of my family, just as I had always done, and came to the line in the prayer where it says, "Thou who has chosen us from among all the peoples," and my children, who were looking at me with innocent and questioning eyes, saw that I was losing my grip. . . . The children did not know or understand why I cried so loudly,

but I knew that it was because I was taking leave of my Germanness; it was my inner separation from my former fatherland, a funeral. I buried forty-three years of my life. . . . [F]rom that day forward I would be German no more.

And then a few days later, in the final dramatic scene of his protracted metaphorical burial, Landau went to the cemetery:

I visited the graves of my parents, grandparents, and great-grandparents and talked to them. I gave them back everything that I had absorbed and cultivated in the way of Germanness over the past three generations. I shouted to them in their graves. "You were mistaken, I too, was misled, but now I understand that I am no longer a German. And what will my children be?" No answer came. The gravestones remained silent.

The propaganda minister, Joseph Goebbels (1897–1945), declared on the day of the boycott, "The year 1789 is hereby eradicated from history." Indeed, the Nazis set out to eliminate the French Revolution, with its ideology of liberty, equality, and fraternity. The Revolution, which had emancipated the Jews, was, for the Nazis, a historic error. It would be corrected methodically, exhaustively, and through the legal system. Each day brought with it new laws and intensified discrimination. From their first day in power, the Nazis began to spin an intricate web of laws—there would eventually be over 400—that ensnared Jews and from which escape was impossible. Over the years, the central government in Berlin, along with municipal authorities, issued hundreds of laws, decrees, and local ordinances, vitiating any form of normal life for Jews whatsoever. The laws do not seem to have followed any logical pattern of implementation but were merely designed to stigmatize and terrorize Jews and reduce their lives to nothing more than the naked struggle for survival. There were "big" laws, such as those that stripped all Jews of their German citizenship, and then there were "small" laws that just applied to a handful, such as the 1938 law that banned Jews from owning guns. The latter category of laws is, in some way, the most revealing, for it is in their passage that we can clearly see the lengths to which the Nazis went to ensure that every last Jew was removed from every aspect of German public life. There were never too few Jews engaged in any one occupation, hobby, or pastime to ignore. The persecution of a handful of Jews was treated with the same urgency and zeal that would eventually be applied to the treatment of millions. This totalizing goal demanded that Jews be victimized on a micro as well as a macro level.

On April 4, the German Boxing Association excluded all Jewish boxers. There were not many such young men and therein lies its significance. No Jew was to be spared exclusion, and no German organization would be spared total Aryanization. April 7, 1933, saw the passage of a law that affected many more Jews. It was the "Law for the Re-Establishment of the Professional Civil Service," and it resulted in the dismissal of all civil servants who were not of "Aryan descent." (On April 11, "non-Aryan" was defined as "anyone descended from non-Aryan, particularly Jewish, parents or grandparents. It suffices if one grandparent is non-Aryan.") In a society that practiced terror and encouraged informing on others, the possibility of coming under suspicion was especially high. The April 7 law led some 2 million state employees and thousands of lawyers, doctors, civil servants, and students to

comb through the historical record to prove, should it have ever been necessary, that they were "pure Aryans." This, in turn, meant thousands of priests, pastors, town clerks, archivists, and hospital administrators—all those in possession of official records—assisted those in search of their racial ancestry. All of them, in other words, became part of a gigantic bureaucracy designed to persecute Jews for the purposes of ensuring Germany's racial purity. The definition of "non-Aryan" formed the foundation for all subsequent persecutions of the Jews.

When Hitler came to power, Jews formed 16 percent of all of Germany's lawyers and 11 percent of all her doctors. Like Jewish business owners, they, too, were subject to the boycott of April 1, 1933, and Brownshirts stood outside Jewish legal offices and medical practices to warn off German clients and patients. In March 1933, the League of National Socialist Lawyers demanded that every law firm in Germany become *Judenrein* (Jew-free). In Prussia, 60 percent of Jewish lawyers lost their licenses on April 7, 1933, but even before this, Jewish lawyers and judges had been beaten up and even dragged from court in the middle of proceedings. Initially, the only Jewish lawyers who could continue to practice were World War I veterans or those who had already been in practice since August 1, 1914. However, they were removed from the national registry of lawyers and put on a special list. On September 27, 1933, even these Jewish lawyers lost their exceptional status. No Jew could practice law in Germany anymore.

Hitler was particularly cautious when it came to Jewish doctors, especially since 50 percent of all the physicians in Berlin were Jewish. (They made up 60 percent of all the doctors in Vienna.) To have dismissed them all at once, when so many German patients depended on them, risked a backlash. As such, the campaign against Jewish doctors occurred in three stages. In the first phase, beginning in 1933, Jewish physicians were expelled from the national insurance scheme and were replaced with "Aryan" doctors, who had long sought a way into the system. Persecution paid off. By 1934, the annual taxable income of "Aryan" doctors had increased by 25 percent. When the financial windfall resulting from the persecution of Jewish physicians is combined with the fact that Nazi Germany organized itself along racial lines and that primacy was given to biology (with doctors serving as arbiters of life and death), it is little wonder that the German Medical Association was the most easily and eagerly Nazified of any professional group. Over 50 percent of German doctors were members of the Nazi Party.

The second phase, which began in the summer of 1938, saw the decertification of all Jewish physicians. Jews could no longer treat Germans and could only refer to themselves by the degrading term "sick-treaters," rather than *physicians*. Due to emigration, forced retirement, incarceration, suicide, death, and murder, a mere 285 Jewish physicians still remained in Germany by early 1939. In the final phase, which covered the war years, health care for Jews was confined to the few remaining Jewish hospitals the Nazis permitted to remain open. Eventually, even these institutions, with the exception of the Jewish Hospital in Berlin, were closed down, and the staff, together with their patients, were deported to ghettos and death camps in the east. There, until their own deaths, Jewish doctors and nurses continued to administer treatment to the sick and dying Jews as best as they could.

In April 1933, the systematic dismissal of Jewish faculty and teaching assistants at the universities began. Even at this early stage, with no inkling of what the future held, mortal fear gripped German Jews. The philologist and professor of Romance languages at Dresden's Technical University, Victor Klemperer, who remained in hiding with his non-Jewish spouse in Dresden throughout the war, recorded in his diary on April 12, 1933: "For the moment I am safe. But as someone on the gallows, who has the rope around his neck, is safe. At any moment a new 'law' can kick away the steps on which I am standing and then I'm hanging." And indeed, new laws kept coming. On April 19, 1933, Jewish cattle dealers in the state of Baden were forbidden to speak their unique patois. Only days later, on April 21, kosher slaughtering of animals was outlawed, while on April 25, the "Law against the Overcrowding of German Schools and Universities" was passed. Jews were not to exceed 5 percent of enrollments.

Figure 5.1 depicts the exodus of the chosen people out of Kassel. Soon after the Nazis came to power in 1933, the persecution of Jews became ritualized and even a form of public entertainment and celebration. In this undated photo, a swim club on the Fulda River won first for this exhibit prize in a People's Fair (Volksfest). It shows members of the team dressed as ragtag Jewish refugees, replete with false beards, odd hats, and big noses, sitting amid their luggage and hanging clothes on board a boat. The sign above them, referring to the pauperization of German Jews and the ordinances that forbade them from engaging in public activities, such as being members of clubs and associations, is written in Hessian dialect: "Dr. Isak, Dr. Isidor Levi and Chana have gone bankrupt. They may no longer

Figure 5.1 Exodus of the chosen people out of Kassel.

Source: Photo Scala, Florence/bpk, Bildagentur fuer Kunst, Kultur und Geschichte, Berlin.

go swimming [in the Fulda] and have been packed off to Palestine."

From the beginning, swimming pools were of particular concern to the Nazis, and they made it a priority to have Jews banned from them. Their fears were driven by the belief that Jewish bathers would pollute the water and thus infect healthy Aryans. Then there was the supposed sexual threat posed by Jews clad only in bathing suits. The public swimming pool was a site that the Nazis used to generate an endless stream of pornographic antisemitism. Jews experienced rapid and abrupt social ostracism. Children were especially affected and confused by how quickly their worlds collapsed. Playmates with gentiles one day, Jewish children were shunned the next. Hilma Geffen Ludomer, a Jewish girl from Berlin, recalled, "Suddenly, I didn't

have any friends. I had no more girlfriends, and many of the neighbors were afraid to talk to us." Martha Appel from Dortmund remembered:

[T]he children had been advised not to come to school on April 1, 1933, the day of the boycott. Even the principal of the school thought Jewish children's lives were in danger. . . . My heart was broken when I saw tears in my younger child's eyes when she had been sent home from school while all others had been taken to a show or some other pleasure. . . . Almost every lesson began to be a torture for Jewish children. There was not one subject anymore, which was not used to bring up the Jewish question. And in the presence of Jewish children the teachers denounced all the Jews, without exception, as scoundrels and as the most destructive force in the country. . . . My children were not permitted to leave the room during such a talk; they were compelled to stay and to listen; they had to feel all the other children's eyes looking and staring at them, the examples of an outcast race.

As the situation grew worse, she noted, "[W]ith each day of the Nazi regime, the abyss between us and our fellow citizens grew larger. . . . Of course we were different . . . since we were hunted like deer." Henny Brenner, in Dresden, recalled how fearful her teachers made her. Her biology teacher taught Nazi racial theory to the children and came into the class looking the part, with "her hair in braids and a big round swastika brooch on her blouse." The teacher, who was new to the school, did not know the students and mistakenly called on Henny, who was blond-haired and blue-eyed, to stand before the class and pronounced: "Here is a [perfect] example of Aryan womanhood." As the students were smirking, Henny, who was not amused, said, "I am Jewish." From that time on, she said, "all hell broke loose." Her math teacher, who also "looked like a prototypical Nazi, big and blond," always wore his SS uniform to class, complete with a "Death's Head" insignia.

On May 10, 1933, at universities across Germany, the public burning of books written by liberal humanists, anti-Nazis, and Jews took place. As the flames leapt into the air, Goebbels declared, "The soul of the German people can again express itself. These flames not only illuminate the final end of an old era; they also light up the new." Increasingly pessimistic Jews recalled the prophetic words of the nineteenth-century German Jewish poet Heinrich Heine, who, in his play *Almansor*, said of book burning, "That was only a prelude; where they burn books they will, in the end, burn human beings too." On July 14, celebrated as Bastille Day in France, the Nazis outlawed all other political parties. On that same day, they also passed "The Law for the Prevention of Genetically Diseased Offspring." It permitted the sterilization of anyone suffering from a host of diseases, including "feeble-mindedness, schizophrenia, manic depression and severe alcoholism." Many who were later involved in the murder of Jews in the death camps "trained" in these sterilization and euthanasia programs.

Local municipalities energetically ostracized Jews, prohibiting them from using public parks, zoos, and beaches. Not long after the regime came to power, Jews were banned from membership in local sports clubs, automobile clubs, choral societies, and the German National Chess Association. The Editor Law, passed on October 4, 1933, called for journalism to be racially purified, which, in turn, led to the dismissal of Jewish journalists and publishing executives and banned Jews from serving as newspaper editors. The law's passage was driven by the fact that Jews were heavily represented in the mass media. While in 1933, the overwhelming majority of Germany's 4,700 newspapers and periodicals were not in Jewish hands, the existence of two Jewish-owned media conglomerates, the House of Ullstein and the House of Mosse, was sufficient proof for the Nazis that there actually existed an entity they dubbed the "Jewish press," whose goal was to brainwash Germans and control the country on behalf of the world Jewish conspiracy.

The year 1934 lulled some Jews into a false sense of security. The anti-Jewish agenda seemed to recede in importance, as the regime was principally concerned with consolidating its power and rooting out political opponents. But in truth, the persecution and suffering of the Jews continued unabated. Widening exclusion and public humiliation were experienced everywhere, while poverty also began to grip this once-comfortable middle-class community. At least 20 percent of German Jewry had by now lost their livelihood.

In 1935, party radicals at the local level ramped up physical attacks against Jewish persons and property, and this was accompanied by the continued issuance of new anti-Jewish laws. That year, Jews were forbidden to be art and antique dealers, as well as authors and musicians. On July 10, 1935, hiking was forbidden to Jews if there were more than 20 of them in a hiking party. At the national level, a new phase in Hitler's assault on the Jews occurred with the passage of the Nuremberg Laws in September 1935. The legislation revoked the German citizenship of Jews and those considered to be "racially" Jewish. Reflecting the obsession with what the Nazis called "race defilement," the laws also forbade intermarriage between Jews and Germans and, in fact, all sexual contact between them. Jews and gentiles accused of having had sex were often publicly humiliated, paraded through the streets with obscene signs hung around their necks proclaiming their "guilt." *The Times* of London called the Nuremberg Laws a "cold pogrom." In practical terms, the laws did not change the lives of German Jews; rather, they ratified the discrimination Jews were already suffering. The point was to exacerbate and further legislate the social divide between Jews and Germans. As Hitler told one of his adjutants, "Out of all the professions, into a ghetto, enclosed in a territory where they can behave as becomes their nature, while the German people look on as one looks at wild animals."

In 1936, the Olympic Games were held in Berlin, and the Nazis ordered that anti-Jewish signs be taken down, for fear of offending visitors to Germany. However, the strategic disappearance of a few signs did nothing to ease the discrimination. On January 11, Jews could no longer work as accountants, while on April 3, they were barred from being veterinarians. On June 8, 1937, all postal workers married to Jewish women had to take early retirement. On July 27, 1938, it was decreed that all streets in Germany named after Jews were to be renamed. On March 22, 1938, Jews were forbidden from owning private vegetable gardens, while on November 12, 1938, a law was enacted that prohibited Jews from attending movies, theaters, the opera, and concerts. Three days later, on November 15, Jewish children could no longer attend public schools. (On June 20, 1942, the law was expanded to include all schools.) November 29 brought with it a law banning Jews from owning carrier pigeons. Robbing Jews, an essential element of the Holocaust, became law on February 21, 1939, when they were ordered to turn in all jewelry made of gold, silver, platinum, and pearls. The dates are revealing, for they show more clearly than anything else that there was no respite for the victims. Each day brought with it new restrictions and more suffering, as German Jews lived under a regime that practiced terror and arbitrariness through the judicial system. This meant that they had no protection and no one to whom they could appeal.

When one year passed into the next and it became certain that the Nazis were not going to disappear, an air of desperation began to swirl around German Jews. On October 27, 1937, Victor Klemperer confided to his diary:

The thought that it makes no difference how I am going to spend the rest of my life is constantly on my mind: I no longer believe there will be any political change. Furthermore, I don't believe a change will help me in any way in my circumstances or in my feelings. Feelings of scorn, disgust and deep distrust towards Germany will never leave me. And until 1933 I was so convinced of my being German.

Responses of German Jews

In their overall persecution of Jews, the Nazis were especially insistent that they play no part in the enjoyment or performance of German culture. Nor were they to earn a living from their involvement in it. In response, a young Jewish theater director, Kurt Baumann, requested that Jews be permitted to form an organization that would cater to their cultural needs. In his memoirs, Baumann noted:

> My idea to found a Jewish cultural circle was based on very simple numbers; at the time, 175,000 Jews alone lived in Berlin, many other big cities had, percentage wise, similar concentrations. I figured that a city of 175,000 inhabitants could have their own theatre, opera, symphony orchestra, museum, lectures, and even *Hochschule* [Institute of Higher Education], and this with the economic proportion of a mid-sized city.

In April 1933, the Nazis agreed to Baumann's request and permitted the formation of the Cultural Association of German Jews (Kulturbund deutscher Juden). Later, the Nazis insisted the organization remove the word "German" from its name, and it was officially renamed the Jewish Cultural Association (Jüdischer Kulturbund). The Nazis had three principal reasons for allowing the Kulturbund to come into existence. First, they could claim that Jews were not being mistreated and were having their cultural needs met; second, the Kulturbund could function as a segregated Jewish cultural space and source of employment for Jews; and finally, the Kulturbund created the framework that ensured the complete cessation of Jewish involvement in German culture.

Beginning with Berlin, the Kulturbund soon blossomed and had branches all over the country. In April 1935, the Nazis placed all of Germany's Jewish cultural societies under one umbrella organization, called the Reich Association of Jewish Cultural Societies. In negotiating the terms of the Kulturbund's activities, the Nazis stipulated that (1) the Kulturbund was to be staffed only by Jewish artists and would be self-funded by charging the all-Jewish audiences a monthly fee of 2.50 reichsmarks; (2) only the Jewish press was allowed to report on Kulturbund events; and (3) no events of any kind could proceed until the Kulturbund's programs were first submitted to Hans Hinkel, head of the Prussian Theater Commission, for approval. Shut out of the cultural life of the nation, Jews active in the Kulturbund were forbidden to perform medieval and Romantic-era works, the classics of German theater such as Schiller and Goethe, while foreign works such as Shakespeare's *Hamlet* were permitted, but not the "To be or not to be" soliloquy. The German musical tradition was also declared off-limits to Jews, and from 1933, Jews were forbidden to play Wagner and Strauss. Beethoven, Brahms, and Bach were added in 1936, and after the Austrian Anschluss of 1938, so too were Mozart and Schubert. Jews were forced to altogether reconfigure their cultural activities in a sphere completely separate from that of Germans. They were confined to a cultural ghetto, one that anticipated the physical ghettos into which Jews would later be herded.

By 1938, the Kulturbund had 76 branches in 100 cities and towns across Germany and had a membership that hovered around 20,000. Under constant and intrusive surveillance by the Gestapo, from its foundation until late 1938, the Kulturbund put on 8,457 different cultural events. The profound involvement of Jews in German culture and a measure of the community's deep well of talent is evidenced by the fact that nationwide, the Kulturbund was able to support three theater companies, two philharmonic orchestras, one opera, one cabaret, one theater school, several choirs and also hosted many lecture series. Attendance at these events was highly regulated. Members were entitled to attend two cultural events per month—alternately, an opera and their choice of a lecture in the fields of philosophy, art, religion, or music in one month, and the next month, a drama and a concert. These activities even occasioned heated debates over the nature of Jewish culture. In September 1936, the Kulturbund held a conference titled "What Is Jewish Music in Nazi Germany?" There was a great difference of opinion. Some musicologists maintained that Jewish music did not yet exist, while others held that all music created by composers of Jewish origin was Jewish music. Others took a middle position and noted that only if a piece of music contained certain characteristics could it then be classified as authentic Jewish music.

The Association was divided over whether to present programs of general culture or those of a specifically Jewish character, as the Zionists insisted upon. It was telling that the very first production of the Kulturbund was Gotthold Ephraim Lessing's play about interfaith tolerance, *Nathan the Wise*. The choice was bold but controversial among Jews and was staunchly defended by Kurt Singer, one of the founders of the Kulturbund. This physician and Weimar-era conductor of the Berlin Opera wrote to a Zionist newspaper in 1933:

> There can be no doubt that *Nathan* should be the very first play [we] produce, precisely because it is a modern, combative work. Its language, its dramatic qualities . . . and its purely human, timeless spiritual nature are all chords that resonate in harmonic unity.

The play's message was a stark contrast to the hateful teachings of the Nazis, but also a bittersweet memento of an earlier, more optimistic moment in the history of German and German Jewish relations. The Zionist response to the play, however, was a clearheaded assessment and warning to Jews not to be seduced by the play's message:

> We Jews regard *Nathan the Wise* as a great work of art and an expression of humanistic ideals. But we also consider it to be a period piece, and we do not want to create the impression that the Kulturbund . . . sees this as the real German spirit, as opposed to another spirit [Nazism], which we label as inauthentic; we are not entitled to instruct the Germans. . . . Rather than comforting ourselves with the knowledge that Lessing wrote *Nathan the Wise* 150 years ago, it is our desire to cope with the current plight of Jews. Should the performance of *Nathan the Wise*, which we welcome as an artistic event, have the explicit or implicit intention of segregating the Jews in an old world of illusions, then we would have to object to such a performance.

The Kulturbund's ultimate significance lies in the fact that it provided a venue for Jews to continue their engagement with culture, a necessary tonic in such bitter circumstances, and it also supplied work for actors, directors, musicians, singers, costumers, set designers, and makeup artists. About 2,500 people earned a modest but desperately needed living as employees of the Kulturbund. On September 11, 1941, the Kulturbund was officially dissolved. With the Nazis now fighting a two-front war against Great Britain and the Soviet Union and having already begun the mass murder of Jews on the eastern front, there was no longer any need to keep up the pretenses.

In September 1933, responding to an idea put forth by a number of Jews, the Nazis established a new central organization for German Jewry, the Reich Representation of German Jews (*Reichsvertretung der deutschen Juden*). It was led by Rabbi Leo Baeck (1873–1956) of Berlin. As was the case with the Kulturbund, in 1935, the organization was forced to change its name to the Reich Representation of Jews in Germany, thus reflecting the idea that according to Nazi ideology, the term "German Jew" was an oxymoron. An ecumenical body, the Reich Representation of Jews in Germany housed all streams of German Jewry and was the one organization permitted to speak for the Jewish community to the Nazi government. Its principal activities were to provide vocational training, especially to those preparing to emigrate, cater to the educational needs of young and old alike, and make available extensive welfare services and economic assistance in the form of labor exchange and small loans. Given that the large number of Jews who had lost their livelihoods were denied social welfare and the right to go to school, the Reich Representation of Jews

in Germany provided invaluable material aid and spiritual encouragement to the increasingly desperate Jews of Germany. It was shut down in 1943 when the last of its leaders were deported to the Theresienstadt concentration camp.

The principal Jewish response to Nazi persecution was to leave Germany. Departure, though, did not take place in a mad rush but, rather, in a steady exodus. Psychological, economic, and demographic factors helped fashion Jewish decision-making when it came to emigration. When the Nazis came to power in 1933, 525,000 Jews lived in Germany. Only 37,000 left that year; in large part, no one could really predict the catastrophe to come. In fact, there was always a sense among Germans who opposed Hitler that once in power, the Nazis would calm down and begin to govern more responsibly. Across the political and cultural spectrum, German Jewry also expressed similar sentiments. In June 1933, the liberal Central Union of German Jews, representing the majority of German Jewry, declared:

> [T]he great majority of German Jews remains firmly rooted in the soil of its homeland, despite everything. There may be some who have been shaken in their feeling for the German Fatherland by the weight of recent events. They will overcome the shock, and if they do not overcome it then the roots which bound them to the German mother earth were never sufficiently strong.

The Orthodox Jewish community wrote to Hitler in October 1933:

> The position of German Jewry today, as it has been shaped by the German people, is wholly intolerable.... [Their economic and social position] means that German Jews

have been sentenced to a slow but certain death by starvation. . . . [But] even if some individuals harbor such an intention, *we do not believe it has the approval of the Führer and the Government of Germany.*

In 1933, the founding proclamation of the Reich Representation of German Jews stated:

In the new State the position of individual groups has changed, even of those which are far more numerous and stronger than we are. Legislation and economic policy have taken their own authorized road, including [some] and excluding [others]. . . . The German Jews will be able to make their way in the new State as a working community that accepts work and gives work. . . . We hope for the understanding assistance of the Authorities, and the respect of our gentile fellow citizens, whom we join in love and loyalty to Germany.

Even the Zionists cautioned against wholesale departure for Palestine, believing that the sight of a mass flight of Jews from Germany would encourage other nations to step up discrimination against Jews in order to encourage their departure. Indeed, like many other factions, Zionists still imagined a future for Jews in Germany, albeit on an entirely new political footing. On May 30, 1933, an article appeared in a Zionist newspaper stating the following:

Only a fraction of the half million German Jews can emigrate; an even smaller percentage have the prospect of settling in Palestine and thus returning to agriculture on their ancestral soil. Undoubtedly one cannot let the Jews of Germany starve, hence German Jewry can make a virtue of necessity—if the State gave them the opportunity. . . . The first step toward integrating the Jews into the new State should be domestic colonisation. Jewish farming villages in Germany are no less

possible than in Argentina or Soviet-Russia. One can assume that the Jewish farmer in Germany will develop certain capabilities peculiar to him, which, without negating his own nature, will be of value to the life of the German Volk.

Welding instruction for prospective Jewish emigrants (1936). The trauma of forced emigration from Nazi Germany was often accompanied by the need for occupational retraining. These men from Berlin are learning the trade of welding. Their activity was sponsored by the Hilfsverein der Juden in Deutschland, the Relief Organization of Jews in Germany. Pursuant to their policy of forcing Jews to leave the country, the Nazis charged the Hilfsverein with facilitating the emigration of Jews, who began fleeing Nazi Germany as soon as Hitler took power. In 1933, there were approximately 525,000 Jews in Germany, and in 1938, the year it was annexed to Nazi Germany, Austria's Jewish population stood at 192,000. By September 1939, approximately 282,000 Jews had left Germany and 117,000 had fled Austria. Between 1933 and 1939 most went to neighboring countries, but were later captured by the Nazis, after their conquest of western Europe in 1940. Between 1933 and 1939, approximately 95,000 emigrated to the United States—60,000 to Palestine, 40,000 to Great Britain, and about 75,000 to Central and South America. Just under 20,000 German and Austrian Jews made their way to Shanghai, in Japanese-occupied China.

While turning Germany's overwhelmingly urban, bourgeois Jews into farmers was unrealistic, the general tenor of the responses of all sectors of German Jewry to Nazism should not be dismissed as naïve or delusional. Jewish history and psychology had made Jews keen observers of political storm clouds on the horizon. Though deeply distressed, most did not panic. Hitler was not the first antisemite in history, and he would not be the last.

Figure 5.2 Welding instruction for prospective Jewish emigrants (1936).

Source: Photo Scala, Florence/bpk, Bildagentur fuer Kunst, Kultur und Geschichte, Berlin.

The historical record showed that the Jewish people had survived all previous antisemitic regimes. Why should this be different? As the German Jewish historian Ismar Elbogen wrote in a Jewish newspaper in 1933: "Think of the history of our forefathers; repeatedly they experienced such catastrophes, yet did not surrender their will to live!" The highly stratified class structure of Germany, as reflected in the elitism of its political culture, also made it difficult for anyone to believe that an ill-educated, loutish Austrian corporal could take control of a nation like Germany for a sustained period of time. Recent politics only gave credence to this view. The average lifespan of a Weimar government was nine months, and most Jews, as well as European statesmen, expected the Nazis to fall sooner rather than later.

German Public Opinion

Germans voiced barely a word of opposition to the persecution of the Jews. Not all,

but most either approved or simply did not care. Widespread enthusiasm for the regime led many to a conviction that the Jews were a problem, if not a "misfortune," for Germany. Often left unarticulated, the widespread feeling was that "something" had to be done about the Jews. Such sentiments cut across gender, class, religious, and educational lines. Lydia Gottschewski was a leader of the Nazi Women's League and implored her sisters to be merciless:

> Often, much too often, one hears . . . "I find the fight against the Jews too severe." . . . Sentimental gush that the other person is also a human being and feels and senses like ourselves. . . . The Jew . . . is a subtle poison since he destroys what is necessary to our life. If we are to be healed as a people . . . and conquer a place in the world that is our due, then we must free ourselves ruthlessly from that parasite.

In 1933, no university professors spoke out when books were burned and their 1,200 Jewish colleagues were dismissed. University students were even more openly antisemitic than their teachers and celebrated the exclusion of Jewish students. As early as January 1933, before the dismissal of Jewish professors, students harassed fellow German students who had attended classes taught by Jews. At the Technical University of Berlin, students brought cameras into classrooms to photograph the German students enrolled in such classes. Outside of the university, no real support for Jewish professors came from the intellectual classes. In the business world, Jews were dismissed from their positions on corporate boards, with the vacancies filled by eager German executives. In some instances, positions were found for Jews overseas, but the majority had no such good fortune. The companies they served did little for their Jewish employees. The Hamburg banker Alwin Muenchmeyer admitted in a rare moment of self-criticism, "We did nothing and we didn't think anything of it."

Jews also waited in vain for the representatives of the Protestant and Catholic Churches to speak out. On April 4, 1933, when taking a public stand was at least still possible, Bishop Otto Dibelius, the leading Protestant clergyman in Germany, showed his support for the regime by declaring, "I have always considered myself an antisemite." In September 1933, the Vatican signed a Concordat with the Nazis, in consequence of which Rome did not protest the persecution of the Jews. Occasionally, both churches expressed concern about the mistreatment of Jewish converts to Christianity. For the most part, although they tended not to be as viciously antisemitic as the Nazis, the clerical and intellectual elites of Germany were enthusiastic about the Nazi revolution. Like the great majority of Germans, they were indifferent to the fate of the Jews.

No one was able to claim with any sincerity that he or she did not know what was going on. Anti-Jewish laws were widely reported in the press, and high-ranking Nazis such as Joseph Goebbels publicly boasted about their campaign to remove the Jews from German life. A consistent trope of this propaganda depicted the Jews as the sworn enemies of the German people. As early as 1928, Goebbels published an article in his newspaper, *Der Angriff (The Attack)*, titled "Why Are We Enemies of the Jews?" He listed several reasons: "The Jew was the cause and beneficiary of [German] enslavement," he was "the real cause for the loss of the Great War," and "it is because of the Jew that [Germans] are pariahs in the world." In short, "the Jews had triumphed over [Germans] and the [German] future. . . . [H]e is the eternal enemy of [German] national honor and [German] national freedom."

A relentless stream of antisemitic propaganda permeated all aspects of daily life and would continue to do so until the end of the war. Germany was dotted with antisemitic billboards and posters, exhibiting vile images of Jews, often bearing captions such as "The Jewish Conspiracy," "The Wire Pullers: They Are Only Jews," and after 1939, "The Jews Wanted the War." Hate-filled radio programs, plays, and movies entertained the masses, while the reading public was offered a steady diet of antisemitic newspapers, magazines, and "scholarly journals." The teaching of hate began in childhood. Books for young readers, such as *The Poisonous Toadstool*, carried hideous images of Jews that were intended to frighten and "educate." In July 1937, the Degenerate Art exhibition opened in Munich, displaying art by Jews and other artists disapproved of by the regime. The Nazis heaped scorn on all elements of modern art, the "degeneracy" of which they blamed on Jews. On November 8, 1937, the German Museum in Munich showed a huge exhibit titled "The Eternal Jew." Through the use of inflammatory pictures and captions, the Nazis sought to depict Jews as thoroughly repellent and, in fact, admitted as much. At the conclusion of a film shown at the exhibition, the chief ideologue of the Nazi Party, Alfred Rosenberg, appeared on the screen and said to the audience, "You are horrified by this film. Yes, it is particularly bad, but it is precisely the one we wanted to show you."

The Economics of Persecution

When Hitler came to power, about 100,000 Jewish-owned enterprises were operational in Germany. Business quickly turned sour. Even though the April 1, 1933, boycott was called off after one day, an unofficial boycott remained in place. Companies refused to deliver goods to Jewish businesses, stormtroopers stood a threatening vigil outside Jewish shops, windows were repeatedly smashed, German welfare recipients were not permitted to use their food stamps in Jewish-owned grocery stores, local newspapers were forbidden to publish advertisements for Jewish businesses, and campaigns discouraging Germans buying products from Jewish-owned enterprises continued unabated. One widespread claim declared, "Whoever buys Nivea products is helping to support a Jewish company."

The economic stranglehold on German Jewry ensured that by 1938, between 60 and 70 percent of Jewish businesses had shut down or become "Aryan property." Businesses in the latter category were most likely to have been stolen through the provisions of the campaign known as Aryanization, which referred to the transfer (under pressure) of Jewish-owned businesses to "Aryan" owners. It occurred in two stages: a "voluntary" period from 1933 to 1938 and then, thereafter, a period of compulsory transfer. Aryanization measures were coordinated by economic advisors to local Nazi leaders, local chambers of commerce, and industry, as well as regional and central tax authorities. Duplicity, threats, intimidation, and violence went hand in hand with the "orderly" mechanics of business transfer, which eventually evolved into the systematic, transcontinental robbing of Jews. In 1935, the head of the program, Herbert Göring, brother of Hermann Göring, outlined one of the strategies for taking over a Jewish-owned firm:

> One method is apparently [for us] to approach Jewish firms with an offer to help them as Party members by joining their board of directors, administrative board, executive board or in some other "advisory" capacity, naturally in return for a fee. . . . Once the ties to the Jewish firm have been firmly established and people have managed in some way to "get inside," then difficulties of a personal or political nature are soon created for the Jewish owner.

On March 26, 1938, a German official wrote with undisguised glee to Hermann Göring regarding the situation in Vienna (recently annexed to the Reich):

> It can be anticipated that the Jews will be ready to sell their stores and companies at the cheapest prices. I think it will be possible, in this way, to bring a large part of Jewish property into Aryan hands under the most favourable economic terms.

After the Kristallnacht of November 1938, all pretense of voluntary ownership transfer was dropped, and the outright theft of Jewish property and businesses became the order of the day. Jewish enterprises that had remained in Jewish hands until that point were put under a government-appointed trustee, whose task was to "Aryanize" them. The frenzy to rob Jews led to internecine Nazi envy, evident in the remarks of the Nazi Party chief of finance of South Westphalia in November 1938:

> As we all know, as of January 1, 1939, no Jew is to be owner of an enterprise any longer. This means that Aryanization will have to be conducted at an extreme[ly] high pace. . . . [P]eople who only recently joined the Party and who in the past were on the other side of the fence, are now taking over Jewish businesses for ridiculous prices. People now talk of Aryanization profiteering—just as they talked in the past about the profiteers from inflation.

The widespread enthusiasm for the regime lay in large part with the fact that Germans became material beneficiaries of the dispossession of the Jews. By first securing loyalty through extremely generous social programs, such largesse was supplemented by theft, first from German Jews, then from foreign Jews and the very nations the Nazis conquered when they exacted tribute and hauled off the booty. Billions of reichsmarks in stolen property were directed into Germany's genocidal war of conquest, alleviating Germans of the cost of the war they instigated. According to historian Götz Aly, "[b]y exploiting material wealth confiscated and plundered in a racial war, Hitler's National Socialism achieved an unprecedented level of economic equality and created vast new opportunities for upward mobility for the German people. That made the regime both popular and criminal."

In 1935, Hitler declared that Germany would be ready to go to war in four years. To do so, however, he believed it imperative to remove Jews from German society so that they could not, in his mind, stab Germany in the back, as he had claimed they had done in World War I. It is for this reason that Hitler's assault on the Jews was intensified as war approached. The year 1938 marks a drastic downturn in the perilous condition of German Jewry. At the start of the year, German Jews had to turn in their passports, with new ones going only to those intending to emigrate. On March 12, 1938, Hitler annexed Austria, the act known as the Anschluss. As he rode into Vienna amid the adoring throng, a further 190,000 Jews fell under Nazi rule. The antisemitic frenzy that ensued in Austria surpassed anything like that which had occurred in Germany. Antisemitism was key to the popular support the Nazis enjoyed in Austria, something that distinguished it somewhat from Germany. Beatings, arrests, and outright theft began immediately, as did public humiliation; Jews were forced to scrub the capital's cobblestone streets while being taunted by the gathering crowds that they had never done an honest day's work. By contrast, the city's most famous Jewish resident, Sigmund Freud, did not have to get down on all fours. His celebrity saved him from that. He was, however, under surveillance, was interrogated, had his apartment broken into, and was robbed by stormtroopers. The Nazis even placed a swastika over the entrance to his apartment building. On June 4, 1938, together with his wife, Martha, and his daughter, Anna, Freud was allowed to leave Austria, but not before Princess Marie Bonaparte paid his hefty ransom, his emigration tax had been paid, and he had signed a declaration stating that he had not been mistreated. He added a sarcastic comment to his signature, addressed, perhaps, to the Austrians themselves: "I can most highly recommend the Gestapo to everyone." While Freud was able to spend the last year of his life in London, his three sisters were less fortunate. Denied exit visas by the Nazis, they all perished in concentration camps.

The attacks on Austrian Jews were so outrageous that the head of the Security Service, the SD, Reinhard Heydrich (1904–1942), the man who would come to have operational responsibility for the "Final Solution," told the head of the Austrian Nazis to better control the mobs who had attacked Jews "in a totally undisciplined way." If he did not, Heydrich said that the Gestapo would arrest them all. Even this threat did not work. The violence continued, as did the theft. Shortly after the Anschluss, the Nazis established the Property Transfer Office. Five hundred bureaucrats worked efficiently and, within 18 months, were able to report to SS chief Heinrich Himmler (1900–1945) that they "had practically completed the task of de-Judaizing the Ostmark [Austrian] economy." Nearly all Jewish-owned businesses had been stolen. Prominent Jewish executives were murdered, and the majority of Jews were rendered penniless.

It is a measure of the Austrian zeal for theft that of the 33,000 Jewish-owned businesses in Austria, 7,000 were stolen even before the Property Transfer Office had been established in May 1938. The Nazis also stole apartments. By the end of 1938, of the 70,000 apartments owned by Jews in Vienna, 44,000 had been taken by gentiles. As Jews moved in with one another, often up to six families per apartment, the overcrowding plunged the persecuted into further distress. On August 20, 1938, the Central Office for Jewish Emigration opened in Vienna. It had been established by Adolf Eichmann (1906–1962), who ran the operation that robbed wealthier Jews in order to finance the forced migration of the poorer majority. Working with ruthless efficiency, the Central Office arranged the forced emigration of 110,000 Jews between August 1938 and June 1939. Eichmann gained valuable experience organizing these mass deportations and went on to establish a similar office in Prague for the deportation of Czech Jewry. Later, his job would involve working out the logistics of the mass murder of European Jewry.

As the situation in Germany and Austria grew increasingly worse and many Jews were attempting to leave, Franklin Roosevelt, president of the United States, called for an international forum to discuss the ensuing refugee crisis. The Evian Conference (July 6–13, 1938) was convened with 32 nations in attendance. Part of the invitation read, "[N]o country would be expected to receive a greater number of emigrants than is permitted by its existing legislation." No special efforts to assist Jewish refugees were expected. Even before the conference began, deals were brokered to ensure that nations would do even less than what they were capable of doing. In this regard, Britain insisted that the possibility of Palestine as a place of refuge not be publicly discussed, while the United States requested that no mention be made of the fact that American immigration quotas went unfilled year after year. Sometimes, outrageously disingenuous claims were made in order to avoid providing a haven for Jews. The Australian delegate to the conference, the cabinet minister Thomas Walter White, declared:

Under the circumstances. . . . Australia cannot do more. . . . undue privileges cannot be given to one particular class of non-British subjects without injustice to others. It will no doubt be appreciated also that, as we have no real racial problem, we are not desirous of importing one.

It was a claim that would have come as a great surprise to Australia's Aboriginal population. In fact, the most unequivocal Australian support for Jews in distress came from Aboriginals. On December 6, 1938, William Cooper led a deputation from the Australian Aborigines' League to the German Consulate in Melbourne. He brought with him a firmly worded resolution, attempting to present "on behalf of the aborigines of Australia, a strong protest at the cruel persecution of the Jewish people by the Nazi Government of Germany." Consul general Dr. R. W. Drechsler refused the delegation admittance. Nonetheless, a group that was itself suffering from racist policies stood up for the Jews of the Third Reich. It was a bold and heroic gesture, and even if without effect, it signaled an attempt to intervene in a way that few nation-states did.

After 1921, Canada began to close its doors to immigrants and, in 1931, effectively bolted them shut. From that time forward, an extremely strict quota system was maintained, largely designed to keep out Jewish refugees. Only 15,800 were granted entry into Canada between 1921 and 1931. As in many countries, especially those hard-hit by the Depression, Canadians were largely opposed to allowing in foreigners during the interwar period. The prime minister, Mackenzie King—who supported British appeasement policies toward the Nazis and met with Hitler, describing him as "a reasonable and caring man . . . who might be thought of as one of the saviors of the world"—shared the common prejudices

of his day. In 1939, ignoring pleas from the Canadian Jewish community to admit Jews and their promises that they would financially support the stranded passengers of the SS *St. Louis*, King refused to grant them asylum. The prime minister's attitudes were echoed by the director of the Immigration Branch of the Department of Mines and Resources, Frederick Charles Blair. In 1938, he wrote to King, boasting, "Pressure by Jewish people to get into Canada has never been greater than it is now, and I am glad to be able to add that after thirty-five years of experience here, that it has never been so carefully controlled." The following year, when asked how many Jewish immigrants Canada would accept after World War II, Blair replied, "None is too many." Groups that were willing to help could not, and those that were in a position to do so would not. Chaim Weizmann summed up the international mood aptly when he observed, "The world was divided into two camps: those that wanted to get rid of the Jews and those that refused to take them in."

Jews wishing to leave Hitler's Germany faced many obstacles. The entry permits of various nations demanded that the immigrants provide proof of their ability to support themselves. However, after they had paid the Nazis the exorbitant flight tax, valued at about 25 percent of one's property value, and exchanged their reichsmarks for foreign currency at terrible exchange rates, little was left over that would prove "sustenance capacity." Another fact that militated against German Jewry leaving en masse was that per head of population, Jews had twice as many people over the age of 60 than the rest of the German population. It was simply harder for older people to leave, learn a new language, and start life afresh in a foreign land. In addition, the chief obstacle to leaving was that there was barely anywhere to go. Still, even though most countries refused to accept Jewish refugees, by the outbreak of World War II, about half of the German Jewish population had managed to leave.

One means by which many escaped was through the Ha'avara Agreement (1933–1939). The German Ministry of the Economy and Zionist representatives in Germany concluded a deal on August 27, 1933, that permitted the transfer of Jewish assets to Palestine in exchange for the export of German goods to Palestine. About 100 million reichsmarks were transferred, and about 60,000 German Jews immigrated to Palestine between 1933 and 1939. Neither side trusted the other. The Zionists were under no illusions that the Nazis were being altruistic, and the Nazis were always ambivalent about Zionism, enticed by the idea that it was a means of ridding themselves of Jews, but also fearful that an independent Jewish homeland would be a bridgehead in the so-called "world Jewish conspiracy." After Evian, the Jewish situation deteriorated across Europe, and the noncommittal nature of the conference made it clear that the plight of the Jews would not become an international cause. Other governments felt free to follow the Nazi lead and pursue antisemitic policies without fear of world censure. In 1938, both Italy and Hungary joined Germany in instituting antisemitic race laws, while other states in eastern Europe continued to discriminate against Jews both legally and socially. The refusal of the world's nations to take in Jewish refugees merely emboldened Hitler, leading him to believe that most countries were in agreement with his policies. An internal SD report on the Evian Conference stated:

[T]he many speeches and discussions show that with the exception of a few

countries that can still admit Jewish emigrants, there is an extensive aversion to a significant flow of emigrants either out of social considerations or out of an unexpressed racial abhorrence against Jewish emigrants.

The headline of a Nazi newspaper was more blunt, screaming, "Nobody wants them!"

On August 17, 1938, all Jews were forced to adopt the additional names, *Israel* for men and *Sara* for women, while on October 5, Heinrich Rothmund, head of the Swiss Alien Police and Switzerland's delegate to the Evian Conference, recommended that passports of Jews be stamped with the letter "J." The Nazis passed the measure into law. The territory of the Third Reich, which had been expanded with the annexation of Austria, was further enlarged when, pursuing a policy of appeasement, the Western powers ceded the Sudetenland to Hitler on October 1, 1938. The German chancellor, who had been initially greeted with considerable skepticism in Germany's elite military circles, was increasingly celebrated as a great conqueror. He had rearmed Germany, brought it international recognition by hosting the Olympic Games in 1936, disenfranchised and robbed the Jews in the absence of meaningful international protest, and expanded the country's territory, all without the German army firing a shot. With his regime consolidated, his personal appeal at record levels, and his justified sense that the world was indifferent to the fate of the Jews, he launched his most massive assault yet.

The Night of Broken Glass

On October 28, 1938, Germany expelled some 17,000 Polish Jews from its territory, dumping them in a no-man's-land across the border. In Paris on November 7, Hershel Grynszpan, the distraught son of two of the deported Jews, entered the German Embassy and shot the third secretary, Ernst vom Rath. Two days later, vom Rath died at 5:30 p.m. Hitler and Goebbels were in Munich that evening to celebrate the 15th anniversary of the November 9, 1923, Beer Hall putsch. When the news arrived of vom Rath's death, the two men conferred quietly, but neither made any public reference about the shooting and vom Rath's death in their speeches. News of his passing was precisely what the two men had been waiting for. Hitler secretly authorized a proposal by Goebbels to unleash "spontaneous" demonstrations against the Jews. Typical of his leadership style, after having given his orders, Hitler receded into the background. If the attack on the Jews was successful, he was prepared to allow Goebbels to enjoy the kudos. If the pogrom was, in some way, to backfire, Hitler had insulated himself, and Goebbels would be entirely responsible. Since the summer of 1938, there had been constant talk in certain upper echelons of the party of the need to carry out a large pogrom. Now the moment had arrived. On the night of November 9–10, SA, party functionaries, and fanatical citizens carried out a series of pogroms throughout the Reich known as the *Kristallnacht*, or Night of Broken Glass. Scores of Jewish homes and 7,500 Jewish-owned shops and businesses were destroyed, and over 1,000 synagogues were looted and ransacked, with about 300 set alight. Ninety-one Jews were killed, hundreds more committed suicide or died later as a result of beatings and other forms of mistreatment, and about 26,000 were rounded up and placed in concentration camps. Goebbels was ecstatic, recording in his diary:

> I see a blood-red [glow] in the sky. The synagogue burns. . . . From all over the

Reich information is now flowing in: 50, then 70 synagogues are burning. The Führer has ordered that 20–30,000 Jews should immediately be arrested. . . . In Berlin, 5, then 15 synagogues burn down. Now popular anger rages. . . . It should be given free rein. As I am driven to my hotel, windowpanes shatter. Bravo! Bravo! The synagogues burn like big old cabins.

The police and fire brigades were ordered by Hitler not to interfere, except when German life and property were in danger.

Not only were commercial establishments and synagogues destroyed, but private apartments were also violated. The Swiss consul reported on the situation in Cologne:

> [O]rganized parties moved through [the city] from one Jewish apartment to another. The families were ordered to either leave the apartment or they had to stand in the corner of a room while the contents were hurled from the windows. Gramophones, sewing machines, and typewriters tumbled down into the streets. One of my colleagues even saw a piano being thrown out of a second-floor window.

While Goebbels was reporting on events that occurred in big cities such as Munich and Berlin, the bloodlust and sadism perpetrated on November 9–10 were just as apparent in small cities and towns. In the western German town of Wittlich, a report on events there tells us that the synagogue was destroyed, and the huge lead-light window crashed to the ground. Then, "a shouting SA man climbed to the roof, waving the rolls of the Torah: 'Wipe your asses with it, Jews,' he screamed while he hurled them like bands of confetti on Karnival."

In Nuremberg, Arnold Blum was 16 years of age and "stood before the burning *shul* [synagogue] and watched as the firemen protected the surrounding buildings, being careful not to put any water on the isolated curls of smoke rising here and there from the devastated sanctuary that was once our *shul*." He was in "deep shock, empty of strength, gutted, as was [their] *shul*." Then his emotions began to change:

> Slowly my senses returned in a wave of anger. I clenched my fists, my eyes filled with tears of outrage. My silence screamed: "Kooma Adonai, veyafootsoo oyvecha. . . ." "Rise up, Lord, and scatter your enemies . . ." But the clouds did not part, the *shofar* did not sound, the strong hand and outstretched arm did not appear. It was not the year of the Lord. He had averted His face.

One of the Jews arrested that night was Max Moses Polke. At that time, he was a 41-year-old lawyer from Breslau. At 10:30 on the morning of November 9, he was on his way home from the train station—he had just arrived back from a trip to Berlin—and despite desperately trying to go unrecognized, he was spotted by someone who knew him:

> I was recognized by a man whom I had defended a few years before. . . . He incited a person standing next to him to start insulting me, with other rowdies joining in. . . . The insults soon gave way to physical abuse. Covered with blood, I attempted to flee to a house entrance but the doorman drove me back.

Polke was then taken to the police station, on the way to which he went "past the burning synagogue. Its great dome stood crooked. Flames shot out of the interior. [He] couldn't help but think of the destruction of the Temple in Jerusalem." At the station, he was taken to the courtyard, where he saw a number of Jews he knew, but "they didn't recognize [him] with [his] swollen and disfigured face. [His] lips were so thick that [he] could hardly speak. Four lower teeth and one upper one were loose." From the police station, he and the other Jewish arrestees were marched out and made to run the gauntlet through an abusive crowd shouting "the vilest insults, of which the choruses of 'Die Jews!' were the mildest." From there they were loaded onto a train and sent to the concentration camp at Buchenwald. Upon their arrival,

> young SS men appeared and welcomed [them] with blows to the head. . . . They lined [him and the other Jewish arrestees] up on the camp's parade ground and made [them] stand still for hours. The famous shaving of [their] heads and beards was almost a pleasant relief because at least [the] could sit down during the ceremony.

Polke had lost his right to practice law, and he and his wife were entirely dependent on the income from her shoe shop. But in the days following the Kristallnacht, the decision was taken to carry out the complete exclusion of Jews from the German economy.

> [And so] my wife had been forced to sell the rest of her inventory to a shoe merchant at dumping prices. According to the new laws, she not only could not have the shattered windowpanes replaced by the insurance company but was actually required to have new ones made with her own money.

On top of this, Polke was forced to pay a tax equal to the amount of 20 percent of his property's value. While terrified and impoverished, they were also fortunate:

> On Tuesday, December 13, 1938, at 10:15 A.M. I received the coveted Palestine Certificate from the English General Consul in Berlin. . . . On December 18, 1938, we left Germany forever. I had to leave my seventy-year-old mother alone in Breslau.

Polke's story encapsulates the tragic situation of German Jewry by 1938. He had been disenfranchised; subjected to violence and humiliation, arbitrary arrest, incarceration in a concentration camp; and forced to watch helplessly as his city's synagogues and Jewish-owned businesses were burned to the ground or were looted or brazenly expropriated.

For five years, discrimination, robbery, and defamation met with popular indifference or approval. The widespread violence and property damage of Kristallnacht, however, was not quite as popular as Goebbels's diaries would indicate. A Nazi report declared that "in viewing the ruins and attendant measures employed, all of the local crowds observed were obviously benumbed over what had happened and aghast over the unprecedented fury of Nazi acts that had been or were taking place with bewildering rapidity." Still, there was barely any protest, which by now had little chance of success anyway. To allay any doubts among the populace about the legal basis for the persecution and to help Germans justify the orgy of destruction to themselves, the Nazis broadcast a radio version of Shakespeare's *Merchant of Venice* not long after the Night of Broken Glass. The message was that Shylock, who stood for all Jews, got his comeuppance, as had the Jews of the Third Reich on Kristallnacht. The November pogrom would be the last time that such a violent outburst against the Jews would take place in full view of the German public.

In the immediate wake of the damage and destruction carried out that night, the question of insurance compensation was especially urgent. To discuss the matter, Göring called a meeting on November 12 for the chiefs of all economic departments of the government. Also in attendance were Goebbels and Heydrich, as well as Eduard Hilgard, a representative of the German insurance companies. He told those in attendance that the major insurance companies could not default on claims without risking their international reputations and business. They had to pay out, especially since some of the policyholders were actually German owners of property that had been rented to Jewish shopkeepers. On the other hand, honoring those claims would have been an astronomical expense. The windows alone that were broken on the Kristallnacht were valued at 6 million dollars, equal to approximately $135,000,000 in 2025.

It was Hitler who formulated the policy Göring was about to announce. He told the meeting that after the insurance companies had paid out to Jewish property owners, the government would then impound the money as part of a 1 billion reichsmarks fine, which they called an "atonement penalty," for the murder of Ernst vom Rath. It was also determined that the Jews were to pay for the cleanup. Having devised this scheme to further cripple the Jewish economy, Hitler and Göring sought to accelerate and complete the process of Aryanization by forcing what remained of Jewish property into the state's coffers. The state would pay the Jewish owner the bare minimum for damaged property and, in turn, sell it to "Aryans" at its real value, thereby pocketing the sizeable difference. Finally, Göring declared that effective January 1, 1939, all Jewish business activity in Germany was to cease. This last stipulation meant that Jews would have to sell their businesses and personal possessions. In the frenzied atmosphere of the meeting, Goebbels insisted on the implementation of further laws making it illegal for Jews to attend theaters, concerts, circuses, and parks and from sitting together with non-Jews on trains. Heydrich suggested revoking the driver's licenses of Jews and denying them access to all resorts, cultural institutions, and even hospitals. Not to be outdone, Göring responded to Goebbels's recommendation that Jews be denied all access to forests by suggesting that some sections be open to them, but the "Alpinists would see to it that the various animals, which damn well looked much like the Jews—the elk too has a hooked nose—go into the Jewish enclosure and settle down among them." All these suggestions became law. Göring concluded the meeting by saying, "Incidentally, I'd like to say again that I would not like to be a Jew in Germany."

Most Jews agreed with Göring's statement, and about 120,000 left in the winter of 1938–1939. For some, leaving turned out to provide only the illusion of relief. On May 13, 1939, a German passenger ship, the SS *St. Louis*, left Hamburg bound for Cuba with 900 Jews aboard. Most were headed for the United States. Cuba had charged each one $150 for an entrance visa, but one week before the ship departed, Cuba declared the visas invalid. And still the *St. Louis* sailed. Upon arrival in Havana, the passengers were denied entrance into the port. The German press, which had fanned the flames of antisemitism in Cuba to orchestrate precisely this response, was overjoyed. Here was further confirmation that no one wanted the Jews. On June 2, the ship set sail for Miami, amid protracted negotiations with the Cuban government. A Jewish welfare agency had provided sustenance to the Jews while they were in Cuba, and still the government would not yield. The US government also refused to admit the *St. Louis*. The ship then had no choice but to return to Europe. Belgium, Holland, Great Britain, and France offered to take the Jews until the United States would admit them. However, the process took too long for those who landed in Belgium, Holland, and France. Trapped during the German invasion, the passengers of the *St. Louis* were deported and murdered in the death camps.

Figure 5.3 depicts the burned-out interior of Berlin's Fasanenstrasse Synagogue after Kristallnacht. As the Jewish population of Berlin's western suburbs grew rapidly from less than 5,000 in 1885 to over 23,000 by 1910, it became necessary to build a new synagogue. The Fasanenstrasse Synagogue, one of the largest in Berlin, was built between 1910 and 1912 and sat 1,720 worshippers. The total cost for the purchase of the land and construction was 1.7 million gold marks. The monumental synagogue was predominantly of Romanesque design, with some Byzantine elements. It was home to a liberal congregation headed by Berlin's last chief rabbi, Leo Baeck. The Nazis closed the Fasanenstrasse Synagogue in 1936, and it was destroyed on Kristallnacht, one of over 1,000 synagogues destroyed on that night. Joseph Goebbels, minister of propaganda, personally gave the order to burn down the synagogue.

Immediately after Kristallnacht, more decrees and laws followed. On November 15, all Jewish children still attending German schools were expelled. A November 23 police ordinance prevented Jews from entering

Figure 5.3   Burned-out interior of Berlin's Fasanenstrasse Synagogue after Kristallnacht.

Source: Leo Baeck Institute.

certain areas and determined the times that Jews could appear in public. On November 29, it became illegal for Jews to keep carrier pigeons, a stunningly petty decree in light of the major assault on Jewish life. On December 3, Heydrich's desire to immobilize Jews became law—they were forbidden to own automobiles and motorbikes and had to turn in their driver's licenses.

At the November 12 meeting, Göring still harbored a desire to "kick the Jew out of Germany." The ultimate goal at this stage remained forced emigration. The Madagascar Plan was the idea of shipping Jews off en masse to the French island. The plan, which was first entertained in the 1930s in both France and Poland, was seriously considered by the Nazi government. At the start of the war, the Nazis toyed with the Nisko Plan, also known as the Lublin Plan, the idea of which was to send Jews to a "reservation" near the city of Radom, some 80 kilometers south of Warsaw. Like the idea of Madagascar, it was shelved as impractical, despite the fact that by January 1940, about 70,000 Jews from Vienna, Czechoslovakia, Germany, and western Poland had already been relocated there.

Hitler was concerned about uninhibited private profiteering from the Aryanization of Jewish businesses and property. On December 6, 1938, Göring warned regional Nazi Party heads that all profits from Aryanization belonged to the Reich and were to be deposited with the finance ministry. Göring offered a most revealing reason for this demand: "[I]t is only thus that the Führer's rearmament program can be accomplished." The forthcoming world war would be partly financed by robbing Jews.

Kristallnacht and its immediate aftermath essentially brought to an end the millennial existence of German and Austrian Jewry. As Hitler's foreign policy became more bellicose, so too did his threats against Jews become increasingly blunt. On January 21, 1939, he told the Czech foreign minister, Frantisek Chvalkovsky, "[W]e are going to destroy the Jews. They are not going to get away with what they did on November 9, 1918. The day of reckoning has come." And then on January 30, 1939, on the sixth anniversary of his accession to power, Hitler told the German parliament, the Reichstag:

> Today I will once more be a prophet: if the international Jewish financiers in and outside Europe should succeed in plunging the nations once more into a world war, then the result will not be the Bolshevization of the earth, and thus the victory of Jewry, but the annihilation of the Jewish race in Europe!

PHASE II: THE DESTRUCTION OF EUROPEAN JEWRY (1939–1945)

World War II broke out on September 1, 1939, when Germany invaded Poland. One week before, on August 23, 1939, Germany and the Soviet Union had signed a nonaggression treaty known as the Molotov–Ribbentrop Pact, named after the foreign ministers of the two countries. The pact included a secret protocol, in which the independent countries of Finland, Estonia, Latvia, Lithuania, Poland, and Romania came under "spheres of influence" of the two nations. The pact ensured Hitler that he would not have to fight a war on two fronts, and Stalin benefited by acquiring vastly expanded territory. After the German invasion of Poland and that of the Soviets from the east on September 17, the country fell after three weeks and was partitioned, for the fourth time since the eighteenth century.

The defeat of Poland on October 6, 1939, also meant its division, as prearranged by the two conquerors. As a consequence, 1.2 million Jews in the east of the country came under Soviet control, and more than 2 million Jews in central and western Poland came under direct Nazi rule. Theft was the handmaiden of murder. Not long after invading, the Germans froze all Jewish bank accounts, safety-deposit boxes, and securities. All these assets were then to be deposited in one bank, and for deposits of over 2,000 zlotys, account holders were prohibited from withdrawing more than 250 zlotys per week to cover living costs.

In November 1939, the Nazis established the Trust Office of the General Government of Poland. Its purpose was to secure confiscated Polish national assets, Jewish assets, and property now deemed ownerless because of the war. In Warsaw alone, Jewish real estate assets amounted to approximately 50,000 properties, valued at 2 billion zlotys. With those confiscations, not only did the owners lose out, but the building superintendents and tradesmen who maintained them—plumbers, carpenters, electricians, and handymen—all lost their livelihoods as well. Literally tens of thousands of small, medium, and large businesses owned by Jews were stolen by the Trust Office, which in turn dismissed the Jewish employees of these enterprises. With so much booty to process, a sub-branch of the Trust was established to sell off the property, clothes, and household items of Jews deported from their communities into the ghettos.

Policies that had been implemented against German Jews after Hitler came to power were now imposed on Polish Jews. An order of December 16, 1939, decreed that Polish Jews in the General Government, the area under Nazi control, no longer had any claims on disability pensions, unemployment insurance, and sickness benefits. Hospitalization for Jews was only permitted in exceptional circumstances, and as of March 6, 1940, Jewish doctors, dentists, and midwives were permitted to treat only Jewish patients, thus severely limiting the ability of the Jewish medical community to earn a living.

Plunder and dispossession were a matter of Nazi policy, though it differed from place to place according to whim and local conditions, but the situation in the small Ukrainian town of Boryslav was rather typical. When the Nazis captured it on July 1, 1941, there were 14,000 Jewish residents. The mayor of the town immediately gave the order to the Ukrainian nationalist militias to prepare for a pogrom. According to Duvid Graysdorf, one of Boryslav's 400 Jewish survivors, the massacre, which occurred on July 4, "took the lives of over 800 people." Jews were then "ordered to wear white armbands with the blue star of David. Heavy ransoms were imposed on the Jewish community . . . and the general confiscation of all Jewish property was put into effect." In August 1941, the Nazis imposed a fine of 20 million rubles on the Jews of the Boryslav. The "justification" given was that Lvov, 61 miles away, had been severely damaged in the war, and because the war was the fault of the Jews, they had the responsibility of paying for the damage. People stood in long queues at the offices of the Jewish Council, paying a lot or just a little. Giving 18 rubles (the figure numerically equivalent to the word *chai*, Hebrew for *life*) was quite common, but all amounts, including payments in kind, were accepted. Jews handed over gold and silver items, watches, brooches, candelabras, and wedding rings. The silverware alone weighed in at over 1,400 kilos. To ensure payment, the Germans, with their Ukrainian collaborators, took Jewish hostages. By August 8, the "contribution," as the Nazis called it, had been paid.

Everywhere, German soldiers, policemen, officials, and even civilians felt entitled to take anything they wanted. In Warsaw and Lodz, military and police forces confiscated the contents of textile and grocery warehouses. In Lodz, the robberies were so brazen and on such a huge scale that senior Nazi officials complained about the "wild confiscations." In February 1940, in the small town of Kutno in central Poland, ethnic Germans robbed Jews of such household items as bedding and furniture. Nearly every Jewish home was plundered. Sometimes, the extortions were for private use by German officials and were very specific. In the Warsaw ghetto, a demand was issued to the chairman of the Jewish council on July 22, 1941, on behalf of Brigitte Frank, wife of Hans Frank, governor-general of occupied Poland. She insisted on being given "a coffee-maker to brew Turkish coffee, one lady's traveling kit, and leather boxes large enough to serve four or six people on a picnic." With the German conquest, arbitrary terror was also immediately inflicted on Poland's Jews. Beatings, shootings, and public humiliation characterized daily life. Szaje Chaskiel, a survivor of the Lodz ghetto, Auschwitz, and Buchenwald, recalled what happened when the Nazis arrived in Czestochowa:

I was 10 years old and had only 4 years of schooling when World War II broke out in Poland in 1939. In January 1940, the Gestapo decided to hang 10 Jewish people in the city square in the town that I lived in with my family. Amongst the 10 was my father's uncle Manus. The Jewish police chose my father as one of the people to go out and hang them. My father refused and fought with the police. One of the Gestapo came into our home and tried again to force my dad to hang these people—again he refused. The Gestapo came back, took my father out and shot him. My sister and I carried our father to a cart and we wheeled him to the cemetery. At the age of 11, I had to dig a hole and bury my father.

In the postwar trials at Nuremberg, David Wajnapel testified about what happened when the Nazi arrived in his hometown:

A few weeks after the entry of the German troops into Radom, police and SS authorities arrived. Conditions became immediately worse. The house in the Zeromski Street, where their headquarters were, became a menace to the entire population. People who were walking in this street were dragged into the gateway and ill-treated by merciless beatings and by the staging of sadistic games. All SS officers, as well as the men, took part in this. Being a physician, I often had the opportunity to give medical help to seriously injured victims of the SS.

A Polish report written in 1940 titled "Activity of the Occupation Authorities on Polish Territory" noted thus: "The Jews are the object of indescribable mental torture. Face slapping; kicking; insulting address; ridicule; stealing furniture, furs, food reserves—these are daily occurrences." Religious Jews, in particular, were favorite targets of the Germans, who delighted in humiliating them. Orthodox Jews were force-fed pork and made to urinate and defecate on Torah scrolls. Jewish men were made to pay to have their beards shaved, or their beards were very often burned off or cut off so brutally that lumps of flesh came away from the face.

Such horrors occurred outside of the two main institutions created by the Nazis to destroy the Jews—the ghettos and the camps. But the randomness of the terror experienced outside those settings remained a constant feature of Jewish life under German occupation until the end of the war. However, the establishment of ghettos and camps facilitated the practice of terror on a far larger, more systematic scale.

The Ghettos

On September 21, 1939, just after Poland's collapse, Reinhard Heydrich ordered the ghettoization of Polish Jewry, a process that took place between October 1939 and April 1941. All Jewish communities of fewer than 500 persons were dissolved, and the inhabitants were herded into nearby ghettos, most of which, according to Heydrich, were "to be located along railroad lines." The goal was the immediate concentration of Jews for the purposes of exploiting them for the German war effort and, as Heydrich said, for a "final aim" yet to be determined but one "which will require an extended period of time."

Heydrich's order also carried the stipulation that each ghetto was to be administered by a Council of Jewish Elders, a *Judenrat*. Each Jewish Council was composed of 24 members drawn from the prewar secular and religious elites. The Jewish Councils led a desperate struggle to provide welfare to Jews—they were responsible for housing, medical care, food distribution, and education, and the latter provision was only permitted in some ghettos, not all—but their principal obligation remained the "exact and punctual execution" of Nazi orders. Their tasks included providing the Nazis with maps of the ghettos and accurate lists of Jews and their professions, slave labor, confiscated Jewish property, valuables, and "contributions." Worst of all, the Jewish Councils were later made responsible for selecting which ghetto inhabitants were to be sent to the gas chambers at extermination camps. By co-opting the councils, the Nazis pursued a strategy of making Jews complicit in their own destruction.

The word *ghetto* is a misnomer, for the ghettos established by the Nazis bore no resemblance to the original ghetto, first established in Venice in 1516. Though intended to separate Jews from the rest of the population, the early modern ghetto never prevented contact between Jews and gentiles and, in fact, never fully inhibited Jewish life. The Nazi ghettos, by contrast, were prisons, locked from the outside and secured by German guards. One incarcerated Jew referred to the ghetto as a "prison without a roof." Surrounded by a fence or a wall, Nazi ghettos were constructed in the poorest sections of towns. The non-Jewish population was moved out, and Jews were transferred in.

There were about 1,150 ghettos, and each varied significantly based on when and where it had been built, the nature of the local economy, the occupational structure, the demographic and cultural makeup of the Jewish community, and the topography of the surrounding area. Ghettoization was not a uniform, centrally planned operation, and much was left to local initiative. Despite the differences between ghettos, all of them were places of terror, overcrowding, starvation, epidemics, and isolation from the outside world.

As accustomed as Polish Jews were to antisemitism, the ferocity of the Nazi version took them by surprise. On March 10, 1940, a Hebrew diarist in the Warsaw ghetto, Chaim Kaplan, made a penetrating and defiant observation:

The gigantic catastrophe which has descended on Polish Jewry has no parallel, even in the darkest periods of Jewish history. First, in the depth of the hatred. This is not just hatred whose source is a party platform. . . . It is a hatred of emotion, whose source is some psychopathic malady. In its outward manifestations it functions as physiological hatred, which imagines the object of hatred to be unclean in body, a leper who has no place within the camp. . . . It is our good fortune that the conquerors have failed to consider the nature and strength of Polish Jewry, and this has kept us alive. . . . But we do not conform to the laws of nature. A certain invisible power is embedded in us and it is this secret which keeps us alive and preserves us in spite of all the laws of nature. . . . The Jews of Poland . . . love life, and they do not wish to disappear from the earth before their time. The fact that we have hardly any suicides is worthy of special emphasis. We have been left naked but as long as that secret power is concealed within us, we shall not yield to despair. The strength of this power lies in the very nature of the Polish Jew, which is rooted in our eternal tradition that commands us to live.

When Kaplan wrote these lines, the Nazi death machine was still not operating at full capacity. The situation would only get worse. In the beginning, aid was made available to those incarcerated in ghettos through the Joint Distribution Committee ("the Joint"), an American organization founded in 1914 to offer material assistance to Jewish communities abroad. The Joint was permitted to send in food parcels and other necessities to ghettos located in the General Government, which it did through the Jewish Social Self-Help (JSS or, in Yiddish, *Aleynhilf*), an organization that was headquartered in Cracow under the leadership of theater director Dr. Michael Veychert. In turn, the JSS distributed the items inside the ghetto directly to individuals or through other mutual aid societies. Known by their Polish or Russian acronyms, these agencies included TOZ, Society for Safeguarding the Health of the Jewish Populace; CENTOS, Society for the Care of Orphans and Abandoned Children; and ORT, Society for Trades and Agricultural Labor.

In Warsaw, the JSS was known as ZETOS and was headed by the distinguished historian of Polish Jewry Emanuel Ringelblum (1900–1944). Under his creative and energetic leadership, ZETOS became a vast organization operating departments that dealt with refugee affairs, housing, clothing, culture, and public kitchens. While the JSS often acted in concert with the Jewish Councils, in Warsaw, ZETOS was continually opposed to the Judenrat. Because of this, and due to the assistance it was able to dole out, ZETOS won the trust of the people and was seen by them as the leading Jewish force in the ghetto. Operating on a budget of about $20,000 per month, the JSS distributed money through "house committees," established in the courtyards of apartment buildings in the ghetto. These committees, which did not exist in other ghettos, attempted to provide for the starving inhabitants' material and spiritual needs by running kitchens and organizing recreational activities, makeshift schools, and religious services. Tenants paid dues that were determined at a public meeting, and means testing saw to it that the wealthier were taxed at a higher rate than the poor. Taxes were supplemented by ongoing fundraising campaigns. In 1940, 788 house committees were serving the needs of 7,500 people, and by 1942, the number of committees had increased to 1,108. The task was overwhelming, and it meant that despite its best efforts, ZETOS was unable to provide sufficient food and other forms of welfare for Jews in the ghetto. In Warsaw, at least 75 percent of the 100,000 Jewish children under the age of 15 required welfare assistance of some kind.

The Joint's relief activities ended when Nazi Germany officially declared war on the United States in December 1941. After that, conditions in the ghettos quickly deteriorated. The first to succumb were the refugees brought into the ghettos from surrounding towns. They had no local contacts and were entirely dependent on a welfare system that was unable to provide even for the native Jews of the city, let alone newcomers. Piotrkow's Jewish population went from 8,000 to 12,000, while in Cracow the prewar Jewish population of 56,000 increased to 68,000, thanks to the arrival of Jewish refugees from neighboring small towns. Warsaw took in as many as 150,000 refugees from at least 700 locales. Overcrowding was a constant problem. The ghettos were large, with the biggest in Warsaw, whose population at its peak was about 450,000, an extraordinary number, given that the prewar Jewish population of the city was 337,000. A German official in Warsaw reported in January 1941, "The Jewish quarter extends over about 1,016 acres. . . . Occupancy

Figure 5.4   Persecution of an Orthodox Jew in Warsaw, 1941.

Source: Photo Scala, Florence/bpk, Bildagentur fuer Kunst, Kultur und Geschichte, Berlin.

therefore works out at 15.1 persons per apartment and 6 to 7 persons per room." In Vilna, a Jew wrote, "About 25,000 persons live in our ghetto in 72 buildings on 5 street sections. This comes to one-and-a-half to two meters per person. Narrow as the grave." Similar conditions prevailed in the Lodz ghetto, which held about 200,000 Jews, and Lvov, with about 120,000, the second- and third-largest ghettos, respectively.

Figure 5.4 depicts the persecution of an Orthodox Jew in Warsaw, 1941. The man is having his beard cut off by two soldiers, while a third looks on, laughing. Just as in Nazi Germany before the war, the persecution of Jews in Poland (and elsewhere) after the war began was characterized by humiliation and

an attempt to shame Jews. It was also a source of "entertainment" for German soldiers, as can be seen in this photograph. Religious Jews, in particular, were singled out for such abusive treatment.

Because of overcrowding, plumbing broke and toilets overflowed, leading to the spread of diseases. Very little heating was available in winter, and water became extremely scarce. Of the 31,271 apartments in the Lodz ghetto, only 725 had running water. Parents were often faced with the insoluble dilemma of whether to use precious water for cooking or for washing lice out of their children's hair. People were caked in lice. In such conditions, typhus, tuberculosis, and dysentery ran rampant. A typhus epidemic that broke out in the Warsaw ghetto in late 1940 claimed 43,239 victims. Starvation became not just a by-product of ghetto life but was the consequence of a deliberate policy of the Nazis. In Lodz, the starving young diarist Dawid Sierakowiak recorded on December 28, 1942:

> The ration for the first ten days of January has been issued. There are no potatoes at all in it, only 5 kilos of vegetables and a bit of marmalade. . . . [T]he prospect of cold and hunger fills me with indescribable terror. . . . Today we went to bed without supper because [my sister] Nadzia portioned out our remaining potato scraps for tomorrow and the day after tomorrow.

Dawid was 18 years old when he died on August 8, 1943, of what was known as "ghetto disease," a combination of tuberculosis, starvation, and exhaustion. For Sara Plagier, a 14-year-old girl also in the Lodz ghetto, food even determined time itself:

> In the ghetto we had no need for a calendar. Our lives were divided into periods

based on the distribution of food: bread every eighth day, the ration once a month. Each day fell into two parts: before and after we received our soup. In this way the time passed.

At the beginning of 1942, in the small southeastern Polish town of Józefów, official rations for the 1,800 Jews were 72 grams (2.5 ounces) of bread per day and 200 grams of sugar a month. Jews sometimes also received 60 grams of soap and 1 liter of paraffin. The daily bread ration in Warsaw was less than a hundred grams (3.5 ounces). There the bread was often made with sand or sawdust. In January 1941, the official total daily caloric intake granted to Warsaw's Jews was 220. By August 1941, it was reduced to 177. Moreover, it had become increasingly unaffordable. A kilogram of bread cost 4 zlotys in 1940, rose to 14 zlotys in May 1942, and was fetching 45 zlotys by the summer. The meager amount and poor quality of the bread, coupled with the rising prices, had the desired effect for the Nazis. In January 1941, 818 people starved to death in the Warsaw ghetto. Month after month the number rose. In August, 5,560 perished from hunger. The situation was so bad that the Jewish ghetto hospital was able to conduct some of the first-ever clinical studies of the effects of hunger on the human body. By January 4, 1942, Chaim Kaplan's tone had changed as he described the hunger, disease, and misery that surrounded him:

It is not at all uncommon on a cold winter morning to see the bodies of those who have died on the sidewalks of cold and starvation during the night. . . . In the gutters, among the refuse, one can see almost naked and barefoot little children wailing pitifully. These are children who were orphaned when both parents died

either in their wanderings or in the typhus epidemic.

Only smuggling prevented even more people from dying, and it was often organized by the prewar Jewish criminal class and executed by children small enough to pass through tight spaces. The young smugglers risked their lives to sneak vegetables past the Jewish police and Nazi guards. They became memorialized in popular song:

Over the wall, through holes, and past the guard,
Through the wires, ruins, and fences,
Plucky, hungry, and determined,
I sneak through, dart like a cat

Smuggling was very dangerous, and the Nazis thought nothing of killing children they had caught, and yet the operations went on undeterred. According to Emanuel Ringelblum:

Among the Jewish victims of the smuggling there were tens of Jewish children between 5 and 6 years old, whom the German killers shot in great numbers near the passages and at the walls. . . .

And despite that, without paying attention to the victims, the smuggling never stopped for a moment. When the street was still slippery with the blood that had been spilled, other [smugglers] already set out, as soon as the "candles" [smuggler look-outs] had signaled that the way was clear, to carry on with the work. . . .

The smuggling took place a) through the walls, b) through the gates, c) through underground tunnels, d) through sewers, and e) through houses on the borders [of the ghetto].

Smuggling, soup kitchens, and rudimentary medical care, as crucial as they were, could not prevent thousands of Jews from dying of starvation and disease in the ghettos. By 1942, it is estimated that at least 80,000 died in this way in the Warsaw ghetto alone.

Early on, Nazi ranks were divided about the purpose of the ghettos. There were two groups: the productionists, who thought ghettos could be effectively exploited for the Nazi war effort, and the attritionists, who were of the opinion that the sole purpose of the ghettos was to destroy the inhabitants. In truth, both policies were pursued, but the attritionists always had the upper hand—and the final say. In fact, the Nazis pointed to the unsanitary ghetto conditions as justification for murdering the inhabitants. As the Nazi Party ideologist Alfred Rosenberg said after visiting the Warsaw ghetto, "seeing this race en masse, which is decaying, decomposing, and rotten to the core, will banish any sentimental humanitarianism." Joseph Goebbels expressed similar sentiments even more bluntly after visiting the Vilna ghetto: "The Jews are the lice of civilized humanity. One has to exterminate them somehow, otherwise they will continue to play their tortuous and annoying role." Cynically, Nazi doctors and party officials embarked on a deliberate policy of spreading disease and then claimed that exterminating the ghetto inhabitants would prevent the spread of contagion.

A prevailing characteristic of ghetto life all over Poland was the sense of isolation Jews felt, as they were cut off from the outside world. As Jurek Becker, who was in the Lodz ghetto, wrote in his novel *Jacob the Liar*: "Well . . . it is evening. Don't ask me what time it is. Only the Germans know that." The Nazis confiscated radios, telephones, and newspapers, declaring the use of such items to be punishable by death. Mail service barely functioned. Even walking was regulated. On August 2, 1941, a Nazi decree forbade Jews in the Vilna ghetto "to use sidewalks" and compelled them to "use only the right hand verges of roadways and walk in single file."

Jewish suffering brought forth a new artistic genre—Holocaust music. The subject matter of the songs was grim and blunt: beatings, shootings, starvation, torture, and the loss of family and home. The songs capture the multiple moods of the doomed. Some were defiant. In Kovno, Jewish slave labor brigades sang:

We don't weep or grieve
Even when you beat and lash us,
But never for a moment believe
That you will discourage and dash us.

Other songs reflected despair tinged with the faintest hope of emerging alive. Workers led from the Radom ghetto used to sing:

Work, brothers, work fast,
If you don't, they'll lash your hide.
Not many of us will manage to last—
Before long we'll all have died.

After his wife's death in 1943, Vilna songwriter and resistance fighter Shmerke Kaczerginski wrote the following Yiddish love song, *Friling* (*Springtime*):

I walk through the Ghetto alone and forsaken,
There's no-one to care for me now.
And how can you live when your love has been taken,
Will somebody please show me how?
I know that it's springtime, and birdsong, and sunshine,
All nature seems happy and free,
But locked in the Ghetto I stand like a beggar,
I beg for some sunshine for me.

After the defeat of Poland, the Nazi war machine swept through western Europe, ensnaring ever more Jews in its grip. Between April and June 1940, the Nazis conquered

Denmark (Jewish population 8,000), Norway (Jewish population 2,000), France (Jewish population 350,000), Belgium (Jewish population 65,000), Luxembourg (Jewish population 3,500), and Holland (Jewish population 140,000). In southeastern Europe in April 1941, the communities of Serbia (Jewish population 75,000) and Greece (Jewish population 77,000) came under Nazi control. Occupation brought roundups of Jews, passage of anti-Jewish laws and ordinances, confiscation of property, and the pressing of Jews into forced labor. Antisemitic legislation was also adopted in countries allied with Nazi Germany, either before the war began or thereafter: Slovakia (Jewish population 135,000), Vichy France (Jewish population 350,000), Italy (Jewish population 57,000), Romania (Jewish population 757,000), Hungary (Jewish population 650,000), Bulgaria (Jewish population 50,000), and Croatia (Jewish population 30,000).

In Germany, the myriad antisemitic decrees continued to mount. On the very day the war broke out, September 1, 1939, a law was passed preventing Jews from leaving their homes after eight o'clock in the evening (nine o'clock in summer). The rationale was that they "used the blackout to harass Aryan women." On September 23, 1939, Jews had to turn in their radios; in July 1940, Jews in Berlin were only permitted to shop for food for one hour per day, from four o'clock to five o'clock in the afternoon, that is, after all the best produce had been sold. In Württemberg at the turn of the year 1939–1940, the minister of food and agriculture forbade Jews from purchasing cocoa and gingerbread. On June 26, 1941, a law was passed that made it illegal for Jews to own soap or shaving cream; in August of 1941, Jews were forbidden to borrow library books, and by February 1942, they could no longer purchase newspapers and magazines.

On February 14, 1942, all bakeries and cake shops had to display signs saying that they cannot sell to Jews. On May 15, 1942, Jews were no longer considered worthy of owning pets, and so that small pleasure was banned. In June 1942, Jews were forbidden to buy eggs, then the next month it was milk, and in September, it was meat. On June 12, 1942, Jews could no longer own "electrical and optical equipment, bicycles, typewriters and records." They all had to be turned in to the authorities. In October 1942, Jews were forbidden to buy books. On November 6, 1942, it was declared illegal for Jews to possess cigars and cigarettes. Increasingly during the war, Jews were moved into "Jews' Houses," separate apartment buildings for them alone. Those Germans writing PhD dissertations were instructed to only quote Jewish authors when it is "unavoidable on scientific grounds." Jewish authors were to be listed in a separate bibliography.

In June 1940, as the Nazis conquered western Europe, the Soviet Union gained control over the Baltic states: Lithuania, Latvia, and Estonia. In addition, the Soviets, through military victories and the terms of the Molotov–Ribbentrop Pact, gained control over Volhynia and eastern Galicia (annexed from Poland in September 1939) and from northern Bukovina and Bessarabia (annexed from Romania in 1940). These additional territories were home to about 2 million Jews, and thus, the Soviet Union's Jewish population went from 3 million in 1939 to 5 million by 1940. These annexed Jewish communities, which had displayed remarkable cultural vibrancy in the interwar period, alarmed the Soviet authorities, who feared that they had inherited millions of Jewish nationalists rather than Soviet patriots. Concerned about their attachment to the various forms of Jewish secular and religious culture, Moscow immediately set about suppressing Jewish cultural and religious institutions. Yiddish newspapers, synagogues, and schools were shut down. Some Zionist and Bundist leaders, as well as religious functionaries, merchants, businessmen, and industrialists, were killed, but most were exiled to Siberia. With this reprieve, the Soviets inadvertently saved a quarter of a million Jews from certain death at the hands of the Nazis by deporting them to the Soviet interior. Whatever ill will the Soviet assault on Jewish life generated among Jews, however, soon subsided with the Nazi attack on the Soviet Union.

Mass Shootings in the Soviet Union

On June 22, 1941, Hitler launched Operation Barbarossa, the war against the Soviet Union. Germany invaded with 134 divisions at full fighting strength, while 73 more divisions were stationed behind the front, ready for deployment. In all, there were more than 3 million German soldiers, supported by 650,000 troops from Germany's allies, beginning with Finnish and Romanian forces, which were later joined by units from Italy, Croatia, Slovakia, and Hungary. The invading forces stretched from the Baltic Sea in the north to the Black Sea in the south, a distance of over 2,200 kilometers. The war with Stalin's Russia was to be the great apocalyptic struggle with Communism, one that Hitler called a "war of annihilation." Given his linking of Jews and Bolshevism, this was to be the race war that antisemites had been predicting since the nineteenth century. Despite the Soviet Union's assault on Jewish life, Jews were under no illusions—their survival depended on Soviet victory. Jews in the territories annexed by the Soviet Union looked upon the Russians as liberators and were especially buoyed by the sight of Jewish Red Army officers. In all, as many as 500,000 Jews served in the Red Army during the war, and about

180,000 of them fell in battle. Non-Jews in these same areas saw things very differently. On the whole, they considered the Soviets as their oppressors, Jews as Bolshevik collaborators, and Germans as liberators. This interpretation of power relations would manifest itself in widespread local complicity with the Nazis in the murder of Jews. Among Soviet Jews, the war also sparked a great awakening. For those Jews who had their Jewish identity attenuated, if not obliterated, by the Bolshevik Revolution, the war against the Nazis rekindled a sense of their ethnic origins. The Jewish writer Ilya Ehrenburg delivered a speech in August 1941 in which he gave voice to a new sentiment:

> I grew up in a Russian city. My native language is Russian. I am a Russian writer. Now, like all Russians, I am defending my homeland. But the Nazis have reminded me of something else: my mother's name was Hannah. I am a Jew. I say this with pride. Hitler hates us more than anyone else. And that does us credit.

Hitler appears to have decided upon the mass murder of Soviet Jewry at some point during the planning phase of the invasion of the Soviet Union. Then, sometime in the last three months of 1941, this was extended to European Jewry as a whole. The exact timing of the order is a point of conjecture among historians because no written and signed document has ever been discovered. It probably never existed. Rather, the decision to destroy the Jews was most likely conveyed orally from Hitler to Himmler. By this time, Hitler no longer really distinguished between the Allies and the Jews; they were one and the same, and both were the enemy. In fact, in light of Hitler's belief in a world Jewish conspiracy, he was convinced that the Jews ran Washington, London, and Moscow. The Jew as enemy was Nazism's most consistent article of faith. On November 18, 1942, in the midst of the slaughter of European Jewry, the Reich Propaganda Directorate of the Nazi Party issued its "Word of the Day": "Who Bears the Guilt for the War? Roosevelt, Churchill, and Stalin Bear Responsibility for the War in the Eyes of History. Behind Them, However, Stands the Jew." Another directive issued that same month bore a picture of Roosevelt with a number of smiling men identified as Jews, implying that the American president was their puppet. Ominously, the caption read: "They Will Stop Laughing!!!" The charges and threats never varied and were publicly known from beginning to end. This was an ideological race war, one to finally rid the world of Jews. For Hitler, it would be history's most decisive moment. The destruction of the Jews was a crucial part of the Nazi quest for *Lebensraum* (living space) in the Soviet Union. The *Lebensraum* policy was based upon killing, deporting, or enslaving the Slavic peoples, whom the Nazis considered inferior; the elimination of the Jews; and the repopulation of the area with at least half a million people of German racial ancestry. Together with the 350,000 ethnic Germans indigenous to eastern Europe, the Germanic colonizers would rule the land, whose natural resources and agricultural richness were to be exploited to meet the needs of Germany.

Between 1939 and 1941, over 300,000 Polish Jews fled east into the Soviet Union. With the German invasion of Russia, as many as 1 million Soviet Jews were able to flee eastward, largely into Soviet Asia. This still left approximately 2 million Jews who were unable to escape the invading Nazis. Close on the heels of the German troops that attacked the Soviet Union were four mobile death squads, the *Einsatzgruppen*. Designated by the letters *A*, *B*, *C*, and *D*, each killing unit was made up of between 600 and 1,000 men and was each further divided into two or three smaller commando squads, which themselves had small subunits that were sent out to murder Jews in small and scattered communities. Composed of SS police battalions, regular German army units, and local collaborators, the Einsatzgruppen fanned out in search of civilians from the Baltic states in the north to the Black Sea region in the south. While the perpetrators came from all walks of life, the leaders of the death squads came from a narrower social spectrum. Handpicked by Heydrich, they were not drawn from Germany's criminal class but, rather, from its educated elite. Three of the first four commanders of the Einsatzgruppen (EG), Franz Walter Stahlecker (EG A), Otto Rasch (EG C), and Otto Ohlendorf (EG D), all held PhDs. Only Arthur Nebe (EG B) did not have a doctorate. Among other death squad leaders, there was a physician, a pastor, and even an opera singer.

The murders followed a similar pattern. Troops would arrive in a town in the early hours of the morning, take their victims by surprise, and march them out of town, where they were robbed and made to strip. The naked Jews were then machine-gunned directly or were dumped into antitank ditches, quarries, gorges, or pits that they had been forced to dig themselves. Killings generally went on from dawn to dusk, the killers often drunk, as they shot their victims without mercy or let. No German was ever forced to participate in the shootings and yet there are hardly any recorded instances of soldiers being demoted or disadvantaged in some way for seeking to be excused. All the killers murdered Jews of their own free will. At first, the Einsatzgruppen mostly targeted Jewish men, but later, women and children were included in the shootings. They also murdered Soviet political commissars, partisan fighters, Roma (Gypsies), the sick, and the disabled. The numbers killed by the death squads were staggering, approximately 100,000 Jews per month for the first five months of operations. In the Baltic states, between June 22 and November 25, 1941, Einsatzgruppe A, the most lethal of the four, killed 135,567 Jews. The killings took place rapidly and on an enormous scale. In two periods of just two days each, November 29–30, 1941, and December 8–9, 1941, Einsatzgruppe A, together with the Latvian SS, the Arjas Kommando, shot 25,000 Latvian Jews from Riga in what was known as the Rumbula Massacre. Einsatzgruppe B, operating in Belarus, had killed 45,467 Jews by mid-November 1941. One of the biggest killing sites was the Blagovshchina forest, southeast of Minsk. Beginning in November 1941, Jews, Soviet prisoners of war, and partisans were shot there by Einsatzgruppe B and local collaborators. The first victims were the 100,000 Jews from the Minsk ghetto. At the start of May 1942, Jews were brought there from Germany, Bohemia and Moravia, Poland, Holland, and Belgium and killed. In addition to shooting, the commanders of Einsatzgruppe B introduced dynamite and then gas vans to murder their victims. Estimates put the number of Jews killed in this region at about 200,000. In one of the most notorious mass killings on the Eastern Front, Einsatzgruppe C shot 33,371 Jews from Kiev at a ravine named Babi Yar, in a two-day slaughter that took place on September 29 and 30, 1941. According to Nazi documents, the belongings of the Jews were sent to the National-Socialist Welfare Association and distributed to needy Germans.

Romania was an ally of Nazi Germany, and in the regions under its control, it largely murdered Jews without German encouragement or even much assistance. These areas were where Einsatzgruppe D was deployed. In retaliation for the Soviets having left a timed explosive device that destroyed Romanian army headquarters in Odessa on October 16, 1941, the Romanian Fascist government ordered the rounding up of Jews. On the morning of October 22, Romanian death squads shot 19,000 of them at Odessa's port. Later in the afternoon, a further 20,000 Jews were marched out of Odessa to the village of Dalnic, where, after being tied together in lots of 45 people, they were shot into antitank ditches. Those in this group not killed in this way were herded into warehouses, which were set alight. Under Romanian administration, it has been estimated that between 270,000 and 370,000 Jews in Bessarabia, Bukovina, Transnistria, and Dorohoi County died or were murdered at Romanian hands during the Holocaust. With reference to Romania, Holocaust scholar Raul Hilberg asserted that "no country, besides Germany, was involved in massacres of Jews on such a scale." While the Romanians were slaughtering Jews in this region, so too were the Germans. Sometimes, smaller Jewish communities in the region of Einsatzgruppe D's operations were wiped out in a day or two. From December 11 to 13, 1941, Einsatzgruppe D killed 11,000 Jews at the Black Sea town of Simferopol. Altogether, this unit, under the command of Otto Ohlendorf, murdered 90,000 Jews from June 1941 to March 1942. With assistance from Lithuanian, Latvian, Estonian, Ukrainian, Romanian, Hungarian, and ethnic German "militia units," the four Einsatzgruppen murdered approximately 1.4 million Jews by the spring of 1943.

Rivka Yosselevska was at the site of a mass shooting on Saturday, August 15, 1942. In May 1961, she delivered her eyewitness testimony at the trial of Adolf Eichmann in Jerusalem. Speaking in Yiddish, she told the courtroom that on the day in question, Germans and Belorussians entered the ghetto in Zagorodski, Belarus. It was early morning, and the Jews had been ordered from their homes and made to go through a roll call that lasted all day. That evening, a truck arrived at the ghetto gates:

Those who were strong enough climbed up by themselves, but the weak ones were thrown in. They were piled into the truck like cattle. . . . The rest they made run after the truck. . . . I was holding my little girl and running after the truck, too. Many mothers had two or three children. All the way we had to run. When somebody fell down, they wouldn't let him get up; they shot him on the spot. All my family was there.

We arrived at the place. Those who had been on the truck had already got down, undressed and stood in a row. . . . It was about three kilometres away from our town. There was a hill and a little below it they had dug something like a ditch. They made us walk up to the hill, in rows of four, and . . . shot each one of us separately. . . . They were SS men. They carried several guns with plenty of ammunition pouches. . . .

[My six-year-old daughter, Merkele, and I] stood there facing the ditch. I turned my head. He asked, "Whom do I shoot first?" I didn't answer. He tore the child away from me. I heard her last cry and he shot her. Then he got ready to kill me, grabbed my hair and turned my head about. I remained standing and heard a shot but I didn't move. He turned me around, loaded his pistol, so that I could see what he was doing. Then he again turned me around and shot me. I fell down. . . .

I felt nothing. At that moment I felt that something was weighing me down. I thought that I was dead, but that I could feel something even though I was dead. I couldn't believe that I was alive. I felt I was suffocating, bodies had fallen on me. . . . I pulled myself up with the last bit of strength. When I reached the top I looked around but I couldn't recognize the place. Corpses strewn all over, there was no end to the bodies. You could hear people moaning in their death agony. . . . The Germans were not there. No one was there.

When he shot me I was wounded in the head. I still have a big scar on my head, where I was wounded by the Germans.

When I saw they were gone I dragged myself over to the grave and wanted to jump in. I thought the grave would open up and let me fall inside alive. I envied everyone for whom it was already over, while I was still alive. Where should I go? What should I do? Blood was spouting. Nowadays, when I pass a water fountain I can still see the blood spouting from the grave. The earth rose and heaved. I sat there on the grave and tried to dig my way in with my hands. I continued digging as hard as I could. The earth didn't open up. I shouted to Mother and Father, why I was left alive. What did I do to deserve this? Where shall I go? To whom can I turn? I have nobody. I saw everything; I saw everybody killed. No one answered. I remained sprawled on the grave three days and three nights.

Hermann Graebe was an engineer and manager of a German construction firm in Ukraine. Traveling around, recruiting construction workers, he had occasion to witness the mass murders of Jews. Determined to do what he could to prevent such killings, Graebe, like Oskar Schindler, sought to use his position to save as many Jews as possible by providing them with work. On one occasion in July 1942, hearing that a massacre was about to take place, he obtained a "writ of protection" from the deputy district commissioner and hastily went to Rovno. Brandishing a gun, and the writ, he managed to secure the release of 150 Jews just before they were to be shot. On October 5, 1942, he accidentally came upon an execution squad killing Jews from the small Ukrainian town of Dubno. After the war, at the Nuremberg trials, Graebe was the only German to testify for the prosecution and gave the following eyewitness testimony of the slaughter of 5,000 Jews (he was the target of such hostility that he left Germany in 1948 and immigrated to San Francisco):

> My foreman and I went directly to the pits. Nobody bothered us. Now I heard rifle shots in quick succession from behind one of the earth mounds. The people who had got off the trucks—men, women and children of all ages—had to undress upon the order of an SS man who carried a riding or dog whip. They had to put down their clothes in fixed places, sorted according to shoes, top clothing and undergarments. I saw heaps of shoes of about 800 to 1000 pairs, great piles of under-linen and clothing.
>
> Without screaming or weeping these people undressed, stood around in family groups, kissed each other, said farewells, and waited for a sign from another SS man, who stood near the pit, also with a whip in his hand. During the fifteen minutes I stood near, I heard no complaint or plea for mercy. I watched a family of about eight persons, a man and a woman both of about fifty, with their children of about twenty to twenty-four, and two grown-up daughters about twenty-eight or twenty-nine. An old woman with snow white hair was holding a one-year-old child in her arms and singing to it and tickling it. The child was cooing with delight. The parents were looking on with tears in their eyes. The father was holding the hand of a boy about ten years old and speaking to him softly; the boy was fighting his tears. The father pointed to the sky, stroked his head and seemed to explain something to him.
>
> At that moment the SS man at the pit started shouting something to his comrade. The latter counted off about twenty persons and instructed them to go behind the earth mound. Among them was the family I have just mentioned. I well remember a girl, slim with black hair, who, as she passed me, pointed to herself and said, "twenty-three years old." I walked around the mound and found myself confronted by a tremendous grave. People were closely wedged together and lying on top of each other so that only their heads were visible. Nearly all had blood running over their shoulders from their heads. Some of the people shot were still moving. Some were lifting their arms and turning their heads to show that they were still alive.
>
> The pit was nearly two-thirds full. I estimated that it already contained about a thousand people. I looked for the man who did the shooting. He was an SS man, who sat at the edge of the narrow end of the pit, his feet dangling into the pit. He had a tommy-gun on his knees and was smoking a cigarette. The people, completely naked, went down some steps, which were cut in the clay wall of the pit and clambered over the heads of the people lying there to the place to which the SS man directed them. They lay down in front of the dead or wounded people; some caressed those who were still alive and spoke to them in a low voice. Then I heard a series of shots. I looked into the pit and saw that the bodies were twitching or the heads lying already motionless on top of the bodies that lay beneath them. Blood was running from their necks. The next batch was approaching already. They went down into the pit, lined themselves up against the previous victims and were shot.

Beginning in 1942, the Nazis sought to hide all trace of the Einsatzgruppen's crimes. They were motivated to do so for three reasons: (1) The Allies had gotten word of the shootings; (2) the bodies began to pose a health problem (in the areas around the death camps, the bodies of the murdered Jews began to contaminate the groundwater); and (3) they were concerned that future generations of

Germans would not be able to understand and appreciate the need for the shootings. Under the direction of SS officer Paul Blobel, special units, Sonderkommandos, all numbered 1,005, began to exhume and cremate the corpses. The work was mainly done by Jews, who were forced to stack the bodies between logs, or metal grates, drench them with gasoline, and then set them alight. Giant bone-crushing machines were then brought in to destroy the remains, and the ashes were scattered or reburied in the pits from which the corpses had been removed. At the completion of the gruesome task, the workers were shot to death.

Despite the vast numbers of Jews murdered by the Einsatzgruppen, the Nazis considered the process laborious, inefficient, and too dependent on valuable manpower. It also proved too emotionally difficult for the Germans to carry out. On November 29, 1941, even as the death squads were functioning at full capacity, Heydrich invited representatives of the government, the Nazi Party, and police agencies to a meeting, "followed by luncheon," to discuss "the remaining work connected with this Final Solution." The meeting took place on January 20, 1942. Known to history as the Wannsee Conference, it was named after the suburb of Berlin in which it was held. Before the 15 invitees, Heydrich began by asserting the authority of Himmler (and, by extension, himself) over what was referred to as the "Final Solution" and then summarized the various methods used against the Jews thus far, indicating that they were insufficient to deal with the "11 million Jews" from across Europe that had been slated for annihilation. Operations on a grander scale were to be employed. He told the participants, "In the course of the practical execution of the final solution, Europe will be combed through from West to East."

The registration, deportation, expropriation, and murder of so many Jews required expert planning and, above all, the cooperation and coordination of all branches of the Nazi government. Heydrich assured those at the meeting that the decision had been taken at the very highest authority and that there was no turning back. The 90-minute Wannsee Conference was the moment when every major minister or senior bureaucrat of the Nazi government became a conspirator, fully complicit in what would come to be known as the Holocaust.

The Extermination Camps

By the time of the Wannsee Conference, the Nazis had already decided to murder all the Jews of Europe, but the realization of this goal required a change in strategy. Hitler, who had taken a keen interest in the "progress" of the Einsatzgruppen, was concerned that the extermination of Europe's Jews could not be carried out expeditiously by shooting. For the mass shootings, the murderers went after the Jews by hunting them down. Now, the Jews would be brought to their executioners and murdered in extermination camps, fixed killing installations, where they were to be gassed to death. While thousands of Nazi concentration and labor camps were spread across Europe, there were only six extermination camps, all located in Poland, because of its large Jewish population and the country's central location. They were Chelmno, Belzec, Sobibor, Treblinka, Lublin-Majdanek, and Auschwitz.

Auschwitz and Majdanek were the most complex of the six because they were composite camps, housing an extermination center and slave labor operations. While thousands were murdered at Majdanek, the current state of research does not permit accurate estimates of the number killed there because of the complex uses to which the camp was put. Jews were usually diverted there when they were on their way to other extermination camps and temporarily spared in order to use them as slave labor. Majdanek was also a killing center for victims who could not be killed elsewhere due to logistical reasons, such as congestion, and finally, it also served as a storage depot for property and valuables taken from the Jewish victims at Belzec, Sobibor, and Treblinka.

The largest extermination camp was Auschwitz-Birkenau in southern Poland, 50 kilometers west of Cracow. Auschwitz was divided into three camps, with 39 subcamps on its periphery. The three main camps were Auschwitz I, Auschwitz II, and Auschwitz III. Auschwitz I functioned more like a concentration camp and was designed for the incarceration and elimination of political enemies and to ensure a steady stream of slave labor. It was also the place that the notorious medical experiments on babies, twins, and dwarfs took place. The enforced sterilization and castration of inmates likewise happened here, as did hypothermia experiments, where victims were placed into large vats of ice and freezing-cold water to see how long they could survive, the stated goal being the desire to learn how long German pilots shot down over places like the North Sea could remain alive. Auschwitz II, or Birkenau, was where the gas chambers in Auschwitz were located. Auschwitz III, known as Buna or Monowitz, housed prisoners who worked at the Buna, synthetic rubber works. By November 1944, over a million Jews and tens of thousands of Roma, Poles, and Soviet prisoners of war had been gassed to death at Auschwitz in four gas chambers by means of the cyanide-based insecticide Zyklon B.

The first gassing of Jews began at Chelmno on December 8, 1941. There, Jewish and Roma (Gypsy) prisoners were gassed by being driven around in vans, with a hose attached to the exhaust pipe, which had been redirected into the passenger compartment. Though deadly, this method proved inefficient, and the Nazis began to construct death camps with gas chambers, in order to implement Aktion Reinhard, the planned murder of all 2 million Jews in the General Government. According to the SS officer in charge of the program, Odilo Globocnik, the aims of Operation Reinhard were (1) to "resettle" (i.e., to kill) Polish Jewry, (2) to exploit the labor of some Polish Jews before killing them, (3) to confiscate the personal property of Jews (clothing, currency, jewelry, and other possessions), and (4) to identify and secure alleged hidden and immovable assets, such as factories, apartments, and land. The killing was undertaken at three specially constructed extermination camps: Belzec, Sobibor, and Treblinka. Unlike Auschwitz and Majdanek, these were pure killing centers that existed for no other purpose than exterminating as many Jews as possible, as quickly as possible. They were constructed and administered by the SS criminal police captain Christian Wirth. More than just an administrator, Wirth was also the first commandant of Belzec and personally participated in the killings and persecution of victims there and at the other camps under his charge. His level of brutality was such—he was notorious for whipping Jews in the face and killing babies—that Wirth epitomized the barbaric Nazi tormentor of Jews. Though little known today, Globocnik and Wirth are two of history's greatest mass murderers.

These facilities were manned and operated by about a hundred people who, like Wirth, had gained experience in institutional mass murder in the euthanasia or T-4 program, which operated in Germany between 1939 and 1941. Its aim was to re-engineer the biological or racial character of society by eliminating the sick and the "inferior" from the gene pool. Categorized as "life not worthy of life," about 100,000 mentally and physically disabled children and adults went to their deaths in six killing facilities in Germany and Austria. Most were gassed with carbon monoxide, a method personally recommended by Hitler. The T-4 operations were not confined to Germany. Early in the war, the SS rounded up and shot at least 17,000 Poles in various hospitals and asylums as part of the program. The link between the euthanasia program and the Holocaust lies in the shared personnel, the similar killing methods, and the ideological justification of eliminating lives deemed worthless or harmful.

Gassing operations at Belzec lasted from March 1942 until December 1942, at Sobibor from May 1942 until October 1943, and at Treblinka from July 1942 until August 1943. Most of the victims were from the Polish ghettos of Lublin, Warsaw, Lvov, Cracow, Czestochowa, Bialystok, and Radom. Deporting Jews to extermination camps was known euphemistically as "resettlement" or "evacuation," and the Nazis used collaborating locals—Ukrainians, Belorussians, Romanians—and helpers from the Baltic states to assist them. Approximately 1.7 million Jews were gassed to death in these three extermination camps. Aktion Reinhard was so comprehensively murderous that a mere 120 people survived Belzec, Sobibor, and Treblinka. (*See* Map 5.1.)

According to Globocnik's own figures, during Aktion Reinhard, the Germans confiscated huge amounts of Jewish property and valuables, worth more than 178 million reichsmarks. Most of the booty was sent to the SS Economic Administrative Main Office, while other items were divided among the Ministry of the Economy, the regular army, the SS,

and ethnic Germans in Nazi-occupied eastern Europe.

Aktion Reinhard officially concluded on November 4, 1943, with Aktion Erntefest (Operation Harvest Festival), the planned murder of the last remaining Jews in the General Government. At the Majdanek, Poniatowa, and Trawniki camps, the Nazis forced Jews to dig their own mass graves and then, on November 3 and 4, carried out simultaneous massacres at all three locations. With music blaring from loudspeakers so as to drown out the cries of the victims, as many as 10,000 Jews were shot at Trawniki and 18,000 at Majdanek on the first day. At Poniatowa, 15,000 Jews were shot to death over the two-day period. On November 30, 1943, Himmler sent Globocnik a thank-you letter: "I express to you my thanks and gratitude for the great and unique merits you have earned by the performance of Aktion Reinhard for the benefit of the entire German nation."

The summer of 1942 was the deadliest in Jewish history. Warsaw's prewar Jewish population of 337,000 made it the largest such community in Europe. It was decimated with astonishing rapidity. Between July 22 and September 21, 1942, mass deportations began from the Warsaw ghetto. In that 52-day period, about 300,000 people were taken and gassed at Treblinka. Of the 450,000 people crammed into the ghetto at its peak, only about 55,000 Jews now remained alive. They were spared because they were either working in German factories within the ghetto or were in hiding. A small remnant of this group would form the core of the resistance that would break out in April 1943. In all the ghettos, the liquidation process was similar. The Nazis would demand of the Jewish Council a specified number of Jews, generally to be delivered the next day. In Warsaw, on July 22,

1942, the quota was set at a minimum of 6,000 per day. The responsibility for this fell on the head of the Council, Adam Czerniakow (1880–1942), the Germans having threatened him that his wife would be shot on the spot if he did not comply. He negotiated for exemptions, in particular for orphans. His requests were turned down, and he refused to sign the "resettlement" order. Consumed by despair, the next day, he committed suicide. He left two suicide notes, one to his wife and the other to his fellow members of the Judenrat, in which he stated bluntly, "I am powerless. My heart trembles in sorrow and compassion. I can no longer bear all this. My act will prove to everyone what is the right thing to do."

Lodz, the second-largest ghetto, with 200,000 Jews, was located in a major industrial city where the incarcerated Jews worked in factories—there were more than 100 by

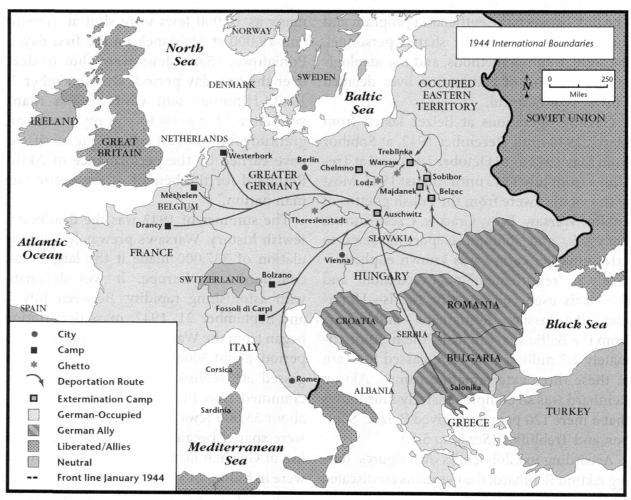

Map 5.1   Deportation routes to death camps, 1942–1944. Of the approximately 6 million Jews who perished in the Holocaust, around 2.75 million were murdered in the six extermination camps that operated in Poland. Trains from all over Europe arrived at the camps on a daily basis. Most Jews were sent to their deaths immediately upon arrival. This was the fate of about 875,000 of Auschwitz's 1 million Jewish victims. At Treblinka, the second-largest death camp, situated 80 kilometers northeast of Warsaw, between 25 and 35 SS men and police and an auxiliary guard unit of between 90 and 150 non-Germans murdered as many as 925,000 Jews between July 1942 and August 1943.

August 1942—for the German war effort. The ghetto leader was Chaim Rumkowski (1877–1944). He repeatedly assured the ghetto inhabitants (and himself) that they would be spared if they kept working and were seen as productive. This led him to make decisions few other ghetto leaders made or perhaps had to make. On September 4, 1942, he spoke to the entire ghetto:

The ghetto has been struck a hard blow. They demand what is most dear to it—children and old people. I was not privileged to have a child of my own and therefore devoted my best years to children. . . . "Brothers and sisters, give them to me! Fathers and mothers, give me your children. . . ." (Bitter weeping shakes the assembled public). . . . Yesterday, in the course of the day, I was given the order to send away more than 20,000 Jews from the ghetto, and if I did not—"we will do it ourselves." The question arose: "Should we have accepted this and carried it out ourselves, or left it to others?" But as we were guided not by the thought: "how many will be lost? but "how many can be saved?" we arrived at the conclusion that however difficult it was going to be, we must take it upon ourselves to carry out of this decree. I must carry out this difficult and bloody operation. I must cut off limbs in order to save the body! I must take away children, and if I do not, others too will be taken, God forbid . . . (terrible wailing).

I cannot give you comfort today. Nor did I come to calm you today, but to reveal all your pain and all your sorrow. I have come like a robber, to take from you what is dearest to your heart. I tried everything I knew to get the bitter sentence cancelled. When it could not be cancelled, I tried to lessen the sentence. Only yesterday I ordered the registration of nine-year-old children. I wanted to save at least one age group—children from nine to ten. But they would not yield. I succeeded in one thing—to save the children over ten. Let that be our consolation in our great sorrow.

There are many people in this ghetto who suffer from tuberculosis, whose days or perhaps weeks are numbered. . . . "Give me these sick people, and perhaps it will be possible to save the healthy in their place." I know how precious each one of the sick is in his home. . . . But at a time of such decrees one must weigh up and measure who should be saved, who can be saved and who may be saved. . . .

A broken Jew stands before you. Do not envy me. This is the most difficult of all orders I have ever had to carry out at any time. I reach out to you with my broken, trembling hands and beg: Give into my hands the victims! So that we can avoid having further victims, and a population of 100,000 Jews can be preserved! So, they promised me: If we deliver our victims by ourselves, there will be peace!!! (shouts from the crowd about other options . . . some saying "We will not let the children go alone—we will all go!!!" and such).

These are empty phrases!!! I don't have the strength to argue with you! If the authorities were to arrive, none of you would be shouting!

Rumkowski remains a controversial figure. His personal manner and his administration of the ghetto were unnecessarily cruel—he rode around the ghetto imperiously in a horse-drawn carriage and had his picture printed on ghetto currency. He was widely reviled by Jews of the ghetto. Yet Lodz remained the last ghetto to be liquidated, perhaps because Rumkowski had made Jewish workers useful to the Germans. They were not, however, indispensable. In August 1944, the Nazis began transporting Jews out of the Lodz ghetto to Auschwitz. At the same time, the Red Army was closing in on Lodz, but it stopped its advance, decamping a mere 75 miles from the city. Still remaining in the ghetto were 70,000 Jews. Had the Soviets continued their march, liberation could have been at hand, and perhaps Rumkowski's theory may have proven correct. Instead, he and his family were placed on one of the last trains to leave the city. It is said that Rumkowski was murdered in Auschwitz by some of his fellow deportees from Lodz.

In addition to the destruction of Polish and Slovakian Jewry in 1942, the Nazis began the wholesale deportation to the gas chambers of Jews from western Europe, beginning with those from Holland, France, and Belgium. Although the number of Jews in the west was far smaller than in eastern Europe, the fact that they had not been corralled into ghettos made their rounding up more complicated. The job was done, however, by collaborationist regimes and local Nazi sympathizers. A report sent to Himmler on September 24, 1942, read, "The new Dutch police squadrons are performing splendidly as regards the Jewish question and are arresting Jews in the hundreds, day and night." In 1939, Holland was home to 140,000 Jews. In two years of deportations, 1942–1944, 107,000 Dutch Jews were gassed in Auschwitz and Sobibor, approximately 75 percent of Holland's prewar Jewish population.

In France, with the biggest Jewish population in western Europe—350,000—the Vichy government instituted antisemitic race laws. The impact on the French Jewish economy was devastating, as confiscations, dismissal from jobs, and the institution of quotas severely restricted the lives of Jews. Of the Jewish population, only 150,000 were French born. The rest were stateless Jews, mostly from Poland, who had come as refugees in the interwar period. When the deportations began, they were taken first. The roundups were almost exclusively conducted by French gendarmes, and by the end of 1942, 42,500 Jews had been deported to Auschwitz from France. By the time of the last deportations in 1944, over 77,000 Jews from France had been murdered in Nazi camps. Over 14 percent of those deported were under the age of 18.

The situation in Belgium differed from that in Holland and France. Despite the fact that over 90 percent of Belgium's 70,000 Jews were foreign-born, Belgians were less compliant with Nazi demands. Large numbers of "ordinary" people helped rescue Jews, while over 25,000 Jews went into hiding, assisted by the Belgian Resistance, which, heavily influenced by Communists, was sympathetic to Jews. Consequently, German military police carried out the deportations between 1942 and 1944. Nearly 25,000 Jews from Belgium were sent to their deaths in Auschwitz.

In all, approximately 60 percent of Holocaust victims were murdered in the six death camps. The killing at these facilities was conducted according to assembly-line methods. It was, says historian Omer Bartov, "industrial murder." Not all the killers were brutal thugs. The huge death toll and the efficiency of slaughter in the camps also required the efforts of respectable, educated people. To make it efficient, the Nazis constantly refined and experimented with varying methods. An army of specialists, among them architects, builders, engineers, accountants, and economists, brought their expertise to bear on the process of killing men, women, and children. Unlike the killing centers of the T-4 program, the extermination camps were not hospitals, nor were they disguised as such; rather, they looked like military encampments with soldiers in uniform, barbed-wire fences, guard towers, barracks, and twice-daily roll calls that lasted for hours, irrespective of the weather.

Jews from the four corners of Europe were packed into sealed cattle cars without food, water, or toilets and shipped to one of the six extermination camps. Sometimes, in the case of the Jews from Greece, the trip to Auschwitz took as long as four days. Many were dead upon arrival. Those still living were ordered off the train, where they were confronted by SS doctors, guards, and snarling dogs. At Auschwitz, the notorious Nazi doctor Josef Mengele awaited the transports. Victims were then directed by him to go either to the left or to the right, that is, to instant death or to a temporary reprieve. Up to the final moment, lying and deception continued. Gas chambers were often disguised as showers, and an orchestra comprised of fellow Jews was ordered to serenade victims on their way to be gassed. At Auschwitz, up to 2,000 people were crammed into each gas chamber, dying an agonizing death in about 20 minutes as people desperately attempted to climb over one another to escape.

If a person was allowed to live, he or she was condemned to either serve as a slave laborer or become the object of ghastly medical experiments. At other times, survival was the arbitrary result of congestion at the gas chambers and crematoria. For those who survived the initial selection, fear, starvation, terror, and a deliberate process of dehumanization began. With shaven heads, striped prison clothes, and a number tattooed on the forearm, inmates were stripped of their individual identities. People were then subject to the camp social hierarchy, which mirrored Nazi racial categories. German political and "asocial" prisoners were on top, then Slavs, and then Jews on the bottom rung.

The killing process was intended to be self-financing. In 1942, Göring declared, "The war must sustain the war!" In the eastern territories, which encompassed the Baltic states, eastern Poland, western Belarus, Ukraine, and Russia, Göring's statement was put into practice with the announcement of October 24, 1942, that Jewish property, "regardless of its worth and usefulness," was to be expropriated. So deeply ingrained was the German belief in the "right" to spoliation of the Jews that directives such as that of October 24 were often superfluous or out of date. Already in August 1942, the Jews of Kovno had been robbed of all possessions and the ghetto had been made to function as a "cashless economy."

Among their many larcenous calculations, Nazi bureaucrats in the Food Ministry took account of the extra food that would be available to Germans with the extermination of the Jews. It was theft that sustained the German war machine. In the camps, those slated for gassing were stripped of their clothes and possessions, including jewelry, watches, eyeglasses, and other items. Work details of prisoners picked through the belongings. Women's hair was shaved off and sent to Germany to make carpet underlay, while clothes and shoes were sent to needy Germans on the home front. Gold teeth were extracted from corpses. These robberies were officially recorded as "general administrative revenues" in the annual budget of the Third Reich, thus hiding the reality, which was that the systematic robbery of the Jewish people (and others) supported the creation of Germany's racist welfare state. During the destruction of Hungarian Jewry in the summer of 1944, around 7,000 Hungarian Jews were being gassed and cremated each day. So frantic was the pace of murder that nearly one-third of the total number of Jews killed at Auschwitz was gassed in a two-month period that summer. To speed up and reduce the costs of the burning process, Nazi engineers designed a means whereby human fat oozing from the burning bodies was channeled back to fuel the flames of the crematoria. In this way, the theft continued even after the Jews were dead.

In the last year of the war, as Germany faced total defeat, Hitler was determined to at least be victorious in his war against the Jews. The Nazis, even at the expense of the war effort, dedicated themselves with great energy to the destruction of those Jews still alive. When the Allied armies began closing in on the Reich in the winter of 1944–1945, the Nazis began to empty the camps of prisoners, sending them by train and on foot back to Germany. They did not want prisoners to fall into the hands of the Allies and provide evidence of Nazi atrocities. The forced marches were brutal, and anyone unable to keep up the hectic pace was simply shot on the spot. Approximately 250,000 Jews and non-Jews died on these death marches. Survivors found themselves interned in concentration camps in Germany, such as Bergen-Belsen, Dachau, and Buchenwald. On January 27, 1945, the Soviet army entered Auschwitz and liberated the 7,000 remaining inmates, while between April and May 1945, the concentration camps in Germany were liberated by British and American forces.

Jewish Resistance

All over Europe, Jews refused to passively accept their fate at the hands of the Nazis and their collaborators and resisted in a variety of ways. These ranged from emigration, when possible, as was the case for about half the Jews in Germany and Austria before the war, to various forms of spiritual resistance and outright armed struggle. In western and eastern Europe, Jews tried to save their children by sending them away to be cared for by non-Jews. About 10,000 Jewish children from the Reich were sent to England on what was called *Kindertransport*. On the continent, when the war began, many parents entrusted their children to convents, where they were saved and raised as Catholics.

In Poland, Emanuel Ringelblum undertook one of the most significant acts of resistance by organizing a secret operation code-named *Oyneg Shabbes* (Sabbath Delight), the goal of which, Ringelblum said, was to gather "materials and documents relating to the martyrology of the Jews of Poland." Documenting ghetto life in as much detail as possible, Ringelblum enlisted the help of dozens of writers, journalists, teachers, rabbis, social scientists, and historians. They wrote reports, collected documents and photographs, commissioned papers and even essays from schoolchildren, and conducted interviews with ghetto dwellers from all walks of life. One worker considered his job "a sacred task," while another, David Gerber, only 19 years old, wrote in his will:

> What we could not cry out to the world, we buried in the ground. May this treasure be delivered into good hands, may it live to see better times, so that it can alert the world to what happened in the twentieth century.

Just prior to the liquidation of the Warsaw ghetto in the spring of 1943, the archive, consisting of thousands of documents, was placed in three milk cans and ten metal boxes and buried in the cellars of several Warsaw buildings. (In 1946, two of the milk cans were unearthed; in 1950, the boxes were found.)

Much of what we know about ghetto life, particularly in Warsaw, comes from Ringelblum's material. Among other things, the Oyneg Shabbes archive revealed the extent of Jewish resistance to the Nazis. We learn that the death rate from hunger would have been even higher were it not for the extensive smuggling activities of children. Cultural programs existed in all ghettos. Poets, painters, writers, and even musicians did their best to carry on their work. Although religious services were banned in most places, including Warsaw, Ringelblum reported the existence of 600 clandestine synagogues. In most ghettos—Lodz was a notable exception—the Nazis forbade Jewish education. In fact, they systematically destroyed libraries and shut down Jewish newspapers and all forms of intellectual life. Still, an illegal Jewish high school functioned in the Warsaw ghetto between 1940 and 1942. Vocational courses, as well as those in pharmacology and technical drawing, were offered. Several university-level courses were available, some in the field of medicine. One of the riskiest undertakings was organized political activity, which was completely banned. Zionist and Bundist youth nevertheless continued to print newspapers and offer spiritual and intellectual comfort to the ghetto inhabitants. When word of mass murders began to spread in the ghettos and the full understanding of the word *deportation* became clear, political youth groups changed tactics and began to concentrate on mounting armed resistance.

For several reasons, armed resistance, though also widespread, was not a viable option for most Jews. Starvation, disease, and terror in the ghettos and the rapidity of Einsatzgruppen executions destroyed the fabric of Jewish existence. Jews had no government-in-exile, as did the Poles, and thus there was no access to information or weapons. The isolation of the ghettos meant Jews had no one upon whom they could rely, nor could they gain the military intelligence necessary to mount armed operations against the Germans. The exclusion of Jews from the civic life of central and eastern European nations before the war meant that there was no formally trained Jewish military officer corps. As such, Jews had no access to arms depots. Many Jews in the ghettos also had difficulty believing the reality of the mass shootings and death camps. In addition, Jewish family life was intensely strong, so many felt great reticence about abandoning family members to go off and join an underground ghetto organization or escape and hook up with partisan groups, many of which were antisemitic. (*See box*, "Resistance in the Vilna Ghetto.")

Given the fact that the Jewish population was composed largely of starving civilians, children, and the elderly, and that so many had been killed over time, the amount of physical resistance is remarkable. Of 5.7 million Soviet prisoners of war, all battle-hardened young men, 3.3 million died at the hands of the Nazis, with barely any resistance mounted at all. Even the leader of the Polish Home Army, General Stefan Rowecki, said on February 5, 1941:

Active warfare against the Nazis can take place in our country, only when the German people will be broken by military defeats, hunger and propaganda. . . . Any attempt by us to take action while the German army is at full strength, regardless of their numbers, . . . will be drowned in a terrible bloodshed.

Jews, who had less to lose, did not wait for the collapse of the German army. Acts of resistance occurred in as many as a hundred ghettos and extermination camps, such as Sobibor, Treblinka, and Birkenau. As many as 30,000 Jews formed their own partisan units or joined up with Soviet partisans operating in forests in the east. Jews also joined with French partisans in western Europe, and with

Italian, Yugoslav, and Greek units in south and southeastern Europe. In those ghettos where chances of survival were negligible, Jewish Councils were more likely to cooperate with underground groups. In Bialystok, Judenrat leader Efraim Barash provided money and work passes for members of the underground. In Minsk, the fourth-largest ghetto, with around 100,000 Jews, about 10,000 fled to the forests with the assistance of the Judenrat. Most of them were killed fighting the Germans, and in the autumn of 1943, the Nazis destroyed the ghetto. By contrast, in those ghettos where Jewish Council members believed that their ghettos might survive, such as in Lodz, there was no cooperation with resistance groups.

The Warsaw Ghetto Uprising of April 1943 represents the most well-known case of Jewish armed resistance to the Nazis. After the end of the mass deportations from the Warsaw ghetto in September 1942, only about 55,000 Jews were left alive. No one over age 80 survived; only 45 people between the ages of 70 and 79 were alive; and of the 31,458 children under age 10 at the start of the deportations, only 498 survived. Feelings of guilt and a burning desire for revenge swept the ghetto.

About 1,000 young people, members of Zionist or Bundist youth movements, formed the Jewish Fighting Organization under the command of Mordechai Anielewicz (1919–1943). As the Germans entered the ghetto to liquidate it on the eve of Passover, April 19, 1943, Jewish resistance fighters were lying in wait. Armed with pistols and Molotov cocktails, they fought pitched battles with the Germans, who were eventually forced to bring in reinforcements and heavy artillery. For three weeks, street battles between Nazi soldiers and Jewish ghetto fighters raged until Anielewicz was killed, Jewish hideouts were discovered, and many arrests were made. On May 16, 1943, SS general Jürgen Stroop reported that Warsaw was completely liquidated. As a mark of his victory, he blew up Warsaw's Great Synagogue.

In the end, whether or not a Jewish Council cooperated with a resistance movement made no difference. Even the fact of resistance made no difference to the final outcome. The rationale behind armed resistance among Jews was different than it was for non-Jews. For the latter, all resistance activity was part of the larger war effort to secure victory against the Nazis. For the Jews, who had lost everything, taking up arms against the Nazis was not part of an overall strategy for military victory; it was about revenge and self-respect. In his last letter, Mordechai Anielewicz wrote, "[T]he fact that we are remembered beyond ghetto walls encourages us in our struggle. . . . Jewish armed resistance and revenge are facts. I have been witness to the magnificent, heroic fighting of Jewish men in battle."

So different was the Jewish situation that even survival was considered with ambiguity, for it brought with it the stark realization of all that had been lost. What did survival even mean in such circumstances? In the Vilna ghetto, the great Yiddish poet and partisan fighter Avrom Sutzkever (b. 1913) darkly pondered what it meant for a Jew to emerge from Hitler's inferno. On February 14, 1943, amid the ruins and remnants, Sutzkever wrote the poem "How?"

How will you fill your goblet on the day of liberation?
And with what?
Are you prepared, in your joy, to feel the dark shrieking of your past where shards of days lie congealed in a bottomless pit?

You will search for a key to fit your old jammed locks.

You will bite into the street like bread, thinking: It used to be better.

And time will quietly gnaw at you like a cricket caught in a fist.

Then your memory will resemble an ancient buried town. And your gaze will burrow down like a mole, like a mole . . .

Awareness of Genocide and Rescue Attempts

What did contemporaries know about the mass murder of the Jews, when did they know it, and in the case of the Allies, what did they do with the information they had? In the pre-war phase, Nazi policy toward Jews was public knowledge. This was, after all, happening to neighbors. Once the war and the subsequent slaughter of European Jewry began, most preferred not to know the details, and the German use of euphemisms helped camouflage reality. But news of the killings was difficult to keep secret. German soldiers and civilians in Poland took pictures of suffering and humiliated Jews, visited the ghettos, and in Warsaw, even filmed what they saw. Pictures and artifacts brought back were shared, providing graphic evidence of what was happening. At official levels, the Nazis published pictures of filthy, lice-ridden ghetto inhabitants to justify German claims that the Jews were subhuman. Photographers accompanied the Einsatzgruppen and recorded for posterity pictures of the mass graves, including dramatic pictures of uniformed killers in the act of shooting Jews. Still, with the nation at war, Germans focused on their own losses, ignoring the fate of a people cast as their mortal enemy.

In the West, definitive news of Hitler's war against the Jews was made known in London and Washington, thanks to a letter dated August 8, 1942, from Gerhart Riegner, a representative of the World Jewish Congress in Geneva. He spoke about "a plan to exterminate all Jews from Germany and German-controlled areas in Europe." In the autumn of 1942, a Polish underground courier, Jan Karski, snuck into the Warsaw ghetto to learn firsthand what was happening. On December 1, 1942, he informed the Polish government-in-exile in London of the extermination of Polish Jewry. Karski's report was then relayed to the Allies. Throughout 1942, the Allies repeatedly threatened the Nazi leadership with severe retribution for its crimes. The leaders of Germany's allies, including Mussolini in Italy, Admiral Horthy of Hungary, Marshal Antonescu of Romania, and President Tiso of Slovakia, were all aware that Jews were being deported to their deaths, as did the collaborationist regime of Vichy France under Marshal Petain and Pierre Laval. On December 17, 1942, a declaration was made in the British Parliament. The Germans "are now carrying into effect Hitler's oft-repeated intention to exterminate the Jewish people in Europe." In April 1944, an eyewitness report came from Auschwitz itself, with the stunning escape of two Jewish inmates, Rudolf Vrba and Alfred Wetzler. Making it to Slovakia, they then dictated to Jewish officials a highly detailed, 32-page account of Auschwitz-Birkenau and the preparations then being made for the arrival and impending destruction of Hungarian Jewry. Little came of this revelation. Fearing that Hungary might make a separate peace with the Allies, Germany occupied Hungary in March 1944. The SS were now in charge of the country, and Adolf Eichmann was dispatched to Budapest to organize the deportation of the Jews. He worked with great haste. Between May 15 and July 7, 1944, 437,000 Hungarian Jews were murdered in Auschwitz. Nearly all were gassed

RESISTANCE IN THE VILNA GHETTO

Beginning on July 4, 1941, the Nazis began shooting Vilna's Jews in massive pits at the nearby forest of Ponary. Employing a rationale used by Chaim Rumkowski in Lodz, the head of the Vilna Judenrat, Jacob Gens, had turned over Jews to the Nazis in the hope that he would be able to save a remnant. Gens believed he, too, could save Jews through a "life-for-work" plan. Addressing the ghetto, he defended his action:

> With hundreds I save thousands; with the thousand that I deliver, I save ten thousand. . . . That there be some remnant, I myself had to lead Jews to their death. And in order for some people to come out of this with a clean conscience I had to put my hands into filth, and trade without conscience.

For those convinced that the goal of the Nazis was to exterminate all Jews, strategies such as Gens's were pointless. On January 1, 1942, with over 30,000 of Vilna's 57,000 Jews already shot, the Hebrew poet and ghetto fighter Abba Kovner (1918–1987) read a declaration to a gathering of youth movement members encouraging resistance:

> Since our last meeting . . . our nearest and dearest have been torn from us and led to death with masses of other Jews. . . . The truth says that we must not believe that those who have been taken from us are still alive, that they have been merely deported. Everything that has befallen us to this point means . . . death.

Yet even this is not the whole truth. . . . The destruction of thousands is only a harbinger of the annihilation of millions. Their death is our total ruin. It is difficult for me to explain why Vilna is bleeding while Bialystok is peaceful and calm . . . [b]ut one thing is clear to me: Vilna is not just Vilna. [The shootings at] Ponary are not just an episode. The yellow patch is not the invention of the local SS commander. This is a total system. We are facing a well-planned system that is hidden from us at the moment.

Is there any escape from it? No. If we are dealing with a consistent system, fleeing from one place to another is nothing but an illusion. . . . Is there a chance that we might be rescued? Cruel as the answer may be, we must reply: no, there is no rescue! . . . Maybe for dozens or hundreds; but for the . . . millions of Jews under the yoke of German occupation there is no rescue.

Is there a way out? Yes. There is a way out: rebellion and resistance.

Within weeks of this speech, Zionist youth leaders and Communists within the ghetto formed the United Partisans Organization (UPO), known in Yiddish as the *Fareynikte Partizaner-Organizatsye.* Led by the Communists Itsik Wittenberg and Abba Kovner, the UPO sought to unite the various resistance groups in the ghetto, carry out acts of sabotage, and encourage widespread resistance. They succeeded in blowing up a German military train, smuggling arms into the ghetto, setting up an illegal printing press outside of

upon arrival. (*See box,* "The Model Concentration Camp: Theresienstadt.")

Though Jews sought assistance from the West as soon as the war began, Jewish leaders had difficulty coming to terms with the Nazi program of genocide. Many found it hard to

believe, and thus, their incomplete knowledge and skepticism hindered their actions. Jews were, the world over, a politically impotent minority. In the United States, they had very little access to power, and given the extent of antisemitism, Jewish leaders were loath to the ghetto, and establishing links with nearby Soviet partisans. The UPO also sent couriers to the Warsaw and Bialystok ghettos to warn Jews about the mass killings of Jews in the occupied Soviet Union. In the numerous songs they sang, Vilna partisans gave expression to their deepest hopes. In the Rudnicki forest, the UPO fighters gathered each morning for reveille and sang their official song in Yiddish, a march titled "Never Say" (*Zog Nit Keyn Mol*):

> Never say that you are walking your final path;
>
> Leaden skies conceal blue days!
>
> The hour we have longed for is so near,
>
> Our step will beat out like a drum. We are here!
>
> From the green land of palms to the
>
> Land of white snow;
>
> We arrive with our pain, with our hurt.
>
> And wherever a spurt of our blood has fallen
>
> Our might and courage will sprout.
>
> The morning sun will gild our today
>
> And yesterday will vanish with the enemy,
>
> But if the sun and the dawn are late in coming,
>
> May this song go from generation to generation like a password.
>
> This song is written with blood and not

> With pencil-lead
>
> It's no song of a free-flying bird,
>
> A people among collapsing walls
>
> Sang this song with pistols in their hands.
>
> Never say that you are walking your final path;
>
> Leaden skies conceal blue days!
>
> The hour we have longed for is so near,
>
> Our step will beat out like a drum. We are here!

When the Nazi secret police, the Gestapo, infiltrated the local Communist underground in July 1943, it learned that Wittenberg was the leader of the UPO. It demanded that the Jewish Council turn him over. After an agonizing debate within the resistance organization, Wittenberg surrendered. He committed suicide with cyanide given him by Jacob Gens.

Gens's attitude to resistance was mixed. Initially, he maintained close connections with the UPO but later concluded that the organization's activities placed the whole ghetto at risk, so he sought to extract concessions from the Germans by turning over Jews for forced labor in Estonia. The ghetto inhabitants were also opposed to the resistance organization, believing that their best hope for survival lay with deportation to Estonian labor camps. Gens was shot and killed by the Gestapo on September 14, 1943, during the final liquidation of the ghetto.

plead the Jewish cause when the national war effort was at stake. In the 1940s, few American parents would have wanted their sons to die saving the lives of European Jews. In Palestine, too, despite family ties to eastern Europe, even the Yishuv did not completely comprehend the events. Beyond this, the Yishuv was weak and had nothing to offer European Jewry in terms of rescue. Non-governmental agencies such as the Red Cross sought to maintain neutrality and turned a blind eye to the extermination process, even after delegations visited

THE MODEL CONCENTRATION CAMP: THERESIENSTADT

On November 24, 1941, the Germans established a "model ghetto"—in reality, a concentration camp—in the Czechoslovakian town of Terezin. It was known by its German name, Theresienstadt, until its liberation on May 8, 1945. Most of the acculturated Jews imprisoned there were German, Czech, Dutch, and Danish. Among them were elderly and prominent Jews and Jewish veterans of World War I.

The Nazis used Theresienstadt for propaganda purposes. They called it a "spa town" and claimed that elderly German Jews had been brought there so that they could "retire" in safety. By 1942, conditions in the ghetto were so bad that thousands perished from starvation and disease. The Nazis built a crematorium there to dispose of 200 bodies a day. Still, the Nazis persisted with their deception and, in June 1944, permitted the International Red Cross, which wanted to investigate rumors of extermination camps, to visit and see conditions for themselves. In preparation, the ghetto was "beautified." Large numbers of Jews were shipped to Auschwitz to avoid the appearance of overcrowding. Gardens were planted, buildings were renovated, and cultural events were staged for the visitors. Theresienstadt had a Judenrat, and the Red Cross delegation was even introduced to the camp's Jewish "mayor," Paul Eppstein. The investigators left satisfied that Jews were being well treated. A propaganda film was made about the "excellent" conditions for Jews in Theresienstadt,

the Nazis having coerced the Jewish prisoner and film director Kurt Gerron to make it. After finishing the film, most of the cast, along with Gerron, who years before had starred alongside Marlene Dietrich in *The Blue Angel*, was deported to Auschwitz, where they were murdered.

Due to the high number of prominent artists interned at Theresienstadt, the Nazis, as part of their elaborate hoax, permitted cultural activities. Painters, writers, academics, musicians, and actors taught classes and put on exhibitions, readings, lectures, concerts, and theater performances. Jewish themes were emphasized. The ghetto even maintained a lending library of 60,000 volumes. The Viennese artist Friedl Dicker-Brandeis (1898–1944) gave art classes and lectures to children, offering them a sophisticated form of art therapy that was designed to allow them to cope with the stress of their situation. Just before she was deported to Auschwitz in September 1944, she filled two suitcases with 4,500 drawings and left them hidden in the camp. Approximately 140,000 Jews were sent to Theresienstadt. About 33,000 died there. Approximately 90,000 were deported from there to Auschwitz, Treblinka, other extermination camps, as well as ghettos farther east and murdered in those places.

Figure 5.5 depicts Jewish money from Theresienstadt. Known as Judengeld, or Jews' money, this 50-kroner banknote was used in the Theresienstadt ghetto (January 1943).

the Theresienstadt ghetto and Auschwitz. Despite being in possession of a steady stream of information concerning the destruction of European Jewry, Pope Pius XII, a man who was deeply hostile to Jews—believing, among other things, that they were behind a Bolshevik plot to destroy Christianity—steadfastly refused to issue any kind of unambiguous condemnation about the murder of European Jewry. Even in quarters where more sympathy could have been expected, such as in the French Resistance, none was forthcoming. In

Figure 5.5 Jewish money from Theresienstadt.
Source: Sergey Goryachev/Shutterstock.

June 1942, a statement in *Cahiers*, the official organ of the French underground, observed, "Antisemitism in its moderate form was quasi-universal, even in the most liberal societies. This indicates that its foundation is not imaginary."

Across Europe, civilian populations were generally indifferent, if not enthusiastic, about the removal of Jews from their respective societies. That said, thousands of Jews were saved by the brave actions of individuals. Raoul Wallenberg, a Swedish diplomat in

ANNE FRANK

Anne Frank was born to Otto and Edith Frank on June 12, 1929, in Frankfurt, Germany. After the Nazis seized power in 1933, the Franks fled to Amsterdam. Anne, who had remained behind in the care of her grandparents, joined the family in Holland in February 1934.

The Germans occupied Amsterdam in May 1940, and the SS installed a civil administration, appointing Arthur Seyss-Inquart as Reich commissar. In January 1941, the German occupation authorities demanded that all Jews be registered. This amounted to a total of 159,806 persons, including 19,561 persons born of mixed marriages. Among the total number of registered Jews were approximately 25,000 Jewish refugees from the German Reich. The Frank family was among this group.

The arrest and deportation of Jews led to a protest strike by Dutch workers in February 1941. This show of support notwithstanding, there was widespread collaboration in Holland with the Nazis. In July 1942, Dutch sympathizers helped round up Jews and concentrate them in Amsterdam while they sent foreign and stateless Jews to the Westerbork transit camp. From there, Jews were deported to Auschwitz and Sobibor.

During the first week in July of 1942, Edith and Otto Frank and their two daughters, Margot and Anne, went into hiding along with four other German Jews, Hermann and Auguste van Pels and their son, Peter, and Fritz Pfeffer. For two years, the eight lived in a secret annex at 263 Prinsengracht Street. They were hidden and given food and clothing by Miep Gies, an employee of Otto Frank, and her social worker husband, Jan. They were assisted by four other Dutch nationals. In her diary, Anne recorded, "Miep is just like a pack mule, she fetches and carries so much. Almost every day she manages to get hold of some vegetables for us [and] brings everything in shopping bags on her bicycle." Thanks to a tip from an anonymous Dutchman, the Gestapo uncovered the hiding place on August 4, 1944, and the Franks were arrested and sent to Westerbork transit camp on August 8.

After the roundup, Miep and another employee of Otto Frank, Bep Voskuijl, went up to the secret annex to see if they could salvage any personal effects. Strewn across the floor were Anne's notebooks and papers. They gathered everything together, and Miep placed Anne's writings in a desk drawer, intending to give them to Anne upon her return. One month after the raid, the Franks and the other Jews who had been hiding with them were deported to Auschwitz.

Budapest, provided 30,000 Jews with Swedish passports, set up "safe houses" for them, and distributed food and medical supplies. In Lithuania, the temporary Japanese consul named Chiune Sugihara saved thousands of Jews. In the summer of 1940, Polish Jewish refugees in Kovno learned that two Dutch colonial islands, Curacao and Dutch Guiana (Suriname), did not require formal entrance visas.

The honorary Dutch consul in Kovno, Jan Zwartendijk, told the refugees that he could stamp their passports with entrance permits to the islands. But to get to them, the refugees would have to pass through the Soviet Union. The Soviet consul was prepared to let them pass on one condition: that in addition to the Dutch entrance permit, they would also have to show a transit visa from the Japanese,

Because they were young and eligible for forced labor, Anne and her sister, Margot, were transferred to the concentration camp Bergen-Belsen in late October 1944. Both of them died of typhus in March 1945, only weeks before the British liberated the camp on April 15, 1945. The only family member to survive the war was Otto Frank. Returning to Amsterdam after the war, Otto went to Miep and Jan's house, where he lived for the next seven years.

Anne wished to become a writer, and in addition to her diary, for which she is most famous, she wrote short stories, fairy tales, essays, and the beginnings of a novel. Anne was between 13 and 15 years of age during her two years in hiding; she was enormously productive during that time, filling five notebooks and writing more than 300 loose, handwritten pages. Her diary, which was published posthumously in 1947 and has been translated into about 70 languages, covers an astonishing array of subjects, from the personal to the political. She was an astute observer, capable of mixing hard-bitten realism with an optimism that bespeaks her profound humanity. Her diary entry for June 20, 1942, clearly gives a sense of the noose tightening around Jewish life, and yet her resilience shines through:

Anti-Jewish decrees followed each other in quick succession. Jews must wear a yellow star, Jews must hand in their bicycles, Jews are banned from trams and are forbidden to drive, Jews are only allowed to do their shopping between three and five o'clock. . . . Jews must be indoors by eight o'clock. . . . Jews are forbidden to visit theaters. . . . Jews may not visit Christians. Jews must go to Jewish schools, and many more restrictions of a similar kind. So we could not do this and were forbidden to do that. But life went on in spite of it all.

On April 17, 1944, Anne wrote what turned out to be her final entry:

I see the world gradually being turned into a wilderness, I hear the ever approaching thunder, which will destroy us too, I can feel the sufferings of millions and yet, if I look up into the heavens, I think that it will all come right, that this cruelty too will end, and that peace and tranquility will return again. In the meantime, I must uphold my ideals, for perhaps the time will come when I shall be able to carry them out.

Anne Frank was one of the more than 1 million Jewish children murdered by the Nazis and their collaborators.

because getting to the Dutch islands required that they transit through Japan. Sugihara requested the transit visas, but the foreign ministry in Tokyo flatly refused. In defiance, from July 31 to August 28, 1940, Sugihara and his wife worked feverishly to write out over 6,000 visas by hand. In France, Pastor Andre Trocme and Daniel Trocme, in the Huguenot village of Le Chambon-sur-Lignon, France,

hid and saved 5,000 Jews. In Holland, a combination of widespread complicity with the Nazis and flat, open terrain, which meant there were neither mountain nor forest hideouts, led to a huge death toll. Of 140,000 Jews in the Netherlands in 1939, 107,000 were exterminated. But at least 25,000 of the survivors owe their lives to their Dutch compatriots who hid them (*see box*, "Anne Frank").

Throughout Poland, too, thousands of individuals hid Jews at great personal risk. There was no promise of reward and only the guarantee of death if caught. A Polish aid organization, Zegota (The Council for Aid to Jews), was set up in 1942 by left-wing political parties that received funds from the Polish government-in-exile. The most dramatic mass rescue of Jews during the Holocaust occurred in occupied Denmark. On the night of October 1, 1943, the Germans began rounding up Jews but found very few because the Danish resistance, the police, the churches, the Danish royal family, and various social organizations had found hiding places for the country's 7,500 Jews. From their hideouts, Jews were shuttled to the coast, where they boarded fishing boats that ferried them to neutral Sweden. Over the course of a month, about 7,200 Jews and 700 of their non-Jewish relatives made it to safety in Sweden. Across Europe, tens of thousands of individuals blessed with courage and conscience saved Jewish neighbors and strangers. Their heroic actions, however, were not enough to stop the genocide.

A particularly contentious issue among historians has been the assessment of Allied behavior—in particular, whether Britain and the United States should have bombed the death camps to stop or at least impede the slaughter. In June 1944, the US War Department said it could not be done, even though it never investigated the possibility of bombing the camps. A variety of excuses were offered. Such an undertaking, according to Assistant Secretary of War John J. McCloy,

> could only be executed by the diversion of considerable air support essential to the success of [the American] forces now engaged in decisive operations and would

in any case be of such doubtful efficacy that it would not amount to a practical project.

Even though requests to bomb the train lines leading to Auschwitz-Birkenau were dismissed as logistically unfeasible, the Americans were bombing factories at and around the extermination camp between August 20 and September 13, 1944. Ironically, it was also claimed that innocent people in the camps would have been killed. It is true that millions of Jews had already been murdered by this time, so bombing the camps would not have prevented the Holocaust. The real value in mounting a sustained campaign to destroy the death factories would have been a symbolic act, but an important one.

On January 13, 1943, outraged by their government's refusal to act decisively to rescue European Jewry, members of the US Treasury Department released a damning document titled "Report to the Secretary on the Acquiescence of This Government in the Murder of the Jews." On January 17, 1944, the report was submitted to President Roosevelt, who responded by establishing the War Refugee Board. It was mandated to negotiate with foreign governments, even enemy ones, to rescue Jews. The whole government was put at the War Refugee Board's disposal, but its efforts were stymied at nearly every turn. The board received little government funding, and President Roosevelt took hardly any personal interest in it. And yet the War Refugee Board was able to save 200,000 Jews, a significant number. A concerted effort, if undertaken earlier, and with more serious support, could have saved even more Jews. In the end, all that stopped the slaughter was Allied victory over Nazi Germany, in particular, the Red Army's conquests of the killing fields of eastern Europe. For 6,000,000 Jews, however, victory came too late.

For Further Reading

On the Holocaust, see Lucy Dawidowicz, *The War against the Jews, 1933–1945* (New York: Holt, Rinehart and Winston,1975); Lucjan Dobroszycki, ed., *The Chronicle of the Łódź Ghetto, 1941–1944* (New Haven, CT: Yale University Press,1984); Christopher R. Browning, *Fateful Months: Essays on the Emergence of the Final Solution, 1941–42* (New York: Holmes & Meier, 1985); Roman Mogilanski, *The Ghetto Anthology: A Comprehensive Chronicle of the Extermination of Jewry in Nazi Death Camps and Ghettos in Poland* (Los Angeles: American Congress of Jews from Poland and Survivors of Concentration Camps, 1985); Alan Adelson and Robert Lapides, eds., *Lodz Ghetto: Inside a Community under Siege* (New York: Viking, 1989); Yitzhak Arad et al., eds., *The Einsatzgruppen Reports: Selections from the Dispatches of the Nazi Death Squads' Campaign against the Jews, July 1941–January 1943* (New York: Holocaust Library, 1989); Ernst Klee et al., eds., *"The Good Old Days": The Holocaust as Seen by Its Perpetrators and Bystanders* (New York: Free Press, 1991); Christopher R. Browning, *Ordinary Men: Reserve Police Battalion 101 and the Final Solution in Poland* (New York: Harper Collins, 1992); Primo Levi, *Survival in Auschwitz* (New York: Touchstone Books, 1996); Isaiah Trunk, *Judenrat: The Jewish Councils in Eastern Europe under Nazi Occupation* (Lincoln: University of Nebraska Press, 1996); Saul Friedländer, *Nazi Germany and the Jews: The Years of Persecution, 1933–1939* (New York: Harper Collins, 1997); Saul Friedländer, *Nazi Germany and the Jews: The Years of Extermination, 1939–1945* (New York: Harper Collins, 2007); Marion A. Kaplan, *Between Dignity and Despair: Jewish Life in Nazi Germany* (New York: Oxford University Press, 1998); Michael Berenbaum and Abraham J. Peck, *The Holocaust and History* (Bloomington: Indiana University Press, 1998); Alan Adelson, *The Diary of Dawid Sierakowiak: Five Notebooks from the Lodz Ghetto* (Oxford, England: Oxford University Press, 1998); Michael Berenbaum and Yisrael Gutman, eds., *Anatomy of the Auschwitz Death Camp* (Bloomington: Indiana University Press, 1998); Nikolaus Wachsmann, *KL: A History of the Nazi Concentration Camps* (New York: Farrar, Straus and Giroux, 2015); Abraham I. Katsh, *Scroll of Agony: The Warsaw Diary of Chaim A. Kaplan* (Bloomington: Indiana University Press, 1999); Yitzhak Arad, Israel Gutman, and Abraham Margaliot, eds., *Documents on the Holocaust: Selected Sources on the Destruction of the Jews in Germany and Austria, Poland, and the Soviet Union* (Lincoln: University of Nebraska Press, 1999); Susan Zuccotti, *Under His Very Windows: The Vatican and the Holocaust in Italy* (New Haven, CT: Yale University Press, 2000); Gulie Ne'eman Arad, *America, Its Jews, and the Rise of Nazism* (Bloomington: Indiana University Press, 2000); Deborah Dwork and Robert Jan van Pelt, *Holocaust: A History* (New York: W. W. Norton, 2002); Alan E. Steinweis, *Kristallnacht 1938* (Cambridge, MA: Belknap Press of Harvard University Press, 2009); and Donald L. Niewyck, ed., *The Holocaust: Problems and Perspectives of Interpretation* (Boston, MA: Wadsworth Cengage Learning, 2011).

CHAPTER 6

INTO THE PRESENT

MOST HOLOCAUST SURVIVORS eventually made their way to countries far from Europe. In Israel, the United States, Australia, Canada, and Latin America, Jewish refugees set about the quietly heroic task of rebuilding their shattered lives. Having escaped their would-be killers, the response of survivors to the nightmare of the Holocaust was to get married, raise a family, and provide for their children. That this is what the overwhelming majority of Jews were able to achieve, irrespective of where they ended up, is one of the great and unsung success stories in Jewish history.

The dissolution of Jewish life in Arab lands also quickened in the postwar world. While some Jewish communities in North Africa were directly touched by the Holocaust, with the Nazis incarcerating thousands of Jews in concentration camps they established there, the majority of Middle Eastern Jewish communities effectively came to an end by 1950 not because of the Nazis but due to local politics. Arab nationalism, antisemitism, and anti-Zionism had been on the rise prior to World War II. In Iraq, occupational and educational discrimination, as well as physical attacks, including murder, became the lot of Iraqi Jews after the country achieved independence in 1932. Such developments culminated

in the Farhud, a pogrom that occurred on June 1 and 2, 1941. Demobilized Iraqi soldiers joined by tribesmen and ordinary Baghdadis went on a rampage and looting spree against the capital's Jews. When it was over, 180 Jews had been killed, and hundreds more had been wounded. Significant numbers of Muslims who came to the aid of their Jewish neighbors were also killed by the mob. With the emergence of the State of Israel in 1948, levels of suspicion and outright persecution increased to such an extent that emigration was the only option. Most Jews chose to go to Israel. The continued existence of Jewish communities elsewhere in Muslim lands—the exceptions were Morocco and Iran (until the Islamic Revolution of 1979)—also became untenable.

Even before the establishment of the State of Israel, Jews all over the Arab world were considered potential traitors and branded as Zionist agents. Life for them had become increasingly difficult and violent. In November 1945, a pogrom in Libya resulted in the murder of 140 Jews and the destruction of five synagogues. In June 1948, amid protests against the new Jewish state, rioters murdered 12 Jews and destroyed 280 Jewish homes. Although emigration was illegal, more than 3,000 Jews left for Israel. When the British legalized emigration in 1949, and in the years

DOI: 10.4324/9781003611608-7

immediately preceding Libyan independence in 1951, further riots prompted the departure of some 30,000 Jews. Over time, and as mandated by Libyan law, Jewish assets were seized and transferred to state ownership. As late as July 1970, the innocuously worded "Law Relative to the Resolution of Certain Assets to the State" held that a state-appointed general custodian would administer the liquid funds of the property of Jews as well as the companies and the company shares belonging to Jews.

The situation was similar in Syria for its 30,000 Jews. The 1947 pogrom in Aleppo caused 7,000 of the town's 10,000 Jews to flee. In 1949, banks were instructed to freeze the accounts of Jews, and all their assets were expropriated. Nearly all Jewish civil servants were dismissed from their jobs, freedom of movement within Syria for Jews was severely curtailed, and frontier posts were established to control the movement of Jews out of the country. In all, approximately 800,000 Jews from Arab lands were displaced and dispossessed after the establishment of the State of Israel.

By the middle of the twentieth century, the ancient Jewish civilizations, in both Christian Europe and the Muslim Middle East, had come to an end through a mixture of voluntary immigration, forced expulsions, and mass murder. As a result, the geographical centers of Jewish settlement shifted. After the war, the Soviet Union, Israel, and the United States emerged as the three countries with the largest Jewish communities in the world. By the end of the twentieth century, the demise of the Soviet Union resulted in a massive exodus of Jews. A century after the first great wave of migration out of eastern Europe, Jewish dispersion from Russia after 1990 again significantly changed the face of Jewish communities across the world.

The emergence of Israel a mere three years after the Holocaust was greeted with unrestrained joy by world Jewry. Even avowedly secular Jews saw Israel as a miracle. Emotionally, the Jewish people had experienced a wild mood swing in a very short period of time, one that saw them go from deep despair to euphoric hope. It was a reversal of national fate that knew no parallels in Jewish history. For individual survivors, however, the postwar experience proved far more complex. Refugees who went to Western Europe or the Americas were mostly welcomed by local communities. Often, they married local Jews but also maintained wide networks of friends among Holocaust survivors. They formed official Holocaust survivor organizations, as well as more informal groups, that provided material aid, comfort, and the opportunity to share stories. The members of one such group used to meet regularly in Melbourne, Australia. They called themselves the "Buchenwald Boys," because when the Buchenwald concentration camp was liberated in April 1945, 60 out of the more than 900 young prisoners made their way to Australia. Mostly orphans, they landed in Melbourne, and with financial and emotional support from the local community, they went about rebuilding their shattered lives. According to Jack Unikowski, one of the survivors, "[a]fter all [they] had been through, [they] came to realize that [they] had arrived in a paradise, too good a life for many Europeans to imagine." Each year, for decades, on the anniversary of their liberation, the Buchenwald Boys celebrated their survival by hosting the Buchenwald Ball. Few, if any, members are still alive. While today, there are about 245,000 Jewish survivors of the Holocaust to be found in about 90 countries—49 percent live in Israel, while 18 percent reside in North America—their overall numbers are rapidly dwindling.

In addition to the impact of the Shoah, the Cold War, decolonization and wars in the Middle East, the collapse of Communism, and the impact of global capitalism are just some of the phenomena that, in reshaping the world, have transformed the Jewish people yet again. Since 1945, the rise of new Jewish centers, the growth of ultra-Orthodoxy, declining birth rates among secular Jews, ongoing assimilation in many quarters, and conversely, Jewish revival in others all characterize a people still undergoing significant social and cultural changes.

IN THE AFTERMATH OF THE HOLOCAUST

Between 1945 and 1952, approximately 250,000 Jews, 80 percent of whom were from Poland, ended up in displaced persons (DP) camps administered by the Allies and the United Nations in Germany, Austria, and Italy. The last DP camp closed in 1957. Much to their dismay and horror, the DPs in Germany found themselves living "among the murderers." Their ultimate goal was to leave Europe, but as was the case before the war, few countries were enthusiastic about opening their doors to refugees. Britain was especially determined that Jews should not reach Palestine, and so it turned many away from there. Nevertheless, from 1945 to 1948, the Brihah (Flight) organization managed to smuggle more than 100,000 Jews into Palestine (see the box "Exodus 1947"). However, most DPs were stuck in camps.

In the DP camps, Jews immediately tried to re-establish a semblance of normality. In the first place, this meant having children. The Nazis left very few Jewish children alive, and so the most fundamental task of the survivors was a procreative one. The birth rate was tremendously high among the DPs. In 1945, the birth rate among non-Jews in Bavaria (the state where most DP camps were located) was 5 births per 1,000 persons. Among Jews in 1946, it was 14.1. Very soon, kindergartens and schools were opened, with teachers coming from Palestine and the United States. Religious services were held, and yeshivot were founded. In 1946, a new edition of the Talmud was published in Munich, the frontispiece showing the camps surrounded with barbed wire and the Jews walking beneath the rays of the sun into the Land of Israel. Denied the practice of religion for so long, Jews in the DP camps created lively religious centers. The DP camps in the American zone of occupation in 1946 were home to 4 yeshivot, 18 rabbis, 16 kosher slaughterers, and significantly, 4 very busy *mohelim* (circumcisers).

The DP camps were also sites of vibrant, secular culture. Starved for information throughout the war, the DPs were voracious consumers of news and literature. Over 170 eclectic publications catered to a wide array of interests and political positions. Theater and musical troupes toured the camps, while 169 sports clubs from the camps played against each other. In addition to soccer, boxing—perhaps not surprisingly—proved especially popular. The DP camps were, of course, only temporary refuges. The majority of survivors wished to leave Europe and start new lives far away from the killing fields.

The Rise of the State of Israel

Despite its bitterness over the 1939 white paper issued by the British government, the leadership of the Yishuv realized that it had no choice but to fight alongside Britain against Germany. Further impetus came from the fact that the grand mufti, an unabashed antisemite, lived in Berlin during the war, had an audience with

Hitler on November 30, 1941, was on close personal terms with Heinrich Himmler, and frequently broadcast Arabic-language messages of support for the Nazi campaign against European Jewry over the radio on Nazi Germany's Oriental Service.

Moreover, as the Germans advanced into Egypt under the command of General Erwin Rommel, the Yishuv had reason to fear that the Holocaust would come to them. Since the summer of 1942, an SS Einsatzgruppen unit had been on standby in Athens, ready to move on Palestine in advance of Rommel's anticipated victory and then begin exterminating the Jews. In May 1942, 600 Zionists gathered in New York's Biltmore Hotel and issued what became known as the Biltmore Program. The document addressed the refugee problem-in-the-making that would follow the war's end. The delegates officially rejected the white paper on behalf of the Zionist movement, as well as plans for partition, demanding immediate Jewish sovereignty in all of Palestine and for it to be considered a "Jewish commonwealth."

In the 1940s, the combined impact of the Holocaust and Britain's obstructionism, which continued to prevent Jewish refugees from getting to Palestine, radicalized certain elements in the Yishuv. The paramilitary organization the Irgun, 2,000 strong and led by Menachem Begin (1913–1992), a future prime minister of Israel, called for a revolt against the British in Palestine. It launched military operations against British installations, as did an even more extreme terror group, the Stern Gang, named after its leader, Avraham Stern (1907–1942). It repeatedly attacked the British, funding itself through criminal activity, including robbing the Histadrut Workers' Bank. After Stern was killed by the British in 1942, some of his followers formed Lehi, an acronym for *Lohamei Herut Yisrael,* or Warriors for the Freedom of Israel. Its leader was Yitzhak Shamir (1915–2012), a future prime minister of Israel. Committed to extremist acts, Lehi was responsible for the 1944 assassination of Britain's minister of state for the Middle East, Lord Moyne, and the 1948 assassination of the United Nations representative in the Middle East, Count Folke Bernadotte. In 1945, the Haganah, the Irgun, and Lehi joined forces to attack the British, who had 100,000 soldiers in Palestine. The British cracked down with a violent operation known as "Black Sabbath." They imposed a curfew on Tel Aviv and Jerusalem, arrested 3,000 Jews, tortured many, and deported some to Africa. One month later, the Jewish response was fierce. In July 1946, the Irgun blew up the King David Hotel in Jerusalem, which served as British military and administrative headquarters. Ninety-one people were killed, most of them British personnel.

By 1947, Britain was no longer an imperial power. "Rule or quit," cried one English newspaper headline. Severely weakened, Britain no longer had the capacity or the will to rule. It was time to leave Palestine. In February, recognizing that it had lost control of the situation, Britain turned the jurisdiction of Palestine over to the United Nations. Pressure on the British to depart also came from the Arab side. After the war, the Arab Higher Committee was reconstituted, expressed vehement opposition to any partition plan, demanded the cessation of Jewish immigration, and called for immediate Palestinian Arab independence. The United Nations (UN) Special Committee on Palestine reiterated the Peel Commission plan for partition. In a tactical concession, Ben-Gurion, the leading political figure of the Yishuv, accepted the recommendation that there be an Arab state and a Jewish state, and he agreed to the placement of Jerusalem under international trusteeship.

Arab states remained opposed. On November 29, 1947, the UN General Assembly put the matter to a vote and received the necessary two-thirds majority: 33 to 13. As the mandatory power, Britain had abstained; the Soviet Union, which saw in the Yishuv a potential socialist ally, voted yes, most likely to curb British influence in the Middle East; and the United States supported partition, as did Latin American nations, who, with no geopolitical considerations at stake, were deeply moved by the plight of the Jews. The resolution was due to take effect in May 1948. Although the partition plan gave the Zionists far less than what they wanted, the vote was a great diplomatic victory, the greatest since the Balfour Declaration of 1917.

The problem was that the vote of November 29 came from a body without the power to enforce it. Diplomacy quickly turned to military struggle between Jews and Arabs. War broke out in two stages between November 1947 and May 1948—initially a civil war, between Jews and Arabs in Palestine. In the first few weeks, more than 80 Jews and 90 Arabs were killed. Arabs attacked Jewish stores and exploded bombs in city centers, while the Haganah attacked Arab villages. Palestinian militia groups killed hundreds of Jews. Jewish Jerusalem was under siege, and some neighborhoods were on the verge of starvation. Palestinian Arabs were soon joined by forces from across the Arab world. The Yishuv was outnumbered two to one. Violent opposition to the partition plan was not confined to Palestine. In Aleppo, Syria, 300 Jewish homes and 11 synagogues were burned to the ground, and 2,000 Jews fled. In Aden, 76 Jews were murdered. In Baghdad, mobs ran riot in Jewish areas, and Chief Rabbi Sassoon Kadoori was forced to issue a statement condemning Zionism. By April 1948, mass demonstrations in the Iraqi capital, Baghdad, brought chants of "Death to the Jews!"

The second phase of fighting in Palestine carried into 1948. In March, the Jewish leadership, in an attempt to secure the borders of a future Jewish state, drove Palestinian guerillas out of the villages from where they were launching attacks. To achieve what was known as Plan D, in many cases, the Jewish authorities sanctioned the expulsion of Arab villagers. One hundred thousand Arabs were forced from their homes with the Israeli conquest of Lydda and Ramle, but these expulsions were not part of a systematic policy. According to the available evidence, Israeli objectives were centered on conquest and not depopulation. There were also massacres, the most notorious of which occurred on April 9, 1948, in the Palestinian village of Deir Yassin, near Jerusalem. There, the Irgun killed approximately 120 Arabs, many of whom were unarmed civilians.

The military victories buoyed Ben-Gurion and his comrades and led them to the conclusion that the time was ripe to declare independence, in full expectation of a multinational Arab invasion. At 4:00 p.m. on May 14, 1948, just hours after the Union Jack was lowered over Palestine, signaling the British departure, Ben-Gurion read the Declaration of Independence from the Tel Aviv Museum. Declaring the establishment of the State of Israel, Ben-Gurion recounted the history of Zionism and the series of international agreements, including the Balfour Declaration, that preceded the UN vote. He stressed the Jewish people's unbroken attachment to the Land of Israel, noted their struggle, in defiance of international restrictions, to get there, and of course, he addressed the impact of the Holocaust. Solemnly, he proclaimed, "By virtue of our natural and historic right and on the strength of the resolution of the United Nations General

Assembly, [we] hereby declare the establishment of a Jewish state in Eretz-Israel, to be known as the State of Israel." That night, the new state was recognized by the United States and, three days later, by the Soviet Union. Ben-Gurion was named prime minister, and Chaim Weizmann became the first president after the honor had been declined by Albert Einstein.

The next day, Arab armies from Egypt, Transjordan, Syria, Lebanon, and Iraq, together with volunteer units from Saudi Arabia and Yemen, attacked, beginning what would be called by Israel the War of Independence. Palestinians would later refer to it as the *Nakba*, or "catastrophe." The Arab invaders numbered about 25,000, while the Yishuv's armed forces consisted of about 35,000 Haganah troops and 3,000 from the Stern and Irgun forces. Israel also had several thousand people who had fought in the British Army in World War II. They were soon joined by 3,500 Jewish and non-Jewish volunteers who had come to Israel from abroad to help defend the new state. These latter two groups were battle-hardened World War II veterans, and their extremely valuable military experience made a significant difference to Israel's fortunes.

Even though Ben-Gurion had already begun a massive stockpiling of weapons in 1946, and the Yishuv had also begun to produce its own light weapons, when the war began, Israel possessed no heavy machine guns, artillery, armored vehicles, antitank or antiaircraft weapons, military aircraft, or tanks. This began to change thanks to Czechoslovakia's violation of the British-initiated United Nations Security Council Resolution 50 (May 29, 1948), which called for an arms embargo on the region. The Czechs began supplying the Jewish state with critical military hardware, including fighter planes. Just three days

before this, a historic development took place. On May 26, 1948, by order of David Ben-Gurion, the Israel Defense Forces (IDF) was officially established. Created as a conscript army, it came into being with the incorporation into the IDF of the Haganah, the Irgun, and the Stern Gang. Two days later, on May 28, the Israel Air Force was formed out of the pre-existing Air Service, the aerial arm of the Haganah. Originally, it used commercial airplanes it converted to military use and a variety of obsolete World War II combat aircraft, including British Spitfires and Czech-built German Messerschmitts. Foreign, particularly American, volunteers were so prominent in flying combat missions during the War of Independence that English, not Hebrew, was the operational language of the air force. Now, with a well-equipped, unified national army and air force, Israel was in a better position to match the (mainly British) heavy equipment and planes already owned by the invading Arab states. The number of Israelis under arms also began to grow significantly, and by the spring of 1949, there were 115,000 Israeli troops, while the Arab forces totaled about 60,000. Shortly after the creation of the State of Israel, its overall military superiority relative to the surrounding Arab countries was firmly established.

After prolonged and fierce fighting for a month, a United Nations–brokered truce in June 1948 made it possible for Israel to regroup and resupply its army. When the Arabs recommenced hostilities in July, Israel fought and won decisively, capturing the western Galilee, territory that was to have gone to the Palestinian Arabs in the partition plan. Israel also took control of the Negev. The new territories enlarged the new state by 20 percent more than the partition plan initially allowed. A Palestinian state did not come into being and, instead, Egypt and Transjordan (later renamed Jordan) seized control of those parts of Palestine they conquered in the war. The UN partitioned Jerusalem between Israel and Jordan, with the latter controlling the most important of Jewish holy sites, the Western Wall.

Better armed, better trained, and more determined than their enemies, Israel had come through its first great life-and-death struggle. The victory saw Israel forge an ethos of embattled heroism, while the values and achievements of the founding generation took on mythical proportions. But a sense of the nation's permanent vulnerability also came to characterize the outlook of Israelis. Even though the Arab forces were poorly coordinated and had fought as separate armies, with very little in the way of real unison of purpose and tactics, they nevertheless inflicted a heavy toll on Israel. In the War of Independence, a total of 6,373 Jews were killed, or 1 percent of the Jewish population. (A further 15,000 were wounded.) The war remains Israel's costliest in terms of lives lost and bodies maimed and had a major impact on the culture and psyche of Israelis and Diaspora Jews thereafter. The war also had catastrophic consequences for the Palestinians. Between 600,000 and 750,000 fled or were expelled from their homes and were turned into refugees.

Only 50 years separated Ben-Gurion's proclamation of the State of Israel and Theodor Herzl's diary entry at the First Zionist Congress in Basel in 1897 when he wrote, "Today I created the Jewish state!" After the War of Independence, Ben-Gurion declared:

> We extend our hand to all neighboring states and their peoples in an offer of peace and good neighborliness. . . . The State of Israel is prepared to do its share in a common effort for the advancement of the entire Middle East.

These intentions have not translated into peaceful coexistence. And when they have, as has been the case with the peace treaties Israel has signed with Egypt and Jordan, relations have been anything but warm.

IN THE STATE OF ISRAEL

The war of 1948 gave birth to the modern Israeli, imagined as a selfless, Hebrew-speaking warrior and pioneer who had returned to the ancestral homeland to till the soil and defend it when necessary. For all of Ben-Gurion's efforts to link the State of Israel with the long, historical experience of the Jewish people, there developed in the 1940s an influential aspect of Israeli culture that sought to establish a clear demarcation between Israeli and Jewish identity.

The Canaanites

Although it had only about two dozen registered members, a new group that called itself the Canaanites touted the contrast between the healthy, suntanned, native-born Israeli, or sabra, and the equally mythical, weak, downtrodden Jew of the Diaspora. The Canaanite activists included poets, authors, journalists, sculptors, and educators. Led by the poet Yonatan Ratosh and the sculptors Binyamin Tammuz and Yitzhak Danziger, the Canaanites rejected Judaism and longed for a return to a Middle Eastern identity that predated both Judaism and Islam. They claimed that large parts of the Middle East, which they named the Land of Kedem (kedem, meaning east or antiquity), constituted an ancient, Hebrew-speaking civilization. They aspired to a Hebrew renaissance, one that would liberate Jews from Judaism and Arabs from Islam. Both religions, they believed, consigned their adherents to medieval superstition, keeping at bay the advances of secular modernity.

Influenced by Fascist culture and the way it both glorified the past and was very much future-oriented at the same time, the Canaanites were radicals who rejected any links to Judaism and Jewish history, preaching instead a Hebrew universalism. Before and during the 1948 war, they objected to the expulsion of Arabs, believing that this constituted only a population transfer from one part of the Land of Kedem to another. Most Jews rejected the Canaanite ideology of "negation of the Diaspora," but its glorification of the new Hebrew man and woman proved appealing within intellectual circles, and the sharp distinction the Canaanites pointed to between Israelis and Diaspora Jews was keenly felt at all levels of Israeli society and helped shape an important element of Israeli culture in the state's formative period.

Despite the self-portrait of heroic self-reliance, the new, fragile state, with approximately 600,000 Jews, not only required the financial and political support of the international community but also desperately needed Jewish immigrants, even though some high-ranking officials complained that Israel could not take in any and all Jews. The minister of finance, Eliezer Kaplan, stated, "We need workers and fighters." Others were concerned about the cultural level of some immigrants, while still others fretted about their political affiliations. Some government officials objected to immigrants based on their countries of origin, while some preferred to make admission contingent upon occupation. Those who came as refugees, without ideological commitment to the Zionist cause, were, in theory, especially unwelcome. But in reality, the losses sustained in the Shoah made sure that the new state could not pick and choose which Jews to accept, and so to facilitate mass immigration, on July 5, 1950, the government promulgated the Law of Return, which endowed "[e]very Jew [with] the right to immigrate to the country." Over the next four years, some 700,000 Jews arrived. The two largest groups included Holocaust survivors from Europe and Jewish refugees from Arab lands. Adjustment for both was difficult.

Approximately 350,000 Holocaust survivors had made their way to Israel by 1949. There they took comfort among one another, with a wide network of groups offering support, and as in the Diaspora, the survivors did a remarkable job of doing the unremarkable—rebuilding family life. Survivors immediately participated in the task of defending and building up the fledgling state, but their political and cultural integration proved very difficult under the circumstances. Many survivors felt that they were the last Jews alive and believed they had an obligation to share their experiences. However, they often faced incredulousness. Michael Goldman was a 17-year-old prisoner in a Polish labor camp near Przemysl. One day he was brought before the camp's commandant, Franz Schwammberger, who proceeded to whip him. Goldman received 80 lashes. His back had been turned into raw meat, and yet astonishingly he survived and eventually made his way to Israel. When he later recounted his story to his relatives, they did not believe him, certain that he was either exaggerating or perhaps hallucinating. Shocked, Goldman declared that his family's response was "the eighty-first blow." His story became symbolic of such encounters, so much so that it was made into a popular Israeli film titled *The Eighty-First Blow*. The mood and the culture of the country meant that few people wanted to listen to such tales of sorrow. The heroic ethos of the new Hebrew warrior promoted a certain social antipathy toward survivors, insofar as the latter physically embodied the weakness Zionist ideology so cruelly claimed was characteristic of Diaspora Jewry. David Ben-Gurion contemptuously referred to Holocaust survivors as "human dust," while others were equally callous. A Mapai (Labor Party) leader said of the survivors, "They must learn love of the homeland, a work ethic, and human morals." However, a more complex rationale informed the official encouragement of silence and the shunning of Holocaust survivors. The presence of survivors evoked the painful realization that contrary to Zionist claims of power and self-reliance, the Yishuv was incapable of rescuing large numbers of Jews, let alone preventing or even putting a stop to the Holocaust. Contempt and incomprehension on the part of Israelis on the one hand and the survivor's sense of estrangement and alienation on the other meant that what most commonly characterized the encounter between survivors and native-born Israelis was awkward silence.

By September 1949, the Jewish population of Israel stood at 957,000. One out of every three Israelis was a survivor. Nearly all those who had come to Palestine prior to the war lost family members in the Holocaust. Many people were wracked with guilt about their escaping in time. For their part, some survivors seethed with anger at the leaders of the Yishuv. Yosef Rosensaft, a leader among the Jewish displaced persons at Bergen-Belsen, berated the Zionists, "You danced the *hora* [a folk dance] while we were being burned in the crematoriums." While relations between survivors and the Yishuv were often tense, Israel nonetheless provided Holocaust survivors with something few other places could—an environment free of antisemitism, the security of being surrounded by fellow Jews, and the chance to be reunited with family members thought to have perished during the war. Thousands of Jews could relate to the experience of Rita Waxman, a Holocaust survivor

who arrived in Israel in the winter of 1949. While shopping in Haifa one day, Waxman caught a glimpse of a soldier queuing up to buy a movie ticket. She stopped dead in her tracks. "Haim?" she called out. As he turned, they stared at each other. Mother and son embraced. Haim was now 21. Separated in Poland when Haim was 14, she, as did he, presumed the other to have been killed. In addition to chance encounters such as this, thousands of Jews were reunited thanks to newspaper advertisements and radio call-in shows.

In addition to Holocaust survivors, very large numbers of Jews from Arab lands also came to Israel mid-century. Altogether, some 260,000 Jews from Arab countries immigrated to Israel between 1948 and 1951, where they made up about 56 percent of the total immigration to the new state. There were also later waves of migration—for example, from Egypt in 1956, and from other North African countries into the 1960s.

Between May 1948 and December 1949, 35,000 Jews came from Yemen. In the next few years, they were joined by a further 14,000. All 49,000 Yemenite Jews arrived in the country on a total of 450 airline flights in what was known as Operation Magic Carpet. Not all politicians were enthusiastic about the arrivals from Yemen, however. The Knesset member Yitzhak Greenbaum declared:

By bringing Yemenites, 70 percent of whom are sick, we are doing no good to anybody. We are harming them by bringing them into an alien environment where they will degenerate. Can we withstand an immigration of which 70 percent are sick?

Others had a very different response, welcoming the Yemenite Jews by romanticizing that they are "a fabulous tribe, the most poetic of the tribes of Israel. Their features bear the ancient Hebrew grace, their hearts are filled with innocent faith and a fervent love of the Holy Land." Ben-Gurion exhibited both tendencies. In November 1950, he wrote of the Yemenite Jews to the chief of staff and later famous archaeologist Yigael Yadin:

> This tribe is in some ways more easily absorbed, both culturally and economically, than any other. It is hardworking, it is not attracted by city life, it has—or at least, the male part has—a good grounding in Hebrew and the Jewish heritage. Yet in other ways it may be the most problematic of all. It is 2,000 years behind us, perhaps even more. It lacks the most basic and primary concepts of civilization (as distinct from culture).

The following year, Ben-Gurion told the Knesset that the government's goal was to inculcate the Yemenite immigrant in the ways of Israel to the extent that he forgets where he came from, just "as [he had] forgotten that [he is] Polish" (see Map 6.1).

One of the largest waves of immigration to Israel was called Operation Ezra and Nehemia (1950–1951), an airlift of 100,000 Jews from Iraq. Although Zionism was never very strong among Iraqi Jews, when the Iraqi government stopped making distinctions between Jews and Zionists after the establishment of the State of Israel, emigration became imperative. When Iraq froze the assets of departing Jews, effectively stealing their property, the Israeli government, which had been directed by the United States and Britain in 1948 to compensate Palestinian refugees, linked the two events, effectively neutralizing both claims. Iraqi Jewish refugees, expecting Israel to compensate them for their losses, were told by Jerusalem to lodge claims with the government of Iraq, the very entity that had robbed them. By the 1970s, discontent among Middle Eastern Jews ran so high that a protest movement was formed, called the Black Panthers.

The absorption of immigrants was a huge and expensive undertaking. In 1949, it was estimated that to provide 230,000 immigrants with housing and employment would cost as much as $700 million. In addition to receiving foreign assistance, the government resorted to inflationary measures and printed money to pay for government services. It also instituted an austerity program, with strict price controls and rationing of food, raw materials, and foreign currency. Modelled on British wartime rationing, the program was intended to ensure a minimum standard of living both for veteran Israelis and for newcomers.

While the goal of providing a minimum standard of living was achieved, the program was extremely unpopular. Women, in particular, bore the brunt of its impact, for it was mostly they who waited in long lines to purchase staples. After queuing for hours, women often went home empty-handed because the food had run out. Oftentimes, certain foodstuffs were declared suddenly available, and women had to go through the routine of returning daily to stores. The situation was worse in summer. Few people owned refrigerators, so food could be bought only in small quantities, lest it spoil. The program bred widespread anger, frustration, and uncertainty. The system also bred corruption, as the government determined which shops would sell what and which suppliers would have the right to provide certain items. Still, some supporters of the plan were even drawn to it for ideological reasons. The poet Uri Zvi Greenberg, then a member of the Knesset, was so enamored of the austerity program

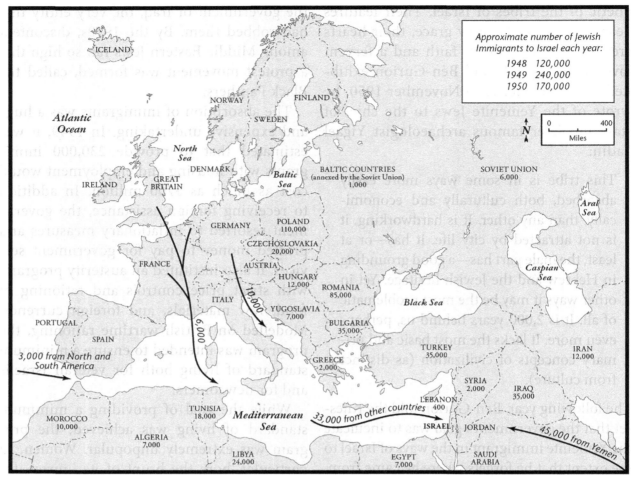

Map 6.1 Jewish immigration to the State of Israel, 1948–1950. By 1950, the two most ancient centers of world Jewry—
Europe and the Middle East—had been decimated by mass murder and forced emigration. For Holocaust survivors in
Europe and Jewish refugees from Muslim lands, the newly created State of Israel proved the most favored destination named
after its American counterpart. They succeeded in calling attention to economic, educational, and social disparities between
Mizrahim (Middle Eastern Jews) and Ashkenazim.

that he wanted it to become Israel's "lifelong
constitution." His was a Zionist celebration
of privation and anti-consumerism. Others
were more pragmatic. The architects of the
plan were certain that, given the challenges
facing the country, there was no other way.
As Ben-Gurion declared in the Knesset, without the austerity program, it would be all but
impossible to carry out the country's three
great tasks: "defence, immigration absorption, and the maintenance of an acceptable
living standard."

Serious social problems notwithstanding, Israel has been enormously successful
in integrating so many people, from so many
different cultures, with a wide variety of religious and political sensibilities. The divisions
among modern Jews that we have charted in
this book have not disappeared. Jews remain
split between secular and religious, left and
right, those of Ashkenazic and those of Sephardic and Middle Eastern background. And
where income distribution among Israelis
was once fairly even, the gap between the

haves and have-nots is widening. Despite and out of the vast differences, however, a nation was forged.

Above all, it was government that provided the solid institutional framework for the new Jewish state. Jewish sovereignty, depicted with a national flag and an anthem, also provided people with a rallying point and sense of belonging and purpose. Organizationally, Israel had long prepared for national independence. With the declaration of statehood in May 1948, government ministries were immediately formed out of the various departments and bureaus that made up the National Council and the Jewish Agency. While national governance was new, administering individual departments was not. Newly created government ministries—such as health, religious affairs, politics, culture, education, finance, immigration, labor, trade, industry, commerce, and foreign affairs—all had fairly experienced leaders from the outset. This is not to say that efficiency was the handmaiden of experience. Assuredly, it was not, for the cabinet ministers presided over a notoriously cumbersome bureaucracy. To make matters worse, the pay and conditions of civil service jobs were abysmal and failed to attract Israel's best and brightest. Yet the necessary infrastructure for successful governance was in place.

Initially, Israel was run by a provisional government. It enjoyed the loyalty of the majority, and its authority to establish a supreme court, issue the nation's currency and postage stamps, and collect taxes went unquestioned. While dissatisfaction accompanied the austerity program, the government's right to install it was also broadly accepted. What was needed was the formation of a permanent government, always intended but postponed due to the War of Independence. Adhering to the principle of universal suffrage, the election of a new government was set for January 25, 1949. Elections continued to employ the long-established system of proportional representation. This had been the case in both Zionist Congresses and in the Yishuv's National Assembly. The Constituent Assembly, which later became the Knesset, was to have 120 members. They were to be elected by voters, irrespective of race, creed, or sex, so long as they were at least 18 years of age. The provisional government, led by Ben-Gurion (Labor), won the first election. Thereafter, the Labor Party held on to the reins of power until 1977.

Elections remain based on the system of proportional representation, in which small parties are crucial for the formation of a government. In this arrangement, majority and minority parties, often with starkly conflicting worldviews, are dependent on one another, and small parties pledge allegiance to the party with the highest number of seats, usually in return for legislative favors. A reflection of the radical and often irreconcilable diversity of modern Jews, this system, with its myriad parties and narrow agendas, while functioning, has also proven to be highly unstable.

The formation of a national government and military was an enormous task, and while foreign aid and donations from world Jewry were crucial, it is what Israelis energetically and creatively did with the assistance that made for the successful absorption of the immigrants and their transformation into modern Israelis. Most notably, through the use of Hebrew as the national language and the integrative impact of compulsory military service, the modern Israeli was formed out of a shared culture and experience. Moreover, Israel achieved statehood and cultivated Israeli identity under the particularly difficult circumstances of near-constant war and

Figure 6.1   Camp trunks. For the most part, Jewish refugees to Israel from Arab lands in the late 1940s and early 1950s were first placed in refugee transit camps prior to their integration into society at large. Here, Iraqi Jews sit with their possessions, contained in the mountains of suitcases and trunks.

economic vulnerability. This further tightened the social and cultural bonds among Israelis, despite the real existence of deep social and cultural fissures.

Israel's Wars

The difficulties of building a state, with meager resources and a highly diverse population, would have been tough enough in a peaceful environment. That Israel did so in a near-constant state of war is a remarkable achievement. After the 1948 War of Independence, Israel fought six wars against Arab nation-states. In the summer of 1949, she signed armistice agreements with Egypt, Jordan, Lebanon, and Syria, but belligerence took other forms, and in August 1949, Egypt closed the Suez Canal to Israeli shipping. In response to a 1951 UN resolution calling on Egypt to open the shipping lanes, the Egyptian government relaxed its prohibition, only to reimpose the ban in 1952. Border skirmishes also took place, and verbal hostility continued to mount. The Egyptian foreign minister, Muhammad Salah al-Din, declared in 1954, "The Arab people will not be embarrassed to declare: We shall not be satisfied except by the final obliteration of Israel from the map of the Middle East." In the Sinai Campaign (1956), Israel fought its second war against the Arabs. In October, with the support of France and Britain, Israel captured the Sinai Peninsula. The US government, previously unaware of the scheme, was furious and publicly rebuked Britain and France. Thereafter, European states would become minor players in Middle Eastern affairs, shadows of their former imperial selves. The United States, by contrast, became the dominant party in brokering Arab–Israeli relations. The United States forced Israel to

THE EICHMANN TRIAL

An important change in Israeli attitudes toward Holocaust survivors took place with the Eichmann trial, which was held in Jerusalem from April 11 to August 16, 1961. Adolf Eichmann, a member of the Nazi SS, was a leading figure in organizing the deportation of Jews to extermination camps. He had escaped from American custody after the war and wandered around Germany until 1950, when, with the help of a Catholic organization dedicated to ferrying ex-Nazis out of Europe, he fled to Argentina. There he lived under the alias Ricardo Klement, until 1960, when agents of the Israeli Security Service (Mossad) abducted Eichmann and brought him to Israel to stand trial. He was indicted on 15 criminal charges, including crimes against humanity, crimes against the Jewish people, and membership in a criminal organization. Three judges presided over the trial while Eichmann sat in a specially constructed bulletproof glass booth in the dock.

The prosecution presented more than 1,500 incriminating documents and 100 witnesses (90 of whom were Nazi concentration and extermination camp survivors). On December 11, 1961, the judges announced their verdict: Eichmann was convicted on all counts. He was hanged at midnight between May 31 and June 1, 1962. His remains were cremated, and his ashes scattered in the sea beyond Israeli territorial waters.

The trial was given wide international coverage, and in Israel, dramatic survivor testimonies, most heard for the very first time, alerted Israelis to the detailed horrors of the Holocaust. A changed attitude and consciousness emerged as empathy for the victims and memory of the event became increasingly central to Israeli culture and sense of self.

surrender the Sinai (a UN force moved in, ensuring Israel's shipping access through the Straits of Tiran), and Israel emerged from the Sinai Campaign with its regional and global reputation enhanced, while Muhammad Salah al-Din's boast appeared to be an empty threat.

Under the powerful Egyptian ruler Gamal Abdul Nasser, plans were again made to launch war against Israel. The Six-Day War (1967) was Israel's third war against the Arab world.

In May of that year, Nasser decided to provoke hostilities by closing the Straits of Tiran to Israeli shipping. He ordered the UN force in the Sinai to leave, and a war of words occupied the world for two tense weeks. The bloodcurdling rhetoric about Israel's imminent obliteration that came from Arab capitals filled Israel's citizens with dread. Following the Eichmann trial, whatever feelings of superiority Israelis may have once felt toward Holocaust survivors had begun to dissipate (see the box "The Eichmann Trial"). In fact, the crisis Israelis were now facing made them identify with the Holocaust more than ever. The possibility of their own defeat and the sense of impending doom were so great that rabbis sanctified public parks in the expectation that the death toll would climb into the hundreds of thousands and the bodies would have to be buried in mass graves.

On June 5, sensing that it could wait no longer, the Israeli air force bombed the airfields of Egypt, Jordan, Syria, and Iraq, destroying their fleets. With lightning speed, Israel then moved into Gaza and Sinai, took the Golan Heights from Syria, occupied the whole west bank of the Jordan River, and captured Jordanian-controlled East Jerusalem. Israel was now 28,000 square miles larger. Although the country had lost 776 soldiers and sustained about 5,200 casualties, the entire Jewish world was electrified by the Israeli victory, especially the sight of Israeli soldiers at the Western Wall. Even the staunch secularist general Moshe Dayan (1915–1981) entered Jerusalem's Old City, proclaiming, "We have returned to all that is holy in our land. We have returned never to be parted from it again."

Amid the euphoria, few gave much thought to the 1 million Palestinians now under Israeli occupation. One who did was the celebrated author Amos Oz, who, in a 1967 article titled "Land of Our Forefathers," warned, "Even unavoidable occupation is a corrupting occupation." One of the direst assessments came from the philosopher and public intellectual Yeshayahu Leibowitz, who, immediately after the war, urged that Israel not hold on to the territories. His advice went unheeded, and he declared, "Israel won the war in six days and lost it on the seventh." Eight Arab nations convened in Khartoum at the end of August 1967, vowing to carry on the struggle against Israel, and declared the following three principles: no peace with Israel, no negotiations with Israel, no recognition of Israel.

Victory in the Six-Day War proved a turning point in the character and nature of Israel, as its domestic life and foreign policy changed. The state began to pursue an agenda of territorial expansion and settlement building on Palestinian land, a policy that has split Israeli Jews and Jewish public

opinion abroad. The settlements are also a focal point of widespread international criticism of Israel.

Israel's fourth war is known as the War of Attrition (1968–1970). It was a conflict of low but constant intensity in which Egypt sought to eject Israel from Sinai. The Soviet Union supported Egypt, with Russian pilots flying sorties in Egyptian planes. The war proved inconclusive, and a truce was signed in 1970. Attempts to sign a formal peace treaty failed, as the Israeli government refused to meet Arab demands for withdrawal from the occupied territories. Terrorist activity of the Palestine Liberation Organization (PLO), which had been founded in 1964, stiffened Israel's resolve not to negotiate a deal. The most infamous terrorist attack was the seizure of Israeli athletes at the 1972 Munich Olympic Games, perpetrated by the Palestinian group Black September, which had close ties to PLO leader Yasser Arafat. After a protracted standoff and a botched rescue operation by German paramilitary troops, 11 of the athletes were killed. The murders of Jews at an event organized to express international goodwill and fellowship, and in Germany of all countries, proved especially shocking.

The fifth Arab–Israeli war was called the Yom Kippur War (1973). After making friendly overtures to Israel, Anwar Sadat, Nasser's successor, planned to attack Israel. Egypt would cross the Suez, and its ally Syria would descend on the Golan Heights. The attack began at 2:00 p.m. on October 6, 1973. With many Israelis fasting and at synagogue, observing Yom Kippur, the country was caught completely by surprise. The attack on the Day of Atonement was only part of the reason for this. Buoyed by the events of 1967, an overconfident Israeli military and intelligence establishment ignored repeated public threats by Sadat and detailed warnings by King Hussein of Jordan and the US Central Intelligence Agency. The 1973 war presented a far graver threat than any previous war. Although Israel ultimately prevailed, the losses were enormous: 2,688 dead, 7,200 wounded, and 294 taken prisoner. The myth of Israeli military invincibility was shattered. Politically and culturally, the country became increasingly factionalized between Right and Left. In the course of this crisis of morale, the fragile political consensus disintegrated. For their part in the Yom Kippur failure, Prime Minister Golda Meir (1898–1978) and Defense Minister Moshe Dayan were forced to resign.

In the international arena, Israel grew increasingly isolated. OPEC, the Arab-led cartel of oil-producing nations, used its control of oil production as a weapon against the West. Tripling the price of petroleum, Arab states applied pressure to Third World countries to break off relations with Israel. The plight of the Palestinians likewise engaged world opinion against the Israeli occupation, especially in Western European left-wing circles. In 1974, the head of the Palestine Liberation Organization, Yasser Arafat, took the podium at the United Nations with an olive branch in one hand and a gun in his holster to make the case to the General Assembly for Palestinian independence. In November 1975, the General Assembly passed a resolution condemning Zionism "as a form of racism," with a vote of 75 for, 35 against, and 32 abstentions. It was a staggering blow.

In Israel, geopolitical tensions brought dramatic political change. In 1977, Menachem Begin, head of the right-wing Likud Party, was swept into office with the electoral support of Jews from Arab lands, dissatisfied with their treatment at the hands of the Ashkenazic establishment, and those alienated by Labor's secularism and its disdain for religious Orthodoxy. This was the Labor Party's first electoral defeat since the founding of the state in 1948. The triumph of the Right was of historic proportions. Menachem Begin was a man of intense political passions, given to demagoguery and histrionics. He repeatedly invoked the legacy of the Holocaust to denounce his political enemies and to justify his policies and personal actions. In addition to his former membership in the Stern Gang and his violent opposition in the early 1950s to Ben-Gurion's willingness to accept financial compensation from the German government for the Holocaust, Begin is also to be remembered for attempting to pursue both peace and Israeli territorial expansion at one and the same time.

When President Anwar Sadat concluded that peace with Israel was possible and desirable, he made the historically monumental decision to come to Israel and meet with Begin. In November 1977, an ecstatic Israeli public welcomed President Sadat. The Knesset also gave the Egyptian leader an enthusiastic reception as he addressed the chamber. The next year, at Camp David, Anwar Sadat, Menachem Begin, and US president Jimmy Carter negotiated a peace treaty, which was signed in 1979. Sadat's decision proved to be a fatal one. Viewed as a traitor for his overture to Israel, Sadat was assassinated by the group Egyptian Islamic Jihad on October 6, 1981. Although his successor, Hosni Mubarak, stuck to the peace treaty with Israel, official circles in Egypt and other Arab countries have done little to change popular sentiment toward Israel and Jews. In the press throughout the Muslim world, the state-controlled media regularly publish hostile articles about Israel, while antisemitic caricatures of Israelis and Jews are standard fare.

Begin's 1977 victory led to the promotion of a "Greater Israel" program, intended to expand the territory of the state through the establishment of Jewish settlements all over the Land of Israel. (It was a policy that left-wing governments also pursued.) Begin stuck to this policy even while signing a peace treaty with Egypt, as, for example, when, during his tenure as prime minister, Israel formally annexed the Golan Heights. The deep divides in Israel's political culture, particularly in response to expansionist policies, began to emerge more fully under Begin's premiership. The distinguished Hebrew University political historian Jacob Talmon wrote to the prime minister in October 1980:

> Mr. Prime Minister . . . [t]he desire at the end of the twentieth century, to dominate and govern a hostile foreign population . . . is like an attempt to revive feudalism. . . . The idea is simply not feasible . . . as France learned in Algeria.

A host of military, labor, and business leaders expressed similar sentiments. Begin and an increasingly strident right wing ignored their warnings. In fact, Begin, together with his minister of defense, Ariel Sharon (b. 1928), launched Israel's sixth Arab–Israeli war, Operation Peace in Galilee (1982). Sharon led Israeli troops into Lebanon to drive the deeply entrenched Palestine Liberation Organization from the country. The ground war resulted in large numbers of casualties, with approximately 600 Israelis killed. Over objections from members of the Israeli military, Sharon recklessly disregarded the original plan to move no farther than 25 miles into Lebanese territory. Instead, he led his troops to the outskirts of Beirut and cut off the city's food, electricity, and water supplies. Deep dismay gripped regular soldiers, who formed a movement named "Soldiers Against Silence." In a newspaper article, former foreign minister Abba Eban wrote that "these six weeks

have been a dark page in the moral history of the Jewish people." It was about to get worse. In seeking to oust Palestinian guerillas from the city and drive the PLO from Lebanon altogether, the Israeli army was assisted by Lebanese Christian forces. Taking advantage of the Israeli presence, Lebanese militia entered the Sabra and Shatila refugee camps, where, on September 16–18, 1982, they massacred as many as 2,300 innocent civilians.

Around the world, the reaction was one of outrage, mostly directed at Israel, but also toward Jews in the Diaspora. Airport workers in Italy boycotted the Israeli national airline, El Al, and synagogues in Rome and Milan were bombed. The Rome bombing caused the death of a 2-year-old. The link between Israel's treatment of the Palestinians and the Nazi treatment of Jews became a common element of anti-Zionist propaganda. But the massacres in Lebanon sparked fury in Israel too. On September 25, 1983, 300,000 Israelis demonstrated in Tel Aviv, demanding to know what role their government had played in the slaughter. Public opinion condemned Sharon and his troops for failing to intervene to stop the killing. An Israeli judicial commission found that while the Israeli army did not participate in the murders, it could and should have stopped them. The commission held that Sharon "bears personal responsibility." The so-called Kahan Commission concluded that Sharon should not hold public office again. (Nevertheless, he later became prime minister.) Begin stayed in office until 1983 and left broken and in disgrace. Even though, for a short while, the objective of driving the PLO from Lebanon and stopping cross-border shelling into northern Israel had been achieved, the Lebanon war had irreparably damaged the domestic credibility of the government as well as Israel's international standing.

With a weakened political system, Israelis opted for a Labor–Likud coalition government with a rotating premiership. In 1983, Yitzhak Shamir of Likud first took office as prime minister for a two-year term. Shamir, a hard-liner who had voted against the peace treaty with Egypt, remained committed to staying in Lebanon despite its enormous costs. He also continued the expansionist settlement policies of his predecessor. True to his own background as a member of the Stern Gang, Shamir condoned the vigilantism of various West Bank settler groups. The unprecedented phenomenon of conscientious objection to military service increased under his administration, while the fragility of the national economy contributed to social unrest. The Lebanon war, the building of settlements, and the implementation of expensive social programs designed to buy popular support were unsustainable. Inflation hit 400 percent per year. Panic selling on the Tel Aviv stock exchange followed, as did a run on banks, with people withdrawing increasingly worthless shekels from savings accounts to buy durable goods.

The government crisis reached its peak in the summer of 1984. New elections were called. The results revealed the weakness of the two major parties, Likud and Labor, and demonstrated that they were powerless to form a government without the assistance of smaller, primarily religious parties. To curry favor, both major parties lavished the smaller parties with all sorts of rewards, out of all proportion to their electoral strength. The stalemate at the polls catapulted Shimon Peres (1923–2016) to the post of prime minister. Peres was a veteran of labor Zionism, a close ally of Ben-Gurion, and an accomplished technocrat. Committed to bringing the troops home, Peres ended the Israeli occupation of southern Lebanon in 1985. Only about 200 Israeli soldiers remained in the southern "security zone." Between 1985 and 1988, many of them were killed as Palestinian militants returned to the area, supported by Hezbollah, a then new militant and political group. With support from Iran, Hezbollah has proven to be an implacable enemy of Israel.

As the years passed, the Israeli occupation of Palestinian territory became more deeply entrenched and institutionalized. In 1987, Palestinians in the occupied territories rebelled, launching the intifada, an Arabic word for "shaking off." The intifada took the form of civil unrest, store closings, tax strikes, mounting barricades, and throwing stones at Israeli soldiers. The minister of defense, Yitzhak Rabin (1922–1995), responded with brutal force, but to little effect. He was unable to quell Palestinian rage and discontent.

Israel's political standing has never fully matched its military power, and the country has sometimes been stymied in dealing with enemies. In the first Gulf War (1990–1991), Iraq fired Scud missiles on Tel Aviv. Fearful that the warheads were tipped with chemical or biological weapons, Israelis donned gas masks and sought safety in underground shelters for nearly two weeks. With Israel prevented by US pressure from retaliating, nothing pointed to increasing Israeli impotence—conjuring up Holocaust images—as starkly as the sight of Jews in Tel Aviv waiting in fear of being gassed. For many, especially Holocaust survivors, the fear they saw among native-born Israelis was vindication that their supposedly passive behavior during the Holocaust was not the result of a flawed Diaspora mentality. On January 25, 1991, an article in the Israeli newspaper *Davar* bore the headline "Yes, It Happened to Us as Well":

Our attitude to the Jews murdered in the Holocaust, an attitude of hard-hearted vanity mixed with insecurity and anxiety, changed considerably. It became more sober, human, and soft, a lot less "Israeli," a lot more "Jewish." The certainty that "it will not happen to us" has turned into a realization that "it did happen to us". . . . In this respect, the recent events are one more step in the process of changing our attitude [to] the Jewish reaction in the [Second World] war. The Jews of Europe took from us, perhaps finally, the status we assumed we deserved, the status of judges sitting, cold and distant, on the high bench, issuing a verdict on millions of Jews. . . . Now we cannot escape the conclusion that it is barely conceivable that a public under stress would react with heroism. . . . The present events will accelerate the process of reconciliation with the past, in which fear was not dandyism—it was a fear of real death.

According to the historian Dina Porat, for many in Israel, the situation created by the Gulf War was analogous to the Holocaust. Saddam was Hitler, the coalition against Iraq was considered the Allies of World War II, while the Palestinians dancing on the rooftops as the Scud missiles hit Tel Aviv reminded some survivors of the joy expressed by Poles at seeing the Warsaw Ghetto burning, and the American soldiers operating the Patriot missiles designed to intercept the Scuds were the Righteous Among the Nations, an honorific used by the State of Israel to describe non-Jews who saved Jews during the Holocaust. Most important of all, the passive role played by Israel, even if forced into it by America, reminded everyone of the helplessness experienced by European Jewry in the Holocaust. Survivors were especially struck by all this. Some were scathing about what they were witnessing. They said the panic reflected the Americanization of Israel, that

it was a society that had gone soft. To Holocaust survivors, the sight of people fleeing Tel Aviv for Eilat, in the far south of the country, or sending their families to friends and relatives in Jerusalem was a marker of the decline of Zionism's ethos of heroism. The tables had now turned. Said one:

We, the survivors [of the Holocaust], are the true Zionists of today, because we know what it means to stand up against fears, against those who attack you, and it certainly means never abandoning your place in Israel, come what may. We know, more than Sabras [native-born Israelis] more than newcomers from other countries and situations, the value of a Jewish state. . . . Each of us witnessed such horrors and suffering, both as a result of a gigantic world war and of the anti-Jewish policies of the Nazis, that now a few bombs that have destroyed a few buildings here and there, or being confined to your home, in your own country, and for just a few weeks, seems to us to be child's play.

In a book on the Gulf War called *Shoah in a Sealed Room: The Shoah in the Daily Press During the Gulf War*, the author stated that while there was no uniform survivor response, "Holocaust survivors and their families show the lowest level of anxiety compared to other groups in the population." Some survivors refused to cower. Said one, "I will never wear a mask," "I lost my ability to be afraid," "Hitler did not wipe me out, and a *pisher* [bed-wetter] like [Saddam] Hussein certainly will not."

A combination of being prevented from striking back at Iraq, Saddam's antisemitism, the threat of being gassed, and the differing reactions of some Holocaust survivors and native-born Israelis to these events all had a profound impact on Israeli attitudes to the Shoah and precipitated a revaluation of previous Zionist assumptions about the Holocaust and Jewish behavior in Europe. On Holocaust Memorial Day (Yom ha-Shoah), April 7, 1992, Ehud Barak, chief of general staff and future prime minister of Israel, headed a delegation of 18 representatives of the Israel Defense Forces to Auschwitz. There, Barak delivered a speech he had written himself. Standing solemnly at this death camp, Barak and his fellow soldiers were in military uniform, a sight whose symbolic importance he was acutely aware of: "There is something symbolic, a kind of circle closing, in the fact that I am here today as the IDF commander." With reference to previous Israeli attitudes to the Shoah, he observed, "We, the first generation of redemption . . . find it difficult to understand the scope and meaning of what happened [in Auschwitz]." But what was now clear was that European Jewry could not have rescued itself, especially since "not even one government was willing or capable of defending or sheltering them." Then, addressing the Jews of Europe as their "deceased brothers," he quoted the Mishnah (Avot 2:4), "[C]ondemn not your fellow man until you stand in his place," and as such, "know that we are, therefore, unable to criticize you." In saying this, Barak challenged the widely held view of those in the Yishuv and the later state of Israel that had they been there, they would have handled the situation differently. Instead, Barak said that Israelis had no right to pass critical judgment because it was now clear that the Jews of Europe had been in an impossible situation. The Gulf War had created a groundswell of empathy and understanding in Israel and brought home to Israelis the idea that the respective fates of Diaspora and Israeli Jews were not as far apart as Zionist ideology had once preached.

The Israeli–Palestinian Peace Process

Barak also pointed to two important lessons for Israel from the Holocaust. The first was that the country needed to remain "very strong" and, second, that it could not depend on military strength alone. Political wisdom and understanding were also required to secure safety and peace. Ever since the 1970s, the term *peace process* has been used to describe the various, mostly American-mediated efforts and proposals to create a lasting peace agreement between the state of Israel and neighboring countries as well as with the Palestinians. Concerning the latter, the goal is a "final status agreement" which would establish a Palestinian state in Gaza and the West Bank in exchange for Palestinians agreeing to accept the existence of the state of Israel and permanently halt attacks against it. It is based on a formula often called "land for peace." However, with the important exceptions of the peace treaties signed with Israel by Egypt in 1979 and Jordan in 1994, formalizing peace agreements between the parties has proven elusive. Indeed, more emphasis has been put on "process" than on "peace," which has effectively resulted in a stalling tactic by all parties for one reason or another in order to buy time and avoid making concessions, the essence of any meaningful peace agreement.

The early 1990s brought about events that promised to be a catalyst for peace. The defeat of Iraq in the Gulf War and the fall of the Soviet Union, both in 1991, and the 1992 Israeli elections that gave left-wing parties 60 out of 120 seats provided Prime Minister Yitzhak Rabin with a diplomatic and political mandate. In secret, his government conducted the first ever face-to-face talks with the PLO. These negotiations ultimately led to the Oslo Accord, which was signed on the White House lawn on September 13, 1993. In a moment that was as awkward as it was historic, President Bill Clinton witnessed PLO leader Yasser Arafat and the Israeli prime minister, Yitzhak Rabin, shake hands.

The Accord stipulated that Israeli troops would withdraw in stages from the West Bank and Gaza, and that a "Palestinian Interim Self-Governing Authority" would be set up for a five-year transitional period, leading to a permanent settlement based on UN resolutions 242 and 338. The agreement spoke of putting "an end to decades of confrontation and conflict" and of each side recognizing "their mutual legitimate and political rights." For his part, Rabin, speaking on behalf of the Israeli people, said, "We who have fought against you, the Palestinians, we say to you today, in a loud and a clear voice, enough of blood and tears . . . enough!" Other than the peace accord signed with Jordan in 1994, various attempts in the early to mid-1990s promised much but delivered precious little. On November 4, 1995, the peace process was set back immeasurably when an Israeli right-wing extremist, Yigal Amir, assassinated Yitzhak Rabin in Tel Aviv.

An important attempt to revive the peace process was made by President Bill Clinton at Camp David in July 2000. Clinton brought Israeli prime minister Ehud Barak and PLO chairman Yasser Arafat together for negotiations that were intended to move beyond process and generalities and deal at a granular and detailed level. Such an approach had no precedent in prior negotiations. However, the details also revealed just how far apart both sides were. The talks were intended to tackle the following issues: territory, the governance of Jerusalem and the Temple Mount, Palestinian refugees and the right of return, security arrangements, and Israeli settlements.

Israel offered the Gaza Strip, a large part of the West Bank, while keeping major settlement blocks and most of East Jerusalem. Israeli negotiators proposed that the Palestinians be granted administration of, but not sovereignty over, the Muslim and Christian quarters of the Old City, with the Jewish and Armenian quarters remaining under Israeli control. The Israelis also proposed Islamic custodianship of the Temple Mount, with Israel retaining control over the Western Wall. The Israelis were not prepared to accept the unconditional right of Palestinian return but did offer that a total of 100,000 refugees would be allowed to return to Israel on the basis of humanitarian considerations or in the interests of family reunification, and they offered to contribute to a fund for Palestinian refugees. For their part, the Palestinians rejected the idea of accepting a state on the West Bank that was not contiguous, because the land was dotted with Israeli settlements. On the issue of East Jerusalem, Barak had told the Americans that he could not extend to the Palestinians anything more than purely symbolic sovereignty over any part of East Jerusalem. As for security issues, Israel demanded that the Palestinian state be demilitarized, with the exception of its security forces, and that it not be permitted to make alliances without Israeli approval. It also demanded use of Palestinian airspace and the right to deploy troops on Palestinian territory in the event of a military emergency. In the end, neither side could accede to the demands of the other, despite each side claiming that it had offered significant concessions. In the end, both sides charged the other with having caused the talks to fail.

Rabin's suppression of the first intifada (1987–1993) had failed, and a second intifada erupted in 2000. It followed, but was not directly caused by, the visit on September

28, 2000, of General Ariel Sharon and an escort of over 1,000 Israeli police officers to the Temple Mount in Jerusalem, site of the Dome of the Rock and the al-Aqsa Mosque. Sharon's deliberately provocative act, in which he declared that the entire complex would remain under perpetual Israeli control, exacerbated the ordinarily high tensions and suspicions attendant to the politics of the Temple Mount.

The violence of the second intifada exceeded that of the first. Palestinian suicide bombings, a tactic first used in the 1980s, were reintroduced with manifest frequency and devastation. Whereas there were 28 such acts between 1989 and 2000, terrorist organizations such as Hamas, Al-Aqsa Martyrs Brigade, Palestinian Islamic Jihad, and the Popular Front for the Liberation of Palestine carried out 40 suicide bombings in 2001, a number that rose to 47 in 2002. In the month of March that year, there were 15 suicide bombings, an average of one every two days. The normality of daily life was shattered. With the "Passover Massacre" on March 27, 2002, when, during a Passover seder at the Park Hotel in Netanya, 30 attendees, mostly elderly tourists, were killed and 140 were injured, Israel struck back by launching Operation Defensive Shield. The largest military operation in the West Bank since the 1967 Six-Day War, it had the stated goal of stopping the terrorist attacks. With a tremendous show of force, the Israeli military destroyed almost the entire Palestinian public administration and re-established full and exclusive military control over the West Bank, including Areas A and B, which were destined to be handed over to the Palestinian Authority according to the terms of the Oslo II Accord. Palestinian leader Yasser Arafat's compound in the city of Ramallah was almost completely destroyed and placed under siege. The death

toll, including both military and civilian, was about 3,000 Palestinians and 1,000 Israelis, as well as 64 foreigners.

In March 2002, when the violence was at its most intense, yet another peace proposal was issued. This time it was an Arab peace initiative sponsored by Saudi Arabia, the first of its kind. Under this plan, Israel would withdraw to the lines of June 1967, a Palestinian state would be established in the West Bank and Gaza, and there would be a "just solution" of the refugee issue. In return, Arab countries would recognize Israel. This plan, like others before it, was not taken up, because the fundamental issues as discussed at Camp David remain the stumbling blocks and the Saudi plan offered no way around them.

It is against the background of the violence in the spring and summer of 2002 that yet another peace plan was proposed. The Quartet on the Middle East—namely, the United States, the European Union, the United Nations, and Russia—sought to salvage what was left of the "peace process" with a new plan, the so-called Roadmap for Peace. The terms of the three-phased plan called for an end to the violence; a halt to Israeli settlement building; the reform of Palestinian institutions; the Palestinian acceptance of Israel's right to exist; the establishment of a viable, sovereign Palestinian state; and that both parties reach a final settlement on all issues by 2005. In November 2003, the United Nations Security Council endorsed the Roadmap in UN resolution 1515, which called for an end to all violence, including "terrorism, provocation, incitement, and destruction." By the end of 2003, the Palestinian Authority had not taken sincere, let alone successful, measures to prevent Palestinian terrorism, while Israel had neither withdrawn from Palestinian areas occupied since September 28, 2000 (the start date of the second intifada), as called for by the Roadmap, nor frozen settlement expansion. These were some of the most important requirements of Phase I of the Roadmap. With the terms unfulfilled, the Roadmap for Peace stalled permanently.

The second intifada, with its very high civilian death toll, saw Israeli armed forces pressed into serving the politics of the occupation. Once engaged with armies of enemy states, they were now reduced to quashing a popular uprising. The site of well-armed Israeli soldiers attacking Palestinians, many of them stone-throwing children, only worsened the image of Israel in world public opinion, a sentiment that reached a crescendo during the Gaza War of 2014. As early as 1984, Alexander Haig, former secretary of state under US president Ronald Reagan and a staunch supporter of Israel, warned, "The sympathy of world opinion which had always before largely belonged to Israel, was in considerable measure transferred to the Palestinian Arabs. Acts of terrorism against Jews . . . aroused less indignation than Israeli acts of reprisal." Haig's analysis has been proven correct, despite the specter of Palestinian suicide bombings, car rammings, and stabbings targeting Israeli civilians. Such attacks over the next decades engendered widespread revulsion among understandably terrified Israelis, including the most vocal critics of the occupation. In response to the suicide bombings, in June 2002, the government of Ariel Sharon began construction of a wall to separate Palestinian and Israeli populations in the West Bank. The respective names for the wall indicate how deep the divide is between the two peoples. Israelis refer to it as a "security fence," while Palestinians and their supporters call it the "Apartheid Wall."

At the US Naval Academy in Annapolis in 2007, President George W. Bush brought together Israeli prime minister Ehud Olmert and Palestinian Authority president Mahmoud Abbas for peace talks. In addition, representatives from the Quartet on the Middle East and more than a dozen Arab countries attended. This was somewhat of a milestone insofar as those countries did not officially recognize the State of Israel. Olmert offered to relinquish parts of East Jerusalem as part of a broader peace settlement, as well as most of the West Bank. Abbas's counteroffer was to let the Israelis keep 1.9 percent of the West Bank in exchange for land in Israel, and he demanded prior to meeting in Annapolis that all six central issues be debated at the conference: Jerusalem, refugees and right of return, borders, settlements, water, and security. As for Olmert's offer, a broad coalition of Israeli right-wing politicians and groups, foreign Jewish organizations, and Christian Zionist groups objected vehemently. On the Palestinian side, Hamas, which had won parliamentary elections and taken control of the Gaza Strip, was not represented and declared it would not be bound by anything decided. Four days before the parties met in Annapolis on November 27, 2008, Hamas held a demonstration in the Gaza Strip, opposing any peace treaty with Israel. Hamas was backed by Iran, which called for a boycott of the conference. Meanwhile, in the West Bank, large demonstrations against the terms of the Annapolis agreement were quelled violently by the PLO's Fatah militants. In other words, hard-liners on both sides were opposed to concessions and, ultimately, to making peace.

Subsequent to Annapolis, all attempts at arriving at a meaningful peace deal have been opposed by uncompromising extremist groups. Hamas, a terrorist organization, is dedicated to the destruction of Israel and is a purveyor of an implacable brand of antisemitism that combines a deep religious belief that the presence of Jews is a pollutant that threatens the pristine Muslim character of Palestine, a belief first articulated by the founder of the Muslim Brotherhood, Hassan al-Banna, and modern Western antisemitic representations of and beliefs about Jews. Many of these ideas are even part of the Palestinian Authority's educational curriculum, constituting a program of childhood indoctrination and incitement. On the other hand, the settler movement in Israel, in tandem with the Likud government and frequently backed by prominent right-wing Jewish voices in the United States, has become increasingly opposed to making any concessions. Indeed, the Israeli right wing has continued to expand settlement building, and there are increasingly loud calls for the formal annexation of the West Bank. If this were to come to pass and Israel were to not grant those Palestinians full citizenship, then the result would be apartheid and thus the end of Israel as a liberal democracy.

Coming into office in 2008, President Barack Obama, like his predecessors, continued the search for a just resolution to the conflict. Under the guidance of Secretary of State John Kerry, direct negotiations between Israelis and Palestinians continued to take place, the ultimate aim of which was to arrive at an official "final status settlement" to the Israeli–Palestinian conflict. The endgame is known as a "two-state solution," with Israel remaining a Jewish state and the establishment of a state for the Palestinian people. That hoped-for scenario seems little more than a pipe dream at this moment in time. Hamas and its supporters, whether other militant groups or non-violent international organizations, such as BDS (Boycott, Divestment, and Sanctions), insist upon claiming that "from the river to the sea Palestine will be free." In other words,

all of historic Palestine is to become the area that would constitute a Palestinian state. Some advocating this position maintain that Jews could live in this Palestinian state, while others make no such guarantee. Either way, this version of a "one-state solution" would see the end of the State of Israel as a Jewish state. By contrast, the one-state solution proposed by strident voices on the Israeli right considers all of historic Palestine to be part of Israel, and thus Jewish. There is no room for a Palestinian state in this scenario, and in order to avoid the apartheid scenario mentioned earlier, some have even advocated the expulsion of the Palestinians. Driven by fundamentalist religious considerations, rampant nationalism, and blind hatred, neither of these one-state solutions constitutes anything more than a recipe for endless injustice and suffering. The unresolved condition of the Palestinians remains the greatest moral and political challenge facing the state of Israel.

The Question of Israel's Jewishness

The great geopolitical issues confronting Israel parallel the domestic tensions that beset Israeli society. The unstable political system, with its reliance on small parties designed to cater to specific interest groups, reflects the cultural fracturing of the Jewish people in the modern period. Should the state be a religious one? If so, what kind of Judaism ought to reign? The divisions and subdivisions defy easy solutions and do not encourage political compromise. Secular sensibilities and practices, reflective of a free democratic society, whether the desire or need to drive in nearby proximity to ultra-Orthodox neighborhoods on a Sabbath or Jewish holiday, operate public transport on such days, or open stores and the like, present irreconcilable problems. How does a liberal state cater to the demands of those who host gay pride marches in Jerusalem without alienating those for whom such a thing is religiously offensive? By the same token, questions surround the protection offered by the state to the marchers themselves, especially in light of the events of 2015, when Yishai Schlissel, an ultra-Orthodox man, attacked participants in a Jerusalem gay pride march. One of his victims, Shira Banki, died from her stab wounds. Schlissel was convicted of murder as well as six counts of attempted murder, his attack on the parade coming a mere three weeks after his completion of a ten-year sentence for a similar attack in 2005.

Debates over the character of the State of Israel reflect the multiple worldviews formed by Jews in the wake of emancipation, acculturation, and the Holocaust. Even identifying as Jewish has been open to contestation in Israel. Zionism's call for an ingathering of Jews put Israel to the test with the large influx of Ethiopian and Russian Jewish immigrants who came to the country in the 1980s and 1990s. An intransigent rabbinic establishment, with a disproportionately important and powerful role in party politics, was loath to believe that all the immigrants were indeed Jewish, or at least Jewish in a way that satisfied Israeli rabbis. In the end, however, these newcomers have been integrated into Israeli society, and in the case of the nearly 1 million Jews from the former Soviet Union, they have noticeably changed the cultural and political landscape of Israel. Zionism has come to mean different things to different Israelis: from liberal conceptions that envision a secular Jewish state living alongside a Palestinian one to the apocalyptic nationalism of the settlers who believe that building the settlements could hasten the Messianic Age. An immigrant society, Israel has known only radical social change. In its first 50 years of existence, Israel's population

has increased from 600,000 to six million. The pioneering ethos has given way to the reality of life in an industrial, largely urban modern welfare state. The farmer and writer Moshe Smilansky (1874–1953), who believed passionately in the redemptive quality of agricultural work in the national Jewish revival, once decried Tel Aviv's "shopkeeping mentality," which, he said, would lead the residents to "hucksterism, assimilation, and apostasy." Earning an honest living in an urban center never led to apostasy in the Diaspora. It is ironic that he predicted it for Israel. Smilansky was wrong, of course. Tel Aviv has been transformed into the world's biggest and liveliest Jewish city. The country as a whole has followed the global trend of urbanization. In the mid-1950s, 16 percent of Israelis worked in agriculture. By 1995, that figure stood at only 3 percent.

Whether they were refugees or motivated Zionists, nearly all Jews who came to build a new life in Israel had either unwillingly or gladly turned their backs on their countries of origin. But by the 1970s and 1980s, changes were afoot. The impact of multiculturalism and ethnic revival prompted Jews from Morocco to celebrate festivals rooted in their North African heritage, while Hasidic Jews began to make devout pilgrimages back to eastern Europe. The nearly one million secular Jews from the former Soviet Union who had come to Israel as of the year 2000 have their own political parties and Russian-language media. A burgeoning Israeli prose literature is written in Russian; movies often feature foreign languages alongside Hebrew. With its largely Georgian script, Dover Koshashvili's *Late Marriage* (2001) relates the culture clash experienced by Georgian immigrants as they encounter modern, secular Israeli mores, while English, Arabic, and some Hebrew form the dialogue in Eran Kolirin's film *The Band's Visit* (2007), the touching and thoughtful story of an Egyptian police orchestra's trip to Israel. The television series *Shtisel*, a family saga centered on the lives of ultra-Orthodox Jews, contained a significant amount of Yiddish dialogue. The multilingual approach also holds true for popular music, where contemporary Israeli groups, such as the Ethiopian hip-hop ensemble Kafeh Shahor Hazak (Strong Black Coffee), sing in Hebrew and Amharic, as does the Idan Raichel Project. Raichel, of eastern European Jewish heritage, uses music as a means of reinvigorating Ethiopian identity in Israel, observing, "I noticed that immigrants from the Ethiopian community changed their names when they got to Israel. They try to assimilate into Western culture and don't keep their roots." He has urged the youth of that community to "remember that they like hip-hop but they are not from Harlem, they like reggae but they are not Bob Marley. The Ethiopians have a great culture that should be cherished." These diverse expressions of creativity, sometimes rooted in an artist's ethnic pride in Diaspora roots, have become important to the changing nature of Israeli identity and have helped redefine Israeli culture, which, in its transformation, is becoming a multilingual polysystem, reminiscent of but in no way identical to the experimental, multilingual culture of interwar Jewish Poland.

In addition, many citizens and residents of Israel are not Jewish at all and are not acculturated into Zionism. A good number are foreign guest workers, and about 20 percent of Israel's total population is of Arab origin. Many are in solidarity with the Palestinians, frustrated that the equality guaranteed them by law does not always translate into social reality. About 25 percent of Jewish Israelis consider themselves religious, and within that group is a sizeable ultra-Orthodox non-Zionist camp. How does Israel go about inculcating a national ethos into an increasingly heterogeneous, and in some sectors non-Zionist and non-Jewish, population? One of the greatest challenges confronting Israel is reconciling its Jewish character and Theodor Herzl's ideal of a "tolerant modern civil state." The story of Israel's Mizrahim illustrates another sort of social challenge altogether.

Mizrahim in Israel

In the middle of the twentieth century, there were about 900,000 Jews known as *Mizrahim* living in Arab lands, as well as in Iran and Turkey. For a host of reasons, their continued residence in those countries was becoming less and less tenable: Poverty, discrimination, outright persecution, Zionist aspirations, messianic longing, and enticement by the State of Israel and Zionist emissaries all served, to one degree or another, to draw Jews from their homes in the Muslim world and to Israel. The waves of migration extended from the middle to the last third of the twentieth century.

The departure of Jews from the Middle East to Israel is highly politicized. The State of Israel has officially considered them to be refugees and has tied their fate to that of the Palestinians in the attempt to draw an equivalency between the fate of the two groups. Some even refer to a "Jewish *nakba*," using the Arabic word Palestinians use to denote their catastrophe of 1948. Many Mizrahim in Israel, however, recoil at being considered refugees. Yehouda Shenhav, an Israeli sociologist of Iraqi heritage, states:

> Any reasonable person, Zionist or non-Zionist, must acknowledge that the analogy drawn between Palestinians and Mizrahi Jews is unfounded. Palestinian refugees did not want to leave Palestine. Many Palestinian communities were

destroyed in 1948, and some 700,000 Palestinians were expelled, or fled, from the borders of historic Palestine. Those who left did not do so of their own volition. . . . In contrast, Jews from Arab lands came to this country under the initiative of the State of Israel and Jewish organizations. Some came of their own free will; others arrived against their will. Some lived comfortably and securely in Arab lands; others suffered from fear and oppression.

Whatever the impetus for their departure, the mass exodus of Mizrahim to Israel began a slow process of sociological, cultural, political, and religious change that continues to have a profound impact on Israeli society. Whereas in demographic terms Israel had been, at the time of its founding, predominantly Ashkenazic (80 percent), the population is now about evenly split. Although the rate of marriage between the two groups continues to rise, this has not led to a diminution, let alone disappearance, of Ashkenazi and Mizrahi ethnic identities into some sort of mythical melting pot. The reason for this is revealed in sociological studies that show that the offspring of these "mixed marriages" interpret and perceive their identity on the basis of markers such as skin color, last name, and place of residence, all of which tend to reveal which group one belongs to or originated from. Moreover, those "mixed" Israelis who are more educated tend to eventually marry Ashkenazi partners, whereas less well-educated "mixed" Israelis tend to marry Mizrahi partners. According to the sociologist Barbara Okun, "such patterns suggest that intermarriage in Israel does not necessarily reduce ethnic differences in socioeconomic status or the salience of ethnicity among disadvantaged groups."

Once the Mizrahim began to arrive in Israel in very large numbers, the Ashkenazic establishment saw these newcomers as backward "orientals" whose traditions and culture were similar to that of Israel's enemies, the Arabs. The attitude of David Ben-Gurion, the first prime minister of Israel, was typical of the Ashkenazic leadership in the early years of the state: "Those [Jews] from Morocco had no education. Their customs are those of Arabs. . . . The culture of Morocco I would not like to have here. . . . We don't want Israelis to become Arabs." In 1949, an official of the Jewish Agency said of the newcomers, "[We] need to teach them the most elementary things— how to eat, how to sleep, how to wash." The view that they were primitive was widespread. In 1949, an incendiary editorial in the newspaper *Ha'aretz* declared:

> [The North African Jews] . . . have almost no education at all, and what is worse is their inability to comprehend anything intellectual. . . . In the . . . [immigrant absorption] camps you find filth, gambling, drunkenness, and prostitution. . . . [There is also] robbery and theft. Nothing is safe from this anti-social element; no lock is strong enough.

The left-wing author of this piece, Aryeh Gelblum, then took a swipe at the future right-wing prime minister Menachem Begin and his political party:

> Perhaps it is not surprising that Mr. Begin and Herut are so eager to bring all these hundreds of thousands at once—they know that ignorant, primitive and poverty-stricken masses are the best raw material for them and could eventually put them in power.

Like Ashkenazic immigrants, particularly Yiddish-speaking ones, Mizrahim were forced to abandon the language and culture of their previous homes and saw that culture maligned. (The denigration of Yiddish culture had the added dimension of being the culture that most of Israel's leaders grew up in, making the ridicule that much more intimate and vicious.) In Israel's version of the "melting pot," Mizrahim were encouraged to conform to a Western, Ashkenazic, Zionist ideal. Public schools and the army were the main institutions that sought to foster the transformation. Young Mizrahim studied Ashkenazic heritage and historical figures and, in the public religious schools, prayed and practiced Judaism according to Ashkenazic customs.

Mizrahim were also victims of systematic housing, occupational, and social discrimination in a way that Ashkenazi immigrants were not. This has led to wide and deeply entrenched socioeconomic gaps between Mizrahim and Ashkenazim and, more recently, among Ashkenazim. The latter is reflective of global trends of inequality, whereas the former has specific and more localized causes rooted in policies and prejudices encountered by Mizrahim upon arrival in Israel. Researchers identify three principal factors that have contributed to the economic disadvantages experienced by Mizrahim: (1) living far from urban centers of power, (2) a poor economic base when starting out as immigrants, and (3) limited educational opportunities. First, like European immigrants, most of those from Arab lands had been highly urbanized, but when they arrived in Israel, they were often sent to squalid tent cities (ma'abarot), with few amenities. When they moved out of the camps, they were settled in Israel's least-developed areas, far from the country's economic, political, and cultural centers. This naturally inhibited their participation in these three areas of national life, thus severely limiting the chances of full integration. Second, in practical terms, geographic marginalization meant economic deprivation, ensuring that the Israeli middle class was made up almost exclusively of Ashkenazim, while Mizrahim, many of whom came to Israel with craft skills, worked in traditionally low-paying artisanal jobs or became manual laborers; many Ashkenazic immigrants had owned their own businesses in their countries of origin and were more commercially adept or were professionals. In addition, many Ashkenazim received assistance from family who had migrated to Palestine years before, while Jews from the Middle East rarely had such sources of support. Many Holocaust survivors also received compensation payments from the German government, and while incommensurate to the pain and suffering they had experienced, these payments provided a valuable extra source of income and, thus, a "leg up" once they were settled in Israel with its small and underdeveloped socialist economy. Mizrahi immigrants, by contrast, largely arrived with few possessions from Arab states, some of which froze their bank accounts, effectively stealing their money. The absence of negotiated compensation payments from those states such as Holocaust survivors received from Germany further widened the economic gap between Mizrahim and Ashkenazim. Third, along with poor housing and low-paying jobs, the educational system into which many Mizrahim were placed was separate and unequal. Insofar as Ashkenazim tended to enroll in secular, Western schools that channeled students toward higher education,

Mizrahim generally went to schools that led to vocational jobs. The divided educational system has led to a divided and inequitable labor market. The totality of this situation led Yosef Amoyal, a North African Jewish cobbler living in Jaffa, to express the sentiments of many poor Mizrahim in a letter he wrote to Prime Minister Ben-Gurion: "I seem to be a stepson to the Israeli people."

In the face of discrimination, Mizrahim have not been silent. There have been significant protest movements, such as the Wadi Salib riots and the Black Panther movement. The former were a series of street protests that took place in the deprived Haifa neighborhood after which the protests were named. They were sparked by the July 9, 1959, police shooting of a Moroccan Jewish immigrant, Ya'akov Elkarif. Two days later, the riots spread to other cities, as demonstrators protested both the shooting and the ethnic discrimination in Israel more generally.

In January 1971, young Mizrahim, referring to themselves as Black Panthers, began protesting outside the Knesset against a lack of educational and employment opportunities and poor, crowded housing conditions. The demonstrations were ongoing, and throughout the following months, activists demonstrated and posted signs around Jerusalem, proclaiming:

Enough! We are a group of exploited youth, and we are appealing to all
Others who feel they are getting a raw deal.
Enough of not having work;
Enough of having to sleep 10 to a room;
Enough of looking at the big apartments they are building for new immigrants
Enough of having to stomach jail and beatings . . . ;
Enough of broken promises from the government;
Enough of being underprivileged;
Enough discrimination.
How long are we going to keep silent?
We are protesting our right to be treated just as any other citizen in the country.

At the core of the protestors' anger was the claim that while new immigrants were awarded benefits that allowed them to buy new houses and cars and have access to good educations, these things came at the expense of veteran Israelis from the Middle East. Protests reached a climax on May 18, 1971. Known as the "The Night of the Panthers," between 5,000 and 7,000 demonstrators gathered in Jerusalem's Zion Square without police permission. When security forces arrived to disperse the crowd, protestors hurled stones and Molotov cocktails, leading to injuries on both sides; 20 people were hospitalized, and police arrested over 100 activists. Throughout the year, protestors gave speeches addressing "the war of the Black Panthers against the Ashkenazi government." Protests in one form or another have continued. In 1997, a group of intellectuals formed *Hakeshet Hademokratit Hamizrachit* (Mizrahi Democratic Rainbow Coalition) to continue the demand for economic and social equality, better jobs, housing, and education.

The long-running protest movements and insistent demands for equality that continue have had a positive impact. Politicians have been responding, and the socioeconomic divide between Ashkenazim and Mizrahim is narrower in the second and third generations than it was in the first. Still, there is a significant gap in educational opportunities between Ashkenazim and Mizrahim. The chances of Mizrahim attaining a higher education are nearly three times lower than for people belonging to any other ethnic group, and whereas 28.8 percent of second-generation Mizrahim have a university or college degree, the figure for Ashkenazim is 49.6 percent.

In its original formulation, the conflict between Mizrahim and Ashkenazim was about access of opportunity and an end to discrimination. With a new middle class, the improvement of the fortunes of the Mizrahim has also been accompanied by a much greater involvement in politics and culture, and Mizrahim are now part of the governing elite. In the cultural realm, while first-generation Mizrahi immigrants were forced to "tone down" open expressions of the cultures they brought with them and become "Israeli," the second and third generations now demand that Oriental Jewish culture be treated on par with Ashkenazi culture. Still, it cannot be overlooked that while the socio-economic inequalities between Mizrahim and Ashkenazim have improved, their persistence remains a serious social ill.

AT HOME IN AMERICA

After World War II, the United States emerged as home to the world's largest and most influential Jewish community. In the past, Jewish communities enjoyed pre-eminence based upon antiquity of settlement or the intellectual prestige of their rabbinate. By contrast, the American Jewish community derived its strength from a combination of demography and economic power. From a class of poor immigrants, American Jews rose rapidly in the postwar era to become middle- and upper-middle-class professionals and businesspeople. By the 1930s, the proportion of Jews working in industry had fallen to 20 percent, while the percentage engaged in commerce and public sector employment had risen to 60 percent. During the interwar period, the percentage of Jews engaged in the liberal professions rose from 3 to 15 percent. The economic advantages from such a rise up the ladder of success have come as a blessing, but also at considerable social and cultural cost.

After World War I, Jews (and other immigrants) who had poured into the United States since 1881 were still newcomers. Many still had relatives in Europe and maintained strong ties to the older centers of Jewish life. Still, the work of building an "American Jewry" was well underway. The great pressure on second-generation American Jews was to enter into the American mainstream. Many Jews in the interwar period sought to rid themselves of many of the markers that most clearly identified them as Jews. Yiddish was the most visible sign of Jewish difference. The 1930 US census indicated that about 1,750,000 Yiddish speakers lived in the United States. The language was as vibrant as the Jewish community itself. But many Jews began to consider that they had to abandon Yiddish to become American. Public school authorities agreed and were even amenable to the demands of Zionist activists, who succeeded in 1931 in having Hebrew become an elective in New York City's public high schools. Ironically, Hebrew-language instruction accompanied increasing Jewish acculturation.

Interwar American Antisemitism

While the public school was the great vehicle for the integration of immigrants into American life, powerful forces were deeply hostile to Jews (and other minority groups). Antisemitism was widespread throughout America in the first half of the twentieth century and was to be found not just in the ideological baggage of hate groups like the Ku Klux

Klan but also in "respectable" society. Clubs and hotels, such as the Hilton chain, refused admission to Jews, and discrimination was evident in employment and housing. Educational institutions were also restricted. After the rush of Jews into the universities in the 1920s, a backlash followed, aimed at curbing the disproportionate presence of Jewish students on campus, and quotas against Jews were put in place. In some Ivy League universities, these quotas were not removed until the early 1960s. In the 1920s, many of the most stridently antisemitic voices were those of prominent and revered Americans. The most famous was the automobile magnate Henry Ford, whose newspaper *The Dearborn Independent* published *The Protocols of the Elders of Zion*. Ford repeatedly spoke of a "Jewish menace," as did another antisemite from Detroit, an infamous Catholic priest named Father Coughlin, who spewed invective against Jews via his Saturday-afternoon radio program that went out to 15 million listeners per week. Into the 1930s, a slew of nativist associations, such as the Daughters of the American Revolution, the American Coalition of Patriotic Societies, the Veterans of Foreign Wars, the American Legion, and in the 1940s the America First Party, all promoted American isolationism, rejection of the New Deal, anti-Communism, and antisemitism. They also lobbied vigorously for immigration quotas on Jews to remain in force. And they had the political power to do so. By the early 1940s, the American Legion had 1.2 million members, of which 28 were senators and 150 were congressmen. The overall atmosphere was such that it was still possible in that age for a Democratic congressman from Mississippi, John Rankin, to make antisemitic speeches in the House of Representatives and use the pejorative word *kike* to refer to Jews.

It is a curious fact of American life that individuals who were beyond the pale of respectable Jewish society stepped into the fight against antisemitism and became, on this one issue, admired heroes. In the 1930s, notorious Jewish gangsters, such as Meyer Lansky and David Berman, broke up Nazi rallies in New York and Minneapolis, respectively. At the same time, the official Jewish establishment preferred to remain quiet, despite repeated requests from rabbis to get such events closed down. While no legal means could prevent such rallies, on one occasion, New York State judge Nathan Perlman personally asked Meyer Lansky to break up a German American Bund rally. His only stipulation was that no one be killed. Years later, Lansky recalled, "I was a Jew and felt for those Jews in Europe who were suffering. They were my brothers." In Minneapolis, David Berman, who controlled the city's illicit gambling, attacked Nazis at a Silver Shirt Legion rally. At an appointed time, Berman and his men burst into the meeting room and beat up the Nazis. Covered in blood, Berman took the microphone and announced, "This is a warning. Anybody who says anything against Jews gets the same treatment. Only next time it will be worse." Berman and his men did the same thing on two more occasions, after which no more Silver Shirt rallies were held in Minneapolis.

A different Jewish response to Fascism and the intolerance that permeated the political culture in the interwar years led to one of the most remarkable contributions of Jews to American—indeed, to world—culture. In 1934, two impoverished Jewish boys in Cleveland, Jerry Siegel and Joe Schuster, brought to life the fictional comic book character Superman. Siegel imagined the discovery of a young child in the Midwest who was born on a distant planet and possessed extraordinary strength. Superman represents a Jewish assimilationist fantasy. Clark Kent, Superman's alter ego, plays the bespectacled nerd. Thoughtful, shy, and "mild-mannered," he was, despite his all-American demeanor, the weak Jew of common stereotype. But for Siegel and Schuster, he had another side—that of the fearless, invincible Superman, the Man of Steel, who fought for "truth, justice, and the American way." Siegel and Schuster worked on their character for four years before Superman made his initial appearance in the fateful year of 1938, when the Nazi menace increasingly threatened Jews and the rest of the free world alike.

Superman was a patently Jewish creation. On the planet Krypton, from which he hails, Superman was known as Kal-El, Hebrew for "Vessel of God." He shared much with the biblical Moses, who also emerged from obscure origins, was discovered as a child, and rose to defeat injustice in the form of Pharaoh, becoming a fighter for truth, justice, and the Jewish way. Siegel and Schuster may also have drawn from Jewish folklore to create their hero, by reworking the tale of the golem, the mythical figure of sixteenth-century Prague who protected the beleaguered Jews of the ghetto. Prior to World War II, this ancient figure of Jewish folklore was widely popularized in books, onstage, and in films, and Superman's protective instincts and great strength recall certain attributes of the golem.

Postwar America

Jewish marginality began to ease in the wake of World War II, in which 550,000 American Jews served, 10,500 were killed, 24,000 were wounded, and 36,000 were decorated for bravery. After the war, American Jewry experienced significant changes in its relationship to America. Like other returning veterans, American Jews were beneficiaries of the GI Bill, as opportunities to pursue higher education increased. But more specifically, victory over the Nazis and American awareness of the Holocaust began to make overt antisemitic sentiments unacceptable. With few exceptions, the social barriers faced by American Jews in the 1920s and 1930s began to disappear, and Jews ascended the socioeconomic ladder. During the process, Jews also began to enter into the American religious consensus. Antisemitism did not entirely disappear but increasingly took political forms, which further contributed to the Jewish embrace of American values. In the aftermath of the espionage trial of Ethel and Julius Rosenberg, executed for treason in 1953, John Rankin, alluding to Jews, said in the House of Representatives:

[C]ommunism is racial. A racial minority seized control in Russia and in all her satellite countries, such as Poland, Czechoslovakia, and many other countries I could name. They have been run out of practically every country in Europe in the years gone by, and if they keep stirring race trouble in this country and trying to force their communistic program on the Christian people of America, there is no telling what will happen to them here.

In response, American Jews reaffirmed their loyalties to America and to Jewish values and asserted the compatibility of the two. One of the great themes that animate the postwar American Jewish experience is the compatibility of secular, bourgeois identity and the assertion of ethnic identity. While the majority of American Jews were no longer religiously observant, they remained identifiably Jewish. They explored a host of cultural possibilities and modes of political expression in the English language that allowed for intense expressions of Jewishness. Indeed, in the postwar period, English became the most important language, after Hebrew, for the production of modern Jewish culture.

Suburbanization

The period between 1948 and 1967 represents a distinct era in the history of the American Jewish experience. During that time, prosperity and suburbanization fostered the creation of a distinctly American Jewish religiosity. In the 1950s, most Jews, especially those in large cities, continued to live in densely populated Jewish neighborhoods. In New York in particular, Jews in parts of the Bronx and Brooklyn felt as though they were living in a majority-Jewish world. For the most part, Jews socialized among themselves and lived in neighborhoods that provided all the amenities required for Jewish life: kosher butcher shops, bakeries, and delis, as well as bookstores, libraries, synagogues, nursing homes, and welfare agencies.

Increasing prosperity, the racial realignment of cities, and a postwar housing shortage encouraged Jews to leave urban areas and move to the suburbs. Some towns had "gentlemen's agreements," legal covenants or deed restrictions between developers and town officials that contained "no Jews" clauses; as a result, Jews tended to congregate in certain neighborhoods where they were welcome. In these new residential areas, they built elaborate synagogues, marking both their success and their intention to stay. Lacking the density of urban life, these new suburban communities did not offer the vast array of secular amenities

previously available to Jews in cities. Instead, the synagogue became the center of communal life (see the box "Rebelling Against American Jewish Suburbia").

Like suburban churches, the new synagogues were hardly places of traditional devotion. American Jews remained secular and confined worship to life cycle and holiday occasions. Synagogue pews sat empty on most days, despite the fact that over half of American Jews held congregational memberships. Most people joined the suburban synagogues for the educational and even recreational programs they offered. Religious practice had little to do with their choice to join. According to the American sociologist Herbert Gans, the synagogues represented "not a return to the observance of traditional Judaism, but a manifestation in the main of a new symbolic Judaism." American "symbolic Judaism" was fully consistent with a genuine commitment to American civil religion. To that end, American Jews wholeheartedly supported the activities of the American Civil Liberties Union and joined the fight to maintain the separation of church and state and to keep religion out of public schools. In so doing, they considered that what was good for them was also good for America.

The Impact of the Holocaust

In the aftermath of the Holocaust, American Jews dedicated themselves to eradicating radical discrimination, particularly that faced by African Americans. Most saw in the fight a direct link to Jewish experience. In a classic essay, the theologian Abraham Joshua Heschel (1907–1972) wrote:

At the first conference on religion and race, the main participants were Pharaoh and Moses. Moses' words were: "Thus says the Lord, the God of Israel, let My people go that they may celebrate a feast to me." While Pharaoh retorted: "Who is the Lord, that I should heed his voice and let Israel go? I do not know the Lord, and moreover I will not let Israel go." The outcome of that summit meeting has not come to an end. Pharaoh is not ready to capitulate. The exodus began, but it is far from having been completed. In fact, it was easier for the children of Israel to cross the Red Sea than for a Negro to cross certain university campuses. Let us dodge no issues. Let us yield no inch to bigotry, let us make no compromise with callousness.

(See the box "The Jews and the Blues.")

It was not just the vicissitudes of ancient Israel that provided inspiration. The Holocaust was of direct significance in forming Jewish responses to the struggle for civil rights. Rabbi Joachim Prinz, a refugee from Nazism, was one of the official representatives of the Jewish community to the March on Washington in 1963. In his address to the crowd, he said:

> When I was the rabbi of the Jewish community in Berlin under the Hitler regime, I learned many things. The most important thing that I learned under those tragic circumstances was that bigotry and hatred are not the most urgent problem. The most urgent, the most disgraceful, the most shameful and the most tragic problem is silence.

Sometimes, those who refused to remain silent paid a terrible price. Andrew Goodman and Michael Schwerner, two Jewish men from New York, together with African American James Chaney, were murdered in 1964 in Mississippi while investigating the bombing of Black churches. Although Goodman and Schwerner never invoked a connection between being Jewish and their civil rights work, American Jews saw them as symbols of a Jewish commitment to social justice and revered them as heroes and martyrs.

But despite Jewish participation in the civil rights struggle, Black–Jewish relations began to falter toward the end of the 1960s over issues related to education. Jewish groups opposed segregation but feared the consequences of social engineering involved in busing. Most Jewish organizations refused to participate in the 1964 boycott of New York City schools by the civil rights movement, which was calling for action to address racial inequalities in education. The urban riots in the summer of 1965 drove another wedge between the communities. Looting and burning of stores in cities, including New York, Philadelphia, and Los Angeles, resulted in the destruction of Jewish property. In Philadelphia, Jews owned 80 percent of the damaged stores.

In the Los Angeles neighborhood of Watts, Jews owned 80 percent of the furniture stores, 60 percent of the food outlets, and 54 percent of the liquor stores that were vandalized and looted. The owners themselves were not affluent people but small shopkeepers besieged by the mob. Jewish organizations were careful to avoid charges of antisemitism, interpreting the riots as a symptom of the larger racial animosities playing themselves out at that time. Embattled Jewish store owners did not always see it that way.

As early as 1965, Black nationalist leader Stokely Carmichael told Whites, and perhaps especially Jews, given their heavy participation in the civil rights movement, that they were to "get off the bandwagon," for they had no role to play in the struggle of African Americans. In the 1970s, official Jewish opposition to racial

REBELLING AGAINST AMERICAN–JEWISH SUBURBIA

In the late 1950s and early 1960s, a rebellion of sorts against the materialism and perceived shallowness of American Jewish suburban culture began. In particular, writers such as Philip Roth, Saul Bellow, and Bernard Malamud wrote of the immigrant Jewish experience with a certain admiration and then more scathingly examined the next step in the transformation of American Jews, which took place in the suburbs. They lamented the cultural loss that such a process entailed.

While Jews were prevalent in every aspect of the entertainment industry, as performers they were especially drawn to stand-up comedy, and the growing revolt against postwar authority and tradition provided grist for the Jewish comedian's mill. Many got their starts in the Jewish holiday resorts of the Catskills in Upstate New York. There, the humor was deeply and openly Jewish. Later, television and Hollywood beckoned, and although Jewish themes were not always part of the material of Jewish comedians, biting social criticism and parody became hallmarks of artists such as Mel Brooks, Larry Gelbart, Carl Reiner, Neil Simon, Woody Allen, and Lenny Bruce. The critical, comedic voice that paid particular attention to language, deploying it in the service of "observational humor," was indelibly associated with Jews.

Lenny Bruce (1925–1966), one of the most important Jewish comedic voices, was born Leonard Alfred Schneider. Early in his career, he was found guilty on obscenity charges but refused to censor his act, wanting to shock and offend with words the America that he held to be prudish and hypocritical. Bruce was, for example, unsparing in his criticism of politics, religion, and the justice system. He also reflected on Jewish assimilation in America by blurring lines of ethnic difference. In one of his most beloved sketches, he praised aspects of gentile culture that he found to be Jewish and was dismissive of Jews he identified as having strayed too far from their roots. In so doing, he both celebrated and ridiculed American and postwar Jewish culture:

Now I neologize Jewish and goyish.

DIG: I'm Jewish. Count Basie's Jewish. Ray Charles is Jewish. Eddie Cantor's goyish.

B'nai B'rith is goyish; Hadassah, Jewish. Marine corps—heavy goyim, dangerous.

Kool-Aid is goyish. All Drake's cakes are goyish. Pumpernickel is Jewish, and, as you know, white bread is very goyish. Instant potatoes—goyish.

Black cherry soda's very Jewish. Macaroons are very Jewish—very Jewish cake. Fruit salad is Jewish. Lime jello is goyish. Lime soda is very goyish. . . .

If you're Italian or Puerto Rican and live in New York or any other big city, you're Jewish. If you're Jewish and live in Butte, Montana, you're going to be goyish even if you're Jewish.

Of course, not everyone has sought to issue such devastating critiques, but rather, in silent recognition of what Lenny Bruce was driving at, some Jews have attempted to reinvigorate American Jewish life and impart to it a meaningfulness that they believed was lost with the process of suburbanization. This has taken many forms— day schools, summer camps, "birthright" trips to Israel, learning Hebrew, a vast Jewish Internet presence, new journals of Jewish opinion, the growth of ultra-Orthodoxy, and the Jewish Renewal movement, among them. One of the most interesting developments has been the creation of what the cultural critic Jeffrey Shandler has called "postvernacular language and culture," by which he refers to the multifarious ways Yiddish continues to provide meaning and purpose even to people who do not have command of the language. He observes that Yiddish serves as "a language of study, as an inspiration for performers and their audiences, as a literature increasingly accessible through translation, as a selective vocabulary sprinkled through the speech of Jews and non-Jews, and as an object of affection." What may have once been an ideological commitment to the language in the immediate postwar years has been transformed into a more positive and creative application of

Yiddish, intended to recapture some of what was lost through genocide, acculturation, and suburbanization. But it constitutes more than an attempt to keep alive that which can never be fully resuscitated. Instead, "postvernacular Yiddish" is a vehicle for entirely new explorations and experimentation in Jewish culture.

Across the United States after World War II, Jews began to leave the deteriorating inner cities for the suburbs. By 1957, approximately 50,000 of Philadelphia's Jews, one-fifth of the total Jewish community, had moved to the northern suburbs. Many of the city's major Jewish institutions were also relocating, among them the Home for the Jewish Aged, the Einstein Medical Center, and Gratz College. By 1965, ten Reform and Conservative congregations were established in and around the suburb of Elkins Park. One of the synagogues to relocate to this area was Temple Beth Sholom, a congregation originally founded in 1919. In 1954, the congregation's rabbi, Mortimer J. Cohen, commissioned the distinguished architect Frank Lloyd Wright to build a new synagogue. Cohen wrote to Wright:

> Our hope is to make Beth Sholom (House of Peace) a symbol for generations to come of the American and the Jewish spirit, a House of Prayer in which all may come to know themselves better as children of the living God.

The complicated design—Cohen wanted a sunken *bimah* (reader's platform) that recalled the passage from Psalms 130, "Out of the depths I cry to Thee, O Lord!" while Wright wanted the building to soar to 100 feet (zoning laws permitted a thrust of only 65 feet). The grand conceptions meant delays and spiraling costs. The only synagogue ever designed by Wright, Beth Sholom finally opened in 1959. While it was an exceptional example of modernist, ecclesiastical architecture, the temple also typified the large, postwar suburban synagogues whose designs owed very little to history and promised a new beginning for postwar Jewish communities. Beth Sholom's main sanctuary seats 1,020 worshipers, while the Sisterhood Sanctuary, located downstairs, replicates the main sanctuary on a smaller scale and seats 242. The building's structure is pyramid-shaped, with three steel tripod girders supporting steeply inclined walls. The design allows for complete freedom from internal support columns and thus provides an entirely open space. The lattice walls of the sanctuary are composed of translucent layers of wire, glass, and plastic. In daylight hours, the glass walls allow natural sunlight to fill the sanctuary, while at night, artificial lighting permits the entire building to glow from within. Wright, who passed away just before the building was completed, described Beth Sholom as a "luminous Mount Sinai."

Figure 6.2   Exterior of Beth Sholom Congregation, Philadelphia.

quotas in university admissions and hiring also further soured relations between the two groups. Later, public expressions of hostility from two prominent African Americans set off a firestorm. In 1984, Jesse Jackson referred to New York City as "Hymietown," while Nation of Islam leader Louis Farrakhan called Judaism a "gutter religion." Farrakhan continues to give virulently antisemitic speeches and interviews. In 1991, the incident in which an African American child, Daren Cato, was accidentally hit and killed by a car driven by a Hasid in Brooklyn led to a full-scale riot—Jews called it a pogrom—in which Yankel Rosenbaum, a visiting yeshiva student from Australia, was stabbed and killed. A widening socioeconomic gap between Blacks and Jews drove them further apart. While both groups continued to publicly voice a similar commitment to ethnic self-assertion and shared aspirations to "social justice," they tended to pursue these goals more separately than together.

While it is true that in the 1960s American Jews began to invoke the Holocaust on behalf of the civil rights crusade, Holocaust memory had begun to play a major role within American Jewish self-understanding as early as the 1950s.

Poems and prayers of remembrance for European Jewry were incorporated into liturgy across the Jewish denominational divide. A Haggadah published in New York in 1950 included a picture of Auschwitz and another of Treblinka in the "Pour Out Your Wrath" section of the Passover seder service. Public monuments to the recent European tragedy were erected as well. Thanks to the Synagogue Council of America, new synagogues that opened in the suburbs throughout the 1950s received ritual objects salvaged from Europe. New communities thus attempted to form direct links to ancient communities that no longer existed. Warsaw ghetto memorial

events were held all over America, and Jewish summer camps chose the midsummer fast of Tisha B'Av, which commemorates the destruction of the two Temples in Jerusalem, to teach children about the recent horrors in Europe.

Just as the Holocaust spurred American Jews' commitment to homegrown civil rights, they discovered another civil rights issue that needed addressing—the plight of Soviet Jewry. With a nagging sense that the United States and American Jews in particular had perhaps not done all they could have done for European Jewry during the war, they now refused to sit idly while another European Jewish community suffered discrimination. The "Free Soviet Jewry" movement became a rallying cry for American Jews, at both the individual and institutional levels. By supporting the desire of many Soviet Jews to emigrate, the campaign also demonstrated the community's loyalties in the Cold War, especially important given the extent to which American Jews identified with the political left, which often brought them under suspicion.

In the 1980s, as the remaining victims of the Holocaust were rapidly beginning to pass away, survivors—Eli Wiesel among them—began to express fears that the memory of the Holocaust would fade away with the eyewitnesses. This has proven to be incorrect. The Six-Day War invigorated Jewish self-consciousness by making American Jews aware of the precariousness of Israel's existence. Its vulnerability occasioned public reflection on the extermination of European Jewry and inspired the ongoing work of commemoration. The aging of the survivors and the multicultural environment of the 1970s and the 1980s that celebrated group difference contributed to propelling the Holocaust to a central place in American Jewish culture. After the fall of Communism in 1989, visits by Jewish groups, especially of young people, to the

THE JEWS AND THE BLUES

A tradition of cultural affinity between Jews and African American culture long predated the advent of the civil rights era. Cultural icons, such as the Russian immigrant Irving Berlin (1888–1989), were especially drawn to ragtime music, even though they did not fully understand the great Scott Joplin's syncopated rhythms. Berlin even wrote songs for black performers. In Hollywood, Al Jolson (1886–1950), who was born in the village of Srednik in Lithuania, appeared in the first talking picture, *The Jazz Singer* (1927). Performing in blackface, Jolson played the son of a cantor—which he was in real life—caught between his father's wish that he follow in his pious musical footsteps and his own wish to sing black music. In an era when singing in blackface elicited far different reactions than is the case today, Jolson was warmly embraced by African Americans. In addition to his close and lifelong personal relationships with African Americans, he was a staunch and vocal advocate of breaking down barriers on Broadway for black performers. When he died suddenly in 1950, some 20,000 people attended his funeral at Temple Israel on Hollywood Boulevard, among them Noble Sissle, the great jazz composer and bandleader, who was the official representative of the Negro Actor's Union. Jolson is buried at Hillside Memorial Park, the elaborate monument at his grave site designed by America's foremost African American architect, Paul Revere Williams. At Jolson's grave, a six-pillar marble structure is topped by a dome, next to which is a three-quarter-size bronze statue of Jolson resting on one knee, arms outstretched, in the familiar pose he used to sing his hit song "Mammy." The inside of the dome features a huge mosaic of Moses holding the Ten Commandments and identifies Jolson as "The Sweet Singer of Israel."

George Gershwin (1898–1938) was deeply influenced by African American music and, in 1924, penned the classic *Rhapsody in Blue*. He followed this with a string of spirituals, rags, and blues, including the American original "I Got Rhythm." The year 1935 saw the premiere of his play *Porgy and Bess*, and Gershwin so perfectly captured the feel and cadence of black life and music in that production that the highly critical *New York Herald-Tribune* review of the play called it "a piquant but highly unsavory stirring-up together of Israel [and] Africa."

Jews also played prominent roles as managers of black artists, when hardly any white promoters dared to cross color lines. Ella Fitzgerald, John Coltrane, Miles Davis, Louis Armstrong, and B. B. King all had Jewish managers. A most significant development took place in the late 1950s, when two Jewish immigrant brothers from Poland, Leonard and Phil Chess, founded Chess records in Chicago. At this hallowed institution, they recorded blues giants, such as John Lee Hooker, Elmore James, Bo Diddley, Etta James, Willie Dixon, Buddy Guy, Howlin' Wolf, and Muddy Waters. Chuck Berry also recorded for Chess in 1950. Many of these performers had no record contracts at the time that the Chess brothers signed them and were poor and little-known outside Chicago's South and West Side club scene. The Chess brothers not only recorded music that suited black tastes but also introduced the most authentic modern American musical tradition to white audiences and performers the world over. What in large measure allowed for the British invasion of the 1960s, spearheaded by the Beatles, the Rolling Stones, and virtuosos such as Eric Clapton, came courtesy of the precious Chess recordings that made their way to England, allowing the young Englishmen to learn from their idols.

In the 1960s, Jewish performers, such as Bob Dylan, were deeply influenced by the blues, again helping introduce an American art form to white American audiences. Jewish musical promoters were also in the forefront of breaking down racial barriers in the 1960s. At the famed Fillmore West in San Francisco and Fillmore East in New York, America's leading concert promoter, Bill Graham, himself a child survivor of the Holocaust, invited black artists such as Jimi Hendrix, Albert King, and B.B. King to take the stage with white performers at a time when most venues in America were still segregated.

death camps in Poland have intensified the public culture of Holocaust awareness among American Jews.

In the immediate postwar period, Holocaust memorialization was conducted by and for Jews. Beginning in the 1970s, however, Holocaust awareness merged into American culture. As American Jews became integrated into public life, many holding elected office, their fellow non-Jewish politicians began to attend Holocaust memorial events. The widely watched 1978 NBC miniseries titled *Holocaust* further intensified American public interest in the event, as did Steven Spielberg's 1993 film *Schindler's List*. The diary of Anne Frank is as well-known to American schoolchildren as any diary by an American citizen. Classes on the Holocaust in high schools and universities are commonplace throughout the United States, as is the phenomenon of Holocaust survivors, an ever-dwindling minority, publicly recounting their experiences to students. Thanks to these transformations, Holocaust memory has taken on an American cast, exemplified by the opening on the Washington Mall of the United States Holocaust Memorial Museum in 1993. What the Americanization of the Shoah will mean for the way the Holocaust is remembered remains to be seen.

American Jewish Cultures

Since the 1960s, the prominence of American Jews in fields such as politics, journalism, entertainment, business, and academia has been so disproportionate that it has become commonplace. Prohibitions or inhibitions against Jews occupying important positions in the public life of the nation are no longer an issue. Senator Joseph Lieberman's run for the office of vice president in 2000 and Bernie Sanders's campaign in 2016 to be the Democratic candidate for the presidency are

a testament to that. The culture or religion of American Jews no longer constitutes a barrier to integration. Film, television, and theater address Jewish themes with such regularity that non-Jewish audiences can see them as universal or even uniquely American. The Jewish aspect of cultural creations does not hinder their massive appeal. High school students across America read Elie Wiesel's Holocaust memoir, *Night*, while the American public warmly received television programs such as *Seinfeld* with several identifiably Jewish characters. NBC initially hesitated to pick up *Seinfeld* for fear that it might be "too Jewish," and then it was delighted to have been proven wrong by the extent to which "Middle America" loved the program.

American Judaisms

Secular Jewish culture, from nineteenth-century Yiddish theater to Hollywood films and television, has outpaced religious innovation on American soil. Institutionally, the three denominations of Judaism—Reform, Conservative, and Orthodox—predominate. While all three have undergone significant changes in America, all trace their aesthetic and doctrinal origins to Europe. Reconstructionism represents one of the few attempts to develop a new form of distinctively American Judaism. Its founder, Mordecai Kaplan (1881–1983), emigrated from Vilna to the United States with his family in 1889. An observant Jew and a graduate of the Jewish Theological Seminary, Kaplan grew increasingly disenchanted with Orthodoxy. He articulated his critique of American Judaism in a work titled *Judaism as a Civilization* (1934), where he rejected the notion of supernatural revelation as a fundamental basis for Judaism and argued instead that Jewishness was a civilization. While he identified beliefs and practices as important to Judaism, Kaplan also assigned great significance to language, culture, literature, ethics, art, history, social organization, symbols, and customs. Kaplan's anthropological approach dovetailed with the needs of second- or third-generation American Jews, moving toward "symbolic Judaism." Kaplan's effort to "reconstruct" or revive Judaism along ethnic lines proved remarkably prescient. Although Reconstructionism failed to win the sympathies of American Jewry to any appreciable extent, perhaps because its stress on Jewish ethnicity alienated American Jews who were seeking acceptance as Americans, Kaplan's idea of the synagogue as a social and cultural center, offering a variety of cultural and educational programs, has won wide acceptance among all streams of Judaism. Kaplan, an egalitarian, also instituted the bat mitzvah ceremony for girls. His daughter Judith was the first celebrant in 1922. This innovation entered Jewish practice the world over.

Kaplan's concerns for the future of Judaism were grounded in his fears of secularization's negative impact on Jews. As early as 1920, he saw American Judaism as stagnant and claimed that its creative developments were initiatives of eastern European Jewish immigrants. "Judaism in America," he wrote, "has not given the least sign of being able to perpetuate itself." While such dire predictions did not come true, American Jewish leaders, especially since the 1960s, have continually expressed their concerns and fears that assimilation is ravaging the Jewish community. They point to Jewish religious and cultural illiteracy, the very small numbers of children attending Jewish day schools, the fact that perhaps half of America's Jews have never been to Israel, the decline in giving to Jewish charities, and above all, the 50 percent intermarriage rate in 2004, which is a dramatic rise from about 9 percent in 1964.

The scholarship on intermarriage takes an ambivalent view of the numbers. There are pessimists and optimists as regards the historical significance of such trends. Intermarriage is a sign of the decline of suspicion and hostility on both sides of the religious divide—hence the ambivalence. Where once religious belief and communal attitudes led Jewish parents to object to intermarriage and even perform the ritual of sitting *shivah* (the custom of mourning the dead), parental interest is now principally concerned with the individual happiness of children. The personal shame and communal stigma that once accompanied intermarriages have largely disappeared. Mutual acceptance, in the most intimate sense, has broken down traditional barriers.

Jewish religious leaders have met the challenges of intermarriage in various ways. The Reform movement has taken the most proactive stance in mounting outreach programs to intermarried couples and by easing conversion. Some Reform rabbis have even performed wedding ceremonies in tandem with Christian clergy to satisfy the needs of both parties to the marriage. This has elicited cries of "assimilation" and "betrayal" from Conservative and Orthodox circles, and even those within the Reform movement have been split over this practice. In 1983, in response to the increasing number of children from mixed marriages, the leaders of the Reform denomination undertook to accept as Jewish anyone who had had a Jewish education and had at least one Jewish parent, mother or father. They also permitted non-Jewish spouses to become synagogue members and to participate in the life of the congregation. In making these changes, American Reform rabbis have made repeated reference to both the social reality of contemporary American Jewish life and the continued impact of the

Holocaust. The Jewish people, they argue, are not in a demographic position to turn anyone away. Reconstructionists typically sided with the Reform movement on this issue, whereas Orthodox Jews have held to the ancient prohibitions against intermarriage. Jews who identified with the conservative movement, as often happens, found themselves somewhere in the middle, not condoning intermarriage but recognizing that it does not necessarily manifest the desire to reject Judaism. Rather, it is a consequence of an open society in which there are no barriers to dating people of a different or of no faith. Indeed, people can often fall in love for reasons that do not reflect a larger cultural or philosophical position. The Conservative movement thus neither officially promotes nor rejects intermarriage. Some congregations have adopted a policy of *kiruv*, drawing intermarried couples nearer without explicitly endorsing such unions. Conversions to Judaism have also changed the nature of American Jewish life and have increased in number together with the rise of intermarriages. In 1954, about 3,000 non-Jews converted to Judaism. At the end of the 1970s, the rate of conversion was about 10,000 per year.

Between 1967 and 2000, American Jewry entered a new period of its postwar history. In the last 30 years of the twentieth century, American Jews tended toward two opposing poles in terms of their Jewish identities. Many developed intense commitments to Jewish culture and engaged in the search for continuity. Many others became more secular and drew further away from organized Jewish life. The latter development has given rise to expressions of great alarm within the Jewish community about the future of American Jewry. Fears about biological continuity have been a feature of the modern Jewish experience. Before World War I, Jewish leaders and

demographers in western and central Europe repeatedly expressed fears that assimilation and a very low birth rate were leading to the demise of Jewish communities. Recent American Jewish expressions of this phenomenon fit into these long-held concerns.

While religious practice among most American Jews remains relatively weak, the Jewish community possesses great reserves of institutional strength and cultural creativity. Unrivalled anywhere else in the Diaspora is the commitment to secular Jewish studies at the highest educational levels. In the 1960s, universities all over America began to fulfill the dreams of the nineteenth-century founders of *Wissenschaft des Judentums* producing cutting-edge research while teaching about Jewish civilization in all its forms to packed classrooms of students from a dizzying array of backgrounds. Secular education is also found in bastions of modern Orthodoxy. Yeshiva University in New York maintains a commitment to observant Jewish practice that is compatible with secular education.

While synagogue membership and attendance at Reform and Conservative congregations may be on the decline, ultra-Orthodoxy, by contrast, began to exhibit extraordinary growth after World War II. These Jewish communities were especially devastated during the war, given that their inability to pass as non-Jews and their lack of close contacts among neighboring gentiles meant that most were unable to be hidden. After the war, the remnants of Hasidic communities began to rebuild life in Israel, Britain, Canada, France, Belgium, Australia, and especially the United States. The postwar story of American Hasidism runs counter to the standard narrative of Jewish acculturation and suburbanization. Instead, Hasidic communities dedicated themselves to rebuilding their numbers and remaining apart from American culture through communal insularity and scrupulous observance of religious ritual to an extent rarely seen before the war.

The postwar growth of American ultra-Orthodoxy was led by the heads of the three major Hasidic courts: Satmar, led by Joel Teitelbaum (1887–1979); Lubavitcher, whose leader was Menachem Mendel Schneerson (1902–1994); and Bobover, the leading figure of which was Shlomo Halberstam (1907–2000). Under their leadership—and that of smaller sects, such as the Belzer, Vishnitzer, Gerer, Skverer, and Bratslaver—the number of American Hasidim has increased significantly. Only a few thousand made their way to the United States after the war. By the year 2000, between 7 and 9 percent of American Jews were Orthodox, and probably half of them, about 350,000, were Hasidim. This constitutes about half the world's estimated 700,000 Hasidim. The growth rate of American Hasidim is approximately 5 percent per year, far in excess of that of secular Jews, which means a doubling of their population every 15 years.

The Hasidic communities in postwar America avoided assimilation by retaining Yiddish for daily speech, maintaining traditional dress—one group can be distinguished from another by such markers as hats, pants, shoe style, and even sock color—and living in densely packed, mostly urban communities, such as Borough Park, Crown Heights, and Williamsburg in Brooklyn, New York, and in Monsey and New Square in Rockland County, New York. In those communities, a vast network of schools, social service agencies, and voluntary associations provides for community members from cradle to grave.

Beyond agreeing upon the need to avoid American culture, Hasidic communities have differed in terms of their relations with the outside world. While most have been extremely insular, especially when it comes to contacts with the rest of American Jewry, Lubavitch or Chabad Hasidism vigorously promotes its form of Judaism among secular Jews. The community sends emissaries out to the wider world, approaching Jewish men on the street to lay tefillin and women to light Shabbat candles, driving around in "mitzvah-mobiles" and beckoning to Jews via megaphones, and instituting Hannukah lighting ceremonies in public squares and even the White House. Especially active among young Jews, by the 1990s, Lubavitch had established more than 900 so-called Chabad Houses on American college campuses, as well as others in 70 different countries. (Even Reform Judaism's late twentieth-century outreach program to unaffiliated Jews owes some measure of inspiration to the success of such programs run by Chabad.) Chabad has also been extremely effective in establishing a vast publishing industry, with Yiddish newspapers, textbooks, and novels, and a communications network, with radio, television, movies, and Internet sites.

In part due to Chabad's success, many among the Lubavitcher rebbe's followers genuinely believed that he was the messiah. For many critics, this was idolatry, some going so far as to claim that Chabad Judaism is Christological in nature. The claims and counterclaims about the Lubavitcher rebbe, as well as the difficulties of leadership succession among both Satmar and Bobover Hasidim, have fostered deep divisions and intense acrimony within ultra-Orthodoxy. In part, this is a consequence of the growth and success of Hasidism in the United States, where communities, now in the tens of thousands, are far more difficult to manage and control than their small predecessors, and even though the ultra-Orthodox world is plagued by genuine poverty, the economic success of some Hasidic communities, such as Chabad, adds a further dimension to various power struggles. In some measure, centralized leadership is giving way to centrifugal forces.

Elsewhere, independent prayer and study groups, new synagogues, and secular Jewish cultural activities have found grassroots support across the United States. Some of them are syncretistic, combining Eastern traditions, such as meditation and chanting, with Judaism, or incorporating Hasidic singing into otherwise secular services. A well-established alternative synagogue in Berkeley, California, called the Aquarian Minyan, was established in 1974. For the High Holidays, it offers "services [that] are co-created and led by members and friends of the Aquarian Minyan community [and] . . . will combine innovative and traditional approaches, including participatory liturgy, music, chanting, meditation, and movement."

The sexual politics of the 1960s also ushered in innovations to American Judaism. Jewish women, an important constituency of second-wave feminism, demanded equal religious rights. In 1972, Sally Priesand (b. 1946) became Reform Judaism's first ordained female rabbi; she was followed in 1974 by Sandy Sasso (b. 1947), who became the first ordained female Reconstructionist rabbi; and finally, in 1985, Amy Eilberg (b. 1954) became the first woman to graduate with rabbinical ordination from the Conservative movement's Jewish Theological Seminary in New York. At an informal level, many new changes and innovations were appearing thanks to feminism. New Jewish rituals were developed, specifically tied to life cycle events, such as giving birth to daughters or menstruation. In some quarters, Rosh Chodesh (new moon) was adopted as a special time for women to study texts and perform Jewish rituals particular to them. Many of the demands put forth by Jewish feminists appeared in the pages of *Lilith*,

a Jewish feminist magazine founded in 1973. Even Orthodox communities have felt the impact of such changes, and women's study groups and access to higher education have become commonplace. Reflecting a desire to finally make their voices heard, gay Jews, who long felt shut out of communal life, began to establish separate synagogues in the 1980s. A perfect microcosm of the broader Jewish community, these congregations ranged from liberal to the liturgically conservative. The place of gay Jews in the ritual life of American synagogues remains a controversial issue in Conservative congregations, is accepted in Reform temples, and is anathema in Orthodox circles.

In contrast to these aforementioned progressive strains, an extreme right-wing Jewish politics was also born in the 1960s. As American Jews became more solidly middle-class, thousands of poor Jews who did not have the means to move to the suburbs remained in the inner cities. Inspired by militant black nationalists and protective of what he called the "little Jews" stranded in hostile neighborhoods, Rabbi Meir Kahane (1932–1990) founded the Jewish Defense League (JDL) in 1968, with its motto "Never Again," a reference to the Holocaust. An aggressive alarmist, Kahane castigated the major American Jewish organizations for not doing all they could to protect American Jews from "another Holocaust." Kahane's vigilantes patrolled the streets with baseball bats and lead pipes, threatening and sometimes carrying out violent acts against those who they thought threatened Jews. In response to the JDL, American Jewish welfare agencies began to take notice of the "little Jews" and engaged in a concerted effort to financially assist Jews who had been left out of the "American dream." The JDL also demonstrated outside the United Nations, Soviet consulates, and Russian artistic performances

Figure 6.3 Logo of Justice for Jews from Arab Countries (JJAC).

on behalf of Soviet Jewry. Its activities presented a model of Jewish political militancy that was novel in the American setting. Kahane settled in Israel and, in 1984, won a seat in the Knesset representing the Kach party, which he founded in the early 1970s. Under Kahane, Kach proposed compensating Arabs to leave Israel and expelling those who refused to do so. Branded as racist by the Knesset, Kach was banned from participating in the 1988 elections. In 1990, an Egyptian militant assassinated Kahane in New York City.

Immigration continues to transform American Jewry. In the period between 1967 and 2000, new Jewish immigrants arrived from Syria, Morocco, Iran after 1979, and Russia.

As was the case in Europe in the interwar period, the rise of Arab nationalism and Muslim fundamentalism in the 1930s and 1940s led to increasing hostility toward Jews. This was exacerbated by the founding of the State of Israel in 1948. At this point, Jewish life

became all but impossible in Arab lands, and approximately 800,000 Jews from across the Middle East left voluntarily, fled, or were displaced and dispossessed. The JJAC, founded in 2002, is a coalition of major American Jewish communal organizations. Its mandate is "[t]o ensure that justice for Jews from Arab countries assumes its rightful place on the international political agenda and that their rights be secured as a matter of law and equity." To that end, the JJAC seeks to educate the public on the historic plight of Jews who were displaced from Arab countries and to advocate for redress after 1991. Native Jews regarded it as their responsibility to integrate the new arrivals and provided considerable community resources for their absorption. While not all the new immigrants wanted to be incorporated into Jewish communities, the presence of so many newcomers added great diversity to religious and neighborhood life. Brighton Beach in Brooklyn became "Little Odessa," while the Pico-Robertson section of Los Angeles, a densely populated enclave of Persian Jews, among others, has acquired all the markings of an authentic, urban Jewish neighborhood.

All over the United States, but especially in New York City and Los Angeles, there is also a very large expatriate Israeli community. They tend to have fewer formal communal affiliations than other immigrant Jewish groups, preferring their own social networks. The sheer number (we do not have precise figures) has had a significant impact on Israel itself, and not just in terms of their absence. Whereas other groups of Jewish immigrants are, for the most part, lost to their home countries forever, the impact of Israeli immigrants, particularly those in the United States, has served to strengthen ties between Israelis and the Diaspora, as vast numbers of them now have relatives living in America.

American Jews and the State of Israel

After 1967, American Jews overwhelmingly defined their Jewishness through support for Israel. At that time, significant numbers of American Jews actively opposed the war in Vietnam and were disproportionately represented in radical student politics. Like others on the Left, they voiced their opposition in terms of their disavowal of "American imperialism." Generally supportive of countries engaged in the postcolonial struggle, American Jews admired Israel as a small heroic bastion of democracy. Israel was seen as a David to its neighboring Goliaths, and not just by Jews, but also by most people on the political left. But in the summer of 1967, the rise of Holocaust consciousness and the continued reverberations in the aftermath of the Eichmann trial produced support for Israel as a specifically Jewish cause. M. Jay Rosenberg, a left-wing radical who had only the most marginal identification with Jewish culture, recalled the impact of the Six-Day War:

> On Monday June fifth [1967], I awoke to the news that Israel was at war. . . . I knew that my concern was not as a leftist or even, at that moment, as an American. I did not fear for Israel because she was "the only democracy in the Middle East" or because she was a "socialist enclave" surrounded by "feudal sheikdoms." I cared because Israel was the Jewish state and I was a Jew. Her anguish was mine, the anguish of my people. I would not forget that.

Rosenberg's view reflected those of many other American Jews. People felt an intimate bond with the fate and future of Israel. This intensified after the Yom Kippur War of 1973, when Israel became increasingly dependent on US aid. American Jewish political groups began to calculate their interests in terms of the impact of certain American policies on Israel and lobbied accordingly. Consensus stifled debate within the American Jewish community regarding Israel's policies, and Israel's embattled status was repeatedly invoked to inhibit critical Jewish voices and dissent. In the early 1980s, progressive groups such as Breira ("Option" or "Choice"); its successor, New Jewish Agenda; and American Friends of Peace Now were hounded and decried from within the Jewish world.

The 1982 Lebanon War was a watershed in the way Israelis began to reassess aspects of state policy. It exercised a similar impact on American Jews. Just as Israelis spoke out against their government, American Jews voiced similar opinions publicly. Young Jews, especially on university campuses, split from the Jewish establishment's uncritical support of Israel. Out of deep and abiding concern, increasing numbers of American Jews expressed objections to the occupation and to the settler movement. That many of the settlers, including some of the most radical, were American added another level of intensity to the protest. American Jewry split over Israel even more bitterly after the Oslo Accords of 1993. While the majority waxed enthusiastic about the prospects for peace, symbolized by the famous handshake between Yitzhak Rabin and Yasser Arafat on the White House lawn, others could not accept the necessary diplomatic accommodations.

While the relationship between American Jewry and Israel remains strong, it is complex, with trends and undercurrents that are reflective not merely of the relationship itself but of larger changes in the political and cultural outlook of American Jewry. Similarly, just as America and American Jewry have changed radically since World War II, Israel has changed dramatically as a country since its founding in 1948. With it, Israel's attitude toward American Jewry and the Diaspora more generally has likewise shifted.

In order to assess the relationship between American Jews and Israel, it is necessary to have a fundamental picture of the sociological and cultural character of American Jewry. It is difficult to generalize about a population of over 5 million, but data gleaned from reputable sources gives us a fairly clear picture and provides us with the best means of examining the relationship. According to an extensive survey undertaken by the Pew Research Center in 2013, American Jews overwhelmingly claim to be proud of being Jewish and feel that they have a strong sense of belonging to the Jewish people. However, 22 percent describe themselves as having no religion. This figure becomes even more revealing when the survey's results are analyzed by generation. Fully 93 percent of Jews in the aging Greatest Generation identify as Jewish on the basis of religion, while only 7 percent describe themselves as having no religion. By contrast, among the youngest generation of American Jewish adults, the millennials, 68 percent identify as Jews by religion, while a full 32 percent describe themselves as having no religion and identify as Jewish on the basis of ancestry, ethnicity, or culture. Compared with Jews by religion, those who identify as having no religion are also less likely to be connected to Jewish organizations or be raising their children Jewish. Reform Judaism is the largest Jewish denomination in the United States, claiming the allegiance of 35 percent of American Jews, while 18 percent identify with Conservative Judaism, 10 percent with Orthodox Judaism, and 6 percent with a variety of smaller groups, such as the Reconstructionist and Jewish Renewal movements.

At a most basic level, this portrait of American Jewry has consequences for its relationship to Israel. There is no doubt that most American Jews still support Israel. According to the survey, about 70 percent of those Jews surveyed say they feel either very attached (30 percent) or somewhat attached (39 percent) to Israel. This figure remains unchanged from the year 2001. In addition, 43 percent of Jews have been to Israel, with 23 percent having gone more than once. (About 40 percent of Israelis have visited the United States at least once.) And despite the fact that 62 percent of those surveyed say that being Jewish is mainly a matter of ancestry and culture, while only 15 percent say it is mainly a matter of religion, 40 percent of Jews say "they believe the land that is now Israel was given by God to the Jewish people." Behind all these figures, there is an important story to be told.

According to a 2016 study of Israeli Jews, a majority feel they share a common destiny with American Jews and have either "a lot of" or "some" things in common with them. American Jews describe their relationship to Israel in different terms, with 70 percent of them saying they support and feel emotionally attached to Israel. However, despite this, the era of unquestioning support for Israel from American Jews is over. Some historians have drawn on the language of romance to suggest that the relationship has progressed from being a "courtship" or a "love affair" into a "marriage," a good one, but with all the ups and downs characteristic of such a long-term relationship. Historically speaking, however, the fact that American Jews are adopting a more critical stance toward Israel does not signal a radical change as much as it is reflective of a return to what had been the normative American Jewish attitude toward Zionism up until World War II. When the state of Israel came into existence in 1948, with the exception of a deeply committed few, most Jews offered it tacit rather than concrete support. This largely remained the case until 1967, the Six-Day War ushering in an era of full-throated American Jewish (and American) support for Israel. At the outset, it needs to be clear that the end of the era of unquestioning support does not mean a desire to end the relationship. The number of Jews who oppose the existence of Israel as a Jewish state is relatively minuscule, confined to a few ultra-Orthodox Jewish sects on the one hand and, on the other, relatively small but growing numbers of left-wing, secular Jews, a significant number to be found on college campuses. The overwhelming majority of American and world Jewry wish to see Israel thrive and be secure. What has changed for the majority of American Jews is not the issue of whether the state should exist but what the state should look like. This in itself is among the oldest of internal Zionist arguments, many of which we have explored earlier in this book. The disputes among American Jews over Israel are driven by what the various camps believe to be in Israel's best interests. Especially for liberal-minded Jews, to be "pro-Israel" no longer necessarily means to support the policies of its government. By contrast, those on the Right tend to consider those whom they would not consider "pro-Israel" to, by definition, be "anti-Israel." Inevitably, of course, the different policies Jews advocate reflect their own brands of Jewishness. Whereas once American Jews believed that only Israelis knew what was best for their country, the inhibition to speak up has now dissipated.

The challenges put to Israel from an increasingly vocal American Jewry crystallize around multiple issues: religion, demography, culture, and politics, to name but some of the most important categories. Of course, they are not distinct from one another and frequently overlap.

Religion

While the majority of religiously affiliated Jews in the United States are liberal, the authority of their main denominations, Reform and Conservative Judaism, is quite severely curtailed in Israel. At the founding of the state, Prime Minister David Ben-Gurion's government ceded authority over religious affairs to the Israeli chief rabbinate, a strictly Orthodox institution. It has remained that way ever since. As such, Orthodox institutions receive state funding while, for the most part, the Reform and Masorti (Conservative) movements have to fund themselves, usually with support from the United States and the Jewish Agency for Israel, which provides relatively small amounts. Crucially, the life cycle events the two religious branches preside over are not recognized by the State of Israel. The Orthodox establishment has control over laws that pertain to marriage, divorce, conversion, burial, and many other areas of life. This situation has real-life consequences—for example, for converts wishing to immigrate to or be buried in Israel. As of June 2017, a bill pending passage in the Knesset states that individuals who convert in Israel under Reform, Conservative, and private Orthodox auspices would not be eligible for citizenship under the Law of Return. It has been reported that leading figures in the pro-Israel lobby group AIPAC (American Israel Public Affairs Committee) have issued stern warnings to Prime Minister Netanyahu about the consequences of a rift between American Jews and Israel if the foregoing forms of Judaism continued to be seen as illegitimate. The religious establishment's disregard for non-Orthodox women's spirituality and piety has also animated a major dispute over egalitarian worship at the Western Wall. The still-unresolved matter has proven a particularly delicate issue for the government of Benjamin Netan-yahu, which has to placate the Orthodox religious establishment and simultaneously not offend American Jewry. That is becoming increasingly difficult in light of the fact that Netanyahu's government has reneged on the agreement. Rabbi Rick Jacobs, president of the Union for Reform Judaism, which represents 850 congregations and nearly 1.5 million members, has stated that the collapse of the deal "will signal a very serious rupture in the relationship between North American Jewry and the State of Israel."

Reform and Conservative Judaism have often been treated with contempt in official circles. In July 2015, Religious Affairs Minister David Azoulay, from the Orthodox Shas Party, said on Israeli radio that "[a] Reform Jew, from the moment he stops following Jewish law, cannot allow [himself] to say that he is a Jew." Even an avowedly secular Jew, such as David Ben-Gurion, had grave misgivings about American Judaism. When, in 1961, prominent American Jews objected to Israel's kidnapping of the Nazi Adolf Eichmann and then putting him on trial in Israel, a country that did not even exist when the Holocaust took place, Ben-Gurion lashed out: "[The] Judaism of Jews of the United States is losing all meaning and only a blind man can fail to see the day of its extinction."

However, the place of non-Orthodox forms of American Judaism is more complicated than just their relation to the official rabbinate. According to Daniel Elazar, founder of the Jerusalem Center for Public Affairs, it is not merely the rabbinate that stymies the Reform and Conservative movements in Israel. Though it is slowly changing, much of the Israeli public—and that includes non-Orthodox Jews—does not consider these American branches of Judaism to be authentic, and the public rejects the changes that these movements have made to traditional Judaism. The marginalization and fundamental lack of respect for the religious sensibilities of most religiously affiliated American Jews are, at heart, a political problem as much as a religious one. With Israel's parliamentary system based upon a system of proportional representation, no party, on either the Right or the Left, can form a government without forming an alliance with some of the religious parties. That fact alone makes the possibility of Israel accepting American styles of Judaism as authentic and religiously binding rather remote. This is further complicated by the fact that at a most basic level, where Israeli Jews are becoming increasingly religious, American Jews are decidedly moving in a secular direction. All the foregoing will have serious cultural, political, and social consequences that, among other things, will have a significant impact on mutual relations between American and Israeli Jews well into the future.

Demography

One reason for the growing divide is a natural, demographic one and, in many ways, applies to almost all Diaspora communities. However, the rather-long settlement of Jews in the United States makes the American case somewhat different. A large percentage of those Jews trace their American origins to the period of mass migration between 1881 and 1920. Now long situated and warmly accepted in American society, the younger generation of American Jews has no firsthand experience of systemic discrimination at a personal level; moreover, barely any country with sizeable Jewish population has a regime of antisemitic laws. Thus, the idea of Israel as a safe haven for persecuted Jews no longer comports with historical reality in the United States or any-where else for that matter. As such, what once animated the Zionism of previous genera-tions of Jews no longer holds true for younger adult American Jews. Moreover, where Jew-ish support for Israel was once motivated by the reality that the country was vulnerable to neighboring nation-states seeking to destroy it, Israel vanquished those enemies in succes-sive wars. Following the Iranian revolution of 1979, only Iran and its non-state proxies remain committed to Israel's destruction. One consequence of this situation is that younger American Jews have never really seen Israel in peril. Rather, it has seen Israel only as a regional military superpower and, for increasing numbers of young Jews, an occupying force. This contrasts with the sen-timent of Israelis, many of whom feel the daily threat of terrorism as well as the danger that emanates from the chaos and violence in neighboring states. Israeli and American Jews, especially young ones, simply do not share the same view of Israel when it comes to geopolitics and Israel as a state actor.

Rabbis, communal leaders, and academic researchers have also pointed to the demo-graphic consequences of intermarriage for the future of American Jewry. Approxi-mately 58 percent of American Jews cur-rently marry outside of the faith, and of that group, 37 percent who have children say that they are not raising them to be Jewish. There are many serious social consequences born of this situation. In simple terms, future generations will see fewer and fewer chil-dren born of such marriages who express attachment to Jews, Judaism, and the State of Israel. On the other hand, the extremely high birth rates among Orthodox Ameri-can Jews will ensure a steady growth of at least one segment of American Jewry with

strong allegiance to Israel. So as one group of American Jews pulls away, another moves toward Israel's embrace.

Culture

On a cultural level, as Israel has grown with age, it has developed a thick Hebrew culture that the majority of American Jews have no access to. Just as American Jews are deeply Ameri-can, Israeli Jews are far more deeply Israeli than ever before. The majority of American and Israeli Jews are no longer from immigrant communities. Most Israeli Jews were born in Israel, while most American Jews were born in the United States. As older generations die off, there are fewer family connections than ever before between the two countries, and with the passage of time, so, too, do shared histori-cal experiences and sentiments disappear. For example, Holocaust survivors in America and those in Israel both shared memories of the "old country" and the horrors of the Shoah so that each had an intuitive understanding of the other even without personally knowing each other. By contrast, the respective life experi-ences and cultural heritage of the native-born American Jew and the native-born Israeli Jew are at great remove from one another. As Yossi Klein-Halevi has correctly noted, "Israeli Jews' identity is inseparable from the military." This is simply not the case for American Jews or, indeed, world Jewry.

To be sure, the estrangement is mitigated by certain important factors, such as increased travel between the two countries, but with increasing numbers of American Jews claim-ing that they are culturally but not religiously Jewish (many secular Israelis feel similarly), then the one tie that would bind each group to the other—namely, religion—is being undone. Moreover, according to author Daniel Gor-dis, "there is a pervasive commitment to the sort of liberalism that embraces universal-ism and rejects particularism which has actu-ally become the religion of young American Jews." By contrast, Israel as a Jewish state was intended to be ethnically and religiously par-ticularistic and, as such, was never supposed to resemble the United States. This strikes increasing numbers of young American Jews as illiberal. As members of one ethnic minor-ity among many, American Jews live, accord-ing to the sociologist Steven M. Cohen, "in a culture that is marked by radical inclusiv-ity, cosmopolitanism and what we call Jewish personalism—they make decisions on how to be Jewish based on personal meaning." By contrast, Cohen observes:

> Israeli Jews have traditional, premodern notions about what it means to be Jewish. They live in a part of the world that has strong group boundaries, is fairly conser-vative with respect to changing norms and locates authority in the traditional rather than the personal sphere.

About 70 percent of American Jews describe themselves as politically liberal, and if they acknowledge a religious dimension to their Jewishness, then that, too, would tend to lean toward the liberal end of the spectrum. By contrast, Israel, since the late 1970s, has, in the political realm as well as the religious sphere, moved sharply to the right. While that stands to alienate many liberal Ameri-can Jews, the changed direction of Israel has attracted the allegiance of increasing num-bers of ultra-Orthodox Jews, many of whom had previously been opposed to a Jewish state for religious reasons. In fact, most American Jews who immigrate to Israel are not secu-lar pioneers, as once was the case, but are Orthodox. They also tend to hold right-wing political views and leave their mark on Israeli

politics and culture in a way that creates fur-ther distance between the majority of Ameri-can and Israeli Jews.

In the cultural realm, there is one other important factor that shapes the current American Jewish relationship to Israel, and it has to do with the country's Ashkenazi–Miz-rahi divide. The Israeli government does not keep statistics on who is "Ashkenazi" and who is "Mizrahi." More religiously, culturally, and politically conservative than Ashkenazi Jews, Mizrahim have recast Israel ever since the right-wing Likud Party, which they largely support, first came to power in 1977. Coming from societies that never experienced a thor-oughgoing critique of religion and reaction against that process, Mizrahim have tended to be more embracing and less hostile toward religion than many secular Ashkenazic Jews. Ironically, this also holds true for secular Miz-rahim, who, for the most part, are also more inclined to incorporate aspects of Jewish reli-gious practice into their daily lives. In the political realm, the second-class status of Jews as *dhimmi* in Arab lands and their dispossess-sion and displacement from those countries after 1948 also color the attitude of Mizrahim toward Palestinians and the rest of the Arab world. Similarly, the discrimination they faced at the hands of the Ashkenazic establishment, especially in the period after 1948, contrib-uted to a Mizrahi political and cultural back-lash against left-wing, secular Zionism. Their culturally and politically conservative views thus place them at odds with the dominant regime of American Jewish political sensibili-ties. The Mizrahim have played a central role in creating today's Israel, and even if Ameri-can Jews do not understand, or if they do but prefer not to acknowledge the reasons behind Israel's social transformation, some of the con-sequences of it are a source of contemporary disquiet and disillusionment for many liberal American Jews.

Politics

Another source of fracture revolves around attitudes toward democracy. The need for an open, democratic society is a sine qua non for nearly all Americans, Jews included. In a 2016 Pew Research survey of Israelis, 76 percent of the population believed it was possible to have a democratic and Jewish society. However, broken down among religious communities, only 58 percent of ultra-Orthodox (*Haredim*) believed this was the case. In fact, while 62 percent of Israeli Jews believe democratic principles should take priority over religious law (*halakhah*), a full 89 percent of ultra-Orthodox Israelis believe that *halakhah* should be given preference if there is a contradiction between the two legal codes. With Israel's rightward trajectory, even a demotion, let alone an abandonment, of democratic principles could lead to a monumental rupture between the majority of American Jews and Israel.

In the political realm, the most important cause of distancing or critique (not necessarily the same thing) of young American Jews from Israel turns on the government's treatment of the Palestinians. The 2016 Pew Research survey of Israelis highlights the radically different ways American and Israeli Jews assess the conflict with the Palestinians. At a most fundamental level, only 38 percent of Jewish Americans compared to 56 percent of Israeli Jews think the Israeli government is making a sincere effort to achieve peace with the Palestinians. On the whole, however, Israeli and American Jews agree that the Palestinians are not sincere in their efforts to achieve peace. As for the impact of West Bank Jewish settlements, 42 percent of Jews in Israel say the continued building of these settlements helps the security of the country, whereas only 17 percent of American Jews agree. In fact, 44 percent of American Jews say the settlements actually imperil Israel's own security interests; that figure for Israeli Jews is only 30 percent.

One source of these differing views of the political situation is rooted in fundamental misperceptions of Israel by American Jews. According to the historian of American Jewry Jonathan Sarna, in the era prior to the advent of the internet, most information that the Jewish world received from and about Israel was "very positive and monochromatic," so much so that Jews "could really project a lot onto Israel, and American Jews liked that. In recent years, American Jews have discovered the real Israel, and that is never as good as the Israel of your imagination." The stark reality of the Occupation is there for all who wish to see it, and as such, the once universally positive representation of Israel by a government office such as the Sochnut (Jewish Agency) is dismissed as so much propaganda by young skeptical American Jews. In view of this, many of the guides on the very popular Taglit-Birthright program that takes young Jewish adults to Israel for the first time present the Palestinian viewpoint so that the American visitors can hear that side of the story as well as the Israeli Jewish one. In fact, the educational guidelines of Taglit call on the programs to "respect the integrity and sensibilities of participants and . . . not attempt to missionize." Taglit even monitors for political bias by sending third-party compliance officers to observe every group and survey its members.

Despite the often heavily manipulated and propagandistic presentation of the plight of the Palestinians under occupation, there is enough reliable documentation of all kinds, many from reputable Israeli sources, to lead increasing numbers of young Jewish Americans to no longer accept at face value Israeli government claims about the situation on the West Bank and in Gaza. Indeed, millennial Palestinians are just as likely to disbelieve official statements that come from the Palestinian Authority as young Israeli and American Jews are to disbelieve official word from Jerusalem. It needs to be recognized that with the advent of social media and alternative news outlets, younger generations across the world have far less faith in official government pronouncements than ever before. Thus, while young American Jews may not accept the Israeli government's view of the situation, they are also highly skeptical of their own government's statements on a whole array of subjects, none of them having anything to do with Israel and the Palestinians. This is a universal phenomenon. The greater democratization of the news demands greater transparency. The widespread disbelief of government and traditional media cannot but color the American Jewish relationship with Israel.

It should also be borne in mind that the growing debate and argument about Israel's policies toward the Palestinians are causing fractures and fault lines within the American Jewish community as well. One important source of the friction is that AIPAC appears to many to have all but abandoned its nonpartisan posture with regard to Israeli and even American politics. Its words and actions bespeak an organization that supports the rightward turn in Israeli politics and Likud policies more specifically. Those views are also increasingly reflected in the far more conservative, Republican-leaning leadership of major American Jewish organizations. However, with a solid 70 percent of American Jews self-identifying as politically liberal and voting Democratic, it appears that the leaders of these organizations are beginning to be less and less reflective of the socioeconomic and political makeup of the overwhelming majority of American Jews. So too does it mean that the views on Israel of rank-and-file young Jews differ significantly from those of the leadership of major Jewish organizations. Nonetheless, it would be wrong to speak of irreparable rupture. AIPAC, despite its conservative tilt, has been very successful in garnering support from younger Jews, but so too has J-Street, a liberal alternative to AIPAC.

In the end, the very real religious, political, and cultural divisions within American Jewry mean that there is no singular American Jewish relationship with Israel. Those fissures bespeak a plurality of voices, opinions, and levels of commitment. For young American Jews, there is also an element of fatigue with the Israeli–Palestinian conflict, its seeming intractability at odds with other historic conflicts around the world that have been resolved. Moreover, millennials live in times marked by instant resolution and gratification. They are also a simple click away from answers to an infinite number of questions. Those posed by Israel and its relationship to the Palestinians; to democracy, liberal values, and egalitarianism; to American Jewry; and to the meaning of Jewish identity and Judaism do not lend themselves to easy answers. Nearly all observers report seeing a waning of interest in Israel on the part of young American Jews, many of whom consider issues of social justice at home in the United States to be of greater relevance and urgency than issues to do with Israel. Just as this situation was not predictable even just a few years ago, so too is the future of the American Jewish and Israeli Jewish relationship impossible to foretell. What is clear is that cultural changes among Jews in the two biggest Jewish populations in the world, together representing about 80 percent of world Jewry, are serving to redefine the nature of the relationship in ways both positive and negative.

At the beginning of the twenty-first century, most American Jews are no longer bound to Judaism or Jewishness by social or communal discipline but out of a conscious choice. While large numbers, perhaps as many as 2 million out of America's 5.5 million Jews, remain unaffiliated, there is still a vast reservoir of talent, creativity, and energy propelling American Jewry in novel directions.

EASTERN EUROPE AFTER THE SHOAH

Soviet Union

The war and the Holocaust exacted a terrible toll on Soviet Jewry. The prewar Jewish population stood at around 3 million. Around half that number was murdered in the Shoah, and untold numbers of Jews died in combat, fighting for the Red Army. In 1945, the total Jewish population of the Soviet Union had been reduced to about 1.5 million. Altogether, Jewish losses during the war were proportionately higher than they were for any other Soviet nationality. Still, with the large number of Jews deported and evacuated deep into Russian territory, as well as the overall Allied victory, the Soviet Union emerged after the war with the largest Jewish population in Europe.

In 1942, the Soviet government permitted the formation of the Jewish Anti-Fascist Committee (JAFC). The goal was to marshal political and financial support for the Soviet war effort from Jewish communities in the West. In 1943, Shlomo Mikhoels (1890–1948), the renowned actor, and the Yiddish poet Itsik

Fefer (1900–1948) traveled to the United States, Canada, and Mexico to garner moral and financial support for the Soviet Union. Ilya Ehrenburg, a prominent Soviet Jewish journalist, writer, and leading member of the JAFC, stayed behind but reminded American Jews, "There is no ocean behind which you can hide. . . . Your peaceful sleep will be disturbed by the cries of Leah from Ukraine, Rachel from Minsk, Sarah from Bialystok—they are weeping over their slaughtered children." The delegation not only met with celebrities such as Albert Einstein, Charlie Chaplin, Eddie Cantor, and Yehudi Menuhin but also addressed large rallies, including one at New York's Polo Grounds, attended by 50,000 people. During the war, Jewish organizations from abroad, mostly in the United States, provided about $45 million in aid to the Soviet war effort. With its own newspaper and through the offer of support to Yiddish artists and writers from Russia, Poland, Romania, and the Baltic, the JAFC was the only official Jewish institution operating in the Soviet Union. It therefore became a focal point of Jewish cultural activities and, for many, a promoter of Jewish nationalism. As such, the JAFC came under suspicion by the regime.

After the war, Joseph Stalin, increasingly paranoid and psychotic, began an antisemitic campaign against "rootless cosmopolitans," a code word for Jews allegedly harboring "anti-patriotic views." Between 1948 and 1953, the Soviet authorities initiated a deliberate campaign to liquidate what remained of Jewish culture. Prior to his own arrest, the celebrated Yiddish author Peretz Markish remarked to a friend, "Hitler wanted to destroy us physically. Stalin wants to do it spiritually." The most well-known of Stalin's victims was the Yiddish actor and de facto head of Soviet Jewry Shlomo Mikhoels. On January 13, 1948, he was murdered by the secret police. They then ran over him with a truck to make it look like an automobile accident. As part of the sham, Mikhoels was even honored with a large state funeral. Not long afterward, Markish went to Mikhoels's dressing room and wrote the opening stanzas of his poem "Sh. Mikhoels—A Memorial Flame at Your Coffin." Courageously declaring that Mikhoels had been murdered, Markish has the anguished voice of Mikhoels state bluntly that he (and the Jewish people) had been murder victims:

> I want eternity to come before your violated threshold
> With murder-marks and blasphemy on my face, The way my people roam five-sixths of the earth—
> Marked by axe and hate—for you to know them by.

With Mikhoel's murder, a campaign was initiated against Jewish culture that saw libraries, publishing houses, research institutes, theaters, and at the end of 1948, the JAFC itself shut down. Such closings were immediate and without warning. Ester Markish, wife of Peretz Markish, recalled the closure of the Soviet Union's last Yiddish publishing house:

> [T]rucks filled with State Security agents pulled up in front of the house. Soldiers in civilian clothes burst into the printing plant and disconnected the machines. Everything came to a standstill; all was silence. "Your publishing house is closed down!" one of the pogromists bellowed.

Hundreds of Yiddish writers, journalists, editors, actors, performers, artists, and musicians were arrested, their state subsidies withdrawn.

Many were sentenced to years of hard labor in the Gulag, the Soviet prison system. Others, such as the distinguished Yiddish authors Itsik Fefer, Dovid Bergelson (1884–1948), along with Peretz Markish (1895–1949), were publicly tried, found guilty of attempting to establish a Zionist state in Crimea, and executed.

When Jews were arrested, the press began to print the original Jewish name of the accused in parentheses after his or her assumed Russian name, thus "exposing" or "outing" those Jews charged with being "anti-patriotic." Descriptions of the charges often carried editorial comment that drew on a nineteenth-century antisemitic trope— namely, that being Jewish precluded fully comprehending the national culture. As a question posed in the official party organ, *Pravda*, asked, "What kind of an idea can Gurvich have of the national character of a Soviet Russian man?"

In the Soviet client state of Czechoslovakia, the campaign against "Zionist cosmopolitans" purportedly in positions of leadership in the Communist Party culminated in November 1952 in the Prague show trials of Rudolf Slánsky and his comrades. "During the investigation," it was announced, "we discovered how treason and espionage infiltrate the ranks of the Communist Party. This channel is Zionism." One of the charges brought against Slánsky was that he used Jewish doctors to assassinate his enemies. On December 1, 1952, Stalin announced to the Politburo:

> Every Jewish nationalist is the agent of the American intelligence service. Jewish nationalists think that their nation was saved by the U.S.A. (there you can become rich, bourgeois, etc.). They think they're indebted to the Americans.

Among doctors, there are many Jewish nationalists.

On December 3, 1952, 13 former Communist leaders of Czechoslovakia, 11 of whom were Jews, were executed.

On January 13, 1953, Stalin, who saw conspiracies everywhere, turned on Soviet Jewish physicians, accusing them of a plot to poison him and Communist Party leaders. That day in *Pravda*, the headline read, "Vicious Spies and Killers Under the Mask of Academic Physicians." The article informed the Soviet public that:

> The majority of the participants of the terrorist group were recruited by a branch-office of American intelligence—the international Jewish bourgeois-nationalist organization called "Joint" (American Joint Distribution Committee). The filthy face of this Zionist spy organization, covering up their vicious actions under the mask of kindness, is now completely revealed. . . . Unmasking the gang of poisoner-doctors [has] struck a blow

against the international Jewish Zionist organization.

The Jewish Anti-Fascist Committee's trip to the United States in 1943 was a huge success, in that it raised large sums of money and garnered much moral support for the Soviet war effort. At the moment that Soviet Jewry was faced with extinction by the Nazi invasion, the JAFC was also a rallying point for Jewish national identity in the Soviet Union. The trip to the United States by Mikhoels and Fefer also helped American and Russian Jews reconnect with each other. Out of the contacts came a decision to publish simultaneously in the United States and the Soviet Union a black book documenting the anti-Jewish crimes of the Nazis. In 1944, the writer Ilya Ehrenburg sent a collection of letters, diaries, photos, and eyewitness accounts to the United States to be used in the book. *The Black Book* was published in New York in 1946, with a preface written by Albert Einstein. No Russian edition appeared.

Figure 6.4   Itsik Fefer, Albert Einstein, and Shlomo Mikhoels (1943).

Initially, nine people were arrested, suspected of taking part in the "Doctors' Plot." In the period from 1948 to 1953, the charges against Jews multiplied, as they were accused of corruption, speculation, and other economic crimes against the state. Retribution was demonstrable. The percentage of Jews in the Central Committee of the Communist Party declined from ten in 1939 to two in 1952. In the Soviet Republics, Jews were removed almost entirely from positions of authority in the party. In addition, Jews were systematically dismissed from leading positions in the armed forces, the press, the universities, and the legal system. To ethnically cleanse the state apparatus of Jews, the Soviets engaged in a massive exercise of "investigative genealogy," studying the backgrounds of leading figures to see if they were of Jewish descent and, thus, enemies of the state.

One month after Stalin's death on March 5, 1953, *Pravda* declared that the Doctors' Plot had been a fraud, and the accused were released from prison. A thaw in relations set in, and the repression eased. Many Jews got their jobs back, which was easier in scientific fields, whereas ideologically sensitive positions in the humanities, as well as in the security apparatus and foreign affairs, remained off-limits. Even though many of those Jews who had been murdered or imprisoned were officially "rehabilitated" when Stalin's successor, Nikita Khrushchev, denounced Stalin in 1956, he never mentioned the campaign against Jews. While Jews gained back some measure of their individual rights, Jewish cultural institutions were never restored, and antisemitism was not officially denounced, as it had been in the 1920s. Some Jews were pleased that the worst excesses of the system were being corrected and attempted to make the best of the situation. Others were less satisfied.

Although deranged, Stalin was not entirely incorrect. The war had indeed fostered the emergence of Jewish nationalism among many Soviet Jews, and that sentiment intensified during the postwar period, with the assault on Jewish culture. The establishment of the State of Israel in 1948, which was initially supported by the Soviet Union, also encouraged—as the Soviets had feared—Zionist sympathy among Soviet Jews. When Golda Meir, Israel's first ambassador to the Soviet Union, arrived in 1948, large demonstrations in support of Israel greeted her at every public appearance. On October 4, Rosh Hashanah, she attended synagogue, and the assembled crowd began shouting "Shalom!" At Yom Kippur services ten days later, a crowd gathered outside the Metropole Hotel to serenade the delegation of Israeli diplomats with the chant "Next Year in Jerusalem!"

The only officially sanctioned and state-supported expression of Jewish culture was the Yiddish newspaper *Sovietish heymland* (*Soviet Homeland*), launched in 1961. But in the more relaxed post-Stalin period, the authorities granted permission for the existence of a large number of unofficial clubs, societies, and organizations dedicated to Jewish culture. Religious life, though severely circumscribed by the Bolshevik Revolution, was never entirely eliminated. Although their numbers were greatly reduced by the mid-1930s, select synagogues continued to function throughout the Soviet period, and religiously committed Jews continued to celebrate Jewish holidays, often in secret. In some cases, the meanings of holidays were reinterpreted in light of current realities. Passover seders, for instance, could commemorate the oppression of Jews under Egyptian slavery while simultaneously acknowledging the current oppression under which Soviet Jews were living. Religious practice was not necessarily an expression of faith among Jews in the Soviet Union; rather, it was just as likely an expression of ethnic solidarity.

The brief period of liberalization under Khrushchev, which saw the opening of a Moscow yeshiva and the publication of a siddur (prayer book), came to an end in 1957. For the next seven years, a widespread campaign against all religions struck with particular ferocity against Judaism because, unlike the similar program in the 1920s, this one went beyond a critique of religion and was plainly antisemitic. The post-revolutionary attack on Judaism in the 1920s was largely conducted in Yiddish because it was meant for internal consumption. During the campaign of the 1950s and 1960s, publications were presented in the major languages of the Soviet Union and were thus accessible to non-Jews. Very often, the attacks were anti-Zionist tirades, with accusations that Zionists actually collaborated with the Nazis during the war. Synagogues were closed, and in 1960, the baking of matzah for Passover was banned. The latter decree was repealed in 1964 in the face of widespread international protest.

Loss of jobs and status, trials against Jews for having committed "economic crimes" in the early 1960s that resulted in a disproportionate number of Jews executed, general economic stagnation, Cold War tensions, and the euphoria aroused by Israel's victory in the Six-Day War led to an increase in the number of Jews wishing to immigrate to Israel. Overrepresented among Soviet dissidents, Jews were increasingly seen as intellectual agitators against the regime. The accusation was not far from the truth. A favorite joke among Soviet Jews revealed where they stood

in relation to Communism, and even in relation to their parents, who had often been true believers.

A political instructor asks Rabinovich:
"Who is your father?"
"The Soviet Union."
"Good. And who is your mother?"
"The Communist Party."
"Excellent. And what is your fondest wish?"
"To become an orphan."

Indeed, Soviet Jews felt like orphans and were treated as such. Discrimination in education and employment increased, but rather than back down, Jews requested exit visas in ever-increasing numbers. Moscow soon began to believe that getting rid of troublesome Jews was preferable to forcing them to remain in the Soviet Union. American political pressure also played an important role in the Kremlin's change of policy. In the early 1970s, the regime began to permit Jews who wished to depart to do so. Not everyone who applied to leave could go, but nearly a quarter of a million went to Israel, the United States, Australia, and Canada. In 1974, the Soviets reversed policy after the US Congress passed the Jackson–Vanick Act, which denied Most Favored Nation status to the Soviet Union unless it liberalized its emigration policies. Rather than capitulate, the Soviet Union hardened its stance, barely permitting any Jews to leave the country between 1980 and 1986.

American Jewish organizations such as the American Jewish Conference on Soviet Jewry and the Anti-Defamation League have tended to credit themselves with bringing about the liberalization of Soviet immigration policy, without fully recognizing the role played by Soviet Jews themselves. While the collective efforts of the "Let My People Go" campaign were far from negligible, increasingly vocal dissent by Soviet Jews, including the attempted hijacking of a plane from Leningrad to Israel in 1970 and the subsequent trial in which the defendants openly expressed Zionist sentiments, likely led to the relaxation of Soviet emigration restrictions in 1971–1972. Many Jews were inspired by the actions of the accused. One Soviet Jew, Dov Goldstein, later recalled of the hijackers, "[H]ere are Jews who don't simply talk about Israel, don't just dream, but they do something, and are not afraid of the danger and the punishment." The Soviet Union seems to have concluded that it was mutually beneficial to simply have Jews leave rather than turn these "Prisoners of Zion," as they were known, into martyrs.

Most important for the massive exodus of Jews from the Soviet Union were the liberalizing reforms of President Mikhail Gorbachev and then the Soviet state's collapse in 1991. Between 1988 and 1994, 776,867 legal emigrants left the Soviet Union. About 200,000 Jews settled in the United States, as many as 100,000 went to Germany, and nearly 500,000 settled in Israel, joining the more than 200,000 Jews who had gone to Israel in the two decades prior to 1988. In total, nearly 1.3 million Jews fled the Soviet Union between 1968 and 1994. In Russia, the Jewish population is shrinking, principally due to immigration and aging, the latter reality reflecting the general demographic decline of Russia. In 2006, the total number of Jews in the areas that had been part of the former Soviet Union (Russia, Ukraine, Belorussia, the Baltic states, Moldavia, Transcaucasia, and Central Asia) was about 345,000. Of this number, 228,000 lived in the Russian Federation.

Poland

After the war, about 250,000 Jews remained in Poland. When attempting to return to their homes, stunned survivors were greeted with hostility and violence. Jewish leaders were convinced that the Church had it in its power to effect a transformation in the public's negative attitude toward Jews. In May 1945, the Central Committee of the Jews in Poland wrote to the then highest-ranking official of the Catholic Church in Poland, Adam Sapieha, the archbishop of Cracow, requesting that he intercede:

> For a long time, we have been receiving alarming and frightening reports from various cities and towns about bestial murders committed by armed bands on the defenseless remnants of the Jewish population. We are even more concerned since sporadic incidents have been recently transformed into systematic and organized action, the goal of which is to annihilate the survivors. . . . We are turning to your Eminence, as to one of the leading representatives of the noble Polish humanitarianism, and we appeal to you to speak in public about the matter.

The Central Committee was right to be fearful. About 1,500 Jews were killed in pogroms that swept through Poland in the postwar period. The largest of these occurred in the town of Kielce on July 4, 1946, in the wake of an accusation that Jews had ritually murdered a Polish child. About 50 Jews were shot or beaten to death with iron bars by the mob, which included policemen and soldiers sent to restore order. Any hope that the Church, which saw itself as the authentic custodian of Polish national interests, might offer solace to the victims came to naught. Cardinal Hlond, primate of Poland, explained away the pogrom as a consequence of Jewish participation in the Communist government:

> The fact that this condition [anti-Jewish violence] is deteriorating is to a great degree due to Jews who today occupy

leading positions in Poland's Government and endeavor to introduce a governmental structure which the majority of the people do not desire. This is a harmful game, as it creates dangerous tensions. In the fatal battle of weapons . . . it is to be regretted that some Jews lose their lives, but a disproportionately large number of Poles also lose their lives.

At various points thereafter, antisemitism entered into political discourse, either as a vestige of Polish Catholicism or for the purposes of discrediting political opponents. In 1968, Communist hard-liners resorted to an antisemitic campaign and rounded up Jewish party functionaries. About 20,000 Jews immigrated, mostly to Israel, between 1968 and 1970. By the late 1970s, only about 5,000, mostly elderly, assimilated Jews were still in Poland, caught in a cultural no-man's-land. Not seen as sufficiently Polish by Poles, they also had no place in the Jewish community.

The second half of the 1970s was an era of political liberalization, during which it became possible to raise the subject of Jewish identity in Poland. Dissident Catholic intellectuals organized Jewish "Culture Weeks," while young Jews opened a forum known as the Warsaw Jewish Flying University. The university did not put out a call for collective Jewish action or promote the idea of reinvigorating Jewish life in Poland. It was aware that was impossible. It was, however, a valuable and meaningful experience for the participants on an individual level. Some of them began to learn Yiddish; others lectured on Jewish subjects to gentile audiences; some considered immigration to Israel, though they never left; while others became religiously observant. When it disbanded in

1981, the university had about 60 members, all of whom developed strong attachments to their Jewish identities.

After 1989, American Jewish organizations began to provide various forms of assistance to Jews in Poland. As a result of American encouragement, large numbers of Polish Jewish youth began to attend Jewish events. Jewish newspapers and an important journal of Jewish opinion, *Midrasz*, began to appear. Each summer, the Cracow Jewish Festival takes place in the old Jewish quarter of the town, the largest Jewish festival of its kind in Europe. A smaller Jewish cultural festival also takes place each year in Wroclaw. The Center for Jewish Culture in Cracow is an extremely active institution, sponsoring lectures, exhibitions, concerts, and summer school programs, with courses in Polish, English, and German on Jewish history and culture. In Cracow in 2004, an independent Jewish youth society, *Czulent* (Cholent), is dedicated to the integration of young Jews from Cracow and its surrounding region. The organization especially caters to the significant number of people in Poland who find out only later in life about their Jewish roots. *Czulent* sets itself the task of reintegrating such people into Jewish life, teaching them Jewish traditions, customs, history, and culture. It also seeks to promote community development and Poland's Jewish heritage and to strengthen Polish Jewish relations.

In 1994, the first Jewish school in Warsaw since 1949 opened. In 2007, the Lauder–Morasha School had an enrollment of 240 students, ranging in age from 3 to 16 years old. The school is a secular Jewish institution; students are taught Hebrew and Jewish tradition and culture, alongside a standard Polish curriculum. The school has a sister school—Lauder Etz Chaim—in the western Polish city of Wroclaw. These schools are part of a larger network of 36 Lauder schools and kindergartens in 16 central and eastern European countries.

Elsewhere in the Eastern Bloc, what remained of Jewish life in the aftermath of the Shoah lay in tatters. The security of Jews was compromised by the presence of Jews in the Communist leadership in the various client states of the Soviet Union. Most of these countries permitted Jewish emigration, and those Jews who could leave did so. Predictably, the elderly and infirmed stayed behind. The largest postwar Jewish populations in Communist Europe were to be found in Romania and Hungary.

Romania

In Romania, 400,000 Jews survived out of a prewar total of 700,000. After that of the Soviet Union, this was the largest Jewish population in postwar Europe. With the abolition of the Romanian monarchy in 1947, a crackdown on Jewish economic, political, and institutional life followed. Over 40 percent of Jews were engaged in commerce; their economic ruin was assured with the nationalization of the economy. Many Jews were rounded up for forced labor. The political inclinations of Romanian Jews both before and after the war were decidedly Zionist. There were 100,000 Romanian members of the Zionist movement, which was banned in 1948 because, according to a government denunciation, "[Zionism] in all its manifestations is a reactionary nationalist movement of the Jewish bourgeoisie, supported by American imperialism, that attempts to isolate the masses of Jewish workers from the people among whom they live." The Jewish Democratic Committee, an arm of the Romanian Communist Party that had assisted with the suppression, was also eliminated.

After 1948, all Jewish communal needs and activities were supplied and coordinated by the Federation of Romanian Jewish Communities. Though the government closed down many communal institutions, the federation was permitted to maintain synagogues and cemeteries and run a yeshiva, ritual bathhouses, kosher slaughterhouses, and kosher bakeries. The Federation also published a Romanian, Yiddish, and Hebrew newspaper. Beginning in 1964, the chief rabbi served as the chairman of the Federation. In the early 1960s, about 100,000 Jews were still in Romania. While all schools were nationalized in 1948 and Jewish schools were closed down, an exception was made for a few Jewish schools with instruction in Yiddish, which remained in operation until 1961. Other exceptions to the closure of many Jewish institutions in 1948 were the State Jewish Theaters in Bucharest and Iasi. They had no connection with the community but nonetheless performed in Yiddish until 1968.

Beginning in 1953, with Stalin's death, Romania began to skillfully carve out greater independence from Moscow, not by rebelling, but by displaying loyalty and exploiting matters of mutual interest. In 1958, Moscow, convinced of Romania's reliability, withdrew Soviet troops, allowing Bucharest greater freedom of movement. It sought closer ties to the West, and the regime, suffering under antisemitic misapprehension, believed that this was to be achieved by currying favor with Jews. Following the Six-Day War, Romania refused to follow Moscow and sign a statement denouncing "Israeli aggression." It also refused to break off diplomatic relations.

In fact, in 1969, Romania and Israel elevated the status of their respective diplomatic missions to the rank of embassies.

Despite certain positive tendencies in foreign and domestic policy with regard to Israel and Jews, the social life of Romanian Jewry continued to disintegrate as a result of aging and poverty. However, the biggest factor in the decline of the community was the departure of the Jews. Between late 1949 and the end of 1989, close to 300,000 Romanian Jews were sold to Israel for hard currency. Under the reign of Nicolae Ceausescu (1965–1989) in particular, these sales for thousands of dollars each were made a priority. A key figure in the postwar life of Romanian Jewry was the talented chief rabbi Moses Rosen. Through skillful maneuvering, he convinced the regime of what it wanted to hear—namely, that it would be to their material advantage to treat Jews well. Knowingly, he observed, "I succeeded in convincing the Romanian Government that, by doing good to the Jews, by meting out justice to them, it could obtain advantages in matters of favourable public opinion, trade relations, political sympathies." Some have seen Rosen as a willing tool of the regime and an apologist for it. Many Romanian Jews, however, were able to exit the country thanks to his intercession with the authorities. Only around 10,000 largely poor Jews are left in Romania, their pensions rendered nearly worthless after the fall of Communism. The community is funded almost entirely by the American Joint Distribution Committee.

Hungary

After World War II, about 80,000 Jews lived in Hungary, organized into about 250 Jewish communities. Many of the smaller rural communities were not viable, and those Jews soon moved to Budapest or emigrated. The Hungarian government abolished anti-Jewish legislation and tried and punished those involved in the Hungarian Holocaust. While isolated pogroms broke out in 1946, the government officially recognized the Jewish community in 1948, offering it financial assistance and guaranteeing freedom of religious practice. Between 1948 and 1952, substantial aid also arrived from the American Jewish Joint Distribution Committee. Zionism was a powerful movement and ran schools and youth groups. In 1948, the Hungarian government established formal diplomatic relations with Israel.

The situation changed drastically after the Communists came to power in 1949. Accused by enemies of being a "Jewish government"—at least nine out of 25 politburo members were Jews, with many more occupying positions of authority at the party's lower levels—the Communists in power meted out particularly harsh treatment toward Jews to allay suspicions of a Jewish Communist conspiracy against Hungary. Many Jewish institutions were closed, religious observance was banned, Jewish activists were arrested, Zionism was outlawed, and emigration was prohibited. In 1951, hardship was increased in the wake of a series of expulsions of "capitalists" and "unproductive elements," wherein about 20,000 Jews, mostly from Budapest, were driven to the provinces. After spending time interned in labor camps, exiled Jews were permitted to return to the capital in 1953. In the wake of the 1956 Hungarian Revolution and its suppression by the Soviets, it is estimated that another 20,000 Jews fled Hungary. After 1956, the more liberal regime of Janos Kadar relaxed restrictions on the economy and loosened censorship. After the 1960s, as they were before the war, Jews were again disproportionately represented among doctors, lawyers, academics, journalists, politicians, and cultural circles.

Jewish communal life was supported with government money, and a broad network of institutions was established, including dozens of synagogues, a hospital, old-age homes, and secular and religious schools. With the collapse of the Communist government in 1989, finances, in large part from abroad, were used to rebuild communal institutions and provide for the needs of east-central Europe's largest Jewish community of 100,000 people.

Ironically, Jewish life in cities such as Cracow, Budapest, and Prague (Jewish population 1,600) gives the impression of being very lively, thanks to tourists visiting Jewish sites. Each summer, throngs of people stand in line to visit Europe's oldest functioning synagogue, the medieval Altneuschul in Prague, or the magnificently ornate Tabakshul in Budapest. In Poland, the majority of the attendees at Europe's largest Jewish summer event, the Jewish Culture Festival in Cracow, are non-Jews, as are the owners of the "Jewish" shops in the city's old Jewish quarter, Kazimiersz. In Poland, statues and pictures of dancing Hasidim are emblazoned on everything from refrigerator magnets to vodka bottles. Jewish kitsch is to be seen everywhere. In this environment, east-central Europe has become the site of "virtual Judaism."

WESTERN EUROPE AFTER THE SHOAH

France

French Jewry suffered terribly during the war at the hands of the collaborationist Vichy regime, and a deep sense of trauma and betrayal gripped postwar French Jews. They wondered how, in the first nation in Europe to emancipate the Jews and a country that was seen by so many as a beacon of liberty, the Holocaust could have occurred with such widespread French complicity. Between the end of the war and the 1970s, the issue was avoided altogether in French public discourse, but between the 1970s and the 1990s, avoidance slowly turned to acceptance of responsibility. In 1995, the government of President Jacques Chirac officially admitted French culpability for the way Jews were treated under Vichy.

Despite having lost one-quarter of its Jewish population during the war, French Jewry began to grow in the postwar period due to the arrival of Jews from North Africa. With over 500,000 Jews, over 50 percent of whom live in Paris, France is home to the third largest Jewish community in the world. In the 1950s, Jews came from Tunisia and Morocco, and then in 1962, almost the entire Jewish community of Algeria migrated to France. Many of the 220,000 North African Jews who came to France in the 1960s arrived as French citizens. As such, they, like other immigrants with French citizenship, were entitled to generous government loans, as well as housing and employment assistance. A Jewish social welfare agency, the Fonds Social Juif Unifié (FSJU), founded in 1949, also offered material assistance and advice to the immigrants.

The Jews who migrated to France tended to be wealthier and spoke French, while the poorer North African Jews generally settled in Israel. Like eastern European Jews who migrated to New York and London at the end of the nineteenth century, North African Jews who went to France also transformed the social and cultural profile of the extant Jewish community. Middle Eastern Jews became the dominant force in Franco-Jewish communal, cultural, and religious life in what had been a predominantly Ashkenazic population. New synagogues, community centers, and schools sprouted. In the 1950s, only ten consistorially supervised kosher butchers could be found in the Paris region. By 1977, that number had increased to 97. In the postwar period, most of the rabbis trained in France were Sephardim of North African origin, as have been the last two grand rabbis, René Sirat and Jacques Sitruk.

There are significant differences in religious attitudes among North African Jews in France. According to one important sociological study that examined the first generation of such immigrants, the Tunisians were the most observant, and the Algerians the least observant, with the Moroccans falling somewhere in between. Despite institutional growth, North African immigrants tended not to participate heavily in the activities of the organized community, preferring to conduct their religious and cultural lives in the home.

Among the postwar North African newcomers, just under 30 percent were working-class, about the same percentage were employees and professionals, and 15 percent were small merchants and artisans. The pattern of upward socioeconomic ascent followed the general pattern among Diaspora Jews. With a rapid reduction of the fertility of North African Jewish immigrants—a 50 percent decline between the years 1957–1961 and 1967–1971—their economic status improved, making it possible for them to provide their children with education. In the postwar period, a greater proportion of Jews in France—Sephardim and Ashkenazim—than non-Jews attend institutions of higher learning.

Jewish immigrants from North Africa introduced a new expression of Jewishness into the French public sphere. Like Jewish elites in Britain, those in France preferred "quiet diplomacy" to vigorous protest. By contrast, North African Jews were more assertive than the Ashkenazic establishment. Politically, North African Jewish immigrants expressed a combative style reminiscent of the interwar Jewish immigrants from eastern Europe, whose ranks and political culture had been decimated by the Holocaust. Still, a more demonstrative style of French Jewish political culture that cuts across the Sephardic–Ashkenazic divide emerged in the late 1960s. It can be attributed to the impact of the Six-Day War, the 1967 slur of Charles de Gaulle that the Jews were "an elite people, sure of themselves, and domineering," his implication of Jewish disloyalty to France, the subsequent realignment of French foreign policy away from Israel in favor of the Arabs, and the student revolt of May 1968, which included many Jewish intellectuals who became more militantly expressive of their Jewishness.

A rise in the number of antisemitic incidents, including cemetery and synagogue desecrations, beatings of Jews, and murderous terrorist attacks, most often perpetrated by Muslims, and the emergence of the political far right under Jean-Marie Le Pen in the 1980s continue to stoke the fears of French Jews.

Most significant in the changing political culture of French Jewry is the extent to which Zionism, repudiated by Jewish organizations before World War II, was warmly embraced after it. However, Zionism was not the only political or cultural form of Jewish expression to emerge. In 1967, the Gaston Crémieux Circle, a Diasporist movement, was inaugurated by Jews of eastern European origin. It celebrated Yiddish culture not in the hope of reviving the language but as a model for French

Jews to articulate a new form of French Jewish identity. Their slogan, *le droit à la différence* ("the right to be different"), was a repudiation of the French Revolution's ideal of the homogenizing impact of national citizenship. Arguing for the right of minority cultures to exist in France, the circle's leader, Richard Marienstras, formed alliances with other national minority groups, such as Bretons and Armenians. Although France did not adopt a presidential committee's report that recommended official state recognition of national minority cultures, the circle was instrumental in leading the French debate on the nature of French identity. In the 1970s and 1980s, both left- and right-wing governments publicly endorsed the right of France's national minorities "to be different."

In 1980, Alain Finkielkraut, a Jewish intellectual whose refugee parents had arrived in France from Poland in the 1930s, articulated another vision of Jewish identity, one that was based on neither Sephardic nor Ashkenazic nostalgia, nor Zionism or Yiddishism. Finkielkraut wished for Jews of his generation to develop forms of identity that were not dependent on the trauma of the Holocaust. He found such an identity to be inauthentic because, as he put it, "[he] inherited a suffering that [he] had not undergone." Deeply sensitive to Jewish history and memory and the centrality of the Shoah, he nonetheless called for a personal, rather than collective, engagement with Jewishness. In addition to Marienstras and Finkielkraut, many other French Jewish intellectuals openly propose reconfigurations of Jewish identity, whether in the form of religious Orthodoxy, Sephardic militancy, or a return to medieval Jewish philosophical traditions in lieu of the perils (to Jews) inherent in Western thought and nationalism.

Germany

In Germany, postwar Jewish life can be divided into two phases: (1) 1945–1951, the era of the displaced persons (DPs) camps, and (2) 1951 to the early twenty-first century. Most of the DPs had left Germany by the early 1950s, taking in-depth knowledge of Judaism and strong Jewish identities with them. Many people stayed behind for a variety of reasons. Some were too old and sick to move or psychologically shattered by recent events. Others felt they simply had nowhere else to go. Some Jews had quickly established businesses and were committed to providing for their families, some had German spouses, and many were simply fearful of another rupture and starting over again. Others who wanted to leave stayed because they felt a deep-seated obligation to help those who could not or would not leave.

After the DP camps closed in the 1950s, about 30,000 Jews lived in Germany, in over 100 different communities. About 12,500 of them had left Germany between 1933 and 1938 and returned after the war. About half the Jews in Germany were of eastern European origin, and the other half were German-born, but this breakdown differed considerably according to region. In Bavaria, over 90 percent of the Jews were from eastern Europe, whereas German Jews made up 70 percent of the community in Berlin. Officially constituted communities also differed greatly in size. Some had only six or seven people, while Berlin had 8,000, and Munich, 3,300.

Deep disagreements often divided community members. In some towns, German Jews refused to accept eastern European Jews as full members of their respective communities. The nature of religious observance also changed, thanks to the encounter between eastern European and native German Jews.

Eastern European Orthodoxy held sway over the Liberal Judaism of German Jews. Different tunes, different customs, different forms of Hebrew pronunciation brought forth old frictions between German and Polish Jews in many towns. Disagreements were even greater over the future of the communities. Generally speaking, eastern European Jews saw their presence in Germany as a temporary stop on their way to Israel, while many German Jews felt a historic obligation to stay and rebuild Jewish life.

The choice to stay was not easy, and certainly, most Polish Jews would have preferred to leave. A spate of ritual murder charges in Bavaria in 1948, the more than 100 Jewish cemetery desecrations that had occurred throughout Germany by 1949, and the daubing of swastikas and antisemitic graffiti on buildings exacerbated Jewish antipathy to being in Germany. Those who remained in Germany often felt like history's remnant, their sense of aloneness worsened, as one scholar has noted, by being "shunned and despised by Jews outside Germany." In July 1948, the World Jewish Congress warned that Jews should never again settle on "blood-soaked German soil." Major Jewish organizations even blocked membership of Jews from Germany into the 1960s. Many who stayed had difficulty explaining to their children why, if the majority of DPs had managed to leave Germany, they remained behind. Children felt as though they unfairly bore the stigma of their parents' wrong decision. While the parents were "suspicious of and ambivalent toward all things German," children often resented being placed in the position of being raised in Germany. There are even problems of categorization for those born in Germany. Who were they? They were not German Jews, for that would suggest a continuation of prewar German Jewry, but rather, they were "Jews in Germany," an ambivalent term of self-description that is still in official use, as the community's governing body, founded in 1950, is named the Central Council of Jews in Germany.

After 1989 and the collapse of the Soviet Union, Germany again became a land of Jewish immigration with the eventual arrival of about 100,000 Jews from Russia. These immigrants provided a demographic boost to the pre-existing Jewish population in Germany of about 30,000 and soon began to take up prominent positions within the communities. In fact, for several years, community business was conducted in Russian and then translated into German. As of 2012, the estimated 200,000 Jews of Germany form the fastest-growing Jewish community in Europe.

While Jewish life in Germany is fraught with the impact of the past, a younger generation of German Jews has its eyes on the future. Increasingly, discussions concerning issues of Jewish identity take place in the public sphere. As a consequence, an exciting new German Jewish culture is in the making. There is a small but growing literary, theater, and film scene that tackles the theme of being a Jew in Germany. Universities likewise contribute to the Jewish discourse. In Munich and Berlin, significant numbers of students, most of them not Jewish, pursue Jewish studies and produce original scholarly research of the highest standards. In both cities, new museums of Jewish history attract large numbers of visitors. Aside from organized Jewish life, informal networks—Jewish study groups, choral societies, the *Tarbut* (Hebrew for "culture") adult education conference, which attracts around 300 participants annually—are evidence of an increasingly vibrant Jewish cultural life in Germany.

Elsewhere in Western Europe, Jewish populations have never been able to recover from the Holocaust, natural demographic decline, emigration, and assimilation. In 1939, the Jewish population of Holland stood at 140,000. In 2005, it was 30,000. Belgium was home to 90,000 Jews on the eve of the war and now has 31,000 Jews. Italy's Jewish population has decreased from 57,000 in 1939 to 28,000 in 2005. In all these countries, basic issues of finding Jewish spouses—less of a problem in Belgium, with its significant Hasidic population—and the absence of Jewish cultural life have resulted in a steady exodus of young Jews to England, the United States, and Israel.

Even in England, beyond the Holocaust's reach, the Jewish population shrank from over 400,000 in the 1950s to under 300,000 by the 1990s. The main reason for the decline is a very low birth rate and high death rate. Middle-class and relatively affluent, with a plethora of communal institutions, British Jewry has enjoyed material success. For a brief period in the 1970s and the 1980s, five Jews served as cabinet ministers in Margaret Thatcher's government. But events in the Middle East plague British Jewry and raise public concern. Groups within the radical left, such as the British Association of University Teachers, which in 2006 called for an academic boycott of Israeli universities, and mainstream liberal institutions, such as the *New Statesman*, the *Guardian*, and the BBC, have, at various times, given expression to virulent anti-Israel sentiments, sometimes indistinguishable from antisemitism. On January 14, 2002, the *New Statesman* ran a story on "excessive" Jewish influence and power and carried a front-page illustration of the Union Jack being pierced with a Star of David with the caption "A Kosher Conspiracy?" Although Jews are not under any threat in England, younger, more dynamic voices have urged the ordinarily quiescent leadership, the Board of Deputies, to be more aggressive when representing the community. This faction felt particularly frustrated and abandoned by traditional leaders at the time of the proposed boycott of Israeli academic institutions. The board's traditional approach of "quiet diplomacy" was, according to Jewish critics, a remnant of an earlier, more insecure time, and what was called for now was a more combative mode of self-defense. The divide over this issue may yet spill over into other areas of Anglo-Jewish life and prove a force for creative and more vocal expressions of Jewish identity.

THE JEWS OF THE SOUTHERN HEMISPHERE

In the eighteenth and nineteenth centuries, Jewish immigrants began to make their way to Latin America, South Africa, and Australia. Stable and settled, these communities were far from centers of tradition and authority.

Latin America is home to approximately 400,000 Jews, with the biggest communities in Argentina and Brazil. In Argentina, Jews have had a very mixed experience since World War II. In 1946, Juan Perón, a Nazi sympathizer and Catholic authoritarian, came to power. While he put an end to Jewish emigration and allowed the country to be a haven for Nazis on the run—Adolf Eichmann was captured there in 1960 by Israeli agents—Perón also established diplomatic relations with Israel in 1949. During the military dictatorship of 1976–1983, Jews were accused of left-wing and sometimes Zionist sympathies and were prominent targets of the junta and secret police. They were kidnapped, tortured, and numbered among the *desaparecidos*, or "the disappeared." During this period, Jews lived in fear and many immigrated to Israel.

When the junta fell in 1983, antisemitic attacks also declined. The Jewish community welcomed the democratically elected government of Raul Alfonsín. But antisemitism had not disappeared, and tragedy struck the community in 1994, when the central Jewish communal offices in Buenos Aires were blown up by terrorists in the pay of the Iranian government. Right-wing Argentine circles also appear to have been involved, their presence in the government helping to explain the deliberate foot-dragging of the investigation. In 2005, the Argentine investigator declared the bombing to have been the work of a Lebanese suicide bomber from Hezbollah. No one has yet been brought to justice. Eighty-seven people were murdered in the attack, and over 100 more were injured.

About 181,000 Jews remain in Argentina. As elsewhere, they are overwhelmingly secular, middle-class, and concentrated in commerce. Once a thriving center of spoken Yiddish culture and publishing, the community is almost entirely Spanish-speaking now, though Yiddish theater is still performed. There is also a wide array of Jewish cultural, sporting, and educational institutions. But the community is anything but secure. The collapse of the community's cooperative banking system in the 1960s still continues to be felt, and the most recent economic crisis produced an increase in poverty rates, so relatively large numbers of Jews have chosen to immigrate to Spain, whose Jewish community has enjoyed something of a boost. In the context of economic and possibly political uncertainty, Argentinean Jews fear the resurgence of antisemitism.

In the interwar period, neighboring Brazil took in approximately 30,000 Jewish immigrants, and about 42,000 Jews were living there

when the Nazis came to power in 1933, after which time Brazil tightened its restrictions on Jews seeking to enter the country. For 20 years after World War II, postwar immigration and natural growth saw the community grow to around 120,000, though some estimates put it at 150,000 Jews. Mostly centered in São Paulo and Rio de Janeiro, the communities came to boast an array of day schools, community centers, museums, and Jewish newspapers. Deeply integrated into the economic and cultural life of the country, Jews also came to hold important political offices at state and federal levels. In contrast to Argentina, antisemitism in Brazil in the postwar period has been negligible. As in many other countries, deep pockets of assimilation and an intermarriage rate perhaps as high as 60 percent reflect the high level of Jewish integration into the dominant society.

Since World War II, in lands of the British Commonwealth, such as Canada, South Africa, and Australia, Jews have enjoyed levels of social acceptance barely matched anywhere else. In Canada, when antisemitism has flared, it has largely been confined to Quebec, linked with Francophone hostility to the Anglo-Protestants. Following World War II, Canada reversed its strict anti-immigration policies, and between 1946 and 1960, 46,000 Jewish immigrants were admitted into Canada, a combination of Holocaust survivors and Jews who fled Hungary after the 1956 uprising. The Jewish population reached 200,000 by 1950.

By 2005, 372,000 Jews lived in Canada, making it the fourth-largest Jewish community in the world. Most Jews are settled in the urban centers of Montreal, Toronto, and Winnipeg. Well integrated into Canadian society, Canadian Jewry, more conservative than its American counterpart, has exhibited a greater degree of insularity (a trait shared by other ethnic groups in Canada) and a much stronger degree of commitment to Jewish traditions than American Jews. Zionism, continuing use of Yiddish after the 1950s, less geographical dispersion, and greater contact with refugees and Holocaust survivors—by 1990, between 30 and 40 percent of Canadian Jews were descendants of Holocaust survivors, compared to 8 percent of American Jews—have made for a tightly knit Jewish community in touch with older traditions.

Jewish life in South Africa thrived both before and in the decades after the war despite considerable difficulties. In 1948, the country adopted apartheid, and South African Jewry had to walk a thin line between protest and acquiescence. The ruling Afrikaner elite was also antisemitic, and South African Jewry was constantly on trial. Not too many Jews expressed their disgust with the system, preferring to keep a low profile while accepting its social benefits. However, two of the most outspoken critics of apartheid were Jews—Helen Suzman (b. 1917–2009) and Joe Slovo (1926–1995). Suzman, an economist, was a member of the liberal Progressive Party and spent 36 years in Parliament as a dogged English-speaking opponent of apartheid in a political chamber full of male Afrikaner Calvinists. Slovo, an immigrant from Lithuania, was head of the South African Communist Party and one of the few white members of the African National Congress. By the 1980s, a host of Jewish groups were working with black Africans to bring an end to apartheid. In 1985, Jews for Justice, located in Cape Town, and Jews for Social Justice, centered in Johannesburg, joined forces to reform South African society and attempt to bring the white and black communities together.

While Afrikaner rule never pursued antisemitism as a matter of policy, Jews nonetheless felt insecure. Some started leaving as early as 1960 in the aftermath of the Sharpeville Massacre, in which 69 black Africans were killed and at least 200 were injured when police opened fire on demonstrators protesting against the pass laws, which dictated where, when, and for how long a person could remain in "white" areas. In the 1970s and 1980s, as racial tensions rose and political conflict seemed unavoidable, many Jews began to leave in fear of violence. Some, especially university students, left to avoid military service on behalf of a regime they disliked and an ideology they loathed. Between 1970 and 1992, more than 39,000 Jews left South Africa for Britain, the United States, and Australia. At its peak in the 1970s, the Jewish community was around 120,000 strong. Due to emigration, this number has shrunk considerably, and as of 2012, only about 67,000 Jews remained.

One of the few postwar communities that continue to grow is Australian Jewry. With 112,000 Jews, Australia is the ninth-largest Jewish community in the world. It has benefited from a very tolerant atmosphere, a strong economy, and since the 1970s, waves of migration from South Africa, Russia, and Israel. As of 2001, 12.5 percent of all Jews in Australia were South African. The two largest communities live in Melbourne and Sydney, both exhibiting different characteristics thanks to the fact that Jewish immigrants to Melbourne, beginning in the 1930s, tended to be Yiddish-speaking Jews from eastern Europe, Poland in particular, while more acculturated German, Austrian, and Hungarian Jews gravitated to

Sydney. In 1933, some 23,000 Jews were living in Australia. Between 1938 and 1961, the arrival of refugees, Holocaust survivors, and Hungarian Jews fleeing the political turmoil of 1956 resulted in a total Jewish population increase to 61,000.

Australian Jewry is deeply committed to Jewish tradition, Zionism, and a particular form of Jewishness best described as *yiddishkayt*, the legacy of Yiddish language, culture, and history. The community takes its particular cast from interwar refugees and postwar Holocaust survivors. After the war, survivors and refugees were intensely concerned with the Jewish future. Given that postwar governments admitted Jews but felt that it was the responsibility of the existing Jewish community to assist the newcomers, an elaborate communal welfare system was established to assist with the integration of survivors. Representatives of the welfare agencies met incoming boatloads of Jews at the ports, organized housing and employment, and provided interest-free business loans. The task of caring for the refugees was a great burden for the small local Jewish community, which in turn requested and received help from American aid agencies, such as the Joint Distribution Committee, the Hebrew Immigrant Aid Society, and the Refugee Economic Corporation. Given the high number of Holocaust survivors in Australia, between 1952 and 1965, significant funding was obtained from the Conference on Jewish Material Claims Against Germany. With its higher percentage of Polish Jews who came to Australia bearing a strong philanthropic and social service tradition, Melbourne Jewry was extremely energetic and proactive in assisting the immigrants. As such, this tended to attract an even greater percentage of Holocaust survivors, 60 percent of whom settled in Melbourne.

The impact of such a high percentage of Jews who either fled from interwar persecution or survived the Nazis came to have a decisive impact on Australian Jewish culture. Seeking to rebuild Jewish life after the devastation of the Holocaust, the community focused attention on its children, pouring its resources and energy into building up what would become the largest and most successful network of Jewish day schools in the Diaspora. By 1943, a German Jewish refugee in Sydney, Elchanan Blumenthal, had already established the North Bondi Jewish Kindergarten and Day School. A newspaper report in the *Hebrew Standard of Australasia* reported on the official opening of the institution, revealing the founders' raison d'être: "Let us sadly remember them, all those who over there on the other side are experiencing the full brunt of mysterious Jewish suffering and all the centers of Jewish learning are lying in ruins." The focal point of the Australian day school system is in Melbourne, home to the world's largest such school, Mount Scopus Memorial College, founded in 1949. By the 1980s, the school had over 3,000 students, spread over several campuses. The immediate success of Mount Scopus served as inspiration to open other Jewish day schools. Such institutions cater to a gamut of modern Jewish ideologies, from ultra-Orthodox to Zionist schools, to a Bundist-inspired Yiddish day school. Jewish day schools exist in all major cities in Australia, and it is estimated that approximately 70 percent of Australian Jewish children are educated in these institutions.

What constitutes an unusual model of modern Jewish identity in Australia is the extent to which Jews have been able to remain insular while being, for the most part, secular. A 1992 survey of attitudes toward religion found that 6 percent of respondents identified themselves as "strictly Orthodox," 33 percent were "traditional religious" (not necessarily observant, but when they do attend synagogue, even if infrequently, they choose an Orthodox one), 15 percent were "Liberal/Reform," 43 percent were "Jewish but not religious," and 3 percent were either opposed to religion or identified as something else. The popularity of Chabad Judaism among otherwise-secular Jews is further testament to a kind of Jewish diversity rarely seen elsewhere and one that reflects an ecumenical spirit among Australia's secular Jews.

CONTEMPORARY ANTISEMITISM

While antisemitism remains a pervasive phenomenon, its intensity and visibility ebb and flow. By various measures—social acceptance, economic well-being, and educational attainments, to name but three—few periods in history have been as good for Jews as the current one. Even religious anti-Judaism is on the wane, in the case of the Catholic Church's *Nostra Aetate* (1965), which not only recognizes that the Church received the wisdom of the Old Testament from the Jews but also admits thus:

> True, the Jewish authorities and those who followed their lead pressed for the death of Christ; still, what happened in His passion cannot be charged against all the Jews, without distinction, then alive, nor against the Jews of today. The Catholic Church is the new people of God, the Jews should not be presented as rejected or accursed by God.

The Church has attempted to build bridges between Catholics and Jews and has sought to come to terms with the disastrous impact of its millennial, anti-Jewish teachings. In 1979, Pope John Paul II went to Auschwitz and paid homage to Jewish Holocaust victims, and in 1986, he became the first modern pontiff to visit the Rome synagogue. Pope Francis has continued this display of goodwill toward Jews.

Despite all this, we are nonetheless currently in a period of antisemitic resurgence. According to an Anti-Defamation League survey of 2012, "disturbingly high levels" of antisemitism were to be found in ten European countries. Since the turn of the twenty-first century, antisemitism has risen to levels not seen since World War II, and while its intensity bears little resemblance to that which occurred in the period between and during the two world wars, understanding the impact and nature of contemporary antisemitism will be sorely compromised if it is measured only against that which was perpetrated by the Nazis and their accomplices. Instead, even as we set about describing and analyzing it on its own terms, we will see that in its modern guise, antisemitism in the twenty-first century relies to a great extent on tropes, accusations, stereotypes, and visual imagery drawn from the entire history of antisemitism. Thus, many of the antisemitic depictions and specific charges in current use will be familiar from earlier chapters of this book, but now they are deployed within an entirely new historical context. There are, however, also some entirely new forms of antisemitism, such as intemperate and incendiary charges leveled at Israel and the attempts to delegitimize its very existence, as well as new arenas for its expression and dissemination, such as at universities and via social media, the latter being the vehicle most singularly responsible for the wild spread of antisemitic charges, especially conspiracy theories.

Nowhere today are Jews in Europe assailed by antisemitism as they are in France, which is home to about 500,000 Jews and 5 million Muslims, the two largest such populations in Europe. Most members of both communities trace their roots to North Africa. Until the late 1960s, some even led lives in France characterized by fraternization and shared cultural memories, language, foods, attire, and even religious traditions. In Paris, they often lived as neighbors, frequently in the poorest, outer suburbs. The tensions produced as a result of the French exit from Algeria led to increasingly racialized notions of Frenchness and a hardening of categories such as "Europeans" versus "Muslims." France's pro-Arab orientation during and after the 1967 Six-Day War meant a realignment of the relationship of Jews to the French state. The increasing anxiety and sense of difference experienced by the two communities were exacerbated by what one historian has called "transnational activism on behalf of both sides in the Israeli-Palestinian conflict." The student unrest of May 1968 and the concomitant emergence of a radical left-wing politics took on a stridently pro-Palestinian and anti-Zionist character. All these developments came together and has led to the rise of an "ethno-religious identity politics" that has divided the two communities.

One notable characteristic of resurgent French antisemitism is that it has frequently been violent and far more so than elsewhere in the Diaspora. The 2002 Lyon car attack was one of the earliest manifestations of the revived antisemitism. In this attack, two cars rammed their way through the main gates of a synagogue and then careened into the main sanctuary. The masked assailants then set fire to the vehicles, causing severe damage to the synagogue. Another ominous characteristic of modern French antisemitism is

the targeting of individual Jews. On January 21, 2006, Ilan Halimi, a young French Jew of Moroccan descent, was kidnapped by a group called the Gang of Barbarians, led by Youssouf Fofana. Over a period of three weeks, Halimi was mercilessly tortured and eventually murdered. From March 11 to March 19, 2012, Mohammed Merah, a Frenchman of Algerian descent, went on three murderous shooting sprees in Toulouse and Montauban. In the third of those attacks, on March 19, four people, including three children, were killed at the Ozat Hatorah Jewish Day School. Four other persons were wounded. Before police eventually killed Merah after a three-day siege, he justified his actions by claiming to have targeted French soldiers because they fought al-Qaeda in Afghanistan, while he murdered the Jewish schoolchildren because "[t]he Jews kill our brothers and sisters in Palestine." In July of 2014, during the height of Israel's war in Gaza against Hamas, the situation reached a boiling point, with blatantly antisemitic demonstrations not only in France but also across Europe. In Berlin, there were calls for Jews to be sent to the gas chambers and demonstrators in other European capitals openly embracing Hitler and his antisemitic policies. Chants of "Death to the Jews!" were commonplace in Paris, an eerie recapitulation of the same chants heard expressed by 100,000 demonstrators in the same streets in the summer of 1898 during the Dreyfus Affair. On Sunday, July 13, 2014, hundreds of protestors stormed into the Marais, Paris's historic Jewish quarter. Armed with axes and iron bars and bearing Hamas and ISIS flags, they made their way to the Don Isaac Abravanel synagogue. Among the 200 worshipers inside was the chief rabbi of Paris. The 300 or so demonstrators trapped the Jews inside the synagogue while hurling epithets, including, "Hitler was right!" and "Jews, get out of

France!" In what was a remarkable display of naïveté and incompetence, a mere six police officers had been assigned to monitor the demonstration that day.

During January 7–9, 2015, radical Islamists went on a murderous rampage at a number of locations in and around Paris. On January 7, at the offices of the satirical magazine *Charlie Hebdo*, 12 people were shot dead and a further 12 were wounded. The justification for the killings was the supposed disrespect the magazine had shown toward Islam. However, on January 9, a terrorist named Amedy Coulibaly entered the Hypercacher kosher supermarket armed with semi-automatic weapons. He murdered Jewish shoppers and took several hostages. During the protracted standoff, Coulibaly described his mission as one to avenge the Prophet and kill the Jews. In other words, unlike the specific reason, as spurious as it was, offered for the *Charlie Hebdo* murders, those at the supermarket were perpetrated simply because the victims were Jews and not for anything they were said to have specifically done. When police finally stormed the grocery store, they shot Coulibaly dead and released the 15 hostages. Lassana Bathily, a Muslim who worked at the supermarket, had acted heroically throughout as he risked his life by hiding people from the gunman in a downstairs refrigerator. These are only the most notorious incidents of such violence in France, where reported antisemitic hate crimes more than doubled, from 423 in 2013 to 851 in 2014. By early 2014, the number of French Jews who had immigrated to Israel surpassed the number of American Jews who had done likewise, and conversations within the Jewish community were largely animated by the constant repetition of the question of whether to leave or stay. This is not only a measure of the palpable fear felt among an increasing number of Jews in France but has also sent shockwaves through the French political establishment. After the Hypercacher supermarket attacks, Prime Minister Emanuel Valls delivered one of the greatest speeches on antisemitism ever given by a leading European politician. To rapt attention, he declared to the National Assembly on January 13, 2015:

> Without its Jews France would not be France. This is the message we have to communicate loud and clear. We haven't done so. We haven't shown enough outrage. How can we accept that in certain schools and colleges the Holocaust can't be taught? How can we accept that when a child is asked, Who is your enemy? the response is The Jew? When the Jews of France are attacked, France is attacked; the conscience of humanity is attacked. Let us never forget it.

In England, a country with a Jewish population half the size of France's and with a comparatively weak tradition of antisemitism in the modern period, there has been a marked increase in expressions and acts of antisemitism since the Gaza War in the summer of 2014. The year 2016 was particularly worrying. According to the Community Security Trust (CST), a British charity established in 1994 to ensure the safety and security of the Jewish community in the United Kingdom, there were 1,309 antisemitic incidents in 2016. This was a 36 percent increase over the 960 incidents recorded by the CST in 2015 and the highest number since such figures began to be compiled in 1984. Of the 1,309 antisemitic incidents, 107 were violent assaults, an increase of 29 percent from the 87 violent incidents recorded in 2015. In addition, there were dozens of incidents of damage and desecration of Jewish property and over 1,000 incidents of abusive behavior, including verbal abuse, antisemitic graffiti, antisemitic abuse via social media, and one-off cases of hate mail. Antisemitism also has a distinct political dimension in the United Kingdom, where the situation was compounded by the attitude of some members of the Labor Party and its one-time leader, the unreconstructed Jeremy Corbyn, who, in the past, has lauded Hamas and referred to them as "friends," without regard to the group's antisemitic ideology, something blatantly enshrined in its 1988 charter. Under Corbyn's leadership, a significant number of Labor politicians were emboldened to make anti-Israel statements that have relied on age-old negative tropes about Jews. This touched off a crisis in Labor, resulting in the expulsion from the party of a number of politicians who had made the offending remarks. Most prominent among them was the ex-mayor of London, Ken Livingstone. In April 2016, he was expelled from the Labor Party following a BBC interview in which he stated, "When Hitler won his election in 1932 his policy then was that Jews should be moved to Israel. He was supporting Zionism before he went mad and ended up killing six million Jews." By simultaneously claiming that Hitler took a pro-Zionist stance and was a mass murderer, Livingstone was implying that Zionism as an ideology is in itself a warrant to commit genocide against the Palestinians. Challenged by members of his own party, Livingstone refused to back down. On March 30, 2017, when entering court for a hearing on his previous comments, Livingstone doubled down. Utterly fabricating history, he stated that "right up until the start of the Second World War," there was "real collaboration" between Jews and Nazis. He offered as "proof" the following: "The [Nazi] SS set up training camps so that German Jews who [were] going to go there [Palestine] could be trained to cope with a very different sort of country." In the summer of 2016, in the midst of the political crisis, a Labor politician, Sadiq Kahn, became the newly elected mayor of London and the first-ever Muslim to hold that post. Addressing the antisemitism that was rife within his own party, he declared:

> I am adopting a strict zero-tolerance approach to anti-Semitism and all hate crime. . . . We need to send the message far and wide that anti-Semitism is totally unacceptable and can never be justified, and I will be encouraging other mayors across the country and Europe to sign the pledge. We must work together to root out anti-Semitism wherever we find it— and, yes—that includes within the Labour Party.

Even countries with tiny Jewish communities are not immune from the scourge of antisemitism. Here, Israel is very much at the center of the discourse, the criticism of which does not automatically amount to antisemitism. This is an important distinction that must not be forgotten, as will be more fully elucidated ahead. However, there is a certain strain of anti-Israel sentiment that collapses the categories of anti-Zionism, anti-Israel sentiment, and antisemitism. At times, medieval anti-Jewish charges have been incorporated into a new form of antisemitic rhetoric. This was precisely the case in August 2009, when, in a modern variant of the ancient blood libel, the Swedish tabloid *Aftonbladet* reported that the Israel Defense Forces kidnapped Palestinian youth and dismembered their bodies for the purpose of selling their organs. Also in Sweden, left-wing politicians have helped foster a climate of indifference to a rise in antisemitic rhetoric, abuse, and violence by the application of spurious analogies and false equivalencies. In the city of Malmö in particular, a onetime mayor of the city, Ilmar Reepalu, set the tone. In a 2010 newspaper interview, he responded to the assertion that antisemitism was on the rise in his city, stating thus: "We accept neither Zionism nor antisemitism. They are extremes that put themselves above other groups, and believe they have a lower value." He also criticized Malmö's Jewish community for supporting Israel: "I would wish for the Jewish community to denounce Israeli violations against the civilian population in Gaza. Instead it decides to hold a [pro-Israeli] demonstration in the Grand Square [of Malmö], which could send the wrong signals." He has, of course, never demanded that Swedes, native-born or immigrants, denounce antisemitism, despite his claim that it was no different from Zionism. While Reepalu did not elucidate on what he meant by "send the wrong signals," it is reasonable to assume an implication of Jewish disloyalty, that a true Swede would, by definition, be opposed to Israel and those holding a rally in support of Israel—namely, Jews in Malmö could not be authentic (in a moral sense) Swedes. In October of 2015, in response to a wave of stabbings of Jews by Arabs in Israel, a rally in Malmö heard chants of "Death to the Jews" and demands for "more stabbings." A number of local politicians, including two members of Parliament, were in attendance and voiced no objection to the chants. The Swedish government, headed by the Social Democratic prime minister Stefan Löfven, is known for its staunch support of the Palestinian cause and its criticism of Israel. There is, of course, nothing intrinsically antisemitic about this, except for the fact that the country's foreign minister, Margot Wallström, suggested that the motivation for the series of terrorist attacks across Paris that took place on November 15, 2015, in which 90 people were killed and hundreds more were wounded, stemmed from the frustration of Palestinians. Statements such as these are commonplace in Swedish political life. Because of the collapsing of categories such as Jews and Israelis, attacks on Jews are justified, or at least tolerated, because it is as if it is Israelis who are being targeted and they, in the logic of Swedish political discourse, are fair game.

Even in Denmark, with its proud history of saving its Jews during World War II, violence struck in 2015. However, here the political climate and response were quite different from that in Sweden. On February 15 of that year, a gunman killed 37-year-old Dan Uzan, a young Jewish man on security duty outside Copenhagen's main synagogue, where, at that time, a bat mitzvah was being celebrated. At the funeral for Uzan, the Danish prime minister, Helle Thorning Schmidt, wiped tears from her eyes, and at a vigil the following day, she told the assembled crowd that "an attack on the Jews of Denmark is an attack on Denmark." Indeed, the murder of Uzan took place only a matter of hours after the same gunman had opened fire at a cultural center that was hosting a debate on Islam and free speech, where he killed one of the featured speakers, Finn Norgaard, a documentary filmmaker. In Norway, just after the attack, hundreds of young Muslims mobilized to form a protective "ring of peace" around Oslo's main synagogue. In contrast to Sweden, no spurious justification or rationalization for an attack on Jews was offered by Danish political elites. Almost all the attacks on European Jews were perpetrated by radical Islamists, most of them born in Europe. On some occasions, they have claimed the attacks are revenge for the Israeli treatment of Palestinians. Doing so, of course, clearly collapses the distinction between Israeli Jews and those from European countries, making a mockery of the distinction between anti-Zionism and antisemitism. For the terrorists, it is a distinction without a difference.

The marked rise in antisemitism in Europe has alarmed the continent's Jews. A survey conducted in 2013 by the European Union Agency for Fundamental Rights showed that almost a third of Europe's Jews have considered emigrating, with numbers as high as 46 percent in France and 48 percent in Hungary. And those figures predate the worst of the violent terrorist attacks against Jews. According to Jeffrey Goldberg of *The Atlantic*, "[i]n 2014, Jews in Europe were murdered, raped, beaten, stalked, chased, harassed, spat on, and insulted for being Jewish." Many Jews have left Europe, while many defiantly proclaim the need to stay and claim their rightful place in Europe, and still others see merit or necessity in doing both. This position was expressed by the French Jewish philosopher Alain Finkielkraut at the time of the Hypercacher murders on January 9, 2015. In an interview, Jeffrey Goldberg asked, "Do you have a bag packed?" Finkielkraut responded pessimistically, "We should not leave," he said, "but maybe for our children or grandchildren there will be no choice."

The situation in Europe has led many to rashly opine that the situation today resembles that found in Europe in the 1930s. That is a gross misunderstanding both of the past and of the present. The greatest difference is that there is not one government in Western Europe actively promoting antisemitism, and neither is there a state seeking to introduce antisemitic laws. Still, the subject of the future of Jews in Europe has reverberated across the Jewish world. Jewish community centers, synagogues, official bodies such as the Anti-Defamation League, and Jewish studies programs at universities in the United States and beyond have held workshops and seminars, hosted lectures, and sponsored research studies on the subject. Until the election of Donald Trump to the presidency of the United States in November 2016, American Jewry's principal concerns about antisemitism were focused on Europe. However, with its race-baiting rhetoric, the Trump campaign in 2015 garnered the open support of white nationalists, as well as the endorsement of the Ku Klux Klan and notorious individuals, such as David Duke. In the first ten days after the November 8 election, the Southern Poverty Law Center (SPLC) recorded 100 antisemitic incidents, which was about 12 percent of the total recorded hate crimes. The same center also reported that, in 2016, there were 917 hate groups active in the United States, up from 892 in 2015. Tellingly, the SPLC categorizes hate groups by type, such as anti-immigrant, anti-LGBT, and anti-Muslim. There is, however, no category for antisemitic groups, according to Mark Potok, a senior fellow at the SPLC. In response to a reporter's question as to why this was the case, Potok said, "The reason we don't have a separate category for anti-Jewish groups is that the vast majority of them are all anti-Semitic." Individual instances of antisemitic abuse, the daubing of swastikas on Jewish institutions and college dormitories housing Jewish students, and cemetery desecrations have increased in frequency.

Donald Trump is, of course, not singly responsible for this situation. Antisemitic hate groups and crimes long pre-existed Trump's entrance into politics. The FBI Hate Crime Statistics Report for 2014 showed that 60 percent of the reported religion-based crimes in the United States were directed against Jews and Jewish institutions. However, there can be little doubt that Donald Trump's presidential campaign contributed to a rising climate of hate, both of his own doing and that of his supporters. For example, in February 2016, Trump twice retweeted from the Twitter feed @WhiteGenocideTM, which regularly posts antisemitic content while the user's location was set as "Jewmerica." Then, on July 2, 2016,

Trump tweeted an image of Hillary Clinton. Next to her was a six-pointed star bearing the words "Most Corrupt Candidate Ever!" Clinton's face was set in front of a backdrop of hundred-dollar bills. The tweet was a nasty brew that equated Jews with money, corruption, and influence pedaling, for it implied that Hillary Clinton had been bought and paid for by Jews. The tweet unleashed a storm of protest and indignation, with the campaign denying that it was, in any way, antisemitic. Trump himself tweeted on July 4, 2016: "Dishonest media is trying its absolute best to depict a star in a tweet as a Star of David rather than a Sheriff's Star, or a plain star!" The next day, it was revealed by *mic.com*, an online publication, that the image had been lifted from an antisemitic internet message board used by members of the alt-right, neo-Nazis, and white supremacists.

Another antisemitic element to emerge from Trump's campaign is the QAnon conspiracy theory. At the heart of the ideology is the belief that there exists a cabal of Democratic politicians who are satanic, cannibalistic child molesters who are operating a global child sex trafficking ring. Those who believe the charge also claim that the Trump administration is engaged in battling the pedophiles and would conduct mass arrests and executions on a day followers of the cult have dubbed "The Storm" or "The Event." At its core, QAnon is deeply antisemitic, drawing upon the medieval charge of Jewish ritual murder and blood libel accusations that held that Jews sacrificed Christian children and used their drained blood to bake matzah. QAnon tirelessly promotes the idea that the Jewish financier George Soros and the Rothschild family are deeply involved in the cabal. The movement quickly metastasized with adherents found across the globe.

During Trump's run for the presidency in 2015, the campaign obliquely, and his followers openly, engaged in the online harassment of Jewish journalists. According to a report by the Anti-Defamation League (ADL) titled "Anti-Semitic Targeting of Journalists During the 2016 Presidential Campaign," between August 2015 and July 2016, at least 800 journalists received some 19,000 antisemitic tweets, sent from 1,600 Twitter accounts. "The top 10 most targeted journalists (all of whom are Jewish) received 83 percent of these anti-Semitic tweets." Most of the messages used words such as "kike," "Israel," and "Zionist" and laid claims to any number of conspiracies Jews are said by antisemites to engage in, the most common being that Jews control the media and global finance and were the ones that carried out the 9/11 terrorist attacks. A common feature of many of the tweets is that they contained ghastly photoshopped images of the journalists in Nazi extermination camps, lining up to go into gas chambers or lying on wooden bunks in camp barracks. In other instances, similar photoshopped pictures were those of the journalists' children. An unusually large number came from self-identified Trump supporters. According to the ADL report, the words that show up most frequently in the bios of Twitter users sending antisemitic tweets to journalists are "Trump," "nationalist," "conservative," "American" and "White."

Jewish journalists who had written articles critical of Trump were particular targets of the tweets. The *Politico* journalist Hadas Gold was sent a picture of herself after being shot in the head; it bore the caption "Don't mess with our boy Trump or you will be first in line for the camp." In another instance, when Julia Ioffe wrote a profile of Donald Trump's wife, Melania, for the May 2016 issue of *GQ* that was perceived by some as unflattering, she became the target of two well-known neo-Nazis, who then encouraged their supporters to flood her

Twitter account, making "sure to identify her as a Jew working against White interests." Jonathan Wiseman of *The New York Times*, another journalist who was especially targeted, was the first to call attention to a tactic employed by those sending out antisemitic tweets: the use of triple parentheses around a Jewish journalist's name. The symbol—(((())))—is a typographical transcription of an echo sound effect used on an antisemitic podcast whenever a Jewish name was mentioned. This tactic carries another echo as well. During Stalin's antisemitic purge between 1948 and 1952, the original Jewish names of the accused were placed in parentheses in the Soviet press. Thus outed, they could no longer hide behind the Russian names they had adopted in service to the Revolution. The current American use of the echo led to a defiant response and repurposing of the symbol by Jewish journalists and those who supported them; they placed the symbol around their own Twitter screen names to identify themselves as Jews. It is a hypermodern version of the call by the German Zionist Robert Weltsch, who, in April 1933, declared to his fellow Jews, "The Yellow Badge—Bear It with Pride!"

Perhaps the most blatant use of antisemitic tropes by the Trump campaign came with its closing television advertisement just before the November 8, 2016, election. It depicted Hillary Clinton and three easily identifiable Jews as archvillains: the financier George Soros; the then chair of the Federal Reserve, Janet Yellen; and Goldman Sachs CEO Lloyd Blankfein. The narrator begins:

> The establishment has trillions of dollars at stake in this election. For those who control the levers of power in Washington [picture of Soros] and for the global special interests [picture of Yellen]. They partner

with these people [picture of Clinton] who don't have your good in mind.

He ominously continues:

> It's a global power structure that is responsible for the economic decisions that have robbed our working-class, stripped our country of its wealth and put that money into the [picture of Blankfein] pockets of a handful of large corporations and political entities.

The use of such well-worn antisemitic charges in a political advertisement for a presidential candidate was as shocking as it was deliberate. As Josh Marshall, journalist for the online website Talking Points Memo, wrote, "[t]his is an ad intended to appeal to anti-Semites and spread anti-Semitic ideas. That's the only standard that really matters. This is intentional and by design. It is no accident." At a press conference in February 2017, President Trump responded to a question from an ultra-Orthodox Jewish supporter about what his government intended to do about the "uptick" in antisemitism in the United States. Defensively and rudely, Trump snapped at the reporter, Jake Turx: "Not a simple question. Not a fair question. Okay, sit down. I understand the question. So here's the story folks. Number One: I am the least antisemitic person that you've ever seen in your entire life."

The antisemitism that pre-existed but was emboldened by Donald Trump's campaign came from the extreme right wing of the political spectrum, mostly neo-Nazis and those who identify as white nationalists. But there has also been a rising tide of left-wing antisemitism, which, while often hurling similar charges and even using some of the same iconographies as those on the right, tends to have a very different social base, one that is more educated and is frequently encountered most openly on college campuses. There are two principal drivers of this phenomenon: race and Israel. The first derives from the underlying character of America's own history of racism. The twin pillars upon which that history and its legacy rest are skin color and underrepresentation; indeed, skin color and underrepresentation have historically gone hand in hand in the United States. As such, it is only reasonable that an American understanding of racism be seen through this lens. The problem is that while this is appropriate for peoples of color in the United States, it is not a universally applicable framework to understand other forms of prejudice, such as antisemitism. First, antisemitism obviously long predates the advent of the United States, with its roots in religious conflict and not an economic system based on slave labor or conquest, as was the case with Native Americans. Second, antisemitism is not predicated on skin color or underrepresentation. In fact, one of the distinguishing features of modern antisemitism is the combination of indistinguishable physical features from a white majority (most Jews being Caucasian) and overrepresentation as the means by which Jews are said to engage in a surreptitious conspiracy to achieve control of the economy or the nation. Beginning in the nineteenth century, especially in Europe, the disproportionate presence of Jews in fields such as medicine, law, commerce, journalism, and the arts led to howls of disapproval by all antisemites. Irrespective of the country they were in, the universal claim was that Jews had "taken over" control of the societies in which they lived. In the United States in the early twentieth century, Ivy League universities imposed quotas on the admission of Jewish students. There were also bans against Jews working in various occupations, such as advertising and banking, while housing covenants prevented Jews from buying homes in certain parts of America. In both Europe and the United States, the antisemitic backlash against Jewish success, which called for boycotts, quotas, and the passage of laws intended to curb Jewish upward mobility, contributed to a climate of hatred. In Europe, it was a necessary precondition to what ended up as genocide. This is echoed today in right-wing cries of Jewish "influence" and "control" over society. On the left, over the last 30 years at least, there has been a growing failure to see the reality of antisemitism because of the assumption that racial prejudice is something that only people of color can suffer, and that overrepresentation, dubbed by the left as "white privilege," is some sort of shield against hatred. However, as history makes abundantly clear, whiteness did not protect Jews in Europe before and during World War II, and it does not today in either Europe, the United States, or anywhere else.

Indeed, it is not even fair to claim that whiteness is always the proper color descriptor for Jews. While most people would consider the majority of American Jews to be white, absolutely no white nationalist would. They are very explicit about this. In the spring semester of 2017, flyers posted on college campuses across America declared, "WHITE MAN are you sick and tired of the Jews destroying your country through mass immigration and degeneracy? Join us in the struggle for global white supremacy at the Daily Stormer." At a meeting of European and American white supremacists held in New Orleans in 2005, David Duke told the 300 participants that European Americans were facing [their] "greatest crisis in history," that there was a "genocide" against every "White nation on earth" as a result of "massive immigration" and "the worldwide power of Jewish supremacism." The claim that Jews promote mass immigration—on certain right-wing websites, there is even the charge that Jews bring radical Muslims into the United States in order to have them destroy it—is a charge with firm historical roots. In an infamous passage in *Mein Kampf,* Hitler wrote of the occupation of the Rhineland region of Germany by French troops after World War I. Among those troops were black soldiers from Senegal and the Congo, about whom Hitler railed:

> It was and it is Jews who bring the Negroes into the Rhineland, always with the same secret thought and clear aim of ruining the hated white race by the necessarily resulting bastardization, throwing it down from its cultural and political height, and himself rising to be its master.

Claims from many on the political left, Jews among them, that Jews enjoy "white privilege" simply ignore the claims of white supremacists like Duke that Jews are not white and thus completely misunderstand and, in fact, contribute to contemporary antisemitism and its very complicated nature.

University campuses, almost all of which champion diversity and inclusion, have frequently become sites of outright antisemitism. In fact, instances of antisemitism by faculty members who would position themselves on the left have occurred at many colleges. A vicious string of antisemitic tweets from assistant professor of rhetoric and composition Joy Karega at Oberlin College led to her dismissal in 2016. Among other incendiary claims about Jews, on December 23, 2014, she posted a picture of Jacob Rothschild, a member of the Jewish banking family, with the caption, "We own your news, the media, your oil, and your government." Thousands of faculty members across the United States signed on to a petition demanding her reinstatement. It is impossible to imagine a racist who targets a group other than Jews being so staunchly defended by college professors. The view of Jews controlling the government can be heard from the more radical anti-Zionist voices on the left who specifically claim that American policy toward Israel, if not all of American foreign policy, is dictated by a cabal of pro-Israel Jewish groups that control the Congress. For example, this view was clearly depicted in a cartoon prominently displayed on the website of the "Islamophobia Research and Documentation Center," housed at the University of California–Berkeley's Center for Race and Gender. The cartoon showed a gigantic male figure with a blue-and-white armband emblazoned with a Star of David (identical to ones the Nazis forced Jews in ghettos to wear) standing behind and just as tall as the dome of the Congress, whispering instructions into its ear while simultaneously pointing menacingly at a young Muslim woman holding a Palestinian flag. The idea that Jews control the Congress, or any nation's government, for that matter, dates from the nineteenth century and is a central feature of the notorious *Protocols of the Elders of Zion.* That such a view would appear on the website of a campus unit under the auspices of an academic research center at one of the world's leading universities tests the genuineness of UC–Berkeley's oft-repeated commitment to creating an environment that is devoid of bigotry and is a safe and welcoming one for all students. It is noteworthy that among conspiracy-minded antisemites, there are times when little separates those on the far left from those on the far right. For example, the Oklahoma City bomber Timothy McVeigh shared the very sentiment expressed in the aforementioned cartoon when he used the acronym ZOG (Zionist-occupied government) to refer to the government of the United States.

Another source of today's antisemitism derives from a virulent hatred of the State of Israel, a sentiment long established on the far right and now deeply entrenched on the far left and, in some cases, even left of center politics. It must be clearly stated that there is a difference between criticism of Israel's policies and behavior and antisemitism. In no way is all such criticism an expression of antisemitism. Indeed, Israel's own political culture invites criticism; it is considered a normative characteristic of a society that guarantees freedom of speech, freedom of the press, and freedom of assembly and has a vigorous parliamentary system of government. Moreover, until World War II and the Holocaust, only a relatively small minority of Jews were Zionists. While Zionism was growing in popularity in the interwar period, especially in Poland, the majority of the world's Jews were either agnostic and far more concerned with integration into their host societies, a position that was most pronounced in Western Europe and the United States, or vehemently hostile to Zionism, the position of the Bundists, the Yiddish, socialist labor movement in Poland and Lithuania, and the most popular Jewish political persuasion before the war. Further to the political left were Jewish Communists in both Europe and the United States who were likewise hostile to Zionism. Whether guided by a Jewish political sensibility or an apolitical Jewish sensibility, a principled Jewish anti-Zionism has long existed that in no way can be considered antisemitic. Similarly, a nonpolitical but nevertheless extreme religiously mandated Jewish anti-Zionism also exists, best expressed by the Neturei Karta, an ultra-Orthodox sect that even lives in Israel,

the creation of which they consider to be a sin. Formed in Jerusalem in 1938, the group calls for a dismantling of the State of Israel, believing that Jews are forbidden to have their own state until the coming of the Jewish messiah. Neturei Karta's views may well be misguided and naïve, but it would be incorrect to claim that these people are antisemites.

However, there are no doubt instances when there is no distinction between anti-Zionism and antisemitism. This phenomenon might manifest itself in three ways. First is when criticism of Israel exists in a near-total vacuum, when accusers single-mindedly and almost obsessively focus on Israel's behavior to the exclusion of any reference to the outrages committed by other state and non-state actors. Such things may be reported on, but rarely do they raise the world's popular ire, and nor do they occupy the world's press to anywhere near the extent that Israel does. University student unions do not call for boycotts of other nations, huge protest rallies against individual nation-states rarely take place, and nor are there sustained, well-funded, well-organized BDS-like campaigns of delegitimization against the existence of any other country. It is as if there is something qualitatively and quantitatively so monstrous about Israel's behavior, or even its mere existence, that it exists alone as an outlier, with no other nation committing injustices that can begin to compare to Israel's. None of this is to deny the negative impact of Israel's occupation of the West Bank and Gaza on both the Palestinians and on Israel itself. However, to ignore the outrages that are perpetrated on a daily basis by countries across the globe and singularly focus on Israel invites skepticism about the motivations of Israel's critics. Second is when Israel's actions are described as "typically Jewish," which necessitates the invocation of a host of antisemitic stereotypes or, conversely and perversely, when Zionism is equated with Nazism and Israelis are depicted as Nazis. For the genuinely implacable haters of Israel, the fixation upon it as the locus of all evil and the principal cause of the world's most important problems sees in that obsession and monomaniacal focus a recapitulation of nearly all of history's antisemitic stereotypes and charges. These include the Jews' supposed innate cruelty, immorality, bloodlust, thievery, sense of chosenness, and control of world governments and institutions. Its opponents now frequently use these terms to describe the State of Israel. Third, hostility to Israel can be antisemitic without being deliberately so, insofar as it can be unconscious, emerging from what the philosopher Bernard Harrison has called "the climate of opinion." In his formulation, this

> climate of opinion is not, after all, the work of an individual mind. It is something formed out of a multitude of spoken and written items—books—articles, news items, pronouncements by television pundits and news anchormen, lectures, stories, in-jokes, stray remarks—of equally multitudinous authorship.

Harrison goes on to say that "when enough people in a given social circle have bought into a given climate of opinion, that climate of opinion becomes dominant in that circle." As this applies to BDS, the legal scholar and founder of the Louis D. Brandeis Center for Human Rights Under Law at Baruch College, Kenneth Marcus, writes, "Whether BDS advocates are aware of it, either consciously or unconsciously, they often spread anti-Jewish stereotypes, images, and myths."

A new type of possibly unconscious antisemitism that seems to be spreading concerns the exclusion of Jews from certain organizations and events that consider themselves as representing a politics of progressive values.

To give but one example, on June 24, 2017, three people carrying Jewish Pride flags were asked to leave the annual "Chicago Dyke March." The Chicago-based LGBTQ newspaper *Windy City Times* quoted one Dyke March collective member as saying the rainbow flag with the Star of David in the middle "made people feel unsafe," and that the march was "pro-Palestinian" and "anti-Zionist." According to one of those asked to leave, Laurel Grauer, "[t]hey were telling [her] to leave because [her] flag was a trigger to people [who] found [it] offensive." Another marcher asked to leave was an Iranian Jew, Eleanor Shoshany-Anderson:

> I was here as a proud Jew in all of my identities. . . . The Dyke March is supposed to be intersectional. I don't know why my identity is excluded from that. I felt that, as a Jew, I am not welcome here.

What is perhaps unconsciously antisemitic here is that the Star of David was not meant to represent the star on the flag of the State of Israel but, rather, the Jewish identities of the flag bearers. Before being asked to leave, the ejected women were not asked about their political views of the Israeli–Palestinian conflict, the problematic nature of which can be set aside were that to have happened. It was simply assumed that the Star of David, a Jewish symbol that dates back to antiquity, was an expression of Zionism and that the women must, by definition, be political enemies of the LGBTQ community.

For actual Zionists or just Jews mistaken for Zionists (as anyone bearing a Star of David flag is), there is simply no space within the orbit of intersectional politics. It has been increasingly the case that self-declared Zionists are not welcome at such events because Zionism, it is believed, is a reactionary, if not fascist, political ideology. To assert such a view requires a significant level of ignorance, or conscious denial, about the left-wing and socialist roots of Zionism and Israel. It also means that LGBTQ Israelis are not considered valued members of that transnational community, their mere citizenship making them a guilty party.

Much of the new antisemitism—namely, that which has arisen since the 1960s and continues to metastasize—allows for an unholy alliance that links the right and the left in a hatred of Israel and Jews. According to the French Jewish leader Roger Cukierman, antisemitism has made possible a "brown-green-red alliance"—that is, among ultra-nationalists, the populist green movement, and the radical left. The anti-globalization movement is one instance that sees a marriage between the left and the right. For the far right, Jews seek to remake and weaken the world through the inevitable race mixing that would occur in globalized societies. Furthermore, globalization would destroy national sovereignty and lead to the creation of one world community, with the global supplanting the local. For the contemporary far left, informed by the pronouncements of nineteenth-century opponents of capitalism, such as the French anarchist Pierre-Joseph Proudhon and the German founder of Communism, Karl Marx, the creation of a global world order is the work of capitalists, headed by a cabal of Jewish financiers. Into the anti-globalization ideological mix came Zionism, for it represented the animating ideology behind the so-called Jewish conspiracy to control world governments, accumulate wealth, and promote the interests and hegemony of Israel, which it sees as a repressive, colonial, racist state. For the French anti-globalization activist Jose Bové, a farmer turned politician, the state of Israel, with the support of the World Bank, was putting in place "a series of neoliberal measures intended to integrate the Middle East into globalized production circuits, through the exploitation of cheap Palestinian labor." As such, to its most extreme opponents, globalization is not so much an organic development emerging out of late twentieth-century technological change but a deliberate plot hatched by Jews, inside and outside of Israel, and the bodies they are said to control, such as the International Monetary Fund, the World Bank, and the World Trade Organization. It is for these reasons that at anti-globalization demonstrations some protestors carry Israeli flags with the Star of David replaced with swastikas. One further characteristic of contemporary European antisemitism, particularly on the left, is its "status as an epiphenomenon of anti-Americanism," something referred to by the sociologist Andrei Markovits as "twin brothers."

The rhetoric of anti-globalization ideology from both the left and the right can sometimes share a position while being in radical disagreement about its meaning. Such is the case with colonialism. For the right, colonialism must be opposed because it leads to miscegenation, race mixing, and the decline of the "white race," something they claim Jews very much seek to promote. For the left, the anti-colonial position necessitates a dogged anti-Zionism, which it brands a racist, colonial-settler movement. These are of course very different rationales for opposing colonialism, the former in the name of racism, the latter supposedly serving the cause of anti-racism; however, to work effectively, both require the demonization of Jews and Israel. At their core, both views share a belief in the limitlessness of Jewish power and malevolence. It is the very malleability of antisemitism that makes all these seemingly contradictory positions an actually coherent ideology with a power so great and insidious that at times it leads to the far right and the far left peddling the same age-old myths and accusations about Jews.

Irrespective of where on the political spectrum contemporary antisemitism comes from, whether it is conscious or unconscious, whether the charges are ancient ones that have been repurposed or are entirely new canards, it is clear that the scourge of antisemitism has resurfaced. It has gained a new lease on life from the internet and social media, as well as from unscrupulous politicians and a professoriate with great influence over their students. The resurgence of antisemitism calls for vigilance from all quarters for both moral and practical reasons. There is, first of all, the imperative to battle all forms of prejudice, but there is also a utilitarian need, for as the ex–chief rabbi of Great Britain, Lord Rabbi Jonathan Sacks, warned, "[a]nti-Semitism was always only obliquely about Jews. They were its victims but not its cause. The politics of hate that begins with Jews never ends with Jews." The combination of rampant conspiracy theories and blatant antisemitism that course through so much of the Muslim world and are central to right-wing extremist ideology, as well as a monomaniacal focus on Israel to the exclusion of all else, only serves to make societies susceptible to simplistic diagnoses of and solutions to their real economic, social, and political problems. Curb the influence of the Jews and economic prosperity, jobs, and even national sovereignty will be returned to those communities and countries that have lost them. Eliminate Israel and most of the Middle East's problems will be solved. These are hallucinatory ideas, for antisemitism, in the words of the British lawyer Anthony Julius, is "a site of collective hatreds, cultural anxieties and resentments . . . a discursive swamp, a resource on which religious and political movements, writers, artists, demagogues, and the variously disaffected, all draw, without ever draining." The central idée fixe of antisemitism is one in which the Jews, as a nefarious and evil force, shape history rather than it being nations along with their political leaders and the decisions they make together. It is, in other words, an abdication of responsibility dressed up as a grand theory of history. However, an attempt to solve the world's problems by attacking Jews will not advance society's collective interests, let alone cure its ills. Sadly, history has demonstrated this all too frequently. Compounding the situation, technology and social media have proven to be a blessing for antisemites of all stripes. With no mechanism to police hate speech other than goodwill, something in short supply, especially if such actions were to cut into the profits of tech companies, there is nothing to prevent the vilest antisemitic rhetoric appearing online and spreading at breakneck pace.

The Road to the Future

Historians are not in a position, nor are they expected, to make predictions about the future. It would be foolhardy to do so. No one writing a history of the Jewish people in 1939 could have imagined that, within six years, two-thirds of European Jewry would be murdered, or that within nine years there would be a Jewish state in Israel. Nor could anyone have predicted that the bulk of the Jewish people would no longer perform the rituals of Judaism and be unfamiliar with many of its fundamental practices and teachings. Secularization and social acceptance have also created unimaginable opportunities as well as unforeseen problems. What we can say with certainty is that the Jews of today bear little resemblance to those Jews with whom we began our long story.

For the overwhelming majority, in a mere 300 years, the places where Jews lived, the languages they spoke, the jobs they performed, the clothes they wore, and even the foods they permitted themselves to eat have all changed. This has happened as a result of their complex encounter with the modern world, both its blessings and its horrors. In their engagement with modernity, Jews fashioned a set of responses that allowed them to transform

general as well as Jewish culture. How these will serve the needs of the Jewish people in the future should be left to succeeding generations of historians to ponder.

For Further Reading

On the survivors in postwar Europe, see Yehuda Bauer, *Flight and Rescue: Brichah* (New York: Random House, 1970); Michael Brenner, *After the Holocaust: Rebuilding Jewish Lives in Postwar Germany* (Princeton, NJ: Princeton University Press, 1997); Lucy S. Dawidowicz, *From That Place and Time: A Memoir, 1938–1947* (New York: W. W. Norton, 1989); and Jan T. Gross, *Fear: Anti-Semitism in Poland After Auschwitz* (New York: Random House, 2006).

On Israel, see Howard M. Sachar, *A History of Israel: From the Rise of Zionism to Our Time* (New York: Knopf, 2001); Anita Shapira, *Israel: A History* (Waltham, MA: Brandeis University Press, 2012); Tom Segev, *1949: The First Israelis* (New York: Free Press, 1986); Tom Segev, *The Seventh Million: The Israelis and the Holocaust* (New York: Owl Books, 1991); Benny Morris, *The Birth of the Palestinian Refugee Problem, 1947–1949* (Cambridge, England: Cambridge University Press, 1987); Yael Zerubavel, *Recovered Roots: Collective Memory and the Making of Israeli National Tradition* (Chicago: University of Chicago Press, 1995); Derek J. Penslar, *Israel in History: The Jewish State in Comparative Perspective* (London: Routledge, 2007); David N. Myers, *Between Arab and Jew: The Lost Voice of Simon Rawidowicz* (Waltham, MA: Brandeis University Press, 2008); Eli Lederhendler, *The Six-Day War and World Jewry* (Bethesda, MD: University Press of Maryland, 2000); Alvin Z. Rubinstein, ed., *The Arab-Israeli Conflict: Perspectives* (New York: Harper Collins, 1991); Alan Dowty, *Israel/Palestine* (Cambridge, England: Polity Press, 2005); Alan Dowty, *The Jewish State: A Century Later* (Berkeley: University of California Press, 1998); Benny Morris, ed., *Making Israel* (Ann Arbor: University

of Michigan Press, 2007); and Cary Nelson and Gabriel Noah Brahm, eds., *The Case against Academic Boycotts of Israel* (Chicago: MLA Members for Scholars' Rights, 2015).

On postwar American Jewry, see Arthur A. Goren, *The Politics and Public Culture of American Jews* (Bloomington: Indiana University Press, 1999); Eli Lederhendler, *New York Jews and the Decline of Urban Ethnicity, 1950–1970* (Syracuse: Syracuse University Press, 2001); Robert M. Seltzer and Norman J. Cohen, eds., *The Americanization of the Jews* (New York: New York University Press, 1995); Marc Dollinger, *Quest for Inclusion: Jews and Liberalism in Modern America* (Princeton, NJ: Princeton University Press, 2000); and Hasia Diner, *The Jews of the United States: 1654–2000* (Berkeley: University of California Press, 2006).

On Soviet Jewry, see Salo W. Baron, *The Russian Jews under Tsar and Soviets* (New York: Schocken Books, 1987); Jeffrey Veidlinger, *The Moscow State Yiddish Theater: Jewish Culture on the Soviet Stage* (Bloomington: Indiana University Press, 2000); Yuri Slezkine, *The Jewish Century* (Princeton, NJ: Princeton University Press, 2004); Anna Shternshis, *Soviet and Kosher: Jewish Popular Culture in the Soviet Union, 1923–1939* (Bloomington: Indiana University Press, 2006); Elissa Bemporad, *Becoming Soviet Jews: The Bolshevik Experiment in Minsk* (Bloomington: Indiana University Press, 2013); Zvi Gitelman, *A Century of Ambivalence: The Jews of Russia and the Soviet Union, 1881 to the Present* (Bloomington: Indiana University Press, 2001); Zvi Gitelman et al., eds., *Jewish Life after the USSR* (Bloomington: Indiana University Press, 2003); and Jeffrey Veidlinger, *In the Shadow of the Shtetl: Small*

Town Jewish Life in Soviet Ukraine (Bloomington: Indiana University Press, 2013).

On Jews in contemporary Europe, see Eliezer Ben-Rafael et al., eds., *Contemporary Jewries: Convergence and Divergence* (Boston: E. J. Brill, 2003); Zvi Gitelman et al., eds., *New Jewish Identities: Contemporary Europe and Beyond* (New York: Central European University Press, 2003); Bernard Wasserstein, *Vanishing Diaspora: The Jews in Europe since 1945* (Cambridge, MA: Harvard University Press, 1996); Sander L. Gilman and Karen Remmler, eds., *Reemerging Jewish Culture in Germany: Life and Literature since 1989* (New York: New York University Press, 1994); and Ethan B. Katz, *The Burdens of Brotherhood: Jews and Muslims from North Africa to France* (Cambridge, MA: Harvard University Press, 2015).

On Jews of the Southern Hemisphere, see Kristin Ruggiero, ed., *The Jewish Diaspora in Latin America and the Caribbean: Fragments of Memory* (Portland, OR: Sussex Academic Press, 2005); Gideon Shimoni, *Community and Conscience: The Jews in Apartheid South Africa* (Hanover, NH: University Press of New England, 2003); and Suzanne D. Rutland, *Edge of the Diaspora: Two Centuries of Jewish Settlement in Australia* (New York: Holmes & Meier, 1997).

INDEX

Note: Page numbers in *italics* refer to figures and boxes.